Microsoft®
Visual C++® 6.0

Microsoft®
Visual C++® 6.0

Don Gosselin

**COURSE
TECHNOLOGY**
™
THOMSON LEARNING

Australia • Canada • Mexico • Singapore • Spain • United Kingdom • United States

COURSE
TECHNOLOGY

THOMSON LEARNING

Microsoft Visual C++ 6.0

is published by Course Technology.

Managing Editor
Jennifer Locke

Product Manager
Margarita Donovan

Acquisitions Editor
Christine Guivernau

Production Editors
Megan Cap-Renzi, Kristen Guevara

Developmental Editor
Marilyn Freedman

Associate Product Manager
Tricia Coia

Associate Marketing Manager
Meagan Walsh

Editorial Assistant
Janet Aras

Cover Designer
MaryAnn Southard

Disclaimer
Course Technology reserves the right to revise this publication and make changes from time to time in its content without notice.

ISBN 0-619-03488-2

<small>BRIEF</small>
Contents

TABLE OF
Contents

Preface

Microsoft Visual C++ 6.0 teaches the skills necessary to create applications in the dynamic Visual C++ development environment. The Visual C++ environment takes the C++ language one step beyond being an object-oriented extension of the C language by adding Microsoft Foundation Classes, or MFCs, the building blocks for Windows applications. *Microsoft Visual C++ 6.0* discusses in detail all of these technologies, while also thoroughly exploring the C++ structure and syntax underlying Visual C++.

Microsoft Visual C++ 6.0 provides coverage of the necessary basics of C++ programming in the first few chapters, and then brings the reader confidently into the Visual environment in the second half of the book.

Organization and Coverage

Microsoft Visual C++ 6.0 contains twelve chapters that present hands-on instruction in the basics of C++ and Windows application programming. In these chapters, students with no previous programming experience learn how to plan and create well-structured programs. By the end of the book, students will have learned how to work with basic C++ syntax, such as how to write functions using repetition and control programming structures. Students also learn more advanced topics, such as how to work with the Windows API and access objects contained in MFCS. Additionally, readers will learn how to create and work with dialog-based and document-based applications, how to create visual interface components, how to work with databases, and how to debug their programs.

Each chapter includes a concept lesson, which introduces programming concepts that are presented in hands-on, step-by-step exercises. Each step-by-step exercise provides an opportunity for the student to apply the knowledge learned in the main text. The combination of text explanations with step-by-step exercises that illustrate the concepts reinforces understanding and improves retention of the material presented. It also provides the student with learning opportunities beyond what might be taught in the classroom.

Readers using *Microsoft Visual C++ 6.0* build applications from the bottom up, rather than using pre-written code. This technique facilitates a deeper understanding of the concepts used in programming with Visual C++ 6.0. When readers complete this book, they will know how to create and modify simple Windows and MFC applications and will have the tools to create more complex applications. Users will also have a fundamental knowledge of programming concepts that will be useful whether they continue to learn more about the C++ language or go on to learn other object-oriented languages.

Approach

Microsoft Visual C++ 6.0 distinguishes itself from other books because of its unique approach, which motivates students by demonstrating why they need to learn the concepts and skills. This book teaches programming concepts using a task-driven, rather than a command-driven approach. By working through the chapters—which are each motivated by a realistic application—students learn how to create programs that solve problems they are likely to encounter in the workplace. This is much more effective than memorizing a list of commands out of context.

In addition, *Microsoft Visual C++ 6.0* uses the following teaching techniques:

- The code examples are short; one concept is featured in each code example.
- Variables, functions, objects, and events are covered earlier than in many other texts, giving users a better understanding of the more advanced concepts and techniques that occur later in the text, and allowing them to work on significant projects from the start.
- Text explanation is interspersed with step-by-step exercises.
- Syntax is introduced throughout the text, as necessary.
- C++ applications are built from the bottom up; the user gains a clear picture of how complex programs are built.
- Programming techniques are presented in easy-to-understand lessons.

Features

Microsoft Visual C++ 6.0 is a superior textbook because it also includes the following features:

- **"Read This Before You Begin" Page** This page is consistent with Course Technology's unequaled commitment to helping instructors introduce technology into the classroom. Technical considerations and assumptions about hardware, software, and default settings are listed in one place to help instructors save time and eliminate unnecessary aggravation.
- **Case Approach** Each chapter addresses programming-related problems that individuals could reasonably expect to encounter in business. Each chapter begins with a demonstration of an application that could be used to solve a problem. Showing users the completed application before they learn how to create it is motivational and instructionally sound. By allowing users to see the type of application they will create after completing the chapter, users will be more motivated to learn because they can see how the programming concepts that they are about to learn can be used and, therefore, why the concepts are important.
- **Step-by-Step Methodology** The unique Course Technology methodology keeps users on track. They always write program code within the context of solving the problems posed in the chapter. The text constantly guides users and lets them know where they are in the process of solving the problem. The numerous illustrations guide individuals to create useful, working programs.

- **Tips** These notes provide additional information—for example, an alternate method of performing a procedure, background information on a technique, a commonly-made error to watch out for, debugging techniques, or the name of a Web site the user can visit to gather more information.

- **Summaries** Following each chapter is a Summary that recaps the programming concepts and commands covered in each section.

- **Review Questions** Each chapter concludes with meaningful, conceptual Review Questions that test users' understanding of what they learned in the chapter.

- **Exercises** Programming Exercises provide users with additional practice of the skills and concepts they learned in the lesson.

CT Teaching Tools

All the teaching tools for this text are found in the Instructor's Resource Kit, which is available from the Course Technology Web site (*www.course.com*) and on CD-ROM.

Electronic Instructor's Manual The Instructor's Manual that accompanies this textbook includes:

- Additional instructional material to assist in class preparation, including suggestions for lecture topics.

- **Solution Files** Solutions to all end-of-chapter materials. (Due to the nature of programming, students' solutions may differ from these solutions and still be correct.)

- **Data Files** Data Files, containing all of the data that students will use for the tutorials and exercises in this book, are provided through Course Technology's Online Companion and on the Instructor's Resource Kit CD-ROM. See the "Read This Before You Begin" section preceding the Overview for more information on Data Files.

Course Test Manager 1.2 Accompanying this book is a powerful assessment tool known as the Course Test Manager. Designed by Course Technology, this cutting-edge Windows-based testing software helps instructors design and administer tests and pre-tests. In addition to being able to generate tests that can be printed and administered, this full-featured program also has an outline testing component that allows students to take tests at the computer and have their exams graded automatically.

PowerPoint Presentations This book comes with Microsoft PowerPoint slides for each chapter. These are included as a teaching aid for classroom presentation, to make available to students on the network for chapter review, or to be printed for classroom distribution. Instructors can add their own slides for additional topics they introduce to the class.

MyCourse.com MyCourse.com is an online syllabus builder and course enhancement tool. Hosted by Course Technology, MyCourse.com adds value to your course by providing additional content that reinforces what students are learning.

Most importantly, MyCourse.com is flexible. You can choose how you want to organize the material—by date, by class session, or by using the default organization, which organizes content by chapter. MyCourse.com allows you to add your own materials, including hyperlinks, school logos, assignments, announcements, and other course content. If you are using more than one textbook, you can even build a course that includes all of your Course Technology texts in one easy-to-use site!

Start building your own course today! Just go to *www.mycourse.com/instructor*.

ACKNOWLEDGEMENTS

A text such as this represents the hard work of many people, not just the author. I would like to thank all of the people who helped make this book a reality. First and foremost, I would like to thank Marilyn Freedman, Development Editor, for her outstanding work and for making me a better writer. Next, I would like to thank Margarita Donovan, Project Manager, for making sure that the production of this book did not include any bloodshed. I would also like to thank Kristen Duerr, Publisher; Christine Guiverneau, Acquisitions Editor; Jennifer Muroff, Senior Product Manager; Megan Cap-Renzi and Kristen Guevara, Production Editors; John Bosco and Nicole Ashton in QA.

Thanks also to my clients for giving me time off to write including Mary Ann O'Brien and Ellie Lottero of Harvard University, Peggy Beckley of RWD Technologies, the folks at DigitalThink, Raphael Serebreny of Serena, Kathleen Hughes of Webster Techwriters, Inc., and Steve Churchill of Taviz Technology, Inc.

Many, many thanks to the reviewers for their invaluable comments and suggestions, including W. Pete Brown, Schoolcraft College; Mary Myers, Edison Community College; Donna Occhifinto, Dover Business College; Gary Savard, Champlain College; and William Smith, Tulsa Community College. You truly made this a better book.

On the personal side, I would like to thank my friends and family for their understanding when I disappear for days and weeks on end including (but not limited to) Daryl Gray, Raymond Hernandez, Neil and Ann Hamilton, Dennis and Mary Bourgault, Cynthia Bourgault, Raymond and Lorraine Bourgault, Raymond Gosselin, Karen and Bruce Richman, my sister Jennifer, my grandparents, my many aunts, uncles, and cousins, and of course, my mother. Thanks to my father for always listening when I needed someone to talk to. A very special thanks to my brother, David, for keeping me humble and always reminding me where I came from.

As always, thanks to my friend and colleague, George T. Lynch, for getting me started. Thanks also goes to my cat, Mabeline, for keeping me company while I write, and to my dog, Noah, for never failing to remind me that a world exists outside of my office. Finally, my most important thanks of all goes to my wonderful wife Kathy for her eternal patience and support.

Don Gosselin
Napa, California

Read This Before You Begin

TO THE USER

Data Disks

To complete the chapters and exercises in this book, you need Data Disks. Your instructor will provide you with Data Disks or ask you to make your own.

If you are asked to make your own Data Disks, you will need 3 blank, formatted high-density disks. You will need to copy a set of folders from a file server or stand-alone computer onto your disks. Your instructor will tell you which computer, drive letter, and folders contain the files you need. The following table shows you which folders go on each of your disks:

Student Disk	Write this on the disk label	Put these folders on the disk
1	Chapters 1 through 8	Chapter.01
		Chapter.02
		Chapter.03
		Chapter.04
		Chapter.05
		Chapter.06
		Chapter.07
		Chapter.08
2	Chapter 9	Chapter.09
3	Chapters 10 through 12	Chapter.10
		Chapter.11
		Chapter.12

When you begin each chapter, make sure you are using the correct Data Disk. Ask your instructor or technical support person for assistance.

Using Your Own Computer

You can use your own computer to complete the chapters and exercises in this book. To use you own computer, you will need the following:

- Visual C++ 6.0. This book assumes installation of Visual C++ Standard Edition or Introductory Edition. The following system requirements apply for both compilers:
  - Personal computer with a 486 or higher processor
  - Microsoft Windows 95 or later or Windows NT 4.0 or later
  - 32 MB of RAM
  - VGA or higher-resolution monitor (Super VGA recommended)
  - 225 MB hard disk space for a typical installation; 305 MB for a maximum installation
  - Microsoft Developer Network installation requirements: 43 MB hard disk space for a typical installation; 493 MB for a maximum installation
  - CD-ROM drive
  - Microsoft Mouse or compatible pointing device

You can also use the Professional or Enterprise editions of Visual C++ with this text. However, you should be aware that these versions include additional features that are not documented in this text. Additionally, the Professional and Enterprise editions have more system requirements than the Standard and Introductory editions.

- Data Files. You can get the Data files from your instructor. You will not be able to complete all the chapters and exercises in this book using your own computer until you have the Data files. The user files may also be obtained electronically at the Course Technology Web site at *www.course.com*.
- Project disk space. You will need approximately 70 MB of disk space to store the projects you create in this text.

Additional materials designed especially for you might be available for your course on the World Wide Web. Go to *www.course.com* and search for this book title periodically for more details.

TO THE INSTRUCTOR

To complete all the exercises and chapters in this book, your users must use a set of Data files. These files are included in the Instructor's Resource Kit. They may also be obtained electronically through the Course Technology website at *www.course.com*. Follow the instructions in the Help file to copy the user files to your server or stand-alone computer. You can view the Help file using a text editor, such as WordPad or Notepad.

Once the files are copied, you can make Data Disks for the users yourself or tell them where to find the files so they can make their own Data Disks. Make sure the files get copied correctly onto the Data Disks by following the instructions in the Data Disk section. This will ensure that users have enough disk space to complete all the chapters and exercises in this book.

Course Technology Data Files

You are granted a license to copy the Data files to any computer or computer network used by individuals who have purchased this book.

1

INTRODUCTION TO PROGRAMMING AND VISUAL C++

In this chapter you will learn about:

♦ Computer programming and programming languages
♦ C/C++ programming
♦ Logic and debugging
♦ Creating a new project in Visual C++
♦ The Visual C++ IDE
♦ Managing the workspace
♦ Visual C++ Help

COMPUTER PROGRAMMING AND PROGRAMMING LANGUAGES

Creating programs, or instructions, that control the operation of a computer is called **computer programming**. Think, for a moment, about an automobile. The automobile is useless without someone to drive it. If you compare an automobile to a computer, you can see that the computer is useless without a program that "drives" its hardware. The instructions used to create computer programs are called **programming languages**. To understand Visual C++ programming and how it relates to the C/C++ programming languages, it is helpful to know a little background about computer programming and how current programming languages evolved.

Machine and Assembly Languages

The electronic circuitry of a computer is controlled by two simple electronic signals, or switches—an on switch and an off switch. A 1 represents the on switch, and a 0 represents the off switch. Telling a computer what to do involves writing programs that set these switches to on or off. **Machine language** is the lowest level of computer languages, and programs written in machine language consist entirely of 1s and 0s that control the computer's on and off switches. For example, a program written in machine language may contain lines similar to the following. Note that the following code is not an actual program; it just serves to give an idea of how difficult it can be to program with machine language.

```
0 0 1 0 1 0 1 0 1
1 0 0 1 1 0 0 1 1
0 0 1 1 0 0 1 1 0
1 0 0 0 0 1 1 1 1
0 0 1 0 1 1 0 1 0
1 0 0 1 1 1 1 0 0
0 0 1 1 0 1 0 0 1
```

Writing a program in machine language is very difficult because you must understand how the exact placement and combination of 1s and 0s will affect your program. Assembly languages provide an easier (although still challenging) method of controlling a computer's on and off switches. **Assembly languages** perform the same tasks as machine languages, but use simplified names of instructions instead of 1s and 0s. To get an idea of how difficult it can be to program with assembly languages, examine the following assembly code, which only performs some simple numeric calculations.

```
Main proc
      mov ax, dseg
A     integer ?
B     integer ?
C     integer ?
cseg segment para public 'code'
assume cs:cseg, ds:dseg
Main proc
      mov ax, dseg
      mov ds, ax
      mov es, ax
      mov A, 3
      mov B, -2
      mov C, 254
      mov ax, A
      add ax, B
      mov C, ax
```

Machine languages and assembly languages are known as **low-level languages** because they are the programming languages that are closest to a computer's hardware. Each type of CPU (central processing unit) contains its own internal machine language and assembly language.

To write programs in machine language, a programmer must know the specific machine language and assembly language for the type of CPU on which a program will run. Since each CPU's machine language and assembly language is unique, it is difficult to translate low-level languages from one CPU to another.

High-Level Programming Languages

Because of the difficulty of working with low-level languages, high-level, or symbolic, languages were developed to make it easier to write computer programs. **High-level programming languages** create computer programs using instructions that are much easier to understand than machine or assembly language code because you use words that more clearly describe the task being performed. Examples of high-level languages include C++, BASIC, and COBOL. To understand the difference between low-level languages and high-level languages, consider the following assembly language code that adds two numbers:

```
mov A, 3
mov B, 2
add A, B
```

Although easier than machine language, the above assembly language code is still difficult to understand. In comparison, the same task is accomplished in a high-level language using a much simpler statement such as `PRINT 3 + 2`.

Programs written in high-level languages must be translated into a low-level language using a program called a compiler. A **compiler** translates programming code into a low-level format. You need to compile a program only once when you are through writing it or after editing an existing program. When you execute the program, you actually execute the compiled, low-level format of the program.

Procedural Programming

One of the most common forms of programming in high-level languages is called procedural programming. In **procedural programming**, the individual statements used in a high-level computer programming language are often grouped into logical units called **procedures**. For example, a checkbook program may contain a series of statements grouped as a procedure named `balanceCheckbook` that balance a checkbook. Another procedure named `sumDeposits` may be used to calculate the total of all deposits made during a single period. A single procedural program may contain hundreds of variables and thousands of statements and procedures.

 Procedures are also referred to as routines, subroutines, or functions.

One of the most important aspects of procedural programming is that it allows you to temporarily store pieces of information, called **variables**, in computer memory locations. The information contained in a specific variable often changes. For example, you may have a program that creates a variable containing the current time. Each time the program runs, the time is different, so the value *varies*. The value of a variable often changes during the course of a program's execution. For example, a payroll program might assign employee names to a variable named `employeeName`. The memory location referenced by the variable `employeeName` might contain different values (a different value for every employee of the company) at different times. In contrast, a **constant** contains information that does not change during the course of program execution. You can think of a constant as a variable with a *constant* value. A common example of a constant is the value of pi (π), which represents the ratio of the circumference of a circle to its diameter. The value of pi never changes from the constant value 3.141592.

Each line in a procedural program that performs an individual task is called a **statement**. The statements within a procedural program are usually executed in a linear fashion, one right after the other. Figure 1-1 displays a simple procedural program written in BASIC that calculates and prints the average of the numbers 1, 2, and 3. The first two statements in the program create variables named SUM and COUNT. During the course of the program's execution, the numbers 1, 2, and 3 are added to the SUM variable. The COUNT variable maintains a record of how many numbers are assigned to the SUM variable. Finally, the average is calculated using the statement SUM / COUNT.

```
LET SUM = 0
LET COUNT = 0
LET SUM = SUM + 1
LET COUNT = COUNT + 1
LET SUM = SUM + 2
LET COUNT = COUNT + 1
LET SUM = SUM + 3
LET COUNT = COUNT + 1
LET AVERAGE = SUM / COUNT
PRINT "The average is "; AVERAGE
```

Figure 1-1   A procedural program writtten in BASIC

Object-Oriented Programming

Procedural-based programs are self-contained; most code, such as variables, statements, and procedures, exist within the program itself. For example, you may have written a small business program that calculates accounts receivables and accounts payables. To add to the program a new function that calculates the interest on a loan, you must include all the required code within the accounting program using variables, statements, and procedures. If you want to use the interest calculation code in another program, you must copy all of its statements into the new program or recreate it from scratch.

Object-oriented programming takes a different approach. **Object–oriented programming (OOP)** refers to the creation of reusable software objects that can be easily incorporated into another program. An **object** is programming code and data that can be treated as an individual unit or component. **Data** refers to information contained within variables, constants, or other types of storage structures. The procedures associated with an object are referred to as **functions** or **methods**. Variables that are associated with an object are referred to as **properties** or **attributes**. Objects can range from simple controls such as a button, to entire programs such as a database application. Object-oriented programming allows programmers to use programming objects that they have written themselves or that have been written by others. One of the most powerful features of object-oriented programming is that it allows programmers to use objects in their programs that may have been created in an entirely different programming language. For example, if you are creating an accounting program in Turbo Pascal, you can use an object named Payroll that was created in C++. You do not need to know how the Payroll object was created in C++, nor do you need to re-create it in Turbo Pascal. You only need to know how to access the functionality of the Payroll object from the Turbo Pascal program.

Objects are **encapsulated**, which means that all code and required data are self-contained within the object itself. Encapsulation is also referred to as a "black box," because of the invisibility of the code inside an encapsulated object. When an object is well written, you cannot see "inside" it—all internal workings are hidden. The code (methods and statements) and data (variables and constants) contained in an encapsulated object are accessed through an interface. An **interface** represents elements required for a source program to communicate with an object. For example, interface elements required to access a Payroll object might be the name of a method within the Payroll object, an employee's name, and rate of pay. You can compare a programming object and its interface to a hand-held calculator. The calculator represents an object, and you represent a program that wants to use the object. You establish an interface with the calculator object by entering numbers (the object's required data) and then by pressing calculation keys (which represent the object's methods.) You do not need to know, nor can you see, the inner workings of the calculator object. As a program, you are concerned only with the results the calculator object returns. Another example of an object and its interface is a Windows word processing program. The word processing program itself is actually a type of object made up of numerous other objects. The program window is called the user interface. The items you see in the word processing window, such as the menu, toolbars, and other elements, are interface items used for executing methods. For example, an icon that you click to bold text is an interface element that executes a bold method. You do not need to know how the method works, only how it executes.

In object-oriented programming, code, methods, attributes, and other information are contained in a structure known as a **class**. Programming objects are created from classes. When you use an object in your program, you actually create an instance of the object's class. An **instance** is an object that has been created from an existing class. As an example, let's return to the Payroll object mentioned earlier. The Payroll object is created from a Payroll class. To use the Payroll class, you create an instance of the class. Particular instances of objects inherit their characteristics from a class. **Inheritance** refers to the ability of an object to take on the characteristics of the class on which it is based. The Payroll object, for instance, inherits all of the characteristics of the Payroll class. As another example, when you create a new word processing document, which is a type of object, it usually inherits the properties of a template on which it is based. The template is a type of class. The document inherits characteristics of the template such as font size, line spacing, and boilerplate text. In the same manner, programs that include instances of objects inherit the object's functionality.

 You will learn about object-oriented programming throughout the course of this text.

C/C++ PROGRAMMING

The term C/C++ refers to two separate, but related, programming languages: C and C++. At Bell Laboratories in the 1970s, Dennis Ritchie and Brian Kernighan designed the procedural C programming language based upon two earlier languages, BCPL and B. In 1985, again at Bell Laboratories, Bjarne Stroustrup created C++ based on the C programming language. C++ is an extension of C that adds object-oriented programming capabilities.

You create C and C++ programs in text files using a text-editing tool such as Notepad. The original program structure you enter into a text file is referred to as **source code**. Once you finish creating your program's source code, you use a compiler to translate it into the machine language of the computer on which the program will run. The compiled machine language version of a program is called **object code**. Once you compile a program into object code, some systems require you to use a program called a **linker**, which converts the object code into an executable file, typically with an extension of .exe. You cannot read object code or the code in an .exe file. The only code format in human-readable form is source code. Note that in Visual C++, you compile and link a program in a single step known as building. You will learn how to build a program later in this chapter.

Remember that each computer contains its own internal machine language. The C/C++ compiler you use must be able to translate source code to the machine language of the computer, or platform, on which your program will run. Numerous vendors market C/C++ compilers for various platforms. Some vendors offer complete development environments containing built-in text editors, compilers, and linkers. Microsoft Visual C++ and Borland C++ Builder are examples of C/C++ professional development environments that contain built-in text editors and compilers, as well as many other development tools.

The C Programming Language

One of the most important programs created with the original C language was the UNIX operating system. Because of its involvement in the creation of UNIX and its subsequent use as the main programming language for the UNIX platform, C was originally used almost exclusively on UNIX platforms. During the 1980s, C compilers were written for other platforms, including personal computers. The first C compilers for other platforms were based on the original version of the language developed by Ritchie and Kernighan. By 1985 numerous C compilers had been created by independent software vendors, many of which did not conform to the original version of the language. To provide a level of standardization for the C language, in 1989 the American National Standards Institute (ANSI) created a standardized version of C that is commonly referred to as **ANSI C**. In 1990 a worldwide standard for the C language named **ANSI/ISO C** was approved by the International Standards Organization (ISO).

One of the great benefits of the C language is that it is much closer to assembly language than other types of high-level programming languages. Being closer to assembly language means that programs written in C often run much faster and more efficiently than programs written in other types of high-level programming languages. Additionally, thanks to the ANSI/ISO standard, the same C program can usually run on many different platforms. However, C's closeness to assembly language can also be a disadvantage. It can make C difficult to use and not ideally suited to certain types of applications, such as graphical applications and object-based programs that you want to use with other programming languages.

The C++ Programming Language

Although C programs are not ideally suited to graphical applications, C++ is a different story. C++ is currently the most popular programming language for developing graphical programs that run on platforms such as Macintosh and Windows. Graphical programs refers to programs with visual components such as dialog boxes, menus, toolbars, and so on. C++ has the ability to create graphical programs because of the object-oriented programming capabilities added by Stroustrup when he first developed the language from its C predecessor. Much of this text explores C++'s object-oriented programming capabilities.

As with the C language, early versions of C++ suffered from a lack of standardization until the worldwide ANSI/ISO C++ standard was approved in 1997. The standardized version of C++ is commonly referred to as **ANSI C++**. The ANSI C++ standard ensures that programs written in C++ are compatible with different compilers and can be run on different platforms.

The ANSI C and ANSI C++ standards define how C/C++ code can be written. The ANSI standards also define **run-time libraries**, which contain useful functions, variables, constants, and other programmatic items that you can add to your programs. The ANSI C++ run-time library is also called the **Standard Template Library** or **Standard C++ Library**. Although the run-time libraries are not actually part of each language's structure, they are required for a compiler to conform to the ANSI C/C++ standards. You can be assured that any of the components of the run-time libraries that you use in your programs will be available to all compilers that support the ANSI C/C++ standard.

Both the C and C++ programming languages are still in use today. In fact, Visual C++ supports both the C and C++ languages. Most of the features of C are also available in C++, which means you can use C++ to write both procedural and object-oriented programs. For this reason, this text focuses primarily on the C++ language.

Microsoft Visual C++

Microsoft Visual C++ is a Windows-based, visual development environment for creating C and C++ applications. Visual C++ contains a built-in text editor, compiler, and other tools for creating programs. You can create both C and C++ applications in Visual C++. The C and C++ language syntax used in Visual C++ conforms to ANSI C/C++ specifications. Actually, Visual C++ itself is *not* a programming language. It is a *development environment* used for creating programs with the C/C++ languages.

The visual aspect of Visual C++ is used for designing the user interface of a program. It displays a C/C++ program in a graphical environment that is easier to work with than numerous text files in a text-editing program. You can also "draw" some parts of your program, such as the controls in a dialog box, using various Visual C++ tools. Although a C/C++ program is displayed in Visual C++ through a graphical user interface, the underlying code is still written in C/C++ syntax. Thus, programmers who have worked with other C/C++ compilers can use their core C/C++ programming skills with Visual C++, and vice-versa.

Visual C++ supports a number of extensions to the ANSI C/C++ run-time libraries. **Extensions** are new or additional features that have been added to the original run-time libraries. Visual C++ extensions may or may not be supported by other C/C++ compilers, so you cannot be absolutely certain that any programs you write that use the extensions will be able to run on other platforms. Visual C++ extends the C++ language by allowing you to include Microsoft Foundation Classes in your programs. **Microsoft Foundation Classes**, or **MFCs**, are libraries of classes that can be used as the building blocks for creating Windows applications with Visual C++. It is very important to understand that any Visual C++ programs you create that utilize MFCs will not conform to the ANSI C/C++ standards, and therefore will not be able to run with other vendor's C/C++ compilers. If you need your C/C++ program to be portable to other platforms, you must use only the standard ANSI C/C++ run-time libraries. Nevertheless, MFCs are an extremely powerful feature of Visual C++, since they allow you to create true Windows applications. Since one of the primary uses of Visual C++ is in the creation of Windows applications, many of the projects you create in this text will include MFCs and therefore will not conform to ANSI C/C++.

 You will learn how to use the various Visual C++ libraries throughout this text.

LOGIC AND DEBUGGING

Each high-level programming language, including Visual C++, has its own **syntax**, or rules of the language. All languages have a specific, limited vocabulary and a specific set of rules for using that vocabulary. For example, you might use the commands *print* or *write* to produce output to the screen. To write a program, you must understand a given programming language's syntax.

To write a program, you must also understand computer-programming logic. The **logic** underlying any program involves executing the various parts of the program in the correct order to produce the desired results. For example, although you know how to drive a car well, you may not reach your destination if you do not follow the correct route. Similarly, you might be able to use a programming language's syntax correctly, but be unable to execute a logically constructed, workable program. Examples of logical errors include multiplying two values when you meant to divide them, or producing output prior to obtaining the appropriate input. The following C++ code contains another example of a logic error:

```
int count = 0;
while (count <= 10) {
    cout << "The number is ";
    cout << count;
}
```

The code in the example uses a **while** statement, which is used to repeat a command or series of commands based on the evaluation of certain criteria. The criterion in the example is the value of a variable named count. The **while** statement is supposed to execute until the count variable is less than or equal to 10. There is no code within the **while** statement's body however, that changes the count variable's value. The count variable will continue to have a value of 0 through each iteration of the loop. In this program, as it is written, a line containing the text string *The number is 0* will print on the screen over and over again.

 Do not worry about how the C++ code in the example is constructed. The example is only meant to give you a better understanding of a logical error.

Any error in a program that causes it to function incorrectly, whether due to incorrect syntax or flaws in logic, is called a bug. **Debugging** describes the act of tracing and resolving errors in a program. Legend has it that the term *debugging* was first coined in the 1940s by Grace Murray Hopper, a mathematician who was instrumental in developing the COBOL programming language. As the story goes, a moth short-circuited a primitive computer that Hopper was using. Removing the moth from the computer *debugged* the system and resolved the problem. Today, a bug refers to any sort of problem in the design and operation of a program.

 Do not confuse bugs with computer viruses. Bugs are errors within a program that occur because of syntax errors, design flaws, and other types of errors. Viruses are self-contained programs designed to "infect" a computer system and cause mischievous or malicious damage. Actually, virus programs themselves can contain bugs if they contain syntax errors or do not perform (or damage) as their creators envisioned.

Many programming languages include commands and other features to assist in locating bugs in a program. Visual C++ contains many debugging commands and features, which you will learn about in Chapter 8. To provide you with some debugging skills prior to Chapter 8, debugging suggestions are offered in the Tips feature throughout this book. As you read the debugging tips however, keep in mind that debugging is not an exact science—every program you write is different and requires different methods of debugging. Your own logical and analytical skills are the best debugging resources you have.

CREATING A NEW PROJECT IN VISUAL C++

In this section, you will learn various techniques for managing the files that compose a Visual C++ application. You will also learn how to work with many of the development environment tools. You will need to store the projects you create in a folder on your hard drive or on a network drive with sufficient disk space. Next, you will create a projects folder named Visual C++ Projects, or some other name that makes sense to you. Regardless of the name you choose in the next exercise for your projects folder, this text refers to it as the *Visual C++ Projects folder* throughout the course of this text.

To create a projects folder for the Visual C++ projects you create in this text:

1. If necessary, start Windows. Open **Windows Explorer** or **My Computer**.

2. Create a folder named **Visual C++ Projects** (or use another name if you like).

3. In your Visual C++ Projects folder, create a folder named Chapter.01 where you will store the projects you create in this chapter.

4. Close **Windows Explorer** or **My Computer**.

Next, you will start creating a new project that you will use for the rest of this chapter to demonstrate the techniques for managing the files that compose a Visual C++ application. The project you create in this section is for demonstration purposes only.

To start creating a new project to demonstrate the techniques for managing the files that compose a Visual C++ application:

1. Click the **Start** button on the taskbar. Point to **Programs** on the Start menu. Point to **Microsoft Visual C++ 6.0** on the Programs menu. Click **Microsoft Visual C++ 6.0**. If the Tip of the Day dialog box appears, click the **Close** button.

 You can prevent the Tip of the Day dialog box from appearing whenever you start Visual C++ by deselecting the Show tips at startup checkbox before clicking the Close button. You can also display the Tip of the Day dialog box at any time by selecting Tip of the Day from the Help menu.

2. Select **New** from the **File** menu or press **Ctrl+N** to display the New dialog box, and then click the **Projects** tab if it is not already selected. The Projects tab of the New dialog box is shown in Figure 1–2.

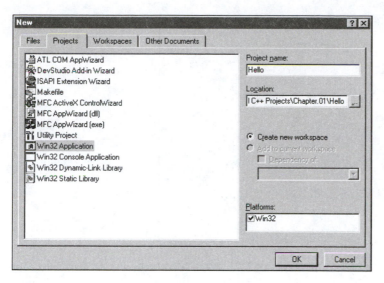

Figure 1-2   Projects tab of the New dialog box

Refer to the appendix for a list of keyboard shortcuts that are available to you when working in Visual C++.

When you first see the New dialog box, you might be intimidated by the many available options. Keep in mind that Visual C++ is a high-level programming environment and that many of the options in the New dialog box are used primarily by professional programmers. By the end of this text, you will understand how to work with many of the options in the New dialog box.

3. In the Projects tab, click **Win32 Application**.

4. Next, click in the **Project name** text box and type **Hello**.

5. Press the **Tab** key to move to the Location text box and type the name of the Visual C++ Projects folder, followed by a backslash and **Chapter.01**, and then followed by another backslash and the text **Hello**. This will create a new folder named Hello in the Chapter.01 folder where the new project will be stored. The Location text box should read `C:\Visual C++ Projects\Chapter.01\Hello`, or something similar if you are using different directory names or drive letters. You can click the button to the right of the Location text box to see the available drives and directories on your computer.

6. Click the **OK** button. The Win32 Application dialog box appears asking what type of windows application you would like to create, as shown in Figure 1-3.

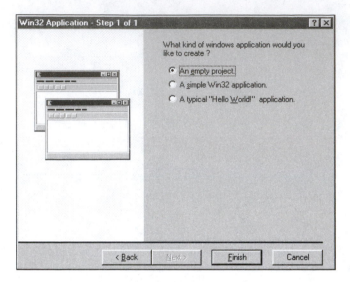

Figure 1-3   Win32 Application dialog box

7. In the Win32 Application dialog box, select the third option, **A typical "Hello World!" application**, and click the **Finish** button. The New Project Information dialog box appears and lists the specifications for your new project, as shown in Figure 1-4.

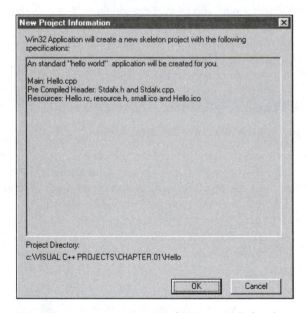

Figure 1-4   New Project Information dialog box

8. In the New Project Information dialog box, click the **OK** button. Visual C++ creates a new project called Hello in the Chapter.01 folder in your Visual C++ Projects folder. The Integrated Development Environment appears.

Visual C++ is part of Microsoft's Visual Studio family of development products. Visual Basic, Visual J++, Visual InterDev, Visual SourceSafe, and the MSDN Library are also members of Visual Studio. The development products in Visual Studio share a common workspace called the **Integrated Development Environment** (IDE). For each instance of the IDE there is a single workspace containing one or more projects. A **project** is the application you are creating. A **workspace** is also an application, but composed of one or more projects. For example, in a large accounting system you may have one project that handles accounts receivables and another project that handles accounts payable. Both projects function as separate applications, but can also be combined to create an accounting workspace. Through the IDE you can simultaneously open projects from any combination of Visual Studio development tools. An example of the Visual C++ IDE is shown in Figure 1–5.

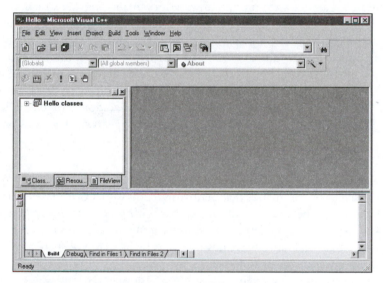

Figure 1-5   Integrated Development Environment

Your screen may not look identical to Figure 1–5.

Projects can be part of one workspace or part of more than one workspace. They can be opened individually within a new workspace or as part of an existing workspace. Any changes to the project itself are reflected in all workspaces in which the project is contained.

THE VISUAL C++ IDE

Visual C++ contains a number of different types of windows and tools used for creating, editing, and managing the various pieces of a project. For now you will concentrate on how to manage windows, projects, and files. You are also going to learn how to use the Text Editor and Output windows.

 To customize various aspects of the Visual C++ IDE, select Options from the Tools menu.

The Main Window

The Visual C++ main window includes the title bar, control menu, control buttons, status bar, menu bar, and toolbars. The **title bar** displays the name of the current workspace, in this case Hello. The control menu and control buttons are used for managing the Visual C++ main window itself. The **control menu** displays a menu of commands for moving, sizing, minimizing, maximizing, and closing the Visual C++ window. Control icons are the Minimize button, Maximize button, and the Close button. The **Minimize** button minimizes the Visual C++ main window; the **Maximize** button maximizes the Visual C++ main window; and the **Close** button exits Visual C++. The **status bar** displays various types of information about the Visual C++ environment or about the current operation. For example, if you highlight a menu command, a description of the command appears in the status bar.

Menu Bar

At the top of the Visual C++ IDE is the menu bar. The **menu bar** is a standard Windows element containing menus of commands that perform various Visual C++ tasks. A menu can be accessed by clicking a menu name in the menu bar with your left mouse button or by holding the Alt key and the menu name's underlined letter simultaneously (for example, Alt+F opens the File menu). Menu commands followed by an arrow display a submenu of additional options. Menu commands followed by an ellipsis (...) display a dialog box that prompts for further information. For example, the New... command on the File menu opens the New dialog box. Menu commands not followed by an ellipsis (...) immediately perform the specified task. For example, selecting Workspace from the View menu immediately displays the Workspace window. An example of the File menu is shown in Figure 1–6.

Figure 1-6   File menu

Menu commands that appear grayed-out, such as the Print command in Figure 1–6, are not available in the current context. In this case, the object that was highlighted when the File menu was clicked cannot be printed.

Toolbars

Toolbars contain buttons representing various Visual C++ commands. To execute a command from a Toolbar button, click the desired button once with your left mouse button. Visual C++ contains a number of built-in toolbars. Each toolbar appears automatically in the appropriate context. You can also manually display or hide each toolbar at any time, although the icons appear grayed-out if they don't apply to the current task. The Standard toolbar is shown in Figure 1–7.

Figure 1-7   The Standard toolbar

To create, delete, or customize toolbars or to change various toolbar options, select **Customize** from the **Tools** menu to display the Customize dialog box, and then select the **Toolbars** tab. An example of the Toolbars tab of the Customize dialog box is shown in Figure 1–8. You can display and hide toolbars by right clicking on an existing toolbar and selecting an item from the shortcut menu.

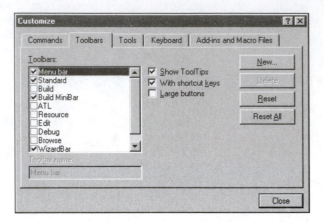

Figure 1-8   Toolbars tab of the Customize dialog box

 To display a description, or **ToolTip**, for a specific toolbar button, hold your pointer over the desired button.

To view, create, delete, or customize toolbars or to change various toolbar options:

1. Select **Customize** on the Tools menu, and then click the **Toolbars** tab. A check mark (✔) next to a toolbar name in the Toolbars list indicates that the toolbar is visible. Toolbar names that do not have a check mark next to them are not currently visible.

2. Click the **Close** button to close the Customize dialog box.

Managing Windows

With so many windows available in the IDE, it is easy for one window to hide another. As you work through this book, you will probably find it necessary to move and resize the windows on your screen. Certain types of windows in the IDE, such as the Workspace and Output window, can be floating or docked. You can drag a floating window to any part of the screen. A window set to docked "snaps" to different positions on the screen. It is usually easier to move a window with the docking property turned off. Figure 1–9 shows examples of docked and floating windows.

1

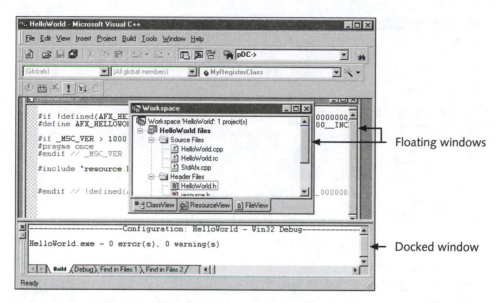

Figure 1-9   Docked and floating windows

 Docking View is not available for editing windows such as the Text Editor window.

 Windows can be arranged automatically using the Cascade, Tile Horizontally, and Tile Vertically commands on the Window menu.

To turn the docking property of a window on or off:

1. Activate a window whose docking property you want to change by clicking on the window or by selecting it from the Window menu, and then select **Docking View** from the **Window** menu. A check mark (✓) next to the Docking View menu item indicates that the property is selected. If there is no check mark next to the Docking View menu item, then the window is floating. An example of how to set a window's docking attribute is shown in Figure 1–10.

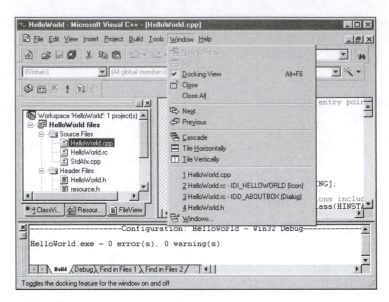

Figure 1-10   Setting a window's docking attribute

 Like windows, toolbars can be floating or docked. To dock a floating toolbar, double-click the toolbar's title bar with your left mouse button. To move a floating toolbar, position your mouse cursor over the toolbar's title bar, then hold your left mouse button and drag the toolbar to the desired position. To move a docked toolbar, position your mouse cursor over the move handle that appears on the left side of the toolbar, then hold your left mouse button and drag to the desired position.

To move a window:

1. Point to a window's **title bar** and hold your left mouse button, then **drag** to the desired position.

To resize a window:

1. Point to the side, corner, top, or bottom of a window, click and hold the left mouse button, and drag to the desired size. Make sure you get a double-arrow pointer before you actually click, hold, and drag. Dragging the top or bottom of a window resizes vertically, dragging the left or right sides resizes horizontally, and dragging a corner resizes horizontal and vertical dimensions simultaneously.

The Workspace Window

Visual C++ projects are normally composed of multiple files representing a specific type of resource or object. Two of the most common file types you will use in Visual C++ are C/C++ source files with an extension of **.cpp** and C/C++ header files with an extension of **.h**. Other types of files used in a Visual C++ project include resource files with an extension of **.rc** that are used for managing visual aspects of a program, such as dialog boxes and toolbars. You use the **Workspace window** in the IDE to manage the various projects and associated files contained in a workspace. Projects, folders, and files in the Workspace window are displayed in a hierarchical list that may remind you of Windows Explorer.

To use the Workspace window to display the contents of the Hello workspace:

1. The Workspace window should have appeared automatically when you first created the Hello project. If it did not, select **Workspace** from the **View** menu. An example of the Workspace window is shown in Figure 1–11.

Figure 1-11   Workspace window

Notice the Plus box or Minus box located to the left of the Hello project folder. The Plus box and Minus box are used for expanding and collapsing folders. The Plus box indicates that an item contains other items that are not currently displayed. The Minus box indicates that all items beneath the associated item are currently visible. Clicking the Plus box displays all files and folders contained within a folder. Clicking the Minus box hides all files and folders that are contained within a folder.

2. Click the **FileView** tab in the Workspace window. The first item in the Workspace list is the Workspace icon. Click the **Plus box** next to the **Hello files** icon located directly beneath the Workspace icon. Then, click the **Plus box** next to the **Source Files** folder. You should see three files listed beneath the Source Files folder: Hello.cpp, Hello.rc, and StdAfx.cpp. For now, do not worry about what these files are used for; we will cover the various files types used in Visual C++ throughout the course of this text.

The Plus box and Minus box are also used in Windows Explorer for expanding and collapsing drives and folders.

This workspace contains only one project named Hello. If it contained additional projects, they would be located in an alphabetical list beneath the Workspace icon.

You can also display the Workspace window by clicking the Workspace button on the Standard toolbar or pressing **Alt+0**.

Notice the three tabs that are visible at the bottom of the Workspace: ClassView, ResourceView, and FileView. The **ClassView** tab displays project files according to their classes, which are arranged as folders in the project directory. The **ResourceView** tab displays the files that are used specifically for building a Windows application. The **FileView** tab is the default view and displays a hierarchical list of all subfolders and files contained in the project's directory structure. You will work mostly with the FileView tab for the next few chapters.

Depending on the type of project, other tabs can appear in the Workspace window. For example, the ResourceView tab appears if your project contains resources such as toolbars, menus, and dialog boxes.

Files can exist within a project's directory structure and *not* be part of the project.

The Text Editor Window

Visual C++ has its own built-in text editor called the **Text Editor** window. The Text Editor window has the same text editing capabilities as other Windows text editors: you can cut and paste, drag and drop, and search for specific text strings. These and other text editing options are available on the Edit menu.

The various types of code elements in the Text Editor window are distinguished by syntax coloring. This color coding makes it easier to understand the structure and code in a C/C++ program. For example, the default syntax coloring for keywords such as `public` is blue. (You will learn about keywords in the next chapter. For now, you should understand that keywords represent some of the most basic parts of a C/C++ program.) If you need to locate a statement containing the keyword `public`, you can start by looking at just the blue text. Of course, if you know the specific text contained in the statement, it can be much easier to use the Find and Replace commands on the Edit menu. If you do not know the specific text, syntax coloring can help you greatly limit the lines that you need to examine. Consider a large word processing document in which you need to locate a piece of text. If you cannot remember the exact text string for which to search, then the Find and Replace command is useless; you would need to examine each line of text in the document manually. Manually searching for text is simpler however, if the specific type of text is indicated by color.

You can change Text Editor options, including syntax color choices, by selecting Options from the Tools menu. The Editor tab in the Options dialog box contains options for the Text Editor itself, while syntax coloring choices can be selected in the Format tab.

The Text Editor window uses a feature called **statement completion** to aid in the creation of C/C++ code. As you are writing code, member lists and parameter information display automatically according to the current object. Members refer to functions and properties that are associated with a particular class. For example, later in this text you will create a class named CCalculator that you will use to create a Windows-based calculator. You will create an object of the class named calc, which you can then use to access the CCalculator class's members. In order to access a class's members, you append a period to an object of the class. Once you append a period to an object of the class, statement completion displays a list of the class's members, as shown in Figure 1-12. You can then let Visual C++ fill in the rest of a member's name for you by double-clicking a name in the list, or by highlighting the name and pressing Enter.

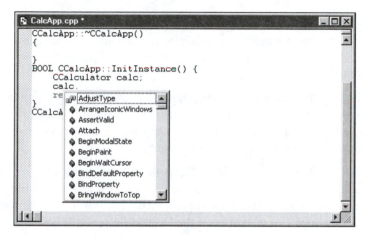

Figure 1-12   Statement completion for a class object

A parameter is a piece of information that is required by a particular function. You enter parameter information into a set of parentheses that follows a function name. Statement completion can help you fill in parameter information. For example, if you type **CreateWindow** and then type the opening parenthesis (, a list of ten parameters accepted by the CreateWindow() function appears. An example of statement completion for the CreateWindow() function's parameters is shown in Figure 1-13.

```
Hello.cpp *                                                    _ □ ×
BOOL InitInstance(HINSTANCE hInstance, int nCmdShow)
{
   HWND hWnd;

   hInst = hInstance;  // Store instance handle in our global variable

   hWnd = CreateWindow(
                       ┌──────────────────────────────────────────────────┐
   if (!hWnd)          │ HWND CreateWindow (LPCTSTR lpClassName, LPCTSTR lpWindowName, DWORD dwStyle,│
   {                   │        int x, int y, int nWidth, HWND hWndParent, HMENU hMenu,│
      return FALSE;    │        HANDLE hInstance, LPVOID lpParam)          │
   }                   └──────────────────────────────────────────────────┘

   ShowWindow(hWnd, nCmdShow);
   UpdateWindow(hWnd);

   return TRUE;
}
```

Figure 1-13 Statement completion for the CreateWindow() function's parameters

 Note Don't worry about the exact meaning of any of the functions we discuss in this chapter, or exactly how to use class members or function parameters. Simply understand that the Text Editor will assist you in the creation of your statements.

To manually display list members for a class or object, place your cursor anywhere in the class or object name and select List Members from the Edit menu or press Ctrl+Alt+T. To manually display parameter information, place your cursor anywhere in a statement and select Parameter Info from the Edit menu or press Ctrl+Shift+Space.

Another tool for writing C/C++ code is **Word Completion**, which is used to automatically complete class names and other elements according to the first few characters you type. For example, if you type the word **Create**, then press Ctrl+Space, a list containing all elements beginning with the word *Create* displays. If the letter or letters you type are unique to a specific element, Visual C++ automatically inserts that element name into your code. For example, if you type **CreateAc**, then press Ctrl+Space, the function name **CreateAcceleratorTable** is inserted into your code since this is the only element that begins with the letters *CreateAc*. You can also use Word Completion by selecting Complete Word from the Edit menu.

Next, you will open a source file in the Text Editor window and examine its contents.

To open a source file in the Text Editor window and examine its contents:

1. Return to the Workspace window in Visual C++ and double-click the filename **Hello.cpp** that should be visible beneath the Hello files icon located directly beneath the Workspace icon. The Hello.cpp source file should open in the Text Editor window as shown in Figure 1-14.

2. Scroll through the document and observe the different color coding that is applied to the various statements in the program. By default, keywords are marked in blue, comments (which are explanatory notes that you place in code) are marked in red, and standard statements are marked in black.

green

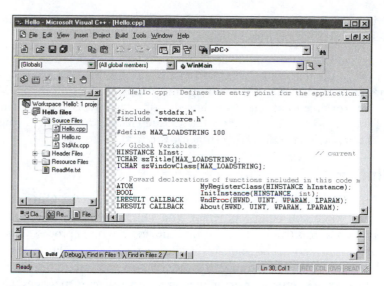

Figure 1-14   Hello.cpp in the Text Editor window

The default color choices on your computer may differ from those mentioned in this text.

3. Twenty lines from the top of the file is a statement that includes a function named WinMain(). Place your cursor anywhere within the function name and press **Ctrl+Shift+Space,** or select **Parameter Info** from the **Edit** menu. A list of parameters for the WinMain() function appears. This exercise serves only to demonstrate how you can display the parameter list after you have finished typing a statement.

4. Press **Escape** to close the Parameter Info list.

5. In about the middle of the file, you will see several statements that begin with **wcex.**. This object is based on the WNDCLASSEX class. Again, don't worry about how to use the WNDCLASSEX class at this point. Our purpose in this section is only to demonstrate the use of the Text Editor window. Place your cursor within any of the wcex object names in any of the statements, and then press **Ctrl+Alt+T,** or select **List Members** from the **Edit** menu. A list of WNDCLASSEX class members should appear. As with the Parameter Info command, this step only serves to demonstrate how to display a class's members after you have finished typing the statement.

6. Press **Escape** to close the member list.

7. Next, try transposing two lines using shortcut keys. Locate the two lines at the top of the file that read #include "stdafx.h" and #include "resource.h". Place your cursor in the bottom line (include "resource.h") and press

Alt+**Shift**+**T** to transpose the two lines. Press **Alt**+**Shift**+**T** again to switch the two lines back to their original positions.

8. Select Keyboard Map from the Help menu for a list of keyboard shortcuts that you can use in the text editor window. Practice using some of the keyboard shortcuts, along with some of the editing commands on the Edit menu. Make any changes you like to the file, including deleting statements and switching the order of statements. You must make a few drastic changes to the file—your file will need to contain at least a few errors for the next exercise.

The Output Window

At the bottom of the IDE is the Output window. Visual C++ uses the **Output window** to display its progress when you build a program. The Output window also displays build messages for any types of errors that Visual C++ finds during the build process. Although we will devote an entire chapter to debugging later in this text, you should know up front that the Output window is your first opportunity to locate bugs in your programs. There are two main types of build messages: compiler error messages and warning messages. **Compiler error messages** occur for any syntax errors in a program. Compiler error messages contain the document name where the error occurred, the line number in the document, and a description of the error. You will learn in the next chapter that functions require an opening and closing brace (}). As an example of a compiler error message, consider the following function that causes a syntax error because it is missing the closing brace (}). Figure 1-15 shows the compiler error message that displays in the Output window.

```
void CErrorsApp::incompleteFunction()
{
    CString szMessage = "Missing closing brace";
    AfxMessageBox(szMessage);
```

Figure 1-15 Output window with compiler error message

Compiler error messages should only be used to find the general location of an error in a program and not as the exact indicator of an error. You cannot always assume that the line specified by an error message is the actual problem in your program. The challenge with the description for the error message shown in Figure 1-15 is that it does not exactly say *function is missing the closing brace*. Instead, the message states *unexpected end of file found*. You need to be able to interpret each message's meaning depending on the given circumstance. In the case of the function's missing closing brace, the compiler searched through the entire source file to locate a matching closing brace for the function. The *unexpected end of file found* message was displayed because the end of the file was reached before the compiler found the closing brace.

You can quickly jump to the line that raised the build error by double-clicking the compiler error message in the Output window. After double-clicking a compiler error message, your cursor will be placed in the line that raised the error and a blue arrow will also point to the line. For example, Figure 1-16 shows the compiler error messages from the Output window in Figure 1-15 along with the Text Editor window containing the source code file. After double-clicking the compiler error message in the Output window, the line in the source file that raised the error is identified—in this case the end of the file.

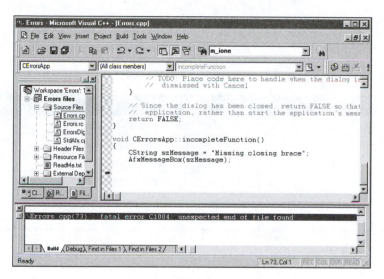

Figure 1-16   Jumping to a statement that raised a compiler error message

Warning messages occur for any potential problems that may exist in your code, but they are not serious enough to cause a compiler error message. One of the more common warning messages you may have seen occurs when you declare a variable, but do not use it in your program. For example, consider the following code:

```
void calculateProfits() {
    int iPayRate = 15;
    int iNumHours = 40;
    double dGrossPay;
    double dNetPay = (iPayRate * iNumHours) / .20;
}
```

Since the dGrossPay variable is never used, the following warning message displays in the Output window:

```
warning C4101: 'dGrossPay' : unreferenced local variable
```

An unused variable is not really a problem in a C++ program. The compiler issues a warning however, about any unused variables and other unused programming elements in order to help you write cleaner and more efficient code.

 You will study functions and variables in the next chapter.

The number and severity of warning messages displayed in the Output window is determined by the Warning Level setting in the C/C++ tab of the Project Settings dialog box. Figure 1-17 lists the warning levels and their descriptions.

Warning Level	Description
None	All warning messages are turned off
Level 1	Displays very severe warning messages
Level 2	Displays less severe warning messages
Level 3	Displays moderately severe warning messages
Level 4	Displays information warnings
Warnings as Errors	Treats all warnings as errors

Figure 1-17   Warning levels

Until you are a more experienced programmer, you should leave your warning level set to the default setting of Level 3. You may even want to consider setting your warning level to Warnings as Errors, which will help you write better code by forcing you to fix all code that raises warnings. If you want to adjust your warning level, select Settings from the Project menu, and then click the C/C++ tab in the Project Settings dialog box. Warning levels are set with the Warning Level drop-down list box and the Warnings as Errors check box. Figure 1-18 shows an example of the C/C++ tab in the Project Settings dialog box.

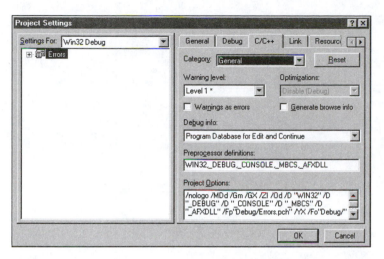

Figure 1-18   C/C++ tab in the Project Settings dialog box

Next, you will build the Hello project and observe the build messages in the Output window. The tools for building and running a program are located on the Build menu. You have two options for compiling and building an application: you can compile C/C++ source files individually using the Compile command, or you can compile all the source files in the program simultaneously and build the executable file using the Build command. You use the Compile command when you want to check your syntax while you are writing code. For small programs, it is usually easier to select the Build command to have the program compiled and built in a single step. The Compile command is useful however, if you have a large program with many C/C++ source files, since it allows you to compile only those files you have modified. Note that even if your file compiles successfully with the Compile command, you must still run the Build command to build the executable file. This text primarily uses the Build command. After running the Build command, you execute a program by selecting the Build menu's Execute command. You will not actually execute any programs in this chapter.

To build the Hello project and observe the build messages in the Output window:

1. Return to the Hello project in Visual C++.

2. Select **Build Hello.exe** from the **Build** menu. During the build process, observe the messages that display in the Output window.

3. Once your project finishes building, you should receive numerous error messages in the Output window. The number and severity of error messages you receive depends on how much editing you did to the file in the previous exercise. Figure 1-19 shows an example of some build messages that may appear in your Output window.

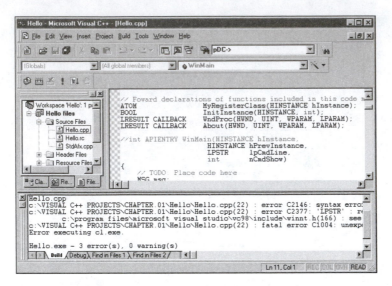

Figure 1-19   Build messages in the Output window

4. Observe the line numbers and descriptions for some of the build messages you receive in your Output window, and try to locate the line in your program that raised the error. You will not attempt to fix any of the errors you entered into your program. The purpose of this exercise is only to demonstrate how to use the Output window to find errors in your program. You will use the Output window extensively in your work with Visual C++.

MANAGING THE WORKSPACE

In this section, you will learn some basic techniques for working with the Visual C++ work-space. You will use these techniques throughout the text, so be sure that you understand them.

Adding Files to a Project

The various resources that make up projects and workspaces are contained in disk files. These include source files and the other types of files that Visual C++ uses in its projects. The files that make up your projects are stored in folders, just like any other files.

It's important that you realize that although a file may be stored in the same folder where other files in a project are stored, the file will not actually be a part of the project until you physically add it to the project. For example, consider the Workspace window displayed in Figure 1-20. The Source Files folder contains several files that are stored in a folder named Greeting files. Each of the files in the Source Files folder has already been added to the project. The Greeting files folder however, may also contain a file named HelloMoon.cpp, that you moved into the folder using Windows Explorer. The Greeting files folder would then contain the files listed in Figure 1-21. Adding the HelloMoon.cpp file to the folder using Windows Explorer does not automatically add the file to the project—you must perform that task manually.

Figure 1-20   Workspace window showing the Source Files folder

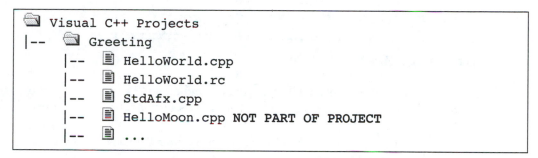

Figure 1-21   Greeting Files folder

Next, you will add a new source file to the project.

To add a new source file to the project:

1. Return to the **Hello** project in Visual C++.

2. Point to **Add To Project** on the Project menu, and then click **New** from the submenu. The New dialog box appears, opened to the Files tab, as shown in Figure 1–22.

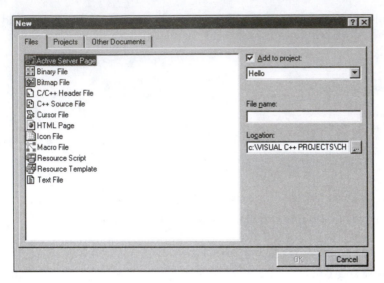

Figure 1-22   Files tab of the New dialog box

3. Click **C++ Source File** from the list, and then click in the File name box. Type **Source2** as the file name and click the **OK** button. The new file opens in the IDE.

 To add an existing file to a project, select New from the Add to Project submenu on the Project menu.

Adding Projects to a Workspace

Workspaces are composed of one or more projects. You can add new or existing projects to a workspace. For example, you may have created a project that organizes your album collection. Now you are creating a more general music collection workspace that organizes all your albums, CDs, and cassettes. Since the album project already exists, you can add it to the music collection workspace, along with the CD and cassette projects you will create. You then combine all three projects to create a single music collection workspace. This workspace is a good example of an object-oriented program. Each project is an object and you are combining them to create a larger object—the workspace.

Next you will add a new project to the current workspace:

To add a new project to the current workspace:

1. Select **New** from the **File** menu, and then click the **Projects** tab in the New dialog box.

2. In the Projects tab, select **Win32 Application**. Then assign a project a name of **Project2** and save it in the Hello folder in the Chapter.01 folder in your Visual

C++ Projects folder. Be sure the **Add to current workspace** radio button is selected beneath the Location box, and then click the **OK** button.

3. In the Win32 Application window, select **A simple Win32 application** and click the **Finish** button. The New Project Information dialog box appears. Click the **OK** button to close the New Project Information dialog box.

4. The new project appears in the Workspace window.

 You can also add a new project by right clicking the Workspace icon in the Workspace window and selecting Add New Project to Workspace from the shortcut menu.

Saving Workspaces, Projects, and Files

As you are developing a project and workspace, you need to compile and execute your programs to make sure they perform as you would like. Unfortunately, even the most well-thought-out code can cause your computer to freeze or even crash. If your computer crashes—and it probably will—you will lose any unsaved changes to your workspace. Therefore, it is good practice to save your workspace at regular intervals and especially before compiling and executing a program.

Recall that a workspace consists of one or more projects, and a project consists of one or more files. If you make changes to a file contained in a project, the file must be saved in order for the changes to be available the next time you access the file. For example, you must save any changes you make to the text in a source file. Properties and other settings for workspaces and projects are also contained in physical files on your computer. Workspace files have an extension of `.dsw` and project files have an extension of `.dsp`. You must also save projects and workspaces if you made any changes to their properties and settings.

To save the Hello workspace:

1. Select **Save Workspace** from the **File** menu.

To save individual files:

1. Activate the window containing the file you want to save or highlight the file name in the Workspace window.

2. Select **Save** from the **File** menu.

 You can also save individual files by clicking the Save icon on the Standard toolbar or by pressing Ctrl+S.

 You can save just the properties and files within an individual project by highlighting the Workspace icon or project name and clicking the Save icon or by selecting Save Workspace from the File menu.

Closing Workspaces, Projects, and Files

As you work with workspaces and projects, you might want to close the current workspace or project before opening new ones. As practice, you will now close the Hello workspace.

To close the Hello workspace:

1. Select **Close Workspace** from the **File** menu.

2. Click **Yes** when you receive a dialog box prompting you to close all document windows.

3. Before closing the workspace, Microsoft Visual Studio displays a dialog box prompting you to save any unsaved files. You will not see this dialog box if all of your files have been saved.

If you have multiple projects and files open, the Visual C++ IDE can become difficult to work with since the screen may become too crowded. Therefore, you may find it necessary to close individual projects and files when you are through working with them.

To close individual projects or files:

1. Activate the window containing the project file you want to close or highlight the project or file name in the Workspace window.

2. Select **Close** from the **File** menu.

Opening Existing Workspaces and Projects

Opening a saved workspace opens all of the projects it contains. You can also open a project independent of any workspace in which it is contained. When you open a project without opening its workspace, you open the project in a blank, empty workspace. Since the Hello workspace you are working on is composed of two projects, you are going to open the workspace instead of the individual project files.

To open the Hello workspace:

1. Select **Open Workspace** from the **File** menu. The Open Workspace dialog box appears, as shown in Figure 1–23.

2. Click the **Hello.dsw file** in the Hello folder in the Chapter.01 folder in your Visual C++ Projects folder, and then click the **Open** button.

3. Now close the workspace by selecting **Close Workspace** from the **File** menu.

1

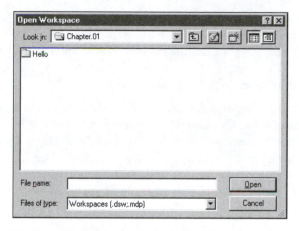

Figure 1-23   Open Workspace dialog box

Before opening a new workspace or project, Microsoft Visual Studio displays a dialog box prompting you to save any unsaved files in the currently open workspace.

You can also open existing workspaces and projects by pressing Ctrl+O. You can select recently opened workspaces and files from the Recent Workspaces submenu and the Recent Files submenu on the File menu.

Exiting Visual C++

You exit the Visual C++ IDE the same way that you exit most other Windows applications.

To exit Visual C++:

1. Select **Exit** from the **File** menu.

2. Before exiting the IDE, Microsoft Visual Studio displays a dialog box prompting you to save any unsaved files in your project. You will not see this dialog box if all of your files have been saved.

You can also exit the Visual C++ IDE by clicking the Close button on the title bar or by pressing Alt+F4.

VISUAL C++ HELP

As you work in Visual C++, there will be plenty of times when you will need to quickly access help on a particular subject. For example, you may not fully understand what a menu command does, may need help with the syntax of a code function, or would simply like to see an overview of a particular subject. At these times, it can be unproductive (and somewhat frustrating) to thumb through a book or reference guide in order to find the information that will help you. Luckily, Visual C++ (and most good Windows applications) provides several types of help resources. The primary help resources available in Visual C++ are ToolTips, the MSDN Library, context-sensitive help, and Internet help.

When you are working with toolbar buttons, it is easy to forget what command a particular button represents. **ToolTips** describe the function a button performs and can be momentarily displayed next to your mouse pointer for individual buttons. To display a ToolTip for a particular button, hold your mouse pointer over a button for a moment. The ToolTip pops up below and just to the right of your mouse pointer and stays visible until you move your mouse pointer off the button. Figure 1-24 displays an example of the ToolTip for the Open Project button on the Standard toolbar.

Figure 1-24   ToolTips

For advanced help and reference information, Visual C++ has an online help system called the **MSDN Library**. All the development tools in Visual Studio share the MSDN Library. As you recall, Visual Studio includes Visual Basic, Visual J++, Visual InterDev, and Visual SourceSafe. The Visual Studio shared online help system can be quite useful if you work with several of these development tools simultaneously or if you are using combinations of the tools to create a single application. For example, you may be developing a C++ application in Visual C++ that includes a project created in Visual InterDev. If you need help with both of these tools while creating your applications, it is much more convenient to use a consolidated help system.

The MSDN Library window contains two panes: the table of contents window and the topic window. The **Table of Contents** window contains four tabs: Contents, Index, Search, and Favorites. The **Contents** tab contains help topics in a table of contents format that is very similar to folders in Windows Explorer or the Workspace window. The **Index** tab is used for browsing a list of key words and topics. The **Search** tab allows you to search for a particular word or phrase. The **Favorites** tab contains your bookmarks for topics of particular interest to you. Help topics selected in any of the Table of Contents window tabs are displayed in the **Topic window**, which is the pane to the right of the Table of Contents window. Also available in the MSDN Library window are a menu bar and toolbar containing various navigation and topic manipulation commands and buttons. Figure 1-25 shows the MSDN Library window opened to the Contents tab and a topic entitled "What's New in Visual C++ Version 6.0."

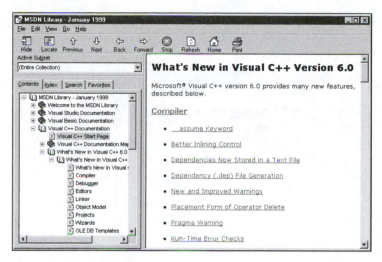

Figure 1-25   MSDN Library

In the following steps, you will open the MSDN Library, locate a topic, and create a book-mark so you can quickly return to it later.

To locate and create a bookmark for a topic in MSDN Library:

1. Start Visual C++ again.

2. Select **Search** from the **Help** menu. The MSDN Library window appears, opened to the Search tab.

 You can also display the MSDN Library's Contents tab by selecting Contents from the Help menu, and the MSDN Library's Index tab by selecting Index from the Help menu.

3. Type **Standard C++ Library** in the **Type in word(s) to search for** box, select the **Match similar words** and **Search titles only** check boxes at the bottom of the Search tab, then click the **List Topics** button. A list of topics appears in the **Select topic** list. Select one of the topics in the list and click the **Display** button. The selected topic appears in the topic window. As Figure 1-26 shows, the words you selected to search for are highlighted.

4. Click the **Favorites** tab. In the **Current topic** box at the bottom of the Favorites tab, replace the topic you selected in the last step with **My Topic** and click the **Add** button. The **My Topic** entry appears in the Topics list.

   In future MSDN Library sessions, use the Display button to show this topic. You can delete the topic by highlighting it and clicking the Remove button. Note that the Remove button does not delete the topic from the MSDN Library data-base—it only deletes the bookmark to the topic.

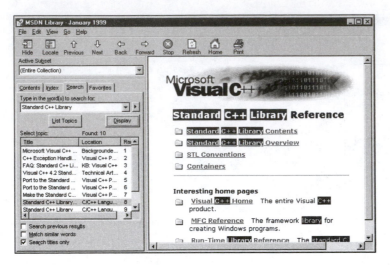

Figure 1-26   Search tab in MSDN Library

Words that are blue and underlined represent hyperlinks to other topics that are associated with the current topic. You can immediately "jump" to another topic by clicking its hyperlink.

MSDN Library also displays **context-sensitive** help for dialog boxes and programming terms. Rather than searching for a help topic yourself, MSDN Library can automatically display the help topic associated with a selected item. You display context-sensitive help by selecting a control in a dialog box, highlighting a property in the Properties window, or placing your cursor in a keyword or function in the Text Editor window and pressing the F1 key. Various windows such as the Workspace window also display context-sensitive help when you press the F1 key, and many dialog boxes contain a context-sensitive Help button. For example, if you press the F1 key or the Help button when the Projects tab of the New dialog box is open, Visual C++ displays context-sensitive help. For certain items, MSDN Library displays a list of context-sensitive help topics from which you can choose. For example, if you press the F1 key in the Text Editor window when your cursor is located somewhere within the `return` keyword, MSDN Library opens and displays the Topics Found dialog box, as illustrated in Figure 1–27.

Visual C++ help is also available on the Internet. Select Microsoft on the Web from the Help menu to access links to several useful Microsoft Web sites, including Online Support and Microsoft Developer Network Online. For a list of support options available from Microsoft, select Technical Support from the Help menu.

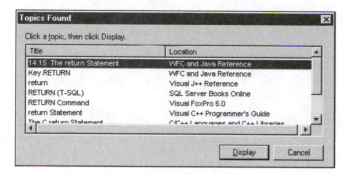

Figure 1-27   Topics Found dialog box

Do not rely too heavily on any single help option. They are all designed for specific purposes. For example, although you could look up a description of a menu command in the online help system, it is much faster to highlight the command and read the Hint displayed in the status bar. Similarly, you could look in online help for a description of a particular toolbar button—although doing so would be difficult if you did not know the function of the button in the first place. Instead, it is easier to hold your mouse pointer over a button until the ToolTip appears.

CHAPTER SUMMARY

- Creating programs or instructions that control the operation of a computer is called computer programming.

- The instructions used to create computer programs are called programming languages.

- Machine languages are the lowest level of computer languages, and programs written in machine language consist entirely of 1s and 0s that control the computer's on and off switches.

- Assembly languages perform the same tasks as machine languages, but use simplified names of instructions instead of 1s and 0s.

- High-level programming languages create computer programs using instructions that are much easier to understand than machine or assembly language code, since you use words that more clearly describe the task being performed.

- A compiler translates programming code into a low-level format.

- With procedural programming, the individual statements used in a high-level computer programming language are often grouped into logical units called procedures.

- One of the most important aspects of procedural programming is that it allows you to temporarily store pieces of information, called variables, in computer memory locations.

❏ A constant contains information, similar to a variable, except that the value contained in a constant does not change during the course of program execution.

❏ Each line in a procedural program that performs an individual task is called a statement.

❏ Object-oriented programming (OOP) refers to the creation of reusable software objects that can be easily incorporated into another program.

❏ An object is programming code and data that can be treated as an individual unit or component.

❏ Data refers to information contained within variables, constants, or other types of storage structures.

❏ The procedures associated with an object are referred to as functions or methods.

❏ Variables that are associated with an object are referred to as properties or attributes.

❏ Objects are encapsulated, which means that all code and required data are self-contained within the object itself.

❏ An interface represents elements required for a source program to communicate with an object.

❏ In object-oriented programming, code, methods, attributes, and other information are contained in a structure known as a class.

❏ An instance is an object that has been created from an existing class.

❏ Inheritance refers to the ability of an object to take on the characteristics of the class on which it is based.

❏ The original program structure you enter into a text file is referred to as source code.

❏ The compiled, machine language version of a program is called object code.

❏ C++ is currently the most popular programming language for developing graphical programs that run on platforms such as Macintosh and Windows.

❏ The standardized version of C++ is commonly referred to as ANSI C++.

❏ The ANSI C++ run-time library is also called the Standard Template Library or Standard C++ Library.

❏ Microsoft Visual C++ is a Windows-based, visual development environment for creating C and C++ applications.

❏ Visual C++ extends the C++ language by allowing you to include Microsoft Foundation Classes in your programs. Microsoft Foundation Classes, or "MFCs", are libraries of classes that can be used as the building blocks for creating Windows applications with Visual C++.

❏ Each high-level programming language, including Visual C++, has its own syntax, or rules of the language.

❑ The logic underlying any program involves executing the various parts of the program in the correct order to produce the desired results.

❑ Debugging describes the act of tracing and resolving errors in a program.

❑ The development products in Visual Studio share a common workspace called the Integrated Development Environment (IDE).

❑ For each instance of the IDE there is a single workspace containing one or more projects.

❑ A project is the application you are creating.

❑ A workspace is also an application, but composed of one or more projects.

❑ The Visual C++ main window includes the title bar, control menu, control buttons, status bar, menu bar, and toolbars.

❑ Projects in Visual C++ are directory based, meaning that all files to be included with a project must reside in a project's root directory or in sub-folders of the root directory.

❑ You use the Workspace window in the IDE to manage the various projects and associated files contained in a workspace.

❑ Visual C++ has its own built-in text editor called the Text Editor window.

❑ Visual C++ uses the Output window to display its progress when you build a program.

❑ Compiler error messages occur for any syntax errors in a program.

❑ Warning messages occur for any potential problems that may exist in your code, but that are not serious enough to cause a compiler error message.

❑ The tools for building and running a program are located on the Build menu.

❑ Although a file may be stored in the same folder where other files in a project are stored, the file will not actually be a part of the project until you physically add it.

❑ Workspaces are composed of one or more projects.

❑ You can add new or existing projects to a workspace.

❑ It is good practice to save your workspace at regular intervals and especially before compiling and executing a program.

❑ As you work with workspaces and projects, you might want to close the current workspace or project before opening new ones.

❑ Opening a saved workspace opens all of the projects it contains. You can also open a project independent of any workspace in which it is contained.

❑ Visual C++ has an online help system called MSDN Library, which all the development tools in Visual Studio share.

❑ Visual C++ help is available on the Internet. Select Microsoft on the Web from the Help menu to access links to several useful Microsoft Web sites including Online Support and Microsoft Developer Network Online.

❑ Select Technical Support from the Help menu for a list of Microsoft support options.

Review Questions

1. Machine languages write programs consisting entirely of _____.

   a. bytes

   b. 1s and 0s

   c. As and Bs

   d. magnetic pulses

2. _____ perform the same tasks as machine languages, but use simplified names of instructions instead of 1s and 0s.

   a. High-level programming languages

   b. 4GL programming languages

   c. Object-oriented machine languages

   d. Assembly languages

3. Programming languages that are closest to a computer's hardware are known as _____ languages.

   a. low-level

   b. entry-level

   c. rudimentary

   d. primitive

4. Low-level languages are _____.

   a. programming languages developed by Microsoft

   b. shared only by Windows operating systems

   c. shared by all operating systems

   d. unique to each type of CPU

5. Programming code is converted into a low-level format using a _____.

   a. modifier

   b. compiler

   c. word processor

   d. systems engineer

6. A(n) _____ translates programming code into object code.

   a. interpreter

   b. filter

   c. compiler

   d. CPU

7. The rules of a programming language are known as its _____.

   a. procedures

   b. assembly

   c. syntax

   d. logic

8. Executing the various statements and procedures of a program in the correct order to produce the desired results is called _____.

   a. reasoning

   b. directional assembly

   c. syntax

   d. logic

9. A(n) _____ refers to programming code and data that can be treated as an individual unit or component.

   a. icon

   b. procedure

   c. concealed unit

   d. object

10. In object-oriented programming, data and procedures are contained in a structure known as a _____.

   a. category

   b. container

   c. class

   d. bucket

11. The Visual C++ user interface shared with all members of Visual Studio is called _____.

   a. Project Explorer

   b. Application Programming Interface (API)

   c. Solution Developer Kit

   d. Integrated Development Environment (IDE)

12. Visual C++ projects are contained within a single _____.

    a. workspace

    b. window

    c. Visual C++ session

    d. project folder

13. _____ is used for managing the various projects and associated files in a workspace.

    a. the Properties Window

    b. Windows Explorer

    c. the Toolbox

    d. the Workspace window

14. Visual C++ uses _____ to display member lists and parameter information.

    a. build statements

    b. statement completion

    c. online help

    d. spell checking

15. Visual C++ displays build messages in the _____ window.

    a. Build

    b. Output

    c. Workspace

    d. Compile

16. _____ errors occur when you enter code that the compiler does not recognize.

    a. Application

    b. Login

    c. Runtime

    d. Syntax

17. When should you save your files?

    a. Only when you are finished

    b. After your computer crashes

    c. At regular intervals

    d. It is unnecessary to save your files

18. If you make changes to files and exit without saving them, Visual C++ _____.

    a. saves them for you

    b. prompts you to save your work

    c. discards your changes

    d. creates new copies of the files that include the changes

19. The Visual C++ online help system, MSDN Library, is shared with _____.

    a. all applications in Windows 95/98

    b. Microsoft Visual Studio

    c. Microsoft Office

    d. all applications in Windows NT

20. ToolTips are displayed for _____.

    a. object properties

    b. toolbar buttons

    c. menu commands

    d. Toolbox controls

21. Words and phrases in MSDN Library that are blue and underlined are called _____.

    a. syntax descriptions

    b. keywords

    c. comments

    d. hyperlinks

EXERCISES

1. What types of information can you think of that could be a constant or a variable? Examples of constants include your name, place of birth, and address, that is unless you move frequently. List constant values that occur in everyday life.

2. Think of a set of common, related tasks that you can create as either a procedural program or an object-oriented program. One example is cleaning your house. First, list the steps in the proper order required to run the program as a procedural program. Next, break the steps into objects that do not have to be performed in sequential order. What are the attributes and functions of these objects? Can the program be simplified by creating an instance of an existing class? What parts of the program must be run in a procedural fashion?

3. Search the Internet and make a list of vendors that market C/C++ compilers. What features are available with different vendor's compilers? Are any free compilers available? Also search online editorials and reviews and make a list of C/C++ development environments such as Visual C++. What are the advantages and disadvantages of the different development environments? Which compilers would you like to use if you were not working with Visual C++ and why?

4. Explain the difference between workspaces and projects.

5. Identify the parts of the Visual C++ IDE that are covered in this chapter. Explain what each element is used for and how it is displayed. Also identify the elements that can be customized.

6. Explain what will happen when you select the following types of menu commands:

   a. A menu command followed by an ellipsis (…)

   b. Menu commands followed by an arrow

   c. Menu commands not followed by an ellipsis (…) or arrow

   d. Grayed-out menu commands

7. Identify the different types of Visual C++ help resources and how they are accessed. Describe situations in which each type of help is most appropriate.

8. Search for the topic "workspace" in the MSDN Library. Before you start your search, select Search titles only. From the list of topics you receive, locate the topic "Viewing the Project Workspace Window " located in the Visual C++ User's Guide. Add a bookmark to the topic called "Visual C++ Workspace Window."

9. Although in this text you will only work with individual projects, your future programming studies or job situations may require that you design workspaces consisting of multiple projects. To learn how to work with a workspace consisting of multiple projects, create a new Win32 Application project named Basketball and save the Basketball project in the Chapter.01 folder on your Data Disk. Now, create a Win32 Application project named Football. When you create the new project, be sure to select the Create a New Workspace radio button before clicking the OK button in the New dialog box. Next, create three additional Win32 Application projects: Baseball, Hockey, and Soccer. When you create a project, a workspace is automatically created using the same name as the project. You can also create your own workspace however, and add existing projects to it. Create your own workspace now by selecting the New command from the File menu. When the New dialog box displays, click the Workspaces tab. In the Workspaces tab, create a new workspace named Sports. After the new workspace is created, add to it each of the sports projects you created.

2

C++ PROGRAMMING BASICS

In this chapter you will learn:

♦ About console applications
♦ About preprocessor directives
♦ About the standard output stream
♦ How to declare variables and constants
♦ How to add comments to a program
♦ About functions and scope
♦ How to work with arrays

PREVIEW: THE HELLO WORLD PROGRAM

When learning a new programming language, an old tradition among programmers is to create a first program that prints or displays the text *Hello World!*. To carry on the tradition, the first program you create in this text will be a Hello World program. The tradition of creating a Hello World program is surprisingly addictive. If you are an experienced programmer, then you have undoubtedly created Hello World programs in the past. If you are new to programming, then you will probably find yourself creating Hello World programs when you learn new programming languages in the future. The Hello World program you create in this chapter builds on the original Hello World program by also saying hello to the Sun and the Moon, as well as printing a line of scientific information about each celestial body.

To preview the Hello World program:

1. Create a **Chapter.02** folder in your Visual C++ Projects folder. (You should have created a Visual C++ Projects folder in Chapter 1.)

2. Copy the **Chapter2_HelloWorld** folder from your Data Disk to the Chapter.02 folder in your Visual C++ Projects folder, and then start Visual C++. If the Tip of the Day dialog box displays, click the **Close** button. Then select **Open Workspace** from the **File** menu and open the **HelloWorld.dsw** file from the Chapter2_HelloWorld folder in the Chapter.02 folder in your Visual C++ Projects folder.

3. Click the **FileView** tab in the Workspace window and expand the Source Files folder. Open the **HelloWorld.cpp** file in the Text Editor window, if it is not already open. The HelloWorld.cpp file contains the C++ code that executes the Hello World program. Figure 2-1 shows the HelloWorld.cpp file. The first lines you see, set off with the symbols /* and */, are called comment lines and are used for adding notes to your program. Words marked in blue in the Text Editor

45

window are called keywords and are part of the C++ programming language. Following the comments is a #include statement that gives your program access to some important run-time libraries that allow programs to display information on the screen. The statement after the #include statement declares a constant. The next three statements are called function prototypes. The statement that begins with **void main()** is a function that is required by every C++ program. You can think of it as your program's starting point. The statements that make up a function are enclosed within curly braces. The main() function's statements declare and initialize variables, call custom functions, and print information to the screen. The last three functions in the file are custom functions that are called by the main() function.

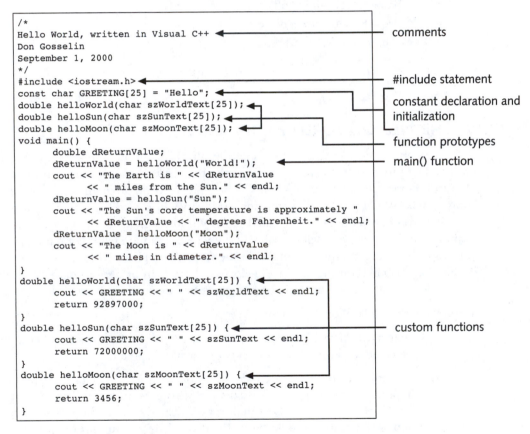

```
/*
Hello World, written in Visual C++                          comments
Don Gosselin
September 1, 2000
*/
#include <iostream.h>                                       #include statement
const char GREETING[25] = "Hello";                          constant declaration and
double helloWorld(char szWorldText[25]);                    initialization
double helloSun(char szSunText[25]);
double helloMoon(char szMoonText[25]);                      function prototypes
void main() {                                               main() function
      double dReturnValue;
      dReturnValue = helloWorld("World!");
      cout << "The Earth is " << dReturnValue
           << " miles from the Sun." << endl;
      dReturnValue = helloSun("Sun");
      cout << "The Sun's core temperature is approximately "
           << dReturnValue << " degrees Fahrenheit." << endl;
      dReturnValue = helloMoon("Moon");
      cout << "The Moon is " << dReturnValue
           << " miles in diameter." << endl;
}
double helloWorld(char szWorldText[25]) {
      cout << GREETING << " " << szWorldText << endl;
      return 92897000;
}
double helloSun(char szSunText[25]) {                       custom functions
      cout << GREETING << " " << szSunText << endl;
      return 72000000;
}
double helloMoon(char szMoonText[25]) {
      cout << GREETING << " " << szMoonText << endl;
      return 3456;
}
```

Figure 2-1   HelloWorld.cpp

4. Build the HelloWorld project by selecting **Build HelloWorld.exe** from the Build menu. When the project finishes building, execute the program by selecting **Execute HelloWorld.exe** from the Build menu. Figure 2-2 shows how the program appears.

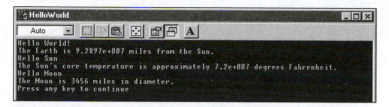

Figure 2-2   Output of Hello World program

5. Press any key to close the Hello World program window.

CONSOLE APPLICATIONS

This chapter introduces the very basics of C++ programming structure. You already know that C++ programs are constructed within text files. Now you can start examining how the actual nuts and bolts of a program are put together. In this chapter you will create C++ console applications in order to learn the basics of C++ programming. A **console application** is a program that runs within an output window, similar to an MS-DOS command prompt window. Console applications do not use any sort of graphical user interface like Windows applications do. Instead, console applications primarily output text to the screen or receive character input from the user's keyboard.

As a beginner, it is easy to become confused by the large amounts of code that are required for creating Windows applications. For this reason, you start with console applications since they are the easiest way to demonstrate simple concepts without the distraction of complex Windows code. Although the goal in this text is the creation of Windows programs, you should understand that there are many uses for console applications, particularly in utility programs that do not need the extra layers of Windows code and graphical user interface elements in order to function. Even within a Windows environment, you have probably seen several examples of console-style applications, such as installation programs and other applications that do not need a Windows interface.

Next, you will create the Hello World console application project.

To create the Hello World console application project:

1. Return to Visual C++.

2. Select **New** from the **File** menu or press **Ctrl+N** to display the New dialog box, and then click the **Projects** tab.

3. In the Projects tab, click **Win32 Console Application**.

4. Type **HelloWorld** in the Project name box. In the Location box, type **c:\Visual C++ Projects\Chapter.02\HelloWorld**, substituting c: with the name of the drive where your Visual C++ Projects folder is stored.

5. Click the **OK** button. The Win32 Console Application dialog box appears asking what type of windows application you would like to create, as shown in Figure 2-3.

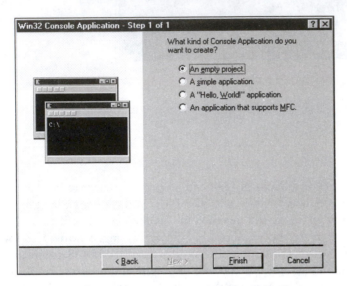

Figure 2-3   Win32Console Application dialog box

6. In the Win32 Console dialog box, select the default option, **An empty project**, and click the **Finish** button. The New Project Information dialog box appears and lists the specifications for your new project.

You may find it confusing that you selected *An empty project* in the Win32 Console Application dialog box, even though one of the choices in the dialog box is *A "Hello World" application*—and a Hello World application is exactly what you are creating in this chapter. Once you gain some basic knowledge of Visual C++, you can use the *A "Hello World" application* and the other choices in the Win32 Console application dialog box to assist you in creating applications, or to use as examples during your learning process. Console applications created with a choice other than *An empty project*, however, include code and statements that can be confusing to beginners. Feel free to experiment on your own with the other types of console application projects.

7. In the New Project Information dialog box, click the **OK** button. Visual C++ creates a new project called Hello World in the HelloWorld directory in your Visual C++ Projects folder, and then displays the IDE.

The project you just created contains no source files; only the project itself has been created. Before you can start writing code, you need to add a source file to the project. Next you will add a new source file to the Hello World program.

To add a new source file to the Hello World program:

1. Point to the **Add to Project** submenu on the **Project** menu, and then select **New**. The New dialog box displays.

2. In the New dialog box, click **C++ Source File** from the list, and then click in the **File name** box. Type **HelloWorld** as the file name. Be sure that the Add to project check box is selected and that the drop-down list beneath the check box is set to HelloWorld. Click the **OK** button. The new file opens in the Text Editor window.

PREPROCESSOR DIRECTIVES

Recall from Chapter 1 that the ANSI standards define run-time libraries, which contain useful functions, variables, constants, and other programmatic items that you can add to your programs. Before you can use any run-time libraries in your program, you must first notify the compiler that you want to use them by adding something called a header file to your program. A **header file**, or **include file**, is a file with an extension of .h that is included as part of a program and alerts the compiler that a program uses run-time libraries. One set of classes you will use extensively in the next few chapters are the iostream classes. The **iostream classes** are used for giving C++ programs input capabilities to, and output capabilities from, the computer screen and disk files, as well as for printing functions. The header file for the iostream classes is `iostream.h`. C++ header files contain information and code that allows you to access the functions, code, and data in run-time library classes. Header files get their name because they are usually placed at the "head" (beginning) of a C++ file.

You add a header file to your program using the #**include statement**. The #include statement is one of several preprocessor directives that are used with C++. The **preprocessor** is a program that runs before the compiler. When it encounters a #include statement, the preprocessor places the entire contents of the designated file into the current file. Preprocessor directives and include statements allow the current file to use any of the classes, functions, variables, and other code contained within the included file.

The syntax for adding a header file is `#include <filename.h>`. You place each preprocessor directive on its own line. You replace the filename portion of the syntax with the name of the file you want to include. The angle brackets (<>) indicate that the file is one of the C++ run-time libraries or an MFC library file. For example, to include the iostream.h file, you use the following statement:

```
#include <iostream.h>
```

Next, you will create the basic structure of the Hello World program by adding the iostream.h header file to the HelloWorld.cpp source file. You will also add a main() function to the source file. Do not worry about understanding how the main() function works. Functions are discussed extensively later in this chapter. For now, you should understand that the main() function is the starting point for every C++ program.

By default, Visual C++ version 6 uses an older version of the Standard C++ Library that requires you to use the .h extension with header files. However, a newer version of the Standard C++ Library is currently available that does not require you to use the .h extension. The new version of the Standard C++ Library includes added features and extensions to the C++ Language. Although Visual C++ version 6 uses the older Standard C++ Library by default, you can use the newer version by excluding the .h extension when you include run-time header files in your programs. For any programs you create with this text, however, you will continue to use the older version of the Standard C++ Library.

To add the iostream.h header file and a main() function to the HelloWorld.cpp source file.

1. Return to the HelloWorld.cpp source file in the Text Editor window in the HelloWorld project.

2. On the first line of the file, type **#include <iostream.h>** and press **Enter**.

3. Type the following code for the main() function:

```
void main() {
    // add code here
}
```

The // add code here statement in the preceding step is called a comment. You will learn about comments later in this chapter.

STANDARD OUTPUT STREAM

Now that you have created the shell of the Hello World program, you will start adding code to make the program work. One of the first coding skills you need to learn when studying a programming language is how to output text to the computer screen. Figure 2-4 shows an example of the output from a simple console application.

Figure 2-4   Simple console application

The text you see in Figure 2-4 is created by sending data to the standard output stream. The **standard output stream** is the destination—usually a screen, file, or printer—for text output. The standard output stream is part of the iostream classes of the standard C++ library. For your purposes, the standard output stream is the console application window.

To send text to the standard output stream, you use the cout (for console output) object. The **cout** object is used for outputting text to the console application window. You must add the

2

iostream.h header file to your program in order to use the C++ standard output stream's cout object. To send data to the standard output stream in C++, you use a statement similar to `cout << "text";`. The insertion operator, `<<`, is used for sending text to an output device, such as a computer screen, file, or printer. It tells the compiler to send the text on the right side of the statement to the standard output stream (represented by cout) on the left side of the statement.

The text portion of the statement is called a text string. A **text string**, or **literal string**, is text that is contained within double quotation marks. The text string that is sent to the cout object is the text that is printed to the standard output stream. When you want to include a quoted string within a literal string, you surround the quoted text with single quotation marks. For example, `cout << "this is a 'text' string";` writes the text *this is a 'text' string* to the standard output stream. You can send multiple text strings to the standard output stream, provided they are separated by `<<` operators. The statement `cout << "My " << "name " << "is " << "Don Gosselin";` writes the text *My name is Don Gosselin* to the screen.

If you want to add line breaks between text that are output to the screen, you use the endl i/o manipulator. The **endl i/o manipulator** is part of the iostream classes and represents a new line character. An **i/o manipulator** is a special function that can be used with an i/o statement.

The abbreviation i/o stands for input/output.

The following code shows how to print multiple statements to the standard output stream, separated by line breaks using the endl i/o manipulator:

```
cout << "Program type: console application" << endl;
cout << "Created with: Visual C++" << endl;
cout << "Programmer: Don Gosselin" << endl;
```

Notice that each statement in the preceding example ends with a semicolon. All statements in C++ must end with a semicolon. A statement is not necessarily a single line of code; large statements can span multiple lines of text. For example, the following statement spans multiple lines of code, yet only includes a single semicolon at the end of the last line:

```
cout << "We, the people of the United States, "
<< "in order to form a more perfect Union, "
<< "establish justice, insure domestic tranquility, "
<< "provide for the common defense, "
<< "promote the general welfare, "
<< "and secure the blessings of liberty "
<< "to ourselves and our posterity, "
<< "do ordain and establish this Constitution "
<< "for the United States of America.";
```

You cannot break text strings; all text strings must exist on the same line and include opening and closing quotation marks. If you insert a break in a text string, you will receive a compiler error.

One of the few types of C++ statements that do not end in semicolons are the preprocessor statements you studied earlier.

You can also place multiple statements on the same line, provided they are separated by semi-colons, as in the following example:

```
cout << "Boston is "; cout << "in Massachusetts.";
```

Next, you will add to the Hello World program several cout statements that print text to the screen. Before you do, it is important to keep in mind that the C++ programming language is case sensitive. For example, the statement `Cout << "My name is Don Gosselin";` will cause an error when you build the project since the compiler does not recognize an object named Cout with an uppercase C; you must enter cout in all lowercase letters. Similarly, the following misspelled statements will cause an error:

```
COUT << "My name is Don Gosselin";
CoUt << "My name is Don Gosselin";
CouT << "My name is Don Gosselin";
```

To add cout statements to the Hello World program.

1. Return to the HelloWorld.cpp source file in the Text Editor window in the HelloWorld project.

2. Replace the `// add code here` statement with the following cout statements:

```
cout << "Hello World!" << endl;
cout << "Hello Sun!" << endl;
cout << "Hello Moon!" << endl;
```

The Hello World program is now essentially complete. Before executing the program, however, you must compile it and build the HelloWorld.exe file.

To build and execute the Hello World program:

1. Return to the HelloWorld project.

2. Select **Build HelloWorld.exe** from the Build menu. You can view the progress of the compilation and build procedures in the Output window at the bottom of the screen. If your program compiles and builds successfully, the Output window displays the message `HelloWorld.exe – 0 error(s), 0 warning(s)`.

If you receive compilation errors, examine the messages displayed in the Output window. Common errors include using the wrong case and forgetting to end each statement with a semicolon.

3. After your project compiles successfully, run the program by selecting **Execute HelloWorld.exe** from the **Build** menu. A command window opens and displays the three text strings, as shown in Figure 2-5.

2

Figure 2-5   Output of Hello World program

4. Press any key to close the command window.

Using cout is the C++ way of writing to the standard output stream, and that is the output method you will use throughout this text. In contrast, in the C language, you write to the standard output stream with the printf() function of the standard input/out (stdio) class. To use the printf() function, you must add the `stdio.h` header file to your program. Although we do not use the printf() function in this textbook, it is important that you understand it because many programmers prefer this method over using the C++ iostream classes. Throughout your career as a C++ programmer, you will certainly see printf() used. If you would like more information on how to use the printf() function, search for the *printf* function topic in the MSDN Library.

VARIABLES

One of the most important aspects of programming is storing and manipulating the values stored in variables. In C++, you create variables using the syntax *type name;*. The *type* portion of the syntax refers to the data type of the variable. The data type used to create a variable determines the type of information that can be stored in the variable. You will learn about data types shortly. For now, you will learn about a single data type, the integer data type, in order to understand and work with variables. The **integer data type** stores positive or negative numbers with no decimal places or the value 0. You declare an integer data type using the `int` keyword.

Reserved words or **keywords** are part of the C++ language syntax. Figure 2-6 lists the C++ reserved words. Reserved words with leading underscores are Microsoft extensions.

__asm	else	main	struct
__assume	enum	__multiple_inheritance	switch
auto	__except	__single_inheritance	template
__based	explicit	__virtual_inheritance	this
bool	extern	mutable	thread
break	false	naked	throw
case	__fastcall	namespace	true
catch	__finally	new	try
__cdecl	float	noreturn	__try
char	for	operator	typedef
class	friend	private	typeid
const	goto	protected	typename
const_cast	if	public	union
continue	inline	register	unsigned
__declspec	__inline	reinterpret_cast	using declaration, using directive
default	int	return	uuid
delete	__int8	short	__uuidof
dllexport	__int16	signed	virtual
dllimport	__int32	sizeof	void
do	__int64	static	volatile
double	__leave	static_cast	wmain
dynamic_cast	long	__stdcall	while

Figure 2-6   C++ reserved words

Using a statement similar to `int myVariable;` to create a variable is called **declaring** the variable. You can assign a value to a variable at declaration using the syntax `int myVariable = value;`. The equal sign in a variable declaration assigns a value to the variable and is called the assignment operator. This usage is different from the standard usage of the equal sign in an algebraic formula. The value you assign to a declared variable must be appropriate for its data type or you will receive an error message when you compile the project. For example, you must assign to an integer variable a positive or negative number with no decimal places using a statement similar to `int myVariable = 100;`. The values you assign to integer data types and other numeric data types are called **literal values**, or **literals**. When assigning literal values to a numeric data type, you do *not* surround the value with quotation marks.

The name you assign to a variable is called an **identifier**, or **variable name**. Identifiers must begin with an uppercase or lowercase ASCII letter or an underscore (_). You can use numbers in an identifier, but not as the first character. You are not allowed to use special characters such as $, &, *, or %.

C++ does not allow you to use a number as the first character in an identifier in order to easily distinguish between an identifier and a literal value.

There are some rules and conventions you need to follow when naming a variable. Reserved words cannot be used for variable names, and you cannot use spaces within a variable name. Common practice is to use an underscore (_) character to separate individual words within a variable name, as in `my_variable_name`. Another common practice is to use a lowercase letter for the first letter of the first word in a variable name, with subsequent words starting with an initial cap, as in `myVariableName`. Figure 2-7 lists examples of some legal and illegal variable names.

Legal Variable Names	Illegal Variable Names
my_variable	%my_variable
MyVariable	1my_variable
MyVariable	#my_variable
_my_variable	@my_variable
my_variable_example	~my_variable
MyVariableExample	+my_variable

Figure 2-7   Examples of legal and illegal variable names

Variable names, like other C++ code, are case sensitive. Therefore, the variable name myVariable contains different values than variables named myvariable, MyVariable, or MYVARIABLE. If you receive an error when compiling a C++ program, be sure that you are using the correct case when referring to any variables you have declared.

Although you can assign a value when a variable is declared, you are not required to do so. Your program may assign the value later, or you may use a variable to store user input. If you do not initialize your variables, however, then they will not contain any data. This can cause problems because you will receive errors if your program attempts to use any variables that have not been initialized. Therefore, it is good practice to always initialize your variables when you declare them. This can be as simple as assigning a value of 0 to a numeric variable at declaration time. Regardless of whether you assign a value to a variable when it is declared, you can change the variable's value at any point in a program using a statement that includes the variable's name, followed by an assignment operator (=), followed by the value you want to assign to the variable. The following code declares an int variable named salary, assigns to it an initial value of 25,000, and prints it using the cout object. The third statement changes the value of the salary variable to 30,000, and the fourth statement prints the new value. The salary variable is declared only once in the first statement.

```
int salary = 25000;
cout << salary << endl;
salary = 30000;
cout << salary << endl;
```

Data Types

Variables can contain many different kinds of values, not just integer values, such as the time, a dollar amount, or a person's name. The values, or data, contained in C++ variables are classified by categories known as data types. A **data type** is the specific category of information that a variable contains. The concept of data types is often difficult for beginning programmers to grasp because in real life you don't often distinguish among different types of information. If someone asks you for your name, how old you are, or what the current time is, it makes no difference to you that your name is a text string and that your age and the current time are types of numbers. However, the specific data type of a variable is very important to a programming language because it helps determine how much memory to allocate for the data, as well as the types of operations that can be performed on a variable. Additionally, data types force you to assign the appropriate value to a variable to help prevent programming errors. For instance, consider a variable named weeklySalary that you use to calculate net pay. If a programming language allowed you to assign an inappropriate value, say the employee's name, to the weeklySalary variable, if you later attempted to use the variable in a calculation you would receive an error message or incorrect result, since text cannot be used in numeric calculations. Data types help prevent these kinds of errors from occurring.

Data types that can be assigned only a single value are called **fundamental types** or **primitive types**. The fundamental types supported in C++ are described in Figure 2-8.

Data Type	Description	Example
bool	An integer type that stores a logical value of true or false.	true or false
char	Any single character contained within single quotation marks or a numeric Unicode character. Char variables occupy one byte.	'A', 'B', 'C', and so on. The letters A, B, and C are represented in Unicode as 65, 66, and 67, respectively.
int, long int	A four byte whole number	A value between −2,147,483,648 and 2,147,483,647
short	A two byte whole number	A value between −32,768 and 32,767
float	A four byte floating point number	A value between −3.4E+38 and 3.4E+38
double, long double	An eight byte floating point number	A value between −1.7E+308 and 1.7E308

Figure 2-8   Fundamental C++ data types and their data ranges on 32-bit Windows operating systems

The values that can be assigned to fundamental types vary according to platform. The values shown in Figure 2-8 are for 32-bit Windows operating systems.

C++ includes many advanced data types including arrays, pointers, references, and structures. Advanced data types can contain multiple values or complex types of information, as opposed to the single values contained in fundamental data types. You will learn about several advanced data types throughout the course of this text.

You may occasionally see data type sizes described using bits instead of bytes. Since eight bits is the equivalent of one byte, a 32-bit int data type is the same as a four byte int data type.

Many programming languages require that you declare the type of data that a variable contains. Programming languages that require you to declare the data types of variables are called **strongly-typed programming languages**. Strong typing is also known as **static typing,** since data types cannot change after they have been declared. Programming languages that do not require you to declare the data types of variables are called **loosely-typed programming languages**. Loose typing is also known as **dynamic typing,** since data types can change after they have been declared. C++ is a strongly-typed programming language. When you declare a variable in C++, you *must* designate a data type. The value contained in a variable can be assigned at declaration or later in the code. You designate a data type by placing the data type name in front of the variable name. The following code illustrates how to declare several different types of variables:

```
int integerVariable = 1157683648;
bool trueOrFalse = true;
char charVariable = 'A';
short shortVariable = 100;
float floatVariable = 2.4e5;
double doubleVariable = 7.2e24;
```

Hungarian Notation

As you learned earlier, you can use any name you like for a variable, provided it doesn't include spaces or special characters, is not a keyword, and starts with a letter or an underscore (_). Variable names, however, do not automatically tell you the variable's data type— and knowing a variable's data type is extremely important when it comes to arithmetic calculations or any type of operation for which you need to assign a new value to a variable. For example, if you attempt to use a char variable in an arithmetic calculation, you will receive a compile error since you cannot perform calculations with text. If you have a very long program, you may find it difficult to remember a variable's data type, or even locate the variable declaration in order to determine the data type. Determining a variable's data type is even more difficult when you are working with a program written by another programmer.

Many C++ programmers use Hungarian notation to easily identify a variable's data type. Dr. Charles Simonyi of Microsoft invented **Hungarian notation** as a variable naming convention for identifying the data types of variables. (Hungarian notation gets its name because Simonyi is Hungarian.) With Hungarian notation, you begin each variable name with a prefix that identifies the data type. For example, the prefix for the integer data type is *i*. If the variable names in a program conform to Hungarian notation then any programmer can clearly identify a variable named, for example, iNetPay as an integer data type. Figure 2-9 lists the common prefixes of Hungarian notation.

Prefix	Data Type
c	char
i	integer
si	short integer
li	long integer
f	float
d	double
s	string of characters
sz	string of characters, terminated by a null character
b	bool
by	single byte
ct	an integer being used as a counter
p	pointer
ar	array
fn, m	function, method

Figure 2-9   Common Hungarian notation prefixes

From this point forward, this text uses Hungarian notation when creating variable names. Remember that Hungarian notation is just a convention; you are not required to use it. You can use any naming convention you like, provided you do not violate any of the rules for identifiers. Hungarian notation, however, is an accepted standard. Using it ensures that other programmers will be able to more easily understand and interpret your code—provided they know the Hungarian notation themselves. Similarly, you will be able to more easily work with other programmer's code if you know the Hungarian notation standard.

Integers

Numeric data types are an important part of any programming language, and are particularly useful when doing arithmetic calculations. C++ supports two numeric data types: integers and floating-point numbers. An **integer** is a positive or negative number with no decimal places. The numbers −250, −13, 0, 2, 6, 10, 100, and 10000 are examples of integers. The data types bool, char, int, long int, and short are all integer data types because they only accept whole numbers with no decimal places. In deciding which integer data type to use, you should always select the smallest type possible in order to conserve memory resources. For example, the short data type takes up only two bytes, while the int data type

2

takes up four bytes. If your variable only needs to store numbers between −32,768 and 32,767, then you should use the short data type instead of the unnecessarily larger int data type.

Although bool and char are considered to be integer data types, the values you can assign to them do not necessarily have to be whole numbers. For example, you can assign a value of *true* to a bool variable. The values assigned to the bool and char data types, however, are converted to whole numbers, or integers, before they are stored.

You will learn more about the bool and char data types later in this section.

By default, integer variables are created with the **signed type modifier**, which allows integers to store both positive and negative numbers. You can specifically designate that an integer is signed using a statement similar to `signed int iVariable;`. However, because integers are signed by default, the statement `int iVariable;` (without the signed type modifier) is equivalent to `signed int iVariable;`.

If you are sure that your integer variable does not need to hold negative numbers, you can used the unsigned type modifier. The **unsigned type modifier** restricts the values assigned to integer variables to positive numbers. To restrict an integer variable to positive numbers, use a statement similar to `unsigned int iVariable;`. Note that when you use the unsigned type modifier, you actually change the range of numbers that can be assigned to the variable. For example, the default range for signed short data types is −32,768 to 32,767. This range means that a short variable can be assigned any of 65,535 numbers—the amount of numbers in the range. However, if you use the unsigned type modifier, which restricts the variable's values to positive numbers, with a short variable using a statement similar to `unsigned short iVariable;`, then the range of numbers that can be accepted by the short variable becomes 0 to 65,535.

Integers can be written as decimal numbers, octal numbers, and hexadecimal numbers. **Decimal numbers** are the standard numbers used in everyday life that are based on a value of ten and do not include a leading 0. Numbers written as decimal integers include 1, 5, 7, 22, and 100. An **octal number** is based on a value of 8 and always begins with a 0 to inform Visual C++ that it is an octal number. Only the numerals 0 through 7 are used with octal numbers. **Hexadecimal numbers** are based on a value of 16 and always begin with the characters 0x or 0X, followed by hexadecimal digits. The numbers 0 through 9 are represented by the numerals 0 through 9 and the numbers 10 through 15 are represented by the letters *A* through *F*. In this text, you will write your integers as decimal numbers.

Floating-Point Numbers

A **floating-point number** contains decimal places or is written using exponential notation. The numbers −6.16, −4.4, 3.17, .52, 10.5, and 2.7541 are all examples of simple floating-point numbers because they contain decimal places. The data types float, double, and long double all contain floating-point numbers. As with the different integer data types, you should use the smallest floating-point type possible in order to conserve memory resources.

Exponential notation, or **scientific notation**, is a way of writing very large numbers or numbers with many decimal places using a shortened format. Numbers written in exponential notation are represented by a value between 1 and 10, multiplied by 10, and raised to some power. The value of 10 is written with an uppercase or lowercase *E*. For example, the number 200,000,000,000 can be written in exponential notation as 2.0e11, which means "2 times 10 to the eleventh power."

The signed and unsigned type modifiers are not used with floating-point variables.

The Character Data Type and Strings

Up to this point, the data types you have seen store only numbers. To store text, you use the **character data type**. You declare a character data type using the reserved word `char`. In contrast to numeric data types, the value you assign to a character data type must be enclosed within quotation marks. To store one character in a variable, you use the char keyword and place the character in single quotation marks. For example, you can assign the letter *A* to a char variable named cLetter using the statement `char cLetter = 'A';`. If you need to declare a char variable that will contain multiple characters without assigning a value to it, you can use the statement `char variable[number];`, replacing *number* with the maximum number of characters that will be assigned to the variable. For example, the statement `char szString[50];` creates a char variable named szString that can contain up to 50 characters.

Although you use the char data type to store characters, it is actually an integer data type. For this reason, values assigned to a char variable are stored as **Unicode characters**, which are numeric representations of all known characters. You can assign a Unicode character directly to a char variable instead of assigning characters contained in single quotation marks. For example, the statement `char cLetter = 65;` assigns the letter *A* to the cLetter variable since the Unicode character for the letter *A* is 65. Note that when you use a Unicode character, you do not place the value within single quotation marks. Regardless of whether you assign a character in single quotation marks or a Unicode character to a char variable, when you retrieve the value of a char variable using a statement such as `cout << cLetter << endl;`, the letter value *A* is returned (assuming *A* was assigned to the cLetter variable).

In most circumstances, it is usually easier to assign a letter in single quotation marks to a char variable rather than having to look up the appropriate Unicode character.

When you assign a text string to a char variable, C++ automatically adds to the end of the string an extra character called a **null character**, which is represented by \0. The null character marks the end of the text string. You need to be aware of the null character because it uses the last character space in the number of characters you designate for your char variables. For example, the following code declares a char variable named szProgramming that can accept up to ten characters. The szProgramming variable is then assigned a value of *Visual C++*, which consists of ten characters.

```
char szProgramming[10]
szProgramming = "Visual C++";
```

If you attempt to compile the preceding code, you will receive an error because there is insufficient space in the variable to store the ten characters of the Visual C++ string, plus the null character. To make the code work, you need to change the szProgramming variable declaration so that it can contain eleven characters instead of ten.

Another reason to be aware of the null character is because it determines the type of prefix you use with the Hungarian notation naming standard. For single char variables, you add a prefix of *c* to the variable name. For string variables that are terminated by a null character, you add a prefix of *sz* to the variable name. The following code contains declarations for both a single char variable and a string char variable:

```
char cLetter = 'J';
char szString[25] = "This is a text string.";
```

Next, you will modify the Hello World program so that the text strings are stored in char variables.

To modify the Hello World program so that the text strings are stored in char variables:

1. Return to the **HelloWorld.cpp** source file in the Text Editor window in the HelloWorld project.

2. Above the first cout statement, add the following statements that declare variables for each of the text strings.

```
char szWorldText[25] = "Hello World!";
char szSunText[25] = "Hello Sun!";
char szMoonText[25] = "Hello Moon!";
```

3. Replace the text strings in each of the three cout statements with the name of the appropriate variable, as follows:

```
cout << szWorldText << endl;
cout << szSunText << endl;
cout << szMoonText << endl;
```

4. Rebuild and execute the program. The console window should appear the same as in Figure 2-5.

5. Press any key to close the console window.

The Escape Character and Escape Sequences

Since the char data type is commonly used to store text strings and you will be using text strings often in your programs, you need to understand a little more of how strings work in C++. As you know, a text string, or literal string, is text that is contained within double quotation marks. Examples of strings you may use in a program are company names, user names, and other types of text. You can use text strings as literal values or assign them to a variable.

If you want to include special characters inside a text string, you need to do so with extra care. Consider the following statement:

```
char szString[100] = "Connecticut's state flower is called
"Mountain Laurel"";
```

This statement causes an error. The Visual C++ compiler assumes that the literal string ends with the double quotation mark before *Mountain*. To get around this problem, you include an escape character before the double quotation marks. An **escape character** tells the compiler or interpreter that the character that follows it has a special purpose. In C++ the escape character is the backslash (\). Placing a backslash in front of a special character tells the C++ compiler that the double quotation mark is to be treated as a regular keyboard character, such as a, b, 1, or 2. The backslashes in the following statement tell the Visual C++ compiler to treat the double quotation marks surrounding *Mountain Laurel* as regular keyboard characters.

```
char cString[100] = "Connecticut's state flower is called
\"Mountain Laurel\"";
```

You can also use the escape character in combination with other characters to insert a special character into a string. When you combine the escape character with other characters the combination is called an **escape sequence**. The backslash followed by a double quotation mark (\") is an example of an escape sequence. Most escape sequences carry out special functions. For example, the escape sequence \t inserts a tab into a string. The null character (\0) you saw earlier is also an example of an escape sequence. Figure 2-10 describes some of the escape sequences that can be added to a string in C++.

Escape Sequence	Character
\b	Backspace
\n	New line
\r	Carriage return
\t	Horizontal tab
\'	Single quotation mark
\"	Double quotation mark
\\	Backslash

Figure 2-10   Escape sequences

Notice that one of the characters generated by an escape sequence is the backslash. Since the escape character itself is a backslash, to include a backslash as a character in a string you must use the escape sequence "\\". For example, to include the path "C:\Visual C++ Projects\" in a string, you must include two backslashes for every single backslash you want to appear in the string, as in the following statement:

```
char cString[100] = "My C++ files are located in C:\\Visual
C++ Projects\\";
```

Figure 2-11 shows an example of a program containing strings with several escape sequences. Figure 2-12 shows the output.

```
#include <iostream.h>
void main() {
    cout << "This line is printed \non two lines." << endl;
    cout << "\tThis line includes a horizontal tab." << endl;
    cout << "My personal files are in c:\\personal." << endl;
    cout << "My dog's name is \"Noah.\"" << endl;
}
```

Figure 2-11   Program containing strings with escape sequences

Figure 2-12   Output of program containing strings with escape sequences

Boolean Values

A **Boolean value** is a logical value of true or false. You can also think of a Boolean value as being *yes* or *no*, or *on* or *off*. In C++, you use the bool data type to contain Boolean values. You can use the words *true* and *false* to indicate Boolean values. You can also use 1 to indicate true or 0 to indicate false. Actually, any integer value other than 0 evaluates to true. However, most programmers use the value 1 or –1 to indicate a value of true. Note that if you use the words *true* or *false*, they are converted to the values 1 or 0 before they are stored in the variable. The following code creates a bool variable and assigns several values to it:

```
bool bVariable;
bVariable = true;    // assigns a value of true
bVariable = false;   // assigns a value of false
bVariable = 1;       // also assigns a value of true
bVariable = 0;       // also assigns a value of false
bVariable = -1;      // also assigns a value of true
```

Boolean values get their name from the nineteenth-century mathematician George Boole, who developed the theories of mathematical logic.

Type Casting

A variable's data type cannot change during the course of program execution. If you attempt to assign a different data type to a variable, you generate an error. If you need to use the contents of a variable as a different data type, you must cast the variable to a new data type. **Casting**, or **type casting**, copies the value contained in a variable of one data type into a variable of another data type. The C++ syntax for casting variables is *variable = new_type (old_variable);*. The new_type portion of the syntax is the keyword representing the type to which you want to cast the variable. Note that casting does not change the data type of the original variable. Rather, casting copies the data from the old variable, converts it to the target variable's data type, and then assigns the value to the new variable. The following code casts an integer variable named *intNumber* to a float variable named *floatNumber*:

```
int iNumber = 100;
float fNumber;
fNumber = float (iNumber);
```

You can also use the older C syntax for casting variables, *variable = (new_type) old_variable;*. This text, however, uses the C++ version.

If you do not explicitly cast a variable of one data type to another data type, then Visual C++ will attempt to automatically perform the cast for you. For example, the following code is identical to the preceding example, except that the intNumber variable is not cast to the float data type before its value is assigned to fNumber. Although you will receive a warning when you compile the program, the value of iNumber will be automatically cast to the float type and assigned to the fNumber variable.

```
int iNumber = 100;
float fNumber;
fNumber = iNumber;
```

How the Visual C++ compiler automatically converts data types is a fairly complex process. If you anticipate that your program will perform operations using multiple data types, you should always manually cast a variable's data type before assigning its value to a variable of another data type.

Regardless of whether your program uses explicit type casting or automatic type casting, you need to be careful when assigning larger data types to smaller ones. For example, the short data type holds values up to 32,768, whereas the int data type holds values up to

2

2,147,483,648. If you attempt to assign the contents of an int variable to a short variable, and the int variable's value is less than or equal to 32,768, then the assignment will be successful. If you attempt to assign to a short variable a value larger than 32,768, however, the value assigned to the short variable will be truncated. Similarly, if you attempt to assign the value of a float variable to an int variable, the float variable value's fractional portion will be lost since the int data type stores only whole numbers.

Constants

As you learned in Chapter 1, a constant contains information that does not change during the course of program execution. There are two methods of creating constants in C++: the #define statement or the const keyword.

The **#define statement** is a preprocessor directive that defines a constant. You place a #define statement at the beginning of a file, just like the #include statement. The syntax for using the #define statement is `#define NAME value`. For example, to create a constant named COMPANY_NAME that contains the constant value *My Company Name*, you use the statement `#define COMPANY_NAME "My Company Name"`. You do not use an equal sign (=) to assign the value to the constant name. Also, as with other preprocessor directives, you do not include a semicolon at the end of the statement. It is common practice to use all uppercase letters for constant names. The following code contains a simple program that defines the COMPANY_NAME constant and outputs the results using cout:

```
#include <iostream.h>
#define COMPANY_NAME "My Company Name"
void main() {
    cout << COMPANY_NAME << endl;
}
```

Next, you will use the #define statement to create a constant containing the text *Hello*. You will then combine the constant with text strings that are output to the console window.

To use the #define statement to create a constant containing the text Hello:

1. Return to the **HelloWorld.cpp** source file in the Text Editor window in the HelloWorld project.

2. Place your cursor at the end of the #include statement, press **Enter** to create a new line, and then add the following #define statement to declare a constant named GREETING:

```
#define GREETING "Hello"
```

3. Remove the word Hello and the space from the three variable declaration statements so they read as follows:

```
char szWorldText[25] = "World!";
char szSunText[25] = "Sun!";
char szMoonText[25] = "Moon!";
```

4. Modify the output statements as follows, so that they output the GREETING constant, a text string consisting of a single space, and the variable:

```
cout << GREETING << " " << szWorldText << endl;
cout << GREETING << " " << szSunText << endl;
cout << GREETING << " " << szMoonText << endl;
```

5. Rebuild and execute the program. The console window should appear the same as it did before you added the constant.

6. Press any key to close the console window.

You can also create a constant by placing the **const keyword** before the data type in a variable declaration. For example, the statement `const char COMPANY_NAME[25] = "My Company";` also creates the COMPANY_NAME constant. The following code contains the same simple program that declares and outputs the COMPANY_NAME constant, but this time using the const keyword:

```
#include <iostream.h>
const char COMPANY_NAME[25] = "My Company";
void main() {
    cout << COMPANY_NAME << endl;
}
```

Next, you will use the const keyword instead of the #define statement to create a constant containing the text *Hello*. You will then combine the constant with text strings that are output to the console window.

To modify the Hello World program so that it creates a constant with the const keyword instead of the with the #define statement:

1. Return to the **HelloWorld.cpp** source file in the Text Editor window.

2. Modify the `#define GREETING "Hello"` so that it reads
   `const char GREETING[25] = "Hello";`.

 Placing a variable or constant declaration outside of a function gives it global scope. You will study scope at the end of this chapter.

3. Rebuild and test the program. The program should function the same as it did with the #define statement constant.

The #define statement is the oldest method of creating constants in C++. However, the const method is the preferred method of creating constants for two reasons. First, the #define method does not allow you to declare the data type of the constant. You will learn in the next section how important data types are to a high-level programming language. Second, the #define method can be confusing since it does not use standard C++ statement syntax, such as an equal sign, to assign the value to the constant name, or a semicolon to end the statement.

The #define statement is discussed here because some programmers still use it to create constants, and you need to be able to recognize it in a program if you ever come across it.

2

ADDING COMMENTS TO A PROGRAM

When you create a program, whether it is with C++ or any other programming language, it is considered good programming practice to add comments to your code. **Comments** are non-executing lines that you place in your code that contain various types of remarks, including the name of the program, your name, and the date you created the program, notes to yourself, or instructions to future programmers who may need to modify your work. When you are working with long programs, comments make it easier to decipher how the program is structured.

Visual C++ supports two types of comments: line comments and block comments. C++ **line comments** are created by adding two slashes // before the text you want to use as a comment. The // characters instruct the compiler to ignore all text to the end of the line. Line comments can appear at the end of a line of code, or they can exist on an entire line by themselves. C-style **Block comments** span multiple lines and are created by adding /* to the first line that is to be included in the block. You close a block comment by typing */ after the last text to be included in the block. The compiler ignores any text or lines between the opening /* characters and the closing */ characters. Figure 2-13 displays a function containing line and block comments.

```
void main() {
    /*
    This line is part of the block comment.
    This line is also part of the block comment.
    */
    cout << "Line comment 1";    // Line comments can
    cout << "Line comment 2";    // follow code statements
    // This line comment takes up an entire line.
}
```

Figure 2-13   Function with line and block comments

Next, you will add comments to the Hello World program.

1. Return to the **HelloWorld.cpp** source file in the Text Editor window.

2. In the HelloWorld.cpp source file, place your cursor above the #include directive, press **Enter**, and add the following comment block. Be sure to replace *your name* and *today's date* with your own name and the date on which you create the program.

```
/*
Hello World, written in Visual C++
your name
today's date
*/
```

 When you create comments in your C++ programs, be sure to use a forward slash (/) and not a backward slash (\). People often confuse these two characters.

3. Above the statement that declares the szWorldText variable, insert a line comment that reads **// variable declarations**.

4. Above the first cout statement, insert another line comment that reads **// output section**. Your code should appear similar to Figure 2-14.

```
/*
Hello World, written in Visual C++
Don Gosselin
September 1, 2000
*/
#include <iostream.h>
void main() {
    // variable declarations
    char szWorldText[25] = "Hello World!";
    char szSunText[25] = "Hello Sun!";
    char szMoonText[25] = "Hello Moon!";
    // output section
    cout << szWorldText << endl;
    cout << szSunText << endl;
    cout << szMoonText << endl;
}
```

Figure 2-14 Hello World project after adding comments

5. Rebuild the project, and then execute the program to confirm that the comments do not display.

FUNCTIONS

Individual statements used in a computer program are often grouped into logical units called procedures. In C++ programming, procedures are called functions. A **function** allows you to treat a logically related group of C++ statements as a single unit. Recall from the last chapter that functions are another name for procedures, routines, and subroutines. Function is the preferred term in C++ programming. An example of a function would be a series of statements in an accounting program that calculate an employee's net pay. You could execute each statement that calculates net pay one statement at a time. However, it is much easier to execute all of the statements at the same time by executing a function that contains them.

2

Before you can use a function in a C++ program, you must first create, or define, it. The lines that compose a function within a C++ program are called the **function definition**. The syntax for defining a function is:

```
return_data_type name_of_function(parameters) {
    statements;
}
```

Note that a function definition consists of four parts:

- A reserved word indicating the return data type of the function's return value

- The function name

- Any parameters required by the function, contained within parentheses following the function name.

- The function's statements enclosed in curly braces { }

You designate a data type for a function because it is common to return a value from a function after it executes. If you do not need to return a value from a function, then you use a data type of **void**.

Following the return data type is the function name. Like variables, the name you assign to a function is called an identifier. The same rules and conventions that apply to variable names apply to function names.

Following the function name are parentheses. Parameters are placed within these parentheses. A **parameter**, or **formal parameter**, is a variable, text string, or literal value that will be used within a function. Later in this section, we will discuss return types and how parameters get their values. For now, we will focus on how functions are structured.

As an example of how to use a parameter, you may write a function named calculate_square_root() that calculates the square root of an integer variable named iNumber. The function name would be written as int calculate_square_root(int iNumber).

Functions can contain multiple parameters separated by commas. To add three separate number parameters to a function named averageResult() that calculates the average of the numbers, you write the function name as int averageResult(int iNumber1, int iNumber2, int iNumber3).

 Functions are not required to contain parameters. Many functions only perform a task and do not require external data.

Following the parentheses containing a function's parameters are a set of curly braces containing the function's statements. A function's statements must be contained within the function's braces. The following code is an example of a function that prints the names of multiple companies.

```
void print_names(char szCoName1[50], char szCoName2[50],
char szCoName3[50]) {
        cout << szCoName1 << endl;
        cout << szCoName2 << endl;
        cout << szCoName3 << endl;
}
```

Notice how the function in the preceding example is structured. The opening curly brace is on the same line as the function name and the closing curly brace is on its own line following the function statements. Each statement between the curly braces is indented using a one-half inch tab. This structure is the preferred format among many programmers. However, some programmers prefer placing the opening curly brace on the line following the function name or using spaces instead of tabs for the indentation of statements. Both formats work exactly the same way. Feel free to use whatever function formatting you prefer. You will see both formats used in this text.

You can set the default formatting for your installation of Visual C++ using the Tabs tab in the Options dialog box.

The main( ) function

The starting point for traditional C++ programs is the main() function. The **main() function** is a special function that runs automatically when a program first executes. All C++ programs must include a main() function. All other functions in a C++ program are executed from the main() function. A main() function is created with the exact same structure as other functions, with the exception that it must be named *main*. The compiler knows that the main() function is the first function to execute when your program first loads. If your program does not include a main() function, then it will not execute.

Defining and Calling Custom Functions

You create your own custom function definitions the same way you create main() functions, except you must use a name other than *main* for the function name. Unlike the main() function, a custom function definition does not execute automatically. Creating a custom function definition only names the function, specifies its parameters, and organizes the statements it will execute. To execute a function, you must invoke, or **call,** it from the main() function.

To call a function, you create a statement that includes the function name followed by parentheses containing any variables or values to be assigned to the function's parameters. The variables or values that you place in the parentheses of the function call statement are called **arguments** or **actual parameters**. Sending arguments to a called function's parameters is called **passing arguments**. The parameters in the called function then take on the value of the arguments that are passed from the calling statement. The values that you pass as arguments must be of the same data type as the function's parameters.

Figure 2-15 shows a C++ program that prints the name of a company. Figure 2-16 shows the output. Notice that the custom print_company_name() function is called from within the main() function. Also notice that the *My Company* text string is passed from the main() function to the szCompanyName parameter, which is of the char data type.

```cpp
#include <iostream.h>
void print_company_name(char szCompanyName[50]) {
    cout << szCompanyName << endl;
}
void main() {
    print_company_name("My Company");
}
```

Figure 2-15   Custom function definition being called from the main() function

Figure 2-16   Output of the custom function definition being called from the main() function

Next, you will modify the Hello World program so that the text strings, *Hello World!*, *Hello Sun!*, and *Hello Moon!* are printed from separate functions. You will also add to the main() function call statements that execute each function. Each new function will contain a char parameter. As you call each function, you will pass to the char parameter the appropriate text to combine with the GREETING constant: *World!*, *Sun!*, or *Moon!*. The program will create the same output that it did before you added the new functions.

To add custom functions to the Hello World program:

1. Open the **HelloWorld** project in Visual C++, if necessary.

2. If necessary, open the **HelloWorld.cpp** source file in the Text Editor window.

3. Delete the following statements from the main() function:

   ```cpp
   char szWorldText[25] = "World!";
   char szSunText[25] = "Sun!";
   char szMoonText[25] = "Moon!";
   ```

4. After the main() function's closing curly brace, add the following function definition for the helloWorld() function.

   ```cpp
   void helloWorld(char szWorldText[25]) {

   }
   ```

5. Move the **cout << GREETING << " " << szWorldText << endl;** statement from the main() function to the helloWorld() function. Be sure to paste the statement between the helloWorld() function's curly braces.

6. After the helloWorld() function's closing curly brace, add the following function definition for the helloSun() function.

```
void helloSun(char szSunText[25]) {

}
```

7. Move the **cout << GREETING << " " << szSunText << endl;** statement from the main() function to the helloSun() function.

8. After the helloSun() function's closing curly brace, add the following function definition for the helloMoon() function.

```
void helloMoon(char szMoonText[25]) {

}
```

9. Move the **cout << GREETING << " " << szMoonText << endl;** statement from the main() function to the helloMoon() function.

10. Delete the following two comment lines from the main() function:

```
// variable declarations
// output section
```

11. Add to the main() function the following three statements, which call the three new functions:

```
helloWorld("World!");
helloSun("Sun!");
helloMoon("Moon!");
```

Before you can successfully compile and execute the modified Hello World program, you need to learn about and add function prototypes.

Function Prototypes

The placement of a custom function definition in your source file is critical, and you must always be aware of the choices. If you place any custom function definitions above the main() function (as shown in Figure 2-15), then your program will compile without the problems that are caused by placement of the custom functions. Many programmers prefer to place the main() function at the beginning of the source file, however, because it is the starting point for all other functions within the file. If you place your main() function above any custom functions in your source file, then you must create a function prototype for each function below the main() function. A **function prototype** declares to the compiler that you intend to use a custom function later in the program. If you attempt to call a custom function at any point in a source file *prior* to where its function prototype or function definition appears, then you will receive an error when you compile the project. Figure 2-17 contains a modified version of the program from Figure 2-15. This time the main() function is placed above the print_company_name() function. If you attempted to compile this program, you would receive an error message since the main() function attempts to call the function prior to its function prototype or function definition.

```
#include <iostream.h>
void main() {
    print_company_name("My Company");
}
void print_company_name(char szCompanyName[50]) {
    cout << szCompanyName << endl;
}
```

Figure 2-17   Company name before adding a function definition

In order for the program in Figure 2-17 to function, you must add a function prototype above the main() function. The syntax for a function prototype is *return_data_type name_of_function(parameters);*. A function prototype is essentially the first line of a function declaration without the opening curly brace. Figure 2-18 shows a correct version of the company name program with a function prototype for the print_company_name() function.

```
#include <iostream.h>
void print_company_name(char szCompanyName[50]);
void main() {
    print_company_name("My Company");
}
void print_company_name(char szCompanyName[50]) {
    cout << szCompanyName << endl;
}
```

Figure 2-18   Company name after adding a function definition

Next, you will add function prototypes to the Hello World program for the helloWorld(), helloSun(), and helloMoon() functions.

To add function prototypes to the Hello World program for the helloWorld(), helloSun(), and helloMoon() functions:

1. Return to the **HelloWorld.cpp** source file in the Text Editor window.

2. Place your cursor after the `const char GREETING[25] = "Hello";` statement, press **Enter**, and then add the following function prototypes:

```
void helloWorld(char szWorldText[25]);
void helloSun(char szSunText[25]);
void helloMoon(char szMoonText[25]);
```

3. Rebuild and execute the Hello World project. The program should function normally.

Return Values

In many instances, you may want one function to receive a value from another function that you can then use in other code. For instance, if you have a function that performs a calculation on a number that is passed to it, you would want to receive the result of the calculation. Consider a function that calculates the average of a series of numbers that you pass to it—the function would be useless if you never saw the result. To return a value to a calling statement, you assign the calling statement to a variable. A variable must be of the same data type as the value being returned from the called function. The following statement calls a function named average_numbers() and assigns any return value to an integer variable named iReturnValue. The statement also passes three literal values to the function.

```
int iReturnValue = average_numbers(1, 2, 3);
```

To actually return a value to a variable, you must include the **return** statement within the called function. The syntax for the return statement is either **return** *value*; or **return(***value***);**. This text primarily uses the first syntax example. The following program contains the average_numbers() function, which calculates the average of three numbers and stores that value in a variable named result. The function then uses the **return** statement to return the value contained in the **iResult** variable to the calling statement in the main() function.

```
#include <iostream.h>
int average_numbers(int iFirstNum, int iSecondNum,
    int iThirdNum);
void main() {
    int iReturnValue = average_numbers(1, 2, 3);
    cout << iReturnValue << endl;
}
int average_numbers(int iFirstNum, int iSecondNum,
    int iThirdNum) {
    int sum_of_numbers = iFirstNum + iSecondNum
        + iThirdNum;
    int iResult = sum_of_numbers / 3;
    return iResult;
}
```

Remember that values passed back and forth between functions must be of the same data type. Notice that at each stage in the preceding code, the values passed and forth are of the integer data type.

The variable name that is returned from a function and the variable name that receives the returned value can be the same. For instance, in the preceding examples, the variable name in the **return** statement in the average_numbers() function and the variable name in the calling statement in the main() function could both be iReturnValue. Also, when you pass

2

variables as arguments to a function, the passed variables and the parameter names within the function itself can also be the same. If you pass variables to the average_numbers() function instead of the literal values used in the main() function, you can use the statement `average_numbers(iFirstNum, iSecondNum, iThirdNum);`, even though the parameter names within the function itself are *a*, *b*, and *c*. However, most programmers usually use unique names to identify specific variables in their code.

Using unique names to identify specific variables makes it easier to understand a program's logic and assists in the debugging process.

You do not need to receive return values from all functions. For example, you would not need to receive a return value from a function that prints an employee's personal information to the screen or performs some other task that does not create or return a useful value. If you do not need to receive a return value from a function, then you are not required to assign the calling statement to a variable. For instance, if you want to call from the main() function the average_numbers() function to calculate the average of the three literal values, *2*, *3*, and *4*, but do not require a return value, you type `average_numbers(2, 3, 4);` without assigning the statement to the `iReturnValue` variable. If you do not want to return a value from a function, then you must use the `void` keyword as the data type in the function's definition. If you use any data type other than void in a function definition, however, then you must return a value from the function.

When a function performs a calculation such as an average, you normally want to receive a return value.

Next, you will modify Hello World so that the helloWorld(), helloSun(), and helloMoon() functions return values. The helloWorld() function will return the distance of the Earth to the Sun (92,897,000 miles), the helloSun() function will return the Sun's core temperature (72,000,000 degrees Fahrenheit), and the helloMoon() function will return the Moon's diameter (3,456 miles). The returned values will be doubles, so you must modify the data type of each function definition, as well as the data type for each function protocol. The individual text strings Hello World!, Hello Sun!, and Hello Moon!, will continue to be printed from each function. However, the return value from each function will be printed from the main() function. You will use a double variable named dReturnType in order to store the value returned from each function. Note that the values returned from a function are often the result of some sort of calculation or expression evaluation. You will not perform any sort of calculation or expression evaluation since your only purpose is to see how values are returned from calling functions.

To add return values to the Hello World program:

1. Return to the **HelloWorld.cpp** source file in the Text Editor window.

2. Change the data type for the three function prototypes to doubles as follows:

```
double helloWorld(char szWorldText[25]);
double helloSun(char szSunText[25]);
double helloMoon(char szMoonText[25]);
```

3. Place your cursor after the main() function's opening curly brace, press **Enter**, and then declare the returnValue integer variable using the statement `double dReturnValue;`.

4. Modify the statement that calls the helloWorld() function so that its return value is assigned to the dReturnValue variable as follows:
`dReturnValue = helloWorld("World!");`.

5. Type the following statement to print the value returned from the helloWorld() function to the screen, along with some descriptive text strings:

```
cout << "The Earth is " << dReturnValue
    << " miles from the Sun." << endl;
```

6. Modify the statement that calls the helloSun() function so that its return value is assigned to the dReturnValue variable as follows:
`dReturnValue = helloSun("Sun");`.

7. Type the following statement to print the value returned from the helloSun() function to the screen, along with some descriptive text strings:

```
cout << "The Sun's core temperature is approximately "
    << dReturnValue << " degrees Fahrenheit." << endl;
```

8. Modify the statement that calls the helloMoon() function so that its return value is assigned to the dReturnValue variable as follows:

`dReturnValue = helloMoon("Moon");`.

9. Type the following statement to print the value returned from the helloMoon() function to the screen, along with some descriptive text strings:

```
cout << "The Moon is " << dReturnValue
    << " miles in diameter." << endl;
```

10. Next, change the data types for the helloWorld(), helloSun(), and helloMoon() functions from void to **double**. Also add a return value of **92897000** to the helloWorld() function, a return value of **72000000** to the helloSun() function, and a return value of **3456** to the helloMoon() function. Each return value should appear as the last statement in each function. The completed helloWorld(), helloSun(), and helloMoon() functions should appear as follows:

```
double helloWorld(char szWorldText[25]) {
    cout << GREETING << " " << szWorldText << endl;
    return 92897000;
}
```

```
double helloSun(char szSunText[25]) {
    cout << GREETING << " " << szSunText << endl;
    return 72000000;
}
double helloMoon(char szMoonText[25]) {
    cout << GREETING << " " << szMoonText << endl;
    return 3456;
}
```

11. Rebuild and execute the program. Your command window should appear similar to Figure 2-19.

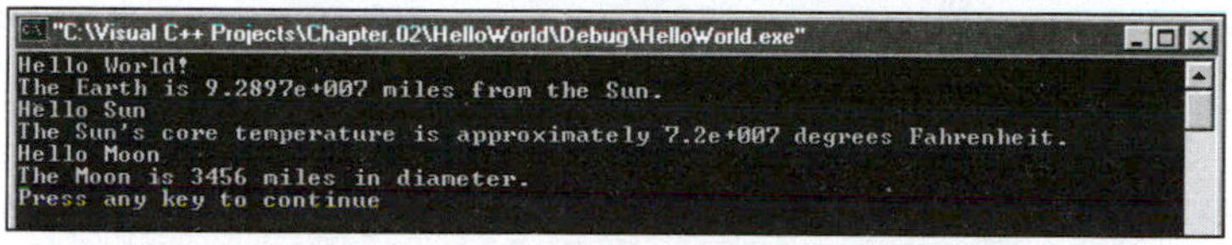

Figure 2-19   Output of Hello World after adding return values

12. Press any key to close the command window.

SCOPE

When you use variables and constants in a C++ program, you need to be aware of their scope. **Scope** refers to where in your program a declared variable or constant can be used. Scope is determined by whether a variable or constant is declared within a function or within a command block. First, you will learn about command blocks.

Command Blocks

The functions you have worked with so far have all consisted of statements contained within a set of braces. Commands contained within a set of braces are known as a command block or a statement block. **Command blocks** are used for grouping statements into a single unit. For example, the following code contains a function whose statements are contained within a command block:

```
void sampleFunction() {
    char szMessage[50] = "This line is part of the command
block.";
    cout << szMessage << endl;
}
```

In the above example, the command block contains all of the function's statements; the statements are then executed as a single unit when the function is called. You can think of a command block as a type of a container that holds a series of statements. In the case of a function, you do not need to execute each statement individually. Rather, you call the command block as a unit using its function name.

Command blocks are not restricted to use with functions. You can use commands blocks at any point in C++ when you want to group statements together into a single unit. For example, the code in Figure 2-20 contains several command blocks that organize sections of C++ code into units:

```
void commandBlocks() {
    {
        char szFirstMessage[50] = "first command block";
        cout << szFirstMessage << endl;
    }
    {
        char szSecondMessage[50] = "second command block";
        cout << szSecondMessage << endl;
    }
    {
        char szThirdMessage[50] = "third command block";
        cout << szThirdMessage << endl;
    }
}
```

Figure 2-20   Command blocks

 Each command block must have an opening brace ({) and a closing brace (}). If a command block is missing either the opening or closing brace, an error will occur.

The command block examples in Figure 2-20 serves no purpose other than to demonstrate the use of command blocks. Note that it is considered poor programming style to include command blocks in your code that serve no purpose. You should only use command blocks in your code for legitimate reasons, such as when you are using control structures and repetition statements. You will study these topics in the next chapter.

Command blocks have a great deal of influence on the scope of functions and variables. Therefore, you need to use command blocks with care and with a good understanding of the logical flow of your program. You will learn about variable scope next.

Variable Scope

A variable can have either global scope or local scope. Variables that have **global scope** are declared outside of any functions or classes and are available to all parts of your program. Variables that have **local scope** are declared inside a function and are available only within the function in which they are declared. Local variables cease to exist when the function within which they are declared ends. If you attempt to use a local variable outside of the function in which it is declared, you will receive an error message when you attempt to compile the program.

Global scope is also referred to as namespace scope or file scope.

 The parameters within the parentheses of a function declaration are considered to be local variables.

The following code includes a global variable, called szGlobalVariable, and a scopeExample() function containing a local variable, called szLocalVariable. When the scopeExample() function is called from the main() function, the global variable and the local variable print successfully from within the scopeExample() function. After the call to the function, the global variable again prints successfully from the main() function. However, if you tried to compile the program, you would receive an error message. The main() function is trying to access a variable, szLocalVariable, that is outside of its scope since szLocalVariable is local to the scopeExample() function.

The main() function also contains a command block that declares a variable named szBlockVariable. The szBlockVariable is available only to the command block and not to the main() function. You can think of szBlockVariable as having *very* local scope. You can print szBlockVariable from inside its command block. However, if you attempt to print it from the main() function, which is outside of the command block, you will receive an error.

```
#include <iostream.h>
  void scopeExample();
  char szGlobalVariable[25] = "First global variable";
  void main() {
       scopeExample();
       cout << szGlobalVariable << endl;      // prints
  successfully
       cout << szLocalVariable << endl;      // error message
       {
            char szBlockVariable[25] = "Command block
  variable."
            print szBlockVariable;      // prints successfully
       }
       print szBlockVariable;    // error message
  }
```

```
void scopeExample() {
    char szLocalVariable[25] = "Local variable";
    cout << szLocalVariable << endl;      // prints
successfully
    cout << szGlobalVariable << endl;     // prints
successfully
}
```

The lifetime of a variable is referred to as the **storage duration**, or **storage class**. There are two types of storage duration: permanent and temporary. **Permanent**, or **static**, storage duration refers to variables that are available for the lifetime of a program. **Temporary**, or **automatic**, storage duration refers to variables that exist only during the lifetime of the command block (such as a function) that contains them. Global variables are always permanent. Local variables are usually temporary.

Although local variables are temporary, they can be made permanent by using the static keyword. When used with a local variable declaration, the **static** keyword changes the variable's storage duration to permanent. A local variable declared with the static keyword is not destroyed after its function or command block finishes executing. To create a static local variable, you use a statement similar to `static int variable;`.

 You can specifically declare variables as temporary with the **auto** keyword using a statement similar to `auto int variable;`. Because all local variables are temporary by default, however, the auto keyword is unnecessary and rarely used.

When a program contains a global variable and a local variable with the same name, the local variable takes precedence when its function is called. In the following code, the global variable szShowDog is assigned a value of *Golden Retriever* before the function that contains a local variable of the same name is called. Once the function is called, the local szShowDog variable is assigned a value of *Irish Setter*. After the function ends, the local szShowDog variable ceases to exist and *Golden Retriever* is still the value of the global szShowDog variable.

```
#include <iostream.h>
void duplicateVariableNames();
char szShowDog[25] = "Golden Retriever";
void main() {
    cout << szShowDog << endl; // prints 'Golden Retriever'
    duplicateVariableNames();
    cout << szShowDog << endl; // prints 'Golden Retriever'
}
void duplicateVariableNames() {
    char szShowDog[25] = "Irish Setter";
    cout << szShowDog << endl; // prints 'Irish Setter'
}
```

ARRAYS

An **array** is an advanced data type that contains a set of data represented by a single variable name. You use arrays to store collections of related data. When you declare an array, you designate the number of elements that you want to store in the array. An **element** is an individual piece of data contained in an array. The syntax for declaring an array is *type name[elements]*;. Notice that when declaring an array, you must declare its data type, just as you would with regular variables. Array names follow the same naming conventions as variable names and other identifiers. Because you are using Hungarian notation, array names will have *ar* prefix. The following statement declares an array named arMyArray of the int data type and designates that it contains three elements:

```
int arMyArray[3];
```

You can use any of the primitive data types as an array's data type. The following statement, for example, declares an array of the char data type with five elements. Remember that the char data type stores single characters unless you specify the number of characters within brackets at the end of the variable name. The examples you see in this section store single char data type characters in an array. In the next chapter, you will learn how to store multi-character strings within the elements of an array.

```
char arStudentGrades[5];
```

The numbering of elements within an array starts with an index number of 0. (This numbering scheme can be very confusing for beginners.) An **index number** is an element's numeric position within the array. You refer to a specific element by enclosing its index number in brackets at the end of the array name. For example, the first element in the arStudentGrades array is arStudentGrades[0], the second element is arStudentGrades[1], the third element is arStudentGrades[2], and so on. You assign values to individual array elements in the same fashion you assign values to a standard variable, except you include the index number for an individual element of the array. The following code assigns values to the five elements within the arStudentGrades array:

```
arStudentGrades[0] = 'A';    // first element
arStudentGrades[1] = 'B';    // second element
arStudentGrades[2] = 'C';    // third element
arStudentGrades[3] = 'D';    // fourth element
arStudentGrades[4] = 'F';    // fifth element
```

You use an element in an array in the same manner you use other types of variables. For example, the following code prints the values contained in the five elements of the arStudentGrades array:

```
cout << arStudentGrades[0] << endl; // prints A
cout << arStudentGrades[1] << endl; // prints B
cout << arStudentGrades[2] << endl; // prints C
cout << arStudentGrades[3] << endl; // prints D
cout << arStudentGrades[4] << endl; // prints F
```

Once you have assigned a value to an array element, you can change it later just like you can change other variables in a program. To change the first element in the arStudentGrades array from *A* to *B*, you include the statement **arStudentGrades[0] = 'B';** in your code.

You can assign values to an array's elements when you first create the array using the syntax *type name[elements] = {value1, value2, ...};*. Be sure to place each value you want assigned to the array inside the curly braces { }, separated by commas, and in the order in which you want them assigned to the array elements. For example, the following code assigns values to the arStudentGrades array when it is created, then prints each of the values using the array's element numbers:

```
char arStudentGrades[5] = {'A', 'B', 'C', 'D', 'F'};
cout << arStudentGrades[0] << endl; // prints A
cout << arStudentGrades[1] << endl; // prints B
cout << arStudentGrades[2] << endl; // prints C
cout << arStudentGrades[3] << endl; // prints D
cout << arStudentGrades[4] << endl; // prints F
```

In the next chapter, you will see some more advanced array examples. You will also learn how to create array elements that contain strings instead of individual characters.

CHAPTER SUMMARY

- ❑ A console application is a program that runs within an output window, similar to an MS-DOS command prompt.

- ❑ A header file, or include file, is a file with an extension of .h that is included as part of a program and alerts the compiler that a program uses run-time classes.

- ❑ You add a header file to your program using the #include statement.

- ❑ The iostream classes are used for giving C++ programs input capabilities to and output capabilities from the computer screen and disk files, as well as for printing functions.

- ❑ The preprocessor is a program that runs before the compiler and places the entire contents of a designated file into the current file.

- ❑ Preprocessor directives and include statements allow the current file to use any of the classes, functions, variables, and other code contained within the included file.

- ❑ The standard output stream is the destination, usually a screen or file, for text output.

- ❑ You send text to the standard output stream in code with the cout (for console output) object. You must add the iostream.h header file to your program in order to use the C++ standard output stream's cout object.

- ❑ The cout object is used for outputting text to the console application window.

- ❑ A text string, or literal string, is text that is contained within double quotation marks.

- ❑ All statements in C++ must end with a semicolon.

2

❑ A statement is not necessarily a single line of code; large statements can span multiple lines of code.

❑ An i/o manipulator is a special function that can be used with an i/o statement.

❑ The endl i/o manipulator is part of the iostream classes and represents a new line character.

❑ The C++ programming languages are case sensitive.

❑ Before executing a program, you must compile and build it. The tools for building and running a program are located on the Build menu in Visual C++.

❑ The C iostream classes do not include an **endl** i/o manipulator to force a line break, as do the C++ iostream classes. Instead, you include the \n escape character as part of the text string to force a line break.

❑ The data type used to create a variable determines the type of information that can be stored in the variable.

❑ The integer data type stores positive or negative numbers with no decimal places.

❑ The character data type stores text.

❑ Reserved words or keywords are part of the C++ language syntax.

❑ Using a statement similar to **int myVariable;** to create a variable is called declaring the variable.

❑ The values you assign to integer data types and other numeric data types are called literal values, or literals.

❑ The name you assign to a variable is called an identifier, or variable name. Identifiers must begin with an uppercase or lowercase ASCII letter or underscore (_). You can use numbers in an identifier, but not as the first character. You are not allowed to use special characters such as $, &, *, or %. Reserved words cannot be used for variable names, and you cannot use spaces within a variable name.

❑ Although you can assign a value when a variable is declared, you are not required to do so. Your program may assign the value later or you may use a variable to store user input.

❑ There are two methods of creating constants in C++: the #define statement or using the const keyword.

❑ A data type is the specific category of information that a variable contains.

❑ The specific data type of a variable is very important to a programming language because it helps determine how much memory to allocate for the data, as well as the types of operations that can be performed on a variable. Additionally, data types force you to assign the appropriate value to a variable to help prevent programming errors.

❑ Data types that can be assigned only a single value are called fundamental types or primitive types.

❏ Programming languages that require you to declare the data types of variables are called strongly-typed programming languages.

❏ Programming languages that do not require you to declare the data types of variables are called loosely-typed programming languages.

❏ When you declare a variable in C++, you must designate a data type.

❏ Hungarian notation is a convention for naming variables so that it is easy to identify their data types.

❏ An integer is a positive or negative number with no decimal places.

❏ By default, integer variables are created with the signed type modifier, which allows integers to store both positive and negative numbers.

❏ The unsigned type modifier restricts the values assigned to integer variables to positive numbers.

❏ Decimal numbers are the standard numbers used in everyday life that are based on a value of 10 and do not include a leading 0.

❏ An octal number is based on 8 and always begin with a 0 to inform Visual C++ that it is an octal number.

❏ Hexadecimal numbers are based on 16 and always begin with the characters 0x or 0X, followed by hexadecimal digits.

❏ A floating-point number contains decimal places or is written using exponential notation.

❏ Values assigned to a char variable are stored as Unicode characters, which are numeric representations of all known characters. You can assign a Unicode character directly to a char variable instead of alphabetic characters contained in single quotation marks.

❏ An escape character tells the compiler that the character that follows it has a special purpose.

❏ When you combine the escape character with other characters the combination is called an escape sequence.

❏ A Boolean value is a logical value of true or false.

❏ You can use the words *true* and *false* to indicate Boolean values. You can also use 1 to indicate true or 0 to indicate false.

❏ Casting, or type casting, copies the value contained in a variable of one data type into a variable of another data type.

❏ If you do not explicitly cast a variable of one data type to another data type, Visual C++ will attempt to automatically perform the cast for you.

❏ Comments are non-printing lines that you place in your code to contain various types of remarks.

2

❑ C++ line comments are created by adding two slashes // before the text you want to use as a comment.

❑ C-style Block comments span multiple lines and are created by adding /* to the first line that is to be included in the block. You close a comment block by typing */ after the last text to be included in the block.

❑ A function allows you to treat a related group of C++ statements as a single unit.

❑ The lines that compose a function within a C++ program are called the function definition.

❑ You designate a data type for a function since it is common to return a value from a function after it executes.

❑ If you do not need to return a value from a function, then you use a data type of **void**.

❑ A parameter, or formal parameter, is a variable, text string, or literal value that will be used within a function.

❑ The main() function is a special function that runs automatically when a program first executes.

❑ You create your own custom function definitions the same way you create main() functions, except you must use a name other than main for the function name.

❑ To execute a function, you must invoke, or call, it from the main() function.

❑ The variables or values that you place within the parentheses of a function call statement are called arguments or actual parameters.

❑ Sending arguments to a called function's parameters is called passing arguments.

❑ A function prototype declares to the compiler that you intend to use a custom function later in the program.

❑ If you attempt to call a custom function at any point in a source file prior to its function prototype or function definition, you will receive an error when you compile the project.

❑ To return a value to a calling statement, you assign the calling statement to a variable. A variable must be of the same data type as the value being returned from the called function.

❑ To actually return a value to a variable, you must include the **return** statement within the called function.

❑ The values passed back and forth between functions must be of the same data type.

❑ Command blocks are used for grouping statements into a single unit.

❑ Scope refers to where in your program a declared variable or constant can be used.

❑ Global scope refers to variables declared outside of any functions or classes and that are available to all parts of your program.

❏ Local scope refers to a variable declared inside a function and that is available only within the function in which it is declared.

❏ The lifetime of a variable is referred to as the storage duration, or storage class.

❏ Permanent, or static, storage duration refers to variables that are available for the lifetime of a program.

❏ Temporary, or automatic, storage duration refers to variables that exist only during the lifetime of the command block (such as a function) that contains them.

❏ The static keyword changes a variable's storage duration to permanent.

❏ An array is an advanced data type that contains a set of data represented by a single variable name.

❏ An element is an individual piece of data contained in an array.

❏ Array names follow the same naming conventions as variable names and other identifiers.

❏ The numbering of elements within an array starts with an index number of 0.

❏ You assign values to individual array elements in the same fashion you assign values to a standard variable, except you include the index for an individual element of the array.

REVIEW QUESTIONS

1. A console application _____.

    a. contains a graphical user interface like Windows applications

    b. is essentially the same as a Web browser

    c. is a development environment used for creating C++ programs

    d. is a program that runs within an output window, similar to an MS-DOS command prompt

2. When does the preprocessor run?

    a. Before a program executes

    b. After a program executes

    c. Before the compiler

    d. After the compiler

3. What is the correct syntax for including in a program a header file that is one of the C++ run-time libraries or an MFC library file?

    a. `#include <header_file.h>`

    b. `#include <header_file.h>;`

    c. `include < header_file.h>`

    d. `include < header_file.h>;`

4. To include a custom header file within your program, you surround the header file name with _____.

   a. single quotation marks

   b. double quotation marks

   c. angle brackets

   d. parentheses

5. Which header file is required to send data to the C++ standard output stream?

   a. output.h

   b. stdin_stdout.h

   c. iostream.h

   d. stdio.h

6. What is the correct syntax for sending quoted text within a literal string to the C++ standard output stream?

   a. `cout << "The cashier said "May I help you?"";`

   b. `cout << 'The cashier said 'May I help you?'';`

   c. `cout << "The cashier said 'May I help you?'";`

   d. `cout << The cashier said "May I help you?";`

7. What is the correct syntax for printing the statements *Birds Fly*, *Horses Run*, and *Fish Swim* on three separate lines?

   a. `cout << "Birds Fly" << "Horses Run" << "Fish Swim";`

   b. `cout << "Birds Fly" << endl << "Horses Run" << endl << "Fish Swim";`

   c. `cout << "Birds Fly";`
      `cout << "Horses Run";`
      `cout << "Fish Swim";`

   d. `cout << "Birds Fly";`
      `<< "Horses Run";`
      `<< "Fish Swim";`

8. Consider the line breaks in the following statement. What will happen if you attempt to compile and execute the code?

   ```
   cout << "A Tree
   Grows "
   << "in Brooklyn";
   ```

   a. The text string is printed on a single line.

   b. The text string is printed on two lines.

   c. The text string is printed on three lines.

   d. You will receive a compiler error.

9. Which header file is required to send data to the C standard output stream?

    a. output.h

    b. stdin_stdout.h

    c. iostream.h

    d. stdio.h

10. What is the correct syntax for declaring a variable named numberVar with an integer data type and assigning to it a value of 100?

    a. `integer numberVar = 100;`

    b. `int* numberVar = 100;`

    c. `int numberVar = 100;`

    d. `integer numberVar = "100";`

11. What is the correct syntax for declaring a variable named textVar with a character data type and assigning to it a value of *I like programming*?

    a. character textVar = "I like programming";

    b. char textVar[15] = "I like programming";

    c. char textVar = "I like programming";

    d. character textVar = "I like programming";

12. Which of the following is a legal name for a variable?

    a. %variableName

    b. 1variableName

    c. variableName

    d. +variableName

13. Identifiers in C++ can begin with an uppercase or lowercase ASCII letter or
    _____.

    a. the dollar sign ($)

    b. an underscore character (_)

    c. a number

    d. the number sign (#)

14. Which is the correct syntax for creating a constant named LAST_NAME with a value of *Morinaga* using the #define preprocessor directive?

    a. #define LAST_NAME = "Morinaga"

    b. #define LAST_NAME "Morinaga"

    c. #define LAST_NAME "Morinaga";

    d. #define(LAST_NAME) = "Morinaga";

15. Which is the correct syntax for creating a constant named LAST_NAME with a value of *Morinaga* using the const keyword?

    a. `#const LAST_NAME = "Morinaga"`

    b. `const LAST_NAME "Morinaga"`

    c. `const char LAST_NAME[25] = "Morinaga";`

    d. `const(LAST_NAME) = "Morinaga";`

16. Data types that can be assigned only a single value are called _____ types.

    a. basic

    b. rudimentary

    c. fundamental

    d. single-value

17. Which of the following is not a fundamental data type?

    a. bool

    b. floating-point

    c. short

    d. array

18. Text that is enclosed within quotation marks is _____.

    a. a literal string

    b. quoted text

    c. a comment

    d. an element

19. A loosely-typed programming language _____.

    a. does not require data types of variables to be declared

    b. requires data types of variables to be declared

    c. does not have different data types

    d. does not have variables

20. Which of the following is not an integer?

    a. 7.6

    b. 12

    c. 0

    d. 1

21. Which of the following is not a floating-point number?

    a. -439.35

    b. 3.17

    c. 10

    d. 1.0

22. Boolean values are stored as the values _____.

    a. minimum and maximum

    b. positive and negative

    c. 0 and 1

    d. true and false

23. Which of the following is the correct syntax for including double quotation marks within a string that is already surrounded by double quotation marks?

    a. `"Some computer's have \"artificial\" intelligence."`

    b. `"Some computer's have "artificial" intelligence."`

    c. `"Some computer's have /"artificial/" intelligence."`

    d. `"Some computer's have ""artificial"" intelligence."`

24. What value will be assigned to the iReturnResult variable in the statement `iReturnResult = "2" + "5";`?

    a. 10

    b. 52

    c. 25

    d. 7

25. You create line comments by adding _____ to a line you want to use as a comment.

    a. `||`

    b. `**`

    c. `//`

    d. `\\`

26. Block comments begin with /* and end with _____.

    a. `*/`

    b. `/*`

    c. `//`

    d. `**`

27. The lines that compose a function within a C++ source file are called the function
    _____.

    a. section

    b. unit

    c. container

    d. definition

28. C++ reserved words can be used as _____.

    a. function names

    b. variables

    c. both of these

    d. neither of these

29. A variable that is contained within a function's parentheses is called a parameter or
    a(n) _____.

    a. field

    b. routine

    c. method

    d. argument

30. A function's statements are located between which characters?

    a. { }

    b. [ ]

    c. < >

    d. ( )

31. If you do not need to return a value from a function, then you use a data type of
    _____,

    a. empty

    b. void

    c. null

    d. You do not specify a data type

32. Which of the following is the correct syntax for a function named carInformation() that does not return a value and that receives three text arguments: make, model, and color?

a.

```
void carInformation(char make[10], char model[10], char
color[10]) {
    statements;
}
```

b.

```
empty carInformation() {
    parameters char make[10], char model[10], char
color[10]
    statements;
}
```

c.

```
function carInformation(char make, char model, char color) {
    statements;
}
```

d.

```
carInformation() {
    char make[10];
    char model[10];
    char color[10];
    statements;
}
```

33. Sending arguments to a called function is called _____ arguments.

a. generating

b. passing

c. routing

d. sending

34. When does the main() function execute?

a. When the program first executes

b. During the compilation process

c. Only when it is called from another function

d. The main() function never executes; its only purpose is for declaring variables and function prototypes

35. Where must a function prototype be declared?

a. Inside a function

b. Before the function is called

c. After the function is called

d. Inside the main() function

2

36. The return statement _____.

   a. exits the program

   b. calls the main() function

   c. restarts the current function

   d. returns a value to the calling function

37. Variables passed back and forth between two functions must _____.

   a. have the same data type

   b. have the same name

   c. be global variables

   d. be constants declared with the const keyword

38. The syntax for using the return statement is `return value;` or _____.

   a. `return(value);`

   b. `return value();`

   c. `value return;`

   d. `value return();`

39. What value is printed from the following code?

```
#include <iostream.h>
int average_numbers(int a, int b, int c);
void main() {
     int returnValue
     returnValue = 0;
     returnValue = average_numbers(1, 2, 3);
     cout << returnValue << endl;
}
int average_numbers(int a, int b, int c) {
     int sum_of_numbers = a + b + c;
     int result = sum_of_numbers / 3;
     returnValue = 1;
     return result;
}
```

   a. 0

   b. 1

   c. 2

   d. 3

40. What value is printed from the bolded line in the following code?

```
#include <iostream.h>
void sportsCar();
void myCar = "Chevrolet";
void main() {
```

```
        char myCar[10] = "Ford";
        {
            char myCar[10] = "Toyota";
        }
        carInformation();
    }
  void carInformation() {
        cout << myCar << endl;
        myCar = "Corvette";
    }
```

a. Chevrolet

b. Ford

c. Toyota

d. Corvette

41. A variable that is declared outside a function is called a(n) _____ variable.

a. local

b. class

c. program

d. global

42. A local variable must be declared _____.

a. before a function

b. with the `global` keyword

c. within a function definition's braces

d. with the `local` keyword

43. The lifetime of a variable is referred to as its storage duration or _____.

a. persistence

b. storage continuance

c. storage class

d. global visibility

44. Which is the correct syntax for declaring an integer variable with permanent storage duration?

a. `permanent int variable;`

b. `static int variable;`

c. `persist int variable;`

d. `global int variable;`

45. What must be added to the following code in order for it to compile properly?

```
#include <iostream.h>
void main() {
      print_company_name("My Company");
}
void print_company_name(char company_name[50]) {
      cout << company_name << endl;
}
```

    a. A #define processing directive

    b. A global declaration of the company_name variable

    c. A function prototype

    d. An #include directive for the stdio.h header file

46. The numbering of elements within an array starts with an index number of _____.

    a. −1

    b. 0

    c. 1

    d. 2

47. What is the correct syntax for creating an integer array with ten elements?

    a. `int arVariable[10];`

    b. `int arVariable = Array(10);`

    c. `arVariable[] = new Array(10);`

    d. `Array[10] arVariable;`

48. Which of the following refers to the first element in an array named iEmployees[]?

    a. iEmployees[0]

    b. iEmployees[1]

    c. iEmployees[first]

    d. iEmployees[a]

EXERCISES

1. Create a console application project named PersonalInfo. Within the main()function, use cout statements to print your name, address, date of birth, and social security number to the screen.

2. Create a console application project named Continents. Within the main()function, use cout statements to print the names of the continents: Africa, Antarctica, Asia, Australia, Europe, North America, and South America.

3. Create a console application project named Initials that uses cout statements to print your initials in large block letters. Build each block letter out of the same initial letter. Figure 2-21 shows an example of how the program output may appear using the initials *DG*.

Figure 2-21   Output of the Initials program

4. Create a console application project named Star that uses cout statements to print a large star to the console window using asterisks. Figure 2-22 shows an example of how the program output may appear.

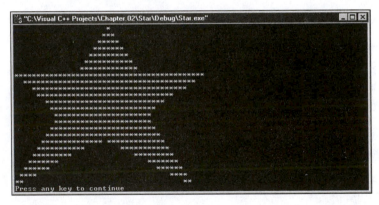

Figure 2-22   Output of the Star program

5. Create a console application project named Chapter2Exercise5. From the main() function, use the cout statement to print the text *This line is created using the C++ standard output stream.* Add comments above the cout statement explaining the printing method.

6. Create a console application project named ExecutiveSalaries. Think of some fictitious names for the top five executive positions at a corporation: Chairman, Chief Executive Officer, Chief Operating Officer, Chief Information Officer, and Chief Financial Officer. Within the main() function, declare three variables for each of the executives; one variable should contain the executive's name, another variable should contain the executive's title, and the last variable should contain the executive's salary. Assign each executive's name, title, and salary to his or her respective variables, and then print all of the variables. Each individual executive's name, title, and salary should be printed on its own lines.

7. Rewrite the following code so that the lines printed from the multiple cout statements are printed from a single statement:

```
#include <iostream.h>
void main() {
cout << "Mark Twain said ";
cout << "'Everybody talks about the weather, ";
cout << " but nobody does anything about it.'" << endl;
}
```

8. Identify the data types of each variable according to Hungarian notation:

- cData _____
- iPeriod _____
- siMonths _____
- liProjectedFigures _____
- fWeeklySalary _____
- dGrossRevenue _____
- szStreetAddress _____
- bHealthBenefits _____
- ctLoop _____

9. Create a program that displays a simplified version of your work history including the names of your former employers, positions within the companies, and dates of employment. Create the employers, positions, and dates of employment in columns. To create line breaks, use an escape character within the string variables. Save the project as WorkHistory.

10. Create a program containing personal information including your name, age, the type of car you have, the mortgage interest on your house or loan interest on your car, and whether you have a dog. Use different data types for each variable. Print each piece of information to the screen. Be sure to create items for the char, int, and floating-point data types. For example, your name will be the string data type, your age will be the int data type, and the mortgage interest on your house will be a floating-point data type. Save the project as PersonalInfo2.

11. Discuss the types of information you think should be used as constants. Explain why you think these types of information should be constants and not variables.

12. Create a console application program named FavoriteFoods. Create four functions that print the names of your favorite foods. For example, you may have a function named *chinese* that contains the statement **cout << "Chinese" << endl;**. Call each of the functions from the main() function, starting with your favorite type of food. Use literal strings in the main() function to describe your favorite foods. For example, to print the line *My favorite food is Chinese*, you use two statements. The first statement should read **cout << "My favorite food is ";**, and the second statement calls the chinese() function, which prints the word *Chinese*.

13. Create a console application project named CarObject. Create an automobile() function with four parameters: make, model, color, and engine. Call the automobile() function from the main() function, and pass to it values for the four parameters. Print each of the parameters to the screen from the automobile() function.

14. Create a console application project named CompanyInfo that includes a function named company(). Include three parameters in the company () function: name, products, and motto. Also create a function named employees() that prints the number of employees. Assign the number of employees to a variable within the employees() function. Call the company() function from the main() function and pass values to the name, products, and motto parameters. Print each of the parameters to the screen. Then call the employees() function from inside the company() function and print the number of employees. Combine each printed variable with a descriptive string. For example, when you print the company name, it should read something like *The company name is MyCompany*.

15. Create a console application project named Favorite Movies that prints the names of your favorite movies. The project should contain two custom functions: one that prints your three favorite comedies and one that prints your three favorite dramas. Name one function comedy() and the other function drama(). Assign each of the movie titles to a local variable within the comedy or drama function, then print each variable. Also create a global variable that will hold the name of your absolute favorite movie. Call the comedy and drama functions from the main() function, then print the name of your absolute favorite movie after the two functions are called.

16. Rewrite the following code so that it functions correctly, but *do not use a function prototype*.

```
#include <iostream.h>
void main() {
    functionA();
}
void print_company_name() {
    cout << "printed from functionA()" << endl;
}
```

17. Explain the difference between the #define preprocessor directive constants and constants created with the const keyword.

18. Think of a type of program that you feel would benefit from the use of command blocks. Explain why you would use command blocks and not separate functions for the code.

19. Modify the following code so that the seven variables are stored in an integer array. Be sure to use the correct Hungarian notation.

```
int iInterestRate1 = .0725;
int iInterestRate2 = .0750;
int iInterestRate3 = .0775;
int iInterestRate4 = .0800;
int iInterestRate5 = .0825;
int iInterestRate6 = .0850;
int iInterestRate7 = .0875;
```

CHAPTER

3

OPERATORS AND CONTROL STRUCTURES

In this chapter you will learn:

♦ About expressions
♦ How to use arithmetic, assignment, comparison, and logical operators
♦ How to work with string functions
♦ About operator precedence
♦ How to work with decision-making statements
♦ How to work with the standard input stream
♦ How to work with repetition statements

PREVIEW: THE CHEMISTRY QUIZ PROGRAM

In this chapter you will learn about, among other topics, expressions and operators, decision-making statements, and flow-control statements. So far, the code you have written has been linear in nature. In other words, your programs start at the beginning and end when the last statement in the program executes. Decision-making and flow-control statements allow you to determine the order in which statements execute in a program. The special types of C++ statements used for making decisions are called decision-making structures. The ability to control the flow of code and to make decisions during program execution is one of the most fundamental skills required in programming. To learn these concepts, you will create a chemistry quiz, using the different decision-making structures and statements available in C++. Keep in mind that a thorough understanding of all of the topics you study in this chapter will be required in order to complete the remainder of the chapters in this text.

To preview the Chemistry Quiz program:

1. Create a **Chapter.03** folder in your Visual C++ Projects folder.

2. Copy the **Chapter3_ChemistryQuiz** folder from the chapter.03 folder on your Data Disk to the Chapter.03 folder in your Visual C++ Projects folder. Then open the **ChemistryQuizFinal** project in Visual C++. If the Tip of the Day dialog box displays, click the **Close** button.

3. Open the **ChemistryQuizFinal.cpp** file in the Text Editor window, if it is not already open. Figure 3-1 shows a partial listing of the file. The file includes the iostream.h header file in order to provide access to the input and output streams. In the last chapter, you worked only with the output stream and cout statements to write information to the screen. In this chapter you will also receive information from the input stream using cin statements. You should recognize the remainder of the statements in Figure 3-1, except for the **for** statement, which is used for managing the repeated execution of statements in a C++ program.

```cpp
#include <iostream.h>

char arUserAnswers[5];

char arCorrectAnswers[5] = {'d', 'a', 'd', 'c', 'b'};

void recordAnswer(int iQuestion, char cAnswer) {

    arUserAnswers[iQuestion-1] = cAnswer;

}

void scoreQuiz() {

    int iTotalCorrect = 0;

    for(int ctCount = 0; ctCount < 5; ++ctCount) {          ⟵——— for statement

        if (arUserAnswers[ctCount]

            == arCorrectAnswers[ctCount])

            ++iTotalCorrect;

    }

    cout << "You scored " << iTotalCorrect

        << " out of 5 answers correctly!" << endl;

}
```

Figure 3-1 ChemistryQuizFinal.cpp

```
void main() {

    char cInput;

    cout << "Chemistry Quiz\n";

    // QUESTION 1

    cout << "1. Which of the following would decrease in
        pH if an" << endl
        << "    equal volume of 0.5M NaOH were to be
            added?" << endl
        << "\ta. Water" << endl
        << "\tb. 0.25M Na2CO3" << endl
        << "\tc. 0.5M HCl" << endl
        << "\td. 0.6M KOH" << endl;
    cout << "Your answer> ";

    cin >> cInput;                              ←——————— cin statement

...
```

Figure 3-1   ChemistryQuizFinal.cpp (continued)

4. Build and execute the Chemistry Quiz program, and then try answering the questions. When you finish answering all of the questions, the scoreQuiz() function executes and uses the **for** statement to score the quiz. Figure 3-2 shows how the program appears in the console window.

5. Press any key to close the Chemistry Quiz program window.

Figure 3-2   Output of the Chemistry Quiz program

Expressions and Operators

Variables and data become most useful when you use them in an expression. An **expression** is a combination of literal values, variables, operators, and other programming elements that can be evaluated by the Visual C++ compiler to produce a result. For example, the Visual C++ compiler recognizes the literal values and variables in Figure 3-3 as expressions.

```
"this is a string variable"    // string literal expression
10                             // integer literal expression
3.156                          // floating-point literal expression
true                           // Boolean literal expression
null                           // null literal expression
iEmployeeNumber                // variable expression
```

Figure 3-3   Literal and variable expressions

You can use operands and operators to create more complex expressions. **Operands** are variables and literals contained in an expression. **Operators** are symbols used in expressions to manipulate operands. You have worked with several simple expressions so far that combine operators and operands. Consider the following statement:

```
iMyNumber = 100;
```

This statement is an expression that results in the value 100 being assigned to the variable iMyNumber. The operands in the expression are the *iMyNumber* variable name and the integer value 100. The operator is the equal sign (=) assignment operator. The equal sign operator is an assignment operator since it *assigns* the value (100) on the right side of the expression to the variable (iMyNumber) on the left side of the expression. Figure 3-4 lists the main types of C++ operators.

3

Operator Type	Description
Arithmetic (+, −, *, /, %, ++,--)	Used for performing mathematical calculations
Assignment (=, +=, −=, *=, /=, %=)	Assigns values to variables
Comparison (==, !=, >, <, >=, <=)	Compares operands and returns a Boolean value
Logical (&&, ||, !)	Used for performing Boolean operations on Boolean operands

Figure 3-4   C++ operator types

 Other types of C++ operators include bitwise operators, which operate on integer values. Bitwise operators treat integers as binary numbers and are a complex topic.

C++ operators are binary or unary. A **binary operator** requires an operand before the operator and an operand after the operator. The equal sign in the statement `iMyNumber = 100;` is an example of binary operator. A **unary operator** requires a single operand either before or after the operator. For example, the increment operator (++), an arithmetic operator, is used for increasing an operand by a value of one. The statement `iMyNumber++` changes the value of the myNumber variable to 101.

 The operand to the left of an operator is known as the left operand and the operand to the right of an operator is known as the right operand.

Next, you will learn about the different types of C++ operators.

Arithmetic Operators

Arithmetic operators are used to perform mathematical calculations, such as addition, subtraction, multiplication, and division. You can also return the modulus of a calculation, which is the remainder left when you divide one number by another number. C++'s binary arithmetic operators and their descriptions are listed in Figure 3-5.

Operator	Description
+ (addition)	Adds two operands
− (subtraction)	Subtracts one operand from another operand
* (multiplication)	Multiplies one operand by another operand
/ (division)	Divides one operand by another operand
% (modulus)	Divides two operands and returns the remainder

Figure 3-5   Arithmetic binary operators

Arithmetic operations can also be performed on a single variable using unary operators. Figure 3-6 lists the unary arithmetic operators available in C++.

Operator	Description
++ (increment)	Increases an operand by a value of one
-- (decrement)	Decreases an operand by a value of one
− (negation)	Returns the opposite value (negative or positive) of an operand

Figure 3-6   Arithmetic unary operators

The increment (++) and decrement (--) unary operators can be used as prefix or postfix operators to increase or decrease values. A **prefix operator** is placed before a variable. A **postfix operator** is placed after a variable. The statements ++iMyVariable; and iMyVariable++; both increase iMyVariable by one. The two statements, however, return different values. When you use the increment operator as a prefix operator, the value of the operand is returned *after* it is increased by a value of 1. When you use the increment operator as a postfix operator, the value of the operand is returned *before* it is increased by a value of 1. Similarly, when you use the decrement operator as a prefix operator, the value of the operand is returned *after* it is decreased by a value of 1. When you use the decrement operator as a postfix operator, the value of the operand is returned *before* it is decreased by a value of 1. If you intend to assign the incremented or decremented value to another variable, then whether you use the prefix or postfix operator makes a difference.

You use arithmetic unary operators in any situation where you want to use a more simplified expression for increasing or decreasing a value by 1. For example, the statement iNumber = iNumber + 1; is identical to the statement ++iNumber;. As you can see, if your goal is only to increase a variable by 1, then it is easier to use the unary increment operator. But remember that with the prefix operator the value of the operand is returned *after* it is increased or decreased by a value of 1, while with the postfix operator, the value of the operand is returned *before* it is increased or decreased by a value of 1.

For an example of when you would use the prefix operator or the postfix operator, consider an integer variable named iStudentID that you would use for assigning student IDs in a class registration program. One way of creating a new student ID number is to store the last assigned student ID in the iStudentID variable. When you need to assign a new student ID, you could retrieve the last value stored in the iStudentID variable and then increase its value by 1. In other words, the last value stored in the iStudentID variable will be the next number that you will use for a student ID number. In this case, you would use the postfix operator to return the expression's value *before* it is incremented by using a statement similar to `iCurrentID = iStudentID++;`. Because you are storing the last assigned student ID in the iStudentID variable, you would want to increment the value by 1 and use the result as the next student ID. With this scenario, you would use the prefix operator, which returns the expression's value after it is incremented using a statement similar to `iCurrentID = ++iStudentID;`.

Assignment Operators

Assignment operators are used for assigning a value to a variable. You have already used the most common assignment operator, the equal sign (=), to assign values to variables. The equal sign assigns an initial value to a new variable or assigns a new value to an existing variable. For example, the following code creates a variable named cMyCar, uses the equal sign to assign it an initial value, then uses the equal sign again to assign it another new value.

```
char cMyCar[10] = "Ford";
cMyCar = "Corvette";
```

C++ includes other assignment operators in addition to the equal sign. These additional assignment operators perform mathematical calculations on variables and literal values in an expression, then assign a new value to the left operand. Figure 3-7 displays a list of the common C++ assignment operators, along with an example of each operator and an example of the fully expressed arithmetic operator.

Operator	Description	Assignment Operators	Arithmetic Operators
=	Assigns the value of the right operand to the left operand	iNum1 = iNum2;	(not applicable)
+=	Combines the value of the right operand with the value of the left operand or adds the value of the right operand to the value of the left operand and assigns the new value to the left operand	iNum1 += iNum2;	iNum1 = iNum1 + iNum2;
-=	Subtracts the value of the right operand from the value of the left operand and assigns the new value to the left operand	iNum1 -= iNum2;	iNum1 = iNum1 - iNum2;
*=	Multiplies the value of the right operand by the value of the left operand and assigns the new value to the left operand	iNum1 *= iNum2;	iNum1 = iNum1 * iNum2;
/=	Divides the value of the left operand by the value of the right operand and assigns the new value to the left operand	iNum1 /= iNum2;	iNum1 = iNum1 / iNum2;
%=	Modulus—divides the value of the left operand by the value of the right operand and assigns the remainder to the left operand.	iNum1 %= iNum2;	iNum1 = iNum1 % iNum2;

Figure 3-7   Assignment operators

Comparison Operators

Comparison operators are used to compare two operands for equality and to determine if one numeric value is greater than another. A Boolean value of true or false is returned after two operands are compared. Figure 3-8 lists the C++ comparison operators.

Operator	Description
== (equal)	Returns true if the operands are equal
!= (not equal)	Returns true if the operands are not equal
> (greater than)	Returns true if the left operand is greater than the right operand
< (less than)	Returns true if the left operand is less than the right operand
>= (greater than or equal)	Returns true if the left operand is greater than or equal to the right operand
<= (less than or equal)	Returns true if the left operand is less than or equal to the right operand

Figure 3-8   Comparison operators

 The comparison operator (==) consists of two equal signs and performs a function different from the assignment operator, which consists of a single equal sign (=). The comparison operator (==) *compares* values, whereas the assignment operator (=) *assigns* values.

Comparison operators are often used within conditional and looping statements such as the **if else, for**, and **while** statements. Although you will not learn about conditional and looping statements until later in this chapter, learning about the conditional operator now will help you better understand how to work with comparison operators. The **conditional operator** executes one of two expressions, based on the results of a conditional expression. The syntax for the conditional operator is (*conditional expression*) ? *expression1*: *expression2*;. If the conditional expression evaluates to true, then *expression1* executes. If the conditional expression evaluates to false, however, then *expression2* executes. The following code shows an example of the conditional operator. In the example, the conditional expression checks to see if the iValue variable is greater than 100. If the value is greater than 100, then the text *iValue is greater than 100* is assigned to the szResult variable. If the value is not greater than 100, then the text *iValue is less than or equal to 100* is assigned to the szResult variable. Since iValue is equal to 150, the conditional statement returns a value of true and *expression1* executes. This results in *iValue is greater than 100* being printed to the screen.

```
int iValue = 150;
char szResult[50];
(iValue > 100) ? szResult = "iValue is greater than 100"
      : szResult = "iValue is less than or equal to 100";
cout << szResult << endl;
```

Logical Operators

Logical operators are used for comparing two Boolean operands for equality. Like comparison operators, a Boolean value of true or false is returned after two operands are compared. Figure 3-9 lists the C++ logical operators.

Operator	Description
&& (AND)	Returns true if the both the left operand and right operand return a value of true, otherwise it returns a value of false.
|| (OR)	Returns true if either the left operand or right operand returns a value of true. If neither operand returns a value of true, then the expression containing the || (OR) operator returns a value of false.
! (NOT)	Returns true if an expression is false and returns false if an expression is true.

Figure 3-9   Logical operators

String Functions

As you work in C++, you will often find it necessary to manipulate text strings. For example, you may find it necessary to combine the values in a char variable named szFirstName and the values in a char variable named szLastName into a single char variable named szName. Or, you may want to assign a new value to a char variable after its initial declaration. One of the drawbacks to using the char data type is that you cannot use the assignment operator to assign a new value to a char variable after its declaration. Many programming languages include operators for manipulating and combining text strings. However, in C++ you must use a **string function** to manipulate char variables. Although string functions are not precisely "operators," you need to understand them because they are vital to working with strings in your programs. Figure 3-10 lists common string functions.

Function	Description
strcat()	Appends one string to another
strchr()	Finds the first occurrence of a specified character in a string
strcmp()	Compares two strings
strcpy()	Replaces the contents of one string with the contents of another
strcspn()	Finds the first occurrence in a string of a specified character within a specified character set
strlen()	Returns the length of a string
strncat()	Appends characters to a string
strncmp()	Compares characters within two strings
strncpy()	Copies characters from one string into another
strpbrk()	Finds the first occurrence in a string of a specified character in another string
strrchr()	Finds the last occurrence in a string of a specified character
strspn()	Finds the first occurrence in a string of a specified substring
strstr()	Finds the first occurrence in a string of another specified string

Figure 3-10   Common string functions

In Windows programming, you can create text strings using the CString class. Text strings created with the CString class are much easier to manipulate than strings assigned to char variables.

The functions listed in Figure 3-10 are contained in the string.h header file. To use the functions, you must add the statement `#include <string.h>` to your program. Two string functions that you will see frequently used in this text are the strcpy() and strcat() functions.

The **strcpy() function** copies a literal string or the contents of a char variable into another char variable using the syntax `strcpy(destination, source);`. The *destination* argument represents the char variable to which you want to assign a new value to while the *source* variable represents the literal string of char variable containing the string you want to assign to the destination variable.

The **strcat() function** combines, or *concatenates* two strings using the syntax `strcat(destination, source);`. The *destination* argument represents the char variable whose string you want to combine with another string. The *source* argument can be either a char variable or a literal string. When you execute strcat(), the string represented by the *source* argument is appended to the string contained in the destination variable.

To successfully assign one string to another using strcpy(), or to concatenate two strings using strcat(), you must make the destination char variable large enough. If you do not make the destination char variable large enough, then you will either lose data when you call the strcpy() or strcat() functions, or you will receive an error when you attempt to run the program.

The following code shows how to use both the strcpy() and strcat() functions with char variables containing a person's name. The first three statements simply declare three char variables: szFirstName, szLastName, and szFullName. Next, the strcpy() function assigns values to both the szFirstName and szLastName variables. The value of the szFirstName variable is then assigned to the szFullName variable using the strcpy() function. Finally, strcat() statements assign a space to the szFullName variable to separate the first and the last names, along with the szLastName variable.

```
char szFirstName[25];
char szLastName[25];
char szFullName[50];
strcpy(szFirstName, "Mike");
strcpy(szLastName, "Okayabashi");
strcpy(szFullName, szFirstName);
strcat(szFullName, " ");
strcat(szFullName, szLastName);
```

See the MSDN Library for the complete syntax of other string functions.

Operator Precedence

When creating expressions in C++, you need to be aware of the precedence of an operator. **Operator precedence** is the order of priority in which operations in an expression are evaluated. Figure 3-11 shows the order of precedence for the most commonly used operators in C++.

Operator	Order of Precedence
++	Post-increment—highest precedence
--	Post-decrement
( )	Function call
[ ]	Array element
->	Pointer to structure member
.	Structure or union member
++	Pre-increment
--	Pre-decrement
!	Logical NOT
–	Unary minus
+	Unary plus
&	Address
*	Indirection
new	Allocate program memory
delete	Deallocate program memory
(type)	Type cast [for example, (float) i]
.*	Pointer to member (objects)
->*	Pointer to member (pointers)
*	Multiply
/	Divide
%	Remainder
+	Add
–	Subtract
<<	Left shift
>>	Right shift
<	Less than
<=	Less than or equal to
>	Greater than
>=	Greater than or equal to

Figure 3-11   Order of precedence for commonly used operators

Operator	Order of Precedence
==	Equal
!=	Not equal
&&	Logical AND
||	Logical OR
? :	Conditional
=	Assignment
*=, /=, %=, +=, -=, <<=, >>=, &=, ^=, |=	Compound assignment
,	Comma—lowest precedence

Figure 3-11　Order of precedence for commonly used operators (continued)

 The preceding list does not include all of the operators that C++ evaluates in the order of precedence. Only the operators discussed in this text are listed.

Expressions are evaluated on a left-to-right basis with the highest priority precedence evaluated first. For example, the multiplication operator (*) has a higher precedence than the addition operator (+). Therefore, the statement 5 + 2 * 8 evaluates to 21. The numbers 2 and 8 are multiplied first for a total of 16, then the number 5 is added. If the addition operator had a higher precedence than the multiplication operator, then the statement would evaluate to 56, because 5 would be added to 2 for a total of 7, which would then be multiplied by 8.

Parentheses are used with expressions to change the order in which individual operations in an expression are evaluated. For example, the statement 5 + 2 * 8, which evaluates to 21, can be rewritten as (5 + 2) * 8, which evaluates to 56. The parentheses tell C++ to add the numbers 5 and 2 before multiplying by the number 8. Using parentheses forces the statement to evaluate to 56 instead of 21. You can find a complete listing of C++ operator precedence in the appendix.

DECISION-MAKING STATEMENTS

When you write a computer program, regardless of the programming language, you often need to execute different sets of statements depending on some predetermined criteria. You may need to execute different sets of code depending on the time of day, information gathered from a user, the evaluation of a conditional expression, and so on. For example, a doctor's office may use a program that sends out different healthcare reminder notices to people depending on their age. For people under the age of 12, a set of code generates a notice reminding them to get their measles vaccination. For people over 65, another set of code generates a notice reminding them to get their flu shots. The process of determining the order in which statements execute in a program is called **decision making** or **flow control**. The special types of C++ statements used for making decisions are called decision-making structures. The most common decision-making structures include `if`, `if...else`, and `switch` statements.

`if` Statements

One of the more common ways to control program flow is a technique that uses the `if` statement. The **`if` statement** is used to execute specific programming code if the evaluation of a conditional expression returns a value of true. The syntax for the `if` statement is as follows:

```
if (conditional expression) {
    statement(s);
}
```

The `if` statement contains three parts: the key word `if`, a conditional expression enclosed within parentheses, and executable statements. Note that you must enclose the conditional expression within parentheses.

If the condition being evaluated in an `if` statement returns a value of true, then the statement (or statements) immediately following the `if` keyword and its condition executes. After the `if` statement executes, any subsequent code executes normally. Consider the following example. The `if` statement uses the equal (==) comparison operator to determine whether iNum is equal to 5. Since the condition returns a value of true, two lines print. The first line is generated by the `if` statement when the condition returns a value of true, and the second line executes after the `if` statement is complete.

```
int iNum = 5;
if (iNum == 5) // CONDITION EVALUATES TO 'TRUE'
     cout << "The variable is equal to '5'." << endl;
cout << "This text is printed after the if statement.";
```

 One method many programmers use in a conditional statement to make it easier to distinguish between the assignment operator (=) and the comparison operator (==) is to reverse the order of the comparison. Instead of writing `iNum == 5` you would write `5 == iNum`. The second example performs the same comparison as the first, but it prevents you from accidentally assigning a value to a variable when you meant to compare them, otherwise, `5 = iNum` will generate a compile error message.

You can use a command block to construct a decision-making structure that executes multiple statements. The following code shows a program that runs a command block if the conditional expression within the `if` statement evaluates to true.

```
int iNum = 5;
if (iNum == 5) {     // CONDITION EVALUATES TO 'TRUE'
     cout << "The condition evaluates to true." << endl;
```

```
        cout << "iNum is equal to 5." << endl;
        cout << "Each of these lines will be printed."
              << endl;
    }
    cout << "This statement always executes after the if -
    statement." << endl;
```

When an `if` statement contains a command block, the statements in the command block execute when the `if` statement's condition evaluates to true. After the command block executes, the code that follows executes normally. When an `if` statement's condition evaluates to false, the command block is skipped and the statements that follow execute. If the conditional expression within the `if` statement in the preceding code evaluates to false, then only the cout statement following the command block would execute.

When you build an `if` statement, remember that after the `if` statement's condition evaluates, either the first statement following the condition executes, or the command block following the condition executes. Any statements following the `if` statement's command or command block execute regardless of whether the `if` statement's condition evaluates to true or false.

It is easy to forget to include all of the statements inside a command block that are to execute, when an `if` statement evaluates to true. For example, consider the following code.

```
    bool bVariable = false;
    char szString[25] = "";
        if (bVariable == true)
            szString = "condition is true";
            cout << szString << endl;
```

At first glance, the code looks correct. In fact, when the condition evaluates to true, the code seems to run correctly. When the condition evaluates to false, however, the cout statement runs anyway, printing either *true or false*, whatever value was assigned to the szString variable when it was first declared. To fix this problem, enclose the two statements following the `if` statement within a command block as follows:

```
    bool bVariable = false;
    char szString = "";
        if (bVariable == true) {
            szString = "condition is true";
            cout << szString << endl;
    }
```

Now if the condition evaluates to false, both statements will be bypassed since they are contained within a command block.

Next, you will start creating the Chemistry Quiz program you saw at the beginning of this chapter. In this version of the program, each question in the Chemistry Quiz will be scored using a unique function. `If` statements within each question's function evaluate the user's answer and print a response of *Correct Answer* or *Incorrect Answer*.

To start creating the Chemistry Quiz program as a console application:

1. Create a new empty Win32 Console Application project named **ChemistryQuiz1**. Save the project in the **Chapter.03** folder in your Visual C++ Projects folder. Once the project is created, add a C++ source file named **ChemistryQuiz1**.

2. Type the processing directive that gives the program access to the iostream library: **#include <iostream.h>**.

3. Press **Enter** and type the following function prototypes for each question's scoring function. Each function receives a single argument containing the response gathered from the user. (You will learn how to gather input from the user after this exercise.)

```cpp
void scoreQuestion1(char cAnswer);
void scoreQuestion2(char cAnswer);
void scoreQuestion3(char cAnswer);
void scoreQuestion4(char cAnswer);
void scoreQuestion5(char cAnswer);
```

4. Add the following empty main() function. We will return to the main() function after discussing how to gather input from the user.

```cpp
void main() {


}
```

5. After the main() function's closing brace, add the following five functions, which score each question. Each function receives a cAnswer variable containing the user's response, which is then evaluated by `if` statements.

```cpp
void scoreQuestion1(char cAnswer) {
    if (cAnswer == 'a')
        cout << "Incorrect Answer" << endl;
    if (cAnswer == 'b')
        cout << "Incorrect Answer" << endl;
    if (cAnswer == 'c')
        cout << "Incorrect Answer" << endl;
    if (cAnswer == 'd')
        cout << "Correct Answer" << endl;
}
void scoreQuestion2(char cAnswer) {
    if (cAnswer == 'a')
        cout << "Correct Answer" << endl;
    if (cAnswer == 'b')
        cout << "Incorrect Answer" << endl;
    if (cAnswer == 'c')
        cout << "Incorrect Answer" << endl;
    if (cAnswer == 'd')
        cout << "Incorrect Answer" << endl;
}
```

3

```cpp
void scoreQuestion3(char cAnswer) {
    if (cAnswer == 'a')
        cout << "Incorrect Answer" << endl;
    if (cAnswer == 'b')
        cout << "Incorrect Answer" << endl;
    if (cAnswer == 'c')
        cout << "Incorrect Answer" << endl;
    if (cAnswer == 'd')
        cout << "Correct Answer" << endl;
}
void scoreQuestion4(char cAnswer) {
    if (cAnswer == 'a')
        cout << "Incorrect Answer" << endl;
    if (cAnswer == 'b')
        cout << "Incorrect Answer" << endl;
    if (cAnswer == 'c')
        cout << "Correct Answer" << endl;
    if (cAnswer == 'd')
        cout << "Incorrect Answer" << endl;
}
void scoreQuestion5(char cAnswer) {
    if (cAnswer == 'a')
        cout << "Incorrect Answer" << endl;
    if (cAnswer == 'b')
        cout << "Correct Answer" << endl;
    if (cAnswer == 'c')
        cout << "Incorrect Answer" << endl;
    if (cAnswer == 'd')
        cout << "Incorrect Answer" << endl;
}
```

6. Build the project. If you receive any compilation errors, fix them, and then recompile. Before you can run the Chemistry Quiz program, you will need to add code that receives input from users.

Standard Input Stream

So far, you have only output information to the console window using the cout object of the standard output stream. There are many instances, however, in which you need to receive information from a user. The **cin** object (pronounced "c in") receives information from the user via the standard input stream. Whereas the standard output stream prints text to the screen or to a file, the **standard input stream** reads information from the keyboard. In other words, the cin object receives keyboard input from the user and returns it to a C++ program. The syntax for using the cin object is *cin >> variable;*. Notice the extraction operator (>>) points towards the variable, in contrast to the syntax for the cout object, cout << "*text*";, in which the insertion operator (<<) points towards the cout object. The **extraction operator** (>>) retrieves information from the input stream. Take a moment to compare the extraction operator (>>) to the insertion operator (<<), which inserts information into the output stream. Essentially, the cout operator sends information towards the cout object (insertion), and the cin object sends information towards a variable (extraction).

A cin statement causes a C++ console application program to pause execution and wait for input from the user. The program starts again once the user presses Enter. Any characters the user entered before pressing Enter are assigned to the designated variable. The keyboard input that can be assigned to a variable using the cin object depends on the variable's data type. For example, the following code declares an int variable named iNumber, and then uses a cin statement to assign a value to the variable:

```
int iNumber;
cin >> iNumber;
```

The user can enter any number between –2,147,483,648 and 2,147,483,647, because that is the valid range for the int data type. If the user enters a floating-point number such as 56.74, however, the number will be truncated to 56 before it is assigned to the iNumber variable since int data types cannot store decimal values. A value of 0 will be assigned if you attempt to assign characters to the iNumber variable. As another example of data types and cin statements, consider the following code:

```
char cLetter;
cin >> cLetter;
```

Because the char data type stores only single characters, if a user types multiple letters, only the first letter typed will be assigned to the cLetter variable in the preceding code. For example, if the user types *Hello* before pressing Enter, then only the letter *H* is assigned to the cLetter variable. If you want to use a cin statement to assign a string to a variable, then you must first declare the number of characters that will be assigned to the variable. For example, the following code declares two char variables, cFirstName and cLastName, to collect a user's name. The variable declaration statements specify 25 as the maximum number of characters to assign to each variable, which should be sufficient to hold the first and last names of most people.

```
char cFirstName[25];
char cLastName[25];
cout << "Enter your first name: ";
cin >> cFirstName;
cout << "Enter your last name: ";
cin >> cLastName;
cout << "Your name is " << cFirstName << " " << cLastName <<
endl;
```

Next, you will add to the ChemistryQuiz1 project cout statements that print questions to the screen and cin statements to receive each response.

To add to the ChemistryQuiz1 project cout statements that print questions to the screen and cin statements to receive each response:

1. Return to the **ChemistryQuiz1.cpp** source file in the Text Editor window in the **ChemistryQuiz1** project.

2. Between the main() function's curly braces, declare a title for the quiz and a char variable to hold the response received from cin statements (which you will create next):

```
char cInput;
cout << "Chemistry Quiz\n";
```

3. Next, add the code for the first question. The code displays the question using cout statements and receives an answer using a cin statement. After the user answers the question, the scoreQuestion1() function executes to score the response. Notice that each answer includes a tab escape character \t so that it is indented beneath the question.

```
// QUESTION 1
cout << "1. Which of the following would decrease in pH if an"
        << endl
<< "   equal volume of 0.5M NaOH were to be added?" << endl
<< "\ta. Water" << endl
<< "\tb. 0.25M Na2CO3" << endl
<< "\tc. 0.5M HCl" << endl
<< "\td. 0.6M KOH" << endl;
cout << "Your answer> ";
cin >> cInput;
scoreQuestion1(cInput);
```

4. Now add the remainder of the questions:

```
// QUESTION 2
cout << "2. Which of the following compounds contain Mangan
ese "
        << endl
<< "   in its highest oxidation state?" << endl
<< "\ta. Mn2O7" << endl
<< "\tb. MnC2O4" << endl
<< "\tc. KMnO5" << endl
<< "\td. K2MnO4" << endl;
cout << "Your answer> ";
cin >> cInput;
scoreQuestion2(cInput);
// QUESTION 3
cout << "3. Select the appropriate classification for the a
ction "    << endl
<< "   of heat on a mixture of sodium benzoate and soda-
lime?"
        << endl
```

```
                   << "\ta. Polymerization" << endl
                   << "\tb. Addition" << endl
                   << "\tc. Condensation" << endl
                   << "\td. Decarboxylation" << endl;
              cout << "Your answer> ";
              cin >> cInput;
              scoreQuestion3(cInput);
              // QUESTION 4
              cout << "4. Select the compound which reacts with aqueous s
              odium "
                        << endl
                   << "   hydroxide but not with aqueous sodium carbonate" << e
              ndl
                   << "\ta. HOCH2CH2OH" << endl
                   << "\tb. CH3CHClCO2H" << endl
                   << "\tc. PhOH" << endl
                   << "\td. CH3(CHOH)CH3" << endl;
              cout << "Your answer> ";
              cin >> cInput;
              scoreQuestion4(cInput);
              // QUESTION 5
              cout << "5. Select the structure possessed by helium, at ro
              om "
                        << endl
                   << "   temperature and atmospheric pressure:" << endl
                   << "\ta. Giant structure of ions" << endl
                   << "\tb. Widely spaced atoms" << endl
                   << "\tc. Widely spaced molecules" << endl
                   << "\td. Giant structure of atoms" << endl;
              cout << "Your answer> ";
              cin >> cInput;
              scoreQuestion5(cInput);
              cout << endl;
```

5. Build and execute the project, then answer the questions. As you select a response for each question, you will immediately learn whether the answer is correct. Figure 3-12 shows the output after answering several questions.

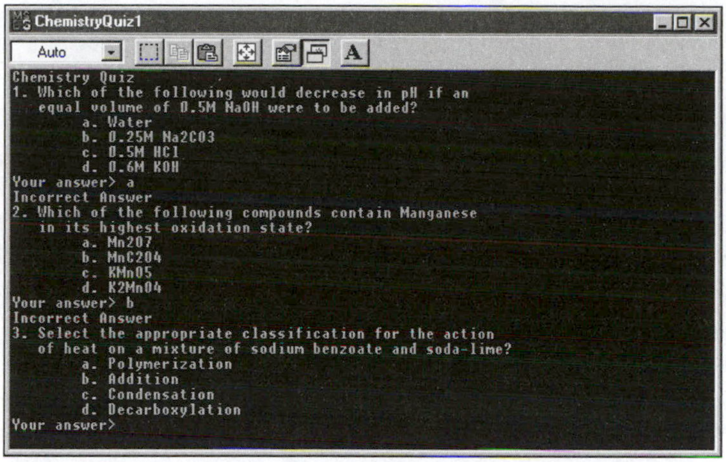

Figure 3-12   Output of ChemistryQuiz1

6. Press any key to close the command window.

if...else **Statements**

When using an **if** statement, you can include an **else** clause to run an alternate set of code if the conditional expression evaluated by the **if** statement returns a value of false. For instance, you may have an investment program that uses an **if** statement whose conditional expression evaluates a Boolean variable named bStockMarket that determines if the user of the program invests in the stock market. If the condition evaluates to true, then the **if** statement prints a list of recommended stocks. If the condition evaluates to false, then the statements in an **else** clause display other types of investment opportunities. An **if** statement that includes an **else** clause is called an **if...else** statement. You can think of an **else** clause as being a backup plan for when the **if** statement's condition returns a value of false. The syntax for an **if...else** statement is as follows:

```
if (conditional expression) {
    statement(s);
}
else {
    statement(s);
}
```

You can use command blocks to construct an **if...else** statement as follows:

```
if (condition) {
    statements;
}
else {
    statements;
}
```

The `else` clause can only be used with an `if` statement. Unlike the `if` statement, the `else` clause cannot be used alone.

A common technique is to combine an **else** structure with another **if** statement. The following code shows an example of a program that gathers a number from a user, assigns it to a variable named iNumber, and then uses an **if...else** structure to determine the size of the number. The opening **if** statement first checks to see if the iNumber variable is less than or equal to 100. If it is, then the statement following the **if** statement executes. If the **if** statement's conditional expression evaluates to false, then an **else** structure combined with an **if** statement determines if the iNumber variable is between 100 and 1000. The final **else** structure executes if the number the user enters does not meet the conditional statements in the **if** and **else...if** structures.

```cpp
int iNumber;
cout << "Please enter a positive number." << endl;
cin >> iNumber;
if (iNumber <= 100) {
    cout << "The number you entered is " << iNumber;
    cout << iNumber << " is between 0 and 100" << endl;
}
else if (iNumber > 100 && iNumber <=100)  {
    cout << "The number you entered is " << iNumber;
    cout << iNumber << " is between 100 and 1000" << endl;
}
else  {
    cout << "The number you entered is " << iNumber;
    cout << iNumber << " is greater than 1000" << endl;
}
```

The C++ code for the ChemistryQuiz1 project you created earlier uses multiple **if** statements to evaluate the results of the quiz. Although the multiple **if** statements function properly, they can be simplified using an **if...else** statement. Next, you will create a new version of the Chemistry Quiz program that contains an **if...else** statement instead of multiple **if** statements.

To create a new version of the Chemistry Quiz program that contains an **if...else** statement instead of multiple **if** statements:

1. Return to the ChemistryQuiz1.cpp source file in the Text Editor window and choose **Select All** from the **Edit** menu. Once the code is highlighted, select **Copy** from the **Edit** menu. You will copy the highlighted code into a new project, rather than retyping it.

2. Create a new empty Win32 Console Application project named **ChemistryQuiz2**. Save the project in the **Chapter.03** folder in your Visual C++ Projects folder. Select the **Create new workspace** radio button before clicking the OK button in the New dialog box. Once the project is created, add a C++ source file named **ChemistryQuiz2**.

3. After the ChemistryQuiz2.cpp file opens in the Text Editor window, select **Paste** from the **Edit** menu to paste the code you copied from the ChemistryQuiz1.cpp file.

4. Because you only need the `if` statement to test for the correct answer, you can group all the incorrect answers in an `else` clause. Modify each of the functions that scores a question so that the multiple `if` statements are replaced with an `if...else` statement. The following code shows how the statements for the scoreQuestion1() function should appear. Modify each score Question()function in a similar fashion.

```cpp
if (cAnswer == 'd')
    cout << "Correct Answer" << endl;
else
    cout << "Incorrect Answer" << endl;
```

5. Build and execute the **ChemistryQuiz2** project. The program should function the same as when it contained only `if` statements.

6. Press any key to close the command window.

Nested `if` Statements

When you make a decision with a control structure such as an `if` or `if...else` statement, you may want the statements executed by the control structure to make other decisions. For instance, you may have a program that uses an `if` statement to ask users if they like sports. If users answer yes, you may want to run another `if` statement that asks users whether they like team sports or individual sports. Because you can include any code you like within the `if` statement or the `else` clause, you can include other `if` or `if...else` statements. An `if` statement contained within another `if` or `if...else` statement is called a **nested** `if` statement. Similarly, an `if...else` statement contained within another `if` or `if...else` statement is called a **nested** `if...else` statement. You use nested `if` and `if...else` statements to perform conditional evaluations in addition to an original conditional evaluation. For example, the following code performs two conditional evaluations before the cout statement executes:

```cpp
int iNumber = 7;
if (iNumber > 5)
    if (iNumber < 10)
        cout << "The number is between 5 and 10." << endl;
```

If either of the conditions in this example evaluate to false, then the program skips the remainder of the `if` statement.

The C++ code in the ChemistryQuiz2.cpp file is somewhat inefficient since it contains multiple functions that perform the same task of scoring the quiz. A more efficient method of scoring the quiz is to use a single function that contains nested decision-making structures. Next, you will create a new version of the Chemistry Quiz program that contains a single function that checks the correct answer for all the questions using nested `if...else` statements.

To create a new version of the Chemistry Quiz program that contains a single function that checks the correct answer for all the questions using nested `if...else` statements:

1. Return to the ChemistryQuiz2.cpp source file in the Text Editor window and choose **Select All** from the **Edit** menu. Once the code is highlighted, select **Copy** from the **Edit** menu. You will copy the highlighted code into a new project rather than retyping it.

2. Create a new empty Win32 Console Application project named **ChemistryQuiz3**. Save the project in the **Chapter.03** folder in your Visual C++ Projects folder. Select the **Create new workspace** radio button before clicking the OK button in the New dialog box. Once the project is created, add a C++ source file named **ChemistryQuiz3**.

3. After the ChemistryQuiz3.cpp file opens in the Text Editor window, select **Paste** from the **Edit** menu to paste the code you copied from the ChemistryQuiz2.cpp file.

4. Replace the five function prototypes with a single function prototype: **void scoreQuestions(int iNumber, char cAnswer);**. The scoreQuestions() function will check all of the answers. You will send an answer argument to the scoreQuestions() function, just like you did with the functions that scored each individual question. You will also send a new argument, *iNumber*, which represents the question number, to the scoreQuestions() function.

5. Delete the five functions that following the main() function.

6. After deleting the five functions, add the scoreQuestions() function constructor after the main() function's closing brace: **void scoreQuestions(int iNumber, char cAnswer) {**.

7. Press **Enter** and add the opening `if` statement that checks to see if the question number is equal to 1. If it is, a nested `if...else` statement evaluates the response.

```
if (iNumber == 1) {
    if (cAnswer == 'd')
        cout << "Correct Answer" << endl;
    else
        cout << "Incorrect Answer" << endl;
}
```

8. Add an `else` clause for question number 2:

```
else if (iNumber == 2) {
    if (cAnswer == 'a')
        cout << "Correct Answer" << endl;
    else
        cout << "Incorrect Answer" << endl;
}
```

3

9. Add an **else** clause for question number 3:

```
else if (iNumber == 3) {
    if (cAnswer == 'd')
        cout << "Correct Answer" << endl;
    else
        cout << "Incorrect Answer" << endl;
}
```

10. Add an **else** clause for question number 4:

```
else if (iNumber == 4) {
    if (cAnswer == 'c')
        cout << "Correct Answer" << endl;
    else
        cout << "Incorrect Answer" << endl;
}
```

11. Add an **else** clause for question number 5:

```
else if (iNumber == 5) {
    if (cAnswer == 'b')
        cout << "Correct Answer" << endl;
    else
        cout << "Incorrect Answer" << endl;
}
```

12. Add a closing brace (**}**) for the scoreQuestions() function.

13. In the main() function, change each question's function call to **scoreQuestions(*number*, cInput);**, changing the *number* argument to the appropriate question number. For example, the function call for question 1 should read: **scoreQuestions(1, cInput);**.

14. Build and execute the ChemistryQuiz3 project. The program should still function the same way it did with the multiple **if** statements and the multiple functions.

15. Press any key to close the command window.

switch Statements

Another C++ statement that is used for controlling program flow is the **switch** statement. The **switch statement** controls program flow by executing a specific set of statements depending on the value returned from an expression. Note that the result returned from an expression must be an integer data type, which includes the bool, char, int, long int, and short data types. The **switch** statement compares the result returned from the expression to a label contained within the **switch** statement's command block. If the value matches a particular label, then statements associated with that label execute. Essentially, a switch statement executes a particular block of statements according to the value returned from an expression.

For example, suppose you have a program that determines which sales rep should handle a new customer, based on the customer's ZIP code. The program may contain an integer variable named iZipCode. A `switch` statement can evaluate the iZipCode variable (which is an expression) and compare it to a label within the `switch` statement. The `switch` statement may contain a label for each ZIP code that you need to evaluate. Statements within each label could then assign the correct sales rep name to a char variable named szSalesRep, along with any other functionality that may be required to set up a new customer account. For instance, if the iZipVariable variable is equal to 94939, then the statements that are part of the 94939 label execute. Although you could accomplish the same functionality using `if` or `if...else` statements, a `switch` statement makes it easier to organize different branches of code that can be executed.

 You will receive a compiler error if the expression you evaluate in a `switch` statement is any data type other than bool, char, int, long int, or short.

A `switch` construct consists of the following components: the keyword `switch`, an expression, an opening brace, a `case` label, the keyword `break`, a `default` label, executable statements, and a closing brace. The syntax for the `switch` statement is as follows:

```
switch (expression) {
    case label :
        statement(s);
        break;
    case label :
        statement(s);
        break;
    ...
    default :
        statement(s);
}
```

The labels within a `switch` statement are called **case labels,** and they identify specific code segments. A `case` label consists of the keyword `case`, followed by a constant value, followed by a colon. For char labels, enclose each character within single quotes, as if you were assigning a new char value to a variable. C++ compares the value returned from the `switch` statement's expression to the literal value or variable name following the `case` keyword. If the comparison yields a match, the `case` label's statements execute. For example, you may have a `case` label similar to `case 3:`. If the value of a `switch` statement's expression equals 3, then the `case 3:` label's statements execute. Similarly, if you use a char variable in the `switch` statement's expression, then you would use a label similar to `case 'A':` for each of the characters you want to evaluate.

 A `case` label can be followed by a single statement or multiple statements. Unlike `if` statements, however, multiple statements for a `case` label do not need to be enclosed within a command block.

Another decision-making structure that works with labels is the goto statement. When C++ encounters a goto statement, program execution is immediately and unconditionally transferred to a specified label. Although supported in C++, it is considered poor programming technique to use the goto statement because it makes program flow extremely difficult to follow. For this reason the goto statement is not discussed in this text, and you are encouraged to avoid using it in your programs.

Another type of label used within **switch** constructs is the **default** label. The **default label** contains statements that execute when the value returned by the **switch** statement's conditional expression does not match a **case** label. A **default** label consists of the keyword **default** followed by a colon.

When a **switch** construct executes, the value returned by the conditional expression is compared to each **case** label in the order in which it is encountered. Once a matching label is found, its statements execute. You can place any statements you like after a case label, and you do not need to use command blocks to surround multiple statements that are placed after a case label. Instead, C++ knows to execute any statements within a given case label until either a new case label is encountered or the **switch** statement's closing brace is encountered. Unlike the **if...else** statement, program execution does not automatically exit the **switch** construct after a particular **case** label's statements execute. Instead, the **switch** statement continues evaluating the rest of the **case** labels in the list. Once a matching **case** label is found, however, evaluation of additional **case** labels is unnecessary. If you are working with a large **switch** construct with many **case** labels, evaluation of additional **case** labels can potentially slow down your program.

It is good programming design to end a **switch** construct once it performs its required task. A **switch** construct ends automatically after C++ encounters its closing brace (}) or when a **break** statement is found. A **break statement** is used to exit **switch** constructs and other program control statements such as **while, do...while**, and **for** repetition statements. To end a **switch** construct once it performs its required task, you should include a **break** statement within each **case** label section.

 You will learn more about repetition statements later in this chapter.

Figure 3-13 displays an example of a program that uses a **switch** construct. The main() function displays a menu of American cities from which users can choose. The number of the selected city is passed to the iAmericanCity variable in the cityLocation() function and evaluated in a **switch** statement. The **switch** statement compares the contents of the iAmericanCity argument to the **case** labels. If a match is found, a string listing the city's state is returned and a **break** statement ends the **switch** construct. If a match is not found, the value *You did not select one of the five cities!* is returned from the **default** label. Figure 3-14 shows the output.

```
#include <iostream.h>
void cityLocation(int iAmericanCity);
void main()
{
    int iCity = 0;
    cout << "Enter a number to find the state where a city
            is located." << endl;
    cout << "1. Boston" << endl;
    cout << "2. Chicago" << endl;
    cout << "3. Los Angeles" << endl;
    cout << "4. Miami" << endl;
    cout << "5. Providence" << endl << endl;
    cin >> iCity;
    cout << endl;
    cityLocation(iCity);
}
void cityLocation(int iAmericanCity) {
    switch (iAmericanCity) {
        case 1:
            cout << "Boston is in Massachusetts"
                    << endl;
            break;
        case 2:
            cout << "Chicago is in Illinois"
                    << endl;
            break;
        case 3:
            cout << "Los Angeles is in California"
                    << endl;
            break;
        case 4:
            cout << "Miami is in Florida" << endl;
            break;
        case 5:
            cout << "Providence is in Rhode Island"
                    << endl;
            break;
        default:
            cout << "You did not select one of the five
                    cities!" << endl;
    }
}
```

Figure 3-13   Program containing a switch statement

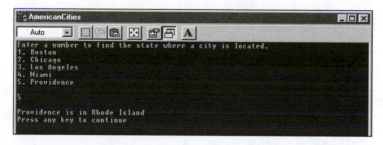

Figure 3-14   Output of program containing a `switch` statement

Next, you will create a new version of the Chemistry Quiz program in which the scoreQuestions() function contains a `switch` statement instead of nested `if...else` statements. Each `case` statement in the modified program checks for the question number from the function's number argument. The `switch` statement makes better programming sense because it eliminates the need to check the question number multiple times, as is necessary with an `if...else` structure.

To create a new version of the Chemistry Quiz program in which the scoreQuestions() function contains a switch statement instead of nested `if...else` statements:

1. Return to the ChemistryQuiz3.cpp source file in the Text Editor window and choose **Select All** from the **Edit** menu. Once the code is highlighted, select **Copy** from the **Edit** menu. You will copy the highlighted code into a new project, rather than retyping it.

2. Create a new empty Win32 Console Application project named **ChemistryQuiz4**. Save the project in the **Chapter.03** folder in your Visual C++ Projects folder. Select the **Create new workspace** radio button before clicking the OK button in the New dialog box. Once the project is created, add a C++ source file named **ChemistryQuiz4**.

3. After the ChemistryQuiz4.cpp file opens in the Text Editor window, select **Paste** from the **Edit** menu to paste the code you copied from the ChemistryQuiz4.cpp file.

4. Change the `if...else` statements within the scoreAnswers() function to the following `switch` statement.

```
switch (iNumber) {
    case 1:
        if (cAnswer == 'd')
            cout << "Correct Answer" << endl;
        else
            cout << "Incorrect Answer" << endl;
        break;
```

```
        case 2:
            if (cAnswer == 'a')
                cout << "Correct Answer" << endl;
            else
                cout << "Incorrect Answer" << endl;
            break;
        case 3:
            if (cAnswer == 'd')
                cout << "Correct Answer" << endl;
            else
                cout << "Incorrect Answer" << endl;
            break;
        case 4:
            if (cAnswer == 'c')
                cout << "Correct Answer" << endl;
            else
                cout << "Incorrect Answer" << endl;
            break;
        case 5:
            if (cAnswer == 'b')
                cout << "Correct Answer" << endl;
            else
                cout << "Incorrect Answer" << endl;
            break;
    }
```

5. Build and execute the ChemistryQuiz4 project. The program should still function the same as it did with the nested `if...else` statements.

6. Press any key to close the command window.

REPETITION STATEMENTS

The statements you have worked with so far execute one after the other in a linear fashion. `If`, `if...else`, and `switch` statements select only a single branch of code to execute, then program execution continues on to the statement that follows. But what if you want to repeat the same statement, function, or code section five times, ten times, or one hundred times? For example, suppose you have a program that prompts users for information such as their name or telephone number. If the user does not enter the correct information, then you may want to keep repeating the prompt statements until the user enters the correct information. A **looping statement** repeatedly executes a statement or a series of statements while a specific condition is true or until a specific condition becomes true. Looping techniques include `while`, `do...while`, `for`, and `continue` statements.

while **Statements**

One of the simplest types of looping statements is the while statement. The **while statement** is used for repeating a statement or series of statements as long as a given conditional expression evaluates to true. The syntax for the while statement is as follows:

```
while (conditional expression) {
    statement(s);
}
```

Like the if...else and switch statements, the conditional expression that the while statement tests for is enclosed within parentheses following the keyword while. As long as the conditional expression evaluates to true, the statement or command block that follows will execute repeatedly. Each repetition of a looping statement is called an **iteration**. Once the conditional expression evaluates to false, the loop ends and the next statement following the while statement executes.

A while statement will keep repeating until its conditional expression evaluates to false. To end the while statement once the desired tasks have been performed, you must include code that tracks the progress of the loop and changes the value produced by the conditional expression. You track the progress of a while statement, or any other loop, with a counter. A **counter** is a variable that increments or decrements with each iteration of a loop statement.

 Many programmers often name counter variables *count*, *counter*, or something similar. The letters *i*, *j*, *k*, and *l* are also commonly used as counter names. Using a name such as *count*, the letter *i* (for *increment*), or a higher letter helps you remember (and lets other programmers know) that the variable is being used as a counter. In this text we will use the Hungarian notation prefix, *ct*, with a variable name.

The following code shows an example of a simple program that uses a while statement. The program declares a variable named ctCount and assigns to it an initial value of 1. The ctCount variable is then used in the while statement's conditional expression (ctCount <= 5). As long as the ctCount variable is less than or equal to five, the while statement will loop. Within the body of the while statement, the cout statement prints the value of the ctCount variable, then the ctCount variable increments by a value of 1. The while statement loops until the ctCount variable increments to a value of 6.

```
int ctCount = 1;
while (ctCount <= 5) {
    cout << ctCount << endl;
    ++ctCount;
}
cout << "You have printed 5 numbers." << endl << endl;
```

The preceding code prints the numbers 1 to 5, which represent each iteration of the loop. Once ctCount reaches 6, the message *You have printed 5 numbers.* is printed to demonstrate when the loop ends. Figure 3-15 shows the output.

Figure 3-15   Output of a simple `while` statement

The preceding example controls the repetitions in the `while` loop by incrementing a counter variable. However, you can also control the repetitions in a `while` loop by decrementing counter variables. Consider the following program code:

```
int ctCount = 10;
while (ctCount > 0) {
     cout << ctCount << endl;
     --ctCount;
}
cout << "We have liftoff." << endl << endl;
```

In this example the initial value of the ctCount variable is 10, and it is decreased by 1 using the decrement operator (--). While the ctCount variable is greater than 0, the statement within the `while` loop prints the value of the ctCount variable. When the value of ctCount is equal to 0, the `while` loop ends and the statement immediately following it prints. Figure 3-16 shows the program's output.

Figure 3-16   Output of a `while` statement using a decrement operator

There are many ways to change the value of a count variable to control the repetitions of a while loop. The following example uses the `*=` assignment operator to multiply the value of the ctCount variable by 2. Once the ctCount variable reaches a value of 100, the `while` statement ends. Figure 3-17 shows the program's output.

```
int ctCount = 1;
while (ctCount <= 100) {
     cout << ctCount << endl;
     ctCount *= 2;
}
cout << endl;
```

Figure 3-17   Output of a `while` statement using the `*=` assignment operator

It is important to include code that monitors a **while** statement's conditional expression. You also need to include code within the body of the **while** statement that changes *some* part of the conditional expression. If you do not include code that changes the value used by the conditional expression, your program will be caught in an infinite loop. An **infinite loop** is a situation in which a looping statement never ends because its conditional expression is never updated or is never false. Consider the following **while** statement:

```
int ctCount = 1;
while (ctCount <= 10) {
    cout << "The number is " << ctCount << endl;
}
```

Although the **while** statement in the above example includes a conditional expression that checks the value of a count variable, there is no code within the **while** statement's body that changes the count variable's value. The count variable will continue to have a value of 1 through each iteration of the loop. In this case, the text *The number is 1* prints over and over again, until you close the console application window.

You can end an infinite loop in a console application by pressing Ctrl+Break.

do...while Statements

Another C++ looping statement that is similar to the **while** statement is the **do...while** statement. The **do...while statement** executes a statement or statements once, then repeats the execution as long as a given conditional expression evaluates to true. The syntax for the **do...while** statement is as follows:

```
do {
    statement(s);
} while (conditional expression);
```

As you can see in the syntax description, the statements execute *before* a conditional expression is evaluated. Unlike the simpler **while** statement, the statements in a **do...while** statement always execute once, before a conditional expression is evaluated.

The following `do...while` statement executes once before the conditional expression evaluates the ctCount variable. Therefore, a single line that reads *The count is equal to 2* prints. Once the conditional expression (ctCount < 2) executes, the `do...while` statement ends since the ctCount variable is equal to 2 and causes the conditional expression to return a value of false.

```
int ctCount = 2;
do {
      cout << "The count is equal to " << ctCount << endl;
      ++ctCount;
} while (ctCount < 2);
```

Note that this `do...while` example includes a counter within the body of the `do...while` statement. As with the `while` statement, you need to include code that changes some part of the conditional expression in order to prevent an infinite loop from occurring.

`for` Statements

You can also use the `for` statement to loop through code. The `for` statement is used for repeating a statement or series of statements as long as a given conditional expression evaluates to true. The `for` statement performs essentially the same function as the `while` statement: if a conditional expression within the `for` statement evaluates to true, then the `for` statement executes and will continue to execute repeatedly until the conditional expression evaluates to false. One of the primary differences between the `while` statement and the `for` statement is that in addition to a conditional expression, you can also include code in the `for` statement's constructor to initialize a counter and change its value with each iteration. The syntax of the `for` statement is as follows:

```
for (initialization expression; condition; update statement) {

      statement(s);

}
```

When C++ encounters a `for` loop, the following steps occur:

1. The initialization expression is started. For example, if the initialization expression in a `for` loop is `int ctCount = 1;`, then a variable named ctCount is declared and an initial value of 1 is assigned to it. The initialization expression is only started once when the `for` loop is first encountered.

2. The `for` loop's condition is evaluated.

3. If the condition evaluation in Step 2 returns a value of true, then the `for` loop's statements execute, Step 4 occurs, then the process starts over again with Step 2. If the condition evaluation in Step 2 returns a value of false, then the `for` statement ends and the next statement following the `for` statement executes.

4. The update statement in the `for` statement's constructor is executed. For example, the count variable may increment by 1.

You can omit any of the three parts of the **for** statement constructor, but you must include the semicolons that separate each section. If you omit a section of the constructor, be sure you include code within the body that will end the **for** statement or your program may get caught in an infinite loop.

The following code displays an example of a **for** statement that prints the contents of an array.

```
#include <iostream.h>
void main() {
    char arStudentGrades[5];
    arStudentGrades[0] = 'A';      // first element
    arStudentGrades[1] = 'B';      // second element
    arStudentGrades[2] = 'C';      // third element
    arStudentGrades[3] = 'D';      // fourth element
    arStudentGrades[4] = 'F';      // fifth element
    for (int ctCount = 0; ctCount < 5; ++ctCount) {
        cout << arStudentGrades[ctCount] << endl;
    }
    cout << endl;
}
```

As you can see in the example, the counter is initialized, evaluated, and incremented within the constructor. You do not need to include a declaration for the ctCount variable before the **for** statement, nor do you need to increment the count variable within the body of the **for** statement. Figure 3–18 shows the output of the program.

Figure 3-18   Output of program with a **for** statement that displays the contents of an array

You can create looping statements that are controlled by counters more efficiently using **for** statements than using **while** statements. Using a **for** statement is more efficient because you do not need as many lines of code. Consider the following **while** statement:

```
int ctCount = 1;
while (ctCount <= 5) {
    cout << ctCount << endl;
    ++ctCount;
}
```

The preceding `while` statement can be created more efficiently using a `for` statement as follows:

```
for (int ctCount = 1; ctCount <= 5; ++ctCount) {
    cout << ctCount << endl;
}
```

There are times, however, when using a `while` statement is preferable to using a `for` statement. If you do not use a counter to update the conditional expression or if the counter must be updated from the body of the looping statement, a `while` construction works better than a `for` construction. The following code relies on a value returned from a cin statement, rather than a counter, for program control.

```
char cKey = 'Y';
while (cKey == 'Y') {
    cout << "Press an uppercase Y to redisplay this text. ";
    cin << cKey;
}
```

You could accomplish the same task using a `for` statement, but in this case the third part of the `for` statement's constructor that updates the counter is unnecessary. Therefore, this code is better written using a `while` statement. If you use a `for` statement instead of a `while` statement in the preceding example, you must leave out the update section from the `for` statement's constructor. You must also remember to leave in the semicolon that separates the conditional section from the update section. If you leave the update section in the constructor, you could create an infinite loop. The following code performs essentially the same task as the preceding `while` example, but causes an infinite loop since the constructor always changes the cKey variable to *Y* with each iteration. No matter how many times you press any key other than *Y*, the `for` constructor reassigns the variable to *Y* each time the code repeats, causing an infinite loop.

```
for (char cKey = 'Y'; cKey == 'Y'; cKey = 'Y') {
    cout << "Press an uppercase Y to redisplay this text: ";
    cin >> cKey;
}
```

To make the above `for` loop function correctly without causing an infinite loop, you must remove the update section from the constructor, as follows:

```
for (char cKey = 'Y'; cKey == 'Y';) {
    cout << "Press an uppercase Y to redisplay this text: ";
    cin >> cKey;
}
```

Next, you will create a final version of the Chemistry Quiz program that uses a single `for` statement containing a nested `if` statement to score the quiz. Although the `for` statement you create is somewhat more complicated than using the `if`, `if...else`, and `switch` statements, it takes up considerably fewer lines of code. You will also include code that scores the entire quiz after a user is finished, instead of grading the quiz answer-by-answer.

To create the final version of the Chemistry Quiz program:

1. Open the ChemistryQuiz4 project, and then open the ChemistryQuiz4.cpp source file in the Text Editor window, if necessary. Once the file is open, choose **Select All** from the **Edit** menu. Once the code is highlighted, select **Copy** from the **Edit** menu. You will copy the highlighted code into a new project, rather than retyping it.

2. Create a new empty Win32 Console Application project named **ChemistryQuizFinal**. Save the project in the **Chapter.03** folder in your Visual C++ Projects folder. Select the **Create new workspace** radio button before clicking the OK button in the New dialog box. Once the project is created, add a C++ source file named **ChemistryQuizFinal**.

3. After the ChemistryQuizFinal.cpp file opens in the Text Editor window, select **Paste** from the **Edit** menu to paste the code you copied from the ChemistryQuiz4.cpp file.

4. Delete the entire scoreQuestions() function, and replace the scoreQuestions() function prototype with the following lines to create two global char arrays: arUserAnswers[] and arCorrectAnswers[]. The arUserAnswers[] array holds the answers selected each time the quiz runs, and the arCorrectAnswers[] array holds the correct response for each of the questions.

```
char arUserAnswers[5];
char arCorrectAnswers[5] = {'d', 'a', 'd', 'c', 'b'};
```

5. Press **Enter** and type the following function, which assigns the response from each question to the appropriate element in the arUserAnswers[] array. The program sends the actual question number (1-5) and answer (a-d) to the function from the main() function. To assign question responses to the correct element, 1 must be subtracted from the question variable because the elements in an array start with 0.

```
void recordAnswer(int iQuestion, char cAnswer) {
    arUserAnswers[iQuestion-1] = cAnswer;
}
```

6. Press **Enter** and type the opening header for the function that scores the quiz: **void scoreQuiz() {**. You will call this function at the end of the main() function.

7. Press **Enter** and type **int iTotalCorrect = 0;** to declare a new int variable and assign to it an initial value of 0. The iTotalCorrect variable will hold the number of correct answers.

8. Press **Enter** and type the opening statement for a **for** loop that scores the quiz: **for(int ctCount = 0; ctCount < 5; ++ctCount) {**. A counter named ctCount initializes to a value of 0 since 0 is the starting index of an array. The conditional expression checks to see if ctCount is less than or equal to the number of elements in the arUserAnswers[] array. Finally, the ctCount variable increments by 1 with each iteration of the loop.

9. Press **Enter** and add the following `if` statement within the `for` loop. The `if` statement compares each element within the arUserAnswers[] array to each corresponding element within the arCorrectAnswers[] array. If the elements match, the iTotalCorrect variable increments by 1.

```
if (arUserAnswers[ctCount] == arCorrectAnswers[ctCount])
    ++iTotalCorrect;
```

10. Add the closing brace for the for loop. Then add a cout statement that shows how many questions were answered correctly:

```
}
    cout << "You scored " << iTotalCorrect
         << " out of 5 answers correctly!" << endl;
```

11. Add a closing brace (}) for the scoreQuiz() function.

12. In the main() function, change the name of the function called after each question from scoreQuestions() to **recordAnswer()**. Be sure to include the question number and cInput arguments. For example, the statement for question 1 should read `recordAnswer(1, cInput);`.

13. Finally, add the statement `scoreQuiz();` that calls the scoreQuiz() function immediately after the last recordAnswer() function call in the main() function.

14. Build and execute the ChemistryQuizFinal project. Test the program by answering all five questions. Your output should appear similar to Figure 3-19, depending on how many questions you answered correctly.

Figure 3-19   Output of ChemistryQuizFinal

15. Press any key to close the command window.

`continue` Statements

Suppose you want a program to loop through the elements of an array containing a list of stocks. For stocks worth more than $10, the program prints information to the screen, such as purchase price, number of shares, and so on. You want the program to skip stocks worth less than $10 and move on to a new stock. Earlier you learned that you could use a break statement to halt execution of a looping statement. But with a break statement, execution leaves the loop altogether and the next statement following the loop executes. Is there a method for stopping and restarting a loop? The **continue statement** halts a looping statement and restarts the loop with a new iteration. You use the `continue` statement when you want to stop the loop for the current iteration, but want the loop to continue with a new iteration. For example, you may have a program that uses a `for` statement to loop through the elements of an array containing a list of stocks. For stocks worth more than $10, you print information to the screen, such as purchase price, number of shares, and so on. However, you use the `continue` statement to skip stocks worth less than $10 and move on to a new iteration. The following code contains a `for` loop containing a **break** statement.

```
for(int ctCount = 1; ctCount <=5; ++ctCount) {
    if(ctCount == 3)
        break;
    cout << ctCount << endl;
}
```

The **for** loops in the preceding examples contain an **if** statement that checks if the current value of ctCount equals 3. When ctCount equals 3, the **break** statement immediately ends the **for** loop. The output for the preceding **for** loop is as follows:

```
1
2
```

The following code displays the same **for** loop from the previous example, but with a `continue` statement.

```
for(int ctCount = 1; ctCount <=5; ++ctCount) {
    if(ctCount == 3)
        continue;
    cout << ctCount << endl;
}
```

In the preceding example, when ctCount equals 3, the **continue** statement stops the current iteration of the **for** loop, and the program skips printing the number 3. However, the loop continues to iterate until the conditional expression **ctCount <= 5** is false. The output is:

```
1
2
4
5
```

CHAPTER SUMMARY

- ❏ An expression is a combination of literal values, variables, operators, and other expressions that can be evaluated by the Visual C++ compiler to produce a result.

- ❏ Operands are variables and literals contained in an expression.

- ❏ Operators are binary or unary symbols used in expressions to manipulate operands.

- ❏ A binary operator requires an operand before the operator and an operand after the operator.

- ❏ A unary operator requires a single operand either before or after the operator.

- ❏ Arithmetic operators are used to perform mathematical calculations, such as addition, subtraction, multiplication, and division in C++.

- ❏ A prefix operator is placed before a variable and returns the value of the operand *after* the operation is performed.

- ❏ A postfix operator is placed after a variable and returns the value of the operand *before* the operation is performed.

- ❏ Assignment operators (=) are used for assigning a value to a variable.

- ❏ Comparison operators are used to compare two operands for equality and to determine if one numeric value is greater than another.

- ❏ Logical operators are used for comparing two Boolean operands for equality.

- ❏ You must use string functions found in the string.h header file to manipulate char variables.

- ❏ The strcpy() function copies the contents of one string into another using the syntax `strcpy(string1, string2);`.

- ❏ The strcat() function combines, or concatenates, two strings.

- ❏ Operator precedence is the order of priority in which operations in an expression are evaluated.

- ❏ The operator with the highest order of precedence is the scope resolution operator (::).

- ❏ Parentheses are used with expressions to change the order in which individual operations in an expression are evaluated.

- ❏ Flow control is the process of determining the order in which statements are executed in a program.

- ❏ The `if` statement is used to execute specific programming code if the evaluation of a conditional expression returns true.

- ❏ After an `if` statement's condition evaluates, either the first statement following the condition executes or the command block following the condition executes.

3

❑ Statements following an `if` statement's command or command block execute regardless of whether the if statement's conditional expression evaluates to true or false.

❑ The cin object reads information from the keyboard via the standard input stream.

❑ The extraction operator (>>) retrieves information from the output stream.

❑ The `else` clause runs an alternate set of code if the conditional expression evaluated by an `if` statement returns a value of false.

❑ In an `if...else` construct, only one set of statements executes: either the statements following the `if` statement or the statements following the `else` clause. Once either set of statements executes, any code following the `if...else` construct executes normally.

❑ An `if` statement contained within another `if` statement is called a nested `if` statement. Similarly, an `if...else` statement contained within an `if` or `if...else` statement is called a nested `if...else` statement.

❑ The `switch` statement controls program flow by executing a specific set of statements depending on the value returned by an expression.

❑ `case` labels within a `switch` statement mark specific code segments.

❑ The `default` label contains statements that execute when the value returned by the `switch` statement's conditional expression does not match a case label. A `default` label consists of only the keyword `default` followed by a colon.

❑ When a `switch` statement executes, the value returned by the conditional expression is compared to each `case` label in the order in which it is encountered. Once a matching label is found, the matching label's statements execute.

❑ A `break` statement is used to exit a `switch` statement.

❑ A looping statement repeatedly executes a statement or a series of statements while a specific condition is true or until a specific condition becomes true.

❑ The `while` statement is used for repeating a statement or series of statements as long as a given conditional expression evaluates to true.

❑ You must include code that tracks the progress of the `while` statement and changes the value produced by the conditional expression once the desired tasks have been performed.

❑ A counter is a variable that increments or decrements with each iteration of a looping statement.

❑ If a counter variable is beyond the range of a `while` statement's conditional expression, then the `while` statement will be bypassed completely.

❑ In an infinite loop, a looping statement never ends because its conditional expression is never updated.

❑ The `do...while` statement executes a statement or statements once, then repeats the execution as long as a given conditional expression evaluates to true.

❑ The `for` statement is used for repeating a statement or series of statements as long as a given conditional expression evaluates to true.

❑ You can omit any of the three parts of the `for` statement constructor, but you must include the semicolons that separate each section. If you omit a section of the constructor, be sure you include code within the body that will end the `for` statement or your program may get caught in an infinite loop.

❑ The `continue` statement halts a looping statement and restarts the loop with a new iteration.

REVIEW QUESTIONS

1. Operators that require an operand before the operator and an operand after the operator are called _____ operators.

   a. unary

   b. binary

   c. double

   d. multiplicity

2. The modulus operator (%) _____.

   a. coverts an operand to base 16 (hexadecimal) format

   b. returns the absolute value of an operand

   c. calculates the percentage of one operand compared to another

   d. divides two operands and returns the remainder

3. What value is assigned to the iReturnValue variable in the statement `iReturnValue = count++;`, assuming the count variable contains the value 10?

   a. 10

   b. 11

   c. 12

   d. 20

4. What value is assigned to the bReturnValue variable in the statement `bReturnValue = "First String" == "Second String";`?

   a. First String

   b. Second String

   c. True

   d. False

5. What value is assigned to the bReturnValue variable in the statement `bReturnValue = 100 != 200;`?

   a. First String

   b. Second String

c. True

d. False

6. What value is assigned to the bReturnValue variable in the statement
`bReturnValue = 50 == "fifty";`?

a. True

b. False

c. 50

d. "fifty"

7. The && (and) operator returns true if _____.

a. the left operand returns a value of true

b. the right operand returns a value of true

c. the left operand and right operand both return a value of true

d. the left operand and right operand both return a value of false

8. The operator that returns true if either its left or right operand returns a value of true
is the _____ operand.

a. ||

b. ==

c. %%

d. &&

9. What value is assigned to the bReturnValue variable in the statement
`returnValue = !x;`, assuming x has a value of true?

a. true

b. false

c. null

d. undefined

10. The order of priority in which operations in an expression are evaluated is known as
_____.

a. prerogative precedence

b. operator precedence

c. expression evaluation

d. priority evaluation

11. The operator with the highest order of precedence in C++ is the _____.

a. assignment operator

b. addition/subtraction operator

c. scope resolution operator

d. parentheses ()

12. What is the value of the expression `4 * (2 + 3)`?

    a. 11

    b. −11

    c. 20

    d. 14

13. The process of determining the order in which statements execute in a program is called _____.

    a. process manipulation

    b. flow control

    c. programmatic configuration

    d. architectural structuring

14. Which of the following is the correct syntax for an `if` statement?

    a.
```
if (myVariable == 10);
cout << "Your variable is equal to 10." << endl;
```

    b.
```
if myVariable == 10
cout << "Your variable is equal to 10." << endl;
```

    c.
```
if (myVariable == 10)
cout << "Your variable is equal to 10." << endl;
```

    d.
```
if (myVariable == 10),
cout << "Your variable is equal to 10." << endl;
```

15. An `if` statement can include multiple statements provided they _____.

    a. execute after the `if` statement's closing semicolon

    b. are not contained within a command block

    c. do not include other `if` statements

    d. are contained within a command block

16. What happens after you execute an `if` statement?

    a. The statement immediately following the `if` statement executes.

    b. The program ends.

    c. The `if` statement continues looping.

    d. The first matching case label in the `if` statement repeats.

17. Which operators can you use with an `if` statement?

    a. Only comparison operators

    b. Only logical operators

    c. Both comparison and logical operators

    d. You cannot use operators with an `if` statement

18. User input is received from _____.
    a. the standard output stream
    b. the standard input stream
    c. the Win32 API
    d. Windows dialog boxes

19. Which is the correct syntax for receiving user input?
    a. `cin << variable;`
    b. `cin >> variable;`
    c. `stdin << variable;`
    d. `stdin >> variable;`

20. Which of the following statements is true?
    a. An `if` statement must be constructed with an `else` clause.
    b. An `else` clause can be constructed without an `if` statement.
    c. An `if` statement can be constructed without an `else` clause.
    d. An `else` clause cannot be constructed with an `if` statement.

21. How many `if` statements can be nested in another `if` statement?
    a. 0
    b. 1
    c. 5
    d. As many as necessary

22. The `switch` statement controls program flow by executing a specific set of statements depending on _____.
    a. the result of an `if...else` statement
    b. the flow control header file that is included in the program
    c. whether an `if` statement executes from within a function
    d. the value returned by a conditional expression

23. The `case` labels within a `switch` statement are used to _____.
    a. mark specific code segments
    b. evaluate a conditional expression
    c. designate code that is to be ignored by the C++ compiler
    d. leave comments for other programmers

24. When the value returned by a `switch` statement's conditional expression does not match a `case` label, then the statements within the _____ label execute.
    a. `exception`
    b. `Else`
    c. `error`
    d. `default`

25. You can exit a `switch` statement using a _____ statement.

    a. `break`

    b. `end`

    c. `quit`

    d. `complete`

26. Each repetition of a looping statement is called a (an) _____.

    a. recurrence

    b. iteration

    c. duplication

    d. re-execution

27. Counter variables _____.

    a. are used to count the number of times a looping statement has repeated

    b. count the number of times a function starts and stops

    c. are used to count how many times a C++ program has been executed

    d. are used only within `if` or `if...else` statements

28. Which of the following is the correct syntax for a `while` statement?

    a.
```
while (ctCount <= 5, ++ ctCount) {
      cout << ctCount << endl;
   }
```

    b.
```
while (ctCount <= 5) {
      cout << ctCount << endl;
      ++ctCount;
   }
```

    c.
```
while (ctCount <= 5);
         cout << ctCount << endl;
         ++ctCount;
```

    d.
```
while (ctCount <= 5; cout << ctCount << endl) {
      ++ ctCount;
   }
```

29. Counter variables _____.

    a. can only be incremented

    b. can only be decremented

    c. can be changed using any conditional expression

    d. do not change

30. An infinite loop is caused _____.

    a. when you omit the closing brace for a decision making structure

    b. when a conditional expression never evaluates to false

    c. when a conditional expression never evaluates to true

    d. whenever you execute a `while` statement

31. If a `do...while` statement's conditional expression evaluates to false, how many times will the `do...while` statement execute?

    a. Never

    b. Once

    c. Twice

    d. Repeatedly—this conditional expression causes an infinite loop

32. Which of the following is the correct syntax for a `do...while` statement?

    a.
    ```
    do while (ctCount < 10) {
        cout << "Printed from a do...while loop." << endl;
    }
    ```

    b.
    ```
    do { while (ctCount < 10)
            cout << "Printed from a do...while loop." << endl;
    }
    ```

    c.
    ```
    do {
            cout << "Printed from a do...while loop." << endl;
            while (ctCount < 10)
    }
    ```

    d.
    ```
    do {
            cout << "Printed from a do...while loop." << endl;
    } while (ctCount < 10);
    ```

33. Which of the following is the correct syntax for a `for` statement?

    a.
    ```
    for (int ctCount = 0; ctCount < 10; ++ ctCount)
            cout << "Printed from a for statement." << endl;
    ```

    b.
    ```
    for (int ctCount = 0, ctCount < 10, ++ ctCount)
            cout << "Printed from a for statement." << endl;
    ```

    c.
    ```
    for {
            cout << "Printed from a for statement." << endl;
    } while (int ctCount = 0; ctCount < 10; ++ ctCount)
    ```

    d.
    ```
    for (int ctCount = 0; ctCount < 10);
            cout << "Printed from a for statement." << endl;
            ++ ctCount;
    ```

34. When is a **for** statement's initialization expression executed?

    a. When the **for** statement begins executing

    b. With each repetition of the **for** statement

    c. When the counter variable is incremented

    d. When the **for** statement ends

35. The _____ statement halts a looping statement, but instead of exiting the loop construct entirely, it restarts the loop with a new iteration.

    a. `proceed`

    b. `reiterate`

    c. `restart`

    d. `continue`

EXERCISES

1. What value is assigned to returnValue for each of the following expressions?

   ❑ `int returnValue = 2 == 3;`

   ❑ `int returnValue = 2 >= 3;`

   ❑ `int returnValue = 2 <= 3;`

   ❑ `int returnValue = 2 + 3;`

   ❑ `int returnValue = (2 >= 3) && (2 > 3) ;`

   ❑ `int returnValue = (2 >= 3) || (2 > 3) ;`

2. Use parentheses to modify the order of precedence of the following code so the final result of iNumber is 581.25. (The result of iNumber using the current syntax is 637.5.)

   ```
   int iNumber = 75;
   iNumber = iNumber + 30 * iNumber / 4;
   ```

3. Identify and fix the logic flaw in the following **if** statement:

   ```
   int iNum = 100;
   if (iNum >= 100);
       cout << "The variable is greater than ";
       cout << "or equal to '100'." << endl;
   ```

4. Add an **else** statement to the **if** statement in the preceding exercise that prints *The variable is less than '100'.* to the screen if the iNum variable is less than 10.

5. Modify the code you used in the two preceding exercises so that it includes a nested **if...else** statement that checks to see if the variable is greater than 50 or less than 50. Print the appropriate text to the screen describing the iNum variable's range. For example, if the iNum variable is less than 100, but greater than 50, you should print two lines to the screen: *The variable is less than '100'.* and *The variable is greater than '50'.*

6. Rewrite the following code using a **switch** statement.

```
:if (szSport == "golf")
    cout << "Golf is played on a golf course." << endl;
else if (szSport == "tennis")
    cout << "Tennis is played on a tennis court." << endl;
else if (szSport == "baseball")
    cout << "Baseball is played on a baseball dia-
mond." << endl;
else if (szSport == "basketball")
    cout << "Basketball is played on a basketball court." <
< endl;
```

3

7. Add code to the **if...else** structure in the preceding exercise that prints the line *I don't recognize your sport* to the screen if none of the conditional expressions in the **if...else** structure returns a value of true.

8. Write a **switch** statement that prints the appropriate grade description to the screen for the grades *A, B, C, D,* and *F.* Use single char variables for each case label. For example, for the *A* case label, print the value *A letter grade of A represents excellent work.*

9. Add code to the following **switch** statement so that after the statements in a case label execute, the **switch** statement ends.

```
switch (iAreaCode) {
    case 617:
        cout << "Boston's area code is "
            << iAreaCode << endl;
    case 212:
        cout << "Manhattan's area code is "
            << iAreaCode << endl;
    case 415:
        cout << "San Francisco's area code is "
            << iAreaCode << endl;
    case 813:
        cout << "St. Petersburg's area code is "
            << iAreaCode << endl;
    case 508:
        cout << "Worcester's area code is "
            << iAreaCode << endl;
}
```

10. Rewrite the **switch** statement in the preceding exercise using an **if...else** statement.

11. Modify the **switch** statement from Exercise 10 so that a default value of *You did not enter a valid area code* prints to the screen if none of the case labels matches the iAreaCode variable.

12. Create a program that determines sales territories by state. Create a decision-making structure that evaluates a state selected by the user and prints the name of the region where the state is located: North, South, East, West, Midwest, Southwest, and so on. Print an output statement to the screen that states the sales territory where the state is located. For example, if a user selects California, then print "The state you entered is in the Western sales region" to the screen. What is the best decision structure to use for this type of a program? Save the project as SalesRegions in the Chapter.03 folder in your Visual C++ Projects folder.

13. Create a program that calculates an employee's weekly gross salary, based on the number of hours worked and hourly wage. Compute any hours over forty as time-and-a-half. Use the appropriate decision structures to create the program. Save the project as Wages in the Chapter.03 folder in your Visual C++ Projects folder.

14. Rewrite the following `while` statement using a `for` loop.

```
int ctCount = 25;
while (ctCount >= 0) {
    cout << "The current number is " << ctCount << endl;
    --ctCount;
}
```

15. The following code should print the numbers 1 through 100 to the screen. The code contains several logic flaws, however, that prevent it from running correctly. Identify and fix the logic flaws.

```
int ctCount = 0;
int arNumbers[100];
while (ctCount >= 100) {
    arNumbers[ctCount] = ctCount;
    ++ctCount;
}
while (ctCount >= 100) {
    cout << arNumbers[ctCount] << endl;
}
```

16. Rewrite the following statement using a `while` loop:

```
for(int ctCount; ctCount <= 15; ++ctCount) {
    if (ctCount == 10)
        break;
    else
        cout << "The current number is " << ctCount << end
l;
}
```

INTRODUCTION TO MEMORY MANAGEMENT AND CLASSES

In this chapter you will learn

♦ About memory management

♦ About object-oriented programming and classes

♦ How to work with pointers and references to objects

♦ About information hiding

♦ How to use access specifiers

♦ About interface and implementation files

PREVIEW: THE RETIREMENT PLANNER PROGRAM

In this chapter and the next few chapters, you will study memory management and classes, which are two of the most important topics in C++ programming. Memory management techniques are introduced here, because they are used extensively when working with classes. You will only touch on the basic concepts of memory management, however, since the primary focus of this chapter is how to work with classes.

Recall from Chapter 1, that classes are structures that contain code, methods, attributes, and other information. In this chapter you will create a Retirement Planner program to learn how to work with basic class techniques.

To preview the Retirement Planner program:

1. Create a **Chapter.04** folder in your Visual C++ Projects folder.

2. Copy the **Chapter4_RetirementPlanner** folder from the Chapter.04 folder on your Data Disk to the Chapter.04 folder in your Visual C++ Projects folder. Then open the **RetirementPlanner** project in Visual C++. If the Tip of the Day dialog box displays, click the **Close** button.

3. The Chapter4_RetirementPlanner folder in the Chapter.04 folder in your Visual C++ Projects folder contains two C++ source files and a C++ header file. First, open the **CalcSavings.cpp** file in the Text Editor window. This file is a Win32 console application with a main() function that displays and gathers information. You should be able to recognize most of the code. The CalcSavings.cpp file will be used for demonstrating how to work with the class that will make up the Retirement Planner program's functionality. Close the **CalcSavings.cpp** source file.

4. Open the **RetirementPlanner.h** header file. This file contains only variable declarations and function prototypes, as illustrated in Figure 4-1. The program also contains some new preprocessor directives, along with two labels—public and private—that determine how functions and variables can be accessed outside of the class. Close the **RetirementPlanner.h** source file. You will also see a function that includes the inline keyword, but that is declared outside of the class declaration. This is known as an inline function and is used with small functions to request that the compiler replace calls to a function with the function definition wherever the function is called in a program.

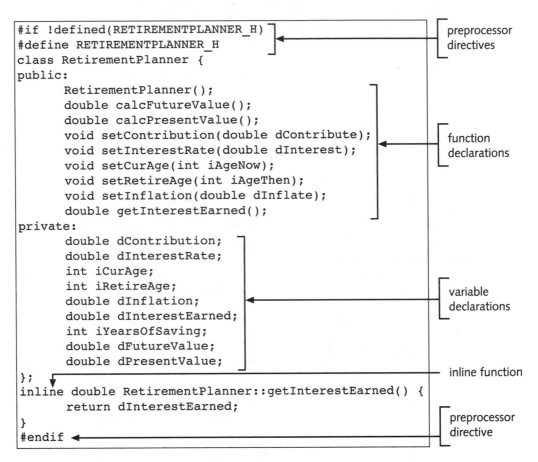

```
#if !defined(RETIREMENTPLANNER_H)          ┐  preprocessor
#define RETIREMENTPLANNER_H                ┘  directives
class RetirementPlanner {
public:
    RetirementPlanner();
    double calcFutureValue();
    double calcPresentValue();
    void setContribution(double dContribute);    function
    void setInterestRate(double dInterest);      declarations
    void setCurAge(int iAgeNow);
    void setRetireAge(int iAgeThen);
    void setInflation(double dInflate);
    double getInterestEarned();
private:
    double dContribution;
    double dInterestRate;
    int iCurAge;
    int iRetireAge;
    double dInflation;                            variable
    double dInterestEarned;                       declarations
    int iYearsOfSaving;
    double dFutureValue;
    double dPresentValue;
};                                                inline function
inline double RetirementPlanner::getInterestEarned() {
    return dInterestEarned;
}                                                 preprocessor
#endif                                            directive
```

Figure 4-1   Chapter6_RetirementPlanner.h

5. Open the **RetirementPlanner.cpp** file. This file contains the actual definitions for the functions declared in the RetirementPlanner.h source file. Figure 4-2 shows a portion of the file. Notice that the file imports the RetirementPlanner.h file using an #include statement, but that the header file name is enclosed in quotation marks instead of brackets. Also notice that each function definition is preceded by RetirementPlanner and the scope resolution operator (::). RetirementPlanner is the name of the class itself. You use the class name and the scope resolution operator to define a function as being part of a particular class.

4

```
#include "RetirementPlanner.h"
RetirementPlanner::RetirementPlanner() {
        dContribution = 0;
        dInterestRate = 0;
        dInterestEarned = 0;
        iYearsOfSaving = 0;
        dFutureValue = 0;
        dPresentValue = 0;
        dInflation = 0;
        iCurAge = 0;
        iRetireAge = 0;
        dInflation = 0;
}
double RetirementPlanner::calcFutureValue() {
        iYearsOfSaving = iRetireAge - iCurAge;
        dFutureValue = 0;
        for(int i=0; i < iYearsOfSaving; i++) {
                dFutureValue += 1;
                dFutureValue *= (1+(dInterestRate/100));
}
...
```

statement including the RetirementPlanner.h file

Function names are preceded by class name and the scope resolution operator

Figure 4-2   RetirementPlanner.cpp

6. Build and execute the Retirement Planner program. Then enter values for each of the variables to calculate retirement savings. Figure 4-3 shows how the program appears in the console window after entering some values.

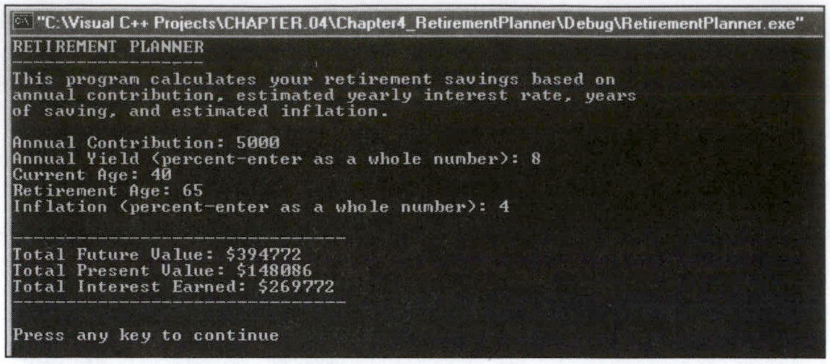

Figure 4-3   Retirement Planner console window

7. Press any key to close the Retirement Planner program window.

MEMORY MANAGEMENT

In order to work with classes and with the Windows programs that you will create later in this text, you need to have a basic understanding of the mechanics of memory management. Managing memory involves the manipulation of the memory addresses where variables are stored. This gives you much greater control over your program and allows you to adjust memory requirements as necessary, which in turn will increase the performance of your program. Memory management, however, is one of the most confusing aspects of C++ programming. The reasons why you need to manage memory are complex and require that you have a thorough understanding of object-oriented programming. Therefore, you will not delve too deeply into the theory behind, or reasons for, memory management. As you will learn in future chapters, Visual C++ automatically sets up many of the memory management aspects of the programs you will create. But, without at least a minimal understanding of what is going on in your code, you will never be able to fully master Visual C++ programming.

Pointers

One of the most commonly used memory management techniques in C++ is the use of pointers. A **pointer** is a special type of variable that stores the memory address of other variables. You use pointers to manipulate a variable and its contents through its memory address instead of through its variable name. Why do you use pointers? Why not just use a variable directly instead of using another variable that points to the original variable's memory address? Working with pointers confers many advantages—all related to the efficiency of your programs—but the most important advantage comes when you need to use functions to work with or modify large variables, such as a complex array.

Later in this chapter, you will learn how to work with class objects, which are another form of variable. Class objects can be very large and pointers allow you reduce the amount of required memory by eliminating the need to duplicate large variables (such as objects) when you need to have multiple functions work on the same variable. For example, you may need to pass a large variable to a function. Once the function receives the variable, it performs some sort of processing on it, and then returns the variable to the calling function. When you pass the variable itself, the program actually makes a copy of the variable to work with, which significantly increases the memory resources required by your program. A more efficient method is to pass only the memory address of the variable using a pointer variable. Using a pointer variable, the function can manipulate the original variable, avoiding the costly memory overhead required to pass a large variable to, and return a large variable from, a function. In addition by using pointers, multiple functions can access and manipulate a single copy of a variable in a program. Pointers also make it easier to work with arrays and allow you to dynamically allocate variables at run time without knowing the data type of a variable.

You declare a pointer with a data type, just like you declare ordinary variables. To declare a variable as a pointer, you place **the indirection operator (*)** after the data type or before the variable name. For example, both of the following statements declare pointer int variables. Notice that the pointer names, pFirstPointer and pSecondPointer, are both prefixed with a *p*, which is Hungarian notation for a pointer variable.

```
int* pFirstPointer;
int *pSecondPointer;
```

Although both of the preceding statements correctly declare pointer variables, you will use the first syntax since that is the syntax used by Visual C++. You should be able to recognize the second statement, however, as being an equally correct method of declaring a pointer.

After you declare a pointer variable, you use the **address of (&)** operator to assign to the pointer variable the memory address of another variable. You place the address of operator in front of the variable whose address you want to assign to the pointer. For example, the first two statements in the following code declare a variable named dPrimeInterest and a pointer named pPrimeInterest. After declaring the pPrimeInterest pointer, the third statement uses the address of operator to assign the dPrimeInterest variable's address to the pPrimeInterest pointer.

```
double dPrimeInterest;
double* pPrimeInterest;
pPrimeInterest = &dPrimeInterest;
```

You can also declare a pointer and assign to it a variable's memory address in the same statement as follows:

```
double dPrimeInterest;
double* pPrimeInterest = &dPrimeInterest;
```

If you were to print the pPrimeInterest pointer variable to the screen using a cout statement, you would see the memory address it stores. If you were to print the memory address of the dPrimeInterest variable (the variable—not the pointer variable) and precede it with the address of the operator, you would see that the address stored in the pPrimeInterest pointer is the same as the address of the dPrimeInterest variable. The following code adds to the dPrimeInterest and pPrimeInterest declaration code cout statements that print the contents of the pPrimeInterest pointer and the address of the dPrimeInterest variable. If you were to execute the code, you would see the output shown in Figure 4-4. In Figure 4-4, the same memory address is printed twice, demonstrating that the pointer variable contains the memory address of the dPrimeInterest variable.

```
double dPrimeInterest;
double* pPrimeInterest = &dPrimeInterest;
cout << "The value stored in the pPrimeInterest "
     << "pointer is: " << pPrimeInterest << endl;
cout << "The memory address of the dPrimeInterest "
     << "variable is: " << &dPrimeInterest << endl;
```

Figure 4-4   Output showing pPrimeInterest value and dPrimeInterest memory address

Once you assign the memory address of a variable to a pointer, to access or modify the contents of the variable pointed to by the pointer, you precede a pointer name in an expression with the **de-reference (*)** operator. It is a little confusing that the de-reference operator (*) happens to be an asterisk, the same as the indirection operator. You can distinguish the two operator types by the fact that the indirection operator is only used when declaring a pointer, while the de-reference operator is used when you need to access or modify the contents of the address pointed to by a pointer. In the following code, which shows the same dPrimeInterest and pPrimeInterest example from before, the fourth statement uses a standard assignment operation to assign the value .065 to the dPrimeInterest variable. The cout statement then prints the value of the dPrimeInterest variable to the screen. Then, the dPrimeInterest variable is assigned the value of .07, this time using the de-reference operator with the pPrimeInterest variable. The last statement prints the dPrimeInterest variable again, demonstrating that you can change the contents of a variable through a pointer to the variable's memory address without directly manipulating the original variable. Figure 4-5 shows the output.

```
double dPrimeInterest;
double* pPrimeInterest;
pPrimeInterest = &dPrimeInterest;
dPrimeInterest = .065;
cout << "The value of dPrimeInterest is: "
     <<dPrimeInterest << endl;
*pPrimeInterest = .07;
cout << "The value of dPrimeInterest is: "
     <<dPrimeInterest << endl;
```

```
"C:\Visual C++ Projects\CHAPTER.04\Pointers\Debug\Pointers.exe"
The value of dPrimeInterest is: 0.065
The value of dPrimeInterest is: 0.07
Press any key to continue
```

Figure 4-5 Output after assigning a new value using the de-reference operator

One very useful pointer that you can use in C++ is a pointer of type char*. When you create a char variable using a statement similar to `char szString[10];`, you are really creating an array of char elements. As you know, in order to assign a string to a char variable, you must know the maximum number of characters that the variable will contain. However, if you declare a char* pointer instead of a char variable, you do not need to specify the maximum number of characters that the variable will contain. For example, up to this point, to declare a char variable named szProgramming that can accept up to ten characters, you have needed to use the format `char szProgramming[10] = "Visual C++";`. In this statement, the szProgramming variable is assigned a value of *Visual C++*.

An easier method of creating a string variable is to use a char* pointer as in the following code. You can assign any string you want to the variable without having to declare the maximum number of characters.

```
char* szProgramming = "Visual C++";
```

 Although char* is a pointer, it is common practice to prefix char* variable names with sz, which is Hungarian notation for a string of characters, terminated by a null character.

Once you create a char* pointer variable, you can use it in the same way you use a standard char variable. Unlike other types of pointers, you do not need to use the address of or de-reference operators to access and modify the contents of a char* pointer variable. The following code shows an example of how you can use a char* pointer variable in a program:

```
char* myDog = "Golden Retriever";
cout << myDog << endl;
mydog = "Irish Setter";
cout << myDog << endl;
```

References

A **reference**, or **reference variable**, is an alias for an existing variable. Compared to pointer variables, references provide a streamlined way to work with passing large variables to, and returning large variables from, a function. You create a reference by appending an ampersand (&) to the data type in a variable declaration and by assigning an existing variable to the new variable name. The syntax for creating a reference is `type& reference_name = variable_name;`. The following code creates a reference named rPrimeInterest that is an alias for the dPrimeInterest variable:

```
double dPrimeInterest;
double& rPrimeInterest = dPrimeInterest;
```

Note that when you first declare a reference, you must assign an existing variable to it or you will receive a compile error. The statement `double& rPrimeInterest;`, for instance, causes a compile error because no variable has been assigned to the rPrimeInterest reference.

Once you create a reference, you can use it exactly as you would use a standard variable. Unlike pointers, you do not need to use any special operators to access or modify the original variable. The following code shows how you can modify the dPrimeInterest variable through the rPrimeInterest reference. Figure 4-6 shows the output.

```
double dPrimeInterest;
double& rPrimeInterest = dPrimeInterest;
rPrimeInterest = .065;
cout << "The value of dPrimeInterest is: "
    <<dPrimeInterest << endl;
rPrimeInterest = .07;
cout << "The value of dPrimeInterest is: "
    <<dPrimeInterest << endl;
```

Figure 4-6   Output after assigning new values through a reference

You are probably asking yourself what the difference is between a pointer and a reference variable. Although they appear similar on the surface, they really are two separate elements. A pointer stores the memory address of a variable, while a reference is an alias for a variable. In reality, a reference also stores the memory address of a variable, but it behaves like a variable. A reference can be easier to work with than a pointer because you do not have to use special operators to access the variable for which the reference is an alias. One of the most common uses of a reference is when you need one function to work with a large variable that is declared in another function. Passing a reference eliminates the memory overhead associated with passing a copy of a large variable. You can pass a pointer, but then you would need to deal with the address of and de-reference operators.

Stack Versus Heap

The local variables and pointers you have seen so far, such as `int iCount;` or `int* iCount;`, are created in an area of memory known as the stack. The **stack** is a region of memory where applications can store data such as local variables, function calls, and parameter information. Recall that local variables have automatic storage duration that refers to their existence only during the lifetime of the command block (such as a function) that contains them. Automatic storage duration refers to C++ automatically adding and removing local variables to and from the stack. You, as the programmer, have no control over the stack; C++ automatically handles placing and removing data to and from the stack. For many situations, storing data on the stack is the best way of managing memory because C++ handles memory allocation and de-allocation for you.

There will be cases, however, in which you will want to have greater control over the allocation and de-allocation of the memory used by your program. For example, you may write a program that needs to allocate memory to a variable, but you will not know the variable's data type or the value it will store until run time. Therefore, you need to know the variable's data type at compile time in order for your program to be able to reserve the correct amount of memory on the stack. To allocate variables at run time, you use an area of memory known as the heap. The **heap**, or the **free store**, is an area of memory that is available to an application for storing data whose existence and size are not known until run time. To add and remove variables to and from the heap, you use the `new` and `delete` keywords.

The `new` Keyword

The **new** keyword creates a variable on the heap and returns the variable's heap memory address. The syntax for using the `new` keyword is *pointer* = new *data_type*;. For example, to declare an int pointer named iPointer that points to a heap variable, you use the following statements:

```
int* pPointer;
pPointer = new int;
```

You can also combine the pPointer declaration with the statement that calls the **new** keyword as follows:

```
int* pPointer = new int;
```

Once you allocate a heap variable, you refer to it in your code the same way you refer to other pointer variables. For example, the following statements declare a new double heap variable named pPrimeInterest and assign to it the value .065. The first cout statement then prints the value of the dPrimeInterest variable (.065) and the second cout statement prints its memory address.

```
double* pPrimeInterest = new double;
*pPrimeInterest = .065;
cout << *pPrimeInterest << endl;
cout << &pPrimeInterest << endl;
```

The delete Keyword

Once you are through working with heap memory, you need to free it so that other parts of your program can use it. You use the **delete** keyword to de-allocate memory that has been reserved on the heap. The syntax for calling the **delete** keyword is **delete pointer_name;**. For example, to delete the heap memory pointed to by the pPrimeInterest pointer, you use the statement **delete pPrimeInterest;**.

It is important to understand that the **delete** keyword does not delete the pointer itself. Rather, it deletes the contents of the heap memory address pointed to by a pointer variable. You can re-use the pointer itself after calling the **delete** keyword. The pointer still exists and points to the same heap memory address that it did before calling the **delete** keyword. For example, the following code declares the pPrimeInterest pointer on the heap and assigns to it a value of .065. Then, the **delete** keyword deletes the heap address that stores the value of .065. Finally, a new value is added to the heap address. If you examine the output in Figure 4-7, you will see that after the **delete** statement executes, the pPrimeInterest pointer still points to the same memory address.

```
double* pPrimeInterest = new double;
*pPrimeInterest = .065;
cout << "The value of pPrimeInterest is: "
    << *pPrimeInterest << endl;
cout << "The memory address of pPrimeInterest is: "
    << &pPrimeInterest << endl;
delete pPrimeInterest;
*pPrimeInterest = .070;
cout << "The value of pPrimeInterest is: "
    << *pPrimeInterest << endl;
cout << "The memory address of pPrimeInterest is: "
    << &pPrimeInterest << endl;
```

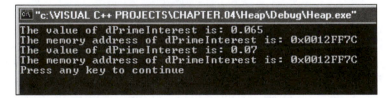

Figure 4-7   Output of program with heap variables

 There is only so much heap memory available to an application. If you fail to delete heap variables, your program may experience something called a memory leak. A memory leak is a condition in which a system's memory is not released after it is used (in other words, it "leaks out" of the heap). If you have a program that continually creates heap variables without deleting them, you will eventually run out of heap memory, causing your program to crash.

You can store arrays on the heap, just as you store other types of variables. To store an array on the heap, you need to use the syntax *type* pointer_name* = new *type*[*elements*];. For example, the following statement creates on the heap an int array named arInvestments consisting of ten elements:

```
int* arInvestments = new int[10];
```

Deleting the contents of an array stored on the heap also requires a slightly different syntax. You must append two brackets to the `delete` keyword using the syntax `delete[] array_name;`. For example, the following statement deletes the heap memory that stores the array pointed to by the arInvestments pointer:

```
delete[] arInvestments;
```

4

OBJECT-ORIENTED PROGRAMMING AND CLASSES

Classes form the basis of object-oriented programming. Object-oriented programming refers to a way of designing and accessing code. The pieces of the programming puzzle—data types, variables, control structures, functions, and so on—are the same as in any other types of programming. What is different is how the puzzle is assembled. You first learned about classes in Chapter 1 in very general terms. For the rest of this chapter, you will learn about classes in detail.

Classes

Classes were defined in Chapter 1 as structures that contain code, methods, attributes, and other information. Now that you are familiar with the basics of a C++ program, let's refine this definition. In C++ programming, **classes** are structures that contain variables along with functions for manipulating the variables. The functions and variables defined in a class are referred to as **class members**. Class variables are referred to as **data members,** and class functions are referred to as **member functions**. To use the variables and functions in a class, you declare an object from that class. When you declare an object from a class, you are said to be **instantiating** an object. When you work with a class object, member functions are often referred to as methods, and data members are often referred to as properties.

Classes themselves are also referred to as user-defined data types or programmer-defined data types. These terms can be somewhat misleading, however, since they do not accurately reflect the fact that classes can contain member functions. Additionally, classes usually contain multiple data members of different data types, so calling a class a data type becomes even more confusing.

One reason classes are referred to as user-defined data types or programmer-defined data types is that you can work with a class as a single unit, or *object*, in the same way you work with a variable. In fact, C++ programmers use the terms *variable* and *object* interchangeably. The term, object-oriented programming comes from the fact that you can bundle variables and functions together and use the result as a single unit (a *variable* or *object*). What this means will become clearer to you as you progress through this text. For now, think of a hand-held calculator as an example. A calculator could be considered an object of a Calculation class. You access all of the Calculation class's functions (such as addition and subtraction) and its data members (operands that represent the numbers you are calculating) through your calculator object. You never actually work with the Calculation class yourself, only with an object of the class (your calculator).

But why do you need to work with a collection of related variables and functions as a single object? Why not simply call each individual variable and function as necessary, without using all of this class business? The truth is you are not required to work with classes; you can create much of the same functionality without classes as you can by using classes. Some simple types of Visual C++ programs you write will probably not need to be created with classes. Classes help make complex programs easier to manage, however, by logically grouping related functions and data and by allowing you to refer to that grouping as a single object. Another reason for using classes is to hide information that users of a class do not need to access or know about. Information hiding helps minimize the amount of information that needs to pass in and out of an object, which helps increase program speed and efficiency. Classes also make it much easier to re-use code or distribute your code to others for use in their programs. (You will learn how create your own classes and include them in your programs shortly.) Without a way to package variables and functions in classes and include those classes in a new program, you would need to copy and paste each segment of code you wanted to re-use (functions, variables, and so on) into any new program.

An additional reason to use classes is that instances of objects inherit their characteristics, such as class members, from the class upon which they are based. This inheritance allows you to build new classes based on existing classes without having to rewrite the code contained in the existing classes. You will learn more about inheritance in the next chapter. But for now, you should understand that an object has the same characteristics as its class.

There are two primary types of classes that you will work with in this text: classes declared with the **struct** keyword and classes declared with the **class** keyword. First, you will learn about classes declared with the **struct** keyword.

Creating Structures

So far you have worked with data types that store single values such as integers, floating-point numbers, and characters. You have also worked with arrays, which contain sets of data represented by a single variable name. One drawback to using arrays is that all elements in an array must be of the same data type. Suppose you have several pieces of related information, such as x, y, and z, that you want to be able to refer to as a single variable, similar to an array. You cannot use an array, however, because the individual pieces of information are of different data types. To store this type of information as a single variable, you use something called a structure. A **structure**, or **struct**, is an advanced, user-defined data type that uses a single variable name to store multiple pieces of related information. Remember that a user-defined data type is another way of referring to a class. This means that a structure is also a class. The individual pieces of information stored in a structure are referred to as **elements**, **fields**, or **members**. You define a structure using the structure keyword and the following syntax:

```
struct structure_name {
    data_type field_name;
    data_type field_name;
    ...
} variable_name;
```

You might also see structures referred to as record structures or data structures.

The structure_name portion of the structure definition is the name of the new, user-defined data type. You can use any name you like for a structure, as long as you follow the same naming conventions that you use when declaring variables and functions. Within the structure's curly braces, you declare the data type and field names for each piece of information stored in the structure, the same way you declare a variable and its data type. The variable_name portion of the structure declaration is optional and allows you to create a variable based on the new structure when the structure is first declared. If you omit variable_name, then you can later declare a new variable in your code using the structure name as the data type. To give you a better idea of how a structure is used, suppose you have a set of employee information that you want to refer to as a single unit. Some of the information may include first name, last name, and salary. The following code declares a structure for the employee information, but does not assign a variable name at declaration since variable_name is omitted:

```
struct employee {
    char* firstName;
    char* lastName;
    long salary;
};
```

After creating the preceding structure, you declare a new variable of type employee using a statement similar to **employee currentEmployee;**. Recall that the terms variable and object are used interchangeably. This means that a variable based on a structure is also an object. To access the fields inside a structure variable, you append a period to the variable name, followed by the field name using the syntax **variable.field;**. When you use a period to access an object's members, such as a structure's fields, the period is referred to as the **member selection operator**. The following code shows the same employee structure definition followed by statements that declare a new employee variable and assign values to the structure fields. Then the code shows statements that print the contents of each field:

```
struct employee {
    char* firstName;
    char* lastName;
    long salary;
};
void main() {
    employee currentEmployee;
    currentEmployee.firstName = "Carmen";
    currentEmployee.lastName = "Aguirre";
    currentEmployee.salary = 60000;
    cout << currentEmployee.firstName << endl;
    cout << currentEmployee.lastName << endl;
    cout << currentEmployee.salary << endl;
}
```

You are not allowed to assign values to the fields inside the structure definition itself. For example, the following code causes a compile error:

```
struct employee {
    char* firstName = "Carmen";
    char* lastName = "Aguirre";
    long salary = 60000;
};
```

You can, however, assign values to a structure's fields when you declare a variable of the structure's type. To do this, you must enclose the values you want assigned to the structure's fields within braces, separated by commas, and in the order in which the fields are declared in the structure definition. For example, the following code contains the employee structure definition, followed by the declaration of the currentEmployee variable, which assigns initial values to the fields:

```
struct employee {
    char* firstName;
    char* lastName;
    long salary;
};
void main() {
    employee currentEmployee = {"Carmen",
        "Aguirre", 60000};
}
```

Note that structures are part of the C programming language. However, they are widely used in Windows programming; in fact, you will use structures extensively when you work with Windows programs later in this text. In order to familiarize you with defining structures, you will now create a simple console application that creates a structure named sportsCar, assigns values to a sportsCar variable, and then prints the variable's contents. The sportsCar structure will define fields in several different data types that will contain the specifications of a particular sports car.

To create a simple console application that creates the sportsCar structure, assigns values to a sportsCar variable, and then prints the variable's contents:

1. Create a new empty Win32 Console Application project named **CarInfo**. Save the project in the **Chapter.04** folder in your Visual C++ Projects folders. Once the project is created, add a C++ source file named **CarInfo**.

2. Type the processing directive that gives the program access to the iostream library: **#include <iostream.h>** and press **Enter**.

3. Next, add a constructor for the main() function: **void main() {**.

4. In the main() function's body, define the following sportsCar structure. Notice that the structure's fields are of different data types.

```cpp
struct sportsCar {
     char* make;
     char* model;
     long year;
     int doors;
     double engine;
};
```

5. After the last statement in the structure definition, press **Enter.** Then, type the following statements, which declare a new sportsCar variable named myCar and assign values to the structure's fields:

```cpp
sportsCar myCar;
myCar.make = "Ford";
myCar.model = "Mustang";
myCar.year = 2000;
myCar.doors = 2;
myCar.engine = 4.5;
```

6. Next add the following statements, which print the values assigned to the structure's fields:

```cpp
cout << "This is my car" << endl;
cout << "---------------" << endl;
cout << "Make: " << myCar.make << endl;
cout << "Model: " << myCar.model << endl;
cout << "Year: " << myCar.year << endl;
cout << "Doors: " << myCar.doors << endl;
cout << "Engine: " << myCar.engine << " liters"
      << endl << endl;
```

7. Finally, type the main() function's closing brace: **}**.

8. Build and execute the CarInfo project. Figure 4-8 shows the output.

9. Press any key to close the command window.

4

Figure 4-8   Output of CarInfo

Creating Classes with the `class` Keyword

The most important type of class used in C++ programming is defined using the **class** keyword. For brevity, from this point forward classes defined with the **class** keyword will be referred to simply as classes. You define classes the same way you define structures, and you access a class's data members using the member selection operator. The following code shows an example of a class named Stocks:

```
class Stocks {
public:
    int iNumShares;
    double dPurchasePricePerShare;
    double dCurrentPricePerShare;
};
void main() {
    Stocks stockValue;
    stockValue.iNumShares = 500;
    stockValue.dPurchasePricePerShare = 10.785;
    stockValue.dCurrentPricePerShare = 6.5;
}
```

The differences between the preceding class and the structure example you saw earlier are the use of the **class** keyword and the **public:** label. The **public:** label determines default accessibility to a class's members. In fact, default accessibility is one of the only differences between structures and classes. For now, you should understand that the accessibility to a class's members is what allows you to hide information, such as data members, from users of your class. You will learn more about accessibility when we discuss information hiding later in this chapter.

Structures are left over from C programming. Classes are unique to C++ programming. In C programming, structures do not support encapsulation since C programming is primarily a procedural programming language, not object-oriented, as is C++. In C++ programming, however, structures do support encapsulation, making them virtually identical to classes. This means that you can substitute the `struct` keyword for any classes declared with the `class` keyword. However, most C++ programmers use the `class` keyword to clearly designate the programs they write as object-oriented C++ programs. And since you are studying C++, you will define your classes with the `class` keyword.

As you saw in the preview, some portions of a class are created in a header file, while other portions are created in C/C++ source files. You will learn about the reasons for separating classes into separate files shortly. For now, you should understand that the declarations in a class, such as variable declarations and function prototypes, are declared in a header file. The actual definitions, however, such as statements that assign values to data members and function definitions, are declared in a C/C++ source file. First you will create the RetirementPlanner.h header file, which declares the RetirementPlanner class.

4

To create the RetirementPlanner.h header file:

1. Return to Visual C++.

2. Create a new empty Win32Console Application project named **RetirementPlanner**. Save the project in the **Chapter.04** folder in your Visual C++ Projects folder.

3. Add a new C/C++ Header File named **RetirementPlanner.h** to the RetirementPlanner project.

4. In the RetirementPlanner.h file, type the following code to declare the RetirementPlanner class. Be sure to include the semicolon after the closing brace.

```
class RetirementPlanner {
};
```

Next you will start creating the CalcSavings.cpp file, which will contain the program's main() function. In the main() function, you will declare a RetirementPlanner object and use that object to access data members and member functions in the RetirementPlanner class.

To start creating the Retirement Planner program:

1. Add a new C++ Source File named **CalcSavings.cpp** to the RetirementPlanner project.

2. Before you can instantiate an object of a class, you must first include the class's header file in your .cpp file, just as you would include any other header files you need in your program. However, with custom classes that you write yourself (as opposed to the runtime classes that are part of Visual C++), you must enclose the header file name within quotation marks instead of brackets. Type the following statements to include the iostream class and the RetirementPlanner class.

```
#include <iostream.h>
#include "RetirementPlanner.h"
```

3. Type the following main() function which includes a single statement that declares a RetirementPlanner object named savings.

```
void main() {
    RetirementPlanner savings;
}
```

Pointers and References to Objects

Memory management is just as important when you work with classes as it is when you work with primitive data type variables. When declaring and using pointers and references to class objects, follow the same rules as you would when declaring and using pointers and references to variables of primitive data types. You use the **new** operator to allocate memory to structures and classes on the heap. Instead of using the member selection operator (.), however, you must use the **indirect member selection operator (->)** to access class members through a pointer to an object either on the stack or on the heap. Figure 4-9 shows two examples of how to access a class's data members through a pointer. Memory is allocated for the stockPick object on the stack along with a pointer to the stockPick object named pStackStock. The pHeapStock pointer is declared for the Stocks object allocated on the heap. Both the pStackStock and the pHeapStock variables are passed to a totalValue() function that calculates the current stock price. The data members are accessed using the indirect member selection operator. Notice that since you pass a Stocks pointer to the totalValue() function, the argument in the totalValue() function definition is also a Stocks pointer.

```cpp
#include <iostream.h>
class Stocks {
public:
    int iNumShares;
    double dPurchasePricePerShare;
    double dCurrentPricePerShare;
};
double totalValue(Stocks* pCurStock);
void main() {
    // allocated on the stack
    // with a pointer to the stack object
    Stocks stockPick;
    Stocks* pStackStock = &stockPick;
    pStackStock ->iNumShares = 500;
    pStackStock ->dPurchasePricePerShare = 10.785;
    pStackStock ->dCurrentPricePerShare = 6.5;
    cout << totalValue(pStackStock) << endl;
    // allocated on the heap
    Stocks* pHeapStock = new Stocks;
    pHeapStock->iNumShares = 200;
    pHeapStock->dPurchasePricePerShare = 32.5;
    pHeapStock->dCurrentPricePerShare = 48.25;
    cout << totalValue(pHeapStock) << endl;
}
double totalValue(Stocks* pCurStock) {
    double dTotalValue;
    dTotalValue = pCurStock->dCurrentPricePerShare
        * pCurStock->iNumShares;
    return dTotalValue;
}
```

Figure 4-9   Program that declares and passes object pointers

The totalValue() function in Figure 4-9 is not a function member of the Stocks class. Rather, it is a standard function that is available to the entire program. You will learn how to work with member functions later in this chapter.

You set references to class objects the same way you set references to other types of variables. Figure 4-10 shows a modified version of the program in 4-9, this time using a single instance of a Stocks object named stockPick. A reference to the stockPick object, rStockPick, is passed to the totalValue() function instead of a pointer. The argument in the totalValue() function definition has also been changed to a reference to a Stocks object instead of a pointer to a Stocks object.

```cpp
#include <iostream.h>
class Stocks {
public:
    int iNumShares;
    double dPurchasePricePerShare;
    double dCurrentPricePerShare;
};
double totalValue(Stocks& rCurStock);
void main() {
    Stocks stockPick;
    Stocks& rStockPick = stockPick;
    rStockPick.iNumShares = 500;
    rStockPick.dPurchasePricePerShare = 10.785;
    rStockPick.dCurrentPricePerShare = 6.5;
    cout << totalValue(rStockPick) << endl;
}
double totalValue(Stocks& rCurStock) {
    double dCurPrice;
    dCurPrice = rCurStock.dCurrentPricePerShare
          * rCurStock.iNumShares;
    return dCurPrice;
}
```

Figure 4-10   Program that declares and passes an object reference

INFORMATION HIDING

One of the most fundamental principals in object-oriented programming is the concept of information hiding. Information hiding gives an encapsulated object its black box capabilities so that users of a class can see only the members of the class that you allow them to see. Essentially, the principal of **information hiding** states that any class members that other programmers, or *clients*, do not need to access or know about should be hidden. Information hiding helps minimize the amount of information that needs to pass in and out of an object, which helps increase program speed and efficiency. Information hiding also reduces the complexity of the code that clients see, allowing them to concentrate on the task of integrating an object into their programs. For example, if a client wants to add to her Accounting program a Payroll object, she does not need to know the underlying details of the Payroll object's member functions, nor does she need to modify any local data members that are used by those functions. The client only needs to know which of the object's member functions to call and what data needs to be passed to those member functions.

Now consider information hiding on a larger scale. Professionally developed software packages are distributed in an encapsulated format, which means that the casual user—or even an advanced programmer—cannot see the underlying details of how the software is developed. Imagine what would happen if Microsoft distributed Excel without hiding the underlying programming details. Most users of the program would be bewildered if they accidentally opened the source files. Obviously, there is no reason why Microsoft would allow users to see the underlying details of Excel, since users do not need to understand how the underlying code performs the various types of spreadsheet calculations. Microsoft also has a critical interest in protecting proprietary information, as do you. The design and sale of software components is big business. You certainly do not want to spend a significant amount of time designing an outstanding software component, only to have an unscrupulous programmer steal the code and claim it as his or her own.

This same principal of information hiding needs to be applied in object-oriented programming. There are few reasons why clients of your classes need to know the underlying details of your code. Of course, you cannot hide *all* of the underlying code, or other programmers will never be able to integrate your class with their applications. But you need to hide most of it.

Information hiding on any scale also prevents other programmers from accidentally introducing a bug into a program by modifying a class's internal workings. Programmers are curious creatures and will often attempt to "improve" your code, no matter how well it is written. Before you distribute your classes to other programmers, your classes should be thoroughly tested and bug-free. With tested and bug-free classes, other programmers can focus on the more important task of integrating your code into their programs using the data members and member functions you designate.

To enable information hiding in your classes you must designate access specifiers for each of your class members. You must also place your class code into separate interface and integration files. You will learn about these topics next.

Access Specifiers

The first step in hiding class information is to set access specifiers for class members. **Access specifiers** control a client's access to data members and member functions. There are four levels of access specifiers: public, private, protected, and friend. You will use the public, private, and friend access specifiers in this chapter. In the next chapter, you will learn about the protected access specifier.

The **public access specifier** allows anyone to call a class's function member or to modify a data member. The **private access specifier** prevents clients from calling member functions or accessing data members and is one of the key elements in information hiding.

Private access does not restrict a class's internal access to its own members; a class's function member can modify any private data member or call any private function member. Private access restricts clients from accessing class members. The private access specifier does not actually hide class member definitions; it only protects them. To hide class member definitions, you must separate classes into interface and implementation files, which you will learn about shortly.

Both public and private access specifiers have what is called **class scope**: Class members of both access types are accessible by any of a class's member functions. In contrast, variables declared inside a function member have local scope to the function only and are not available outside the function, even if the function is declared with the public access specifier.

You place access specifiers in a class definition on a single line followed by a colon, similar to a **switch** statement's case labels. An access specifier that is placed on a line by itself followed by a colon is called an **access label**. The access privilege of any particular access label is applied to any class members that follow, up to the next label. For example, the following code contains a public and a private access label. The public label declares two public data members, iNumShares and dPurchasePricePerShare, and the private label declares a single private data member, dCurrentPricePerShare.

```
class Stocks {
public:
    int iNumShares;
    double dPurchasePricePerShare;
private:
    double dCurrentPricePerShare;
};
```

Access labels can be repeated, although most programmers prefer to organize all of their public class members under a single public access label, and all of their private class members under a single private access label. However, the following code organization with its two public access labels is legal:

```
class Stocks {
public:
    int iNumShares;
private:
    double dCurrentPricePerShare;
public:
    double dPurchasePricePerShare;
};
```

It is common practice to list public class members first in order to clearly identify the parts of the class that can be accessed by clients.

The default access specifier for classes is private. If you exclude access specifiers from your class definition, then all class members in the definition are private by default. For example, since the following class definition does not include any access labels, the three data member definitions are private by default:

```
class Stocks {
    int iNumShares;
    double dPurchasePricePerShare;
    double dCurrentPricePerShare;
};
```

If you have some reason for making all of your class members private, you should include a private access label to make it clear how you intend for the class members to be used. Many programmers prefer to make all of their data members private to prevent clients from accidentally assigning the wrong value to a variable or from viewing the internal workings of their programs. Or, they simply want to prevent curious clients from modifying the various parts of their program. Even if you do not need to make it clear for yourself, you should include an access label in case other programmers need to modify your work.

 Default class member access is one of the major differences between classes and structures in C++. Access to classes is private by default. Access to structures is public by default.

Even if you make all data members in a class private, you can still allow clients of your program to retrieve or modify the value of data members by using accessor functions. **Accessor functions** are public member functions that a client can call to retrieve or modify the value of a data member. Because accessor functions often begin with the words *get* or *set*, they are also referred to as get or set functions. Get functions retrieve data member values; set functions modify data member values. To allow a client to pass a value to your program that will be assigned to a private data member, you include arguments in a set function's header definition. You can then write code in the body of the set function that validates the data passed from the client, prior to assigning values to private data members. For example, if the Payroll class includes a private data member containing the current state income-tax rate, then you could write a public accessor function named getStateTaxRate() that allows clients to retrieve the variable's value. Similarly, you could write a setStateTaxRate() function that performs various types of validation on the data passed from the client (such as making sure the value is not null, is not greater than 100%, and so on) prior to assigning a value to the private state tax rate data member.

Next you will add public and private labels to the RetirementPlanner.h file, along with some declarations for private data members.

To add public and private labels to the RetirementPlanner.h file, along with some declarations for private data members:

1. Return to the **RetirementPlanner** project and open the **RetirementPlanner.h** file in the text editor window.

2. Modify the RetirementPlanner.h file as follows. Later you will add member function declarations to the public section that will modify and retrieve the data members declared in the private section.

```
class RetirementPlanner {
public:
private:
        double dContribution;
        double dInterestRate;
        double dInterestEarned;
        int iYearsOfSaving;
        double dFutureValue;
        double dPresentValue;
        double dInflation;
        int iCurAge;
        int iRetireAge;
};
```

Interface and Implementation Files

Although the first step in information hiding is to assign private access specifiers to class members, private access specifiers only designate which class members a client is not allowed to call or change. Private access specifiers do not prevent clients from seeing class code. To prevent clients from seeing the details of how your code is written, you place your class's interface code and implementation code in separate files. The separation of classes into interface and implementation files is a fundamental software development technique since it allows you to hide the details of how your classes are written and makes it easier to modify programs.

Interface code refers to the data member and function member declarations inside a class's braces. Interface code does not usually contain definitions for function members, nor does it usually assign values to the data members. Declarations are statements that only declare data members without assigning a value to them, such as **double dCurrentPricePerShare;**, or function prototypes such as **double totalValue();**. You create interface code in a header file with an .h extension—the same types of header files you have been including with your programs since Chapter 2. The interface code should be the only part of your class that a client can see and access. In effect, the interface is the "front door" to your program.

Implementation code refers to a class's function definitions and any code that assigns values to a class's data members. In other words, implementation code contains the actual member functions themselves and assigns values to data members. You add implementation code to standard C++ source files with an extension of .cpp. You give the implementation code access to the interface code by importing the header file into the C++ source file using an #include directive, just as you would import any other header file.

C++ source files are distributed in compiled format, while header files are distributed as plain text files. Thus, clients who use your code can see only the names of data members and member functions. Clients can use and access public class members, but they cannot see the details of how your code is written. Without this ability to hide implementation details, clients could easily get around restrictions you place on class members with the private access specifier by copying your code into a new class file, and changing private access specifiers to public.

 If you are only using classes to make your own code more efficient and have no intention of distributing your classes to others, you can place both the declarations and definitions into a .cpp file. This is not considered good programming practice, however, since the separation of interface and implementation is a fundamental software development technique. Additionally, if you change your mind and decide to distribute your class to others, you would need to go back and separate the class into interface and implementation files.

You have already created the Retirement Planner program's interface file, RetirementPlanner.h, including the necessary class member declaration statements. Now you will start creating the implementation file, RetirementPlanner.cpp. Note that some of the examples of implementation files you have seen in this chapter have included their own main() functions. Although you can add executable class code by including a main() function in an implementation file, you are not required to. For example, the RetirementPlanner.cpp implementation file will not include a main() function. Instead, the RetirementPlanner.cpp implementation file will be called by the CalcSavings.cpp file's main() function.

To start creating the RetirementPlanner.cpp implementation file:

1. Return to the RetirementPlanner project.

2. Add a new C++ Source File named **RetirementPlanner.cpp** to the RetirementPlanner project.

3. After the RetirementPlanner.cpp file opens in the Text Editor window, import the RegistrationPlanner.h header file by typing the statement `#include "RetirementPlanner.h"`.

Modifying a Class

Hiding implementation details is reason enough for separating a class's interface from its implementation. But, another important reason for separating a class into interface and implementation files is to make it easier to modify a program at a later date. When you modify a class, interface code, such as class member declarations, should change the least. The implementation code normally changes the most when you modify a class. This rule of thumb is not carved in stone since you may find it necessary to drastically modify your class's interface. But for the most part, the implementation is what will change.

No matter what changes you make to your implementation code, the changes will be invisible to clients if their only entry point into your code is the interface—provided the interface stays the same. Designing your code so that modifications are made to the implementation code and not the interface code means that if you make any drastic changes or improvements to your class, you only need to distribute a new .cpp file to your clients, not a new interface file. Be aware, however, that if you modify class member declarations or add new declarations to expand the program's functionality, you may also need to distribute a new header file.

4

If the public interface class members stay the same, then clients do not need to make any changes to *their* code in order to work with your modified class. For instance, consider the Payroll object we discussed earlier. The Payroll object may contain a public function member named calcFederalTaxes() that calculates a paycheck's federal tax withholding based on income-tax percentages published by the Internal Revenue Service. If the Internal Revenue Service changes any of the income-tax percentages, then you will need to modify the private data members within the calcFederalTaxes() function. Clients, however, do not need to be concerned with these details; they will continue to call the public calcFederalTaxes() function as usual. For these types of changes, you would not need to distribute a new interface file to your clients. You would need to distribute only a new implementation file containing the modified calcFederalTaxes() function.

Preventing Multiple Inclusion

Larger class-based programs are sometimes composed of multiple interface and implementation files. With larger programs, you need to ensure that you do not include multiple instances of the same header file when you compile the program, since multiple inclusions will make your program unnecessarily large. Multiple inclusions of the same header usually occur when you include one header into a second header, and then include the second header in an implementation file.

Visual C++ generates an error if you attempt to compile a program that includes multiple instances of the same header. To prevent multiple inclusions prior to compilation, however, most C++ programmers use the #define preprocessor directive with the #if and #endif preprocessor directives in header files. You first learned how to use the #define preprocessor directive in Chapter 2 to define a constant. The **#if** and **#endif preprocessor directives** determine which portions of a file to compile depending on the result of a conditional expression. All statements located between the #if and #endif directives are compiled if the conditional expression evaluates to true. Each #if directive must include a closing #endif directive.

 The #if and #endif preprocessor directives are similar to the if statements you learned how to use in Chapter 4.

The following code shows the syntax for the #if and #endif preprocessor directives. Notice that unlike the conditional expression for standard if statements, the conditional expression for #if and #endif directives is not enclosed within parentheses.

```
#if conditional expression
    statements to compile;
#endif
```

To prevent multiple inclusions of header files, you use the #define directive to declare a constant representing a specific header file. Each time the compiler is asked to include that header file during the build process, it uses the defined constant expression with the #if directive to check if a specific header file's constant exists when you build a project. The **defined constant expression** returns a value of true if a particular identifier is defined or a value of false if it is not defined. The syntax for the defined constant expression is #defined(*identifier*). To see if an identifier has *not* been defined, add the not operator (!) before the defined expression.

Common practice when defining a header file's constant is to use the header file's name in uppercase letters appended with _H. For example, the constant for the stocks.h header file is usually defined as STOCKS_H.

If a header file's constant has not been defined, statements between the #if and #endif directives define the constant, and any statements preceding the #endif directive are compiled. If a header file's constant has already been defined, however, all statements between the #if and #endif directives are skipped, preventing a multiple inclusion. Figure 4-11 shows how to add code to the header file that prevents multiple inclusions of the Stocks class.

```
#if !defined(STOCKS_H)
#define STOCKS_H
class Stocks {
private:
     int iNumShares;
     double dPurchasePricePerShare;
     double dCurrentPricePerShare;
};
#endif
```

Figure 4-11   Header file with preprocessor directives

Next you will add preprocessor directives to the RetirementPlanner.h file in order to prevent multiple inclusions.

To add preprocessor directives to the RetirementPlanner.h file in order to prevent multiple inclusions:

1. Return to the RetirementPlanner project and open the RetirementPlanner.h file in the Text Editor window.

2. Modify the RetirementPlanner.h file by adding the following bolded statements. The private data members, which you included in the file earlier, will be used by member functions that you will add later.

```
#if !defined(RETIREMENT_H)
#define RETIREMENT_H
class RetirementPlanner {
public:
private:
     double dContribution;
     double dInterestRate;
     double dInterestEarned;
     int iYearsOfSaving;
     double dFutureValue;
     double dPresentValue;
     double dInflation;
};
#endif
```

MEMBER FUNCTIONS

Because member functions perform most of the work in a class, you will learn about the various techniques associated with them. As you saw earlier, you declare functions in an interface file, but define them in an implementation file. Member functions are usually declared as public, but they can also be declared as private. Public member functions can be called by anyone, while private member functions can be called only by other member functions in the same class.

You may wonder what good a private function member would be since a client of the program cannot access a private function. Suppose your program needs some sort of utility function that clients have no need to access. For example, your program may need to determine an employee's income-tax bracket by calling a function named calcTaxBracket(). To use your program, the client does not need to access the calcTaxBracket() function. By making the calcTaxBracket() function private, you protect your program and add another level of information hiding.

Although member functions are usually defined in an implementation file, they can also be defined in an interface file. Functions defined inside the class body in an interface file are called **inline functions**. To conform to information hiding techniques, only the shortest function definitions should be added to the interface file. Even better, you should add function prototypes to the interface file, and write the function definitions in the implementation file. The following code shows an example of a public inline function definition in the Stocks class for a function member named getTotalValue(). The getTotalValue() function accepts two arguments from the client: the number of shares and the current price. The arguments are assigned to private data members, and then the price is calculated and returned.

```
class Stocks {
public:
    double getTotalValue(int iShares, double dCurPrice){
        iNumShares = iShares;
        dCurrentPricePerShare = dCurPrice;
        dCurrentValue = iNumShares
            * dCurrentPricePerShare;
        return dCurrentValue;
    }
private:
    int iNumShares;
    double dCurrentPricePerShare;
    double dCurrentValue;
};
```

In order for your class to identify which functions in an implementation file belong to it (as opposed to standard function definitions), you precede the function name in the function definition header with the class name and the scope resolution operator (::).

For example, to identify the getTotalValue() function in an implementation file as belonging to the Stocks class, the function definition header should read `double Stocks:: getTotalValue(int iShares, double dCurPrice){`. Figure 4-12 shows both the interface and implementation files for the Stocks class. The getTotalValue() function's prototype is declared in an interface file named stocks.h, while the getTotalValue() function definition is placed in an implementation file named stocks.cpp.

```
// stocks.h
class Stocks {
public:
    double getTotalValue(int iShares, double dCurPrice);
private:
    int iNumShares;
    double dCurrentPricePerShare;
    double dCurrentValue;
};
// stocks.cpp
#include "stocks.h"
double Stocks::getTotalValue(int iShares,
    double dCurPrice){
    iNumShares = iShares;
    dCurrentPricePerShare = dCurPrice;
    dCurrentValue = iNumShares * dCurrentPricePerShare;
    return dCurrentValue;
}
```

Figure 4-12   Stocks class interface and implementation files

Even though the member functions of a class may be defined in an implementation file separate from the interface file, as long as the functions include the class's name and the scope resolution operator, they are considered to be part of the class definition. Just think of the declarations and definitions that compose your class as being "spread out" across multiple files.

Next you will add function prototypes to the RetirementPlanner.h file and their corresponding function definitions to the RetirementPlanner.cpp file. The RetirementPlanner class uses five functions for setting the values of private data members: setContribution(), setInterestRate(), setCurAge(), setRetireAge(), and setInflation(). Two other functions, calcFutureValue() and calcPresentValue(), perform the actual calculations that give the Retirement Planner program its functionality. The calcFutureValue() function returns the future value of an investment based on the amount invested each year, the yearly annual interest on the investment, and the number of years spent saving for retirement. The number of years spent saving for retirement is calculated by subtracting the age you started saving from the age you retire. The calcPresentValue() function adjusts the future value of an investment for inflation. An accessor function, getInterestEarned(), returns the total amount of interest earned on retirement savings. The getInterestEarned() function is a typical *get* function that returns to the client the value of a private data member. Note that you will not learn any detail on how the functions perform the calculations since algebra is not the purpose of your studies. If you examine the formulas closely, you will see that they are structured using typical C++ operators.

First, you will add the function prototypes to the RetirementPlanner.h file.

To add the function prototypes to the RetirementPlanner.h file:

1. Return to the **RetirementPlanner.h** file in the Text Editor window.

2. Add to the RetirementPlanner.h file the following bolded function prototypes.

```
#if !defined(RETIREMENT_H)
#define RETIREMENT_H
class RetirementPlanner {
public:
    double calcFutureValue();
    double calcPresentValue();
    void setContribution(double dContribute);
    void setInterestRate(double dInterest);
    void setCurAge(int iAgeNow);
    void setRetireAge(int iAgeThen);
    void setInflation(double dInflate);
    double getInterestEarned();
private:
    double dContribution;
...
```

Next you add the member functions to the RetirementPlanner.cpp implementation file.

To add the member functions to the RetirementPlanner.cpp implementation file:

1. Return to the **RetirementPlanner.cpp** file in the Text Editor window.

2. First, add the calcFutureValue() function member after the #include statement, as follows:

```
#include "RetirementPlanner.h"
double RetirementPlanner::calcFutureValue() {
    iYearsOfSaving = iRetireAge - iCurAge;
    dFutureValue = 0;
    for(int i=0; i < iYearsOfSaving; i++) {
        dFutureValue += 1;
        dFutureValue *= (1+(dInterestRate/100));
    }
    dFutureValue *= dContribution;
    dInterestEarned = dFutureValue -
        (dContribution * iYearsOfSaving);
    return dFutureValue;
}
```

3. Next add the calcPresentValue() function member after the calcFutureValue() function:

```
double RetirementPlanner::calcPresentValue() {
    double dFutureValue = calcFutureValue();
    for(int i = 0; i < iYearsOfSaving; i++) {
        dFutureValue /= (1 + (dInflation/100));
    }
    dPresentValue = dFutureValue;
    return dPresentValue;
}
```

4. Finally, add the set functions and the getInterestEarned() function member after the calcPresentValue() function as follows:

```
void RetirementPlanner::setContribution(double dContribute)
{
    dContribution = dContribute;
}
void RetirementPlanner::setInterestRate(double dInterest) {
    dInterestRate = dInterest;
}
void RetirementPlanner::setCurAge(int iAgeNow) {
    iCurAge = iAgeNow;
}
void RetirementPlanner::setRetireAge(int iAgeThen) {
    iRetireAge = iAgeThen;
}
void RetirementPlanner::setInflation(double dInflate) {
    dInflation = dInflate;
}
double RetirementPlanner::getInterestEarned() {
    return dInterestEarned;
}
```

To call a public member function of an instantiated object, append the function name to the object name with the member selection operator, followed by parentheses containing any arguments required by the function. For example, the first statement in the following code declares a Stocks object named stockPick. The second statement executes the getTotalValue() function, passing to it the number of stocks and the current price per share.

```
void main() {
    Stocks stockPick;
    stockPick.getTotalValue(100, 10.875);
}
```

Member Lists

Once you type the member selection operator following an instantiated object, Visual C++ displays a class's data members and member functions in the member list. (You first learned about member lists in Chapter 1.) Figure 4-13 shows an example of the member selection list for the Stocks class that includes both data members and member functions.

```cpp
#include "stocks.h"
#include <iostream.h>
double Stocks::dPortfolioValue = 0;
double Stocks::getPortfolioValue() {
    return dPortfolioValue;
}
double Stocks::getTotalValue(int iShares, double dCurPrice){
    iNumShares = iShares;
    dCurrentPricePerShare = dCurPrice;
    dCurrentValue = iNumShares * dCurrentPricePerShare;
    dPortfolioValue += dCurrentValue;
    return dCurrentValue;
}
void main() {
    Stocks stockPick1;
    Stocks stockPick2;
    Stocks stockPick3;
    cout << stockPick1.getTotalValue(100, 10.875) << endl;
    cout << stockPick2.getTotalValue(200, 64.25) << endl;
    cout << stockPick3.
    cout << Stocks::           dCurrentPricePerShare      << endl;
}                                 dCurrentValue
                                  dPortfolioValue
                                  getPortfolioValue
                                  getTotalValue
                                  iNumShares
```

Figure 4-13   Stocks class member selection list

After typing or selecting an object's function member, you receive an onscreen prompt listing the argument types required by the function, as shown in Figure 4-14.

```cpp
#include "stocks.h"
#include <iostream.h>
double Stocks::dPortfolioValue = 0;
double Stocks::getPortfolioValue() {
    return dPortfolioValue;
}
double Stocks::getTotalValue(int iShares, double dCurPrice){
    iNumShares = iShares;
    dCurrentPricePerShare = dCurPrice;
    dCurrentValue = iNumShares * dCurrentPricePerShare;
    dPortfolioValue += dCurrentValue;
    return dCurrentValue;
}
void main() {
    Stocks stockPick1;
    Stocks stockPick2;
    Stocks stockPick3;
    cout << stockPick1.getTotalValue(100, 10.875) << endl;
    cout << stockPick2.getTotalValue(200, 64.25) << endl;
    cout << stockPick3.getTotalValue(
    cout << Stocks::getPortfolioValue  double getTotalValue (int iShares, double dCurPrice)
}
```

Figure 4-14   Function member's argument list

To access member lists for pointers to objects, replace the member selection operator in the preceding code with the indirect member selection operator. The following code declares a pointer to the stockPick object and also instantiates a new Stocks object on the heap. Both pointers then use the indirect member selection operator to call the getTotalValue() function:

```
void main() {
    Stocks stockPick;
    Stocks* pStackStock = &stockPick; // stack pointer
    Stocks* pHeapStock = new Stocks; // heap pointer
    cout << pStackStock->getTotalValue(200, 64.25)
        << endl;
    cout << pHeapStock->getTotalValue(100, 17.5)
        << endl;
}
```

Next you will add code to the CalcSavings.cpp file that accesses the RetirementPlanner class's functions. You will use cout statements to display instructions to users and cin statements to gather data. You will assign the data returned from the cin statements to variables, which you will then pass to the RetirementPlanner class's function members. Finally, you will calculate and display the results using the calcFutureValue(), calcPresentValue(), and getInterestEarned() functions.

To add code to the CalcSavings.cpp file that accesses the RetirementPlanner class's functions:

1. Open the **CalcSavings.cpp** file in the Text Editor window.

2. Add the following statements after the **RetirementPlanner savings;** statement. The statements declare variables that you will use to hold the values retrieved from the user with the cin statements. The variables will then be passed to the RetirementPlanner class member functions.

```
double dContribute = 0;
double dInterest = 0;
int iAgeNow = 0;
int iAgeThen = 0;
double dInflate = 0;
```

3. Press **Enter** and add the following cout statements that explain the program to the user:

```
cout << "RETIREMENT PLANNER" << endl;
cout << "-------------------" << endl;
cout << "This program calculates your "
    << "retirement savings based on" << endl;
cout << "annual contribution, estimated "
    << "yearly interest rate, years " << endl;
cout << "of saving, and estimated inflation."
    << endl << endl;
```

4. Press **Enter** again and add the following statements that gather values from the user, assign the values to variables, then pass the variables to the member functions.

```
cout << "Annual Contribution: ";
cin >> dContribute;
savings.setContribution(dContribute);
```

```
cout << "Annual Yield (percent-enter as a whole number): ";
cin >> dInterest;
savings.setInterestRate(dInterest);
cout << "Current Age: ";
cin >> iAgeNow;
savings.setCurAge(iAgeNow);
cout << "Retirement Age: ";
cin >> iAgeThen;
savings.setRetireAge(iAgeThen);
cout << "Inflation (percent-enter as a whole number): ";
cin >> dInflate;
savings.setInflation(dInflate);
cout << endl;
```

5. Press **Enter** a final time and add the following statements that display the calculated savings results to the user:

```
cout << "---------------------------------" << endl;
cout << "Total Future Value: $" <<
savings.calcFutureValue() << endl;
cout << "Total Present Value: $" <<
savings.calcPresentValue() << endl;
cout << "Total Interest Earned: $" <<
savings.getInterestEarned() << endl;
cout << "---------------------------------" << endl << endl;
```

6. Build and execute the RetirementPlanner project. Then, test the program. When you
enter percentages for either Annual Yield or Inflation, enter the numbers as whole
numbers, not with a decimal point. For example, to enter 10%, type 10, not *.10*.

The `this` Pointer

With some types of programs, you may need to instantiate multiple objects based on the
same class. For example, if you are calculating stock values with the Stocks object, you may
instantiate a new Stocks object for each stock in your investment portfolio. Remember that
because objects are encapsulated, each object contains its own copies of a class's members.
When your programs call a class's function member, the compiler knows which object
instance called the function through the `this` pointer. The **this** pointer is a pointer that
identifies the object instance that called a function. C++ uses the `this` pointer to be sure
that a function member uses the correct set of data members for a given object.

By default, the `this` pointer is implied, meaning that a function member automatically
knows that the `this` pointer points to the calling object. Therefore, it is not usually necessary to use the `this` pointer with your data members. It is, however, occasionally used to
return a pointer to the current object. In other instances it is used to return the memory
address of the current object. For these reasons, you should be able to identify the `this`
pointer if you encounter it.

The following code shows an example of the getTotalValue() function of the Stocks class. Each data member is referenced using the **this** pointer with the indirect member selection operator:

```
double Stocks::getTotalValue(int iShares,
    double dCurPrice){
    this->iNumShares = iShares;
    this->dCurrentPricePerShare = dCurPrice;
    this->dCurrentValue = this->iNumShares
        * this->dCurrentPricePerShare;
    return this->dCurrentValue;
}
```

Since the **this** pointer is implied by default, the following version of the getTotalValue() function is equally correct:

```
double Stocks::getTotalValue(int iShares,
    double dCurPrice){
    iNumShares = iShares;
    dCurrentPricePerShare = dCurPrice;
    dCurrentValue = iNumShares
        * dCurrentPricePerShare;
    return dCurrentValue;
}
```

You will not use **this** pointers, unless you need to return the address of the current object.

Inline Functions

When you define a function in an implementation file separate from the interface file, the interface file must make a separate call to the implementation file whenever it wants to execute the function. This organization will be slower than if the function were defined as an inline function within the implementation file. Although you will often want to create function definitions in your implementation code for the purposes of implementation hiding, you will probably also want the speed benefits of inline code.

For small functions, you can use the **inline** keyword to request that the compiler replace calls to a function with the function definition wherever the function is called in a program. You place the **inline** keyword at the start of a function header. For example, to mark the getTotalValue() function as an inline function, its function header should read **inline double getTotalValue(int iShares, double dCurPrice)**. Additionally, you must place the function definition for a function declared with the **inline** keyword in the header file—not the implementation file. If you do add the **inline** keyword to a function that is not declared within a class header file, you will receive a compile error.

When the compiler encounters the **inline** keyword, it performs a cost/benefit analysis to determine whether replacing a function call with its function definition will increase the program's speed and performance. If the compiler's cost/benefit analysis determines that there will be no significant speed or performance gain by replacing a given function call with its function definition, then the `inline` keyword is ignored. Therefore, you should only use the `inline` keyword for small functions whose implementation you want to hide. Figure 4-15 illustrates how the compiler replaces a function call with its function definition.

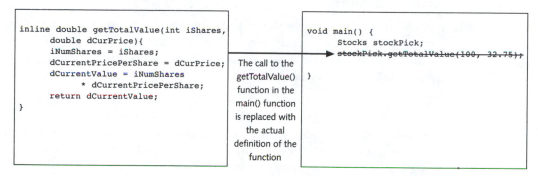

```
inline double getTotalValue(int iShares,
    double dCurPrice){
    iNumShares = iShares;
    dCurrentPricePerShare = dCurPrice;
    dCurrentValue = iNumShares
        * dCurrentPricePerShare;
    return dCurrentValue;
}
```

The call to the getTotalValue() function in the main() function is replaced with the actual definition of the function

```
void main() {
    Stocks stockPick;
    stockPick.getTotalValue(100, 32.75);
}
```

Figure 4-15   Compilation of a function marked with the inline keyword

Implementation hiding is still enforced when you use the `inline` keyword, since nobody can read the compiled version of a program. For functions whose implementations you do not need to hide, simply include the function in the interface file as an inline function.

 You can also use the `inline` keyword with global functions. As with member functions, however, the global functions you define as inline should be relatively small.

Next you will add the `inline` keyword to the getInterestEarned() function, which is small and stable enough that it can be defined as inline. You will also move the getInterestEarned() function definition to the header file so that the program compiles correctly.

To define the getInterestEarned() function as inline:

1. Open the **RetirementPlanner.cpp** file in the Text Editor window.

2. Highlight the **getInterestEarned()** function definition and cut it to the Clipboard by selecting **Cut** from the **Edit** menu.

3. Open the **RetirementPlanner.h** file in the Text Editor window.

4. Paste the getInterestEarned() function after the class's closing brace and semi-colon but above the `#endif` directive by selecting **Paste** from the **Edit** menu.

5. Modify the getInterestEarned() function definition so that it reads `inline double RetirementPlanner:: getInterestEarned()`. Note that you do not need to add the `inline` keyword to the function declaration in the class body.

6. Rebuild and execute the RetirementPlanner project. The program should function the same as it did before you added the `inline` keyword to the getInterestEarned() function.

Constructor Functions

When an object is first instantiated from a class, you will often want to assign initial values to data members or perform other types of initialization tasks, such as calling a function member that may calculate and assign values to data members. In a C++ program, you simply assign a value to a variable in the main() function using a statement such as `int iCount = 1;`.

Although classes are "mini-programs," they do not include a main() function in which you can assign initial values to data members or call initialization functions. Instead, you use a constructor function. A **constructor function** is a special function with the same name as its class that is called automatically when an object from a class is instantiated. You define and declare constructor functions the same way you define other functions, although you do not include a return type since constructor functions do not return values. For example, the following inline constructor function for the Payroll class initializes the dFedTax and dStateTax data members, which are respectively assigned a federal tax rate of 28% and a state tax rate of 5%:

```
class Payroll {
public:
    Payroll() {
        dFedTax = .28;
        dStateTax = .05;
    };
private:
    double dFedTax;
    double dStateTax;
};
```

You can also include just a function prototype in the interface file for the constructor function, and then create the function definition in the implementation file. The following code shows an example of how you implement the Payroll constructor function in an implementation file. It may look unusual, but when you define a constructor function in an implementation file, be sure to include the class name and scope resolution operator in order to identify the function as a class member.

```
Payroll::Payroll() {
    dFedTax = .28;
    dStateTax = .05;
};
```

In the next chapter you will learn about some advanced constructor techniques, as well as how to use the opposite of a constructor, a *destructor*.

Next you will add a constructor to the RetirementPlanner class. The constructor you will add will initialize all of the private data members to 0. Initializing private data members to 0 ensures that the calculations within the member functions have a value to work with in the event that a client fails to provide one of the values when executing any of the member functions.

To add a constructor to the RetirementPlanner class:

1. First, open the **RetirementPlanner.h** file in the Text Editor window.

2. Add a constructor prototype to the public section as follows:

```
#if !defined(RETIREMENTPLANNER_H)
#define RETIREMENTPLANNER_H
class RetirementPlanner {
public:
      RetirementPlanner();
...
```

3. Next, open the **RetirementPlanner.cpp** file in the Text Editor window.

4. Add a constructor function definition that initializes the data members to 0:

```
#include "RetirementPlanner.h"
RetirementPlanner::RetirementPlanner() {
     dContribution = 0;
     dInterestRate = 0;
     dInterestEarned = 0;
     iYearsOfSaving = 0;
     dFutureValue = 0;
     dPresentValue = 0;
     dInflation = 0;
     iCurAge = 0;
     iRetireAge = 0;
}
double Retirement::calcFutureValue(double dAmount,
     double dYield, int iCurAge, int iRetireAge) {
     dContribution = dAmount;
     dInterestRate = dYield;
     ...
```

5. Rebuild and execute the RetirementPlanner project. The program should function the same as it did before you added the constructor function.

friend Functions

When you use the public access modifier with a class member, the entire world has access to that class member. In contrast, only members of the same class can access private class members. What if you want to selectively allow access to class members, yet still maintain a level of information hiding? In these situations, the friend access modifier comes into play. The **friend** access modifier allows designated functions or classes to access a class's hidden members. Only a class itself can designate the function and class friends that can access its private members; external functions and classes cannot make themselves friends of a class. In other words, your class has to give friend access to external functions and classes. You declare a friend function by including the function's prototype in an interface file, preceded by the keyword `friend`.

 You can place a friend declaration anywhere inside the class, except within a function definition. You can even place a friend declaration within the declarations for public and private class members. It is good practice, however, to keep all definitions for a specific type of access modifier together.

Here's an example of how to declare a friend function. Suppose you want to allow an external function named getStateTax() to access in the Payroll class a private data member that contains a current state tax rate. Figure 4-16 shows the Payroll interface file and its implementation file. The interface file includes three private data members, dFedTax, dStateTax, and dNetPay. The dFedTax and dStateTax data members are respectively assigned a federal tax rate of 28% and a state tax rate of 5%. Both data members receive their initial values from the Payroll() constructor function. A public function member named calcNetPay() calculates the net pay for an employee based on the pay rate and number of hours passed as arguments from the client. The class also includes a declaration for a friend function named getStateTax() that is defined in the implementation file. Note that even though the getStateTax() function is defined in the class's implementation file, it is not part of the class since its header declaration does not include the name of the class and the scope resolution operator. The implementation file also includes a main() function, which, again, is not part of the class itself, that instantiates a new Payroll object on the heap and calls the calcNetPay() function. The next statement passes the Payroll object's pointer to the getStateTax() function. Because the getStateTax() function is declared as a friend of the Payroll class, it is allowed to retrieve the value assigned to the private dStateTax data member. Note that the double variables declared within the calcNetPay() function are local variables, not class data members. Figure 4-17 shows the program's output.

```
// Payroll.h
class Payroll {
public:
    double calcNetPay(double dPay, double dHours);
    Payroll();
private:
    double dFedTax;
    double dStateTax;
    double dNetPay;
    friend double getStateTax(Payroll* pStateTax);
};
// Payroll.cpp
#include <iostream.h>
#include "Payroll.h"
double getStateTax(Payroll* pStateTax) {
    return pStateTax->dStateTax;
}
```

Figure 4-16   Payroll class declaring and defining a friend function

4

```cpp
void main() {
    Payroll* pCalcPayroll = new Payroll;
    double dPay = 25.5;
    double dHours = 40;
    cout << "Your hourly wage is $" << dPay << endl;
    cout << "You worked " << dHours << " hours" << endl;
    cout << "Your net pay is $";
    cout << pCalcPayroll->calcNetPay(dPay, dHours)
        << endl;
    cout << "The current state tax rate is ";
    cout << getStateTax(pCalcPayroll) << endl;
}
double Payroll::calcNetPay(double dPay, double dHours) {
    double dGrossPay = dPay * dHours;
    double dCurFedTaxes = dGrossPay * dFedTax;
    double dCurStateTaxes = dGrossPay * dStateTax;
    double dNetPay = dGrossPay - (dCurFedTaxes
        + dCurStateTaxes);
    return dNetPay;
}
Payroll::Payroll() {
    dFedTax = .28;
    dStateTax = .05;
}
```

Figure 4-16   Payroll class declaring and defining a friend function (continued)

```
"c:\Visual C++ Projects\Chapter.05\Payroll\Debug\Payroll.exe"
Your hourly wage is $25.5
You worked 40 hours
Your net pay is $683.4
The current state tax rate is 0.05
Press any key to continue
```

Figure 4-17   Output of payroll program

To designate all functions within another class as friends of the current class, you create a declaration in the current class using the syntax `friend class name`, replacing *name* with the name of the class containing the functions you want to mark as friends. For example, to allow all the functions in a Benefits class to access the private members in the Payroll class, add the declaration `friend class Benefits` to the Payroll class's interface file as follows.

```
class Payroll {
public:
    double calcNetPay(double dPay, double dHours);
    Payroll();
private:
    double dFedTax;
    double dStateTax;
    double dNetPay;
    friend double getStateTax(Payroll* pStateTax);
    friend class Benefits;
};
```

CHAPTER SUMMARY

- A pointer is a special type of variable that stores the memory address of other variables.

- You declare a variable as a pointer by placing the indirection operator (*) after the data type or before the variable name.

- You use the address of operator (&) to assign to the pointer variable the memory address of another variable.

- Once you assign the memory address of a variable to a pointer, you precede a pointer name in an expression with the de-reference operator (*) in order to access or modify the contents of the variable pointed to by the pointer.

- A reference, or reference variable, is an alias for an existing variable.

- The stack is a region of memory where applications can store data such as local variables, function calls, and parameter information.

- The heap, or the free store, is an area of memory that is available to an application for storing data whose existence and size are not known until run time.

- The **new** keyword creates a variable on the heap and returns a pointer to the variable's heap address.

- You use the **delete** keyword to de-allocate memory that has been reserved on the heap.

- In C++ programming, classes are structures that contain variables along with functions for manipulating that data.

- The functions and variables defined in a class are referred to as class members.

- Class variables are referred to as data members, while class functions are referred to as member functions.

❏ Classes are referred to as user-defined data types or programmer-defined data types because you can work with a class as a single unit, or object, in the same way you work with variables.

❏ When you declare an object from a class, you are said to be instantiating an object.

❏ A structure, or struct, is an advanced, user-defined data type that uses a single variable name to store multiple pieces of related information.

❏ The individual pieces of information stored in a structure are referred to as elements, fields, or members.

❏ When you use a period to access an object's members, such as a structure's fields, the period is referred to as the member selection operator.

❏ Structures are part of the C programming language and are not limited to use with Windows programs.

❏ Default accessibility is the only difference between structures and classes in C++.

❏ Most C++ programmers use the **class** keyword to clearly designate the programs they write as object-oriented C++ programs.

❏ When declaring and using pointers and references to class objects, follow the same rules as you would when declaring and using pointers and references to variables of primitive data types.

❏ You use the indirect member selection operator (->) to access class members through a pointer to an object either on the stack or on the heap.

❏ The principal of information hiding states that any class members that other programmers, or clients, do not need to access or know about should be hidden.

❏ Access specifiers control a client's access to data members and member functions. There are four levels of access specifiers: public, private, protected, and friend.

❏ The public access specifier allows anyone to call a class's function member or to modify a data member.

❏ The private access specifier is one of the key elements in information hiding since it prevents clients from calling member functions or accessing data members.

❏ Both public and private access specifiers have what is called class scope in that class members of both access types are accessible by any of a class's member functions.

❏ You place access specifiers in a class definition on a single line followed by a colon, similar to a **switch** statement's case labels.

❏ An access specifier that is placed on a line by itself followed by a colon is referred to as an access label.

❑ Many programmers prefer to make all of their data members private in order to prevent clients from accidentally assigning the wrong value to a variable or from viewing the internal workings of their programs.

❑ Accessor functions are public member functions that a client can call to retrieve or modify the value of a data member.

❑ The separation of classes into separate interface and implementation files is considered to be a fundamental software development technique since it allows you to hide the details of how your classes are written and makes it easier to modify programs.

❑ The interface refers to the data member and function member declarations inside a class's braces.

❑ The implementation refers to a class's function definitions and any code that assigns values to a class's data members.

❑ Multiple inclusions of the same header usually occur when you include one header into a second header, and then include the second header in an implementation file.

❑ The #if and #endif preprocessor directives determine which portions of a file to compile depending on the result of a conditional expression.

❑ The defined constant expression returns a value of true if a particular identifier is defined or a value of false if it is not defined.

❑ You can create function member definitions in either the interface file or the implementation file.

❑ Function member definitions in an interface file are referred to as inline functions.

❑ Even though the member functions of a class may be defined in separate files from the class declarations, as long as the function includes the class's name and the scope resolution operator, then it is considered to be part of the class definition.

❑ The GetWindowText() function is a Win32 API function that retrieves either the value displayed in a control or the title text for windows that are not controls.

❑ The `this` pointer is a pointer that identifies the object instance that called a function.

❑ By default, the `this` pointer is implied, meaning that a function member automatically knows that the `this` pointer points to the calling object.

❑ For small functions, you can use the inline keyword to request that the compiler replace calls to a function with the function definition wherever the function is called in a program.

❑ A constructor function is a special function with the same name as its class that is called automatically when an object from a class is instantiated.

❑ The friend access modifier allows designated functions or classes to access a class's hidden members.

REVIEW QUESTIONS

1. You can create a pointer using the syntax *type* pointer;* or _____.

    a. `type *pointer;`

    b. `*type pointer;`

    c. `type pointer*;`

    d. `type& pointer;`

2. Which operator do you use to assign to the pointer variable the memory address of another variable?

    a. `&`

    b. `*`

    c. `%`

    d. `=`

3. Which operator do you use in order to access or modify the contents of the variable pointed to by the pointer?

    a. `&`

    b. `*`

    c. `%`

    d. `=`

4. Which of the following is the correct syntax for assigning a string to a char* pointer named szCalifornia?

    a. `*szCaliforniaCapital = "Sacramento";`

    b. `char* szCaliforniaCapital[25] = "Sacramento";`

    c. `char* szCaliforniaCapital = "Sacramento";`

    d. `char szCaliforniaCapital = "Sacramento";`

5. Which of the following correctly declares a reference named rBucks that is an alias for a variable named iDollars, assuming the iDollars variable already exists?

    a. `int& rBucks = iDollars;`

    b. `int rBucks& = iDollars;`

    c. `int rBucks = &iDollars;`

    d. `int& rBucks;`
    `   rBucks = iDollars;`

6. When you declare a standard variable using a statement similar to
   `int iCount = 0;`, where in memory is the variable stored?

   a. stack

   b. heap

   c. free store

   d. iostream

7. Which of the following statements is the correct syntax for declaring a variable on
   the heap?

   a. `double dPrice = new double;`

   b. `double* dPrice = new double;`

   c. `double* dPrice = double;`

   d. `*double dPrice = new double;`

8. Which keyword do you use to remove a variable from the heap?

   a. `remove`

   b. `delete`

   c. `kill`

   d. `purge`

9. Which of the following terms does not refer to class functions?

   a. member functions

   b. global functions

   c. user-defined data types

   d. programmer-defined data types

10. The term *object* is used interchangeably with the word(s) _____.

    a. *function*

    b. *variable*

    c. *statement*

    d. *data type*

11. You define a structure using the _____ keyword.

    a. structure

    b. struct

    c. record

    d. data

12. Which statement best describes how you store data types in a structure?

    a. All variables in a structure must be of the same data type.

    b. You must use all numeric data types or all character data types.

    c. You can use any mix of data types.

    d. Structures do not directly declare data types, only variable names that are later assigned a specific data type.

13. Which of the following is the correct syntax for declaring a variable named accountingInfo based on a structure named accounting?

    a. `accounting accountingInfo;`

    b. `currentEmployee accountingInfo;`

    c. `accountingInfo currentEmployee();`

    d. `accountingInfo = new currentEmployee();`

14. When you use a period to access an object's members, such as a structure's fields, the period is referred to as the _____.

    a. object selector

    b. member selection operator

    c. field indicator

    d. structure operand

15. Examine the following structure declaration and determine why it will cause a compiler error:

    ```
    struct accounting {
        char* period = "1st Quarter";
        long fiscalYear = 2000;
        double curTaxRate = .15;
    };
    ```

    a. The name of the structure must be followed by parentheses, the same as a function definition.

    b. You are only allowed to use a single data type within a structure definition.

    c. You are not allowed to assign values to the fields inside the structure definition itself.

    d. The structure must be declared using the structure keyword.

16. Which of the following statements declares a Boat object named sailBoat on the stack with a pointer to the sailBoat object?

    a. Boat sailBoat;
    ```
    Boat* pSailBoat = &sailBoat;
    ```

    b. Boat sailBoat;
    ```
    Boat* pSailBoat = sailBoat;
    ```

    c. Boat sailBoat;
    ```
    Boat pSailBoat = &sailBoat;
    ```

    d. Boat sailBoat;
    ```
    Boat pSailBoat = sailBoat;
    ```

17. Which of the following statements declares a Boat object named sailBoat and a reference to the Sailboat object?

    a. Boat sailBoat;
    ```
    Boat& rSailBoat = *sailBoat;
    ```

    b. Boat sailBoat;
    ```
    Boat rSailBoat = &sailBoat;
    ```

    c. Boat sailBoat;
    ```
    Boat& rSailBoat = sailBoat;
    ```

    d. Boat sailBoat;
    ```
    Boat* rSailBoat = &sailBoat;
    ```

18. What is the accessibility of the data members in the following class?
    ```
    class Boat {
          int iLength;
          double dEngineSize;
          char cClass;
    }
    ```

    a. public

    b. private

    c. friend

    d. protected

19. What is the accessibility of the data members in the following structure?
    ```
    struct Boat {
          int iLength;
          double dEngineSize;
          char cClass;
    }
    ```

    a. public

    b. private

    c. friend

    d. protected

20. Member functions that are defined within an interface file are referred to as
    _____ functions.

    a. member

    b. inline

    c. embedded

    d. compiled

4

21. Which of the following preprocessor directives is used for preventing multiple header
    file inclusion?

    a. #multiple

    b. #define...#!define

    c. #include...#stop_include

    d. #if and #endif

22. Which of the following elements is not considered part of a class's scope?

    a. implementation files

    b. interface files

    c. constructor functions

    d. a main() method

23. How else can you write the statement `this->iLength = 10;` in a function member, assuming the iLength variable is a data member of the same class?

    a. `this.iLength = 10;`

    b. `class.iLength = 10;`

    c. `self.iLength = 10;`

    d. `iLength = 10;`

24. Which of the following keywords forces the compiler to replace calls to a function
    with the function definition wherever the function is called in a program?

    a. include

    b. inline

    c. replace

    d. insert

25. Which statement is the correct definition in an implementation file for the constructor function for a class named Boat, assuming the construct function does not accept any arguments?

    a. `Boat () {`

    b. `Boat:Boat () {`

    c. `function Boat::Boat () {`

    d. `class Boat::Boat () {`

26. The _____ access modifier allows designated functions or classes to access a class's hidden members.

a. public

b. private

c. friend

d. protected

EXERCISES

1. What is the difference between a class and a structure? How do the two class types differ between C and C++?

2. Rewrite the following structure as a class. Be sure to assign the same access to the data members as they have in the structure.

```
struct CourseInfo {
    double dTuition;
    int iCourseID;
    char cGrade;
}
```

3. To the main() function in the following code, add cout statements that print each of the carInfo object's data members.

```
struct Transportation {
    double dCarEngineSize;
    int iMotorcycleCCs;
    int iSemiNumberofAxels;
}
void main() {
    Transportation vehicleInfo;
    vehicleInfo.dCarEngineSize = 3.1;
    vehicleInfo.iMotorcycleCCs = 750;
    vehicleInfo.iSemiNumberofAxels = 6;
}
```

4. Rewrite the struct in Exercise 3 as a class. Also rewrite the main() function so that the object is declared on the heap instead of on the stack. Be sure to correctly modify in the main() function the statements that reference each data member.

5. What is the difference between a class's interface file and its implementation file?

6. Recall that accessor functions, which assign values to and retrieve values from private data members, are often referred to as get and set functions. Write the appropriate

implementation file for the following class declaration and create get and set functions so that they assign values to and retrieve values from the private data members.

```
class MutualFund {
public:
     void setNumberOfShares();
     void setAnnualYield();
     int getNumberOfShares();
     double getAnnualYield();
private:
     int iNumberOfShares;
     double dAnnualYield;
}
```

7. Write a main() function that sets, retrieves, and prints the values of the private data members in the MutualFund class.

8. Add a friend function to the MutualFund class. Design the friend function so that it sets, retrieves, and prints all of the MutualFund class's private data members. Also, rewrite the main() function so that instead of setting, retrieving, and printing the private data members directly, it passes to the friend function a pointer to a MutualFund object.

9. Write the appropriate interface file for the following class implementation.

```
#include " DistanceConversion.h"
DistanceConversion:: DistanceConversion () {
     dMiles = 0;
     dKilometers = 0;
}
double DistanceConversion::milesToKilometers(double
     dMilesArg) {
     dMiles = dMilesArg;
     dKilometers = dMiles * 1.6;
     return dKilometers;
}
double DistanceConversion::kilometersToMiles(
     double dKiloArg) {
     dKilometers = dKiloArg;
     dMiles = dKilometers * .6;
     return dMiles;
}
```

10. Find two ways to modify the DistanceConversion class so that the member function is compiled inline. Create separate versions of the class for each of your solutions.

11. Create a BaseballTeam class with appropriate data members such as team name, games won, games lost, and so on. Write appropriate get and set functions for each data member. Instantiate a number of BaseballTeam objects and assign appropriate values to each private data member using the get functions. Finally, use the get statements to retrieve and print the values in each private data member.

12. Create an Automobile class. Include private data members such as make, model, color, and engine, along with the appropriate get and set functions for setting and retrieving private data members. Use cin and cout statements to gather and display information.

13. Create a class-based temperature conversion program that converts Fahrenheit to Celsius and Celsius to Fahrenheit. To convert Fahrenheit to Celsius subtract 32 from the Fahrenheit temperature, then multiply the remainder by .55. To convert Celsius to Fahrenheit multiply the Celsius temperature by 1.8, then add 32. Use cin and cout statements to gather and display information.

14. Create a CompanyInfo class that includes private data members such as the company name, year incorporated, annual gross revenue, annual net revenue, and so on. Write set and get functions to store and retrieve values in the private data members. Also, create a friend function that calculates the company's operating costs by subtracting net revenue from gross revenue. Use cin and cout statements to gather and display information.

15. Create a BankAccount class that allows users to calculate the balance in a bank account. The user should be able to enter a starting balance, and then calculate how that balance changes when they make a deposit, withdraw money, or enter any accumulated interest. Add the appropriate data members and member functions to the BankAccount class that will enable this functionality. Also, add code to the class that ensures that the user does not overdraw his or her account. Be sure that the program adheres to the information hiding techniques that were discussed in this chapter. Use cin and cout statements to gather and display information. You will need to use a decision-making structure that continually displays a menu from which the user can select commands to manage his or her account.

5

OBJECT MANIPULATION

> **In this chapter you will learn:**
> - About default constructors
> - How to create parameterized constructors
> - How to work with initialization lists
> - How to create copy constructors
> - How to work with destructors
> - How to overload operators
> - About static class members
> - About constant objects

PREVIEW: THE BUILDING ESTIMATOR PROGRAM

The Building Estimator program is a console application that calculates the cost of building a home for three separate customers. The program allows users to select a home style, the number of bedrooms, and the number of bathrooms. Then it calculates the estimated cost of building the home based on preset amounts. The Building Estimator program is a fairly simple example of the type of program that building contractors and architects might use in real life to estimate the cost of building an entire housing development. Although the program allows you to estimate costs for only three customers, it provides a sufficient demonstration of the object manipulation techniques discussed in this chapter.

To preview the Building Estimator program:

1. Create a **Chapter.05** folder in your Visual C++ Projects folder.

2. Copy the **Chapter5_BuildingEstimator** folder from the Chapter.05 folder on your Data Disk to the Chapter.05 folder in your Visual C++ Projects folder. Then open the **Estimator** project in Visual C++. If the Tip of the Day dialog box displays, click the **Close** button.

3. The Estimator project contains two files: Estimator.h and Estimator.cpp. You should recognize both of these files as the interface and implementation files for a class. Open the **Estimator.h** file in the Text Editor window. Notice some of the unfamiliar declarations. Figure 5-1 briefly explains each of these declarations. (Some of the declarations in Figure 5-1 are placed on the same line to save space.)

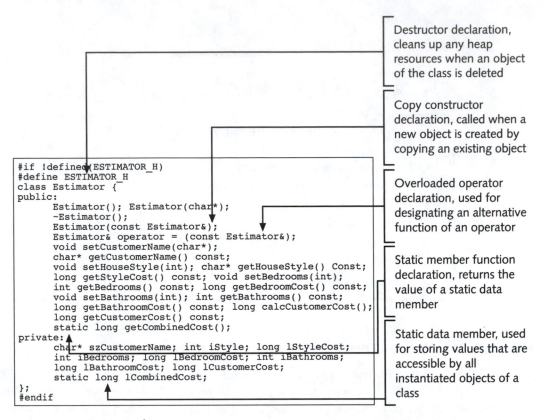

Destructor declaration, cleans up any heap resources when an object of the class is deleted

Copy constructor declaration, called when a new object is created by copying an existing object

Overloaded operator declaration, used for designating an alternative function of an operator

Static member function declaration, returns the value of a static data member

Static data member, used for storing values that are accessible by all instantiated objects of a class

```cpp
#if !defined(ESTIMATOR_H)
#define ESTIMATOR_H
class Estimator {
public:
    Estimator(); Estimator(char*);
    ~Estimator();
    Estimator(const Estimator&);
    Estimator& operator = (const Estimator&);
    void setCustomerName(char*);
    char* getCustomerName() const;
    void setHouseStyle(int); char* getHouseStyle() Const;
    long getStyleCost() const; void setBedrooms(int);
    int getBedrooms() const; long getBedroomCost() const;
    void setBathrooms(int); int getBathrooms() const;
    long getBathroomCost() const; long calcCustomerCost();
    long getCustomerCost() const;
    static long getCombinedCost();
private:
    char* szCustomerName; int iStyle; long lStyleCost;
    int iBedrooms; long lBedroomCost; int iBathrooms;
    long lBathroomCost; long lCustomerCost;
    static long lCombinedCost;
};
#endif
```

Figure 5-1   Estimator.h

4. Close the **Estimator.h** interface file and open the **Estimator.cpp** implementation file. Estimator.cpp is a fairly long file containing various C++ code segments that you should recognize. Figure 5-2 shows the class member definitions whose declarations were called out in Figure 5-1.

```
#include "Estimator.h"

...

Estimator::Estimator(const Estimator& sourceObject) {

     szCustomerName = new char[50];

     strcpy(szCustomerName, sourceObject.szCustomerName);

}

Estimator::~Estimator() {

     delete[] szCustomerName;

}

Estimator& Estimator::operator = (const Estimator& operand) {

     szCustomerName = new char[50];

     strcpy(szCustomerName, operand.szCustomerName);

     iStyle = operand.iStyle;

     lStyleCost = operand.lStyleCost;

     iBedrooms = operand.iBedrooms;

     lBedroomCost = operand.lBedroomCost;

     iBathrooms = operand.iBathrooms;

     lBathroomCost = operand.lBathroomCost;

     lCustomerCost = operand.lCustomerCost;

     return *this;

}
...

long Estimator::getCombinedCost() {

     return lCombinedCost;

}
```

Copy constructor definition

Destructor definition

Overloaded operator definition

Static member function definition

Figure 5-2   Estimator.cpp

5. Build and execute the Building Estimator program. Enter values for each of the variables that calculate building estimates. Figure 5-3 shows the output from a completed version of the Building Estimator program after entering some data for the first customer.

Figure 5-3   Output of Building Estimator program

6. Press any key to close the Building Estimator program window.

INTRODUCTION

In the last chapter you learned about object-oriented programming techniques and basic class concepts. This chapter continues the discussion of class concepts by introducing various techniques for manipulating objects.

Classes are a fundamental, yet complex, feature of C++, and the topics in this chapter cover more advanced aspects of classes. As you work through this chapter, remember that your ultimate goal is creating Visual C++ programs using Microsoft Foundation Classes, not creating C++ programs that use standard classes. Although class concepts theory is invaluable in helping you understand advanced programming concepts and progressing further in computer science, this chapter mainly focuses on *how* to use some advanced class concepts in your programs. Having a basic understanding of how to implement the topics presented in this chapter will enable you to work with Microsoft Foundation Classes, which make use of advanced class features.

ADVANCED CONSTRUCTORS

In the last chapter, you touched on the subject of constructors in order to provide a mechanism for initializing data members. Constructors, however, can do more than initialize data members. They can execute member functions and perform other types of initialization routines that a class may require when it first starts. The following constructor techniques will be discussed:

- default constructor
- parameterized constructors
- initialization lists
- copy constructor

First, you will learn about the default constructor.

Default Constructor

The **default constructor** does not include any parameters, and is called for any declared objects of its class to which you do not pass arguments. But, before diving into default constructors, review what you already know about constructor functions. You define and declare constructor functions the same way you define other functions, although you do not include a return type since constructor functions do not return values. For example, in Figure 5-4 the constructor function for the Payroll class initializes the dFedTax and dStateTax data members, which are respectively assigned a federal tax rate of 28% and a state tax rate of 5%. The constructor function prototype is declared in the interface file, while the constructor function itself is declared in the implementation file.

```cpp
// Payroll.h
class Payroll {
public:
    Payroll();
private:
    double dFedTax;
    double dStateTax;
};
// Payroll.cpp
#include "Payroll.h"
Payroll::Payroll() {
    dFedTax = .28;
    dStateTax = .05;
};
```

Figure 5-4   Constructor function for the Payroll class

The constructor function in Figure 5-4 is an example of a default constructor. You instantiate an object based on a default constructor function using the syntax *classname object_name;*. For example, to declare an object named currentEmployee using the Payroll object's default constructor function, you use the statement **Payroll currentEmployee;**.

Notice that default constructors, which do not accept parameters, are not instantiated with parentheses. You simply use a statement such as **Payroll currentEmployee;**. If you attempt to use parentheses when you instantiate an object based on a default constructor, you will receive a compile error when the compiler encounters a statement that attempts to use that object. For example, the statement **Payroll currentEmployee();** is incorrect. Figure 5-5 shows an example of the compile error that is raised in Visual C++ when an empty pair of parentheses are used when instantiating an object based on the Payroll class's default constructor. The Output window has been scrolled to the right so you can see the description of the error.

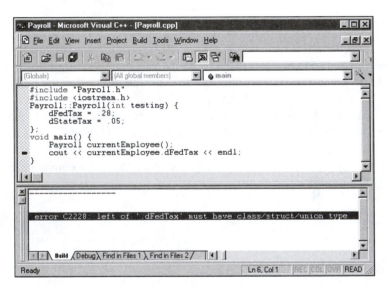

Figure 5-5   Incorrectly instantiated default constructor causing a compile error

In addition to initializing data members and executing member functions, default constructors perform various types of behind-the-scenes class maintenance. For this reason, if you do not declare and define one in your code, Visual C++ automatically supplies a default constructor. Good programming technique dictates, however, that you should always create a default constructor for your class, even if you do not need to write your own default constructor to initialize data members and perform other initialization tasks. You need to supply a default constructor because once you create a parameterized constructor, the Visual C++-supplied default constructor is no longer available. If you create a parameterized constructor for your class but not a default constructor, a client will receive a compile error if he or she attempts to instantiate an object based on your class using the default constructor. Figure 5-6 shows an example of the Payroll class that contains a single parameterized constructor that accepts federal and state income tax percentages. The statement in the main() function is illegal since it attempts to instantiate an object using the missing default constructor.

```
// Payroll.h
class Payroll {
public:
    Payroll(double dFed, double dState);
private:
    double dFedTax;
    double dStateTax;
};
// Payroll.cpp
#include "Payroll.h"
#include <iostream.h>
Payroll::Payroll(double dFed, double dState) {
    dFedTax = dFed;
    dStateTax = dState;
};
void main() {
    Payroll employee; // illegal
    ...
}
```

Figure 5-6   Payroll class missing default constructor function

If you do not need the default constructor, simply leave the function body empty. For example, to include an empty default constructor for the Payroll class, include the statement `Payroll();` in the interface file and the following definition in the implementation file:

```
Payroll::Payroll() {
    // empty function body
};
```

Figure 5-7 shows a corrected version of the Payroll class with an empty default constructor function.

```
// Payroll.h
class Payroll {
public:
    Payroll();
    Payroll(double dFed, double dState);
private:
    double dFedTax;
    double dStateTax;
};
// Payroll.cpp
#include "Payroll.h"
#include <iostream.h>
Payroll::Payroll() {
    // empty function body
};
Payroll::Payroll(double dFed, double dState) {
    dFedTax = dFed;
    dStateTax = dState;
};
void main() {
    Payroll employee;
    ...
}
```

Figure 5-7   Payroll class after adding empty default constructor function

Next you will start creating the Building Estimator program. To create the Estimator.h interface file:

1. Create a new empty Win32 Console Application project named **BuildingEstimator**. Save the project in the **Chapter.05** folder in your Visual C++ Projects folders.

2. Add a new C/C++ Header File named **Estimator.h** to the Building Estimator project.

3. In the Estimator.h file, type the opening preprocessor directive to prevent multiple inclusion of the class file, along with the opening class declaration statement:

```
#if !defined(ESTIMATOR_H)
#define ESTIMATOR_H
class Estimator {
```

4. Add the public declaration section, which declares a constructor and various functions for setting and retrieving data members in the Estimator class. For example, the setCustomerName() function sets the customer name in the szCustomerName variable (which you will create next) using a char* parameter.

You retrieve the value in the szCustomerName variable using the getCustomerName() member function.

```
public:
      Estimator();
      void setCustomerName(char*);
      char* getCustomerName();
      void setHouseStyle(int);
      char* getHouseStyle();
      long getStyleCost();
      void setBedrooms(int);
      int getBedrooms();
      long getBedroomCost();
      void setBathrooms(int);
      int getBathrooms();
      long getBathroomCost();
      long calcCustomerCost();
      long getCustomerCost();
```

5. Next, add the private declaration section with various private data members. Each of these data members stores a specific piece of information that relates to a customer's estimate. For example, the szCustomerName data member stores the customer name in a string, while the iStyle variable contains an integer representing the selected building style.

```
private:
      char* szCustomerName;
      int iStyle;
      long lStyleCost;
      int iBedrooms;
      long lBedroomCost;
      int iBathrooms;
      long lBathroomCost;
      long lCustomerCost;
```

6. Finally, close the class declaration and the #if preprocessor directive:

```
};
#endif
```

Next, you will create the Estimator.cpp implementation file. Included on your Data Disk is a basic version of the Estimator.cpp file that you can add to your project so you do not have to spend too much time typing. If you do not have access to a data disk, then type the program as shown in the figures in the following steps.

To create the Estimator.cpp implementation file:

1. Copy the **Estimator.cpp** file from your Data Disk to the BuildingEstimator folder in the Chapter.05 folder in your Visual C++ Projects folder.

2. Add the **Estimator.cpp** file to the BuildingEstimator project by pointing to **Add to Project** on the **Project** menu, and then clicking **Files**.

Once the file is added, open it in the Text Editor window. The first four lines of the file are #include statements that import several header files that are required by the program, including the Estimator.h interface file. Following the #include statements are constructor function definitions and definitions for the set and get functions. The constructor function initializes the program's variables, and the set and get functions are used for setting and retrieving data member values. Figure 5-8 shows the #include statements and class functions.

```
#include "Estimator.h"
#include <iostream.h>
#include <ostream.h>
#include <string.h>
Estimator::Estimator() {
    szCustomerName = new char[50];
    iStyle = 0;
    lStyleCost = 0;
    iBedrooms = 0;
    lBedroomCost = 0;
    iBathrooms = 0;
    lBathroomCost = 0;
    lCustomerCost = 0;
}
void Estimator::setCustomerName(char* szCustName) {
    strcpy(szCustomerName, szCustName);
}
char* Estimator::getCustomerName() {
    return szCustomerName;
}
void Estimator::setHouseStyle(int iHouse) {
    iStyle = iHouse;
    switch (iHouse) {
        case 1: // A-Frame
            lStyleCost = 35000;
            break;
        case 2: // Cape Cod
            lStyleCost = 45000;
            break;
        case 3: // Colonial
            lStyleCost = 60000;
            break;
        case 4: // Cottage
            lStyleCost = 32000;
            break;
        case 5: // Ranch
            lStyleCost = 28000;
            break;
        default:
            lStyleCost = 0;
    }
}
```

Figure 5-8   Estimator class member function definitions

```
long Estimator::getStyleCost() {
     return lStyleCost;
}
char* Estimator::getHouseStyle() {
     switch (iStyle) {
          case 1: // A-Frame
               return "A-Frame";
               break;
          case 2: // Cape Cod
               return "Cape Cod";
               break;
          case 3: // Colonial
               return "Colonial";
               break;
          case 4: // Cottage
               return "Cottage";
               break;
          case 5: // Ranch
               return "Ranch";
               break;
     }
     return "";
}
void Estimator::setBedrooms(int iBeds) {
     iBedrooms = iBeds;
     lBedroomCost = 5000 * iBeds;
}
int Estimator::getBedrooms() {
     return iBedrooms;
}
long Estimator::getBedroomCost() {
return lBedroomCost;
}
void Estimator::setBathrooms(int iBaths) {
     iBathrooms = iBaths;
     lBathroomCost = 2500 * iBaths;
}
int Estimator::getBathrooms() {
     return iBathrooms;
}
long Estimator::getBathroomCost() {
     return lBathroomCost;
}
long Estimator::calcCustomerCost() {
     lCustomerCost = lStyleCost + lBedroomCost + lBathroomCost;
     return lCustomerCost;
}
long Estimator::getCustomerCost() {
     return lCustomerCost;
}
```

Figure 5-8   Estimator class member function definitions (continued)

3. Scroll down in the file until you see the code following the curCustomerCost()
member function definition. You will see two global function prototypes and a
global variable declaration, followed by the main() function. The main() method
instantiates an Estimator object and then calls the two global functions. The first
global function, curCustomerName() (located directly below the main() function),
is used for building the global szName variable with the client's first and last names
after the names are received from the user via the cin statement. The second
global function, curCustomerEstimate(), uses cin statements to gather building
preferences from the user. You pass to the curCustomerEstimate() function a
reference to the currently instantiated object. The Estimator class's members are
then called through the object reference. The curCustomerEstimate() function
may be intimidating at first. Actually, it is mostly composed of cout statements
for displaying information from the user. (Several of the cout statements include
\t escape characters to better format the output to the screen.) The important
statements with which you need to be concerned in the curCustomerEstimate()
function are bolded in Figure 5-9.

```cpp
void curCustomerName();
void curCustomerEstimate(Estimator&);
char szName[50];
void main() {
    cout << "New Home Building Estimator" << endl;
    cout << "-----------------------------------"
        << endl << endl;
    cout << "Customer 1" << endl << endl;
    curCustomerName();
    Estimator customer1;
    customer1.setCustomerName(szName);
    curCustomerEstimate(customer1);
}
void curCustomerName() {
    char szInput[25];
    cout << "First name: " ;
    cin >> szInput;
    strcpy(szName, szInput);
    strcat(szName, " ");
    cout << "Last name: ";
    cin >> szInput;
    strcat(szName, szInput);
    cout << endl;
}
```

Figure 5-9 Estimator program's main() and global functions

```cpp
void curCustomerEstimate(Estimator& curCustomer) {
    int iInput;
    cout << "House Styles \tCost" << endl;
    cout << "1. A-Frame \t$35,000" << endl;
    cout << "2. Cape Cod \t$45,000" << endl;
    cout << "3. Colonial \t$60,000" << endl;
    cout << "4. Cottage\t$32,000" << endl;
    cout << "5. Ranch \t$28,000" << endl << endl;
    cout << "Select a house style by number: ";
    cin >> iInput;
    curCustomer.setHouseStyle(iInput);
    cout << "Number of bedrooms: ";
    cin >> iInput;
    curCustomer.setBedrooms(iInput);
    cout << "Number of bathrooms: " ;
    cin >> iInput;
    curCustomer.setBathrooms(iInput);
    cout << endl;
    cout << "The following building estimate
        was prepared for "
    << curCustomer.getCustomerName() << ":"
        << endl << endl;
    cout << "House Style: " << curCustomer.getHouseStyle()
        << "\t$" << curCustomer.getStyleCost() << endl;
    cout << "Total Bedrooms: "
        << curCustomer.getBedrooms()
        << "\t$" << curCustomer.getBedroomCost()
            << "\t ($5,000 per bedroom)" << endl;
    cout << "Total Bathrooms: "
        << curCustomer.getBathrooms()
        << "\t$" << curCustomer.getBathroomCost()
        << "\t ($2,500 per bathroom)" << endl;
    cout << "\t\t\t=========" << endl;
    cout << "    TOTAL BUILDING COST\t$"
        << curCustomer.calcCustomerCost() << endl;
    cout << endl;
    cout << endl;
}
```

Figure 5-9 Estimator program's main() and global functions (continued)

4. Build and execute the project. Enter a customer's first and last name, and select
   the style house and the number of bedrooms and bathrooms. After entering the
   required information, the total estimate for the customer's house appears. After
   the program finishes executing, press any key to return to Visual C++.

The basic functionality of the program is fairly simple in order to allow you to concentrate on the class techniques presented in this chapter. The program does not include any error checking or ways of validating user input. Therefore, if you try to crash the program, you will probably succeed.

Parameterized Constructors

Although constructor functions do not return values, they can accept parameters that a client can use to pass any initialization values to your class. The constructor function in Figure 5-4 assigns default values to the dFedTax and dStateTax data members. Instead of assigning default values, you can allow a client to pass in the values for these data members by designing the constructor function with parameters. First, you include a function prototype such as `Payroll(double dFed, double dState);` in the interface file. Then, you write the constructor function definition in the implementation file as follows:

```
Payroll::Payroll(double dFed, double dState) {
    dFedTax = dFed;
    dStateTax = dState;
};
```

Because you should always keep your data members private, the Payroll() constructor function in the preceding code assigns the parameters passed by the client to the private dFedTax and dStateTax data members.

Any type of C++ function, whether a standard function or member function, can be overloaded. An **overloaded function** refers to multiple functions within a program that share the same name, but that accept different parameters. Each version of an overloaded function must accept different parameters or you will receive a compiler error. You overload functions when you want to execute a different set of statements depending on the parameters and data types that are passed to the function. For example, you may have a function named downPayment() that calculates the down payment required for purchasing a home. You may have one version of the downPayment() function that accepts a single parameter consisting of the purchase price. Statements within the body of the downPayment() function assume the down payment will be 10% and calculate the amount accordingly. The following code shows an example of the downPayment() function that accepts a single parameter:

```
double downPayment(double dPrice) {
    double dPercentDown = .1;
    return dPrice * dPercentDown;
}
```

You can overload the downPayment() function so that a second version of the function will be called if you supply a second parameter consisting of the percent that the function should use to calculate the down payment. The following code shows the overloaded downPayment() function that accepts two parameters:

```
double downPayment(double dPrice, double dPercent) {
    double dPercentDown = dPercent;
    return dPrice * dPercentDown;
}
```

Visual C++ knows which version of the overloaded downPayment() function to execute and responds to the parameters that you pass to the function. For example, if you execute the statement `downPayment(185000);`, then Visual C++ calls the overloaded downPayment() function that accepts only a single parameter. If you execute the statement `downPayment(185000, .2);`, however, then Visual C++ calls the overloaded downPayment() function that accepts two parameters.

Constructor functions can be overloaded, just like other functions. This means that you can instantiate different versions of a class, depending on the supplied parameters. Since constructors are called automatically when an object is instantiated, you only need to supply the correct number of arguments in order to call the correct overloaded constructor function. To instantiate an object based on a class constructor that accepts parameters, you append parentheses and the necessary parameters to the variable name when you instantiate the object. For example, if a constructor function for the Payroll class accepts a double parameter, then you can instantiate an object based on that constructor function using a statement similar to `Payroll currentEmployee(.12);`.

To instantiate an object on the heap using a parameterized constructor, you append parentheses and the necessary parameters to the class name in the right operand. For example, the statement `Payroll* currentEmployee = new Payroll(.12);` declares a Payroll object on the heap and passes to it a single floating-point parameter. Note that you are not limited to instantiating objects using parameterized constructors; you can also call the default constructor by leaving the parentheses in the class name in the right operand empty, as in the statement `Payroll* currentEmployee = new Payroll();`.

Being able to overload a constructor function allows you to instantiate an object in multiple ways. For example, a client using the Payroll class, which calculates an employee's net pay, may live in a state that has no state income tax. For states without an income tax, clients would not have a value to pass into the dStateTax data members. To avoid this problem, you could rewrite the class so that it does not require state tax information. But the rewritten class would be useless to clients who live in states that have an income tax. A better solution is to overload the constructor by adding a function that accepts only a federal income-tax parameter. Figure 5-10 shows a modified version of the Payroll class with two parameterized constructor functions: one for states that have a state income tax and one for states that do not have a state income tax. The first statement in the main() function instantiates an object named employeeFL, for an employee in Florida where there is no state income tax. The second statement in the main() function instantiates an object named employeeMA, for an employee in Massachusetts where there is a 5.95% state income tax. Notice that the class also includes an empty default constructor function. This default constructor function assigns default values to the data members in the event that a client fails to call one of the parameterized constructor functions.

```cpp
// Payroll.h
class Payroll {
public:
    Payroll(); // default constructor
    Payroll(double dFed);
    Payroll(double dFed, double dState);
private:
    double dFedTax;
    double dStateTax;
};
// Payroll.cpp
#include "Payroll.h"
#include <iostream.h>
Payroll::Payroll() {
    dFedTax = .28;
    dStateTax = .05;
}
Payroll::Payroll(double dFed) {
    dFedTax = dFed;
};
Payroll::Payroll(double dFed, double dState) {
    dFedTax = dFed;
    dStateTax = dState;
};
void main() {
    Payroll employeeFL(.28);
    Payroll employeeMA(.28, .0595);
}
```

Figure 5-10   Parameterized constructor functions

Next you will add to the Building Estimator program a parameterized constructor for the customer's name.

To add a parameterized constructor for the customer's name to the Building Estimator program:

1. Open the **Estimator.h** file in the Text Editor window.

2. Add a member function declaration for the parameterized constructor, shown in bold, after the default constructor, as shown in the following code:

```
#if !defined(ESTIMATOR_H)
#define ESTIMATOR_H
class Estimator {
public:
     Estimator();
     Estimator(char*);
     void setCustomerName(char*);
     char* getCustomerName() const;
     void setHouseStyle(int);
...
```

3. Next, open the **Estimator.cpp** file in the Text Editor window and add the parameterized constructor function definition immediately after the default constructor function definition. The parameterized constructor function definition includes the same statements as the setCustomerName() member function. The first statement creates the szCustomerName variable on the heap, and the second statement uses the strcpy() function to copy the szCustName parameter variable into the szCustomerName variable. The rest of the statements initialize the class's other data members.

```
Estimator::Estimator(char* szCustName) {
     szCustomerName = new char[50];
     strcpy(szCustomerName, szCustName);
     iStyle = 0;
     lStyleCost = 0;
     iBedrooms = 0;
     lBedroomCost = 0;
     iBathrooms = 0;
     lBathroomCost = 0;
     lCustomerCost = 0;
}
```

4. Modify the statements in the main() function that instantiate a new Estimator object so that the customer's name is passed as a parameter rather than assigned through the setCustomerName() function:

```
void main() {
     cout << "New Home Building Estimator" << endl;
     cout << "--------------------------------"
          << endl << endl;
     cout << "Customer 1" << endl << endl;
     curCustomerName();
     Estimator customer1(szName);
     curCustomerEstimate(customer1);
}
```

5. Rebuild and execute the program. The program should function the same as it did when you first built it.

Initialization Lists

Initialization lists, or **member initialization lists**, are another way of assigning initial values to a class's data members. An initialization list is placed after a function header's closing parentheses, but before the function's opening curly brace. You start an initialization list with a single colon, followed by assignment statements separated by commas. The assignment statements in an initialization list must be in functional notation. **Functional notation** is another way of assigning a value to a variable using the syntax *variable_name(value)*;. For example, instead of using the statement iCount = 10; to assign an integer of 10 to a variable named iCount, you can use the functional notation statement iCount(10);.

Consider the following simple constructor that assigns parameter values to the Payroll class's dFedTax and dStateTax data members.

```
Payroll::Payroll(double dFed, double dState) {
    dFedTax = dFed;
    dStateTax = dState;
};
```

Instead of using the preceding code to assign the parameter values to the data members, you can use the following initialization list:

```
Payroll::Payroll(double dFed, double dState)
    : dFedTax(dFed), dStateTax(dState) {
};
```

Next, you will convert the Estimator class's constructor functions so that the numeric data members are initialized through initialization lists.

To convert the Estimator class's constructor functions so that the numeric data members are initialized through initialization lists:

1. Return to the **Estimator.cpp** file in the Text Editor window.

2. Modify the default constructor as follows. However, leave the initialization statement for the szCustomerName variable as it is.

```
Estimator::Estimator()
    : iStyle(0), lStyleCost(0), iBedrooms(0),
    lBedroomCost(0), iBathrooms(0), lBathroomCost(0),
    lCustomerCost(0) {
    szCustomerName = new char[50]
}
```

3. Modify the parameterized constructor so that it includes an initialization list, and leave the initialization statements for the szCustomerName variable as they are.

```
Estimator::Estimator(char* szCustName)
    : iStyle(0), lStyleCost(0), iBedrooms(0),
    lBedroomCost(0), iBathrooms(0), lBathroomCost(0),
    lCustomerCost(0) {
    szCustomerName = new char[50];
    strcpy(szCustomerName, szCustName);
}
```

4. Build and execute the program. You should not notice a change in functionality.

Initialization lists can make more efficient use of memory since they do not require additional statements within the body of a constructor. The functional notation required by initialization lists, however, can be confusing because it resembles function calls. Therefore, except for the preceding exercise, you will continue to use standard assignment statements within the body of constructor statements for classes you create throughout the rest of this text. As you create larger and more complex programs, and become more comfortable with C++, you may want to experiment with initialization lists to see if they make your programs run more efficiently.

Copy Constructor

There will be times when you want to instantiate a new object based on an existing object. For example, you may have a class named Registration that is used for registering students in training classes. The Registration class may contain data members for the student's name, social security number, and so on, along with a data member representing the course for which the student is registering. Essentially, each object represents a single student enrollment into a single course. If a student registers for a second course, you do not necessarily want to go through the process of adding the student's vital statistics to a new object's data members. Instead, it is easier to make a copy of the existing object and change only the course to the new course for which the student wants to register.

There are two ways to create a new object from an existing object. You can use either the syntax *class new_object = existing_object;* or the syntax *class new_object(old_object);*. The first syntax declares a new object of the designated class and assigns to it the existing object. To use the first syntax to copy an existing Registration object named firstCourse to a new Registration object named secondCourse, you use the statement `Registration secondCourse = firstCourse;`.

The second syntax for copying an object resembles the syntax for instantiating an object based on a parameterized constructor. Instead of passing a variable or literal value, however, you pass an object. Recall from the previous chapter that an object is actually a type of variable. Since you can pass a variable to a function, you can pass an object as well. Both syntax examples execute the default copy constructor, which you will learn about shortly. To use the second syntax to copy an existing Registration object named firstCourse to a new Registration object named secondCourse, you use the statement `Registration secondCourse(firstCourse);`.

Regardless of which syntax you use to copy an object, it is important to understand that *no default constructor executes for the new object.* Instead, C++ uses a copy constructor to exactly copy each of the first object's data members into the second object's data members in an operation known as **memberwise copying.** A **copy constructor** is a special constructor that is called when a new object is instantiated from an old object. Just as Visual C++ supplies a default constructor if you fail to write one yourself, it also supplies a **default copy constructor** that automatically copies the members of the original object to the new object. Figure 5-11 shows how data members are copied with the default copy constructor using the Registration class as an example.

firstClass object   **secondClass object**

Data Members   **Data Members**
char szName[20] = "Mike Morinaga"   Registration secondCourse =   char szName[20] = "Mike Morinaga"
char szCourse[20] = "Biology"   firstCourse;   →   char szCourse[20] = "Biology"
double dFee = 300   →   OR   double dFee = 300
bool bAudit = false;   Registration   bool bAudit = false;
                                            secondCourse(firstCourse);

Figure 5-11   Memberwise copying with the default copy constructor

A default copy constructor executes only when you initialize a new object based on an existing object, and not when you assign one existing object to another existing object. Initialization differs from assignment because initialization creates something new, while assignment assigns a new value to an object that already exists. For example, the default copy constructor is invoked for the statement `Registration secondCourse = firstCourse;` since a new object is actually being initialized, based on the old object. In contrast, the first two statements in the following code each perform object instantiations, executing the class's default constructor, not the copy constructor. The third statement only assigns the firstCourse object to the existing secondCourse object; it does not instantiate anything. The third statement does *not* execute the default copy constructor, or any other constructor for that matter.

```
Registration firstCourse;
Registration secondCourse;
secondCourse = firstCourse; // simple assignment statement
```

Later in this chapter you will learn how to overload the assignment operator in order to call the copy constructor during the assignment of one object to another.

The default copy constructor is sufficient for most purposes. It is not sufficient, however, when you need to use pointers to dynamically allocate memory. The memberwise copy operation that is performed by the default copy constructor exactly copies all members of an existing object to a new object, including memory addresses stored in pointers. The memberwise copy operation does not copy the information in the memory address, only the memory address itself. If you use the default copy constructor to create a new object from an existing object that is based on a class containing pointers, the new object and the existing object will contain pointers to the same memory addresses. When new and existing objects contain pointers to the same memory addresses, multiple objects in your program will share the same information. Objects that attempt to store and access information in the same memory address can cause chaos in your program. Figure 5-12 illustrates this scenario by showing how two char* pointers share the same memory address after you create a new Registration object by copying an existing Registration object.

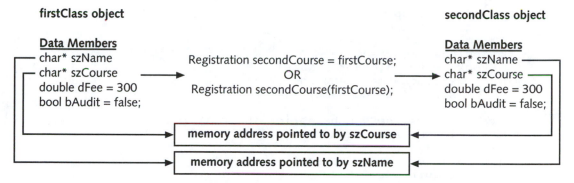

Figure 5-12   Objects with pointers to the same memory address

As an example of copied objects that contain pointers to the same memory address, examine the modified Stocks class in Figure 5-13. The interface file declares a character pointer named szStockName that will point to the address of a string containing the stock's name. The constructor function accepts a single parameter representing the name of a stock, and then dynamically allocates memory for the szStockName. The value of the stock name parameter is then copied using the strcpy() method to the address pointed to by the szStockName pointer. The class also includes methods for getting and setting data members, along with a method for calculating the total value of a stock. The program's main() function instantiates a new Stocks object named stockPick1, passing to the constructor function the value *Cisco*. Then a new Stocks object named stockPick2 is copied from the stockPick1 object. The program then attempts to assign a new value of *Lucent* to the stock name of the stockPick1 object using the setStockName() function. Since both the stockPick1 and stockPick2 objects contain pointers to the same memory address for the stock name, the value of *Cisco* is overwritten by *Lucent*. Figure 5-14 shows the output.

```
:// Stocks.h
class Stocks {
public:
     Stocks(char* szName);
     void setStockName(char* szName);
     char* getStockName() const;
     void setNumShares(int);
     int getNumShares() const;
     void setPricePerShare(double);
     double getPricePerShare() const;
     double calcTotalValue();
private:
     char* szStockName;
     int iNumShares;
     double dCurrentValue;
     double dPricePerShare;
};
// Stocks.cpp
#include "stocks.h"
#include <string.h>
#include <iostream.h>
Stocks::Stocks(char* szName) {
     szStockName = new char[25];
     strcpy(szStockName, szName);
};
void Stocks::setNumShares(int iShares) {
     iNumShares = iShares;
}
int Stocks::getNumShares() {
     return iNumShares;
}
void Stocks::setPricePerShare(double dPrice) {
     dPricePerShare = dPrice;
}
double Stocks::getPricePerShare() {
     return dPricePerShare;
}
void Stocks::setStockName(char* szName) {
     strcpy(szStockName, szName);
}
char* Stocks::getStockName() {
     return szStockName;
}
double Stocks::calcTotalValue() {
     dCurrentValue = iNumShares * dPricePerShare;
     return dCurrentValue;
}
```

Figure 5-13   Stocks class program with objects containing pointers to the same memory address

```
void main() {
    Stocks stockPick1("Cisco");
    stockPick1.setNumShares(100);
    stockPick1.setPricePerShare(68.875);
    /* The following statement creates a new object
    by copying an existing object */
    Stocks stockPick2(stockPick1);
    stockPick2.setStockName("Lucent");
    stockPick2.setNumShares(200);
    stockPick2.setPricePerShare(59.5);
    cout << "The current value of your stock in "
        << stockPick1.getStockName() << " is $"
        << stockPick1.calcTotalValue()
            << "." << endl;
    cout << "The current value of your stock in "
        << stockPick2.getStockName() << " is $"
        << stockPick2.calcTotalValue()
            << "." << endl;
}
```

5

Figure 5-13 Stocks class program with objects containing pointers to the same memory address (continued)

 The Stocks class in Figure 5-13 does not include a default constructor so that you can focus on the use of the copy constructor. Remember that it is good programming practice, however, to always include a default copy constructor in your classes.

Figure 5-14 Output of Stocks class program with objects containing pointers to the same memory address

To prevent copied objects in your program from sharing pointers to the same memory address, you must write your own copy constructor. Copy constructors are identical to standard constructors, except they must accept a single call-by-reference parameter to an object preceded by the **const** keyword to indicate to the compiler that the original object is not to be modified in any way. The syntax for a copy constructor declaration is *class_name*(const *class_name*& *object_name*);. The call-by-reference object parameter in a copy constructor represents the object being copied. When an object reference parameter in a member function is preceded by the const keyword, the parameter is referred to as a **constant parameter**. You use a constant parameter in a copy constructor to assign values to a new object's data members. Once an object has been passed by reference to a function, you can refer to its data members using the parameter name and the member selection operator.

 Constant parameters are not restricted to use with copy constructors; you can use them with any object reference in a member function. The use of constant parameters in a member function is considered good programming practice since they clearly indicate which objects should not be modified by a member function. You can almost think of constant parameters as a "reminder" in the event that you forget that an object should not be modified. If you accidentally attempt to modify a constant parameter in a member function, you will receive a compile error.

The following code shows an example of a constructor function for the Stocks class that dynamically allocates new memory for the stock name for any new Stocks objects created by copying an existing object. Like the code in the constructor function, memory is dynamically allocated for the szStockName pointer. Since you do not yet know the name of the new stock, however, the old name is copied to the new memory address using the strcpy() method. Although both Stocks objects will initially be assigned the same stock name, each name will be stored in its own memory address where you can safely manipulate it without affecting the data members of the other object.

```
// Stocks.h
...
    Stocks(const Stocks&); // copy constructor declaration
...
// Stocks.cpp
Stocks::Stocks(const Stocks& sourceStock) {
            szStockName = new char[25];
      strcpy(szStockName, sourceStock.szStockName);
}
```

Figure 5-15 shows a new version of the Stocks class with a copy constructor, and Figure 5-16 shows the program's output.

```cpp
// Stocks.h
class Stocks {
public:
    Stocks(char* szName);
    Stocks(const Stocks&); // copy constructor declaration
    void setStockName(char* szName);
    char* getStockName() const;
    void setNumShares(int);
    int getNumShares() const;
    void setPricePerShare(double);
    double getPricePerShare()const;
    double calcTotalValue();
private:
    char* szStockName;
    int iNumShares;
    double dCurrentValue;
    double dPricePerShare;
};
// Stocks.cpp
#include "stocks.h"
#include <string.h>
#include <iostream.h>
Stocks::Stocks(char* szName) {
    szStockName = new char[25];
    strcpy(szStockName, szName);
};
Stocks::Stocks(const Stocks& sourceStock) {
            szStockName = new char[25];
    strcpy(szStockName, sourceStock.szStockName);
}
void Stocks::setNumShares(int iShares) {
    iNumShares = iShares;
}
int Stocks::getNumShares() {
    return iNumShares;
}
void Stocks::setPricePerShare(double dPrice) {
    dPricePerShare = dPrice;
}
double Stocks::getPricePerShare() {
    return dPricePerShare;
}
void Stocks::setStockName(char* szName) {
    strcpy(szStockName, szName);
}
char* Stocks::getStockName() {
    return szStockName;
}
double Stocks::calcTotalValue() {
    dCurrentValue = iNumShares * dPricePerShare;
    return dCurrentValue;
}
```

Figure 5-15   Stocks class program with a copy constructor

```
void main() {
    Stocks stockPick1("Cisco");
    stockPick1.setNumShares(100);
    stockPick1.setPricePerShare(68.875);
    Stocks stockPick2(stockPick1);
    stockPick2.setStockName("Lucent");
    stockPick2.setNumShares(200);
    stockPick2.setPricePerShare(59.5);
    cout << "The current value of your stock in "
        << stockPick1.getStockName() << " is $"
        << stockPick1.calcTotalValue()
            << "." << endl;
    cout << "The current value of your stock in "
        << stockPick2.getStockName() << " is $"
        << stockPick2.calcTotalValue()
            << "." << endl;
}
```

Figure 5-15   Stocks class program with a copy constructor (continued)

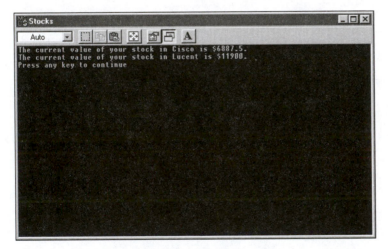

Figure 5-16   Output of Stocks class program with a copy constructor

Next, you will instantiate a second object in the Building Estimator program by copying the first object.

To instantiate a second object in the Building Estimator program by copying the first object:

1. Return to the **Estimator.cpp** file in the Text Editor window.

2. Add to the end of the main() function the following code, which instantiates a new Estimator object named customer2 by copying the customer1 object. The curCustomerName() global function is called to gather the second customer's name into the szName global variable, which is then passed to the setCustomerName() member function. Finally, the curCustomerEstimate() function is called to collect the building information for the second customer.

```
cout << "Customer 2" << endl << endl;
Estimator customer2(customer1);
curCustomerName();
customer2.setCustomerName(szName);
curCustomerEstimate(customer2);
```

3. To the end of the main() function, add the following statements, which print each customer's name and estimate to the screen.

```
cout << "Customer, Estimate" << endl;
cout << "--------------------" << endl;
cout << customer1.getCustomerName() << ", $"
     << customer1.getCustomerCost() << endl;
cout << customer2.getCustomerName() << ", $"
     << customer2.getCustomerCost() << endl;
```

4. Build and execute the program. Notice that when the customer names get printed at the end, the second customer's name prints twice. Since you have not yet added a copy constructor, calling the setCustomerName() member function in Step 2 overwrites the first customer's name because both object's szCustomerName data members point to the same memory address. Figure 5-17 shows the output after adding some sample names. The second name added in the example is *Erica Miller*.

Figure 5-17 Output of Building Estimator program before adding a copy constructor

Since the Building Estimator program includes a data member (szCustomerName) for which memory is dynamically allocated, you also need to add a copy constructor.

To add a copy constructor to the Building Estimator program:

1. Open the **Estimator.h** file in the Text Editor window.

2. After the declarations for the default and parameterized constructor, add a declaration for the copy constructor as follows:

```
public:
    Estimator();
    Estimator(char* szCustName);
    Estimator(const Estimator&);
...
```

3. Open the **Estimator.cpp** file in the Text Editor window.

4. Add the following copy constructor function definition after the parameterized constructor definition. The statements you need to add are bold and are identical to the statements in the parameterized constructor function that dynamically allocates memory to the szCustomerName data member.

```
Estimator::Estimator(const Estimator& sourceObject) {
            szCustomerName = new char[50];
    strcpy(szCustomerName, sourceObject.szCustomerName);
}
```

5. Rebuild and execute the project. The szCustomerName data members for both objects should now be assigned and printed properly, as shown in Figure 5-18.

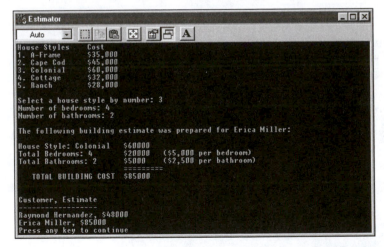

Figure 5-18   Output of Building Estimator program after adding a copy constructor

DESTRUCTORS

Just as a default constructor is called when a class object is first instantiated, a default destructor is called when the object is destroyed. A **default destructor** cleans up any resources allocated to an object once the object is destroyed. The default destructor is sufficient for most classes, except when you have allocated memory on the heap. Recall that variables you declare on the heap using the **new** operator must be manually removed with the delete operator. Even though an object may be destroyed, any variables declared on the heap would still exist, taking up valuable memory resources unless you manually destroy them. To delete any heap variables declared by your class, you must write your own destructor function.

 Deleting heap variables is not the only task that destructor functions perform. You can also use destructor functions to complete any pending tasks or perform other types of system cleanup before an object is destroyed.

You create a destructor function using the name of the class, the same as a constructor function, preceded by a tilde ~. Destructor functions cannot be overloaded or accept parameters. Therefore, you can write only one destructor function for any given class. As with constructor functions, destructor functions are not defined with a data type since they do not return values. Figure 5-19 shows an example of a destructor declaration and definition for the Stocks class.

```
// Stocks.h
class Stocks {
public:
    ~Stocks();
...
};
// Stocks.cpp
Stocks::~Stocks() {
    // destructor statements;
};
```

Figure 5-19   Destructor declaration and definition for the Stocks class

A destructor is called in two ways: when a stack object loses scope when the function in which it is declared ends or when a heap object is destroyed with the delete operator. Examine the modified version of the Stocks.cpp file in Figure 5-20. The main() function declares two Stocks objects, one on the stack and one on the heap. The constructor for the class declares a heap variable to contain the name of the stock. Since you have declared two Stocks objects, two stock name heap variables will be created. To delete the stock name heap variables, a destructor has been added that uses the statement `delete[] szStockName;`. Two brackets have been appended to the delete operator since the szStockName heap variable is an array. So you can see when the destructor is called, the destructor includes a cout statement that prints *Destructor called*. Figure 5-21 shows the output.

```cpp
// Stocks.cpp
#include "stocks.h"
#include <string.h>
#include <iostream.h>
Stocks::Stocks(char* szName) {
    szStockName = new char[25];
    strcpy(szStockName, szName);
};
Stocks::~Stocks() {
    delete[] szStockName;
    cout << "Destructor called" << endl;
};
Stocks::Stocks(const Stocks& sourceStock) {
    szStockName = new char[25];
    strcpy(szStockName, sourceStock.szStockName);
}
void Stocks::setNumShares(int iShares) {
    iNumShares = iShares;
}
int Stocks::getNumShares() {
    return iNumShares;
}
void Stocks::setPricePerShare(double dPrice) {
    dPricePerShare = dPrice;
}
double Stocks::getPricePerShare() {
    return dPricePerShare;
}
void Stocks::setStockName(char* szName) {
    strcpy(szStockName, szName);
}
char* Stocks::getStockName() {
    return szStockName;
}
double Stocks::calcTotalValue() {
    dCurrentValue = iNumShares * dPricePerShare;
    return dCurrentValue;
}
```

Figure 5-20 Stocks class with a destructor

```
void main() {
     Stocks stockPick1("Cisco"); // stack object
     stockPick1.setNumShares(100);
     stockPick1.setPricePerShare(68.875);
     Stocks* stockPick2 = new Stocks("Lucent"); // heap object
     stockPick2->setNumShares(200);
     stockPick2->setPricePerShare(59.5);
     cout << "The current value of your stock in "
          << stockPick1.getStockName() << " is $"
          << stockPick1.calcTotalValue()
               << "." << endl;
     cout << "The current value of your stock in "
          << stockPick2->getStockName() << " is $"
          << stockPick2->calcTotalValue()
               << "." << endl;
}
```

Figure 5-20   Stocks class with a destructor (continued)

Figure 5-21   Output of Stocks class with a destructor

Notice in Figure 5-21 that the destructor function is called only once. The stockPick1 object calls the destructor function when it is destroyed by the main() function going out of scope. The stockPick2 object does not call the destructor function since it is declared on the heap and must be deleted manually. To delete the stockPick2 object manually, add the statement `delete stockPick2;` to the main() function, as shown in Figure 5-22. Figure 5-23 shows the output.

```
// Stocks.cpp
void main() {
     Stocks stockPick1("Cisco");
     stockPick1.setNumShares(100);
     stockPick1.setPricePerShare(68.875);
     Stocks* stockPick2 = new Stocks("Lucent");
     stockPick2->setNumShares(200);
     stockPick2->setPricePerShare(59.5);
     cout << "The current value of your stock in "
          << stockPick1.getStockName() << " is $"
          << stockPick1.calcTotalValue()
               << "." << endl;
     cout << "The current value of your stock in "
          << stockPick2->getStockName() << " is $"
          << stockPick2->calcTotalValue()
               << "." << endl;
     delete stockPick2;
}
```

Figure 5-22   Stocks class main() function after adding a delete statement

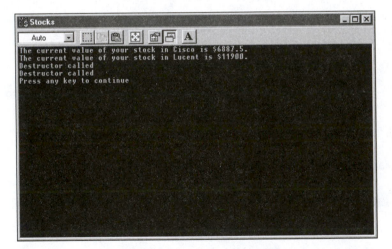

Figure 5-23   Output of Stocks class main() function after adding a delete statement

The Estimator class creates the szCustomerName data members on the heap. Therefore, you need to add a destructor function to delete them. You will also instantiate another Estimator object on the heap to represent a third customer. The third Estimator object instantiated on the heap will demonstrate how the destructor function is called when a heap object is deleted. The two Estimator objects instantiated on the stack will demonstrate how the destructor function is called when an object goes out of scope.

To add a destructor function and a heap object to the Estimator class:

1. Open the **Estimator.h** file in the Text Editor window.

5

2. Add the destructor function declaration after the copy constructor function declaration, as shown below:

```
public:
     Estimator();
     Estimator(char*);
     Estimator(const Estimator&);
     ~Estimator();
...
```

3. Open the **Estimator.cpp** file in the Text Editor window.

4. Add the following destructor function definition after the copy constructor definition. The destructor function contains two statements. The first statement deletes the szCustomerName data member, and the second statement prints the text *Estimate deleted* to the screen. Since szCustomerName is an array, brackets are appended to the delete keyword.

```
Estimator::~Estimator() {
     delete[] szCustomerName;
     cout << "Estimate deleted" << endl;
}
```

5. Finally, modify the main() function as follows so that a third object is instantiated. Unlike the other two objects, this third object is instantiated on the heap. The final statement deletes the heap object, which calls the destructor function.

```
void main() {
     cout << "New Home Building Estimator" << endl;
     cout << "---------------------------------"
          << endl << endl;
     cout << "Customer 1" << endl << endl;
     curCustomerName();
     Estimator customer1(szName);
     curCustomerEstimate(customer1);
     cout << "Customer 2" << endl << endl;
     Estimator customer2(customer1);
     curCustomerName();
     customer2.setCustomerName(szName);
     curCustomerEstimate(customer2);
     cout << "Customer 3" << endl << endl;
     curCustomerName();
     Estimator* customer3 = new Estimator(szName);
     curCustomerEstimate(*customer3);
     cout << "Customer, Estimate" << endl;
     cout << "------------------" << endl;
     cout << customer1.getCustomerName() << ", $"
          << customer1.getCustomerCost() << endl;
     cout << customer2.getCustomerName() << ", $"
          << customer2.getCustomerCost() << endl;
     cout << customer3->getCustomerName() << ", $"
          << customer3->getCustomerCost() << endl << endl;
     delete customer3;
}
```

6. Rebuild and execute the program. After entering data for all three customers, *Estimate deleted* should print three times, one for each object that was destroyed.

OPERATOR OVERLOADING

In C++, operators, such as the addition operator, are really internal C++ functions. For example, for the addition operator, the left and right operands are being passed as arguments to the internal addition operator *function,* which performs the actual addition operation. Since operators are really functions, you can overload them just as you can overload other types of functions. **Operator overloading** refers to the creation of multiple versions of C++ operators that perform special tasks required by a class in which an overloaded operator function is defined. You overload an operator when you want the operator to perform different operations, depending on the situation. For example, the default operation of the increment operator is to increase an operand by a value of 1. In stock trading, it is common to buy shares in blocks of 100. When you work with a Stocks class, you can overload the increment operator so that it increases a value by 100 only when used with objects of the Stocks class. The original implementation of the increment operator that increases values by 1 still functions when used with variables that are not objects of the Stocks class. You will see an example of how to overload the increment operator for the Stocks class later in this section. As another example, you may want to overload the greater-than operator > in the Payroll class so that it performs the same function as the indirect member selection operator -> when used with an object of the class that overloads it.

After writing the appropriate statements in an overloaded operator function for the greater-than operator > in the Payroll class, both of the following statements would allow you to access the calcNetPay() member function in the Payroll class through a pointer to the class named curEmployee:

```
curEmployee->calcNetPay();
curEmployee>calcNetPay();
```

You can overload almost any C++ operator, with the exception of the operators listed in Figure 5-24.

Figure 5-24   C++ operators that cannot be overloaded

Operator	Name
.	Member selection
.*	Pointer-to-member selection
::	Scope resolution
? :	Conditional
#	Preprocessor symbol
##	Preprocessor symbol

You create an overloaded operator function as either a class member function or a friend function of a class. The following operators must be overloaded as member functions:

- = assignment
- -> indirect member selection operator
- () function call
- [] subscript

There are no other special rules as to whether you create overloaded operator functions as member functions or friend functions. You are also not required to create an overloaded operator function as either a member function or a friend function. Overloaded operator functions can simply be created as global functions within your program. It is common practice, however, to create an overloaded operator function as either a member function or a friend function since overloaded operator functions usually need access to a class's private data members.

Overloaded operator functions defined as member functions and overloaded operator functions defined as global functions or friend functions have different parameter requirements. For example, if you overload the addition operator as a member function, then you need to include only a single parameter. However, if you overload the addition operator, as either a global function or as a friend function, then you need to include two parameters. The syntax used in this chapter is for overloaded operator functions defined as global functions or friend functions.

 To see a list of rules for creating overloaded functions, search for the Operator Overloading topic in the MSDN Library, and then select the General Rules subtopic.

An overloaded operator function executes if the data types for each operand within a statement match the data types in the overloaded operator function's parameter list. At least one of the overloaded operator function's parameters must be of a class type. If you use an overloaded operator in your program, but do not include the correct data types or class types for each operand in your statement, then the operator's default operation is performed. For example, you might overload the multiplication operator * to perform some special operation required by your class, provided that the left operand is of the Stocks data type and the right operand is of the double data type. However, if a statement in your programs uses the multiplication operator, but does not include a Stocks data type as the left operand and a double data type as the right operand, then the default, multiplication, is performed.

Each type of operator (binary, unary, comparison, and so on) requires a slightly different type of function definition in order to overload an operator. Once you understand how to overload binary and unary operators, you should be able to figure out on your own how to overload other types of operators.

Overloading Binary Operators

A binary operator requires an operand before the operator and an operand after the operator. The equal sign in the statement `iMyNumber = 100;` is an example of a binary operator. Suppose in the Payroll class you want to create two overloaded operator functions for the binary addition operator +. Suppose also that you have instantiated three Payroll objects, ytdPay, firstWeekJan, and secondWeekJan, and that you have assigned values to their data members. The first overloaded addition operator function will add the dNetPay data members of two Payroll objects and assign the result to the dNetPay data member of a third Payroll object. The second overloaded addition operator function will add a double value to the dNetPay data member of one Payroll object and assign the result to the dNetPay data member of another Payroll object. After writing the overloaded operator functions, you will be able to use the addition operator in the following three ways.

```
// standard addition operation
int iNum = 20 + 30;
// adds the dNetPay data members of two Payroll objects
// and assigns the result to the dNetPay data member
// of a third object
ytdPay = firstWeekJan + secondWeekJan;
// adds a double value to the dNetPay data member
// of a Payroll object
ytdPay = ytdPay + 1000.00;
```

To overload a binary operator as a global or friend function, you use the following overloaded function syntax:

```
type operator binary_operator (const class&
    leftOperand, const class& rightOperand) {
}
```

An overloaded operator function is defined with a type, just like other functions. The **operator** keyword designates a function definition as an overloaded operator function. The preceding syntax represents a binary overloaded operator, such as the addition operator. The first parameter in the parameter list represents the *left* operand, and the second parameter in the parameter list represents the *right* operand. When using an object as a parameter you include a reference to the class type and you must declare each parameter as a constant parameter.

In our example, the overloaded addition operator function will essentially build a new Payroll object and assign to its dNetPay data member the combined values of the two object operand's dNetPay data members. The new object is then returned to the statement that calls it. Since you are returning a Payroll object, the function is defined to return a data type of Payroll. Recall that classes are really user-defined data types. Since classes are actually data types, you can use them as a function's return value. The first statement in the function body instantiates a new Payroll object named ytdPay. The second statement uses the standard addition operator to add the values of the dNetPay data members of the leftOperand object reference and the rightOperand object reference and assign the result to the dNetPay data member of the ytdPay object. Finally, the third statement returns the ytdPay object. To overload the addition operator + in the Payroll class, with each operand being of a Payroll object, you use the following code.

```
friend Payroll operator + (const Payroll& amount1,
    const Payroll& amount2) {
    Payroll ytdPay;
    ytdPay.dNetPay = amount1.dNetPay
        + amount2.dNetPay;
    return ytdPay;
}
```

To execute the preceding overloaded operator, you use a statement similar to `ytdPay = firstWeekJan + secondWeekJan;`. Note that you do not append the data members to each operand since the overloaded operator function needs to receive a reference to an object, not a data member.

Remember that at least one parameter must be of a class type. In the case of binary operators, one of the parameters in an overloaded operator function can be of another data type. For example, you use the following function definition if you want the right operand in the preceding example to be of the double data type:

```
friend Payroll operator + (const Payroll& amount1,
    const double dAmountz) {
    Payroll ytdPay;
    ytdPay.dNetPay = amount1.dNetPay + amount2;
    return ytdPay;
}
```

The preceding overloaded operator may be used with the Payroll class if you want to add a holiday bonus or other type of additional compensation to the dNetPay data member of the ytdPay object. To execute the preceding overloaded operator and add a bonus of $1000 to the dNetPay data member of the ytdPay object, you would use a statement similar to the following:

```
ytdPay = ytdPay + 1000.00;
```

The following statement, however, would not execute the overloaded operator because the left and right operands are not of the correct data type. The left operand should be of the Payroll data type and the right operand should be of the double data type.

```
ytdPay = 1000.00 + ytdPay;
```

Figure 5-25 shows a completed version of the Payroll class with two overloaded addition operators. Figure 5-26 shows the output.

```
// Payroll.h
class Payroll {
public:
     Payroll();
     double calcNetPay(double dPay, double dHours);
     double getNetPay() const;
     friend Payroll operator + (const Payroll&,
          const Payroll&);
     friend Payroll operator + (const Payroll&,
          const double);
private:
     double dFedTax;
     double dStateTax;
     double dNetPay;
};
// Payroll.cpp
#include <iostream.h>
#include "Payroll.h"
Payroll::Payroll() {
     dFedTax = .28;
     dStateTax = .05;
}
double Payroll::calcNetPay(double dPay, double dHours) {
     double dGrossPay = dPay * dHours;
     double dCurFedTaxes = dGrossPay * dFedTax;
     double dCurStateTaxes = dGrossPay * dStateTax;
     dNetPay = dGrossPay - (dCurFedTaxes + dCurStateTaxes);
     return dNetPay;
}
double Payroll::getNetPay() {
     return dNetPay;
}
Payroll operator + (const Payroll& amount1,
     const Payroll& amount2) {
     Payroll ytdPay;
     ytdPay.dNetPay = amount1.dNetPay
          + amount2.dNetPay;
     return ytdPay;
}
Payroll operator + (const Payroll& amount1,
     const double dAmount2) {
     Payroll ytdPay;
     ytdPay.dNetPay = amount1.dNetPay + dAmount2;
     return ytdPay;
}
```

Figure 5-25 Payroll class with two overloaded addition operators

```
void main() {
     Payroll firstWeekJan;
     Payroll secondWeekJan;
     Payroll ytdPay;
     cout << "Net pay for the 1st week in January is $";
     cout << firstWeekJan.calcNetPay(25.5, 40) << endl;
     cout << "Net pay for the 2nd week in January is $";
     cout << secondWeekJan.calcNetPay(25.5, 37.5) << endl;
     // calls overloaded + operator
     // with two Payroll object parameters
     ytdPay = firstWeekJan + secondWeekJan;
     cout << "Year-to-date net pay is $";
     cout << ytdPay.getNetPay() << endl;
     // calls overloaded + operator with one Payroll object
     // parameter and one double value parameter
     ytdPay = ytdPay + 1000.00;
     cout << "Year-to-date net pay with bonuses is $";
     cout << ytdPay.getNetPay() << endl;
}
```

5

Figure 5-25   Payroll class with two overloaded addition operators (continued)

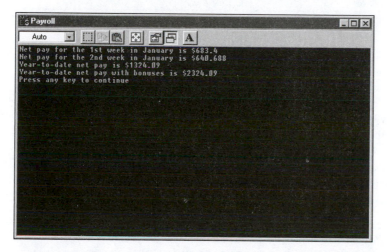

Figure 5-26   Output of Payroll class with two overloaded addition operators

Overloading Unary Operators

A unary operator requires a single operand either before or after the operator. For example, the increment operator (++), an arithmetic operator, is used for increasing an operand by a value of 1. If you have a variable named myNumber that contains the value 100, then the statement ++iMyNumber changes the value of the myNumber variable to 101. When you overload a unary operator, the overloaded function definition includes only a single parameter in the parameter list since unary operators use only single operands. The syntax for an overloaded unary operator function is as follows:

```
class operator unary_operator (const class& operand) {
}
```

The unary operators that you can overload are listed in Figure 5-27. Note that when overloading of increment and decrement operators is discussed in this section, only an explanation of how to overload the prefix forms of these operators is offered. Overloading postfix increment and decrement operators requires some special coding techniques, which are too advanced for your purposes.

Figure 5-27   Unary operators that can be overloaded

Operator	Description
!	Logical NOT
&	Address-of
~	One's complement
*	Pointer de-reference
+	Unary plus
++	Increment
–	Unary negation
––	Decrement

To see how to overload a unary operator, overload the increment operator (++) in the Stocks class so that it increases the number of shares of a particular Stocks object by 100, instead of by the default value of 1. The default increment operator will still function if used with any type of variable other than a Stocks object. When used with the Stocks object, however, the increment operator will increase the iNumShares data member by a value of 100. The overloaded function definition for the increment operator that increases a Stocks object operand by a value of 100 is as follows:

```
Stocks operator ++ (const Stocks& operand) {
    Stocks roundLot;
    roundLot.iNumShares = operand.iNumShares + 100;
    return roundLot;
}
```

The preceding function includes a single parameter that refers to the Stocks operand used with the increment operator. In the function body, a new Stocks object (roundLot) is instantiated. Its iNumShares data member is assigned the value of the operand object reference's iNumShares data member, plus 100. The roundLot Stocks object is then returned to the calling statement.

Figure 5-28 contains a simplified version of the Stocks program you have seen throughout this chapter, including the overloaded increment operator. Figure 5-29 shows the output. Notice that in the overloaded increment operator function, the values of both data members of the Stocks object, iNumShares and dPricePerShare, are being assigned to the roundLot object. Since we are building a new object with the overloaded function, you must be sure to copy all of the data members from the original object to the new object that is being returned.

```cpp
// Stocks.h
class Stocks {
public:
    friend Stocks operator ++ (const Stocks&);
    void setNumShares(int);
    int getNumShares() const;
    void setPricePerShare(double);
    double getPricePerShare() const;
    double calcTotalValue();
private:
    int iNumShares;
    double dCurrentValue;
    double dPricePerShare;
};
// Stocks.cpp
#include "stocks.h"
#include <string.h>
#include <iostream.h>
Stocks operator ++ (const Stocks& operand) {
    Stocks roundLot;
    roundLot.iNumShares = operand.iNumShares + 100;
    roundLot.dPricePerShare = operand.dPricePerShare;
    return roundLot;
}
void Stocks::setNumShares(int iShares) {
    iNumShares = iShares;
}
int Stocks::getNumShares() {
    return iNumShares;
}
void Stocks::setPricePerShare(double dPrice) {
    dPricePerShare = dPrice;
}
double Stocks::getPricePerShare() {
    return dPricePerShare;
}
double Stocks::calcTotalValue() {
    dCurrentValue = iNumShares * dPricePerShare;
    return dCurrentValue;
}
```

Figure 5-28   Stocks class with an overloaded increment operator

```
void main() {
    Stocks stockPick1;
    stockPick1.setNumShares(100);
    stockPick1.setPricePerShare(68.875);
    cout << "The value of your stock is "
        << stockPick1.calcTotalValue() << "." << endl;
    stockPick1 = ++stockPick1;
    cout << "After purchasing 100 additional shares, "
        << endl << "the value of your stock is $"
        << stockPick1.calcTotalValue() << "." << endl;
}
```

Figure 5-28   Stocks class with an overloaded increment operator (continued)

Figure 5-29   Output of Stocks class with an overloaded increment operator

Overloading the Assignment Operator

Next, you will overload the assignment operator so that it can be used to assign the data members of one object to the data members of another object of the same class. The overloaded operator examples you have seen in this section have instantiated new objects of a particular class, assigned values to the new object's data members, and then returned the object itself to the calling statement.

Overloading the assignment operator requires a slightly different set of steps. You declare the assignment operator's overloaded function with a class *reference* data type instead of a class data type. When you write an overloaded assignment operator function, a temporary object representing the left operand of the assignment statement is instantiated each time you call the function. Instead of returning an entire object from the function, you return just the value of this temporary object using the `this` pointer. Recall that the `this` pointer identifies the object instance that called a function. In the case of an overloaded assignment operator function, the `this` pointer refers to the temporary object instance created by the function itself. Since the `this` pointer is implied, you can refer to the temporary object's data members directly.

To overload the assignment operator in the Estimator class:

1. Open the **Estimator.h** file in the Text Editor window.

2. Add the following overloaded assignment operator function declaration after the destructor function declaration.

   ```
   Estimator& operator = (const Estimator&);
   ```

 Remember that the assignment operator must be created as a member function, not as a friend function or a global function.

3. Open the **Estimator.cpp** file in the Text Editor window.

4. Add the following definition for the overloaded assignment operator after the destructor definition. Notice that the data members of the operand object are being assigned to the overloaded assignment operator function's temporary Estimator object. A reference to the temporary object is then returned using the `return *this;` statement.

   ```
   Estimator& Estimator::operator = (const Estimator& operand)
   {
           szCustomerName = new char[50];
       strcpy(szCustomerName, operand.szCustomerName);
       iStyle = operand.iStyle;
       lStyleCost = operand.lStyleCost;
       iBedrooms = operand.iBedrooms;
       lBedroomCost = operand.lBedroomCost;
       iBathrooms = operand.iBathrooms;
       lBathroomCost = operand.lBathroomCost;
       lCustomerCost = operand.lCustomerCost;
       return *this;
   }
   ```

5. In the main() function, replace the statement `Estimator customer2 (customer1);` with the following two statements that demonstrate the overloaded assignment operator.

   ```
   Estimator customer2;
   customer2 = customer1;
   ```

6. Rebuild and execute the program. Although you should not see any difference in the way the program functions, you can see how useful overloading the assignment operator can be.

5

STATIC CLASS MEMBERS

When you first studied variables in Chapter 2, you learned how to use the **static** keyword when declaring a variable. When used with a local variable declaration, the **static** keyword changes the variable's storage duration to permanent. A local variable declared with the **static** keyword is *not* destroyed after its function or command block finishes executing. Instead, a static variable exists for the lifetime of the program.

You can also use the **static** keyword when declaring class members. Static class members, however, are somewhat different from static variables. When you declare a class member to be static, only one copy of that class member is created during a program's execution, regardless of how many objects of the class you instantiate. In contrast, each class object receives its own individual copies of non-static class members. Figure 5-30 illustrates the concept of static and non-static data members with the Payroll class by making the dFedTax and dStateTax data members static. It is much more efficient to make dFedTax and dStateTax static data members. The values of these data members will be exactly the same for all Payroll objects. Having them be non-static class members would create unnecessary duplication of information.

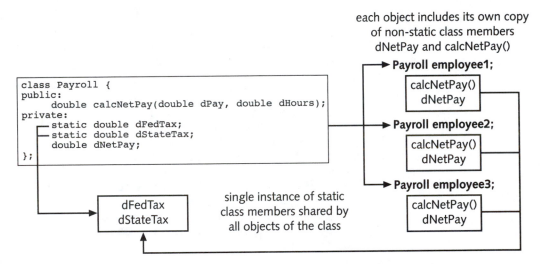

Figure 5-30   Multiple class objects with static and non-static data members

Next, you will learn about static data members and static member functions.

Static Data Members

You declare a static data member in your implementation file using the syntax `static type name`, similar to the way you define a static variable. Static data members are bound by access specifiers, the same as non-static data members. This means that public static data members are accessible by anyone, while private static data members are available only to other functions in the class or to friend functions. When a program executes, each instantiated object can access the static data member, just as it would access non-static data members.

By default, static data members are assigned an initial value of 0. What happens if you want to assign a different initial value to a static data member? You could use a statement in the class constructor, although doing so will reset a static variable's value to its initial value each time a new object of the class is instantiated. Instead, to assign a value to a static data member, you add a global statement to the implementation file using the syntax `type class::variable = value;`. Initializing a static data member at the global level ensures that it is only initialized when a program first executes—not each time you instantiate a new object. The type portion of the statement indicates the variable's data type as declared in the interface file. The `class::variable` portions of the statement are the class name, scope resolution operator, and the name of the variable (as declared in the interface file). Notice that even though the static data member's statement is similar to the data member declaration in the interface file, it does not include the static keyword.

As an example of declaring and initializing a static data member, consider one of the most common uses of static data members: counting the number of a class's instantiated objects. To declare in the Stocks class a static data member named iStockCount, you add the statement `static int iStockCount` to the interface file. Since a static data member is not associated with any particular object, you cannot initialize it in any constructor functions or the variable would be reinitialized each time you instantiated a new object of the class. To initialize the iStockCount data member to 0, you add to the implementation file the statement `int Stocks::iStockCount = 0;` at a global level, outside of any function definitions. To increment the iStockCount static data member by 1 each time a new Stocks object is instantiated, you add a statement to the constructor function similar to `++iStockCount;`. In order for the value stored in iStockCount to be valid, however, you must add code to the destructor function that decrements the iStockCount variable each time a Stocks object is destroyed. Figure 5-31 contains an example of the Stocks class, with the iStockCount static data member. Statements in the constructor and destructor increment and decrement the iStockCount variable each time a new Stocks object is created or destroyed. Figure 5-32 shows the program's output.

```
:// Stocks.h
class Stocks {
public:
    Stocks();
    ~Stocks();
    void setNumShares(int);
    int getNumShares() const;
    void setPricePerShare(double);
    double getPricePerShare() const;
    double calcTotalValue();
    // static data member declaration
    static int iStockCount;
private:
    int iNumShares;
    double dCurrentValue;
    double dPricePerShare;
};
// Stocks.cpp
#include "stocks.h"
#include <string.h>
#include <iostream.h>
// global static data member initialization
int Stocks::iStockCount = 0;
Stocks::Stocks() {
    iNumShares = 0;
    dCurrentValue = 0;
    dPricePerShare = 0;
    // increment the static data member each time a
    // new object is instantiated
    ++iStockCount;
}
Stocks::~Stocks() {
    // decrement the static data member each time a
    // new object is destroyed
    --iStockCount;
}
void Stocks::setNumShares(int iShares) {
    iNumShares = iShares;
}
int Stocks::getNumShares() {
    return iNumShares;
}
void Stocks::setPricePerShare(double dPrice) {
    dPricePerShare = dPrice;
}
double Stocks::getPricePerShare() {
    return dPricePerShare;
}
```

Figure 5-31   Stocks class with a static data member that counts the number of a class's instantiated objects

```
double Stocks::calcTotalValue() {
     dCurrentValue = iNumShares * dPricePerShare;
     return dCurrentValue;
}
void main() {
     Stocks stockPick1;
     Stocks stockPick2;
     Stocks stockPick3;
     stockPick1.setNumShares(100);
     stockPick1.setPricePerShare(10.875);
     stockPick2.setNumShares(200);
     stockPick2.setPricePerShare(64.25);
     stockPick3.setNumShares(100);
     stockPick3.setPricePerShare(17.5);
     cout << stockPick1.calcTotalValue() << endl;
     cout << stockPick2.calcTotalValue() << endl;
     cout << stockPick3.calcTotalValue() << endl;
     cout << "There are " << Stocks::iStockCount
          << " instantiated Stocks objects." << endl;
}
```

Figure 5-31 Stocks class with a static data member that counts the number of a class's instantiated objects (continued)

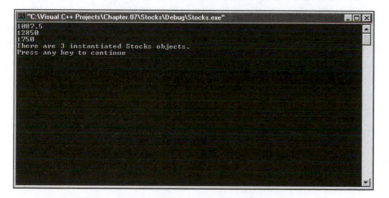

Figure 5-32 Output of Stocks class with a static data member that counts the number of a class's instantiated objects

In a member function, you can refer to a static data member directly, the same as you refer to other data members directly. For example, to assign a value of 10 to the iStockCount variable from inside one of the Stocks class's member functions, you simply use the statement iStockCount = 10;. To refer to a static data member from outside a member function, you precede the variable name with the name of the class and the scope resolution operator. For example, to assign a value of 10 to the iStockCount static data member from within a main() function, you use the statement `Stocks::iStockCount = 10;`.

 You can refer to a static data member by appending its name and the member selection operator to *any* instantiated object of the same class, using syntax such as `stockPick.iStockCount`. By using the class name and the scope resolution operator instead of any instantiated object of the class, however, you more clearly identify the data member as static. Clearly identifying data members as static makes working with a program easier when you have not worked with it in a long time or when another programmer needs to modify your application.

As another example, consider a static Stocks class data member named dPortfolioValue that keeps track of the total value of all instantiated stocks. Instead of updating the dPortfolioValue data member in each object's constructor function, you will update it each time the calcTotalValue() member function is called. Figure 5-33 shows an example of the Stocks class program with the dPortfolioValue static data member. The dPortfolioValue static data member is assigned an initial value of 0 in the implementation file. The main() method in the implementation file now instantiates three Stocks objects: stockPick1, stockPick2, and stockPick3. As the calcTotalValue() function executes for each object, stockPick1's value returns as 1087.50, stockPick2's value returns as 12850, and stockPick3's value returns as 1750. Each time the calcTotalValue() function executes, it increments the dPortfolioValue static data member by the value of each stockPick object. The dPortfolioValue static data member's total value of 15687.5 prints after each individual stock's value prints. (Note that the code that declared and modified the iStockCount data member from the previous example has been removed for simplicity.) Figure 5-34 shows the program's output.

```
// stocks.h
class Stocks {
public:
    Stocks();
    void setNumShares(int);
    int getNumShares() const;
    void setPricePerShare(double);
    double getPricePerShare() const;
    double calcTotalValue();
    static double dPortfolioValue;
private:
    int iNumShares;
    double dCurrentValue;
    double dPricePerShare;
};
```

Figure 5-33   Stocks class with a static data member that keeps track of the total value of all instantiated stocks

```cpp
// stocks.cpp
#include "stocks.h"
#include <string.h>
#include <iostream.h>
double Stocks::dPortfolioValue = 0;
Stocks::Stocks() {
    iNumShares = 0;
    dCurrentValue = 0;
    dPricePerShare = 0;
}
void Stocks::setNumShares(int iShares) {
    iNumShares = iShares;
}
int Stocks::getNumShares() {
    return iNumShares;
}
void Stocks::setPricePerShare(double dPrice) {
    dPricePerShare = dPrice;
}
double Stocks::getPricePerShare() {
    return dPricePerShare;
}
double Stocks::calcTotalValue() {
    dCurrentValue = iNumShares * dPricePerShare;
    dPortfolioValue += dCurrentValue;
    return dCurrentValue;
}
void main() {
    Stocks stockPick1;
    Stocks stockPick2;
    Stocks stockPick3;
    stockPick1.setNumShares(100);
    stockPick1.setPricePerShare(10.875);
    stockPick2.setNumShares(200);
    stockPick2.setPricePerShare(64.25);
    stockPick3.setNumShares(100);
    stockPick3.setPricePerShare(17.5);
    cout << stockPick1.calcTotalValue() << endl;
    cout << stockPick2.calcTotalValue() << endl;
    cout << stockPick3.calcTotalValue() << endl;
    cout << Stocks::dPortfolioValue << endl;
}
```

Figure 5-33   Stocks class with a static data member that keeps track of the total value of all instantiated stocks (continued)

Figure 5-34   Output of Stocks class with a static data member that keeps track of the total value of all instantiated stocks

Next, you will add to the Estimator class a static data member that stores the combined total of each customer's estimate.

To add to the Estimator class a static data member that stores the combined total of each customer's estimate:

1. Open the **Estimator.h** file in the Text Editor window.

2. Add the declaration **static long lCombinedCost;** to the end of the private declaration section.

3. Open the **Estimator.cpp** file in the Text Editor window.

4. Initialize the lCombinedCost static data member by adding the statement **long Estimator::lCombinedCost = 0;** after the #include <string.h> statement, but above the constructor function. Be sure to add the statement at the global level, outside of any function definitions so that the static data member is not reinitialized each time you instantiate a new object.

5. The calcCustomerCost() member function calculates the building cost estimate for each customer. Modify the function as follows so that each customer cost is added to the static lCombinedCost data member:

```
long Estimator::calcCustomerCost() {
    lCustomerCost = lStyleCost + lBedroomCost
        + lBathroomCost;
    lCombinedCost += lCustomerCost;
    return lCustomerCost;
}
```

To access the lCombinedCost static data member, you will use a static member function, which you will study next.

Static Member functions

Static member functions are useful for accessing static data members. Like static data members, they can be accessed independent of any individual class objects. This is useful when you need to retrieve the contents of a static data member that is declared as private, such as when you need to find out the current number of a class's instantiated objects. Static member functions are somewhat limited since they can only access other static class members or functions and variables located outside of the class. You declare a static member function similar to the way you declare a static data member by preceding the function declaration in the interface file with the **static** keyword. You do not include the **static** keyword, however, in the function definition in the implementation file.

Like static data members, you need to call a static member function's name only from inside another member function of the same class. If you use a static member function outside of the same class, you precede its name with the class name and scope resolution operator, or you append the function name to an existing object of the class using the member selection operator. For example, to access a function without using an instantiated object, call a static function named getPortfolioValue() of the Stocks class using the statement **Stocks::getPortfolioValue();**. Alternatively, if you have an instantiated object of the Stocks class (stockPick, for example), then you can use the statement **stockPick.getPortfolioValue();**.

You can execute static member functions even if no objects of a class are instantiated. Therefore, you can use a static member function to check the value of a static data member, even if no objects of the class exist. For example, you may write code that uses a static member function with a static counter data member that automatically exits the program once a user closes the last object of a class.

One use of static member functions is to access private static data members. Recall that many programmers prefer to hide all of a class's data members. If you decide to hide your static data members, you can access them with a static member function. Figure 5-35 shows a modified version of the Stocks program in which the dPortfolioValue static data member has been made private. A new static getPortfolioValue() function has been added that returns the value of the dPortfolioValue static data member. Note that you are not allowed to use the **const** keyword with a static member function, even if the member function does not modify any data members.

```
// stocks.h
class Stocks {
public:
    Stocks();
    void setNumShares(int);
    int getNumShares() const;
    void setPricePerShare(double);
    double getPricePerShare() const;
    double calcTotalValue();
    static double getPortfolioValue();
private:
    static double dPortfolioValue;
    int iNumShares;
    double dCurrentValue;
    double dPricePerShare;
};
// stocks.cpp
#include "stocks.h"
#include <string.h>
#include <iostream.h>
double Stocks::dPortfolioValue = 0;
double Stocks::getPortfolioValue() {
    return dPortfolioValue;
}
Stocks::Stocks() {
    iNumShares = 0;
    dCurrentValue = 0;
    dPricePerShare = 0;
}
void Stocks::setNumShares(int iShares) {
    iNumShares = iShares;
}
int Stocks::getNumShares() {
    return iNumShares;
}
void Stocks::setPricePerShare(double dPrice) {
    dPricePerShare = dPrice;
}
double Stocks::getPricePerShare() {
    return dPricePerShare;
}
double Stocks::calcTotalValue() {
    dCurrentValue = iNumShares * dPricePerShare;
    dPortfolioValue += dCurrentValue;
    return dCurrentValue;
}
```

Figure 5-35   Stocks class with a static data member and static member function

```
void main() {
    Stocks stockPick1;
    Stocks stockPick2;
    Stocks stockPick3;
    stockPick1.setNumShares(100);
    stockPick1.setPricePerShare(10.875);
    stockPick2.setNumShares(200);
    stockPick2.setPricePerShare(64.25);
    stockPick3.setNumShares(100);
    stockPick3.setPricePerShare(17.5);
    cout << stockPick1.calcTotalValue() << endl;
    cout << stockPick2.calcTotalValue() << endl;
    cout << stockPick3.calcTotalValue() << endl;
    cout << Stocks::getPortfolioValue() << endl;
}
```

Figure 5-35   Stocks class with a static data member and static member function (continued)

Next, you will add to the Estimator class a static member function that returns the value of the static lCombinedCost data member.

To add to the Estimator class a static member function that returns the value of the static lCombinedCost data member:

1. Open the **Estimator.h** file in the Text Editor window.

2. Add the member function declaration **static long getCombinedCost();** to the end of the public declaration section.

3. Open the Estimator.cpp file in the Text Editor window.

4. Add the following definition for the static getCombinedCost() member function after the getCustomerCost() member function definition:

    ```
    long Estimator::getCombinedCost(){
        return lCombinedCost;
    }
    ```

5. Finally, add the following statements to the main() function, *above* the last statement that deletes the customer3 object. The statements call the static getCombinedCost() member function, which returns the value of the lCombinedCost static data member.

    ```
    cout << "The combined cost for all three customers is $"
        << Estimator::getCombinedCost() << endl;
    ```

6. Rebuild and execute the program. After entering data for all three customers, your screen should appear similar to Figure 5-36:

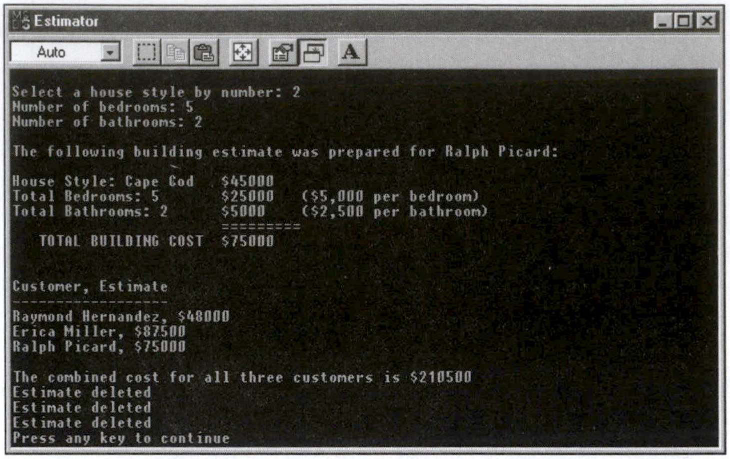

Figure 5-36   Output of final version of Building Estimator program

CONSTANT OBJECTS

If you have any type of variable in a program that does not change, you should always use the **const** keyword to declare the variable as a constant. Constants are an important aspect of good programming technique since they prevent clients (or you) from modifying data that should not change. Since objects are also variables, they too can be declared as constants. As with other types of data, however, you only declare an object as constant if it does not change. For example, you may have a class that instantiates an object representing the current date. If you will not need to modify any of the object's data members, then you should declare the object as constant. To declare an object as constant, place the **const** keyword in front of the object declaration. For example, to declare a constant object named currentDate from a class named Date using the default constructor, you use the statement **const Date currentDate;**.

Constant data members in a class cannot be assigned values using a standard assignment statement within the body of a member function. Therefore, you must use an initialization list to assign initial values to these types of data members. Consider the Payroll class again. Assume that it may be more efficient to use constants for the dFedTax and dStateTax data members.

The following code shows how to declare the dFedTax and dStateTax data members as constants in the interface file and how to initialize their values using an initialization list in the default constructor:

```cpp
// Payroll.h
class Payroll {
public:
     Payroll();
private:
     const double dFedTax;
     const double dStateTax;
};
// Payroll.cpp
#include "Payroll.h"
#include <iostream.h>
Payroll::Payroll()
     : dFedTax(.28), dStateTax(.05) {
};
```

In contrast, the following code raises several compile errors since constants must be initialized in an initialization list:

```cpp
// Payroll.h
class Payroll {
public:
     Payroll();
private:
     const double dFedTax;
     const double dStateTax;
};
// Payroll.cpp
#include "Payroll.h"
#include <iostream.h>
Payroll::Payroll() {
     dFedTax = .28; // illegal
     dStateTax = .05; // illegal
};
```

Another good programming technique is to always use the **const** keyword to declare get functions that do not modify data members as constant functions. The **const** keyword makes your programs more reliable by ensuring that functions that are *not* supposed to modify data *cannot* modify data. To declare a function as constant, you add the **const** keyword after a function's parentheses in both the function declaration and definition. For example, in the last chapter you saw a function named getStateTax() that only returns the current state tax rate stored in the dStateTax data member. Since the getStateTax() function does not modify any data, it should be a constant function. The following code shows the declaration and definition for a constant version of the getStateTax() function. Notice that the **const** keyword has been added after the function's parentheses.

```
// Payroll.h
double getStateTax(Payroll* pStateTax) const;
// Payroll.cpp
double Payroll::getStateTax(Payroll* pStateTax) const {
    return pStateTax->dStateTax;
}
```

Next, you will define the Estimator class's get functions as constant.

To define the Estimator class's get functions as constant:

1. Open the **Estimator.h** file in the Text Editor window.

2. In the public section, add the **const** keyword after each of the get function's parentheses. The following code shows the function declarations that you need to modify, along with where you need to place the **const** keyword.

```
char* getCustomerName() const;
char* getHouseStyle() const;
long getStyleCost() const;
int getBedrooms() const;
long getBedroomCost() const;
int getBathrooms() const;
long getBathroomCost() const;
long getCustomerCost() const;
```

3. Open the **Estimator.cpp** file in the Text Editor window.

4. In each of the get function definitions corresponding to the function declarations you modified in Step 2, add the **const** keyword after each of the function's parentheses.

5. Rebuild and execute the program. The program should function the same as it did in the previous set of steps.

Chapter Summary

◻ The default constructor is the constructor that does not include any parameters and that is called for any declared objects of its class to which you do not pass arguments.

◻ Visual C++ automatically supplies a default constructor, even if you do not declare and define one in your code.

◻ An overloaded function refers to multiple functions within a program that share the same name, but that accept different parameters.

◻ Although constructor functions do not return values, they can accept parameters that a client can use to pass initialization values to your class.

◻ Initialization lists, or member initialization lists, are another way of assigning initial values to a class's data members.

❏ Functional notation is another way of assigning a value to a variable.

❏ A copy constructor is a special constructor that is called when a new object is instantiated from an old object.

❏ C++ supplies a default copy constructor that automatically copies the members of the original object to the new object.

❏ A copy constructor executes only when you initialize a new object based on an existing object, not when you simply assign one existing object to another existing object.

❏ If you use the default copy constructor to create a new object from an existing object that is based on a class containing pointers, the new object and the existing object will contain pointers to the same memory addresses.

❏ To prevent copied objects in your program from sharing pointers to the same memory address, you must write your own copy constructor using the syntax
class_name(const *class_name*& *object_name*);.

❏ When an object reference parameter in a member function is preceded by the **const** keyword, the parameter is referred to as a constant parameter.

❏ A default destructor cleans up any resources allocated to an object once the object is destroyed.

❏ To delete any heap variables declared by your class, you must write your own destructor function.

❏ A destructor is called in two ways: when a stack object loses scope when the function in which it is declared ends, or when a heap object is destroyed with the delete operator.

❏ Operator overloading refers to the creation of multiple versions of C++ operators that perform special tasks required by the class in which an overloaded operator function is defined.

❏ You create an overloaded operator function as either a class member function or a friend function of a class.

❏ An overloaded operator function executes if the data types for each operand within a statement match the data types in the overloaded operator function's parameter list. At least one of the overloaded operator function's parameters must be of a class type.

❏ When you declare a class member to be static, only one copy of that class member is created during a program's execution, regardless of how many objects of the class you instantiate.

❏ You must use an initialization list to assign initial values to constant data members.

❏ A good programming technique is to always use the **const** keyword to declare get functions that do not modify data members as constant functions.

REVIEW QUESTIONS

1. Which is the correct syntax for declaring a stack object of the Students class using the default constructor?

    a. Students curStudent;

    b. Students curStudent();

    c. Students curStudent = new Students;

    d. Students curStudent = new Students();

2. How many parameters can you include in a default constructor?

    a. 0

    b. 1

    c. 2

    d. 5

3. Which of the following statements is true of an overloaded function?

    a. Each version of an overloaded function must accept different parameters.

    b. Each version of an overloaded function must accept identical parameters.

    c. The parameters accepted by the different versions of an overloaded function make no difference, provided each version contains different sets of statements in its function body.

    d. Overloaded functions cannot accept parameters.

4. What happens if you write a parameterized constructor for the Students class, but not a default constructor, and you attempt to instantiate a new object of the class using the default constructor?

    a. The compiler automatically supplies a default constructor.

    b. The compiler converts the statement into a format that can be used with a parameterized constructor.

    c. You will receive a compiler error because the automatically supplied default constructor is no longer available.

    d. The compiler prompts you to enter the appropriate value for the parameterized constructor.

5. If the following constructor function definition is declared in an implementation file, what is the correct statement for the member function declaration in the interface file:

```
double Students::Students(double dGPA) {
    dGradePointAverage = dGPA;
```

a. `Students() = double;`

b. `Students::Students(double dGPA);`

c. `Students();`

d. `Students(double);`

6. How do you modify the following constructor and data member initialization statements into an initialization list?

```
double Students::Students(double dGPA) {
    dGradePointAverage = dGPA;
    iStudentID = 0;
    iClassCode = 0;
    dClassFee = 0;
```

a. `double Students::Students(double dGPA) {`
   `: dGradePointAverage = dGPA, iStudentID = 0,`
   `iClassCode = 0, dClassFee = 0`

b. `double Students::Students(double dGPA)`
   `: dGradePointAverage = dGPA, iStudentID = 0,`
   `iClassCode = 0, dClassFee = 0 {`

c. `double Students::Students(double dGPA`
   `: dGradePointAverage = dGPA, iStudentID = 0,`
   `iClassCode = 0, dClassFee = 0) {`

d. `double Students::Students(double dGPA) {`
   `: dGradePointAverage = dGPA; iStudentID = 0;`
   `iClassCode = 0; dClassFee = 0 {`

7. How can you initialize constant data members?

a. Within the body of parameterized constructor functions

b. Within the body of default constructor functions

c. Using initialization lists

d. Within the parameter list of a member function declaration

8. _____ is another way of assigning a value to a variable.

a. Bit-wise assignments

b. Data transformation

c. Functional notation

d. Dynamic variable generation

9. You can create a new Students object named newStudent by copying the existing curStudent object using the statement `Students newStudent = curStudent;` or by using the statement _____.

   a. `newStudent = curStudent;`

   b. `curStudent = newStudent;`

   c. `Students newStudent(curStudent);`

   d. `Students curStudent(newStudent);`

10. When you create a new object by copying an existing object, data members of the original object are automatically copied to the new object using _____.

   a. the default constructor

   b. the default copy constructor

   c. a parameterized constructor

   d. the default destructor

11. Which is the correct syntax for a copy constructor?

   a. `class_name(const class_name object_name);`

   b. `class_name(class_name& object_name);`

   c. `class_name(const class_name&);`

   d. `class_name(const class_name& object_name);`

12. What is one reason for writing your own copy constructor function?

   a. When you declare an object on the stack

   b. When your project includes friend functions

   c. If you have multiple classes in a project

   d. When you need to use pointers to dynamically allocate memory

13. When an object reference parameter in a member function is preceded by the const keyword, the parameter is referred to as a _____.

   a. dynamic variable

   b. constant parameter

   c. static data member

   d. dynamic parameter

14. A _____ cleans up any resources allocated to an object once the object is destroyed.

   a. parameterized destructor

   b. copy constructor

   c. system administrator

   d. default destructor

15. A destructor is called when a stack object loses scope, when the function in which it is declared ends, or _____

    a. when a heap object is destroyed with the delete operator

    b. when you call the kill operator

    c. when you manually remove the object from the stack by calling the ~stack() function

    d. when you explicitly call the destructor function

16. Which is the correct destructor function definition for the Students class?

    a. `Students~();`

    b. `~Students();`

    c. `!Students();`

    d. `*Students();`

17. Which of the following operators must be overloaded as a member function?

    a. `->`

    b. `+`

    c. `&`

    d. `!`

18. What is the correct syntax for overloading a binary operator?

    a. `type binary_operator (const class& leftOperand, const class& rightOperand) { }`

    b. `operator binary_operator (const class& leftOperand, const class& rightOperand) { }`

    c. `type operator binary_operator (const class leftOperand, const class rightOperand) { }`

    d. `type operator binary_operator (const class& leftOperand, const class& rightOperand) { }`

19. How many parameters are used in the parameter list for an overloaded unary operator?

    a. 0

    b. 1

    c. 2

    d. It depends on the operator

5

20. What is the correct function declaration for overloading the assignment operator in the Students class?

    a. `Students* operator = (const Students* operand);`

    b. `Students & operator = (const Students& operand);`

    c. `Students operator = (const Students operand);`

    d. `Students operator = (const Students& operand);`

21. To instruct a class to create only one copy of a class member, regardless of how many objects of that class you instantiate, you precede the class member declaration with the keyword _____.

    a. fixed

    b. single

    c. permanent

    d. static

22. What is the correct syntax for declaring a constant object named astronomyClass from a class named Syllabus?

    a. `const Syllabus astronomyClass;`

    b. `Syllabus const astronomyClass;`

    c. `Syllabus astronomyClass const;`

    d. `astronomyClass const Syllabus;`

23. When do you declare a class's member functions as constant?

    a. If the function is a static data member

    b. Whenever the function operates on a static data member

    c. For set functions that modify data

    d. For get functions that do not modify data

24. Which of the following is the correct declaration for a constant function named returnGPA() that returns an int value?

    a. `int returnGPA(int iStudentID) const;`

    b. `int const returnGPA(int iStudentID);`

    c. `const int returnGPA(int iStudentID);`

    d. `int returnGPA(const int iStudentID);`

EXERCISES

1. Add a constructor function to the following class so that instead of calling the set functions to assign values to the data members, the values are passed as parameters when an object of the class is instantiated. Also, rewrite the statements in the main() method so that they use the new parameterized constructor instead of the default constructor.

```cpp
// MutualFund.h
class MutualFund {
public:
    MutualFund();
    void setFundName(char*);
    void setFundShares(int);
private:
    char* szFundName;
    int iFundShares;
}
// MutualFund.cpp
#include <string.h>
#include "MutualFund.h"
MutualFund::MutualFund() {
    szFundName = new char[50];
    iFundShares = 0;
}
void MutualFund::setFundName(char* szName) {
    strcpy(szFundName, szName);
}
void MutualFund::setFundShares(int iShares) {
    iFundShares = iShares;
}
void main() {
    MutualFund curFund;
    curFund.setFundName("Janus");
    curFund.setFundShares(500);
}
```

2. Rewrite the following code segment so that its data members are initialized in an initialization list.

```cpp
// DistanceConversion.h
class DistanceConversion {
public:
    DistanceConversion();
    double milesToKilometers(double);
    double kilometersToMiles(double);
```

```
private:
double dMiles;
double dKilometers
}
// DistanceConversion.cpp
#include " DistanceConversion.h"
DistanceConversion:: DistanceConversion () {
    dMiles = 0;
    dKilometers = 0;
}
double DistanceConversion::milesToKilometers(
    double dMilesArg) {
    dMiles = dMilesArg;
    dKilometers = dMiles * 1.6;
    return dKilometers;
}
double DistanceConversion::kilometersToMiles(
    double dKiloArg) {
    dKilometers = dKiloArg;
    dMiles = dKilometers * .6;
    return dMiles;
}
```

3. Write the appropriate copy constructor for the following class:

```
// Auto.h
class Auto {
public:
    Auto (char*, double);
    ...
private:
    char* szCarMake;
    double dCarEngine;
}
// Auto.cpp
#include " Auto.h"
#include <string.h>
Auto::Auto(char* szMake, double dEngine) {
    szCarMake = new char[25];
    strcpy(szCarMake, szMake);
    dCarEngineSize = dCarEngine;
}
void main() {
    Auto oldCar("Chevy", 351);
    Auto newCar(oldCar);
}
```

4. Add an appropriate destructor to the class in Exercise 3.

5. When you write an overloaded assignment operator, there is the possibility that a client will attempt to assign an existing object to itself. For example, if you have a Students object named curStudent, the statement `curStudent = curStudent;` will attempt to assign the same object to itself. Rewrite the following overloaded assignment operator so that it checks whether the temporary object created when you call the overloaded assignment operator function is the same as the object parameter. If they are the same, simply return the current object instead of reassigning new values to the temporary object. Hint: you will need to use a decision-making structure and the `this` reference.

```
MutualFund& MutualFund::operator
    = (const MutualFund& operand) {
    szFundName = new char[50];
    strcpy(szFundName, operand.szFundName);
    iFundShares = operand.iFundShares;
    return *this;
}
```

6. Create an Auction class that contains data members appropriate for an auction including itemName, highBidder, lowBidder, and reserve price. Store the itemName, highBidder, and lowBidder fields as heap variables. Instantiate an Auction object on the heap. Allow two people to play an "auction game" using a console application. Once one of the bidders meets the reserve price, end the auction and print the high bidder's name to the screen. Also write a destructor function that cleans up the heap variables and prints AUCTION CLOSED once the reserve price is reached.

7. Create a CompanyInfo class that includes private data members such as the company name, year incorporated, annual gross revenue, annual net revenue, and so on. Use a parameterized constructor to obtain the company name. Write set and get functions to store and retrieve values in the private data members. Copy the original object into a subsidiary company object and create an appropriate copy constructor function. Use static data members to store the combined gross revenue for both companies. Output each company's information in a console application, using a static member function to retrieve the static combined gross revenue data member. Be sure to include a destructor.

8. Overload the subtraction operator for the stocks class so that one class's number of shares is subtracted from another class's number of shares.

9. Create a FootballGame team class with appropriate data members such as team name, home city, quarterback, mascot, and so on. Write an overloaded increment operator that increments a static currentScore data member by six points (the number of points earned for a touchdown) each time a team makes a touchdown. Write the appropriate set and get functions for the class. Use a console application to output an imaginary "play-by-play" description of the game (be creative) similar to what you might hear a radio commentator read. You do not have to output hundreds of lines—just enough lines to demonstrate the functionality of the class. Each time a touchdown is scored, call the overloaded increment operator. Be sure to write a destructor to clean up any data members stored on the heap.

10. Modify the FootballGame class so that several teams compete in the playoffs. Add a static data member that keeps track of all of the touchdowns scored in the playoffs. Also, write a static member function that lists the total touchdowns scored as the last line that is "read" by the sports commentator.

11. Create an Investment class that includes the appropriate data members for various types of investments. Write appropriate get and set functions for each data member. Also include a data member that holds the investment's total value. Use a parameterized constructor to receive the name of each investment in a char* pointer. Be sure to include a destructor to clean up the heap when each object is destroyed. Also include a static data member and a static member function that calculates the total worth of an investment portfolio by adding together the total value of data members for each instantiated object. Add the Investment class to a console application, and then instantiate an Investment object and initialize its data. Create two additional Investment objects by copying the original object. You will need to write a copy constructor for when you duplicate objects. Retrieve and print the data members for each object. Also print out the contents of the static data member using a statement similar to "Your investments are worth a total of $100,000."

6

INHERITANCE

In this chapter you will learn:

♦ About base classes and derived classes

♦ About access specifiers and inheritance

♦ How to override base class member functions

♦ About constructors and destructors in derived classes

♦ About polymorphism and how to use virtual functions and virtual destructors

♦ How to create abstract classes

PREVIEW: THE CONVERSION CENTER PROGRAM

One of the most important features of C++ is the ability of one class to use the member functions and data members of another class through a process known as inheritance. Although inheritance is an important feature of C++ (or any object-oriented programming language), it is a critical feature of Microsoft Foundation Classes. You *must* use inheritance techniques in order to work with Microsoft Foundation Classes later in this text, so it is vital that you understand the concepts presented in this chapter.

To study the inheritance techniques presented in this chapter, you will work on a Conversion Center program that performs temperature, distance, and household measurement conversions. You will work with four classes to perform the conversions: Conversion, Temperature, Distance, and Household.

To preview the Conversion Center program:

1. Create a **Chapter.06** folder in your Visual C++ Projects folder.

2. Copy the **Chapter6_ConversionCenter** folder from the Chapter.06 folder on your Data Disk to the Chapter.06 folder in your Visual C++ Projects folder. Then open the **ConversionCenter** project in Visual C++. If the Tip of the Day dialog box displays, click the **Close** button.

3. Open the Conversion class interface file, **Conversion.h**, in the Text Editor window. The Conversion class is a base class file on which the other class files in the program are based. The file contains two unfamiliar elements: function declaration statements that begin with the **virtual** keyword, and the protected access specifier. Notice that one function declaration statement beginning with the **virtual** keyword includes **=0** at the end of the statement. This type of function is known as a pure virtual function and is used when you need to force a new class that inherits the characteristics of your class in order to provide its own implementation of a given function. The Conversion interface file is shown in Figure 6-1.

```
#if !defined(CONVERSION_H)
#define CONVERSION_H

class Conversion {
public:
     Conversion();
     virtual ~Conversion();
     double getResult() const;
     virtual void setResult(double) = 0;◄─── virtual function declaration
     char* getConversionType() const;
protected: ◄────────────────────────────── protected access specifier
     char* szCurConversion;
     double dResultAmount;
};
```

Figure 6-1   Conversion interface file

4. Open the **Conversion.cpp** implementation file and examine its contents. It contains some standard function definitions, including definitions for the functions that were declared with the virtual keyword.

5. The other three classes on your Data Disk, Temperature, Distance, and Household, are standard classes that perform different types of data conversion operations. Open the Temperature.h file. Above the class declaration is a #include statement that makes the Conversion class available to the Temperature class. The class declaration itself also includes the code **: public Conversion**, which allows the Temperature class to inherit the characteristics of the Conversion class. The Temperature.h file is shown in Figure 6-2. The other class interface files contain similar statements. You can examine them on your own.

```
#if !defined(TEMPERATURE_H)
#define TEMPERATURE_H

#include "Conversion.h"          statement that includes the Conversion class

class Temperature : public Conversion {
public:
     Temperature();
     virtual ~Temperature();          modifiers that allow the Temperature class to
     void setResult(double);          inherit the characteristics of the Conversion class
     void convertToCelcius(double);
     void convertToFahrenheit(double);
};

#endif
```

Figure 6-2   Temperature.h

6. Finally, open the Temperature class's implementation file, Temperature.cpp, in the Text Editor window and examine its contents. The function definitions are fairly straightforward. Notice that the file contains a definition for the virtual function that was declared in the Conversion interface file.

7. Build and execute the Conversion Center program, and then test the calculations. Figure 6-3 shows the output for a completed version of the Conversion Center program after performing a distance conversion.

8. Press any key to close the Conversion Center program window.

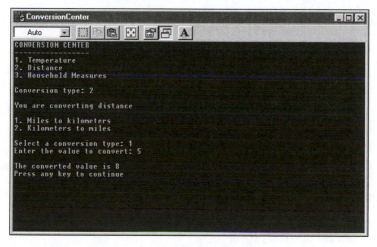

Figure 6-3   Output of the Conversion Center program

BASIC INHERITANCE

In the previous two chapters you studied how to create classes and use them as objects in C++ programs. You learned only how to create and manipulate individual classes, one at a time. There will be times, however, when you have a particular class that does not quite contain all of the class members you need in your program. Nonetheless, the class contains *some* member functions and data members that exactly match the requirements of your program. One option is to recreate all of the original class's functionality—provided you have access to the implementation file—and add any additional class members you need. Another option is to use inheritance to give a new class access to the original class's class members and create only the new class members you need in your program. **Inheritance** is the ability of one class to take on the characteristics of another class.

To explore the topic of inheritance, you will examine a program for allocating grant money that might be written for a School of Anthropology at a college or university. The school administration might need to keep track of grant money that is allocated to each anthropologist for his or her research. In the Grant Allocation program, a basic Anthropology class, such as the class shown in Figure 6-4, handles much of the program's functionality, such as recording the name of each anthropologist, calculating the amount of grant money each anthropologist needs, and so on.

```cpp
// Anthropology.h
#if !defined(ANTHROPOLOGY_H)
#define ANTHROPOLOGY_H
class Anthropology {
public:
    Anthropology();
    Anthropology(char*);
    ~Anthropology();
    void setAnthropologistName(char*);
    char* getAnthropologistName() const;
    void setGrantAmount(double);
    double getGrantAmount() const;
    void setResearchDuration(int);
    int getResearchDuration()const;
private:
    char* szAnthropologist;
    double dAmountGranted;
    int iResearchDuration; // in months
};
#endif
// Anthropology.cpp
#include "Anthropology.h"
#include <string.h>
#include <iostream.h>
Anthropology::Anthropology() {
    szAnthropologist = new char[50];
}
Anthropology::Anthropology(char* szName) {
    szAnthropologist = new char[50];
    strcpy(szAnthropologist, szName);
}
```

Figure 6-4 Anthropology class

```
Anthropology::~Anthropology() {
    delete[] szAnthropologist;
}
void Anthropology::setAnthropologistName(char* szName) {
    strcpy(szAnthropologist, szName);
}
char* Anthropology::getAnthropologistName() const {
    return szAnthropologist;
}
void Anthropology::setGrantAmount(double dGrantAmount) {
    dAmountGranted = dGrantAmount;
}
double Anthropology::getGrantAmount() const {
    return dAmountGranted;
}
void Anthropology::setResearchDuration(int iDuration) {
    iResearchDuration = iDuration;
}
int Anthropology::getResearchDuration() const {
    return iResearchDuration;
}
```

Figure 6-4   Anthropology class (continued)

The School of Anthropology is divided into two departments, Physical Anthropology and Cultural Anthropology. (Physical anthropology deals with the physical study of humans and related species such as apes; cultural anthropology deals with cultural aspects of humans such as language and archaeology.) Each department head wants the Grant Allocation program to record information that is specific to his or her discipline. Rather than write separate, unrelated classes for each department that duplicate the functionality of the Anthropology class, you can write classes that inherit the characteristics of the Anthropology class. Then to each new class, you can add member functions and data members that are specific to each department. For example, a new Physical class may be created for the Physical Anthropology department, and a Cultural class may be created for the Cultural Anthropology department. The Physical class needs to store a data member for the amount of grant money reserved for primate care. The Cultural class needs to store data members for the amount of grant money allocated for two separate purposes: the purchase of Egyptian antiquities, and cassette tapes to record speech patterns. Assuming that each class will inherit the members of the Anthropology class, you would need only the class declarations and definitions shown in Figures 6-5 and 6-6. Note that these two classes do not yet inherit the characteristics of the Anthropology class. We will discuss how to implement inheritance in the next section.

```
// Physical.h
#if !defined(PHYSICAL_H)
#define PHYSICAL_H
#include "Anthropology.h"
class Physical {
public:
     Physical();
     void setPrimateCare(double);
     double getPrimateCare() const;
private:
     double dPrimateCare;
};
#endif
// Physical.cpp
#include "Physical.h"
Physical::Physical() {
     dPrimateCare = 0;
}
void Physical::setPrimateCare(double dCost) {
     dPrimateCare = dCost;
}
double Physical::getPrimateCare() const {
     return dPrimateCare;
}
```

Figure 6-5   Physical class

```
// Cultural.h
#if !defined(CULTURAL_H)
#define CULTURAL_H
#include "Anthropology.h"
class Cultural {
public:
     Cultural();
     void setAntiquitiesCost(double);
     double getAntiquitiesCost() const;
     void setCassettesCost(double);
     double getCassettesCost() const;
private:
     double dAntiquitiesCost;
     double dCassettesCost;
};
#endif
// Cultural.cpp
#include "Cultural.h"
Cultural::Cultural() {
     dAntiquitiesCost = 0;
     dCassettesCost = 0;
}
```

Figure 6-6   Cultural class

```
void Cultural::setAntiquitiesCost(double dCost){
    dAntiquitiesCost = dCost;
}
double Cultural::getAntiquitiesCost() const {
    return dAntiquitiesCost;
}
void Cultural::setCassettesCost(double dCost) {
    dCassettesCost = dCost;
}
double Cultural::getCassettesCost() const {
    return dCassettesCost;
}
```

Figure 6-6   Cultural class (continued)

6

Next, you will start creating the Conversion Center program. The three types of conversions, temperature, distance, and household measurements, require slightly different types of functions. They share some common features, however, that can be inherited from a main Conversion class. For example, the Conversion class contains member functions such as getResult() and setResult() that are used to set and retrieve the results of a dResultAmount data member. These member functions and the dResultAmount data member can be inherited by the Temperature, Distance, and Household classes. Another data member that can be inherited is szCurConversion, which contains a string describing the current type of conversion. Included on your Data Disk are basic versions of the four interface files and the four implementation files used in the Conversion Center program. You can add these files to your project so you do not have to spend too much time typing. If you do not have access to a Data Disk, then type the program as shown in the figures in the following steps. First, you will create the interface files, which contain standard declarations for the various member functions and data members required by each class.

To create the Conversion Center program's interface files:

1. Return to Visual C++.

2. Create a new empty Win32 Console Application project named **ConversionCenter**. Save the project in the **Chapter.06** folder in your Visual C++ Projects folder.

3. Copy the **Conversion.h**, **Temperature.h**, **Distance.h**, **Household.h**, **Conversion.cpp**, **Temperature.cpp**, **Distance.cpp**, **Household.cpp**, and **Main.cpp** files from your Data Disk to the ConversionCenter folder in the Chapter.06 folder in your Visual C++ Projects folder.

4. Add the **Conversion.h**, **Temperature.h**, **Distance.h**, and **Household.h** interface files to the ConversionCenter project by pointing to **Add To Project** on the **Project** menu, and then clicking **Files**. If you do not have access to a Data Disk, then create new header files by entering the code for each of the interface files, as shown in the following four figures.

```
#if !defined(CONVERSION_H)
#define CONVERSION_H

class Conversion {
public:
     Conversion();
     ~Conversion();
     double getResult() const;
     void setResult(double);
     char* getConversionType() const;
private:
     char* szCurConversion;
     double dResultAmount;
};

#endif
```

Figure 6-7   Conversion.h

```
#if !defined(TEMPERATURE_H)
#define TEMPERATURE_H

class Temperature {
public:
     Temperature();
     ~Temperature();
     void convertToCelsius(double);
     void convertToFahrenheit(double);
};

#endif
```

Figure 6-8   Temperature.h

```
#if !defined(DISTANCE_H)
#define DISTANCE_H

class Distance {
public:
     Distance();
     ~Distance();
     void convertToMiles(double);
     void convertToKilometers(double);
};

#endif
```

Figure 6-9   Distance.h

```
#if !defined(HOUSEHOLD_H)
#define HOUSEHOLD_H

class Household {
public:
     Household();
     ~Household();
     void teaspoonsToTablespoons(double);
     void tablespoonsToTeaspoons(double);
     void cupsToQuarts(double);
     void quartsToCups(double);
};

#endif
```

Figure 6-10   Household.h

Next, you will create the implementation files.

To add the implementation files to the Conversion Center program:

1. Add the **Conversion.cpp**, **Temperature.cpp**, **Distance.cpp**, and **Household.cpp** implementation files to the ConversionCenter project by pointing to **Add To Project** on the **Project** menu, and then clicking **Files**. If you do not have access to a Data Disk, then create new implementation files by entering the code for each of the files shown in the following four figures.

```cpp
#include "Conversion.h"
Conversion::Conversion() {
    dResultAmount = 0;
}
Conversion::~Conversion() {
}
char* Conversion::getConversionType() const {
    return szCurConversion;
}
void Conversion::setResult(double dAmount) {
    dResultAmount = dAmount;
}
double Conversion::getResult() const {
    return dResultAmount;
}
```

Figure 6-11   Conversion.cpp

```cpp
#include "Temperature.h"
#include "string.h"
Temperature::Temperature() {
    szCurConversion = "temperature";
}
Temperature::~Temperature() {

}
void Temperature::convertToCelsius(double dTemperature) {
        dResultAmount = dTemperature - 32 * .55;
        setResult(dResultAmount);
}
void Temperature::convertToFahrenheit(double dTemperature) {
        dResultAmount = dTemperature * 1.8 + 32;
        setResult(dResultAmount);
}
```

szCurConversion, dResultAmount(), and setResultAmount() are inherited from the Conversion class

Figure 6-12   Temperature.cpp

6

```
#include "Distance.h"
#include "string.h"
Distance::Distance() {
    szCurConversion = "distance";
}
Distance::~Distance() {

}
void Distance::convertToMiles(double dKilometers) {
    dResultAmount = dKilometers * .6;
    setResult(dResultAmount);
}
void Distance::convertToKilometers(double dMiles) {
    dResultAmount = dMiles * 1.6;
    setResult(dResultAmount);
}
```

> szCurConversion, dResultAmount(), and setResultAmount() are inherited from the Conversion class

Figure 6-13   Distance.cpp

```
#include "Household.h"
#include "string.h"
Household::Household() {
    szCurConversion = "household measures";
}
Household::~Household() {

}
void Household::teaspoonsToTablespoons(double dMeasure) {
    dResultAmount = dMeasure * .33;
    setResult(dResultAmount);
}
void Household::tablespoonsToTeaspoons(double dMeasure) {
    dResultAmount = dMeasure * 3;
    setResult(dResultAmount);
}
void Household::cupsToQuarts(double dMeasure) {
    dResultAmount = dMeasure * .25;
    setResult(dResultAmount);
}
void Household::quartsToCups(double dMeasure) {
    dResultAmount = dMeasure * 4;
    setResult(dResultAmount);
}
```

> szCurConversion, dResultAmount(), and setResultAmount() are inherited from the Conversion class

Figure 6-14   Household.cpp

Base Classes and Derived Classes

When you write a new class that inherits the characteristics of another class, you are said to be **deriving** or **subclassing** a class. An inherited class is referred to as the **base class,** and the class that inherits a base class is referred to as a **derived class**. A class that inherits the characteristics of a base class is also said to be **extending** the base class, since you often *extend* the class by adding your own class members.

Professional programmers, as well as other texts on C++, use several other terms that describe base classes and derived classes. Base classes are also called parent classes, ancestor classes, or superclasses. Derived classes are also called child classes, descendent classes, or subclasses. This book, however, uses the terms base class and derived class.

When a class is derived from a base class, the derived class inherits all of the base class's data members and all of its member functions, with the exception of the following member functions:

- Constructor functions
- Copy constructor functions
- Destructor functions
- Friend functions
- Overloaded assignment operator (=) functions

A derived class must provide its own implementations of these functions. Note that even though a derived class does not inherit constructor, copy constructor, destructor, friend, or overloaded assignment operator functions from a base class, a base class's constructor and destructor functions still execute when you instantiate or destroy an object of a derived class that extends the base class. You will further explore this topic later in this chapter.

Figure 6-15 shows the hierarchy of the Physical and Cultural classes when they are derived from the Anthropology base class. Both the Physical and Cultural derived classes inherit the class members of the Anthropology base class. Each derived class also includes its own unique class members. A derived class's members are not available to the base class or to other classes that are derived from the same base class. They are available only to the derived class itself or to other derived classes to which it may be a base class.

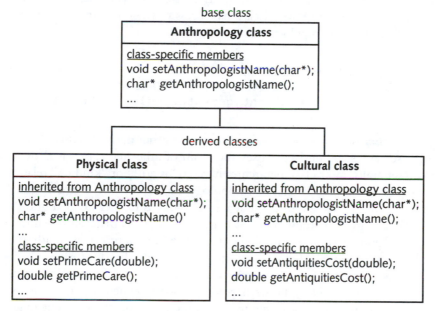

Figure 6-15   Base class and derived classes

You derive a class by including the base class in the derived class's interface file with a #include statement. You must also append a colon to the header declaration statement in the interface file, followed by an access modifier and the name of the base class. The access modifiers and base class names following the colon in a class's header declaration statement are known as the **base list**. To modify the interface file for the Cultural class so that it inherits the characteristics of the Anthropology class, you modify the class header declaration statement as follows:

```
class Cultural : public Anthropology
{
public:
    Cultural();
    ...
```

 By including multiple access modifiers and base class names separated by commas in the base list, you can add multiple inheritance to your programs. Multiple inheritance, however, is an advanced topic that you will learn about later.

Once you extend a base class, you can access its class members directly through objects instantiated from the derived class. For example, the following main() function declares a Physical object named currentGrant and then calls several member functions. If you refer back to Figure 6-5 you will see that the Physical class does not include setAnthropologistName() or getAnthropologistName() member functions. Even so, once you extend the Anthropology class in the Physical class, the Physical class has access to these member functions since they are inherited from the Anthropology class.

```
void main() {
    Physical currentGrant;
    currentGrant.setAnthropologistName("Richard Leakey");
    cout << currentGrant.getAnthropologistName() << endl;
}
```

Derived classes themselves can serve as base classes for other derived classes. When you build a series of base classes and derived classes, the chain of inherited classes is known as a **class hierarchy**. Generally, most class hierarchies have an "is a(n)" or "kind of" relationship. For example, the Physical class "is an" Anthropology class. Consider a larger class hierarchy. Within Anthropology, the field of cultural anthropology is further divided into three major subfields: archaeology (the study of a past culture through its material remains), linguistics (the study of languages), and ethnology (the study of cultures). As with the Physical Anthropology and Cultural Anthropology departments, the heads of each sub-department might also want to record unique information in the Grant Allocation program for their specific subfields. For example, the Archaeology sub-department might want to record in which country an archaeologist is digging, the Linguistics sub-department might want to record the name of a linguist's primary language of study, and the Ethnology department might want to record which culture an ethnologist is studying. You can derive each of these subfields as classes in the Anthropology class hierarchy for the Grant Allocation program. Each new class, representing each subfield, "is a" Cultural class, which "is an" Anthropology class. The more detailed Anthropology class hierarchy is shown in Figure 6-16.

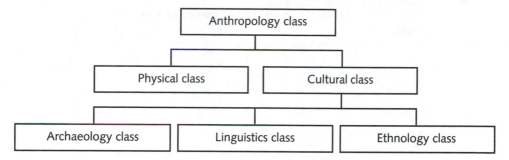

Figure 6-16   Anthropology class hierarchy

Each class in a class hierarchy cumulatively inherits the class members of all classes that precede it in the hierarchy chain. For example, in the class hierarchy shown in Figure 6-16, the Cultural class inherits the class members of the Anthropology class. The Archaeology, Linguistics, and Ethnology classes that derive from the Cultural class inherit the class members of the Cultural class, as well as the class members of the Anthropology class. A class that directly precedes another class in a class hierarchy and that is included in the derived class's base list is called the **direct base class**. A class that does not directly precede a class in a class hierarchy and therefore is not included in the class's base list is called an **indirect base class**. In Figure 6-16, the Cultural class is the direct base class of the Archaeology, Linguistics, and Ethnology classes. The Anthropology class is the indirect base class for those classes.

Next, you will modify the Temperature, Distance, and Household classes so that they derive from the Conversion base class.

To modify the Temperature, Distance, and Household classes so that they derive from the Conversion base class:

1. Modify the Temperature.h file as follows:

```
#if !defined(TEMPERATURE_H)
#define TEMPERATURE_H
#include "Conversion.h"
class Temperature : public Conversion {
public:
     Temperature();
...
};
#endif
```

2. Modify the Distance.h file as follows:

```
#if !defined(DISTANCE_H)
#define DISTANCE_H
#include "Conversion.h"
class Distance : public Conversion {
public:
        Distance();
...
};
#endif
```

3. Modify the Household.h file as follows:

```
#if !defined(HOUSEHOLD_H)
#define HOUSEHOLD_H
#include "Conversion.h"
class Household : public Conversion {
public:
        Household();
...
};
#endif
```

Next, you will add to the Conversion Center program a new C++ source file, named Main.cpp, that imports all three of the derived classes. The Main.cpp file also includes the program's main() function and uses numerous cout and cin statements to communicate with the user. Note that you do not need to import the Conversion base class since it is already imported by the three derived classes.

The Main.cpp file also imports a header file that you have not seen before, cstdlib.h. The cstdlib.h header file includes the exit() function, which allows you to end a console application early. The syntax for using the exit() function is **exit(*integer*);**. An integer of 1 indicates that the program should exit; an integer of 0 indicates that the program should continue running. You will use the exit() function in case a user does not enter the correct number for one of the Conversion Center program's options.

To add a new C++ source file named Main.cpp to the Conversion Center program:

1. Add to the ConversionCenter project the **Main.cpp** file that you copied earlier to the ConversionCenter folder in the Chapter.06 folder in you Visual C++ Projects folder. You add existing files to a project by pointing to **Add To Project** on the **Project** menu, and then clicking **Files**. If you do not have access to a Data Disk, then create a new Main.cpp file and enter the code for the file as shown in Figure 6-17. The #include statements import the Temperature, Distance, and Household classes, along with the iostream.h and cstdlib.h files. The first part of the main() function prompts the user to enter a number representing the type of conversion he or she wants to perform: Temperature, Distance, or Household Measures. Then an **if** statement is called that instantiates the correct

object based on the user's selection. Within the `if` statement are additional `if` statements that narrow the user's conversion choices. Other than the somewhat lengthy cout and cin statements, the only tasks that the main() function performs are to find out which conversion the user wants to perform, gather a number from the user and store it in the dValue variable, and pass the dValue variable to the appropriate class's member function. If you examine the .cpp files, you will see that the derived class objects are calling several member functions that are defined in the Conversion base class including the getResult() and getConversionType() member functions. The important statements in Figure 6-17 are bolded.

```cpp
#include <iostream.h>
#include <cstdlib>
#include "Temperature.h"
#include "Distance.h"
#include "Household.h"
void main() {
    int iSelection;
    double dValue;
    cout << "CONVERSION CENTER" << endl;
    cout << "----------" << endl;
    cout << "1. Temperature" << endl;
    cout << "2. Distance" << endl;
    cout << "3. Household Measures" << endl << endl;
    cout << "Conversion type: ";
    cin >> iSelection;
    cout << endl;
    if (iSelection == 1) {
        Temperature temp;
        cout << "You are converting "
            << temp.getConversionType()
            << endl << endl;
        cout << "1. Celsius to Fahrenheit" << endl;
        cout << "2. Fahrenheit to Celsius"
            << endl << endl;
        cout << "Select a conversion type: ";
        cin >> iSelection;
        cout << "Enter the value to convert: ";
        cin >> dValue;
        cout << endl;
        if (iSelection == 1)
            temp.convertToFahrenheit(dValue);
        else if (iSelection == 2)
            temp.convertToCelsius(dValue);
        else {
            cout << "You did not select a correct
                number!" << endl;
            exit(1);
        }
```

Figure 6-17   Main.cpp

```
cout << "The converted value is "
          << temp.getResult() << endl;
}
else if (iSelection == 2) {
     Distance distance;
     cout << "You are converting "
          << distance.getConversionType() << endl;
     cout << endl;
     cout << "1. Miles to kilometers" << endl;
     cout << "2. Kilometers to miles" << endl << endl;
     cout << "Select a conversion type: ";
     cin >> iSelection;
     cout << "Enter the value to convert: ";
     cin >> dValue;
     cout << endl;
     if (iSelection == 1)
          distance.convertToKilometers(dValue);
     else if (iSelection == 2)
          distance.convertToMiles(dValue);
     else {
          cout << "You did not select a correct
               number!" << endl;
          exit(1);
     }
     cout << "The converted value is "
          << distance.getResult() << endl;
}
else if (iSelection == 3) {
     Household measure;
     cout << "You are converting "
          << measure.getConversionType() << endl;
     cout << endl;
     cout << "1. Teaspoons to tablespoons" << endl;
     cout << "2. Tablespoons to teaspoons" << endl;
     cout << "3. Cups to quarts" << endl;
     cout << "4. Quarts to cups" << endl << endl;
     cout << "Select a conversion type: ";
     cin >> iSelection;
     cout << "Enter the value to convert: ";
     cin >> dValue;
     cout << endl;
     if (iSelection == 1)
          measure.teaspoonsToTablespoons(dValue);
     else if (iSelection == 2)
          measure.tablespoonsToTeaspoons(dValue);
     else if (iSelection == 3)
          measure.cupsToQuarts(dValue);
     else if (iSelection == 4)
          measure.quartsToCups(dValue);
```

Figure 6-17 Main.cpp (continued)

```
        else {
            cout << "You did not select a correct
                number!" << endl;
            exit(1);
        }
        cout << "The converted value is "
            << measure.getResult() << endl;
    }
    else {
        cout << "You did not select a correct number!"
            << endl;
        exit(1);
    }
}
```

Figure 6-17   Main.cpp (continued)

2. Build the **ConversionCenter** project. You should receive a number of compile errors that are the result of the derived classes not having access to the base class's private members. Next you will learn how to fix this problem by using protected access specifiers.

Access Specifiers and Inheritance

Even though a derived class inherits the class members of a base class, the base class's members are still bound by its access specifiers. Private class members in the base class can be accessed only by the base class's member functions. The private class members of a base class are instantiated with an object of the derived class—you just do not have access to them. For example, the szAnthropologist data member in the Anthropology class is private. If you write the following member function in the Cultural class, which attempts to directly modify the szAnthropologist data member, you will receive a compile error.

```
void Cultural::setAnthropologistName(char* szName) {
    strcpy(szAnthropologist, szName);
}
```

Instead, to access the szAnthropologist data member you must call the Anthropologist class's setAnthropologistName() member function, which is public. Alternatively, you can declare the szAnthropologist data member with the protected access specifier. The **protected access modifier** restricts class member access to the class itself, to classes derived from the class, or to friend functions and friend classes. You declare class members as protected in an interface file in the same fashion that you declare public and private class members: by placing the protected access specifier on a line by itself followed by a colon, followed by the class members. The following code shows a modified version of the Anthropology class's interface file in which the private access modifier has been changed to protected. A member function in the Cultural class that attempts to directly modify the szAnthropologist data member will function correctly since the Cultural class is a derived class of the Anthropology class and the szAnthropologist data member is now declared as protected.

```
class Anthropology {
public:
    Anthropology();
    Anthropology(char*);
    ...
protected:
    char* szAnthropologist;
    double dAmountGranted;
...
};
```

The access specifier included in a class header declaration's base list is another important facet of inheritance. You saw that a public access modifier was used when the base list was first introduced.

```
class Cultural : public Anthropology
{
public:
    Cultural();
    ...
```

Using a public access modifier in the base list gives the derived class public access to each of the base class's public members. If you use the private access modifier in the base list, then the base class's public members become private. In this case, clients of your class will not be able to access any public members of the base class. There are few compelling reasons for hiding a base class's public members from clients of a derived class, so you should normally use the public access specifier in the base list.

Although you should always use an access specifier in the base list, you are not required to. Remember, however, that a class's default access is private. If you fail to include an access specifier in the base list, your base class's public members become private to clients of your derived class. For example, the following Cultural class header declaration, which extends the Anthropology class, hides the Anthropology class's public data members from clients of the Cultural class:

```
class Cultural : Anthropology
{
public:
    Cultural();
    ...
```

Next, you will modify the Conversion.h interface file's private class members so that they are protected class members:

To modify the Conversion.h interface file's class members so that they are protected instead of public:

1. Open the **Conversion.h** file in the Text Editor window.

2. Change the private access modifier to protected as follows:

```
class Conversion {
public:
...
protected:
      char* szCurConversion;
      double dResultAmount;
};
```

3. Rebuild the **ConversionCenter** project and execute the program. You should now be able to call any of the conversion routines.

Overriding Base Class Member Functions

Derived classes are not required to use a base class's member functions. You can write a more suitable version of a member function for a derived class when necessary. Writing a member function in a derived class to replace a base class member function is called **function overriding**. As an example of when you would override a function, consider a base class named Expenses that includes a function named calcExpenses(). The calcExpenses() function in the base class calculates the total expenses that an employee incurs in a monthly period. However, you may derive a class named TravelExpenses from the Expenses base class that only needs to calculate an employee's monthly travel expenses, not their total monthly expenses. In this case, you would implement in the derived TravelExpenses class your own version of the calcExpenses() function that calculates just travel expenses.

 You cannot override a data member.

In order to override a base class function, the derived member function declaration must exactly match the base class member function declaration, including the function name, return type, and parameter. However, the statements in the body of each function definition can be entirely different. If the derived class member function declaration does not match the base class member function declaration, overriding does not occur; you simply create a new member function in the derived class. For example, the following code shows setGrantAmount() function declarations in both the Anthropology class and in the Cultural class. The Cultural class version of the function definition does not override the Anthropology class version since the two functions return different data types:

```
// Anthropology.h
...
void setGrantAmount(double);
...
// Cultural.h
...
double setGrantAmount(double);
```

6

The difference between function overriding and function overloading can be somewhat confusing. Essentially, function overriding allows you to create new behavior for a base class member function. Function overloading allows you to create multiple versions of the same function (possibly with different behavior) with different parameter lists. Figure 6-18 shows an example of overriding the setGrantAmount() member function in the Physical class derived from the Anthropology class. The setGrantAmount() member function in the Anthropology class simply assigns the value passed to the double parameter to the dAmountGranted data member. The Physical Anthropology department, however, automatically assigns 25% of all grant amounts to a dPrimateFund data member that ensures enough grant money is reserved for the care of primates being studied. The overridden setGrantAmount() member function in the Physical class performs the necessary calculations to deduct 25% from the grant money and assign it to the dPrimateFund data member. Of that grant money, 75% is then assigned to the dAmountGranted data member.

```cpp
// BASE CLASS
// Anthropology.h
...
public:
...
    void setGrantAmount(double dGrantAmount);
...
// Anthropology.cpp
void Anthropology::setGrantAmount(double dGrantAmount) {
    dAmountGranted = dGrantAmount;
}
// DERIVED CLASS
// Physical.h
...
public:
...
    void setGrantAmount(double dGrantAmount);
...
// Physical.cpp
void Physical::setGrantAmount(double dGrantAmount) {
    dPrimateCare = dGrantAmount * .25;
    dAmountGranted = dGrantAmount * .75;
}
```

Figure 6-18   Overridden member function in a derived class

You can also override overloaded functions in a class definition. If you override an overloaded function, however, you need to create a separate function definition in the derived class for each version of the overloaded function.

If you instantiate both a base class object and a derived class object on the stack, the compiler will know which version of an overridden function to call for each stack object. If a stack object of the base class calls the function, then the base class version of the function executes. If a stack object of the derived class calls the function, then the derived class's version of the function executes.

If you use pointers to class objects, the compiler may not automatically know which version of an overridden function to execute. If you anticipate that clients of your class hierarchy will use pointers to objects of your base and derived classes, then you need to declare any overridden functions as virtual. You will learn about virtual functions later in this chapter in a section on polymorphism.

There may be times when you want a derived class object to call a base class version of an overridden function. To force a derived class object to use the base class version of an overridden function you precede the function name with the base class name and the scope resolution operator using the syntax *object.base_class*`::function();`. Figure 6-19 shows an example of a main() function that instantiates three objects: one object of the Anthropology class, and two objects of the Physical class. All three objects call the setGrantAmount() function and pass to it a grant amount of 10,000. When the Anthropology class object, grant1, calls the setGrantAmount() member function, the Anthropology base class version of the function executes. When the first Physical class object, grant2, calls the setGrantAmount() member function, the derived Physical class version of the function executes. The second Physical object, grant3, calls the base class version of the setGrantAmount() member function using the Anthropology class name and the scope resolution operator. Since the first Physical object, grant2, is the only object to call the overridden function, it is the only object to assign an amount of 7,500 to the dAmountGranted data member. The other two objects assign the full grant amount of 10,000 to the dAmountGranted data member since they called the Anthropology base class version of the overridden function. The output shown in Figure 6-20 shows that each object called the correct version of the function.

```
void main() {
    Anthropology grant1;
    Physical grant2;
    Physical grant3;
    grant1.setGrantAmount(10000);
    grant2.setGrantAmount(10000);
    grant3.Anthropology::setGrantAmount(10000);
    cout << "The grant amount for grant1 is $"
        << grant1.getGrantAmount() << endl;
    cout << "The grant amount for grant2 is $"
        << grant2.getGrantAmount() << endl;
    cout << "The grant amount for grant3 is $"
        << grant3.getGrantAmount() << endl;
}
```

Figure 6-19   Calling the base class and overridden versions of an inherited function

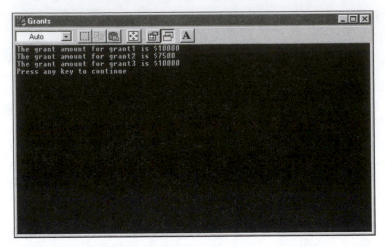

Figure 6-20   Output of program that calls the base class and overridden versions of an inherited function

Next, you will override the setResult() function in each of the Conversion Center program's derived classes. You do not actually need to override the setResult() function, because each of the derived classes does not need a unique implementation of the function. You're overriding the function for practice.

To override the setResult() function in each of the Conversion Center program's derived classes:

1. Open the **Conversion.h** interface file in the Text Editor window.

2. Copy the **setResult()** function declaration statement.

3. Open the **Temperature.h** interface file in the Text Editor window and paste the setResult() function declaration statement into the public section as follows:

```
class Temperature : public Conversion {
public:
      Temperature();
      ~Temperature();
      void convertToCelsius(double);
      void convertToFahrenheit(double);
      void setResult(double);
};
```

4. Open the **Distance.h** interface file in the Text Editor window and paste the setResult() function declaration statement into the public section as follows:

```
class Distance : public Conversion {
public:
      Distance();
      ~Distance();
```

```
        void convertToMiles(double);
        void convertToKilometers(double);
        void setResult(double);
};
```

5. Open the **Household.h** interface file in the Text Editor window and paste the setResult() function declaration statement into the public section as follows:

```
class Household : public Conversion {
public:
        Household();
        ~Household();
        void teaspoonsToTablespoons(double);
        void tablespoonsToTeaspoons(double);
        void cupsToQuarts(double);
        void quartsToCups(double);
        void setResult(double);
};
```

6. Next, open the **Conversion.cpp** file in the Text Editor window and copy the setResult() function definition.

7. Open the **Temperature.cpp** file in the Text Editor and paste the setResult() function definition after the destructor. After you paste the function, be sure to change the Conversion class reference preceding the scope resolution operator to Temperature, as follows.

```
void Temperature::setResult(double dAmount) {
        dResultAmount = dAmount;
}
```

8. Open the **Distance.cpp** file in the Text Editor and paste the setResult() function definition after the destructor. After you paste the function, be sure to change the Conversion class reference preceding the scope resolution operator to Distance, as follows.

```
void Distance::setResult(double dAmount) {
        dResultAmount = dAmount;
}
```

9. Open the **Household.cpp** file in the Text Editor and paste the setResult() function definition after the destructor. After you paste the function, be sure to change the Conversion class reference preceding the scope resolution operator to Household, as follows.

```
void Household::setResult(double dAmount) {
        dResultAmount = dAmount;
}
```

10. Rebuild the project and execute the program. The program should function the same as before you overrode the setResult() function.

CONSTRUCTORS AND DESTRUCTORS IN DERIVED CLASSES

When you derive one class from another class, you can think of any instantiated objects of the derived class as having two portions: the base class portion and the derived class portion. During the instantiating process, the base class portion of the object is instantiated, and then the derived class portion of the object is instantiated. Two constructors execute for a single derived class object: the base class constructor and the derived class constructor. Earlier you learned that a derived class does not inherit a base class's constructor or destructor. This is true, but it does not mean that the base class's constructor and destructor do not execute. In fact, every constructor in a class hierarchy for classes above a specific derived class execute when you instantiate an object based on the derived class. If the currently instantiated object has three base classes above it in a class hierarchy, then four constructors execute, one for each of the three base classes and one for the current derived class. Just as each constructor in a class hierarchy executes when a derived class object is instantiated, each destructor in a class hierarchy executes when a derived class object goes out of scope or is destroyed.

When a derived class object instantiates, constructors begin executing at the top of the class hierarchy. First, the base class constructor executes, then any indirect base class's constructors execute. Finally, the derived class's constructor executes. When an object is destroyed, class destructors are executed in the reverse order. First, the derived class's destructor is called, then the destructors for any indirect base classes, and finally, the destructor for the base class. Figure 6-21 illustrates this process using a class hierarchy with four levels.

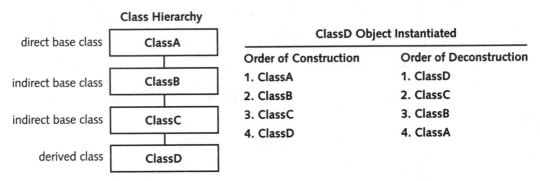

Figure 6-21   Execution of constructors and destructors in a class hierarchy

The order of construction makes sense, since it allows base classes to perform any initialization on class members that may be used by derived classes. And the order of destruction ensures that any base class members required by derived classes are not destroyed until all objects of any derived classes are destroyed first. For example, the Anthropology base class constructor allocates memory on the heap for the szAnthropologist pointer. Derived classes of the Anthropology base class can then use the inherited setAnthropologistName() and getAnthropologistName() member functions to store and retrieve an anthropologist's name. If a derived class's constructor were called before the Anthropology base class constructor, then the derived class could conceivably try to call the setAnthropologistName() member function before space is allocated on the heap for the szAnthropologist pointer, causing an error. Similarly, if the Anthropology base class destructor were called and deleted the szAnthropologist pointer before a derived class's destructor is called, the derived class could try to store or retrieve the value pointed to by the szAnthropologist pointer, again causing an error.

Figure 6-22 shows modified versions of the constructors and destructors for the Anthropology base class and the derived Physical class, along with a main() function, that demonstrate the order of execution for the constructors and destructors. Output statements have been added to each constructor and destructor that print a line of text describing when each function is called. Figure 6-23 shows the output when you execute the main() function.

6

```cpp
// Anthropology.cpp
...
Anthropology::Anthropology() {
    szAnthropologist = new char[50];
    cout << "Base class constructor called."
        << endl;
}
Anthropology::Anthropology(char* szName) {
    szAnthropologist = new char[50];
    strcpy(szAnthropologist, szName);
    cout << "Base class constructor called." << endl;
}
Anthropology::~Anthropology() {
    delete[] szAnthropologist;
    cout << "Base class destructor called." << endl;
}
...
// Physical.cpp
...
Physical::Physical() {
    dPrimateCare = 0;
    cout << "Derived class constructor called." << endl;
}
Physical::~Physical() {
    cout << "Derived class destructor called." << endl;
}
...
void main() {
    Physical grant1;
    grant1.setAnthropologistName("Richard Leakey");
    cout << "The anthropologist's name is "
        << grant1.getAnthropologistName() << endl;
}
```

Figure 6-22   Order of construction and destruction for the Anthropology base class and the derived Physical class

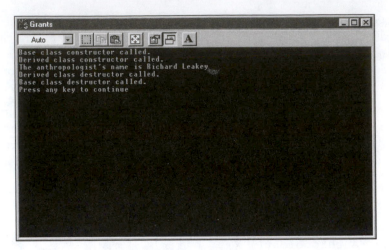

Figure 6-23   Output showing the order of construction and destruction for the Anthropology base class and derived Physical class

Parameterized Base Class Constructors

Notice that the main() function in Figure 6-22 executes the default constructor for both the Anthropology class and the Physical class since the statement that instantiates the Physical object, grant1, does not include parentheses or parameters. There will be times, however, when you will need to execute a base class's parameterized constructor instead of its default constructor. For example, rather than calling the setAnthropologistName() function to assign a value to the Anthropology class's szAnthropologist data member, you may want to simply assign a value to the szAnthropologist data member by calling the parameterized base class constructor when you first instantiate the grant1 object. You execute a base class's parameterized constructor using an initialization list in a derived class's parameterized constructor. For example, the parameterized constructor for the Anthropology base class accepts a single char* parameter containing an anthropologist's name. You create a parameterized constructor for the Physical class that also accepts a single char* parameter, and you include an initialization list that passes the char* parameter to the Anthropology class's parameterized constructor. This forces the Anthropology class's parameterized constructor to execute instead of its default constructor.

Figure 6-24 shows a parameterized Physical class constructor with an initialization list that calls the Anthropology class's parameterized constructor, along with a modified main() function. Notice that the szName parameter is not used in the body of the constructor; it is only passed to the base class parameterized constructor. The output of the modified program is the same as Figure 6-23.

```
// Physical.cpp
...
Physical::Physical(char* szName) : Anthropology(szname) {
    dPrimateCare = 0;
    cout << "Physical derived class constructor called." <<
endl;
}
...
void main() {
    Physical grant1("Richard Leakey");
    cout << "The anthropologist's name is "
        << grant1.getAnthropologistName() << endl;
}
```

Figure 6-24   Physical class constructor with an initialization list

6

Base Class Copy Constructors

When you create a new derived class object by copying an existing derived class object, if the base class constructor allocates memory on the heap, you need to call a base class copy constructor. You do this to ensure that the new base class object and the existing base class object do not contain pointers to the same memory addresses. You call a base class copy constructor using an initialization list with the derived class copy constructor, the same as when you call a parameterized base class constructor. The main() method in Figure 6-25 creates a new Physical object named grant2 by copying the existing grant1 object. The Physical derived class's copy constructor includes an initialization list that passes the derived copy constructor's object parameter to the Anthropology class copy constructor. Notice that in this case the derived class's copy constructor only serves to pass the object parameter to the Anthropology class copy constructor (although it also prints some text to the screen saying it was called).

If you execute the Grant Allocation program with the code in Figure 6-25, you will see the output in Figure 6-26. Notice that the class constructors are called for the grant1 object and that the copy constructors are called for the grant2 object.

```
// Anthropology.cpp
...
Anthropology::Anthropology(const Anthropology&
    sourceObject) {
    szAnthropologist = new char[50];
    strcpy(szAnthropologist,
        sourceObject.szAnthropologist);
    cout << "Base class copy constructor called." << endl;
}
...
// Physical.cpp
...
Physical::Physical(const Physical& sourceObject)
    : Anthropology(sourceObject) {
    cout << "Derived class copy constructor called."
        << endl;
}
...
void main() {
    Physical grant1("Richard Leakey");
    Physical grant2(grant1);
    grant2.setAnthropologistName("Dianne Fossey");
    cout << "The first anthropologist's name is "
        << grant1.getAnthropologistName() << endl;
    cout << "The second anthropologist's name is "
        << grant2.getAnthropologistName() << endl;
}
```

Figure 6-25   Calling a base class copy constructor

Figure 6-26   Anthropology base class and Physical derived class after adding
copy constructors

POLYMORPHISM

As you learned earlier, member functions in a base class can be overridden by derived classes. Thus, you will have multiple versions of the same function available to your program. The ability to override base member functions in derived classes is called **polymorphism**, which means "many forms." As a more general object-oriented programming term, polymorphism refers to a programming language's ability to process objects differently depending on their data type.

When declaring objects with overridden functions on the stack, you do not need to worry about polymorphism since the compiler can figure out which overridden function object to execute based on the class type of each object. When you use pointers to objects, however, the compiler can become confused by the class type of an object and call the wrong version of an overridden function. Recall that an object of a derived class "is an" object of its base class. For this reason, a pointer to an object of a base class can also point to an object of a derived class. It does not work the other way: A pointer of a derived class cannot point to a base class object. As an example, look at the overridden setGrantAmount() member function again. In the following code, a Physical class object is declared on the stack using the default constructor. Then, an Anthropology pointer is declared and assigned the address of the Physical class object. Finally, the overridden setGrantAmount()member function is called.

```
void main() {
    Physical aGrant("Richard Leakey");
    Anthropology* pGrant = &aGrant;
    pGrant->setGrantAmount(10000);
    cout << "The grant amount for "
        << pGrant->getAnthropologistName()
        << " is $" << pGrant->getGrantAmount() << endl;
}
```

In the preceding code, how does the compiler know which version of the overridden setGrantAmount()function to execute? Should it execute the base class version of the function, since that is the data type of the pointer, or should it execute the derived class version, since that is the data type of the object being pointed to? Unfortunately, the incorrect Anthropology class version of the function executes, which does not reserve 25% of the grant amount to the Physical class's dPrimateCare data member. If you were to execute the code, the output statement in the console window would read *The grant amount for Richard Leakey is $10000* instead of correctly reading *The grant amount for Richard Leakey is $7500.*

The problem with the preceding code is that the decision about which class's version of the function to execute is decided at compile time, when you first build the project. The compiler uses the base class version of the function, not the inherited class that the object points to, since the base class version of the function is the only thing it sees during the compilation process. Deciding which class members to use at compile-time is called **early binding**. With polymorphism, however, you want decisions about which class members to use to be made at run-time, based on an object's class type. Deciding which class members to use at run-time is called **dynamic binding**, or **run-time binding**. To enable dynamic binding, you declare an overridden member function as virtual.

Virtual Functions

There will be times when you know that a function you implement in your base class will need to be overridden in any derived classes. For example, the calcExpenses() function in the Expenses class that you learned about earlier will probably always need to be overridden to create a version of the function tailored to the needs of any derived classes. In order to be sure that the compiler knows which version of a function to execute, the base class version or a derived class version, you declare the base class version as virtual. A **virtual function** instructs the compiler to decide at run-time which version of an overridden function to call. In other words, a virtual function ensures that the compiler knows which version of a function to execute. To declare an overridden function as virtual, you add the `virtual` keyword at the beginning of the member function declaration in the base class. You do not need to add the `virtual` keyword to the base class function definition or the derived class function declaration or definition. Figure 6-27 shows a modified version of the Grant Allocation program. This time the base class declaration of the overridden function includes the `virtual` keyword. Now when you execute the main() function with the heap objects, the correct derived class version of the overridden function is called. Figure 6-28 shows the output.

```cpp
// BASE CLASS
// Anthropology.h
...
public:
...
    virtual void setGrantAmount(double dGrantAmount);
...
// Anthropology.cpp
void Anthropology::setGrantAmount(double dGrantAmount) {
    dAmountGranted = dGrantAmount;
}
// DERIVED CLASS
// Physical.h
...
public:
...
    void setGrantAmount(double dGrantAmount);
...
// Physical.cpp
void Physical::setGrantAmount(double dGrantAmount) {
    dPrimateCare = dGrantAmount * .25;
    dAmountGranted = dGrantAmount * .75;
}
...
void main() {
    Physical aGrant("Richard Leakey");
    Anthropology* pGrant = &aGrant;
    pGrant->setGrantAmount(10000);
    cout << "The grant amount for "
        << pGrant->getAnthropologistName()
        << " is $" << pGrant->getGrantAmount() << endl;
}
```

Figure 6-27   Grant Allocation program with a virtual overridden member function

Next, you will modify the object declarations in the Main.cpp file so that the objects are instantiated on the heap. So that the correct overridden version of the setResult() function executes, you will modify the setResult() function declaration in the Conversion class so that it is virtual.

To instantiate the class objects in the Main.cpp on the heap and to modify the overridden setResult() function in the Conversion class so that it is virtual:

1. Open the **Main.cpp** file in the Text Editor window.

Figure 6-28   Output of Grant Allocation program with a virtual overridden member function

2. Modify the **if** statement that instantiates the Temperature object so that it is instantiated on the heap as follows. Be sure to change the member selection operators to indirect member selection operators and to add a statement to the end of the **if** block that deletes the heap object.

```
if (iSelection == 1) {
    Temperature* temp = new Temperature;
    cout << "You are converting "
         << temp->getConversionType() << endl << endl;
    cout << "1. Celsius to Fahrenheit" << endl;
    cout << "2. Fahrenheit to Celsius" << endl << endl;
    cout << "Select a conversion type: ";
    cin >> iSelection;
    cout << "Enter the value to convert: ";
    cin >> dValue;
    cout << endl;
    if (iSelection == 1)
        temp->convertToFahrenheit(dValue);
    else if (iSelection == 2)
        temp->convertToCelsius(dValue);
    else {
```

6

```
                    cout << "You did not select a correct number!"
                        << endl;
                    exit(1);
            }
            cout << "The converted value is " << temp->getResult()
                << endl;
            delete temp;
    }
```

3. Modify the `if` statement that instantiates the Distance object so that it is instantiated on the heap as follows. Be sure to change the member selection operators to indirect member selection operators and to add a statement to the end of the `if` block that deletes the heap object.

```
else if (iSelection == 2) {
    Distance* distance = new Distance;
    cout << "You are converting "
        << distance->getConversionType() << endl;
    cout << endl;
    cout << "1. Miles to kilometers" << endl;
    cout << "2. Kilometers to miles" << endl << endl;
    cout << "Select a conversion type: ";
    cin >> iSelection;
    cout << "Enter the value to convert: ";
    cin >> dValue;
    cout << endl;
    if (iSelection == 1)
        distance->convertToKilometers(dValue);
    else if (iSelection == 2)
        distance->convertToMiles(dValue);
    else {
        cout << "You did not select a correct number!"
            << endl;
            exit(1);
    }
    cout << "The converted value is "
        << distance->getResult() << endl;
    delete distance;
}
```

4. Modify the `if` statement that instantiates the Household object so that it is instantiated on the heap as follows. Be sure to change the member selection operators to indirect member selection operators and to add a statement to the end of the `if` block that deletes the heap object.

```
else if (iSelection == 3) {
    Household* measure = new Household;
    cout << "You are converting "
        << measure->getConversionType() << endl;
    cout << endl;
    cout << "1. Teaspoons to tablespoons" << endl;
```

```
        cout << "2. Tablespoons to teaspoons" << endl;
        cout << "3. Cups to quarts" << endl;
        cout << "4. Quarts to cups" << endl << endl;
        cout << "Select a conversion type: ";
        cin >> iSelection;
        cout << "Enter the value to convert: ";
        cin >> dValue;
        cout << endl;
        if (iSelection == 1)
             measure->teaspoonsToTablespoons(dValue);
        else if (iSelection == 2)
             measure->tablespoonsToTeaspoons(dValue);
        else if (iSelection == 3)
             measure->cupsToQuarts(dValue);
        else if (iSelection == 4)
             measure->quartsToCups(dValue);
        else {
             cout << "You did not select a correct number!"
                  << endl;
             exit(1);
        }
        cout << "The converted value is "
             << measure->getResult() << endl;
        delete measure;
}
```

5. Open the **Conversion.h** file in the Text Editor window.

6. Add the `virtual` keyword to the start of the setResult() function declaration as follows:

```
class Conversion {
public:
...
    virtual void setResult(double);
    char* getConversionType() const;
protected:
    char* szCurConversion;
...
};
```

7. Rebuild and execute the program. The program should execute normally.

Virtual Destructors

As mentioned earlier, a base class pointer can point to an object of a derived class. Why would you use a base class pointer to point to a derived class object? Why not just create a pointer of the correct derived class type? Well, you may not know which derived class type to use until run-time. Therefore, it is easier to create a more generic pointer of the base class type that can point to multiple derived class types. Consider a Shape base class from which multiple other classes derive, such as a Rectangle class, a Square class, and a Circle class. Clients using the Shape class hierarchy may allow users of their program to select a specific shape to be drawn on screen. Because a client cannot know what shape a user will select, he or she may use a Shape pointer to point to an object that corresponds to the selected shape.

As with overridden functions, when you use a base class pointer to point to a derived class, the compiler will not know at compile time which destructor to call: the pointer class type or the class type of the object pointed to. By default, the compiler will use early binding and call only the base class destructor. However, with a base class pointer that points to a derived class, you need to call the destructor for both classes. To force the compiler to use dynamic binding with a destructor, you use the **virtual** keyword with the base class destructor declaration, the same as for virtual functions. A **virtual destructor** instructs the compiler to decide at run-time which destructor, or multiple destructors, to call. You do not need to add the **virtual** keyword to the base class destructor definition or the derived class destructor declaration or definition. Figure 6-29 shows a modified version of the Grant Allocation program's main() function that executes the setGrantAmount() member function. In this version, an Anthropology pointer is declared and points to a Physical object. The figure also shows the destructors for both the Anthropology class and the Physical class. Notice there is a problem in the output in Figure 6-30: The destructor is called only once.

```cpp
// BASE CLASS
// Anthropology.h
...
public:
...
    ~Anthropology();
...
// Anthropology.cpp
Anthropology::~Anthropology() {
    delete[] szAnthropologist;
    cout << "Base class destructor called." << endl;
}
// DERIVED CLASS
// Physical.h
...
public:
...
    ~Physical();
...
// Physical.cpp
void Physical::setGrantAmount(double dGrantAmount) {
    dPrimateCare = dGrantAmount * .25;
    dAmountGranted = dGrantAmount * .75;
}
Physical::~Physical() {
    cout << "Derived class destructor called." << endl;
}
...
```

Figure 6-29   Grant Allocation program with an Anthropology pointer to a Physical object

```
void main() {
    Anthropology* aGrant = new Physical("Richard Leakey");
    aGrant->setGrantAmount(10000);
    cout << "The grant amount for "
        << aGrant->getAnthropologistName()
        << " is $" << aGrant->getGrantAmount() << endl;
    delete aGrant;
}
```

Figure 6-29   Grant Allocation program with an Anthropology pointer to a Physical object (continued)

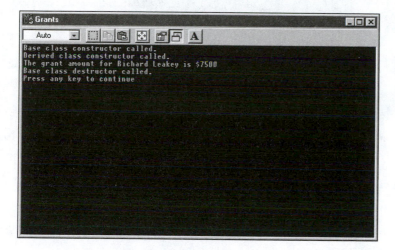

Figure 6-30   Output of Grant Allocation program with an Anthropology pointer to a Physical object

In order to correct the problem and call the destructors for both the base class and the derived class, add the **virtual** keyword to just the base class function declaration as follows:

```
// Anthropology.h
...
public:
...
    virtual ~Anthropology();
...
```

Now when you execute the program, both the base class destructor and the derived class destructor execute, as shown in the output in Figure 6-31.

You will not have any problems with the destructor for the Conversion Center program since the object declarations in the Main.cpp file of the Conversion Center program do not use base class pointers to point to derived class objects. It is possible, however, that a client of the Conversion Center program may need to use a Conversion pointer to point to an object of one of the derived classes. For this reason, you will add the **virtual** keyword to the Conversion base class destructor.

Figure 6-31   Output of Grant Allocation program with an Anthropology pointer to a Physical object after adding a virtual destructor

To add the **virtual** keyword to the Conversion base class destructor:

1. Open the **Conversion.h** file in the Text Editor window.

2. Add the **virtual** keyword to the destructor declaration statement as follows:

```
class Conversion {
public:
     Conversion();
     virtual ~Conversion();
...
protected:
     char* szCurConversion;
...
};
```

3. Rebuild and execute the program. The program should execute normally.

ABSTRACT CLASSES

You may have a base class in a class hierarchy that exists only as a template from which other classes are derived. For example, you may have a generic Aviation class from which you want to derive other types of aviation classes such as Airplanes or Helicopters. Or, the base class may contain members that you want to make sure are implemented only in other derived classes, almost as a set of guidelines that derived classes of your base class should follow. Clients should not be able to instantiate objects from these types of classes, only use them as a basis from which to derive other classes. Classes from which you cannot instantiate an object and that serve only to enforce a design protocol for derived classes are called **abstract classes**.

You create an abstract class by including one or more pure virtual functions in the class definition. A **pure virtual function** is a member function that is declared in an abstract class, but defined in a derived class. You declare a function as virtual by including =0 at the end of the function declaration statement in an abstract class. For example, to declare as a pure virtual function, a function named calcTravelCosts() that returns a double value, you use the statement `virtual double calcTravelCosts() = 0;`. As with function overriding, you must be sure that the return value and parameter list of a derived class's definition of a pure virtual function exactly match the return value and parameter list of the pure virtual function declaration in the abstract class.

Abstract classes can also include standard member functions that derived classes can use or override as necessary. A class derived from an abstract base class, however, must provide a definition for all of the abstract class's pure virtual functions or the derived class itself will also be an abstract class.

Why would you use an abstract class? Consider the Cultural class discussed earlier that represents the Cultural Anthropology department of the School of Anthropology. The Cultural class in the Anthropology class hierarchy could be used as a base class to derive three "subdepartment" classes: Archaeology, Linguistics, and Ethnology, as illustrated in Figure 6-32.

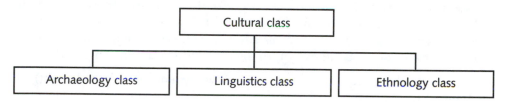

Figure 6-32   Cultural class hierarchy

Suppose that as you are designing the Cultural class, you learn that another programmer has been hired to write the Archaeology, Linguistics, and Ethnology classes. The head of the Cultural Archaeology department wants each of the subdepartments to record the miscellaneous expenses associated with a particular grant. Each department has different types of expenses due to the differences in its fields of study, so you cannot write a single function that can be used by all three departments. You want to make sure that the new programmer writes a unique definition of the setExpenses() member function for each subdepartment. Therefore, you make the Cultural class abstract by writing a pure declaration for the setExpenses() function.

Figure 6-33 shows the interface file for an abstract Cultural class containing two pure virtual functions: calcTravelCosts() and setExpenses(). Notice that both pure virtual function declarations end with =0. A definition file for the Cultural class is not shown since it would not contain definitions for the pure virtual functions. Instead, the pure virtual functions are defined in the Archaeology, Linguistics, and Ethnology classes that derive from the Cultural class.

```
#if !defined(CULTURAL_H)
#define CULTURAL_H
#include "Anthropology.h"
class Cultural : Anthropology
{
public:
     Cultural();
     // pure virtual function declarations
     double calcTravelCosts() = 0;
     double setExpenses() = 0;
     void setAntiquitiesCost(double);
     double getAntiquitiesCost();
     void setCassettesCost(double);
     double getCassettesCost();
private:
     double dAntiquitiesCost;
     double dCassettesCost;
};
#endif
}
```

Figure 6-33   Cultural class interface file with pure virtual functions

The one function in the Conversion Center program that should be defined in all derived classes is the setResult() function. In fact, since the Conversion class does not perform any calculations itself, no object should be instantiated from it. Therefore, you will make it into an abstract class. Because you have already added setResult() function definitions to each of the derived classes, you can easily turn the Conversion class into an abstract class.

To turn the Conversion class into an abstract class by modifying the setResult() function into a pure virtual function:

1. Return to the **Conversion.h** file in the Text Editor window.

2. Convert the setResult() function into a pure virtual function by adding =0 to the end of the setResult() function definition as follows:

```
class Conversion {
public:
...
     virtual void setResult(double) = 0;
     char* getConversionType() const;
protected:
     char* szCurConversion;
...
};
```

3. Open the **Conversion.cpp** file in the Text Editor window.

4. Delete the setResult() function definition since pure virtual functions cannot be defined in a base class.

5. Rebuild and execute the program. The program should execute normally.

CHAPTER SUMMARY

- Inheritance refers to the ability of one class to take on the characteristics of another class.

- When you write a new class that inherits the characteristics of another class, you are said to be deriving or subclassing a class.

- An inherited class is called the base class, and the class that inherits a base class is called a derived class.

- A class that inherits the characteristics of a base class is also said to be extending the base class since you often extend the class by adding your own class members.

- A derived class must provide its own implementations of constructor, copy constructor, destructor, friend, and overloaded assignment operator functions.

- You derive a class by including the base class in the derived class's interface file with an #include statement. You must also append a colon to the header declaration statement in the interface file, followed by an access modifier and the name of the base class.

- The access modifiers and base class names following the colon in a class's header declaration statement are called the base list.

- Once you extend a base class, you can access its class members directly through objects instantiated from the derived class.

- When you build a series of base classes and derived classes, the chain of inherited classes is known as a class hierarchy.

- Each class in a class hierarchy cumulatively inherits the class members of all classes that precede it in the hierarchy chain.

- A class that directly precedes another class in a class hierarchy, and that is included in the derived class's base list, is called the direct base class.

- A class that does not directly precede a class in a class hierarchy, and therefore is not included in the class's base list, is called an indirect base class.

- Even though a derived class inherits the class members of a base class, the base class's members are still bound by its access specifiers.

- The protected access modifier restricts class member access to the class itself, to classes derived from the class, or to friend functions and friend classes.

6

- ❑ Using a protected access modifier in the base list gives the derived class public access to each of the base class's public members.

- ❑ Writing a member function in a derived class to replace a base class member function is called function overriding.

- ❑ To override a base class function, the derived member function declaration must exactly match the base class member function declaration, including the function name, return type, and parameters.

- ❑ To force an object of a derived class to use the base class version of an overridden function, you precede the function name with the base class name and the scope resolution operator using the syntax `object.base_class::function();`.

- ❑ During the instantiating process the base class portion of the object is instantiated, and then the derived class portion of the object is instantiated.

- ❑ You execute a base class's parameterized constructor using an initialization list in a derived class's parameterized constructor.

- ❑ You call a base class copy constructor using an initialization list with the derived class copy constructor.

- ❑ The ability to override base member functions in derived classes is referred to as polymorphism, which means "many forms."

- ❑ Deciding at compile-time which class members to use is called early binding.

- ❑ Deciding at run-time which class members to use is called dynamic binding or run-time binding.

- ❑ A virtual function instructs the compiler to decide at run-time which version of an overridden function to call.

- ❑ A virtual destructor instructs the compiler to decide at run-time which destructor, or multiple destructors, to call.

- ❑ Classes from which you cannot create an object and that only serve to enforce a design protocol for derived classes are called abstract classes.

- ❑ You create an abstract class by including one or more pure virtual functions in the class definition.

- ❑ A pure virtual function is a member function that is declared in an abstract class, but defined in a derived class.

REVIEW QUESTIONS

1. A class that inherits the characteristics of a base class is also said to _____ the base class.

   a. evolve

   b. extend

   c. transform

   d. override

2. Which of the following terms does not refer to a base class?

   a. Superclass

   b. Subclass

   c. Ancestor

   d. Parent

3. Which of the following types of functions does a derived class inherit?

   a. member functions

   b. constructor functions

   c. destructors functions

   d. friend functions

4. The access modifiers and base class names following the colon in a class's header declaration statement is/are known as _____.

   a. access specifiers

   b. inheritance specifiers

   c. the class list

   d. the base list

5. The Students class includes a member function named getStudentID(). Assuming the Freshman class derives from the Students class, which of the following is the correct syntax for calling the getStudentID() member function from a Freshman object named curStudent?

   a. `curStudent.Student.getStudentID();`

   b. `curStudent.Student(getStudentID());`

   c. `curStudent.getStudentID();`

   d. `curStudent.getStudentID(Student);`

6

6. When you build a series of base classes and derived classes, the chain of inherited classes is known as a class hierarchy or a(n) _____

   a. inheritance chain

   b. abstract data structure

   c. base pyramid

   d. object model

7. How would you describe the Undergraduate class in the following class hierarchy?

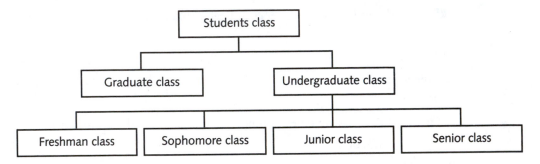

   a. base class

   b. indirect base class

   c. derived class

   d. subclass

8. What is the correct syntax for using the exit() function of the cstdlib.h header file to end a console application early?

   a. `exit(0);`

   b. `object.exit();`

   c. `exit(1);`

   d. `exit(0);`

9. Which of the following does not have access to a base class's protected members?

   a. classes derived from the base class

   b. friend functions of the base class

   c. friend classes of the base class

   d. global functions

10. What access does the Sophomore class have to the Students class in the following class declaration?

```
class Sophomore : Students
{
...
}
```

a. private

b. public

c. protected

d. friend

11. What is the correct syntax to force an Undergraduate object named curStudent to use the Students base class version of the overridden getStudentID() function?

a. `curStudent.Students::getStudentID();`

b. `curStudent.Students(getStudentID());`

c. `Students.curStudent::getStudentID();`

d. `curStudent.Students.getStudentID();`

12. What will the output be from the main() function in the following code?

```
// Auto.h
class Auto {
public:
       Auto();
       void setCarName();
       char* getCarName();
private:
       char* szCarName;
}
// Auto.cpp
Auto::Auto() {
       szCarName = new char[50];
}
void Auto::setCarName() {
       strcpy(szCarName, "American");
}
char* Auto::getCarName() {
       return szCarName;
}
// MyCar.h
class MyCar : public Auto {
public:
       MyCar();
       void setCarName();
}
// MyCar.cpp
```

```
MyCar::MyCar() {
    strcpy(szCarName, "Foreign");
}
void MyCar::setCarName(char* car) {
    strcpy(szCarName, "Chevrolet");
}
void main() {
    MyCar chevy;
    chevy.setCarName();
    cout << chevy.getCarName() << endl;
}
```

a. American

b. Chevrolet

c. Foreign

d. Nothing

13. If you have a base class and a derived class, what is the sequence of construction and destruction when you instantiate an object of the derived class?

a. Base class constructor
Derived class constructor
Derived class destructor
Base class destructor

b. Derived class constructor
Base class constructor
Base class destructor
Derived class destructor

c. Derived class constructor
Derived class destructor
Base class constructor
Base class destructor

d. Base class constructor
Base class destructor
Derived class constructor
Derived class destructor

14. What is the correct syntax to execute a parameterized constructor for the Students base class from an Undergraduate class constructor, assuming the constructor includes one int parameter?

a.
```
Students::Students(int iStudentID) : Students() {
      // statements
}
```

b.
```
Students::Students(int iStudentID) : Students(int) {
      // statements
}
```

c.
```
Students::Students(int iStudentID) {
      Students(iStudentID);
      // statements
}
```

d.
```
Students::Students(int iStudentID) : Students(iStudentID) {
      // statements
}
```

15. What is the correct syntax to execute a base class copy constructor for the Students base class from an Undergraduate class constructor, assuming the constructor includes one int parameter?

a.
```
Students::Students(const Physical& sourceObject)
      : Students(const Physical& sourceObject) {
      // statements
}
```

b.
```
Students::Students(const Physical& sourceObject)
      : Students(sourceObject) {
      // statements
}
```

c.
```
Students::Students(const Physical& sourceObject)
      : Students() {
      // statements
}
```

d.
```
Students::Students()
      : Students(const Physical& sourceObject) {
      // statements
}
```

16. The ability to override base member functions in derived classes is referred to as

_____.

a. multiplicity

b. polymorphism

c. inheritance

d. derivation

17. Deciding at compile-time which class members to use is referred to as _____.

   a. early binding

   b. dynamic binding

   c. precompilation

   d. pseudo-binding

18. Deciding at run-time which class members to use is referred to as _____, or run-time binding.

   a. early binding

   b. dynamic binding

   c. post compilation

   d. pseudo-binding

19. When do you need to use virtual overridden functions and destructors?

   a. When a base class pointer points to a derived class object

   b. When a derived class pointer points to a base class object

   c. Whenever you instantiate an object on the stack

   d. Whenever you instantiate an object on the heap

20. Where do you add the virtual keyword when declaring functions as virtual?

   a. In the base class function declaration

   b. In the base class function declaration and definition

   c. In the base class function declaration and definition, and in the derived class function declaration

   d. In the base class function declaration and definition, and in the derived class function declaration and definition

21. Which of the following declares the void setCarName() function as a pure virtual function?

   a. pure virtual void setCarName();

   b. virtual void setCarName();

   c. void setCarName() = 0;

   d. virtual void setCarName() = 0;

22. What type of class includes pure virtual functions?

   a. base class

   b. indirect base class

   c. abstract class

   d. derived class

EXERCISES

1. Modify the following Residential class definition so that it derives from the RealEstate class. Also, modify the code so that the Residential class can access the private members of the RealEstate class.

```
class RealEstate() {
public:
     RealEstate();
     RealEstate(char*);
     void setCustomerName(char*);
     char* getCustomeName();
private:
     char* szCustomerName;
}
class Residential {
public:
     Residential();
private:
}
```

2. Override the setNumberOfWheels() function so that the Motorcycle class assigns two wheels to the iNumWheels data member instead of four. Also modify the Motorcycle class so that it derives from the Transportation class.

```
// Transportation.h
class Transportation {
public:
     Transportation();
     voidsetNumberOfWheels();
     int getNumberOfWheels();
private:
      int iNumWheels;
}
// Motorcycle.h
class Motorcycle {
public:
     Motorcycle();
private:
}
// Transportation.cpp
#include "Transportation.h"
Transportation::Transportation() {
     setNumberOfWheels();
}
void Transportation::setNumberOfWheels() {
     iNumWheels = 4;
}
```

```
    // Motorcycle.cpp
    Motorcycle::Motorcycle() {
    }
    void main() {
        Motorcycle myBike;
        myBike.setNumberOfWheels()
        cout << "My vehicle has "
            << myBike.getNumberOfWheels();
    }
```

3. Add a statement to the main() function in Exercise 2 so that the base class version of the overridden setNumberOfWheels() function is called in addition to the derived class version.

4. Modify the following derived Residential class constructor so that the parameterized base class constructor executes instead of the default base class constructor.

```
    // RealEstate class parameterized constructor
    RealEstate::RealEstate(char* szName) {
        szCustomerName = new char[50];
        strcpy(szCustomerName, szName);
    }
    Residential::Residential() {
    }
```

5. The main() method in the following code creates a Residential object by copying an existing object. Write a derived copy constructor for the Residential class that calls the RealEstate base class copy constructor.

```
    #include "Residential.h"
    void main() {
        Residential curCustomer("Mike McGillicudy");
        Residential nextCustomer(curCustomer);
        curCustomer.setCustomerName("Susan Osakawa");
    }
```

6. Explain the difference between function overriding and function overloading.

7. Describe when you would need to declare functions and destructors as virtual.

8. Modify the following code so that the overridden setSound() function executes correctly with the statements in the main() method and so that both the base class destructor and the derived class destructor are called.

```
// Instruments.h
class Instruments {
public:
     Instruments();
     ~Instruments();
     void setSound(char*);
     char* getSound();
protected:
     char* szSound;
}
// Instruments.cpp
#include "Instruments.h"
#include "string.h"
#include<iostream.h>
Instruments::Instruments() {
     szSound = new char[25];
}
Instruments::~Instruments() {
     cout << "Everything is " << getSound() << endl;
}
void Instruments::setSound(char* szSound) {
     szSound = "quiet";
}
char* getSound() {
     return szSound;
}
// Percussion.h
#include "Instruments.h"
class Percussion : public Instruments {
public:
     Percussion();
     ~Percussion();
     void setSound(char*);
private:
}
// Percussion.cpp
#include "Percussion.h"
#include "iostream.h"
Percussion::Percussion() {
}
Percussion::~Percussion() {
     cout << "I repeat, the drum goes "
          << getSound() << endl;
}
```

```
void Percussion::setSound(char* szSound) {
    szSound = "boom";
}
void main() {
    Instruments* drums = new Percussion;
    drums->setSound();
    cout << "The drum goes " << drums getSound() << endl;
}
```

9. Modify the code in the Exercise 8 so that the Instruments class is abstract.

10. Describe why you would create an abstract base class.

11. Create a console application project that is based on the class hierarchy of a publishing company. Publishing companies are separated into divisions that publish different types of books such as fiction, nonfiction, business, self-help, and so on. Create an abstract base class from which several book division classes derive. Include pure virtual functions that need to be implemented by all of the divisions, such as author's name and book title. Also, use a parameterized base class constructor for the customer name. Assume that the program will be part of an ordering system that customers can use to place orders. Because you do not know in advance what type of book a customer wants, use a Publishing class pointer to point to a derived class object. Each division's destructor should print a message thanking the customer for visiting the division. Finally, the Publishing class destructor should print a message thanking the customer for his or her order.

12. Create a console application that uses a four-class hierarchy of a hospital emergency room. The Emergency base class should represent the emergency room, the first derived class represents the Stable unit, the next derived class represents the Serious unit, and the last derived class represents the Critical unit. The base class should be an abstract class with a parameterized base class function that stores the patient's name. The pure virtual function for the abstract base class should be used to track a patient's condition. Be sure that all three levels of the emergency room record the patient's current condition in a string variable named szCondition. In the program's main() function, use an Emergency class pointer object to point to objects of the three derived classes. The three pointer objects you create should represent three patients checking into the emergency room. You will essentially "plot" the admission and discharge of the three patients. The constructor for each class should print text describing the unit to which the patient is being moved. For example, the constructor for the Serious unit should print *The patient is being upgraded to serious condition*. Also, the destructor for each class should print text describing the patient's downgraded condition. For example, the destructor for the Serious unit should print *The patient is being downgraded to stable condition*. The last destructor for the Emergency class itself should print *The patient has been discharged*. Note that it is actually poor programming practice to use output statements in constructors and destructors. Output statements are used here, however, in order for you to better understand the execution sequence of constructors and destructors.

7

INTRODUCTION TO WINDOWS PROGRAMMING

In this chapter you will learn:

♦ About Windows programming with Visual C++

♦ About Windows architecture

♦ About the Windows API

♦ How to create a WinMain() function

♦ About events and messages

PREVIEW: INTRODUCTION TO WINDOWS PROGRAMMING

The next steps toward mastering Visual C++ programming are to understand the basics of Windows programming. Creating a Windows program is quite a bit different from creating console applications, because you need to write code that your application can use to communicate with the Windows operating system itself. In order to write a Windows application, you need to understand the basics of Windows architecture and how to work with the Windows API, which your program uses to communicate with the Windows operating system. Additionally, you will need to know how to work with events and messages, which Windows uses to inform your application that it needs to perform some sort of task. To help you understand the basics of Windows programming, in this chapter you will create a Windows calculator program that performs basic arithmetic calculations.

To preview the calculator program:

1. Create a **Chapter.07** folder in your Visual C++ Projects folder.

2. Copy the **Chapter7_Calculator** folder from the Chapter.07 folder on your Data Disk to the Chapter.07 folder in your Visual C++ Projects folder. Then open the **Chapter7_Calculator** project in Visual C++. If the Tip of the Day dialog box displays, click the **Close** button.

3. Open the **Chapter7_Calculator.cpp** file in the Text Editor window and examine the code. You will notice that the code looks quite a bit different from the C++ programs you have created so far. There are several new data types, which you have not learned about yet, and there is no main() function, as you would find in a console application. Instead, there is a WinMain() function, which is the entry point for all Windows applications. In Windows programming, the WinMain() function is used primarily for setting up and displaying new windows. Much of a program's functionality actually executes in a special function called the window procedure. At the end of the WinMain() function is a special **while** loop that is used for handling the application's events and messages. Scroll to the end of the file to see the calculator program's window procedure, which is a function named MainWndProc(). Figure 7-1 shows portions of the Chapter7_Calculator.cpp file.

```
#include <windows.h>
#include <string.h>
long WINAPI MainWndProc(HWND, UINT, WPARAM, LPARAM);
...
HWND hWnd;                                              ──── new data types
HWND hwndEdit;
HWND hwndButtonPlus;
HWND hwndButtonMinus;
HWND hwndButtonMultiply;
HWND hwndButtonDivide;
HWND hwndButton9;
...
int WINAPI WinMain(HINSTANCE hInstance,                 ──── WinMain() function
     HINSTANCE hPrevInstance,
     LPSTR lpCmdLine, int nCmdShow) {
     WNDCLASS wc;
     wc.lpszClassName = "CalculatorClass";
     wc.lpfnWndProc = MainWndProc;
     wc.style = CS_OWNDC | CS_VREDRAW | CS_HREDRAW;
     wc.hInstance = hInstance;
     wc.hIcon = LoadIcon( NULL, IDI_APPLICATION );
     wc.hCursor = LoadCursor ( NULL, IDC_ARROW );
     wc.hbrBackground = (HBRUSH) ( COLOR_WINDOW+1 );
     wc.lpszMenuName = "";
     wc.cbClsExtra = 0;
     wc.cbWndExtra = 0;
     RegisterClass ( &wc );
```

Figure 7-1   Chapter7_Calculator.cpp

```
    MSG msg;
    while(GetMessage(&msg, NULL, 0, 0)) {          while loop for processing
          TranslateMessage(&msg);                  events
          DispatchMessage(&msg);
    }
          return msg.wParam;
}
long WINAPI MainWndProc(HWND hWnd, UINT msg,       window procedure
    WPARAM wParam, LPARAM lParam) {
    HWND hwndCtl = (HWND) lParam;
    switch (msg) {
          case WM_COMMAND:
              switch (wParam) {
```

Figure 7-1   Chapter7_Calculator.cpp (continued)

4. Build and execute the Calculator program, and then test the calculations. Figure 7-2 shows the calculator window that the program generates. The window is similar to other types of windows you will find in the Windows operating system environment.

Figure 7-2   The calculator program

5. Click the Close button to close the Calculator program window.

WINDOWS PROGRAMMING WITH VISUAL C++

At this point in the text, you begin to move into the creation of Windows programs that use a graphical user interface instead of the command-line interfaces found in console applications. The ability to create Windows programs is one of the most important aspects of the Visual C++ environment. Of course, there are plenty of reasons why you may need to create command-line interfaces with console applications, but creating Windows programs is what Visual C++ is really all about.

There are two ways to create Windows programs in Visual C++: with C or C++ and the Windows application programming interface, or with C++ and the Microsoft Foundation Class. This chapter discusses how to create Windows programs with C or C++ and the Windows application programming interface. An **application programming interface**, or **API**, is a library of methods and code that allows programmers to access the features and functionality of an application or operating system. The **Windows API** allows you to write programs for Windows operating systems. The Windows API is the foundation for creating all Windows programs using *any* type of programming language, such as Visual Basic, Fortran, Pascal, as well as C or C++. The Windows API is really a very large collection of code written in the C programming language. Windows operating systems themselves are actually written mostly in the C programming language. You create Windows programs by combining code written in a source programming language with calls to the Windows API. Figure 7-3 illustrates this concept.

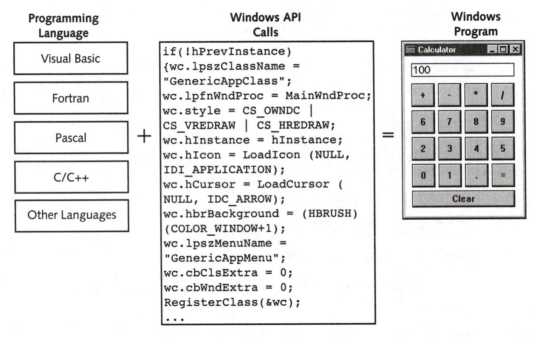

Programming Language		Windows API Calls		Windows Program
Visual Basic				
Fortran				
| Pascal | + | ```
if(!hPrevInstance)
{wc.lpszClassName =
"GenericAppClass";
wc.lpfnWndProc = MainWndProc;
wc.style = CS_OWNDC |
CS_VREDRAW | CS_HREDRAW;
wc.hInstance = hInstance;
wc.hIcon = LoadIcon (NULL,
IDI_APPLICATION);
wc.hCursor = LoadCursor (
NULL, IDC_ARROW);
wc.hbrBackground = (HBRUSH)
(COLOR_WINDOW+1);
wc.lpszMenuName =
"GenericAppMenu";
wc.cbClsExtra = 0;
wc.cbWndExtra = 0;
RegisterClass(&wc);
...
``` | = | |
| C/C++ | | | | |
| Other Languages | | | | |

Figure 7-3 Building a Windows program

Mastering Windows API programming involves a steep learning curve. Not only must you thoroughly understand C programming, but you must also learn how to choose from the literally thousands of functions (as well as other types of code elements, such as constants) that make up the Windows API. Some experts on the subject claim that true mastery over the Windows API requires a year or more of study. Don't be alarmed, however. In this chapter, you will learn only the basics you need to get started. Even though you are studying only the basics, keep in mind that mastery over the Windows API will significantly improve your
```

ability to create professional quality Windows programs. Additionally, the more you know about Windows API programming, the better you will be at working with Microsoft Foundation classes since they are based on the Windows API.

Although you can create Windows programs using C/C++ and the Windows API, with Visual C++ the preferred method of creating Windows programs is to use C++ with the Microsoft Foundation Class. The Microsoft Foundation Class assists C++ programmers in writing Windows programs by hiding much of the underlying details of the C code that makes up the Windows API. The Microsoft Foundation Class also organizes Windows API code so that it can be accessed using object-oriented programming techniques. You will learn about and work with object-oriented programming in the next chapter and throughout the remainder of this text.

This is the only chapter in which you will directly create Windows applications using C/C++ and the Windows API. If the Microsoft Foundation Class makes the task of writing Windows programs with Visual C++ much easier, why bother to spend time learning how to create Windows API applications? The answer is because Microsoft Foundation Class programming is built on Windows API programming. In this chapter you will learn key Windows programming concepts that are vital to your success working with Microsoft Foundation Class programming. This chapter presents fundamental information on how Windows programs are designed, and this information will help you when you tackle the Microsoft Foundation Class and throughout your programming career.

You should already be more than familiar with the graphical user interface of Windows environments. A **graphical user interface**, or GUI (pronounced "gooey"), is a graphically based environment that you use to interact with applications. Some components that are common to most GUI environments include menus, icons to represent files and applications, a desktop, and the ability to interact with the environment using a mouse. In a nutshell, Windows programs do not run in console windows, but exist as separate floating windows in the Windows environment. Windows programs include minimize, maximize, and close buttons, along with title bars containing descriptive text. Many Windows programs also include menu bars, toolbars, scroll bars, and other elements, and they are often resizable. The types of Windows programs can range from the simple calculator program you will create in this chapter to large applications such as Visual C++. To help you clearly understand what a Windows program is, you will now create and examine a simple Windows API program that displays the text *Hello World*. You will not actually write the code that creates the program. Instead, you will allow Visual C++ to create the code for you.

To create a simple Windows API program that displays the text *Hello World*:

1. Return to Visual C++.

2. Select **New** from the **File** menu or press **Ctrl+N** to display the New dialog box, and then click the **Projects** tab.

3. In the Projects tab, click **Win32 Application**.

4. Type **HelloWorld** in the Project name box. In the Location box, type **c:\Visual C++ Projects\Chapter.07\HelloWorld**, substituting c: with the drive where your Visual C++ Projects folder is stored.

5. Click the **OK** button. The Win32 Application dialog box appears asking what type of windows application you would like to create, as shown in Figure 7-4.

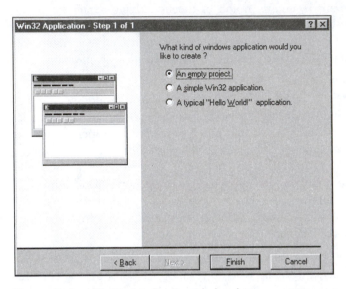

Figure 7-4   Win32 Application dialog box

6. In the Win32 dialog box, select **A typical "Hello World" application**, and click the **Finish** button. The New Project Information dialog box appears and lists the specifications for your new project.

7. In the New Project Information dialog box, click the **OK** button. The new project opens in the IDE.

8. Open the **HelloWorld.cpp** file in the Text Editor and examine the code. The program contains various Windows data types, a WinMain() function, and a window procedure, similar to the calculator program you saw in the preview.

9. Next, build the program by selecting **Build HelloWorld.exe** from the **Build** menu, and then run the program by selecting **Execute HelloWorld.exe** from the **Build** menu. Figure 7-5 shows how the application window should appear. The figure also identifies standard Windows elements.

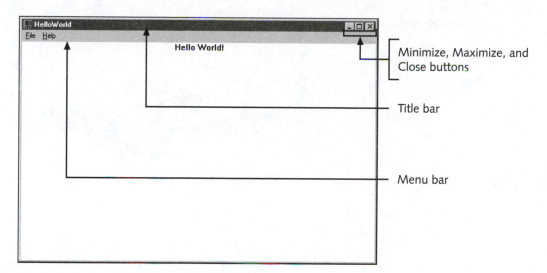

Figure 7-5   HelloWorld.exe application window

10. Close the **HelloWorld.exe** application window by selecting **Exit** from the **File** menu or by clicking the **Close** button in the title bar.

WINDOWS ARCHITECTURE

Before getting into the specifics of how Windows API programs are constructed, it helps to understand the basics of Windows architecture. You have probably heard the term "bit" many times, as in 16-bit, 32-bit, and so on. The term **bit** refers to a binary number of 0 or 1. (Recall from Chapter 1, that machine languages are written entirely in 0s and 1s.) Computers are classified according to how many bits can be transmitted simultaneously into the microprocessor, or CPU. The **bus**, or **data bus**, refers to the electronic path that the bits travel into the microprocessor. You can think of the data bus as the number of roads leading into a microprocessor. The wider the data bus, the more information (bits) can be sent simultaneously to the microprocessor, and the faster a program runs. The actual speed with which information is processed also depends on several other factors, including the microprocessor architecture (80386, i486, Pentium, and so on) and the megahertz at which the microprocessor operates. The 80386 and i486 microprocessors have 32-bit wide data buses, whereas the Pentium family of microprocessors has 64-bit wide data buses. Figure 7-6 illustrates bits being transmitted along the data bus into a microprocessor.

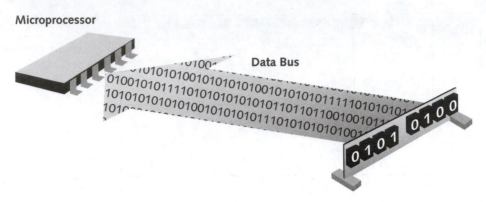

Figure 7-6   A data bus

There are Windows operating systems specifically designed to work with each width of data bus: 16-bit, 32-bit, and 64-bit. The older (and essentially obsolete) Windows 3.1 operates at 16 bits. Windows NT, Windows 95, Windows 98, and Windows CE are 32-bit operating systems. At the time of this writing, Windows 2000 is the only 64-bit Windows operating system. The number of bits in a data bus that an operating system can access simultaneously depends on the operating system or application that is accessing the microprocessor. Windows 3.1 can operate on 80386, i486, and Pentium microprocessors, but can use only 16 bits of each data bus, even though the 80386 and i486 microprocessors are 32-bits wide and the Pentium microprocessor is 64-bits wide. Similarly, Windows NT can operate on 64-bit Pentium computers, but can take advantage of only 32 bits of the data bus. Windows 2000, however, can take advantage of all 64 bits of a Pentium microprocessor, making it run faster than 16-bit and 32-bit Windows operating systems.

A separate Windows API exists for each generation of Windows operating systems. The Windows API for Windows 3.1 was originally called the Win API, but is now usually referred to as the Win16 API to avoid confusion with later versions of the Windows API.

All 32-bit Windows operating systems share the same Windows API, known as the Win32 API. Because Windows NT, Windows 95, Windows 98, and Windows CE share the same Windows API, you can write one application using the Win32 API that can run on all three versions of the operating system. There are some exceptions to this rule in that functionality unique to one operating system is not necessarily available to another operating system. For example, Windows NT contains advanced network security features that are not available on other 32-bit Windows platforms. However, with the exception of operating system-specific features such as Windows NT security, you can be assured that Win32 applications will run successfully on all Win32 operating systems.

One of the problems with the different generations of Windows operating systems is that applications written specifically for one generation will not usually work with earlier Windows operating systems. For example, if you write a true 32-bit Windows application, then that application will not run on the 16-bit Windows 3.1 operating system. A major goal in the development of Windows 2000 was that applications written for 64-bit Windows operating systems would also be able to run on 32-bit Windows operating systems. To accomplish this goal, Microsoft made the Win64 API almost identical to the Win32 API, but with some important changes to data types that allow 64-bit applications to run on 32-bit Windows operating systems. Because of the similarities between the two APIs, this text uses the term *Windows API* to refer to both the Win32 and Win64 APIs.

THE WINDOWS API

A C++ program can access the Windows API by importing the `windows.h` header file, which is included as part of the Visual Studio development environment. The `windows.h` header file includes all of the functions, variables, and other programming elements that make up the Windows API. You import the `windows.h` header file into your program using the `#include` statement, just as you would any other header file.

The `windows.h` header file is also included as part of the Microsoft Platform Software Development Kit (SDK), or Platform SDK. The Platform SDK contains header files, sample code, tools, and information for building applications using the Windows API. The Platform SDK was previously known as the Win32 SDK. However, to allow developers to create one set of code that runs on both Win32 and Win64 platforms, the Win32 SDK was redesigned to support both the older Win32 platform and the current Win64 platform. It was then renamed to the Platform SDK. You can download the Platform SDK from http://msdn.microsoft.com/downloads.

If you would like to learn more about Windows API programming, the Platform SDK is the best place to start. You can also find extensive information on Windows API programming in the MSDN Library.

The Windows API defines its own data types in the `windows.h` header file. You can identify Windows data types by their uppercase letters. For example, the char data type definition in the Windows API is written as CHAR. Some of the Windows API data types, such as CHAR, INT, and BOOL, are identical to their C or C++ language counterparts. Many other Windows API data types have no equivalents in C or C++. You will not see the Windows API data types listed here since there are literally hundreds of them. The Windows API data types used in this chapter will be explained as you encounter them. If you would like to see a list of all the Windows API data types, you can find them in the MSDN Library.

The Windows API includes hundreds of data types so that it can control the information passed to it from source programming languages (such as C, C++, Visual Basic, and so on), and correctly execute a program according to different types of computers. One category of Windows API data types you will use in this chapter are pointer data types. Unlike C and C++, the Windows API includes data types that are used only to declare pointers. A **pointer data type** declares the type and name of a Windows API pointer. In comparison, you declare C and C++ pointers using standard variable data types, such as int and char. Most Windows API pointer data types begin with a prefix of *P* or *LP* (*P* stands for *Pointer* and *LP* stands for *Long Pointer*).

Another category of Windows API data types you will use in this chapter are handle data types. A **handle** is used to access an object that has been loaded into memory. A handle is essentially the same thing as a C++ pointer. Windows API programming, however, uses the term *handles* instead of *pointers* since you typically use a handle to control and manipulate a window (in other words, you use a handle to "handle a window"). Handle data types begin with a prefix of *H*. You already understand that all Windows applications are contained within their own window. An important concept to grasp, however, as you start creating Windows API programs is that all individual controls (such as buttons) and user interface components are also windows, each requiring its own handle. For example, the buttons and edit box in the calculator program you saw in the preview are all considered to be their own windows. Each of these components is a child window within the parent window of the calculator program. A **child window** always appears within the area defined by a parent window. A **parent window** is a primary application window containing one or more child windows. Figure 7-7 uses the calculator program to illustrate the concept of parent and child windows.

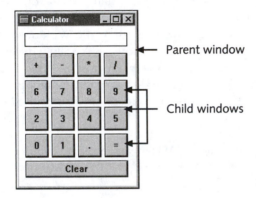

Figure 7-7   Parent and child windows

Next, you will start creating the calculator program by creating a new project and importing the `windows.h` header file.

To start creating the calculator program:

1. Create a new empty Win32 Application project named **Calculator**. Save the project in the **Chapter.07** folder in your Visual C++ Projects folders. Once the project is created, add a C++ source file named **Calculator**.

2. Type the processing directive that gives the program access to the windows.h header file: `#include <windows.h>`.

3. Save the **Calculator.cpp** file by selecting **Save** from the **File** menu. We will return to the Calculator.cpp file later.

THE WINMAIN() FUNCTION

Just as the main() function is the starting point for any C++ program, the **WinMain() function** is the starting point for any Windows API program. The syntax for the WinMain() function definition is as follows:

```
int WINAPI WinMain( HINSTANCE hInstance,
                    HINSTANCE hPrevInstance,
                    LPSTR lpCmdLine,
                    int nCmdShow ) {
    statements;
}
```

The parameters in the preceding WinMain() function definition are written on separate lines for clarity.

The WinMain() function declaration must be declared with type int. The WINAPI portion of the function declaration is a Windows API data type that is required in all Windows API functions. Each of the WinMain() function's four parameters is declared using Windows API data types. The first and second parameters are of the HINSTANCE data type, which represents a handle to a window instance. An **instance** is a particular copy of a window, program, or other type of object that happens to be running. You can execute most Windows programs multiple times and have several copies of the same program running simultaneously. Each of these copies is considered to be an instance of the program. Figure 7-8 demonstrates the concept of instances by showing multiple running copies of the game Minesweeper (which is installed with most versions of Windows). Each copy of Minesweeper is an instance of the application.

The first HINSTANCE parameter, named hInstance, is the handle that represents the current instance of the program's parent window. The second HINSTANCE parameter, named hPrevInstance, represents a previously created instance of the program. The hPrevInstance parameter is left over from 16-bit Windows 3.1, when a program needed to be aware of other instances of itself in order to avoid memory conflicts and other system problems. 32-bit and 64-bit Windows operating systems do not have the same memory conflicts as Windows 3.1 and therefore do not use the hPrevInstance parameter.

The third parameter, named lpCmdLine, is of the LPSTR data type, which is a pointer to a string. The lpCmdLine parameter points to the command line string that executes the program. For example, if you execute the calculator program from a directory named MyProjects on your C: drive, then the lpCmdLine parameter will contain the string **c:\MyProjects\calculator.exe**. The lpCmdLine parameter is often used for gathering additional pieces of information entered at the command line or that might be part of a Windows shortcut. For example, a Windows program may require the user to enter a password at the command line. For these types of programs, you can extract the password from the lpCmdLine parameter for validation purposes.

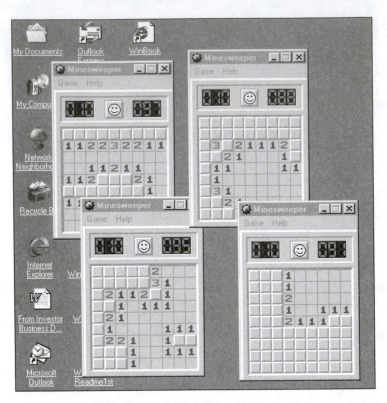

Figure 7-8 Multiple instances of Minesweeper

The last parameter, named nCmdShow, is of the int data type. The nCmdShow parameter returns a constant representing the window's startup mode (minimized, maximized, and so on). Window constants begin with the prefix SW_, followed by a description of the window mode. For example, SW_NORMAL indicates the window is to open normally, and SW_MAXIMIZE indicates that the window is to open maximized. Typically, the window constant is passed by the operating system from a selection made in a Windows shortcut. Your program then checks the value and determines how to display the program's window.

The names assigned to each of the WinMain() function's parameters are arbitrary. You can use any name you like, provided you follow the standard C++ rules for naming identifiers. Many Windows API programmers, however, routinely use the names hInstance, hPrevInstance, lpCmdLine, and nCmdShow to identify these parameters.

Next, you will add a WinMain() function definition to the calculator program.

To add a WinMain() function definition to the calculator program:

1. Open the **Calculator** project in Visual C++. If necessary, open the **Calculator.cpp** file in the Text Editor window.

2. After the processing directive, add the following WinMain() function.

```
int WINAPI WinMain(HINSTANCE hInstance, HINSTANCE hPrevInstance,
    LPSTR lpCmdLine, int nCmdShow) {
}
```

One of the most important tasks performed by the WinMain() function (other than being an entry point for all Windows applications) is the creation and instantiation of windows. The steps involved in creating and instantiating windows are as follows:

1. Define the window class by creating an object of the WNDCLASS structure, and notify Windows of the new class using the RegisterClass() method

2. Create the program's main (parent) window, along with any child windows, using the CreateWindow() method

3. Display the program using the ShowWindow() method

You will now examine each of these steps in detail.

Defining the Window Class

To create and display a window, you must first define and register its window class. The **window class** defines the characteristics of a program's main window. Some examples of characteristics include the style of window and what type of icon will be used to represent the window. Do not confuse the term *window class* with the C++ *classes* you learned about in previous chapters. A window class refers only to the information used to create a window. The classes you learned about in the previous chapters are a separate topic that are the basis of object-oriented programming.

The predefined **WNDCLASS structure** is used for defining the characteristics of a window class. The following code shows the WNDCLASS structure definition. Notice that all but two of the fields are of Windows API data types. You will not actually see the WNDCLASS structure definition in your program since it is already defined in the **windows.h** header file. However, you will instantiate an object based on the WNDCLASS structure.

```
struct _WNDCLASS {
    UINT     style;
    WNDPROC  lpfnWndProc;
    int      cbClsExtra;
    int      cbWndExtra;
    HANDLE   hInstance;
    HICON    hIcon;
    HCURSOR  hCursor;
    HBRUSH   hbrBackground;
    LPCTSTR  lpszMenuName;
    LPCTSTR  lpszClassName;
};
```

Each of the fields in the WNDCLASS structure determines various characteristics of a window. Figure 7-9 lists the WNDCLASS structure fields with a description of what the field controls.

Field	Description
style	The window class style
lpfnWndProc	Pointer to the window procedure
cbClsExtra	The number of extra bytes to allocate following the window class structure
cbWndExtra	The number of extra bytes to allocate following the window class instance
hInstance	The handle to the instance containing the window procedure (lpfnWndProc) for the window class
hIcon	A handle to the icon resource, which displays whenever the program is minimized
hCursor	A handle to a cursor resource
hbrBackground	A handle to the class background brush
lpszMenuName	A pointer to a null-terminated string containing the menu resource for the window class
lpszClassName	A pointer to a null-terminated string representing the window class name

Figure 7-9   WNDCLASS structure fields

Most of the WNDCLASS structure's fields are fairly advanced—too advanced for your brief study of Windows API programming in this chapter. Therefore, this text will not go into depth on most of them. The appropriate values for each field will be listed for you in the examples and exercises you encounter in this chapter.

You do need to understand two fields: the hInstance and the lpfnWndProc fields. The hInstance field contains the handle to the current program, so you assign to the hInstance field the hInstance argument of the WinMain() class. You will use a statement similar to `wc.hInstance = hInstance`, which may be a little bit confusing. Just remember that you are assigning the value of the hInstance *argument* to the hInstance *field*.

The lpfnWndProc field contains a pointer to the name of a special function known as the window procedure that will handle messages. For now, you will assign the value *MainWndProc* to the lpfnWndProc field. You will learn about messages and create the window procedure later in this chapter. Note that although the value *MainWndProc* represents the name of a function, you do not include the function's parentheses when assigning the value to the field.

If you would like more information on the fields in the WNDCLASS structure, search for the WNDCLASS topic in the MSDN Library.

The following code shows how to declare a new variable named wc, based on the WNDCLASS structure. Again, do not worry about understanding the values assigned to the fields, except for the lpfnWndProc and hInstance fields. The lpfnWndProc field is assigned the function named MainWndProc, and the hInstance field is assigned the hInstance parameter of the WinMain() function. The hInstance parameter in the WinMain() function declaration and the statements that assign values to the lpfnWndProc and hInstance fields in the body of the function are bolded so that you can quickly locate them.

```
int WINAPI WinMain(HINSTANCE hInstance, HINSTANCE hPrevInstance,
    LPSTR lpCmdLine, int nCmdShow) {
    WNDCLASS wc;
    wc.style = CS_HREDRAW | CS_VREDRAW;
    wc.lpfnWndProc = MainWndProc;
    wc.cbClsExtra   = 0;
    wc.cbWndExtra = 0;
    wc.hInstance = hInstance;
    wc.hIcon = LoadIcon(hInstance, (LPCTSTR)IDI_EXAMPLE);
    wc.hCursor = LoadCursor(NULL, IDC_ARROW);
    wc.hbrBackground = (HBRUSH)(COLOR_WINDOW+1);
    wc.lpszMenuName = (LPCSTR)IDC_EXAMPLE;
    wc.lpszClassName = "szWindowClass";
    wc.hIconSm = LoadIcon(wcex.hInstance, (LPCTSTR)IDI_SMALL);
}
```

Next, you will define the calculator program's window class.

To define the calculator program's window class:

1. Return to the Calculator.cpp file in the Text Editor window.

2. Insert a new line above the WinMain() function's closing brace, and type **WNDCLASS wc;** to declare a variable named wc, based on the WNDCLASS structure.

3. Press **Enter** and type the following statements to assign values to the window class fields:

```
wc.lpszClassName = "CalculatorClass";
wc.lpfnWndProc = MainWndProc;
wc.style = CS_OWNDC | CS_VREDRAW | CS_HREDRAW;
wc.hInstance = hInstance;
```

```
wc.hIcon = LoadIcon( NULL, IDI_APPLICATION );
wc.hCursor = LoadCursor( NULL, IDC_ARROW );
wc.hbrBackground = (HBRUSH)( COLOR_WINDOW+1 );
wc.lpszMenuName = "";
wc.cbClsExtra = 0;
wc.cbWndExtra = 0;
```

Once you have defined the WNDCLASS structure, you need to use the **RegisterClass() function**, which informs the operating system about the newly-defined window class. The RegisterClass() function accepts a single variable consisting of the address of the WNDCLASS structure you defined. For example, the statement `RegisterClass(&wc);` registers the wc object from the preceding example by using the address operator (&) to pass its address to the operating system.

Next, you will register the calculator program's window class.

To register the calculator program's window class:

1. Insert a new line above the WinMain() function's closing brace, and type `RegisterClass(&wc);` to register the wc window class.

Creating New Windows

The WNDCLASS structure and RegisterClass() function only define the characteristics of a window; they do not actually create and display the window. After declaring a WNDCLASS structure and calling the RegisterClass() function, you must call the CreateWindow() function to create a new window based on the window class. The **CreateWindow() function** creates a new window based on several parameters including window class, size, position, and style. The value returned from the CreateWindow() function is a handle to the newly created window, which you assign to a variable of the HWND data type. You can then use the handle to refer to and control the window. The following code shows the CreateWindow() function syntax. The data types for each parameter are shown in comments.

```
handle = CreateWindow(
    lpClassName,     // LPCTSTR
    lpWindowName,    // LPCTSTR
    dwStyle,         // DWORD
    x,               // int
    y,               // int
    nWidth,          // int
    nHeight,         // int
    hWndParent,      // HWND
    hMenu,           // HMENU
    hInstance,       // HINSTANCE
    lpParam          // LPVOID
    );
```

All windows must be created using their own CreateWindow() functions. For example, in the calculator program, you must create the main program window with a CreateWindow() function, and then use separate CreateWindow() functions for each of the program's controls.

To understand how to use the CreateWindow() function, you need to understand each of the function's parameters. Note that not all of the parameters are required. When parameters are not required, you use a value NULL as a placeholder to maintain the CreateWindow() function's parameter order. As with other Windows API code in this chapter, do not expect to become an expert based on the examples included here; remember there is a steep learning curve to the Windows API. Your goal here is trying to develop a general understanding of how the CreateWindow() function operates.

lpClassName

The **lpClassName parameter** is a pointer to a text string representing the name of the class upon which you want to base the new window. You can assign to the lpClassName parameter either the name of the window class you created with the WNDCLASS structure and RegisterClass() function, or a predefined control class. **Predefined control classes** represent standard types of window controls such as buttons, edit boxes, and scroll bars. You will use several predefined control classes in the calculator program. Figure 7-10 lists the predefined control classes that can be assigned to the lpClassName parameter.

Name	Description
BUTTON	A command button such as an OK or Cancel button
COMBOBOX	An edit box (text box) that also contains a list of selectable choices
EDIT	A single line text box
LISTBOX	A list of selectable choices
MDICLIENT	A Multiple Document Interface (MDI) client window. You will learn about MDI programs in later chapters.
RichEdit	A Rich Edit version 1.0 control that allows users to enter and edit text with character and paragraph formatting
RICHEDIT_CLASS	A Rich Edit version 2.0 control that allows users to enter and edit text with character and paragraph formatting
SCROLLBAR	Scroll bars that are used for navigating within a parent window
STATIC	A static text label used for providing information or describing parts of a parent window

Figure 7-10   Predefined control classes

lpWindowName

The **lpWindowName parameter** is a pointer to a text string containing a name for the window. If the window being created contains a title bar, then the value pointed to by the lpWindowName parameter is used as the title bar text. If the window is a control such as a button or a check box, the lpWindowName parameter specifies the text of the control. For example, if you pass the text *Click Me* to the lpWindowName parameter for a button, then *Click Me* appears as the text on the button's face.

dwStyle

The **dwStyle parameter** determines the specific window styles that will be applied to the new window. Figure 7-11 lists the values that can be passed to the dwStyle parameter. Note that you can quickly identify window styles because they are prefixed with WS_.

Style	Description
WS_BORDER	Window includes a thin-line border
WS_CAPTION	Window includes a title bar
WS_CHILD or WS_CHILDWINDOW	Creates a child window
WS_CLIPCHILDREN	When drawing occurs within the parent window, the areas occupied by child windows are excluded
WS_CLIPSIBLINGS	When drawing occurs within a child window, any overlapping areas of other child windows are excluded
WS_DISABLED	Window is initially disabled
WS_DLGFRAME	Window includes a border style similar to a dialog box window
WS_GROUP	Determines the first control within a group of controls
WS_HSCROLL	Window includes a horizontal scroll bar
WS_MAXIMIZE	Window is initially maximized
WS_MAXIMIZEBOX	Window includes a maximize box
WS_MINIMIZE	Window is initially minimized
WS_MINIMIZEBOX	Window includes a minimize box
WS_OVERLAPPED or WS_TILED	Creates an overlapped window, which includes a title and a border
WS_OVERLAPPEDWINDOW or WS_TILEDWINDOW	Creates an overlapped window with the WS_OVERLAPPED, WS_CAPTION, WS_SYSMENU, WS_THICKFRAME, WS_MINIMIZEBOX, and WS_MAXIMIZE BOX styles
WS_POPUP	Creates a pop-up window
WS_POPUPWINDOW	Creates a pop-up window with WS_BORDER, WS_POPUP, and WS_SYSMENU styles
WS_SIZEBOX or WS_THICKFRAME	Window includes a sizeable border
WS_SYSMENU	Window includes a window menu in the title bar
WS_TABSTOP	The control can receive keyboard focus when the user presses the Tab key
WS_VISIBLE	Window is initially visible
WS_VSCROLL	Window includes a vertical scroll bar

Figure 7-11 Window styles

You can pass multiple window styles to the dwStyle property by separating them with a pipe |. For example, to create a window that includes both minimize and maximize boxes, you pass both values to the dwStyle parameter using the format: `WS_MINIMIZEBOX | WS_MAXIMIZEBOX`.

x, y, nWidth, and nHeight

The **x** and **y** parameters represent the starting position of a window's upper-left corner. The **nWidth** and **nHeight** parameters represent the window's lower-right corner. When the nWidth and nHeight parameters are based on the starting positions of the x and y parameters, all four parameters together determine the window's size. Note that for parent windows, the x, y, nWidth, and nHeight positions are measured from the upper-left corner of your monitor. For child windows, the four parameters are measured from the upper-left corner of the parent window.

A window's position and size are measured in pixels. Remember, a **pixel** (short for **pic**ture **el**ement) represents a single point on a computer screen. The number of pixels available depends on a computer monitor's resolution— 640 columns by 480 rows of pixels on a VGA monitor, and 1,024 columns by 768 rows of pixels on a Super VGA monitor. You reference a window's pixels with x-axis and y-axis coordinates, beginning in the upper-left corner of the screen at an x-axis position of 0 and a y-axis position of 0. Pixel measurements are usually written in the format x, y, which means that the starting point in the upper-left corner of the screen is written as position 0, 0. As you move right from the upper-left corner of the screen along the x-axis, or down along the y-axis, the pixel measurements increase. Therefore, a pixel position that is 100 pixels to the right along the x-axis and 200 pixels down on the y-axis is written as 100, 200.

Figure 7-12 shows an example of the pixel positions for a simple parent window containing a button, which is a child window. It also shows the pixel positions for the button, relative to the parent window.

You can use the value CW_USEDEFAULT with the x and nWidth parameters. When CW_USEDEFAULT is used with the x parameter, the system sets the window to the default position and ignores the y parameter. When CW_USEDEFAULT is used with the nWidth parameter, the system sets the window to the default size and ignores the nHeight parameter. CW_USEDEFAULT is valid only for overlapped windows. If you use CW_USEDEFAULT with a pop-up or child window's x parameter, both the x and y parameters are set to 0, which sets the window's starting position to the upper-left corner of the screen. Similarly, if you use CW_USEDEFAULT with a pop-up or child window's nWidth parameter, both the nWidth and nHeight parameters are set to 0.

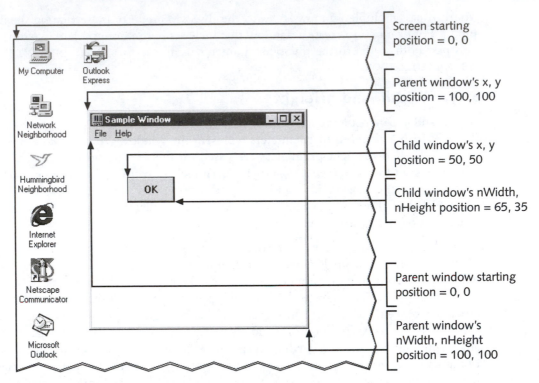

Figure 7-12   Pixel positions

hWndParent

The **hWndParent parameter** specifies a handle to a parent window and tells the system the correct window within which a child window should be created. If the window is a top-level parent window (such as the calculator program's main window), set the hWndParent parameter to NULL. Setting the hWndParent parameter to NULL informs the system that the window is a parent window and should be created directly on the screen instead of within the context of a parent window. For child windows, you set the hWndParent parameter to the handle of the parent window. For example, suppose you have a parent window that you created with its own CreateWindow() function and assigned to a handle named hMainWindow. In the child window's CreateWindow() function, you use hMainWindow for the hWndParent parameter to specify the child window's parent.

hMenu

The **hMenu parameter** specifies a handle to a menu. You will set this value to NULL since you do not need to work with menus in the calculator program.

hInstance

The **hInstance parameter** informs the system in which application instance the window should be created. In most cases, you use the HINSTANCE argument declared in the WinMain() function declaration. For example, if you declared in the WinMain() function declaration an HINSTANCE argument of hMyProgram, then you assign hMyProgram to the hInstance parameter to inform the system that you want the window created in the application designated by the hMyProgram instance handle.

lpParam

The **lpParam parameter** points to either a value passed through the CREATESTRUCT structure or to a CLIENTCREATESTRUCT structure. This is a somewhat advanced parameter that you will not use in the calculator program, so you will set its value to NULL.

The following code shows a complete example of a CreateWindow() function whose return value is assigned to a handle named hSampleWnd. The lpClassName parameter is assigned a class named szWindowClass and the lpWindowName parameter is assigned the text *Sample Window*. The dwStyle parameter is passed a single style, WS_OVERLAPPEDWINDOW. Since the x and hWidth parameters are assigned CW_USEDEFAULT, the y and hHeight parameters are assigned values of NULL. The window being created is a parent window, so hWndParent is assigned a value of NULL instead of the handle to another window. The hMenu parameter is also NULL, because the window will not include a menu. Finally, the hInstance parameter is assigned an application handle named hCurInstance and lpParam is assigned a value of NULL.

```
HWND hSampleWnd;
hSampleWnd = CreateWindow(
        "szWindowClass",
        "Sample Window",
        WS_OVERLAPPEDWINDOW,
        CW_USEDEFAULT,
        NULL,
        CW_USEDEFAULT,
        NULL,
        NULL,
        NULL,
        hCurInstance,
        NULL
        );
```

7

Next, you will create the windows that make up the calculator program, including the main calculator window and the individual controls that make up the calculator program's interface.

To create the windows that make up the calculator program:

1. Above the WinMain() function and after the windows.h processing directive, add the following bolded declarations that create variables based on the HWND data type:

```
#include <windows.h>
HWND hWnd; HWND hwndEdit; HWND hwndButtonPlus;
HWND hwndButtonMinus; HWND hwndButtonMultiply;
HWND hwndButtonDivide; HWND hwndButton9;
HWND hwndButton8; HWND hwndButton7;
HWND hwndButton6; HWND hwndButton5;
HWND hwndButton4; HWND hwndButton3;
HWND hwndButton2; HWND hwndButton1;
HWND hwndButton0; HWND hwndButtonPoint;
HWND hwndButtonEquals; HWND hwndButtonClear;
int WINAPI WinMain(HINSTANCE hInstance, HINSTANCE hPrevInstance,
      LPSTR lpCmdLine, int nCmdShow) {
...
```

2. Insert a new line above the WinMain() function's closing brace, and type the following statement to create the main calculator window and assign it to the hWnd handle. Notice that the lpClassName parameter is assigned a value of CalculatorClass, which is the name you assigned to the window class earlier in the WinMain() function. Also notice that the hWndParent parameter is assigned a value of null since this is the top-level parent window.

```
hWnd = CreateWindow("CalculatorClass", "Calculator",
WS_OVERLAPPEDWINDOW, CW_USEDEFAULT, CW_USEDEFAULT, 185,
265, NULL, NULL, hInstance, NULL);
```

3. Press **Enter** and add the following statement to create the calculator's edit box and assign it to the hwndEdit handle. The lpClassName parameter is assigned the predefined EDIT control class, and the hWndParent parameter is assigned a value of hWnd to identify that window as the edit box's parent window.

```
hwndEdit = CreateWindow("EDIT", NULL, WS_VISIBLE |
WS_CHILD | WS_BORDER | ES_LEFT, 10, 10, 155, 20, hWnd,
NULL, hInstance, NULL);
```

4. Press **Enter** again and add the statements to create the calculator's buttons. Each button is assigned to an appropriately named handle, such as hwndButtonPlus for the plus button. The lpClassName parameters are assigned the predefined BUTTON control class, and the hWndParent parameter is assigned a value of hWnd to identify that window as each button's

parent window. If you prefer not to type all of the code, you can copy it from the Chapter7_Calculator.cpp file in the Chapter7_Calculator folder in the Chapter.07 folder in your Visual C++ Projects folder.

```
hwndButtonPlus = CreateWindow( "BUTTON", "+", WS_VISIBLE |
WS_CHILD | BS_DEFPUSHBUTTON, 10, 40, 35, 35, hWnd, NULL,
hInstance, NULL);
hwndButtonMinus = CreateWindow( "BUTTON", "-", WS_VISIBLE
| WS_CHILD | BS_DEFPUSHBUTTON, 50, 40, 35, 35, hWnd, NULL,
hInstance, NULL);
hwndButtonMultiply = CreateWindow( "BUTTON", "*",
WS_VISIBLE | WS_CHILD | BS_DEFPUSHBUTTON, 90, 40, 35, 35,
hWnd, NULL, hInstance, NULL);
hwndButtonDivide = CreateWindow( "BUTTON", "/", WS_VISIBLE
| WS_CHILD | BS_DEFPUSHBUTTON, 130, 40, 35, 35, hWnd,
NULL, hInstance, NULL);
hwndButton6 = CreateWindow( "BUTTON", "6", WS_VISIBLE |
WS_CHILD | BS_DEFPUSHBUTTON, 10, 80, 35, 35, hWnd, NULL,
hInstance, NULL);
hwndButton7 = CreateWindow( "BUTTON", "7", WS_VISIBLE |
WS_CHILD | BS_DEFPUSHBUTTON, 50, 80, 35, 35, hWnd, NULL,
hInstance, NULL);
hwndButton8 = CreateWindow( "BUTTON", "8", WS_VISIBLE |
WS_CHILD | BS_DEFPUSHBUTTON, 90, 80, 35, 35, hWnd, NULL,
hInstance, NULL);
hwndButton9 = CreateWindow( "BUTTON", "9", WS_VISIBLE |
WS_CHILD | BS_DEFPUSHBUTTON, 130, 80, 35, 35, hWnd, NULL,
hInstance, NULL);
hwndButton2 = CreateWindow( "BUTTON", "2", WS_VISIBLE |
WS_CHILD | BS_DEFPUSHBUTTON, 10, 120, 35, 35, hWnd, NULL,
hInstance, NULL);
hwndButton3 = CreateWindow( "BUTTON", "3", WS_VISIBLE |
WS_CHILD | BS_DEFPUSHBUTTON, 50, 120, 35, 35, hWnd, NULL,
hInstance, NULL);
hwndButton4 = CreateWindow( "BUTTON", "4", WS_VISIBLE |
WS_CHILD | BS_DEFPUSHBUTTON, 90, 120, 35, 35, hWnd, NULL,
hInstance, NULL);
hwndButton5 = CreateWindow( "BUTTON", "5", WS_VISIBLE |
WS_CHILD | BS_DEFPUSHBUTTON, 130, 120, 35, 35, hWnd, NULL,
hInstance, NULL);
hwndButton0 = CreateWindow( "BUTTON", "0", WS_VISIBLE |
WS_CHILD | BS_DEFPUSHBUTTON, 10, 160, 35, 35, hWnd, NULL,
hInstance, NULL);
hwndButton1 = CreateWindow( "BUTTON", "1", WS_VISIBLE |
WS_CHILD | BS_DEFPUSHBUTTON, 50, 160, 35, 35, hWnd, NULL,
hInstance, NULL);
hwndButtonPoint = CreateWindow( "BUTTON", ".", WS_VISIBLE
| WS_CHILD | BS_DEFPUSHBUTTON, 90, 160, 35, 35, hWnd,
NULL, hInstance, NULL);
```

7

```
hwndButtonEquals = CreateWindow( "BUTTON", "=", WS_VISIBLE
| WS_CHILD | BS_DEFPUSHBUTTON, 130, 160, 35, 35, hWnd,
NULL, hInstance, NULL);
hwndButtonClear = CreateWindow( "BUTTON", "Clear",
WS_VISIBLE | WS_CHILD | BS_DEFPUSHBUTTON, 10, 200, 155,
25, hWnd, NULL, hInstance, NULL);
```

Displaying New Windows

The final step in creating a new window is to display it. The CreateWindow() function does not actually display a window; it only creates a new window in memory. The **ShowWindow() function** displays a window onscreen that was created with the CreateWindow() function. The ShowWindow()function accepts two arguments: the handle to a window and the nCmdShow argument that was passed to the WinMain() function. (As you may recall, the nCmdShow argument specifies the startup mode for the window: minimized, maximized, and so on.) For example, to display the window assigned to the hSampleWnd handle, you use the statement `ShowWindow(hSampleWnd, nCmdShow);`. When you first execute a Windows program, you only need to use the ShowWindow() function to display the program's main parent window since child windows are displayed automatically when the parent window is displayed.

Next, you will add a single ShowWindow() function to the calculator program.

To add a ShowWindow() function to the calculator program:

1. Insert a new line above the WinMain() function's closing brace and type `ShowWindow(hWnd, nCmdShow);`. Although the code that creates and displays the calculator program's windows is now complete, you cannot run it just yet. First, you need to learn about events and messages.

EVENTS AND MESSAGES

One of the most powerful aspects of Windows programs is that they are driven by events. An **event** is a specific circumstance that is monitored by Windows. Some of the most common events are actions that users take, such as clicking a button in a Windows application. Other types of events occur behind the scenes and do not involve user interaction. For example, when one window that was obscured by another window becomes visible again, an event occurs that causes Windows to redraw the newly visible portions of the previously obscured window. A common use of events is to add interactivity between your Windows program and its users. The calculator program, for instance, uses button click events to execute the appropriate code segments that give the program its functionality.

When an event occurs, Windows sends a message to the program associated with the event. A **message** is a set of information about a particular event, such as where and when the event occurred. You refer to messages in code using predefined Windows constants beginning with a prefix of WM_ (*WM* stands for Windows Messaging). One of the more commonly used messages is the **WM_COMMAND message**, which is generated for events involving menus and buttons, such as when a user clicks a button. There are literally hundreds of Windows messages. You will be introduced to the messages used in this chapter as necessary. Figure 7-13 illustrates the concept of how Windows generates a message when a user clicks a button in an application.

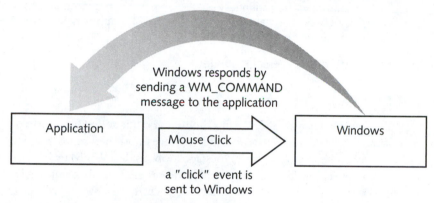

Windows responds by
sending a WM_COMMAND
message to the application

Application

Mouse Click

Windows

a "click" event is
sent to Windows

Figure 7-13   Processing of an event

 You can find a complete listing of Windows messages in the MSDN Library.

Every 32-bit Windows application has its own **message queue** where messages are placed until they are processed by the application. To process a message in an application's message queue, you must perform the following two steps:

1. Write a message loop that retrieves messages from the queue and sends them to the window procedure.

2. Add code to the window procedure code that performs an appropriate action depending on the generated event.

Figure 7-14 illustrates how these two steps work.

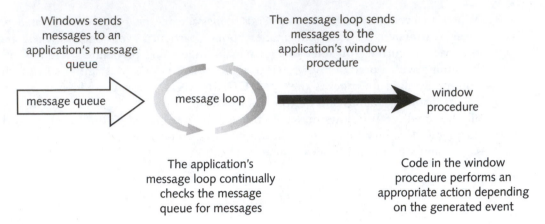

Figure 7-14   Processing of the message queue

Message Loops

Windows applications need a way of checking the message queue for new messages. A **message loop** continually checks the queue for new messages, and then sends any new messages found to the window procedure. You place a message loop inside a WinMain() function so that it starts running (and checking for messages) when the program first executes. Message loops usually use a `while` statement, along with an MSG structure variable and the GetMessage(), TranslateMessage(), and DispatchMessage() Windows API functions. The **MSG structure** contains information about the current message in the application's message queue. The following code is a typical example of a message loop created with a `while` statement that you would place inside a WinMain() function. The first statement in the following code declares a variable of the MSG structure type in order to access the current message information:

```
MSG msg;
while(GetMessage(&msg, NULL, 0, 0 )) {
    TranslateMessage(&msg);
    DispatchMessage(&msg);
}
return msg.wParam;
```

The **GetMessage() function** retrieves messages from an application's message queue and is called as the `while` loop's conditional expression. Note that you can include any type of a statement within a conditional expression, so long as it returns a Boolean value of true or false. You pass to the GetMessage() function the address of the MSG variable, along with several other parameters, which you will not learn about in detail. What is important for you to understand is what keeps the `while` loop iterating. Remember that a looping statement, such as a `while` statement, will continue to iterate as long as its conditional expression evaluates to true. The GetMessage() function returns a value of true for all messages except for one, the WM_QUIT message. The **WM_QUIT message** is generated when an application closes, such as when a user clicks the main application window's close icon. Since WM_QUIT returns a value of false, the message loop ends, which also ends the program. Note that when there are no messages in the message queue, the message loop will continue looping until a new message is generated.

The body of the `while` loop contains the TranslateMessage() and the DispatchMessage() functions. The **TranslateMessage() function** converts keyboard messages into a format Windows can understand. The **DispatchMessage() function** sends messages to the window procedure for processing.

How does the DispatchMessage() function know which function to send a message to? Recall that when you defined the window class, you defined a lpfnWndProc field with a pointer to the name of the window procedure that will handle messages. The function name you assigned to the lpfnWndProc field in the example and in the calculator program was MainWndProc. (You will create the MainWndProc() window procedure in the next section.) The following code contains a partial listing of the window class definition for the example you created earlier, with the lpfnWndProc field highlighted.

```
WNDCLASS wc;
wc.style = CS_HREDRAW | CS_VREDRAW;
wc.lpfnWndProc = MainWndProc;
wc.cbClsExtra  = 0;
wc.cbWndExtra = 0;
...
}
```

For an application to close properly, the WinMain() function's return statement should return the wParam field of the MSG structure. When the WM_QUIT message executes, the wParam field of the MSG structure contains an exit code that should be returned to Windows as the return value from the WinMain() function.

Next, you will add a message loop to the calculator program.

To add a message loop to the calculator program:

1. Insert a new line above the WinMain() function's closing brace and type **MSG msg;** to declare the MSG variable.

2. Press **Enter** and type the `while` structure for the message loop:

```
while(GetMessage(&msg, NULL, 0, 0 )) {
     TranslateMessage(&msg);
     DispatchMessage(&msg);
}
```

3. After the `while` statement's closing brace, add the statement **return msg.wParam;**, which returns the value of the MSG structure's wParam field to the operating system.

Window Procedures

A **window procedure**, or **windproc**, is a special function that processes any messages received by an application. You may also see window procedures referred to as *callback functions* since they give Windows a way of "calling back" your application once it generates an event and message. Essentially, your application "calls" Windows by generating an event, and Windows "calls back" your application and gives it the message in the message queue. The message loop then forwards the message to the window procedure that Windows is trying to reach (or "call back"). You can really think of the window procedure as the heart of a Windows API program since that is where the majority of the program's functionality resides. Figure 7-15 illustrates the concept of a callback function, using an expanded version of the message queue figure you saw earlier.

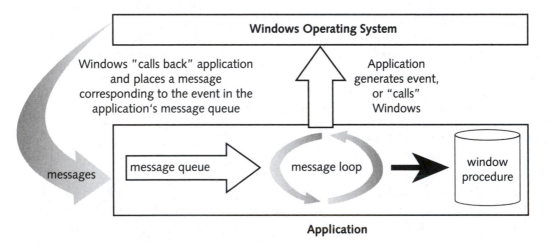

Figure 7-15 Callback function

The following code is a typical function declaration for a window procedure named MainWndProc(). The function declaration declares a return type of long and includes the WINAPI data type, similar to the WinMain() function. The hWnd parameter represents a handle to the application window that generated the message. The msg parameter is an identifier representing the current message. The wParam and lParam parameters both contain additional pieces of information about the current message.

```
long WINAPI MainWndProc(
    HWND hWnd,
    UINT msg,
    WPARAM wParam,
    LPARAM lParam){
    // statements
}
```

Next, you will add a window procedure to the calculator program.

To add a window procedure to the calculator program:

1. First, insert a new line after the `#include <windows.h>` statement and type the following function prototype for the window procedure:

```
long WINAPI MainWndProc(HWND, UINT, WPARAM, LPARAM);
```

2. Now add the following function declaration after the WinMain() function's closing brace. The function contains a single return statement, which returns a value of 0 to indicate that any calls to the window procedure executed normally.

```
long WINAPI MainWndProc(HWND hWnd, UINT msg,
    WPARAM wParam, LPARAM lParam) {
    return 0;
}
```

The primary purpose of a window procedure is to execute the appropriate code, or handler, for a specific message. A **handler** is a segment of code within a window procedure that executes for a specific message. You use a `switch` structure to determine the type of message contained in the msg parameter of the window procedure's function definition. `Case` labels within the `switch` statement contain the handlers or call the appropriate handler functions for each message.

The following code contains a `switch` structure that evaluates the contents of the msg parameter.

```
switch(msg) {
    case WM_COMMAND:
        ...
        break;
    case WM_DESTROY:
        PostQuitMessage(0);
        return 0;
default:
        return DefWindowProc(hWnd, msg, wParam, lParam);
}
```

The preceding code contains `case` labels for two messages: WM_COMMAND and WM_DESTROY. As mentioned previously, WM_COMMAND is generated for events involving menus and buttons. The **WM_DESTROY message** is generated when a window is being destroyed. The handler for the WM_DESTROY message needs to call the PostQuitMessage() function, which generates the WM_QUIT message that tells the message loop to end the program. If you do not include in the window procedure a WM_DESTROY message that calls the PostQuitMessage() function to generate a WM_QUIT message (and perform any other processing before the application's windows are destroyed), then the application will not close properly.

Notice the `default` label in the `switch` statement. The `switch` statement in window procedures must include a default label that calls the Windows API DefWindowProc() function (Def WindowProc stands for *Default Window Procedure*), to which you pass the four parameters that were received by the window procedure itself (hWnd, msg, wParam, lParam). The **Def WindowProc() function** calls the default window procedure for any message for which you do not provide a handler. In other words, if you do not provide handlers for a message, the DefWindowProc() function hands the message back to Windows. It is important to understand that although there are hundreds of Windows messages, you are not required to write handlers for each one. As mentioned previously, Windows processes many types of events behind the scenes—some of which are aimed directly at your application. However, you only need to write code that responds to the events for which your program needs to take specific action, such as to perform the calculation when the equal sign button is pressed in the calculator program (generating a WM_COMMAND message). Windows first checks to see if you have written a handler for a specific message. If you have written a handler for a specific message, then Windows uses it to process the message. If not, the DefWindowProc() function sends the message to Windows, which performs its own default processing.

You may be wondering what the default processing is for many types of events, such as when the WM_COMMAND message is generated for a button click. In some cases, Windows does nothing by default. For example, if you fail to write code that handles a button click, then when a user clicks a button in your program, Windows performs its own default processing—which is to do nothing.

Next, you will add a `switch` statement to the window procedure. The `switch` statement for the calculator program requires a WM_COMMAND message handler, a WM_DESTROY message handler, and a default label that calls the default window procedure.

To add a `switch` statement to the window procedure:

1. Insert a new line above the window procedure's return statement, press **Enter**, and then type the `switch` statement and the `case` label for the WM_COMMAND message.

```
switch (msg) {
    case WM_COMMAND:
        break;
    case WM_DESTROY:
        PostQuitMessage(0);
        return 0;
    default:
        return DefWindowProc(hWnd, msg, wParam, lParam);
}
```

2. Build and execute the **Calculator** project. Figure 7-16 shows how the application window appears. Although you can click the buttons in the program, nothing will happen since you still need to add code to the WM_COMMAND handler. In the next section you will add the final code to the WM_COMMAND handler.

Figure 7-16   Calculator application window

7

3. Close the **Calculator** window.

For the calculator program, you are using the WM_COMMAND message to notify the program when one of the calculator buttons is clicked once. However, there are numerous events associated with buttons, not just single click events. For example, the double-click event is another commonly used button event. You can identify a specific event using the wParam parameter that is passed to the window procedure. For button events, the wParam parameter contains notification codes that identify specific button event types. For example, when a button is double-clicked the wParam parameter will contain the value BN_DBLCLK. Similarly, when a button is clicked once, the wParam parameter will contain the value BN_CLICKED.

Check the MSDN Library for a complete listing of button events.

Next, you will add to the handler for the WM_COMMAND message a **switch** statement that evaluates the wParam parameter.

To add a **switch** statement for the WM_COMMAND message:

1. Above the **break** statement in the **case** label for the WM_COMMAND message, add the following **switch** statement.

```
switch (wParam) {
        case BN_CLICKED:
}
```

Since you are only checking for BN_CLICKED events in the calculator program, you could use an if statement instead of a switch statement. Most programs use a switch statement, however, when checking for notification codes since they usually use multiple types of WM_COMMAND events. Although the calculator program uses only one WM_COMMAND event, you are using a switch statement since programs you create in real life will probably use multiple WM_COMMAND events. Additionally, using a switch statement makes it easier to add support for other types of WM_COMMAND events in the future.

COMPLETING THE CALCULATOR PROGRAM

To complete the calculator program, you need to understand how to calculate numbers in C++. The functionality of the program is not very complex and does calculations with only two numbers (operands) using a single operator (+, -, *, or /). For example, the program can calculate 1 + 2, or 10 / 5, or 15 * 14, and so on. To perform the calculation, you will capture the three parts of an equation in three separate variables: one for the left operand, one for the operator, and one for the right operand. The calculation will use two methods, setNumbers() and runCalculation(). You will learn about each function in turn.

The calculator program requires several string manipulation functions in order to set and retrieve the values that will appear in the edit box. Therefore, before creating the setNumbers() and runCalculation() functions, you need to add a processing directive that gives the program access to the string.h header file.

You also need to add variable declarations to the calculator program that are necessary to perform the calculations, along with function prototypes for the setNumbers() and runCalculation() functions.

To add a processing directive, variable declarations, and a function prototype to the Calculator program:

1. Place your cursor after the windows.h processing directive, press **Enter**, and type the processing directive for the string.h header file: **#include <string.h>**.

2. Place your cursor after the function prototype declaration for the window procedure, press **Enter**, and add the following two function prototype declarations for the setNumbers() and runCalculation() functions:

```
void setNumbers(char szCurNum[10]);
void runCalculation();
```

3. Finally, declare the following variables. The first variable will determine the type of operation being performed (addition, subtraction, multiplication, or division). The next two variables are a char variable and a double variable for the left operand in the equation. The last two variables are a char variable and a double

variable for the right operand in the equation. The char variable will temporarily store the numbers when you display them and retrieve them in the edit box, while the double variables will be used to perform the actual calculations.

```
char cOperation = '0';
char szFirstNum[10] = "";
double dFirstNum = 0;
char szSecondNum[10] = "";
double dSecondNum = 0;
```

Next, you will learn about the setNumbers() function.

Setting the Calculation Variables

The setNumbers() function displays the operands in the calculator's edit box. You cannot place the contents of number variables into the edit box since an edit box accepts only text. For this reason, in the last set of steps you will declare two global variables for each operand: one as a char data type and the other as a double data type. The setNumbers() function uses the char version of each operand variable. In the runCalculation() function you will convert the values in the char variables to numeric values, copy the numeric values into the double data type versions of the operand variables, and then carry out the calculation.

To determine which value to display in the edit box, you need to be able to determine which button was clicked. You will do this by comparing each button's window handle to the handle that was passed to the window procedure's lParam parameter. First, you must convert the value contained in the lParam parameter from text to a handle by casting the lParam parameter to the HWND data type using the following statement:

```
HWND hwndCtl = (HWND) lParam;
```

After adding the preceding statement to the program you can use **if** statements to compare the hwndCtl handle to the handles for each of the buttons to see which one generated the click event.

Next, you will add to the window procedure a statement to declare the hwndCtl handle. You will also add statements for each of the numeric buttons to the BN_CLICKED label that call the setNumbers() function when a particular button is clicked and pass to it the value represented by the button.

To add code to the window procedure that compares the handle in the lParam parameter to each numeric button handle:

1. Place your cursor after the window procedure's opening brace, press **Enter**, and type the statement that declares a new window handle variable named hwndCtl: **HWND hwndCtl = (HWND) lParam;**.

2. Next, add the following bolded **if...else** block to the BN_CLICKED label. Each **if** statement compares the value of the hwndCtl handle to each button's handle. If a match is found, then the setNumbers() function is called and is passed a text string with the appropriate value for each button. For example, if the

hwndCtl handle matches the hwndButton1 handle (the button for the number 1), then a value of "1" is passed to the setNumbers() function using the statement setNumbers("1");.

```
case BN_CLICKED:
if (hwndCtl == hwndButton1)
     setNumbers("1");
else if (hwndCtl == hwndButton2)
     setNumbers("2");
else if (hwndCtl == hwndButton3)
     setNumbers("3");
else if (hwndCtl == hwndButton4)
     setNumbers("4");
else if (hwndCtl == hwndButton5)
     setNumbers("5");
else if (hwndCtl == hwndButton6)
     setNumbers("6");
else if (hwndCtl == hwndButton7)
     setNumbers("7");
else if (hwndCtl == hwndButton8)
     setNumbers("8");
else if (hwndCtl == hwndButton9)
     setNumbers("9");
else if (hwndCtl == hwndButton0)
     setNumbers("0");
else if (hwndCtl == hwndButtonPoint)
     setNumbers(".");
```

Next, you will create the setNumbers() function. Figure 7-17 shows how the function is set up.

```
void setNumbers(char szCurNum[10]) {
     if (cOperation == '0') {
          strcat(szFirstNum, szCurNum);
          SetWindowText(hwndEdit, szFirstNum);
}
else {

          strcat(szSecondNum, szCurNum);
          SetWindowText(hwndEdit, szSecondNum);
     }
}
```

Figure 7-17   setNumbers() function

The value passed to the function is assigned to a char array variable named szCurNum that consists of a single element. You must use a char array instead of a single char variable since the value passed to the function is a string, even though you are passing only a single character. Since a null character is appended to the single character when it passed to the setNumbers() function, the passed information becomes a string instead of a single character.

The **if** statement checks the value of the cOperation variable. If its value is equal to 0, the initially assigned value, then the user is currently building the left operand and the **if** block's statements execute. If the value is not equal to 0, then the user is currently building the right operand and the **else** block's statements execute. (If cOperation does not contain a value of 0, then it will contain a value of +, -, *, or /.) Both the **if** and **else** clauses build the value displayed in the edit box by using the strcat() function to add the value of the szCurNum variable to either the szFirstNum or szSecondNum variables. Recall that the strcat() function is used for combining the contents of one string with another.

Following the strcat() statement is a statement that executes the SetWindowText() function. The **SetWindowText() function** is a Windows API function that changes either the value displayed in a control or the title text for windows that are not controls. The syntax for the SetWindowText() function is `SetWindowText(handle, text);`. You will pass to the SetWindowText() function the handle of the edit control (hwndEdit) along with either the szFirstNum or szSecondNum variable, depending on whether the **if** or **else** clauses are executing.

To create the setNumbers() function:

1. After the closing brace for the window procedure, add the function header:

```
void setNumbers(char szCurNum[10]) {
```

2. Next, add the **if** block:

```
if (cOperation == '0') {
    strcat(szFirstNum, szCurNum);
    SetWindowText(hwndEdit, szFirstNum);
}
```

3. Finally, add the **else** block and the function's closing brace:

```
else {
    strcat(szSecondNum, szCurNum);
    SetWindowText(hwndEdit, szSecondNum);
}
}
```

The final step in setting the calculation variables is to add handlers that determine the type of operation being performed: addition, subtraction, multiplication, or division. When any of these buttons is clicked, the program will assign its associated value (+, -, *, or /) to the cOperation variable.

Additionally, the left operand value currently displayed in the edit box will be assigned to the double data type version of the variable. However, you cannot directly assign a text value to a numeric value. Instead you must use a data conversion routine. The data conversion routine you will use is the **atof() function**, which converts strings to floating-point numbers. The syntax for the `variable = atof(string);`.

See the MSDN Library for a list of other data conversion routines.

To add handlers that determine the type of operation being performed:

1. Modify the **case BN_CLICKED:** label in the MainWndProc() function by adding the following bolded **else...if** statements for the operator variables. The conditional expressions check to see if the hwndCtl handle is equal to the handle for each operation. Within each **else...if** block, the first statement assigns the appropriate value to the cOperation variable, while the second statement uses the atof() function to assign the value of the szFirstNum variable to the dFirstNum variable.

```
case BN_CLICKED:
    ...
  else if (hwndCtl == hwndButtonPoint)
      setNumbers(".");
  else if (hwndCtl == hwndButtonPlus) {
      cOperation = '+';
      dFirstNum = atof(szFirstNum);
  }
  else if (hwndCtl == hwndButtonMinus) {
      cOperation = '-';
      dFirstNum = atof(szFirstNum);
  }
  else if (hwndCtl == hwndButtonMultiply) {
      cOperation = '*';
      dFirstNum = atof(szFirstNum);
  }
  else if (hwndCtl == hwndButtonDivide) {
      cOperation = '/';
      dFirstNum = atof(szFirstNum);
  }
}
```

Adding the Calculation Code

The calculation is performed when the equal sign button is clicked, which assigns the value of the second operand to the dSecondNum variable and executes the runCalculation() function. The runCalculation() function contains the code that actually performs the calculation. First, you will add handler code for the equal-sign button. You will also add handler code that resets the program's variables to their default values when the Clear button is clicked.

To add handler code for the equal-sign button and Clear button:

1. After the **else...if** statement that compares the hwndCtl handle to the division button handle, add the following **else...if** statements for the operator variables. The conditional expressions check to see if the hwndCtl handle

is equal to the handle for each operation. Within the `else...if` block, the first statement uses the atof() function to assign the value of the szSecondNum variable to the dSecondNum variable, while the second statement calls the runCalculation() function.

```
else if (hwndCtl == hwndButtonEquals) {
    dSecondNum = atof(szSecondNum);
    runCalculation();
}
```

2. Finally, add the last `else...if` statement, which resets the program's variables to their original values when the Clear button is clicked.

```
else if (hwndCtl == hwndButtonClear) {
    cOperation = '0';
    strcpy(szFirstNum, "");
    dFirstNum = 0;
    strcpy(szSecondNum, "");
    dSecondNum = 0;
    SetWindowText(hwndEdit, "");
}
```

The last step, before you can use the calculator program, is to create the runCalculation() function. The runCalculation() function will examine the contents of the cOperation variable, and then perform the appropriate calculations. For example, if the cOperation variable is equal to +, then the dFirstNum and dSecondNum variables will be added together. Once the result is calculated, it will be converted to a string using the _gcvt()function. The **_gcvt() function** is a data conversion function that converts floating-point values to string values. The syntax for the _gcvt() function is `_gcvt(floating-point value, digits, char array);`. The digits portion of the function determines the number of digits to convert from the floating-point value to the string value. Number of digits does not mean the number of decimal places, but the number of characters that compose the number. For example, the number 10.8765 is the equivalent of seven digits. You will use a value of 10, which should be sufficient for most simple calculations.

To create the runCalculation() function:

1. After the closing brace for the setNumbers() function, add the runCalculation() function header:

```
void runCalculation() {
```

2. Press **Enter** and add the following two variable declarations. The dResult variable will contain the result of the numeric calculation, while the szResult variable will contain the result after it has been converted using the _gcvt() function.

```
double dResult = 0;
char szResult[10];
```

3. After the second variable declaration, add the following `if...else` block, which evaluates the cOperation variable and then performs the appropriate calculation:

```
if (cOperation == '+') {
    dResult = dFirstNum + dSecondNum;
}
else if (cOperation == '-') {
    dResult = dFirstNum - dSecondNum;
}
else if (cOperation == '*') {
    dResult = dFirstNum * dSecondNum;
}
else if (cOperation == '/') {
    dResult = dFirstNum / dSecondNum;
}
```

4. Insert a new line after the closing brace for the last `else...if` clause and add the following two statements. The first statement uses the _gcvt() function to assign the value of dResult variable to the szResult variable. The second statement uses the SetWindowText() function to place the results of the calculation in the edit box.

```
_gcvt(dResult, 10, szResult);
SetWindowText(hwndEdit, szResult);
```

5. Press **Enter** and add the following statements that reset the variables to their default values:

```
cOperation = '0';
strcpy(szFirstNum, szResult);
dFirstNum = 0;
strcpy(szSecondNum, "");
dSecondNum = 0;
```

6. Press **Enter** again and add the function's closing brace: }.

7. Build, execute, and test the project. If you have problems building the project, or if the calculations do not perform correctly, then compare your code to the Chapter5_Calculator.cpp file on your Data Disk.

CHAPTER SUMMARY

❏ An application programming interface, or API, is a library of methods and code that allows programmers to access the features and functionality of an application or operating system.

❏ The Windows API allows you to write programs for Windows operating systems.

❏ A graphical user interface, or GUI (pronounced *gooey*), is a graphically based environment that you use to interact with applications.

❏ The term bit refers to a binary number of 0 or 1.

❏ Computers are classified according to how many bits can be transmitted simultaneously into the microprocessor, or CPU. The bus, or data bus, refers to the electronic path that the bits travel into the microprocessor.

❏ A separate Windows API exists for each generation of Windows operating systems.

❏ All 32-bit Windows platforms share the same Windows API, known as the Win32 API.

❏ Microsoft made the Win64 API almost identical to the Win32 API, but with some important changes to data types that allows 64-bit applications to run on 32-bit Windows platforms.

❏ The `windows.h` header file includes all of the functions, variables, and other programming elements that make up the Windows API.

❏ The Windows API defines its own data types in the `windows.h` header file.

❏ The Windows API includes many data types in order to control the information passed to it from source programming languages (such as C, C++, Visual Basic, and so on) and to correctly execute a program on different types of computers.

❏ A pointer data type declares the type and name of a Windows API pointer.

❏ A handle is used to refer to a resource or object that has been loaded into memory.

❏ A child window always appears within the area defined by a parent window.

❏ A parent window is a primary application window containing one or more child windows.

❏ The WinMain() function is the starting point for any Windows API program.

❏ An instance is a particular copy of a window or other type of object that happens to be running.

❏ The window class defines the characteristics of a program's main window.

❏ The predefined WNDCLASS structure is used for defining the characteristics of a window class.

❏ The RegisterClass() function informs the operating system about a newly-defined window class.

❏ The CreateWindow() function creates a new window based on several parameters, including window class, size, position, and style.

❏ The lpClassName parameter of the CreateWindow() function is a pointer to a text string representing the name of the class upon which you want to base the new window.

❏ Predefined control classes represent standard types of window controls such as buttons, edit boxes, and scroll bars.

❏ The lpWindowName parameter of the CreateWindow() function is a pointer to a text string containing a name for the window.

❏ The dwStyle parameter of the CreateWindow() function determines the specific window styles that will be applied to the new window.

❏ The nWidth and nHeight parameters of the CreateWindow() function represent the window's lower-right corner, which, when based on the starting positions of the x and y parameters, determine the window's size.

❏ The hWndParent parameter of the CreateWindow() function specifies a handle to a parent window and tells the system the correct window where a child window should be created.

❏ The hMenu parameter of the CreateWindow() function specifies a handle to a menu.

❏ The hInstance parameter of the CreateWindow() function informs the system in which application instance the window should be created.

❏ The lpParam parameter of the CreateWindow() function points to either a value passed through the CREATESTRUCT structure or to a CLIENTCREATESTRUCT structure.

❏ The ShowWindow() function displays a window onscreen that was created with the CreateWindow() function.

❏ An event is a specific circumstance that is monitored by Windows.

❏ A message is a set of information about a particular event, such as where and when the event occurred.

❏ The WM_COMMAND message is generated for events involving menus and buttons, such as when a button is clicked by a user.

❏ Every 32-bit Windows application has its own message queue where messages are placed until they are processed by the application.

❏ A message loop continually checks the queue for new messages, and then sends the message to the window procedure.

❏ You place a message loop inside a WinMain() function so that it starts running (and checking for messages) when the program first executes.

❏ The MSG structure contains information about the current message in the application's message queue.

❏ The GetMessage() function retrieves messages from an application's message queue and is called as a message loop's conditional expression.

❏ The WM_QUIT message is generated when an application closes.

❏ The TranslateMessage() function converts keyboard messages into a format Windows can understand.

❏ The DispatchMessage() function sends messages to the window procedure for processing.

❑ When the WM_QUIT message is raised, the wParam field of the MSG structure contains an exit code that needs to be returned to Windows as the return value from the WinMain() function.

❑ A window procedure, or windproc, is a special function that processes any messages received by an application.

❑ A handler is segment of code within a window procedure that executes for a specific message.

❑ The WM_DESTROY message is generated when a window is being destroyed.

❑ If you do not include in the window procedure a WM_DESTROY message that calls the PostQuitMessage() function to generate a WM_QUIT message (and perform any other processing before the application's windows are destroyed), then the application will not close properly.

❑ The DefWindowProc() function calls the default window procedure for any message for which you do not provide a handler.

❑ You can identify a specific event using the wParam parameter that is passed to a window procedure.

❑ For button events, the wParam parameter contains notification codes that identify specific button event types.

❑ The SetWindowText() function is a Windows API function that changes either the value displayed in a control or the title text for windows that are not controls.

❑ The atof() function converts strings to floating-point numbers.

❑ The _gcvt() function converts floating-point values to string values.

REVIEW QUESTIONS

1. Which of the following best describes how Windows programs are created?

   a. You can only write Windows programs using standard C programming syntax.

   b. You create Windows programs by combining code written in a source programming language with calls to the Windows API.

   c. You can only write Windows programs using standard C++ programming syntax with calls to the Windows API.

   d. Visual C++ is the only current programming environment capable of writing Windows programs because it allows programmers to combine C and C++ syntax.

2. Computers are classified according to how many bits can be _____.

   a. saved to a single local hard drive

   b. saved to a local floppy disk

   c. stored into random access memory (RAM)

   d. transmitted simultaneously into the microprocessor, or CPU

3. The bus, or _____, refers to the electronic path that bits travel into the microprocessor.

   a. truck

   b. road

   c. electronic highway

   d. data bus

4. When operating on a 64-bit Pentium computer, Windows NT can operate at _____.

   a. 16-bits

   b. 32-bits

   c. 64-bits

   d. 128-bits

5. What is the name of the API that is shared by all 32-bit Windows operating systems?

   a. Win32 SDK

   b. Platform SDK

   c. Win API

   d. Win32 API

6. Support for programming in the Windows API is defined _____.

   a. in the `windows.h` header file

   b. in Visual C++

   c. in the Win API

   d. automatically by each Windows operating system

7. Which of the following statements is true?

   a. The Windows API uses the exact same data types as Visual C++.

   b. The Windows API defines its own data types.

   c. The Windows API does not use data types.

   d. The Windows API only uses C data types.

8. Most Windows API pointer data types begin with a prefix of *P* or _____.

   a. LP

   b. POINT

   c. PNT

   d. PT

9. A handle _____.

    a. refers to the Windows API version to which a program conforms

    b. is another way of referring to a Windows program's executable file

    c. is the area of the screen where an application window is drawn

    d. is used to refer to a resource or object that has been loaded into memory

10. All individual controls and user interface components in a Windows API program, such as buttons and edit boxes, are also _____.

    a. handles

    b. windows

    c. programs

    d. variables

11. Which of the following statements is true about parent and child windows?

    a. Child windows are generated by the Windows operating system itself, while parent windows are created by applications written in C++ that make calls to the Windows API.

    b. Parent windows are generated by the Windows operating system itself, while child windows are created by applications written in C++ that make calls to the Windows API.

    c. Parent windows are larger than 100 x 100 pixels, while child windows are smaller than 100 x 100 pixels.

    d. A parent window is a primary application window containing one ore more child windows.

12. A(n) _____ is a particular copy of a window or other type of object that happens to be running.

    a. representation

    b. depiction

    c. instance

    d. object

13. Which WinMain() function parameter is the handle that represents the current instance of the program's parent window?

    a. hInstance

    b. hPrevInstance

    c. lpCmdLine

    d. nCmdShow

7

14. Which WinMain() function parameter is not used in 32-bit and 64-bit Windows operating systems?

    a. hInstance

    b. hPrevInstance

    c. lpCmdLine

    d. nCmdShow

15. The _____ structure is used for defining the characteristics of a window class.

    a. WINDOWCLASS

    b. WNDCLASS

    c. WCLASS

    d. WDCLASS

16. Which window class field is a pointer to the window procedure?

    a. cbWndExtra

    b. lpszClassName

    c. hInstance

    d. lpfnWndProc

17. The _____ parameter of the CreateWindow() function determines whether the new window is based on a custom window class definition or a predefined window class.

    a. lpClassName

    b. lpWindowName

    c. hWndParent

    d. hInstance

18. What should you assign to the hWndParent parameter of the CreateWindow() function for a top-level window?

    a. ""

    b. HINSTANCE

    c. hInstance

    d. NULL

19. The window styles you assign to the dwStyle parameter of the CreateWindow() function are prefixed with _____.

    a. DW_

    b. WS_

    c. STYLE_

    d. WIN_

20. To position a window in the default position, you set the x parameter of the CreateWindow() function to _____.

    a. USEDEFAULT

    b. DEFAULT

    c. CW_USEDEFAULT

    d. CW_DEFAULT

21. What must you do in order to display a new window after creating it with the CreateWindow() function?

    a. Add a message loop.

    b. Write the window procedure.

    c. Call the ShowWindow() function

    d. Nothing. The window displays automatically.

22. The _____ message is generated for events involving menus and buttons, such as when a button is clicked by a user.

    a. WM_COMMAND

    b. WM_EXECUTE

    c. WM_SELECT

    d. WM_CLICK

23. What type of control structure is most commonly used to create a message loop?

    a. `if`

    b. `while`

    c. `do...while`

    d. `switch`

24. Which function retrieves messages from the message queue?

    a. GetMessage()

    b. RetrieveMessage()

    c. NextMessage()

    d. Message()

25. The _____ function converts keyboard messages into a format Windows can understand.

    a. ConvertMessage()

    b. TranslateMessage()

    c. EncodeMessage()

    d. DecipherMessage()

7

26. What does the DispatchMessage() function do?

    a. Cancels any message that cannot be converted into a format Windows can understand

    b. Returns a notification message to the Windows operating system

    c. Executes the appropriate handler

    d. Sends messages to the window procedure for processing

27. A window procedure is also referred to as _____.

    a. the program entry point

    b. a callback function

    c. the WinMain() procedure

    d. a message structure

28. A _____ is a segment of code within a window procedure that executes for a specific message.

    a. handler

    b. prototype function

    c. structure

    d. message function

29. The case label for the WM_DESTROY message should call the _____ function, which generates the WM_QUIT message that tells the message loop to end the program.

    a. MessageLoop()

    b. MessageQueue()

    c. Destroy()

    d. PostQuitMessage()

30. Which function must be included in the default label of a window procedure's **switch** statement in order to return messages that are not handled by your window procedure to the Windows operating system for processing?

    a. DefWindowProc()

    b. WindowProc()

    c. WindowHandler()

    d. RetWindows()

31. The window procedure's _____ parameter contains notification codes that identify specific button event types.

    a. hWnd

    b. msg

    c. wParam

    d. lParam

32. The _____ function is a Windows API function that changes either the value displayed in a control or the title text for windows that are not controls.

    a. WindowText()

    b. SetWindowText()

    c. WindowValue()

    d. SetValue()

33. Which data type conversion routine converts strings to floating-point numbers?

    a. atof()

    b. _gcvt()

    c. parseFloat()

    d. parseString()

34. Which data type conversion routine converts floating-point values to string values?

    a. atof()

    b. _gcvt()

    c. parseFloat()

    d. parseString()

7

EXERCISES

1. Create five different Win32 Application projects. Within each project, use five different visual styles from Figure 7-11, such as WS_BORDER, when creating the application's parent window. Each project's main window should include at least one style attribute that is not included in the other projects. Use a static window to describe styles used in the parent window. For example, if an application includes a minimize button, then a static window should contain the text *This window includes a minimize button*. Save the projects as Style1, Style2, Style3, Style4, and Style 5 in the Chapter.07 folder in your Visual C++ Projects folder.

2. Create a Win32 Application that allows users to play a simple guessing game. In the game, users try to guess a number between 0 and 100. Assign the correct number and the user's guess to variables. Set up an edit box for users to input the number they are guessing. Also create a button named Guess. Use a static window to provide instructions to users and to inform them if they guessed the number correctly.

3. Create a Win32 Application that calculates an employee's weekly gross salary, tax withholding (which is 15% of gross pay), and net pay, based on the number of hours worked and hourly wage. Compute any hours over 40 as time-and-a-half. Use the appropriate decision structures to create the program. Display the weekly gross pay, tax withholding, and net pay in static windows.

4. Create a math quiz for a sixth grade class as a Win32 Application. Include five questions in the program's parent window, and store the answers to the quiz in global variables. Within the parent window, add a button named Score Quiz. When students click the Score Quiz button, determine if they have answered all the questions. If they have answered all the questions, score the quiz using the answers in the global variables and display the score in a static window. If they have not answered all the questions, display a message in the static window that instructs them to answer all of the questions before selecting the Score Quiz button.

5. Create a Win32 Application project with sections for each of your last three jobs. Include edit boxes listing the employer's name, salary, and the number of years you worked there. Next, add four buttons: Highest Salary, Lowest Salary, Longest Employment, and Shortest Employment. Write handler code for each button that determines the appropriate value. After you click a button, display the result in a static window, along with the name of the associated employer.

6. Create a Win32 Application that determines the cost of carpeting a room, based on the room's dimensions and the cost per square foot of carpet. Include edit boxes in the program that allow users to enter the room's length and width in feet, along with an edit box in which they can enter the price per square foot of carpet. Also include a Calculate button that calculates the correct dimensions and total cost. Display the total cost in a static window using explanatory text and the variables. For example, "The total cost to carpet a room is $460."

7. Create a Win32 Application version of the Retirement Planner program you created in Chapter 4. Save the project as RetirementPlanner in the Chapter.07 folder in your Visual C++ Projects folder.

8. Use functions found in the math.h header file to create a more advanced version of the calculator program. Refer to the MSDN Library on the methods available in math.h that you can use in your calculator including the exp() (exponential value) function and the sqrt() (square root) function.

CHAPTER

8

MICROSOFT FOUNDATION CLASSES

In this chapter you will learn:

♦ About Microsoft Foundation Class programming

♦ How to write basic MFC programs

♦ How to work with resources

♦ How to work with Visual C++ class tools

♦ About the CString class

♦ How to create dialog-based applications

♦ How to work with message maps

♦ How to build an application framework with AppWizard

PREVIEW: THE MFC CALCULATOR PROGRAM

In this chapter you will create a calculator program—the same calculator program you worked with in the last chapter—as a Microsoft Foundation Class program. Creating the calculator program as both a Windows API program and a Microsoft Foundations Class program will help you understand how a Microsoft Foundation Class program compares to a standard Windows API program.

To preview the MFC Calculator program:

1. Create a **Chapter.08** folder in your Visual C++ Projects folder.

2. Copy the **Chapter8_Calculator** folder from the Chapter.08 folder on your Data Disk to the Chapter.08 folder in your Visual C++ Projects folder. Then open the **MFCCalculator** project in Visual C++. If the Tip of the Day dialog box displays, click the **Close** button.

3. Individually open the **CalcApp.h** and **Calculator.h** files in the Text Editor window. The CalcApp.h file represents an application class named CCalcApp, and the Calculator.h file represents a dialog window class named CCalculator. The extra *C* in front of the class names identifies the classes as Microsoft Foundation Classes. These files contain some fairly typical code that is found in most header files. In the class header declaration statements, you can see the Microsoft Foundation Classes from which both of these classes are derived; the CCalcApp class is derived from the CwinApp class, and the CCalculator class is derived from the CDialog class.

4. Next, open the **Calculator.rc** file, which represents the visual portion of a dialog box window. This file opens the ResourceView tab in the Workspace window, which is used for managing the graphic components of a Microsoft Foundation Class program. In the ResourceView tab, expand the Dialog folder and double-click the IDD_CALCULATOR icon. The Visual C++ Dialog Editor opens, which is used for graphically creating windows and other elements. You can see that the dialog box resembles the calculator you created in the last chapter. The CCalculator dialog window class manipulates the dialog box window.

5. Click the FileView tab in the Workspace window and open the CCalculator dialog window class's implementation file, **Calculator.cpp**, in the Text Editor window. When you look through the code, you will notice that some of the statements are highlighted in gray. These statements are controlled by ClassWizard, which is used to help create and modify Microsoft Foundation Class programs. You can see that the dialog window class contains a number of member function definitions and other standard elements found in classes. You will also see that the file includes two statements: BEGIN_MESSAGE_MAP() and END_MESSAGE_MAP(). These statements are called macros and declare a "message map" that will be added to the implementation file in order to process Windows messages. The statements between the two macros are under the control of ClassWizard (note they appear in gray) and are used for processing Windows messages. The following code shows an example of the Calculator.cpp file's message map:

```
BEGIN_MESSAGE_MAP(CCalculator, CDialog)
    //{{AFX_MSG_MAP(CCalculator)
    ON_BN_CLICKED(IDC_ONE, OnOne)
    ON_BN_CLICKED(IDC_CLEAR, OnClear)
    ON_BN_CLICKED(IDC_PLUS, OnPlus)
    ON_BN_CLICKED(IDC_MINUS, OnMinus)
    ON_BN_CLICKED(IDC_MULTIPLY, OnMultiply)
    ON_BN_CLICKED(IDC_DIVIDE, OnDivide)
    ON_BN_CLICKED(IDC_ZERO, OnZero)
    ON_BN_CLICKED(IDC_TWO, OnTwo)
    ON_BN_CLICKED(IDC_THREE, OnThree)
    ON_BN_CLICKED(IDC_FOUR, OnFour)
    ON_BN_CLICKED(IDC_FIVE, OnFive)
    ON_BN_CLICKED(IDC_SIX, OnSix)
    ON_BN_CLICKED(IDC_SEVEN, OnSeven)
    ON_BN_CLICKED(IDC_EIGHT, OnEight)
    ON_BN_CLICKED(IDC_NINE, OnNine)
    ON_BN_CLICKED(IDC_POINT, OnPoint)
    ON_BN_CLICKED(IDC_EQUALS, OnEquals)
    //}}AFX_MSG_MAP
END_MESSAGE_MAP()
```

6. Next, open the **CalcApp.cpp** file. This class implementation file represents the application as a whole and is required by all Microsoft Foundation Class programs. An application class includes an InitInstance() function that is used for displaying the windows used in the program. An application class must also include

a global statement that instantiates an object based on the application class itself. Figure 8-1 shows an example of the application class implementation file. You can see in the InitInstance() function that an object of the CCalculator dialog window class is instantiated. The DoModal() function is what actually displays the dialog box window.

```
CCalcApp::CCalcApp()
{

}

CCalcApp::~CCalcApp()
{

}
BOOL CCalcApp::InitInstance() {        InitInstance() function that displays the
        CCalculator calc;               CCalculator window
        calc.DoModal();
        return FALSE;
}
CCalcApp theApplication;               global application class object
```

Figure 8-1   Application class implementation file

7. Build and execute the **MFCCalculator** project, and then test the calculations. Figure 8-2 shows an example of the dialog box window that appears when you run the MFC Calculator program. The program should function the same as the calculator you created in the last chapter.

Figure 8-2   MFC Calculator program window

8. Click the **Close** button to close the Calculator program window.

MICROSOFT FOUNDATION CLASSES

Virtually all of the code and programming examples you have seen so far in this text have used standard C++ syntax that can be used with Visual C++ and with almost any other C++ compiler. This chapter begins discussing Microsoft Foundation Class programming techniques. The **Microsoft Foundation Classes**, or MFC, is a class library that assists programmers in creating Windows-based applications. Perhaps two of the most important aspects of MFC programming are as follows:

- MFC adds object-oriented programming capabilities to Windows API programming.

- MFC encapsulates the Windows API into a logically organized class hierarchy.

 MFC programming is not exclusive to Microsoft Visual C++. Other C++ programming environments that support Microsoft Foundation Classes include Symantec C++, Inprise C++ Builder, and Watcom C/C++.

One of Microsoft's main goals in designing MFC was to create a C++ object-oriented class library for building Windows API applications. Prior to MFC, programmers had to design their programs so that they conformed to the C language requirements of the Windows API. This means that they could not use the object-oriented capabilities of C++, which are not found in C. Recall from the last chapter, the Windows API consists of thousands of C functions and other types of code elements. To successfully program with the Windows API, you must know which of these functions to choose from and you must also understand the fairly complex requirements for structuring a Windows program using a WinMain() function and a window procedure that processes messages. MFC assists C++ programmers in writing Windows programs by encapsulating into logically organized classes the C functions and other code that make up the Windows API. MFC classes also provide much of the functionality required by a Windows API program. The WinMain() function, for instance, is already written within an MFC class. By including or inheriting MFC classes in your program, you inherit the prewritten WinMain() function. When a Windows API program is written with MFC, Visual C++ automatically calls the inherited WinMain() function for you when your program executes. Your main responsibility when writing an MFC program is to derive your own classes from the MFC classes. Once you derive your classes from an MFC class, you then add code to give the program its functionality.

Visual C++ is designed to make writing MFC programs a relatively easy process. When you use Visual C++ to write an MFC program, you use a tool called AppWizard that walks you through the steps involved in creating an MFC application. After running AppWizard, Visual C++ provides something called the **Microsoft Foundation Class framework**, or framework for short, which is basically a skeleton application created from MFC classes that you can use as a basis for your program. You can then use another tool, ClassWizard, to modify the framework. You can also use the New Class command, available on the Insert menu or WizardBar, to create a framework for you. The New Class command sets up the constructor and destructor declarations and definitions (the framework) for you in the new class's interface and implementation files. It is then up to you to fill in the required code for the constructor and destructor functions. (You will learn about WizardBar later in this section.)

AppWizard and ClassWizard perform almost all of the rudimentary work associated with an MFC program for you, by setting up your classes so that they derive from the appropriate MFC classes, including the correct header files in the various C++ files, and performing various other tasks. Your job as a programmer is to find the hooks in the framework that you can use to give your program its functionality. A **hook** is a location in a program where a programmer can insert code that adds functionality. Visual C++ provides plenty of comments to help you find the hooks. For example, Figure 8-3 shows the window that is generated for a simple MFC framework created with AppWizard.

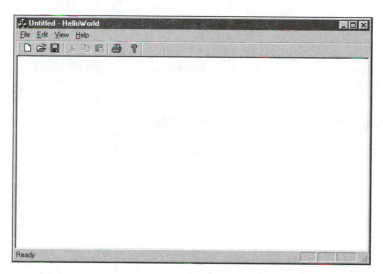

Figure 8-3   Window generated by a simple MFC framework

In order to understand just what a hook is, examine the MFC OnDraw() function, which is used for adding graphical elements to a window. For now, do not worry about understanding exactly how the OnDraw() function works. Simply understand that the framework includes places for you to add your own code that gives your program its functionality. To display the text *Hello World* in the window shown in Figure 8-3, you need to locate the OnDraw() function shown below.

```
void CHelloWorldView::OnDraw(CDC* pDC)
{
        CHelloWorldDoc* pDoc = GetDocument();
        ASSERT_VALID(pDoc);
        // TODO: add draw code for native data here
}
```

The hook in the preceding code is the // TODO: comment located above the function's closing brace. To output *Hello World* in the window, you replace the // TODO: comment with a call to the TextOut() function, as shown in the following example. The TextOut() function graphically adds text to a window.

```
void CHelloWorldView::OnDraw(CDC* pDC)
{
        CHelloWorldDoc* pDoc = GetDocument();
        ASSERT_VALID(pDoc);
        pDC->TextOut(100, 100, "Hello World");
}
```

 You will study both the OnDraw() and TextOut() functions later in this text.

Now, when you execute the program, the window will include *Hello World*, as shown in Figure 8-4.

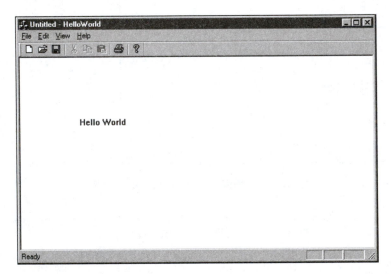

Figure 8-4   Window generated by a simple MFC framework after adding the TextOut() function

Finding the hooks in a framework might seem like an easy task based on this example, but it is, unfortunately, not so simple. Although MFC programs are written using C++ and object-oriented programming techniques, they still ultimately end up as Windows API programs. You still need to use some special techniques for setting up your classes and source files and for working with MFC programs in general. If you do not know these techniques, you will be hopelessly lost when you try to find the hooks you need.

Even the simplest MFC program created with AppWizard consists of at least eight separate files and dozens of lines of code. Many experienced C++ programmers have attempted to jump right into MFC programming by building a program with AppWizard. Once they examine the large amounts of unfamiliar and confusing code, it is not uncommon for some programmers to simply abandon the new program, exit Visual C++, and vow never to work with MFC programs again. To avoid such a scenario, you will start by building your MFC Calculator program from scratch instead of by using AppWizard. Building your MFC Calculator program from scratch will allow you to examine MFC programming techniques. At the end of this chapter, you will build an MFC program with AppWizard and examine the framework. At that point, you should have a fairly clear idea of what each piece of the program does.

As with traditional Windows API programming, MFC programming is a large topic. Even though the thousands of Windows API functions (and other code) are encapsulated in the MFC library, each of those functions still exists and needs to be understood before you can use it in your program. The MFC library is composed of over two hundred classes. The remainder of this text discusses the most basic Windows API programming techniques that use only a handful of the MFC classes.

If you would like to continue your studies of MFC, the MSDN Library contains vast amounts of information. Numerous texts also exist that are devoted exclusively to the study of MFC programming. Remember as you study MFC programming, or any programming language for that matter, that programming is a large and complex topic. Few people exist who have memorized the entire language structure of large programming languages such as C++ and MFCs— although there are some. The majority of professional programmers have only a solid understanding of the basics of a particular programming language, and rely on excellent reference material when they encounter unfamiliar or rarely-used topics. Do not feel that you must memorize or understand every programming topic associated with a particular language. Have a basic understanding, but most important, know where you can find the information you need.

Next, this text discusses the MFC class library, which is at the heart of MFC programming. Then, you will learn about MFC notation.

MFC Class Library

The MFC class library consists of two major sections:

- the MFC class hierarchy
- Global functions and macros

MFC Class Hierarchy

The simple class hierarchy examples you saw in the Inheritance chapter were relatively small. In contrast, the MFC class hierarchy is surprisingly large. The MFC class library contains over two hundred classes, so this text cannot list the entire hierarchy here. Figure 8-5, however, shows a partial listing of the class hierarchy, highlighting some of the more important classes.

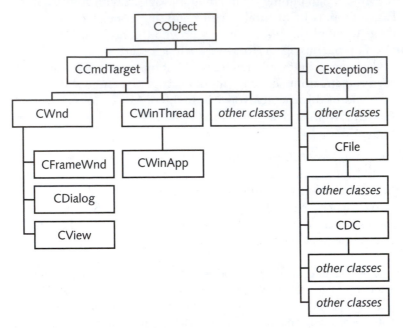

Figure 8-5   Partial listing of the MFC class hierarchy

 You can find a complete listing of the MFC class hierarchy in the MSDN Library.

At the top of the MFC class hierarchy is the **CObject base class.** You will indirectly work with members of the CObject class since its functionality is inherited by its derived classes. The CObject class also includes members for writing data to disk files in a process known as serialization. You will use the CObject class later in this text to serialize data to disk files. For now you should understand that every MFC class inherits the functionality of the CObject base class.

The most important branch of the MFC class hierarchy is the **CCmdTarget class**, which encapsulates the messaging features of the Windows API. Derived from the CCmdTarget class are several other important classes including the CWinApp class and the CWnd class. One class derived from CCmdTarget that you will work with in this chapter is the CDialog class, which creates dialog boxes. Since CDialog is derived from CCmdTarget, CDialog inherits all of CCmdTarget's messaging features. This means that you can add events that generate messages to a dialog class. Later, you will learn how to add events and messages to a dialog class, and how to handle them in your program.

The **CWinApp class**, also known as the **application class**, is responsible for initializing, starting, running, and stopping an MFC windows application. When you run any type of MFC application, it is up to the application class to manage the execution of that application.

The **CWnd class** encapsulates the various Windows API functions, data types, and other code used for creating and instantiating windows. Derived from the CWnd class are more specialized types of window classes such as the **CFrameWnd class**, which creates a standard type of window known as a frame window, and the **CDialog class** for creating dialog boxes. You will learn about each of these classes throughout this chapter; and additional MFC classes in future chapters.

Global Functions

If a function is not a member of an MFC class, then it is a global function that is available to all MFC classes, regardless of their position in the MFC class hierarchy. All MFC global functions begin with a prefix of `Afx`. Although most of the MFC functions and variables you work with will be a member of a class, some will not. For example, one commonly used global function is the AfxMessageBox() function that displays a simple message box to the user. The basic syntax for the AfxMessageBox() function involves passing a single string argument containing the text you want to be displayed in the message box. For example, the statement `AfxMessage Box("Hello World");` displays a message box containing the text *Hello World*. Figure 8-6 shows an example of a message box created with the AfxMessageBox() function.

Figure 8-6 Message box

Normally, to display a simple message box, you would use the MessageBox() member function of the CWnd class, which is almost identical to the AfxMessageBox() function. (Recall that the CWnd class encapsulates the window functionality of the Windows API.) However, you cannot use a class's member function before an object of the class is instantiated. In some cases, you may need to use a message box before a CWnd class object is instantiated in your program. Because you cannot use a class's member function before an object of the class is instantiated, you must use a global function.

 You can pass several other parameters to both the AfxMessageBox() function and the MessageBox() member function. These additional parameters determine the style of the message box and other attributes. For your studies, however, you will display only a simple text string to demonstrate functionality. If you would like more information on message box parameters, search for AfxMessageBox() and MessageBox() in the MSDN Library.

Macros

A programming element that is commonly used in MFC programming is a macro. A **macro** represents C++ code, constants, and other programming elements and is defined using the #define preprocessor directive. You will not actually create any macros in this chapter since the macros you need already exist in the MFC library. Even though you won't be creating macros, it helps to understand what they are when you use them.

The first thing you need to understand, is that a macro in C++ is different from a macro you may see in other environments. End user applications such as Word and Excel allow you to record a set of steps you would like to execute later. For example, in Word, you can record the necessary steps to search for a specific text string, copy the text string, move it to a different location in the document, paste it into the new location, and then bold and underline the text. Word and Excel refer to these types of recorded steps as macros. However, a macro in C++ is a name that represents C++ code and other programming elements that you would like to execute simply by calling the macro name, very similar to the way you call a function name. There are actually many similarities between macros and functions. Understanding when to use a macro and when to use a function, however, requires a more advanced understanding of C++ programming. If you would like further information on when to use a macro and when to use a function, search for the topic *Choosing Between Functions and Macros* in the MSDN Library.

Essentially, during preprocessing a macro name is replaced by the code and other programming elements that it represents. This process is very similar to using the `inline` keyword to request that the compiler replace calls to a function with the function definition wherever in a program the function is called. One of the main differences between inline functions and macros is that in addition to functions macros can represent other programming elements such as constants.

Macro names in the MFC library are in all-uppercase letters. Two of the more common macros you will use are BEGIN_MESSAGE_MAP() and END_MESSAGE_MAP(), which are used for handling messages. Macros can accept parameters, just like functions, so they are followed by parentheses. Unlike functions, however, when you place a macro on a line in a C++ source file you do not use a semicolon. The following code shows an example of the BEGIN_MESSAGE_MAP() and END_MESSAGE_MAP() macros, along with the ON_COMMAND() macro.

```
BEGIN_MESSAGE_MAP(CHelloWorldApp, CWinApp)
    //{{AFX_MSG_MAP(CHelloWorldApp)
    ON_COMMAND(ID_APP_ABOUT, OnAppAbout)
        // NOTE - the ClassWizard will add
            and remove mapping macros here.
        //    DO NOT EDIT what you see in these
            blocks of generated code!
    //}}AFX_MSG_MAP
    // Standard file based document commands
```

```
      ON_COMMAND(ID_FILE_NEW, CWinApp::OnFileNew)
      ON_COMMAND(ID_FILE_OPEN, CWinApp::OnFileOpen)
      // Standard print setup command
      ON_COMMAND(ID_FILE_PRINT_SETUP,
            CWinApp::OnFilePrintSetup)
   END_MESSAGE_MAP()
```

The preceding code is from a framework that was created with AppWizard. You will examine the parts of the code shortly in the Message Maps section.

MFC Notation

All MFC class names begin with *C*. Additionally, data members of MFC classes are prefixed with *m_*. Following the underscore character in an MFC data member name is a Hungarian notation character representing the data member's type. For example, m_hWnd and m_pMainWnd are both examples of MFC data members. The m_hWnd data member is a Windows API handle data type, and the m_pMainWnd data member is a Windows API pointer data type.

As you derive classes from the MFC classes, you should also begin your class names with a *C* and your data members with *m_* in order to identify your program as an MFC program. In fact, both the Add Member Variable dialog box of the ClassWizard and the New Class dialog box encourage you to use MFC notation when you add data members and new classes to your project. When you select the Add Variable button in ClassWizard, the Add Member Variable dialog box displays and automatically enters the prefix *m_* for you in the Member Variable Name text box, as shown in Figure 8-7.

Figure 8-7   Add Member Variable dialog box

When you add a class using the New Class dialog box, Visual C++ automatically assumes that your new class name will begin with a *C*. However, you do not normally use the *C* prefix for the file name. Therefore, Visual C++ strips the C prefix off the suggested class file name. Figure 8-8 shows an example of the New Class dialog box when you add an MFC class named CCalculator. Notice in the File Name box that the suggested name for the class file is *Calculator.cpp*, not *CCalculator.cpp*. If you want to include the *C* prefix in your class file name, then you can do so by clicking the Change button and adding *C* to the suggested file name. For the classes you create in this text, however, you will accept the file names suggested by Visual C++.

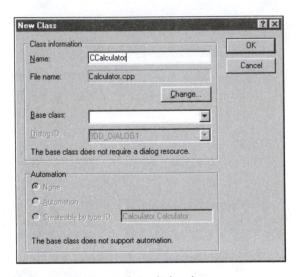

Figure 8-8   New Class dialog box

Basic MFC Programs

You can easily create the framework for an MFC program using AppWizard. Unless you understand the basic structure of an MFC program, however, the framework created by AppWizard will be of little use to you. Therefore, examine the basic structure of an MFC program.

The classes that turn a standard C++ program into an MFC program derive from MFC classes. As you start deriving classes from the MFC classes, remember that the MFC classes are part of a class hierarchy, and, therefore, inherit various data members and member functions. Although you will override a few of the inherited functions, you will most often use a function's base class version along with inherited data members. And, keep in mind that you can always create standard classes to give your program its functionality.

Most of the MFC classes are defined in the afxwin.h file, so you must include that file in the header files of any classes you want to derive from MFC. Later, you will see how the AppWizard manages afxwin.h and other MFC header files using the stdafx.h header file. But for now, just use afxwin.h

By default, Win32 Application projects do not support MFC programming. In order to enable MFC support in a Win32 Application project, you must select the Use MFC in a

Shared DLL setting in the Microsoft Foundation Classes combo box in the General tab of the Project Settings dialog box. Next, you will start creating the MFC Calculator program based on a Win32 Application project and modify the project so that is supports MFC.

To start creating the MFC Calculator program:

1. Return to Visual C++.

2. Create a new empty Win32 Application project named **MFCCalculator**. Save the project in the **Chapter.08** folder in your Visual C++ Projects folders.

3. By default, Win32 Application projects do not support MFC programming. To change this, display the Project Settings window by selecting **Settings** from the **Project** menu. If necessary, click on the General tab. Figure 8-9 shows the General tab of the Project Settings window.

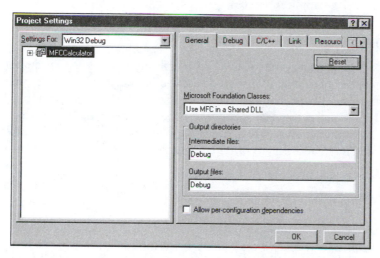

Figure 8-9 General tab of the Project Settings window

4. Select **Use MFC in a Shared DLL** in the **Microsoft Foundation Classes** combo box.

5. Click the **OK** button to close the Project Settings dialog box.

At their most basic level, all MFC programs require an application class and a window class. MFC programs also require message maps to handle Windows messages, but you will learn about that later. As you know, MFC is built on the Windows API, which runs on the Windows platform. Conceptually, you can think of the application class as being the MFC class that sits on top of the Windows API, while the window class sits on top of the application class. The structure of an MFC program and its application class and window class as they relate to the Windows API are illustrated in Figure 8-10.

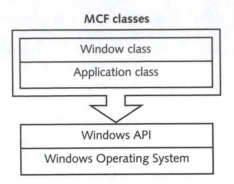

MCF classes

Figure 8-10   MFC application structure

First, you will examine the application class.

The Application Class

An application class is the starting point of any MFC application. You derive an application class from the CWinApp class. The application class object you instantiate in an MFC program represents the application as a whole. Through the application class object you can initialize, start, run, and stop the MFC application. The application class does not actually create anything visible that you can see. Rather, it is used for instantiating window class objects and displaying the windows they represent, in addition to other tasks such as initializing application variables.

When you derive an application object, you must:

- Override the virtual InitInstance() function
- Instantiate a global object of your application class

The InitInstance() function is called by the inherited WinMain() function each time a new instance of your MFC program starts. Remember that MFC provides the WinMain() function for you, and you do not need to write or override it. However, you must override the InitInstance() function in order to display your program's windows. The following code shows an InitInstance() function declaration. Notice that the InitInstance() function declaration is of the BOOL data type and that it includes the virtual keyword to instruct the compiler at runtime which version of the overridden InitInstance() function to use. It returns a value of TRUE if the function is successful and a value of FALSE if it is unsuccessful.

```
virtual BOOL InitInstance();
```

What actually executes the WinMain() function, which calls the InitInstance() function in turn, is the instantiation of a global application class object. You can instantiate only one global application class object, and it is usually instantiated within the application class's definition file. Figure 8-11 shows an example of a basic application class named CBasicApp.

```
// BasicApp.h
#include <afxwin.h>
class CBasicApp : public CWinApp {
public:
    CBasicApp();
    virtual ~CBasicApp();
    virtual BOOL InitInstance();
};
// BasicApp.cpp
#include "BasicApp.h"
CBasicApp::CBasicApp () {
}
CBasicApp::~CBasicApp () {
}
BOOL CBasicApp::InitInstance() {
    statements
    return TRUE;
}
CBasicApp theAppObject; // global object
```

Figure 8-11 Basic application class

8

Next, you will create the application class for the MFC Calculator program. Because you cannot display any windows until you learn about the window class, you will place a global AfxMessageBox() function in the InitInstance() function in order to demonstrate when the application class executes.

To create the application class for the MFC Calculator program:

1. Select the **New Class** command from the **Insert** menu.

2. In the New Class dialog box, type **CCalcApp** as the name of the class and click the **OK** button. Visual C++ creates two files called CalcApp.h and CalcApp.cpp.

3. Open the **CalcApp.h** header file in the Text Editor window.

4. Modify the CalcApp.h header file by adding the following boldface code, which includes the afxwin.h file and derives the class from the CWinApp class. The code also adds a public declaration for the InitInstance() function.

```
#include <afxwin.h>
class CCalcApp  : public CWinApp
{
public:
    CCalcApp();
    virtual ~CCalcApp();
    virtual BOOL InitInstance();
};
```

5. Next, open the **CalcApp.cpp** file in the Text Editor window and add the following InitInstance() function after the destructor function. The InitInstance()

function includes an AfxMessageBox() statement that displays a message box with the text *Application Started*.

```
BOOL CCalcApp::InitInstance() {
    AfxMessageBox("Application Started");
    return TRUE;
}
```

6. Finally, add the statement **CCalcApp theApplication;** after the InitInstance() function's closing brace to instantiate the application object.

7. Build and execute the project. You should see a message box displaying the text *Application Started*.

8. Close the message box, which also stops the application.

The Window Class

The MFC classes that derive from the CWnd class are used for creating the different types of windows that are visible to the user. The class you will use in this section is the **CFrameWnd class**, which creates a simple window with a frame, title bar, control menu, and control buttons. These windows are called frame windows because they usually "frame" an application, acting as a primary window that includes other windows such as view windows, toolbars, and status bars. Almost all MFC programs include a window class derived from the CFrameWnd class, with the exception of dialog-based applications (which you will study next).

With a basic MFC program like the one you are creating, there is little you need to do with the window class other than create its class declaration and definition files and derive the class from the CFrameWnd class. With more complex window classes, you need to write the code that manages the layout of various child windows of the frame class and that processes messages for its child windows. One task that is required for all window classes is calling the inherited Create() function from the class constructor. The **Create() function** creates the window itself when an object of the window class is instantiated. The basic syntax for the Create() function is **Create(NULL, *title*);**. The first parameter of 0 creates the window using default parameters, and the second parameter is a string that is used in the window's title bar. The Create() function also accepts additional parameters that determine the size, formatting, and position of the window. In fact, the Create() function is equivalent to the CreateWindow() function you studied in the last chapter and accepts many of the same parameters. For your basic MFC program, however, you only need to use the first two parameters of the Create() function. Figure 8-12 shows an example of a basic window class named CBasicFrameWnd derived from the CFrameWnd class.

```
// BasicFrameWnd.h
#include <afxwin.h>
class CBasicFrameWnd : public CFrameWnd {
public:
     CBasicFrameWnd();
     virtual ~CBasicFrameWnd();
};
// CBasicFrameWnd.cpp
#include "BasicFrameWnd.h"
CBasicFrameWnd::CBasicFrameWnd () {
     Create(NULL, "Basic MFC Program");
}
CBasicFrameWnd::~CBasicFrameWnd () {
}
```

Figure 8-12   Basic window class

As you recall from the last chapter, creating a window does not actually display it. In standard Windows API programming, you use the ShowWindow() function to display a window. MFC programming also uses a ShowWindow() function to display windows. It is important that you understand that the ShowWindow() function is *not* called from the window class. Instead, you call the ShowWindow() function from the application class's InitInstance() function using an instantiated object of the window class. For example, examine the following modified version of the CBasicApp class implementation file:

```
#include "BasicApp.h"
#include "BasicFrameWnd.h"
...
BOOL CBasicApp::InitInstance() {
     m_pMainWnd = new CBasicFrameWnd;
     m_pMainWnd->ShowWindow(m_nCmdShow);
     m_pMainWnd->UpdateWindow();
     return TRUE;
}
CBasicApp theAppObject; // global object
```

The preceding code includes the BasicFrameWnd.h header file in order to access the members in the window class. The first statement in the InitInstance() function instantiates a new CBasicFrameWnd object on the heap and assigns to it the pointer to the inherited m_pMainWnd data member (which is a pointer data type—note the *p* in the variable name). Notice that the InitInstance() function does not include a statement that deletes the m_pMainWnd object from the heap. You do not need to delete the m_pMainWnd pointer yourself since the inherited WinMain() function automatically deletes it.

The second statement in the InitInstance() function calls the ShowWindow() function, which displays the frame window that was created in the CBasicFrameWnd class. The MFC ShowWindow() function is virtually identical to the Windows API ShowWindow() function you studied in the last chapter, except that you do not pass to it a window handle.

Instead, you pass only the inherited m_nCmdShow data member that is inherited from the CWinApp class. The m_nCmdShow data member is equivalent to the Window API nCmdShow parameter, which represents the window's startup mode. The first time you call the ShowWindow() function in your MFC program you *must* pass to it the m_nCmdShow data member.

After a program's first call to ShowWindow(), you can use the function to manage a window's show state by passing a display constant. For example, if you want to programmatically maximize the window, you can pass to the ShowWindow() function the SW_MAXIMIZE constant using the statement **m_pMainWnd->ShowWindow(SW_MAXIMIZE);**. Look up the ShowWindow topic in the MSDN Library for a listing of other display constants.

The third statement in the InitInstance() function calls the UpdateWindow() function, which is used for updating the display in the window. The UpdateWindow() function is required by almost every MFC program, although it is not necessary for the basic MFC application you are creating. If you were to compile an MFC project that contained the CBasicApp class and the CBasicFrame class, and then execute the program, you would see the window shown in Figure 8-13.

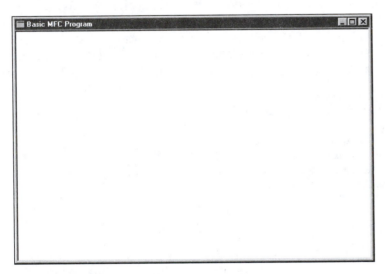

Figure 8-13 Basic MFC program window

An important concept to understand is that m_pMainWnd object is not the window itself. All objects that display windows are not the windows themselves. The window is only a visual representation of the object. Closing a window does not delete the object itself. In fact, all of the object's data members will still be available in case you need to redisplay the window. The object is only destroyed when it is deleted by the inherited WinMain() function when the InitInstance() function goes out of scope.

Next, you will add a window class to the MFC Calculator program.

To add a window class to the MFC Calculator program:

1. Select the **New Class** command from the **Insert** menu.

2. In the New Class dialog box, type **CCalcFrame** as the name of the class and click the **OK** button.

3. Open the **CalcFrame.h** header file in the Text Editor window.

4. Modify the file to include the afxwin.h file and derive the class from the CBasicFrame class as follows:

```
#include <afxwin.h>
class CCalcFrame : public CFrameWnd
{
public:
    CCalcFrame();
    virtual ~CCalcFrame();
};
```

5. Next, open the **CalcFrame.cpp** file in the Text Editor window and add a Create() function statement to the class constructor function as follows.

```
CCalcFrame::CCalcFrame()
{
    Create(NULL, "MFC Calculator");
}
```

6. Open the **CalcApp.cpp** file and add **#include "CalcFrame.h"** after the **#include "CalcApp.h"** statement to give the application class access to the frame class.

7. Replace the AfxMessageBox() statement in the InitInstance() function with the following three statements that instantiate a new CCalcFrame object, and then show and update the window:

```
BOOL CCalcApp::InitInstance() {
    m_pMainWnd = new CCalcFrame;
    m_pMainWnd->ShowWindow(m_nCmdShow);
    m_pMainWnd->UpdateWindow();
    return TRUE;
}
```

8. Rebuild and execute the program. You should see a basic frame window, similar to Figure 8-13.

9. Close the frame window by clicking the **Close** button in the title bar.

8

RESOURCES

This chapter introduces new programming elements called resources that are exclusive to Windows API programming. A **resource** is a graphical user interface element that allows a user to interact with an application. Figure 8-14 lists the standard Windows API resources.

Resource	Description
Accelerator tables	Keyboard shortcut keys
Bitmaps	Icons and other image files
Cursors	Alternate mouse cursors that can be used in place of the standard Windows arrow cursor
Dialog boxes	Dialog boxes, such as Open and Save dialog boxes
HTML pages	Web page documents
Menus	Menus of commands contained in the Windows menu bar
String tables	IDs, values, and captions that are required by an application
Toolbar resources	Graphical elements that execute commands after being clicked by the mouse
Version information	Company and product identification, a product release number, and copyright and trademark notification

Figure 8-14   Standard Windows API resources

Resources are defined in special files called **resource scripts**. Resource scripts have an extension of .rc and are written in C preprocessor language. When you build a project, all of the project's resources are compiled into a file with an extension of .res. You refer to resources in an MFC program using a resource ID. A **resource ID** is a constant declared with the #define preprocessor directive and is used for programmatically referring to a resource. It is common practice to declare all resource constants in an interface file named resource.h in order to make it easier to reference them in your program. Visual C++ automatically creates a resource.h file for you whenever you add a resource script to a project, which occurs automatically when you run AppWizard. If you do not use AppWizard to create an MFC project, then you must manually include the resource.h file in the header file of any MFC-derived classes that use resources.

Although resource files are written in C preprocessor language, you do not actually need to write any code. Instead, you use a Visual C++ Resource editor. When a Visual C++ project includes resources, the Workspace window includes a ResourceView tab that allows you to quickly open a resource in a resource editor. Additionally, you can use the Properties dialog box for modifying various attributes of a resource.

Resource Editors

Resource editors allow you to quickly create and modify resources in a graphical environment. You can still edit a resource file's C preprocessor code, although there is little reason to do so since Visual C++ does an excellent job of writing the code for you. As an example of a resource editor, consider the Dialog Editor, which you will use extensively in this chapter. The Dialog Editor contains a number of tools along with an editing pane where you can graphically draw the dialog box's controls. As you draw the controls, Visual C++ automatically writes the C preprocessor code for you. Figure 8-15 shows a simple dialog box in the Dialog Editor, and Figure 8-16 shows the C preprocessor code that represents the same dialog box. You can also see the Dialog Editor tools in Figure 8-16.

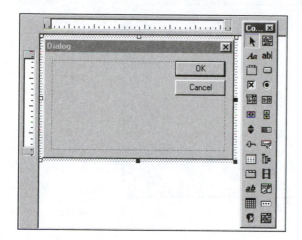

Figure 8-15   Dialog Editor

```
///////////////////////////////////////////////////////////////
//
// Dialog
//

IDD_DIALOG1 DIALOG DISCARDABLE  0, 0, 186, 95
STYLE DS_MODALFRAME | WS_POPUP | WS_CAPTION | WS_SYSMENU
CAPTION "Dialog"
FONT 8, "MS Sans Serif"
BEGIN
    DEFPUSHBUTTON    "OK",IDOK,129,7,50,14
    PUSHBUTTON       "Cancel",IDCANCEL,129,24,50,14
END
```

Figure 8-16   Dialog box C preprocessor code

 You can view and edit a resource's C preprocessor code by selecting Open from the File menu to display the Open dialog box. Select the resource file and select *Text* from the Open As drop-down list box.

ResourceView

Once you add a resource to a project, a new ResourceView tab appears in the Workspace window. ResourceView contains folders representing the different resource types. You can use ResourceView to quickly open a resource in a resource editor. To view a particular resource in its editor, expand its resource folder and double-click on the resource name. Figure 8–17 shows the IDE after expanding the Toolbar folder on the ResourceView tab and double-clicking on the IDR_MAINFRAME resource.

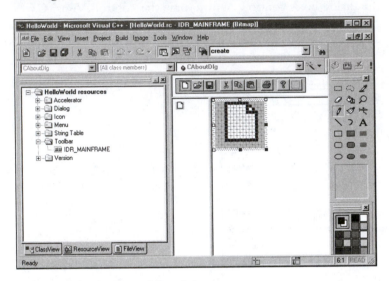

Figure 8-17 ResourceView tab

 You will not see the ResourceView tab if your project does not include any resources.

Properties Dialog Box

The Properties dialog box in Visual C++ (and other Visual Studio tools) is used for modifying the resource ID, setting the caption, and managing the appearance of resources. Different types of resources have different options available in their Property dialog boxes. You use the Properties dialog box to modify a button's resource ID, set the text that appears on the button's face (its caption), and set the style of the button. Figure 8–18 shows the General tab and the Styles tab of the Properties dialog box for a button.

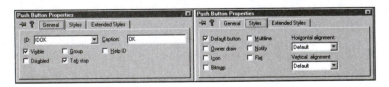

Figure 8-18 Properties dialog box tabs for a button

VISUAL C++ CLASS TOOLS

In this section, you will learn about some tools that are available in Visual C++ for working with classes. You have already seen the ClassView tab in the Workspace window. Two other tools that you can use are ClassWizard and WizardBar.

ClassWizard

Visual C++ provides a tool called **ClassWizard** to assist you in creating and working with MFC-derived classes. Some of the tasks you can perform with ClassWizard include working with Windows messages, adding new classes, and defining member variables that work with the data a user enters into your application's interface elements. You execute ClassWizard by selecting the ClassWizard command on the View menu. Figure 8-19 shows an example of ClassWizard.

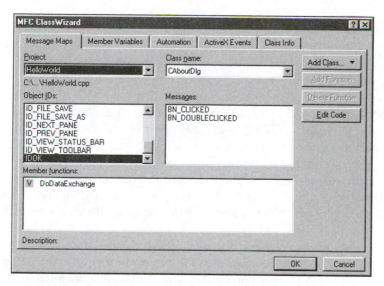

Figure 8-19   ClassWizard

ClassWizard can only be used with MFC programs.

ClassWizard is available only if your project includes a resource script and if it includes a ClassWizard database file with an extension of .clw. When you use AppWizard to build a framework, a resource script is always included and the ClassWizard database file is built by default. If you build a project from scratch and add resources later, Visual C++ will walk you through the steps to create a new ClassWizard database file the first time you run ClassWizard after adding a resource script. Also, be aware that most of the commands in ClassWizard are available only to framework classes created when you use AppWizard to create a new MFC application.

After you add a new class using ClassWizard, you will see some special comment blocks similar to the following:

```
//{{AFX_DATA_MAP
...
//}}AFX_DATA_MAP
```

Comments such as these mark the locations in a MFC program that ClassWizard controls and edits. ClassWizard never modifies code located outside of these comment sections. Normally, you should not need to make any changes to code located within ClassWizard comments, although there may be some occasions when you need to. Be careful when you edit any code accompanied by ClassWizard comments, especially when you see other comments warning you not to edit ClassWizard comments and code.

WizardBar

Another Visual C++ tool you will use when working with classes is WizardBar. **WizardBar** is a toolbar that is used for working with classes in Visual C++. You will find three combo boxes on WizardBar: the Class List, the Filter List, and the Members List. The Class List combo box displays the classes in your project and allows you to quickly navigate to a class by selecting its name in the list. The Filter List combo box is used with MFC programs and allows you to apply a filter to your class using specific resource IDs. The Member List combo box displays a class's members, according to the selection in the Filter List combo box, and allows you to quickly navigate to a class member by clicking its name in the list. One of the most important tools you will find on WizardBar is the Action Control. The Action Control contains two parts: the Action menu on the right and the Action Button on the left. The Action menu contains numerous commands for working with classes while the Action button executes the default action on the Action menu. The default action depends on which combo box on WizardBar has the focus as well as the selected contents of the combo boxes. You can tell the default action by looking on the Action menu for the bolded item. Figure 8-20 shows an example of WizardBar, with the Action menu displayed. Notice that the default action on the Action menu is the Go To Function Declaration command. Clicking the Action button executes the Go To Function Declaration command.

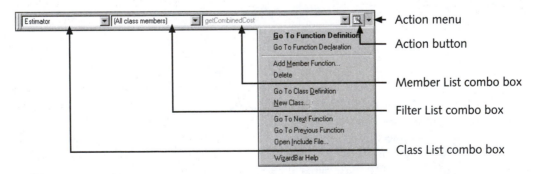

Figure 8-20 WizardBar

You actually could have used WizardBar earlier in this text when you first started working with classes. However, it was important that you first understood how a class was constructed before using Visual C++'s automated tools. You will use ClassWizard and WizardBar throughout the rest of this text.

THE CSTRING CLASS

An important MFC class that you need to know about since you will use it in the next section is the **CString class**, which is used for manipulating strings in MFC programs. You will find that it is much easier to work with strings using the CString class than it is by using char[] arrays and char* pointers. You create a string variable with the CString class using a statement similar to `CString myString;`. You can also assign a string directly to the variable name using a statement such as `CString myString = "This is a text string.";`. There is no need to declare the number of characters you want to store or use a char* pointer. Once you have instantiated two CString variables, you can assign the contents of one variable to the other using the assignment operator, in the same way the assignment operator is used with numeric data types. The following code shows an example of how to assign the contents of one CString variable to another CString variable:

```
CString firstString = "This is a text string";
CString secondString;
secondString = firstString;
```

You can also use several operators with CString variables including the + operator, the += assignment operator, and the == comparison operator. When used with strings, the plus sign is known as the concatenation operator. The **concatenation operator** (+) is used to combine two strings of the CString class. The following code combines a CString variable and a literal string and assigns the new value to another variable:

```
CString firstString = "San Francisco ";
CString newString;
newString = firstString + "is in California";
```

The combined value of the firstString variable and the string literal that is assigned to the newString variable is *San Francisco is in California*.

You can also use the += assignment operator to combine two strings. The following code combines the two text strings, but without using the newString variable:

```
CString firstString = "San Francisco ";
firstString += "is in California";
```

Note that the same symbol—a plus sign—serves as the concatenation operator and the addition operator. When used with numbers or variables containing numbers, expressions using the plus sign will return the sum of the two numbers. However, if you use the concatenation

8

operator with a string value and a number value, the string value and the number value will be combined into a new string value, as in the following example:

```
CString textString = "The legal voting age is ";
CString votingAge = 18;
newString = textString + votingAge;
```

The new value of the newString variable in the preceding example is *The legal voting age is 18.*

The comparison operator is useful with CString variables to determine if they contain the same text. For example, the following code contains an `if` statement that compares the values of two CString variables. Since the variables do not contain the same string values, the message box in the `if` statement does not display.

```
CString firstCity = "San Francisco";
CString secondCity = "Los Angeles";
if (firstCity == secondCity)
    AfxMessageBox("Same cities");
```

DIALOG-BASED APPLICATIONS

One of the more common types of windows used in Windows applications is the dialog box. A **dialog box** is a window that is used to display information or to gather information from users. The message box you have seen in this chapter is an example of a dialog box. Some standard Windows dialog boxes, which are shared by many different types of Windows applications, are called common dialog boxes, and they include the Open and Save dialog boxes, Print dialog boxes, and Font dialog boxes. Figure 8-21 shows the Open dialog box that is shared by many Windows applications.

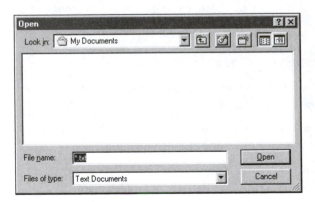

Figure 8-21   Open dialog box

Windows includes a common dialog box library from which you can include common dialog boxes into your applications, regardless of the programming language you use. Using common dialog boxes ensures that the standard dialog box types used by all Windows applications are consistent from one Windows application to another. Also, using common dialog boxes means that you do not have to waste time creating your own versions of each dialog box type. You will work with some common dialog boxes in later chapters. In this chapter, you will learn how to create your own custom dialog boxes.

All dialog boxes—whether standard or custom—are created using two components: a dialog resource and a dialog class derived from the CDialog class. The dialog resource represents the visual aspect of the dialog box, and the dialog class provides programmatic access to the dialog box. The CDialog class is a window class since it derives from the CWnd class, the same as the CFrameWnd class. Most dialog boxes are usually associated with a CFrameWnd class, or another class derived from CWnd. For example, an application that includes a frame window often calls various CDialog class windows in order to display information or to gather information from the user. However, you can also use a dialog box as an application's primary interface window. Applications that use a dialog box as their primary interface window are called **dialog-based applications**. The MFC Calculator program is a dialog-based application.

Next, you will add a dialog resource and a dialog class to the MFC Calculator program. Before you can add the dialog resource, you must add a resource script to the program.

To add a resource script to the MFC Calculator program:

1. Point to **Add To Project** on the **Project** menu, and then click **New** to display the New dialog box.

2. Select **Resource Script** from the **Files** list.

3. Type **Calculator** as the file name and click the **OK** button. A single folder icon labeled Calculator.rc replaces the Text Editor portion of the screen. This folder represents the folder that will contain your project's resources.

4. When you added the resource script to your project, a resource.h file was created in your project directory. You need to add that resource.h file to your project. Point to **Add To Project** on the **Project** menu, and then click **Files** to display the Insert Files into Project dialog box. Select the resource.h file from the file list in the Insert Files into Project dialog box and click the **OK** button.

Now that you have added a resource script, you can add a dialog resource.

To add a dialog resource to the MFC Calculator project:

1. Select **Resource** from the **Insert** menu to display the Insert Resource dialog box.

2. Click the **Dialog** resource type and click the **New** button. A new dialog resource with an OK button and Cancel button appears in the Dialog Editor.

3. With the dialog box selected in the Dialog Editor, select **Properties** from the **View** menu to display the Properties window.

8

4. In the Properties window, change the default resource ID from IDD_DIALOG1 TO **IDD_CALCULATOR**. Also, change the dialog caption from Dialog to **MFC Calculator**.

5. Close the Properties window by clicking the **Close** button on the title bar.

Now you will use ClassWizard to add a dialog class to the project that will provide programmatic access to the dialog resource.

To add a dialog class that provides programmatic access to the dialog resource:

1. First, delete the **CalcFrame.h** and **CalcFrame.cpp** files from your project by selecting each file in the Workspace window and pressing delete. You will no longer need these files since the MFC Calculator program will be dialog-based. Remember from Chapter 1 that deleting a file from the Workspace window does not delete it from your hard drive. Therefore, you also need to open Windows Explorer and delete the files from your project folder. When you are through, return to Visual C++.

2. Select **ClassWizard** from the **View** menu. You will receive a dialog box warning you that the ClassWizard database file, Calculator.clw, does not exist. Click **Yes** to build it from your source files.

3. You will see a dialog box similar to an Open dialog box asking you to select the source files that are included in your project. By default, the three source files, CalcApp.h, CalcApp.cpp, and resource.h, should already be placed in the Files in Project list. If these three files are not listed in the Files in Project list, highlight them in the file list box and click the **Add** button. Click the **OK** button to continue. The MFC ClassWizard dialog box appears.

 Depending on the length of your path, you may not be able to see the entire filenames listed.

4. In the MFC ClassWizard dialog box, click the **Add Class** button and then click the **New** option to display the New Class dialog box. Notice that when you execute the New Class dialog box from ClassWizard, you can select an MFC base class for your new class, among other options.

5. In the New Class dialog box, type **CCalculator** as the name of the class and then select CDialog as the base class. You use the Dialog ID list box to associate the new class with a dialog resource. The IDD_CALCULATOR resource ID should already be selected in the Dialog ID list box. Click the **OK** button.

6. After the New Class dialog box closes, click the **OK** button to close the ClassWizard dialog box.

7. Open the **Calculator.h** file in the Text Editor window and add the following #include statements above the class header declaration:

```
#include <afxwin.h>
#include "resource.h"
```

8. Open the **Calculator.cpp** file in the Text Editor window and delete the **#include "stdafx.h"** statement. ClassWizard adds this statement automatically, although you cannot use it with the MFC Calculator program since you are creating the MFC files from scratch. You will learn about the stdafx.h file at the end of this chapter.

Before you can add code that displays the dialog box, you need to understand the difference between modal and modeless dialog boxes.

Modal and Modeless Dialog Boxes

Modal dialog boxes require users to close or cancel the dialog box before they can continue working with an application. The message boxes you have worked with are examples of modal dialog boxes. Once a modal message box appears on your screen, you cannot access any other window in the application until you close the message box. Simple modal message boxes contain only a single OK button. More complex modal dialog boxes usually contain a Cancel button in addition to an OK button. For example, Figure 8-22 shows the modal Font dialog box for WordPad, a simple word processing program supplied with Windows operating systems. Since the Font dialog box is modal, you cannot click on the main WordPad window until you either select the desired font information and click the OK button, or close the dialog box by clicking the Cancel button.

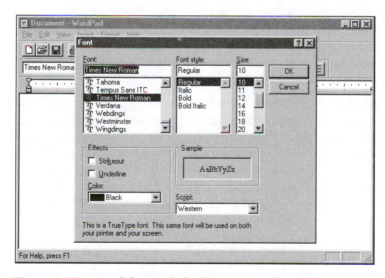

Figure 8-22   Modal Font dialog box in WordPad

The OK button in some types of modal dialog boxes may be a more descriptive button, depending on the dialog box's function. For example, the Open dialog box includes an Open button instead of an OK button, and the Save dialog box includes a Save button instead of an OK button.

In comparison to a modal dialog box, **modeless dialog boxes** do not need to be closed before you return to another window in the application. Modeless dialog boxes function more like frame windows and other types of primary application windows. For dialog based applications like the MFC Calculator program, you can usually use either modeless or modal dialog boxes. If your dialog-based application uses other dialog boxes to gather information that is then used in the main dialog window, you would probably want your main dialog window to be modeless and any other dialog boxes that are called by the main dialog window to be modal.

Modeless dialog boxes require quite a bit more work than modal dialog boxes. Much of the behind-the-scenes work, such as closing and destroying the dialog window, is handled automatically with modal dialog boxes. With modeless dialog boxes, however, especially in dialog-based applications, you need to override several inherited member functions. Overriding the inherited member functions allows you to correctly close and destroy the dialog window. Additionally, overriding inherited member functions allows you to be sure the dialog box functions correctly within the context of the application window. Because of these complexities, you will concentrate on working with modal dialog boxes.

Displaying Modal Dialog Boxes

You display a modal dialog box from an application's InitInstance() method, the same as how you display a frame window. You instantiate an object of the dialog class and use the inherited **DoModal() function** to display the modal dialog box. By default, if a user clicks a button containing a resource ID of IDOK or IDCANCEL, the dialog box closes. The IDOK resource ID represents the OK button and the IDCANCEL resource ID represents the Cancel button.

The DoModal() function returns an integer value representing the resource ID that caused the dialog box to close. You use these resource IDs in an `if` statement to take the appropriate action, depending on whether the user pressed the OK button or the Cancel button. For example, if your dialog box prompts the user for his or her name, then you would use the OK branch of the `if` statement to assign the name to a data member. By default, the IDCANCEL resource ID causes the dialog box to be destroyed. However, you may find it necessary to use the cancel branch of the `if` statement to make sure the user wants to close the dialog box or to save any unsaved data.

The following code shows an example of an application class's InitInstance() function that displays a modal dialog box based on a dialog class named CHelloWorldDlg. The DoModal() function returns the resource ID to an int variable named nResponse. The `if` statement then checks the value of nResponse and executes the appropriate code block. Notice that the

InitInstance() function returns a value of FALSE. Since this is a dialog-based application, you return a value of FALSE from the InitInstance() method in order to exit the application.

```
BOOL CHelloWorldApp::InitInstance() {
    CHelloWorldDlg dlg;
    int nResponse = dlg.DoModal();
    if (nResponse == IDOK) {
        // OK button statements
    }
    else if (nResponse == IDCANCEL) {
        // Cancel button statements
    }
    return FALSE;
}
```

Next, you will add code to the MFC Calculator application class's InitInstance() function, that displays the MFC Calculator program's dialog box as a modal dialog box. Since the MFC Calculator program does not require OK and Cancel buttons, you will delete them from the dialog box. You can close the application by clicking the Close button or by pressing the Escape key. Also, since the dialog box will not include OK and Cancel buttons, there is no need to include the `if` statement. Thus, you can simply call the DoModal() function using a statement similar to `dlg.DoModal();`, without assigning the return value to an integer variable.

To add code to the MFC Calculator application class's InitInstance() function that displays the MFC Calculator program's dialog box as a modal dialog box:

1. Open the **IDD_CALCULATOR** resource in the Dialog Editor by clicking the ResourceView tab, expanding the Dialog folder, and then double-clicking the IDD_CALCULATOR icon. Then delete the **OK** and **Cancel** buttons by clicking each button once and pressing **Delete**.

2. Open the **CalcApp.cpp** file in the Text Editor window.

3. Modify the #include statement that includes the deleted CalcFrame.h file so that it includes the **Calculator.h** file instead.

4. Modify the InitInstance() function by adding the following bolded code so that it declares a new Calculator object named *calc* and calls the DoModal() function. Be sure to delete the statements that instantiated the frame window and modify the return statement so that it returns a value of FALSE.

```
BOOL CCalcApp::InitInstance() {
    CCalculator calc;
    calc.DoModal();
    return FALSE;
}
```

5. Rebuild and execute the program. You should see the dialog box shown in Figure 8-23.

8

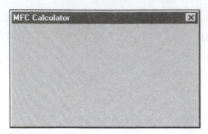

Figure 8-23   Dialog box created by MFC Calculator program

6. Close the dialog box by clicking the **Close** button in the title bar or by pressing **Escape**.

Working with Controls

Dialog boxes typically contain groups of controls through which a user interacts with an application. **Controls** are user interface items such as check boxes, command buttons, text boxes, and other objects. You add controls to a dialog box using the Controls toolbar in the Dialog Editor. To see a description of each toolbar button, hold your mouse over a button until the button's ToolTip appears. Figure 8-24 shows the Controls toolbar with the Edit Box control ToolTip displayed.

Figure 8-24   Controls toolbar

The ability to easily add controls is one of the greatest benefits of using dialog boxes. You can also add controls as child windows to frame windows and other windows, but not as easily as you can add them to dialog windows. With dialog windows you use the Dialog Editor to draw the controls you need onto your dialog box; Visual C++ then enters the correct code in the program's resource script. Dialog windows are the only windows that you can create with a resource editor such as the Dialog Editor. With other types of windows, you need to manually add the code for each control.

You can add the following three types of controls to MFC programs:

- Windows common controls
- MFC controls
- ActiveX controls

Windows common controls are the standard controls, such as edit boxes, buttons, check boxes, and so on, you see in common dialog boxes. Windows common controls are actually provided by the Windows operating system itself, not by Visual C++ or MFC.

MFC controls are provided by MFC and are not part of the Windows operating system. There are three MFC controls: the Bitmap Button control, the Checklist Box control, and the Drag List Box control. The Bitmap Button control is similar to a standard command button except that it displays a bitmap image on its face. The Checklist Box control displays a list of items, such as filenames, that a user can check or uncheck. The Drag List Box control allows users to reorder lists of items, such as a filename list.

ActiveX is a technology that allows programming objects to be easily re-used with any programming language that supports Microsoft's Component Object Model. The **Component Object Model**, or **COM**, is an architecture for cross-platform development of client/server applications. **ActiveX controls** are objects that are placed in Web pages or inside programs created with COM-enabled programming languages. ActiveX controls are very popular in Windows programming; you can literally find thousands of types of ActiveX controls in various places on the Web. However, they are somewhat advanced for your studies. You will work with Windows common controls for the rest of this text.

Recall from the last chapter that individual controls are actually windows, the same as frame windows and dialog windows. Since controls are windows, they can be controlled programmatically using classes derived from the CWnd class. Figure 8-25 lists the Windows common controls, along with a description of each control and its associated MFC class.

Control	Description	MFC Class
animation	AVI video player	CAnimateCtrl
Button	Command button	CButton
combo box	Combination edit box/list box	CComboBox
date and time picker	Date and time selection control	CDateTimeCtrl
edit box	Single line text box	CEdit
extended combo box	Combo box control that is capable of displaying images	CComboBoxEx
header	Button that appears above a column of text and controls the width of the displayed text	CHeaderCtrl
hotkey	Shortcut keys that allows user to quickly perform a task	CHotKeyCtrl
image list	Lists of icons or bitmaps	CImageList

Figure 8-25   Windows common controls and MFC classes

Control	Description	MFC Class
list	Selectable list of text strings with icons	CListCtrl
list box	Selectable list of text strings	CListBox
month calendar	Monthly calendar control	CMonthCalCtrl
progress	Progress bar that tracks the completion of a task	CProgressCtrl
rebar	Toolbar capable of containing control child windows	CRebarCtrl
rich edit	Multi-line edit box with character and paragraph formatting	CRichEditCtrl
scroll bar	Control that scrolls the display of a dialog window	CScrollBar
slider	Selection bar with optional tick marks	CSliderCtrl
spin button	Increment or decrement a value	CSpinButtonCtrl
static-text	Explanatory text	CStatic
status bar	Informational control that displays at the bottom of an application window	CStatusBarCtrl
tab	Dialog box control that divides a dialog box into multiple sections	CTabCtrl
toolbar	List of commands represented by image buttons	CToolBarCtrl
tool tip	Pop-up window that describes a toolbar button	CToolTipCtrl
tree	Hierarchical list of items	CTreeCtrl

Figure 8-25 Windows common controls and MFC classes (continued)

You do not usually need to derive classes for individual controls placed on a dialog box. Remember that controls are usually placed as child windows within a dialog box parent window. Therefore, you can have the dialog box class manage the functionality for each individual control. For example, the controls in the MFC Calculator program you are creating do not need to be controlled using individual MFC classes. Instead, the dialog class will use messages generated by each control to execute the functions that give the program its functionality.

More complex types of controls must be controlled using an associated MFC class. For example, the status bar control is used for displaying various kinds of status information about an application. You will not find a status bar control on the Controls toolbar. Instead, you must use the CStatusBarCtrl class to declare a status bar object, and then use member functions of the CStatusBarCtrl class to format the display of the status bar and assign the various types of status information you want to see displayed. Any required class syntax for controls will be introduced as you encounter them in the text.

Before you start adding controls to the MFC Calculator program's dialog window, you need to think about some interface design issues. Professional programming departments are often separated into two groups: programmers who write code and programmers who design interfaces. Although there is some overlap between these two disciplines, programmers who specialize in interface design often have additional training in graphic design techniques.

When trying to design an interface, you may find yourself growing frustrated because your controls may not line up perfectly, you may not be satisfied with your color choices, and so on. As you start designing visual interfaces, remember that you are studying only the basics. Your goal is to learn the essentials of MFC programming and make the MFC Calculator program function—not necessarily to win design awards. Be patient as you develop your interface design skills.

When you activate the Dialog Editor window, a new menu item, Layout, appears to assist you in designing your dialog window. The Layout menu contains various commands that will assist you in arranging, organizing, and spacing the controls placed on your dialog box. One very useful command that you will use in the next exercise is the Test command, which allows you to see a preview of your dialog box exactly as it will appear when you execute the application.

Next, you will add controls to the MFC Calculator program's dialog resource. You will create the text box using the Edit Box control and the calculator buttons using the Button control. If you are not sure which buttons on the Control toolbar represent the control types, hold your mouse over each button to display its ToolTip. Use the finished calculator shown in Figure 8-26 as a model for how your dialog box should appear.

Figure 8-26   MFC Calculator dialog box

To add controls to the MFC Calculator program's dialog resource:

1. Open the **IDD_CALCULATOR** resource in the Dialog Editor. As you adjust the placement and size of your dialog box and its controls in this exercise, occasionally select the Test command on the Layout menu to see a preview of your dialog box that is exactly as it will appear when you execute the application.

2. The dialog window should appear with squares at its corners and sides that are used for resizing the window. You resize the window by pointing at one of these handles, holding your left mouse button, and dragging to the desired size. Resize your calculator window so that it matches Figure 8-26.

3. Next, add the Edit Box control. Click once on the **Edit Box** control on the Control toolbar and hold your mouse over the approximate location in the dialog

window of the upper-left corner of the control. Holding your left mouse button down, drag to the approximate location of the lower-right corner of the control, and then release your mouse button. The new edit box appears with the same sizing handles you saw around the dialog window. Use the sizing handles to adjust the size of the control, if necessary.

4. Click once on the **Edit Box** control that you just added and select **Properties** from the **View** menu to display the Properties window. When the Properties window displays, click the **General** tab. Change the control's default resource ID from IDC_EDIT1 to **IDC_DISPLAY**.

5. Click the **Styles** tab in the Properties window. The MFC Calculator program's functionality will be through its buttons, so you do not want users to be able to click in the IDC_DISPLAY Edit Box control and type numbers. On the Styles tab, click the **Read-only** check box, which will prevent users from being able to enter any data into the edit box. Close the Properties window.

6. Next, add the calculator buttons using the Button control. You can also use sizing handles to adjust the size of a Button control after adding it to the dialog window.

7. Click once on each button and select **Properties** from the **View** menu to display the Properties window. For each button, use the caption shown in Figure 8-27. Also, change each button's resource ID to the IDs shown in Figure 8-27.

Caption	Resource ID
+	IDC_PLUS
–	IDC_MINUS
*	IDC_MULTIPLY
/	IDC_DIVIDE
.	IDC_POINT
=	IDC_EQUALS
Clear	IDC_CLEAR
0	IDC_ZERO
1	IDC_ONE
2	IDC_TWO
3	IDC_THREE
4	IDC_FOUR
5	IDC_FIVE
6	IDC_SIX
7	IDC_SEVEN
8	IDC_EIGHT
9	IDC_NINE

Figure 8-27   Button captions and resource ID

Dialog Data Exchange

To set and retrieve control values in an MFC application, you can use the same SetWindowText() and GetWindowText() Windows API functions that you learned about in the last chapter. MFC provides a special mechanism, however, called **dialog data exchange**, or **DDX**, to handle the exchange of values between controls and variables. You do not need to call the SetWindowText() and GetWindowText() functions in an MFC program since DDX handles the exchange of information for you. A related mechanism called **dialog data validation**, or **DDV**, assists in the validation of data as it is exchanged between controls and variables.

DDX is enabled by an inherited DoDataExchange() function that works with data members that are under the control of ClassWizard. You may have already seen the DoDataExchange() function that ClassWizard automatically added when it created the CCalculator class. To use DDX, you use the Member Variables tab in ClassWizard to create a data member and associate it with a control's resource ID. ClassWizard also allows you to initialize values for the data member. Figure 8-28 shows an example of the ClassWizard Member Variables tab.

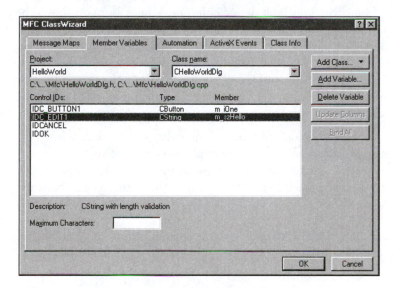

Figure 8-28   ClassWizard Member Variables tab

After you close ClassWizard, initialization statements for each data member are placed in the dialog class's constructor and the appropriate DDX functions for setting the data member's value in the associated control are added to the DoDataExchange() function in the HelloWorldDlg class. The following code shows an example of the constructor and DoDataExchange() function for a dialog class named HelloWorldDlg. ClassWizard automatically added the bolded code between the ClassWizard comments. The constructor initializes a m_szHello data member using the _T() function, which is a special data mapping function that assigns a text string to the m_szHello data member. The only thing you need to do with the _T() function is change the text that it passes as an argument. The DoDataExchange() function contains a single statement that uses a function named DDX_Text() to initialize the IDC_EDIT1 control with the value assigned to the m_szHello data member.

```
CHelloWorldDlg::CHelloWorldDlg(CWnd* pParent /*=NULL*/)
    : CDialog(CHelloWorldDlg::IDD, pParent) {
    //{{AFX_DATA_INIT(CHelloWorldDlg)
    m_szHello = _T("Hello");
    //}}AFX_DATA_INIT
}
void CHelloWorldDlg::DoDataExchange(CDataExchange* pDX) {
    CDialog::DoDataExchange(pDX);
    //{{AFX_DATA_MAP(CHelloWorldDlg)
    DDX_Text(pDX, IDC_EDIT1, m_szHello);
    //}}AFX_DATA_MAP
}
```

When your MFC program initializes, an inherited function named OnInitDialog() is called, which in turn calls the UpdateData() function. The UpdateData() function then calls the DoDataExchange() function. This is all done behind the scenes, but you should be aware of the process. The **UpdateData() function** either initializes dialog box controls using associated data members, or it copies the current control values back into the associated data members. The UpdateData() function calls the DoDataExchange() function when it is passed a value of FALSE by the OnInitDialog() function. When the user closes a modal dialog box by clicking the OK button, the UpdateData() function is called and passed a value of TRUE, which copies the control's current values into the associated data members.

You can also use the UpdateData() function to quickly assign a dialog box's control values to their associated data members. For example, if you want to use in your code the most recent value a user entered into an edit control named IDC_EDIT1, you first call the statement `UpdateData(TRUE);`, which copies the most recent control values to their associated data members.

 Never call the DoDataExchange() function directly; always call it using the UpdateData() function.

Next, you will add a DDX data member to the MFC Calculator program. You will add a DDX data member only for the IDC_DISPLAY control since that is the only control for which you need to set and retrieve values.

To add a DDX data member to the MFC Calculator program:

1. Start **ClassWizard** by selecting it from the View menu, and select the **Member Variables** tab.

2. Select **IDC_DISPLAY** in the Control IDs list, and click the **Add Variable** button. The Add Member Variable dialog box appears.

3. In the Add Member Variable dialog box, type **m_szDisplay** as the name of the variable. Leave the value in the Category drop-down list box as Value and the value in the Variable Type drop-down list box as CString.

4. Click the **OK** button to close the Add Member Variable dialog box, and then click the **OK** button to close ClassWizard.

5. Next, open **Calculator.cpp** in the Text Editor window and examine the constructor and DoDataExchange() functions. The statement `m_szDisplay = _T("");` has been added to the constructor to initialize the m_dDisplay variable. The statement `DDX_Text(pDX, IDC_DISPLAY, m_szDisplay);` has been added to the DoDataExchange() function to set the IDC_DISPLAY control's value to the value of m_szDisplay upon initialization. Change the `m_szDisplay = ("");` statement in the constructor to `m_szDisplay = ("0");` so that an initial value of 0 is assigned to the IDC_DISPLAY control.

8

MESSAGE MAPS

As with Windows API programs, in MFC programs, messages are raised for events that occur. In MFC programs, you do not need to create a window procedure to process messages. Instead, the framework handles the processing of messages using message maps. The inherited Run() function of the CWinApp class automatically retrieves queued messages and sends each message to the appropriate window. Each individual window in an MFC application handles its own messages using a message map. A **message map** associates messages with message handler functions. All windows derived from CCmdTarget can include message maps. Since CWnd derives from CCmdTarget, any of the child class windows of CWnd can include their own message maps.

You add a message map to a window by first adding the DECLARE_MESSAGE_MAP() macro to the class interface file. Then, you must add a message map block to the class implementation file starting with the BEGIN_MESSAGE_MAP() macro and ending with the END_MESSAGE_MAP() macro. ClassWizard automatically added the message map for you when you created the CCalculator class since it derives from the CDialog class, which includes CCmdTarget as an indirect base class. The BEGIN_MESSAGE_MAP() macro accepts two parameters: the class name for which the message map is defined, and the base class to search if the class for which the message map is defined does not include a handler function for the message. The following code shows the message map macros that ClassWizard placed in the CCalculator class. Notice in the implementation file that the first parameter sent to the BEGIN_MESSAGE_MAP() macro is CCalculator, which is the class name for which the message map is defined. The second parameter, CDialog, is CCalculator's base class. The framework searches the CDialog class if the CCalculator class does not include a handler function for a message.

```
// Calculator.h
class CCalculator : public CDialog
{
// Construction
public:
...
protected:
...
    DECLARE_MESSAGE_MAP()
};
// Calculator.cpp
...
BEGIN_MESSAGE_MAP(CCalculator, CDialog)
    //{{AFX_MSG_MAP(CCalculator)
        // NOTE: the ClassWizard will add
            message map macros here
    //}}AFX_MSG_MAP
END_MESSAGE_MAP()
```

 If a class interface file includes a DECLARE_MESSAGE_MAP() macro, then its implementation file must include the BEGIN_MESSAGE_MAP() and END_MESSAGE_MAP() macros.

Inside the BEGIN_MESSAGE_MAP() and END_MESSAGE_MAP() macros you place other macros that represent messages you want a specific window to handle. One of the more common message macros you will use is the **ON_COMMAND macro**, which represents the events that are raised when a user selects a menu option or presses a shortcut key. The ON_COMMAND macro takes two parameters: a resource ID and the name of a message handler function. When the Run() function sends a message to the appropriate window, it also passes the resource ID of the element that raised the event. The message map then searches its list for a macro that matches the message type and that includes the correct resource ID as its first parameter. If the message map finds a matching macro, then it executes the function specified as the macro's second parameter.

The following code shows an example of a message map that includes two ON_COMMAND macros, one for a menu resource ID named ID_FILE_NEW (the New command on a File menu), and one for a resource ID named ID_FILE_OPEN (the Open command on a File menu). The ON_COMMAND macro for the ID_FILE_NEW resource executes a message handler named OnFileNew(), and the ON_COMMAND macro for the ID_FILE_OPEN resource executes a message handler named OnFileOpen(). Both message handlers are inherited functions that are being called directly from the CWinApp class. Notice that you do not include semicolons following a handler function's name.

```
BEGIN_MESSAGE_MAP(CExample, CDialog)
    //{{AFX_MSG_MAP(CExample)
    ON_COMMAND(ID_FILE_NEW, CWinApp::OnFileNew)
    ON_COMMAND(ID_FILE_OPEN, CWinApp::OnFileOpen)
    //}}AFX_MSG_MAP
END_MESSAGE_MAP()
```

Message maps can be somewhat tedious to work with—remembering the various message macros alone is a challenge. You can make the task of working with message maps much easier by using the Message Maps tab in ClassWizard. The Message Maps tab lists the messages that are available for individual resources and creates the message maps and handler definitions for you. Figure 8-29 shows the ClassWizard Message Maps tab.

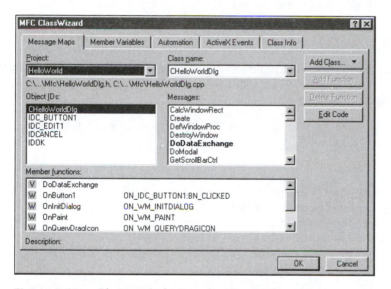

Figure 8-29   ClassWizard Message Maps tab

To give the MFC Calculator program its functionality, you will use the **BN_CLICKED macro**, which is raised for the BN_CLICKED event. The BN_CLICKED event occurs when a user clicks a button. Using a message map with the BN_CLICKED macro is much easier than the technique used in Windows API programming, in which you need to compare each button's window handle to the handle that was passed to the window procedure's lParam parameter.

The Windows API version of the Calculator program also uses the global setNumbers() and runCalculation() functions to give the program its functionality. In the MFC program, you create these functions as member functions of the CCalculator class. Additionally, the global variables used by the setNumbers() and runCalculation() functions are created as data members of the CCalculator class. Message handler functions for each of the buttons execute the setNumbers() and runCalculation() functions and execute other required code. Another major change in the functions is that they now include UpdateData() functions to handle the exchange of data between the IDC_DISPLAY edit box and the m_szDisplay variable.

 Note that with the MFC version of the Calculator program, you could have converted the char data members into CString data members. In order to concentrate on how to make the program work in MFC, however, you will leave the char variables as is.

To give the Calculator program its functionality, first you will add the required data members along with the setNumbers() and runCalculation() member functions.

To add the required data members along with the setNumbers() and runCalculation() member functions:

1. Open the **Calculator.h** file in the Text Editor window.

2. First add **#include <string.h>** after the **#include "resource.h"** statement. The member functions will need access to the string manipulation functions found in the string.h header file.

3. Above the class's closing brace, add a new private section with the following data member declarations:

```
private:
    char cOperation;
    char szFirstNum[10];
    char szSecondNum[10];
    double dResult;
    char szResult[10];
    double dFirstNum;
    double dSecondNum;
```

4. Select **Add Member Function** from the **WizardBar Actions** menu. The Add Member Function dialog box appears.

5. In the Add Member Function dialog box, enter **void** in the Function Type text box and **setNumbers(CString szCurNum)** in the Function Declaration text box. Leave the radio button in the Access group set to Public, and leave the Static and Virtual checkboxes unchecked. Click the **OK** button. The Calculator.cpp file opens to the setNumbers() function definition.

6. Add to the body of the setNumbers() function definition the following statements that build the left and right operands. Notice that instead of including the SetWindowText() function as you did in the Windows API program, this MFC version assigns the value of the current operand to the m_szDisplay variable, and then updates the display in the dialog box by passing a value of FALSE to the UpdateData() function.

```
void CCalculator::setNumbers(CString szCurNum)
{
    if (cOperation == '0') {
        strcat(szFirstNum, szCurNum);
        m_szDisplay = szFirstNum;
    }
    else {
        strcat(szSecondNum, szCurNum);
        m_szDisplay = szSecondNum;
    }
    UpdateData(FALSE);
}
```

7. Return to the **Calculator.h** file in the Text Editor window and select **Add Member Function** from the **WizardBar Actions** menu. The Add Member Function dialog box displays.

8. In the Add Member Function dialog box, enter **void** in the Function Type text box and **runCalculation()** in the Function Declaration text box. Leave the radio button in the Access group set to Public, and leave the Static and Virtual checkboxes unchecked. Click the **OK** button and the Calculator.cpp file opens to the runCalculation() function definition.

9. Add to the body of the runCalculation() function definition the following statements that perform the calculation. This function is virtually identical to the function you created in the Windows API program, except that the dResult and szResult variables are now declared as data members. Also, instead of using the SetWindowText() function to update the display in the dialog box, the m_szDisplay variable is now used with the UpdateData() function.

```
void CCalculator::runCalculation()
{
    if (cOperation == '+') {
        dResult = dFirstNum + dSecondNum;
    }
    else if (cOperation == '-') {
        dResult = dFirstNum - dSecondNum;
    }
    else if (cOperation == '*') {
        dResult = dFirstNum * dSecondNum;
    }
    else if (cOperation == '/') {
        dResult = dFirstNum / dSecondNum;
    }
    _gcvt(dResult, 10, szResult);
    m_szDisplay = szResult;
    UpdateData(FALSE);
    cOperation = '0';
    strcpy(szFirstNum, "");
    dFirstNum = 0;
```

8

```
        strcpy(szSecondNum, "");
        dSecondNum = 0;
    }
```

10. Finally, initialize the data members by modifying the CCalculator constructor function in the Calculator.cpp file as follows:

```
CCalculator::CCalculator(CWnd* pParent /*=NULL*/)
    : CDialog(CCalculator::IDD, pParent)
{
    cOperation = '0';
    strcpy(szFirstNum, "");
    strcpy(szSecondNum, "");
    dResult = 0;
    strcpy(szResult, "");
    dFirstNum = 0;
    dSecondNum = 0;
    //{{AFX_DATA_INIT(CCalculator)
    m_szDisplay = _T("0");
    //}}AFX_DATA_INIT
}
```

Next, you will use ClassWizard to add functions for each button message handler that execute the setNumbers() and runCalculation() functions and other required code.

To use ClassWizard to add message handler functions for each of the buttons that execute the setNumbers() and runCalculation() functions and other required code:

1. Start **ClassWizard** and click the **Message Maps** tab.

2. Select **IDC_CLEAR** in the Object IDs list and **BN_CLICKED** in the Messages list. Then click the **Add Function** button. The Add Member Function dialog box appears.

3. In the Add Member Function dialog box, accept the suggested name of OnClear and click the **OK** button.

4. Click the **Edit Code** button in ClassWizard. The Calculator.cpp file opens to the OnClear() handler function. Replace the // TODO comment with the following bolded code that resets each of the data members and sets the IDC_CLEAR control to a value of 0 by calling the UpdateData() function as follows:

```
void CCalculator::OnClear()
{
    cOperation = '0';
    strcpy(szFirstNum, "");
    dFirstNum = 0;
    strcpy(szSecondNum, "");
    dSecondNum = 0;
    m_szDisplay  = "0";
    UpdateData(FALSE);
}
```

5. Repeat Steps 1 through 4 to add BN_CLICKED message handler functions for the rest of the buttons in the dialog window. Use the name that ClassWizard suggests for each button. After creating each message handler function, add the appropriate code to each function definition as follows:

```cpp
void CCalculator::OnPlus()
{
     cOperation = '+';
     dFirstNum = atof(szFirstNum);
}
void CCalculator::OnMinus()
{
     cOperation = '-';
     dFirstNum = atof(szFirstNum);
}
void CCalculator::OnMultiply()
{
     cOperation = '*';
     dFirstNum = atof(szFirstNum);
}
void CCalculator::OnDivide()
{
     cOperation = '/';
     dFirstNum = atof(szFirstNum);
}
void CCalculator::OnZero()
{
     setNumbers("0");
}
void CCalculator::OnOne()
{
     setNumbers("1");
}
void CCalculator::OnTwo()
{
     setNumbers("2");
}
void CCalculator::OnThree()
{
     setNumbers("3");
}
void CCalculator::OnFour()
{
     setNumbers("4");
}
void CCalculator::OnFive()
{
     setNumbers("5");
}
```

8

```
void CCalculator::OnSix()
{
    setNumbers("6");
}
void CCalculator::OnSeven()
{
    setNumbers("7");
}
void CCalculator::OnEight()
{
    setNumbers("8");
}
void CCalculator::OnNine()
{
    setNumbers("9");
}
void CCalculator::OnPoint()
{
    setNumbers(".");
}
void CCalculator::OnEquals()
{
    dSecondNum = atof(szSecondNum);
    runCalculation();
}
```

6. Rebuild and execute the program, and then test the calculator to see if the calculations function correctly. Your program should function the same as the Windows API program you created in the last chapter.

7. Close the MFC Calculator window by clicking the **Close** icon in the title bar or by pressing **Escape**.

BUILDING AN APPLICATION FRAMEWORK WITH APPWIZARD

You have now examined several of the most important pieces of an MFC framework. Although there are other important aspects of the framework that you still need to explore, at this point you should be able to understand the parts of a simple dialog-based application created with AppWizard. Therefore, you will now use AppWizard to create a dialog-based application so that you can examine the automatically generated code and classes. After all of the work you put into building the MFC Calculator program from scratch, you might wish that you had just skipped right to this section of the chapter! Remember, however, that in order to understand the framework as a whole, you first need to understand its individual pieces.

After you create the dialog-based application using AppWizard, you still might not recognize much of what you see in the framework. However, much of the framework code is automatically created and controlled by ClassWizard, so you do not need to worry about it.

Parts of the framework that you will not recognize include error-checking functions, message handlers, and other code that you will examine in later chapters. You should be able to recognize the application class, the window class, and the dialog resource file and class.

One important aspect of MFC programs that you will not find in an AppWizard-generated program is AfxWin.h include files. Instead, the StdAfx.h file manages the inclusion of AfxWin.h and other MFC headers. By allowing AppWizard and ClassWizard to use StdAfx.h to manage the inclusion of the required MFC header files, you never need to worry about making sure you have included AfxWin.h or any other MFC header into your classes.

To create a dialog-based application using the AppWizard:

1. Create a new project named **AppWizardExample** using the MFC AppWizard (exe) option. Save the project in the **Chapter.08** folder in your Visual C++ Projects folders.

2. AppWizard executes and starts to walk you through the steps involved in creating an MFC program. In Step 1, select **Dialog based** from the application choices and click **Next**.

3. Step 2 allows you to select the features you want to include in your program. Clear all of the check boxes except for the **3D controls** checkbox. Also, change the dialog title to **Dialog-Based Application** and click **Next**.

4. Step 3 asks you what style of project you would like. The only option available to dialog-based applications is **MFC Standard**. Step 3 also asks if you want source code comments generated for the code created by AppWizard. Leave the default option set to **Yes, please** and click **Next**.

5. Step 4 displays the classes that will be created for you and allows you to change the suggested name of your derived classes. Leave the default settings as they are and click **Finish**.

6. Click **OK** when you see the New Project Information box that lists your project's specifications.

7. The project should immediately open to the Dialog Editor and display an automatically created dialog box. Before you do anything else, build the project and execute the program. The program will run and display the dialog box that appears in the Dialog Editor. AppWizard did all the work for you by creating the application class, the dialog class, and the other code required by the program. Click **OK** or **Cancel** to close the program.

8. Now examine the source files listed in the FileView tab of the Workspace window. The AppWizardExample.cpp file is the application window, the AppWizardExample.rc file is the dialog resource file, and the AppWizardExampleDlg.cpp file is the dialog class for the dialog resource file. The StdAfx.cpp file is used by the StdAfx.h file to manage the inclusion of the required MFC header files.

8

9. Although you will not examine every file in detail, at least look at the application class files. First, open the application class header file, **AppWizardExample.h**, in the Text Editor window. You should recognize the code in this file, including the InitInstance() function declaration and the DECLARE_MESSAGE_MAP() macro. Also notice the AppWizard-generated source code comments that explain the different code segments and warn of specific code blocks that you should not edit. Figure 8-30 shows a portion of the AppWizardExample.h file.

```
class CAppWizardExampleApp : public CWinApp
{
public:
     CAppWizardExampleApp();

// Overrides
     // ClassWizard generated virtual function overrides
     //{{AFX_VIRTUAL(CAppWizardExampleApp)
     public:
     virtual BOOL InitInstance();
     //}}AFX_VIRTUAL

// Implementation

     //{{AFX_MSG(CAppWizardExampleApp)
          /7 NOTE - the ClassWizard will add and
               remove member functions here.
          //     DO NOT EDIT what you see in
               these blocks of generated code !
     //}}AFX_MSG
     DECLARE_MESSAGE_MAP()
};
```

AppWizard-generated comments

InitInstance() declaration

macro declaration

Figure 8-30   AppWizardExample.h

10. Now open the **AppWizardExample.cpp** file in the Text Editor window. Although you may not be able to recognize all of the code and macros, you should be able to recognize most of it, including the message map declaration and the code within the InitInstance() function that instantiates and displays the dialog window. Figure 8-31 shows a portion of the AppWizardExample.cpp file.

```
...
BEGIN_MESSAGE_MAP(CAppWizardExampleApp, CWinApp)◄──────────── Message map
    //{{AFX_MSG_MAP(CAppWizardExample2App)
        //T NOTE - the ClassWizard will add and remove
                    mapping macros here.
        //    DO NOT EDIT what you see in these blocks of
                    generated code!
    //}}AFX_MSG
    ON_COMMAND(ID_HELP, CWinApp::OnHelp)
END_MESSAGE_MAP()
...
/////////////////////////////////////////////////////////////////
////////////////
// The one and only CAppWizardExampleApp object

CAppWizardExampleApp theApp;  ◄──────────── Application object
                                             declaration

/////////////////////////////////////////////////////////////////
////////////////
// CAppWizardExampleApp initialization

BOOL CAppWizardExampleApp::InitInstance()  ◄──────────── InitInstance() definition
{
    // Standard initialization
    ...
    CAppWizardExampleDlg dlg;  ◄──────────── Declaring and displaying
    m_pMainWnd = &dlg;                        dialog object
    int nResponse = dlg.DoModal();
    if (nResponse == IDOK)  ◄──────────── if statement handling the
    {                                      response returned from the
        // TODO: Place code here to handle when the dialog   dialog object
        //  is dismissed with OK
    }
    else if (nResponse == IDCANCEL)  ◄────────────
    {
        // TODO: Place code here to handle when the dialog
        //  is dismissed with Cancel
    }

    // Since the dialog has been closed, return FALSE so that
        we exit the
    //  application, rather than start the application's
        message pump.
    return FALSE;  ◄──────────── Since the application is
}                                dialog-based, FALSE is
                                 returned from the
                                 InitInstance() method to
                                 close the application
```

Figure 8-31   AppWizardExample.cpp

Now that you understand the basics of how MFC programs function, in future chapters you will use AppWizard to build new programs.

CHAPTER SUMMARY

- The Microsoft Foundation Classes, or MFC, is a class library that helps programmers create Windows-based applications.

- Visual C++ provides the Microsoft Foundation Class framework, or "framework," for short, which is basically a skeleton application created from MFC classes that you can use as a basis for your program.

- AppWizard is a Visual C++ tool that walks you through the steps involved in creating an MFC application.

❑ A hook is a location in a program where a programmer can insert code that enhances functionality.

❑ The CCmdTarget class encapsulates the messaging features of the Windows API.

❑ The CWinApp class, also known as the application class, is responsible for initializing, starting, running, and stopping an MFC windows application.

❑ The CWnd class encapsulates the various Windows API functions, data types, and other code used for creating and instantiating windows.

❑ Derived from the CWnd class are specialized types of window classes such as the CFrameWnd class, which creates a standard type of a window known as a frame window, and the CDialog class, which creates dialog boxes.

❑ All global functions begin with a prefix of **Afx**.

❑ The AfxMessageBox() function displays a simple message box to the user.

❑ A macro represents C++ code, constants, and other programming elements and is defined using the #define preprocessor directive.

❑ All MFC class names begin with C.

❑ Data members of MFC classes are prefixed with m_.

❑ An application class is the starting point of any MFC application.

❑ You derive an application class from the CWinApp class.

❑ When you derive an application object, you must override the virtual InitInstance() function and instantiate a global object of your application class.

❑ The MFC classes that derive from the CWnd class are used for creating the different types of windows that are visible to the user.

❑ The CFrameWnd class creates a simple window with a frame, title bar, control menu, and control buttons.

❑ The Create() function creates the window itself when an object of the window class is instantiated.

❑ MFC programming uses a ShowWindow() function to display windows. You call the ShowWindow() function from the application class's InitInstance() function using an instantiated object of the window class.

❑ A resource is a graphical user interface element that allows a user to interact with an application.

❑ Resources are defined in special files called resource scripts. Resource scripts have an extension of .rc and are written in C preprocessor language.

❑ A resource ID is a constant declared with the #define preprocessor directive and is used for programmatically referring to a resource.

❏ Resource editors allow you to create and modify resources in a graphical environment quickly.

❏ ClassWizard assists you in creating and working with MFC-derived classes.

❏ ClassWizard is only available if your project includes a resource script and if it includes a ClassWizard database file with an extension of .clw.

❏ WizardBar is a toolbar that is used for working with classes in Visual C++.

❏ The CString class is used for manipulating strings in MFC programs.

❏ The concatenation operator (+) is used to combine two strings of the CString class.

❏ A dialog box is a window that is used to display information or to gather information from users.

❏ Dialog boxes are created using two components: a dialog resource and a dialog class derived from the CDialog class.

❏ Applications that use a dialog box as their primary interface window are called dialog-based applications.

❏ Modal dialog boxes require users to close or cancel the dialog box before they can continue working with the application.

❏ Modeless dialog boxes do not need to be closed before returning to another window in the application.

❏ You instantiate an object of the dialog class and use the inherited DoModal() function to display a modal dialog box.

❏ Controls are user interface items such as check boxes, command buttons, text boxes, and other objects. In Visual C++, you add controls to a dialog box using the Controls toolbar in the Dialog Editor.

❏ Windows common controls are the standard controls you see in common dialog boxes such as edit boxes, buttons, check boxes, and so on.

❏ MFC controls are controls that are provided by MFC and are not part of the Windows operating system.

❏ MFC provides a special mechanism called dialog data exchange, or DDX, to handle the exchange of values between controls and variables.

❏ DDX is enabled by an inherited DoDataExchange() function that works with data members that are under the control of ClassWizard.

❏ The UpdateData() function either initializes dialog box controls using associated data members, or copies the current control values back into the associated data members.

❏ A message map associates messages with message handler functions.

8

❑ You add a message map to a window by first adding the DECLARE_MESSAGE_MAP() macro to the class interface file. Then, you must add a message map block to the class implementation file starting with the BEGIN_MESSAGE_MAP() macro and ending with the END_MESSAGE_MAP() macro.

❑ The ON_COMMAND macro represents the events raised when a user selects a menu option or presses a shortcut key.

❑ The BN_CLICKED macro represents the BN_CLICKED event, which occurs when a user clicks a button.

REVIEW QUESTIONS

1. A _____ is a location in a program where a programmer can insert code that enhances functionality.

    a. block

    b. plug

    c. hook

    d. gap

2. At the top of the MFC class hierarchy is the _____ base class.

    a. CObject

    b. CCmdTarget

    c. CWnd

    d. CWinApp

3. The _____ class encapsulates the messaging features of the Windows API.

    a. CObject

    b. CCmdTarget

    c. CWnd

    d. CWinApp

4. The _____ class is responsible for initializing, starting, running, and stopping an MFC windows application.

    a. CObject

    b. CCmdTarget

    c. CWnd

    d. CWinApp

5. The _____ class encapsulates the various Windows API functions, data types, and other code used for creating and instantiating windows.

   a. CObject

   b. CCmdTarget

   c. CWnd

   d. CWinApp

6. Which of the following is a global MFC function?

   a. `Create();`

   b. `UpdateData();`

   c. `MessageBox();`

   d. `AfxMessageBox();`

7. A _____ represents C++ code, constants, and other programming elements and is defined using the #define preprocessor directive.

   a. global function

   b. MFC data member

   c. macro

   d. script

8. MFC class names begin with _____.

   a. MFC

   b. MF

   c. C

   d. W

9. MFC class data members are prefixed with _____.

   a. mfc_

   b. m_

   c. mf_

   d. w_

10. Most of the MFC classes are defined in the _____ file.

    a. mfcwin.h

    b. mfcclass.h

    c. afxwin.h

    d. mfcapi.h

8

11. Which is the correct declaration for the InitInstance() function?

    a. `virtual WND InitInstance();`

    b. `virtual BOOL InitInstance();`

    c. `virtual void InitInstance();`

    d. `virtual HWND InitInstance(CString);`

12. Where must you declare an application class object?

    a. at the global level of the application class

    b. inside the InitInstance() function

    c. in the application class constructor

    d. in the application interface file

13. Which function creates the window itself when an object of the window class is instantiated?

    a. Open()

    b. Initiate()

    c. Start()

    d. Create()

14. What is the name of the inherited data member to which you assign an instantiated window class object?

    a. mfc_Window

    b. m_pMainWnd

    c. w_MainWnd

    d. mfc_FrameWnd

15. From where must you call the ShowWindow() function?

    a. the application class constructor

    b. the window class constructor

    c. the InitInstance() function

    d. the window class interface file

16. A resource script is defined in a file with an extension of _____.

    a. .h

    b. .cpp

    c. .rc

    d. .rs

17. A resource script is written in _____.

   a. VBScript

   b. C/C++

   c. Fortan

   d. C preprocessor language

18. You assign a resource ID to a resource using _____.

   a. a class data member

   b. a global variable

   c. the const keyword

   d. the #define preprocessor directive

19. It is common practice to declare all resource constants in an interface file named _____ in order to make it easier to reference them in your program.

   a. resource.rc

   b. resource.h

   c. recource.cpp

   d. recource.rs

20. What do you use to modify the resource ID, caption, and other settings of a resource?

   a. AppWizard

   b. ClassWizard

   c. The Workspace window

   d. The Properties window

21. ClassWizard is only available if your project includes a resource script and if _____.

   a. it includes a ClassWizard database file with an extension of .clw

   b. you have compiled the project

   c. you have added an application class to your program

   d. you have added a window class to your program

22. The _____ class is used for manipulating strings in MFC programs.

   a. CString

   b. CText

   c. CTextString

   d. CMFCString

8

23. You create a dialog box using a dialog resource and _____.

    a. the AfxMessageBox() function

    b. a window resource

    c. a dialog class derived from the CFrameWnd class

    d. a dialog class derived from the CDialog class

24. Applications that use a dialog box as their primary interface window are called _____.

    a. dialog box programs

    b. message box programs

    c. dialog-based applications

    d. utility functions

25. _____ dialog boxes require the user to close or cancel the dialog box before they can continue working with the application.

    a. Modal

    b. Modeless

    c. Primary

    d. Stateless

26. _____ do not need to be closed before returning to another window in the application.

    a. Modal

    b. Modeless

    c. Primary

    d. Stateless

27. You display a dialog box window using the _____ function.

    a. Dialog()

    b. ShowWindow()

    c. DoModal()

    d. ShowDialog()

28. Which of the following is *not* one of the control types you can add to an MFC application?

    a. Windows common controls

    b. MFC controls

    c. ActiveX controls

    d. C/C++ controls

29. Which mechanism does MFC provide to handle the exchange of values between controls and variables?

    a. Dialog Data Exchange

    b. Dialog Data Validation

    c. Data Extraction Protocol

    d. Control Value Exchange

30. What is the correct syntax to use with the UpdateData() function to transfer values from control data members to the dialog box controls?

    a. `UpdateData(TRUE);`

    b. `UpdateData(FALSE);`

    c. `UpdateData(SEND);`

    d. `UpdateData(RECEIVE);`

31. Which macro must you place in an interface file to declare a message map?

    a. DECLARE_MESSAGE_MAP()

    b. START_MESSAGE_MAP()

    c. MESSAGE_MAP()

    d. OPEN_MESSAGE_MAP()

32. The first parameter of the BEGIN_MESSAGE_MAP() macro designates the class name for which the message map is defined. What is the second parameter of the BEGIN_MESSAGE_MAP() macro?

    a. The base class from which the current class derives

    b. The function to execute for any messages the message map does not handle

    c. The base class to search if the class for which the message map is defined does not include a handler function for a message

    d. The BEGIN_MESSAGE_MAP() macro does not take a second parameter

8

EXERCISES

1. Modify the following class so that it is an application class. Be sure to add the appropriate functions and declarations to the implementation file.

```
// RealEstate.h
class CRealEstateApp {
public:
     CRealEstateApp();
     virtual ~ CRealEstateApp();
};
// RealEstate.cpp
#include "RealEstate.h"
```

```
CRealEstate:: CRealEstate () {
}
CRealEstate::~CRealEstate () {
}
```

2. Modify the following class so that it is a window class that derives from CFrameWnd:

```
// RealEstateFrameWnd.h
class CRealEstateFrameWnd {
public:
    CRealEstateFrameWnd();
    virtual ~ CRealEstateFrameWnd();
};
// RealEstateFrameWnd.cpp
#include "RealEstateFrameWnd.h"
CRealEstateFrameWnd::CRealEstateFrameWnd() {
}
CRealEstateFrameWnd::~ CRealEstateFrameWnd () {
}
```

3. Modify the implementation file for the application class you created in exercise 1 so that it displays a window from the window class you created in exercise 2.

4. Add to the following InitInstance() function appropriate code that displays a modal dialog window based on a class named CTransportationDlg. Also include an **if** statement that checks to see whether the user clicked the OK button or the Cancel button. If the user clicks the OK button, display a message box with the text *You clicked OK*. If the user clicks the Cancel button, display a message box with the text *You clicked Cancel*.

```
BOOL CTransportationApp::InitInstance() {
}
```

5. Create a modal dialog-based application project. In the main dialog resource, include a single OK button whose caption reads *Close Application*. Also, add a second dialog box resource to the project. The second dialog box should display the text *Are you sure you want to close the application?* and include an OK button that closes the application, and a Cancel button that displays the main dialog window. When the user clicks the Close button in the main dialog window, display the second dialog window.

6. Create a dialog-based application that displays the names of state capitals. In the dialog box window include one Edit Box control and three Button controls. Change the caption of each Button control to the name of a state in your area of the country. When the user clicks a button, display that state's capital in the Edit Box control.

7. Create a dialog-based application to be used as a software development bug report. Use as many types of controls as you can including Static Text, Edit Box, Button, and Check Box controls. Look in the MSDN Library for information on how to use individual control types. For example, you may include a Check Box control for the different types of software installed on a system. Format the Edit Box controls so that they are read-only, and only allow users to fill in values by selecting the various controls on the dialog box. Change each control's resource ID to a value that matches the

purpose of each control. Once users finish filling out the bug report and click the OK button, display all of their entries in another dialog box window before closing the application.

8. Create a dialog-based application to be used for tracking, documenting, and managing the process of interviewing candidates for professional positions. Include Edit Box controls such as candidate's name, business knowledge, and the interviewer's comments. Also, include other controls, such as Check Box and Radio Button, for recording information such as professional appearance and computer skills. Change each control's resource ID to a value that matches the purpose of each control. Once the interviewer completes the interview and clicks the OK button, display the candidate's information in another dialog box window before closing the application.

9. Create a dialog-based math quiz program for a sixth grade class. Use data members for the answers to the quiz. Change the caption of the dialog box's OK button to *Score Quiz*. Also, change each control's resource ID to a value that matches the purpose of each control. When students click the Score Quiz button, use a message map to first determine whether they have answered all the questions. If they have answered all the questions, display a message box with the number of questions they answered correctly. If they have not answered all the questions, redisplay the main dialog box window using the answers saved in the data members, and display a message box that instructs them to answer all the questions before selecting the Score Quiz button.

10. Create an MFC version of the Retirement Planner program you created in Chapter 4. Use a single dialog window for the application. Gather the calculation figures using five Edit Box controls: Annual Contribution, Annual Yield, Current Age, Retirement Age, and Inflation. Also use three Button controls to calculate the values: Total Future Value, Total Present Value, and Total Interest Earned.

11. Create an MFC version of the Building Estimator program you created in Chapter 5. Use separate dialog boxes for each customer, but use a single dialog box to display the estimates for all three customers.

12. Create an MFC version of the Conversion Center program you created in Chapter 6. Use the main dialog window as a "menu" from which the user can select the type of conversion he or she wants to perform. Use separate dialog windows for each of the conversion types. Allow the user to perform multiple conversions within the same window. For example, for the temperature conversion, include a single Edit Box control where the user can enter the temperature he or she wants to convert. Also include two Button controls, one that converts from Celcius to Fahrenheit and another that converts from Fahrenheit to Celcius. Display the results in a read-only Edit Box control.

8

DEBUGGING AND EXCEPTION HANDLING

In this chapter you will learn:

♦ About debugging concepts

♦ How to use basic debugging techniques

♦ About the Visual C++ debugger

♦ How to trace program execution with step commands

♦ How to trace variables and expressions with debug windows

♦ How to use the Call Stack window

♦ About Visual C++ language bugs and debugging resources

PREVIEW: VISUAL C++ DEBUGGING TOOLS

In this chapter, you will not create any new programs. Instead, you will learn how to use the Visual C++ debugging tools to locate errors in an existing MFC dialog–based program named Moving Estimator. The Moving Estimator program could be used by a shipping company to calculate the costs of moving a household from one location to another, based on distance, weight, and several other factors. The program is fairly simple and uses various member functions to calculate the various types of moving costs, along with a function named calcTotalEstimate() that totals the estimate. You can examine a completed version of the program in the MovingEstimatorNoBugs folder on your Data Disk. You should be able to figure out on your own how the program operates.

The only part of the program you will not recognize is the ON_EN_KILLFOCUS macro, which is raised when a control such as an edit box loses the "focus." When you click on a control or press your Tab key to move to a control, that control is said to have the focus. Focus refers to the control that is currently active in the window. When you click off the control or press your Tab key to move to another control, the original control is said to lose focus. The Moving Estimator program uses the ON_EN_KILLFOCUS macro to recalculate the cost of the move each time a new number is entered into an edit box and that edit box loses focus. Figure 9-1 shows an example of the Moving Estimator program's dialog window.

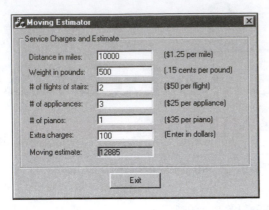

Figure 9-1 Moving Estimator program's dialog window

You will not be working with the version of the program contained in the MovingEstimatorNoBugs folder. Rather, you will work with a version of the program, located in the MovingEstimatorWithBugs folder that contains bugs. You need to use the "buggy" version in order to learn this chapter's debugging techniques. If you get stuck, however, you can use the no-bugs version as a reference.

Some of the most important debugging tools are the "step" tools that help you trace the flow of execution in your program as it executes. Figure 9-2 shows the Moving Estimator program in the IDE as it is paused in break mode. Break mode refers to a temporary pause in program execution. Your program enters break mode once Visual C++ encounters a break point that you set on a statement. Once in break mode, you use the step commands to walk through your program and monitor the results of each statement as it executes. Notice that the Moving Estimator program is still running in the background while you monitor the effects of each statement in break mode. Visual C++ also includes a Debug window, a Debug toolbar, and several debugger windows that assist you in monitoring the values of specific variables in your programs in order to assess their behavior during program execution.

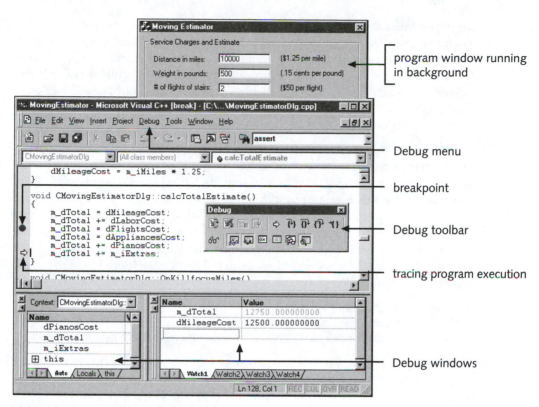

Figure 9-2   Moving Estimator program in break mode

UNDERSTANDING DEBUGGING

Regardless of experience, knowledge, and ability, all programmers create errors in their programs at one time or another. As you learned at the start of this textbook, debugging describes the act of tracing and resolving errors in a program. Debugging is an essential skill for any programmer, regardless of the programming language and the programmer's level of experience. In this chapter, you will learn techniques and tools to help you trace and resolve errors in your Visual C++ programs.

Error Types

Three main types of errors can occur in a Visual C++ program: syntax errors, run-time errors, and logic errors. **Syntax errors** occur when you enter code that the compiler does not recognize. Syntax errors in C++ include invalid statements or statements that are entered incorrectly, such as when a closing parenthesis for a function is missing. Other types of syntax errors include incorrectly spelled or mistyped words. For example, if you were to enter the statement `coute << "Hello World" << endl;`, you would receive a syntax error when you build the program because the cout statement is misspelled as *coute*. Similarly, the statement `Cout << "Hello World" << endl;` also causes a syntax error because the cout object is incorrectly entered with an uppercase *C*. (Remember, C++ is case sensitive.) As you are aware, when you build a project you will receive a build message if your program includes a syntax error. You have probably seen more than your fair share of compiler error build messages in the programs you have been creating. You will examine how to interpret build messages shortly.

If your Visual C++ program encounters a problem while it is executing, the problem is called a **run-time error**. Run-time errors differ from syntax errors in that they do not necessarily represent C++ language errors. Instead, run-time errors occur when your program encounters code that it cannot handle. Some of the most common types of run-time errors occur for numeric calculations. For example, run-time errors occur if you attempt to divide by 0. You will not receive a warning or error message, but the result of the division calculation will be incorrect or erratic. For example, the following code causes a run-time error since the iNumberOfHours variable is set to 0. The dGrossHourlyPay variable is assigned an unusable value of *1.#INF*.

```
double dGrossPay = 1000;
int iNumberOfHours = 0;
double dGrossHourlyPay = dGrossPay / iNumberOfHours;
```

The Visual C++ compiler will warn you of other types of potential run-time errors. For example, another typical run-time error occurs if you attempt to divide by a variable that has not been initialized. You can still execute the program, but you run the risk of raising a run-time error. The following code causes a run-time error because the iNumberOfHours variable is not initialized:

```
double dGrossPay = 1000;
int iNumberOfHours;
double dGrossHourlyPay = dGrossPay / iNumberOfHours;
```

The compiler warns you of the run-time error in the preceding code by raising the following warning message when you build the program:

```
warning C4700: local variable 'iNumberOfHours' used without
having been initialized
```

Later in this section you will examine compiler errors and messages at length.

Logic errors are problems in the design of a program that prevent it from running as you anticipate it will run. The logic behind any program involves executing the various statements and procedures in the correct order to produce the desired results. For example, when you do the laundry, you normally wash, dry, iron, and then fold. If a laundry program irons, folds, dries, then washes, you have a logic error and the program executes incorrectly. One example of a logic error in a computer program includes multiplying two values when you mean to divide them, as in the following code:

```
int iDivisionResult = 10 * 2;
cout << "Ten divided by two is equal to "
     << iDivisionResult << endl;
```

Another example of a logic error is the creation of an infinite loop, in which a loop statement never ends because its conditional expression is never updated or is never false. The following code creates a `for` statement that results in the logic error of an infinite loop since the third argument in the `for` statement's constructor never changes the value of the iCount variable.

```
for(int iCount = 10; iCount >= 0; iCount) {
    cout << We have liftoff in " + iCount);
}
```

Because the iCount variable is never updated in the preceding example, it will continue to have a value of 10 through each iteration of the loop, resulting in the repeated output of the text *We have liftoff in 10*. To correct this logic error, you need to add a decrement operator to the third argument in the `for` statement's constructor, as follows:

```
for(int iCount = 10; iCount >= 0; --iCount) {
    cout << We have liftoff in " + iCount);
}
```

Interpreting Build Messages

The first line of defense against bugs in C++ programs are the build messages that appear in the Output window when the Visual C++ compiler encounters an error during the build process. There are two main types of build messages: compiler error messages and warning messages. **Compiler error messages** occur for any syntax errors in a program. Compiler error messages contain the name of the file in which the error occurred, the line number in the file, and a description of the error. Consider the following function, which causes a syntax error because it is missing the closing brace (}). Figure 9-3 shows the compiler error message that displays in the Output window.

 The Output window in Figure 9-3 has been scrolled to the right so you can see more of the error description.

```
void CErrorsApp::incompleteFunction()
{
    CString szMessage = "Missing closing brace";
    AfxMessageBox(szMessage);
```

Figure 9-3   Output window with compiler error message

 If you click once on a compiler error message in the Output window, the description portion of the message appears in the status bar.

Note that you do not receive compiler error messages for logic errors since computers are not smart enough (yet) to identify a flaw in your logic. For example, if you create an infinite loop with a **for** statement, the interpreter has no way of telling whether you really wanted to continually execute the **for** statement's code. Later in this chapter, you will learn how to trace the flow of your program's execution in order to locate logic errors.

Compiler error messages should only be used to find the general location of an error in a program and not as the exact indicator of an error. You cannot always assume that the line specified by an error message is the actual problem in your program. Your best bet is to carefully examine not just the line specified by the error message, but also the lines immediately above and below the line that raised the error message. The challenge with the description for the error message shown in Figure 9-3 is that it does not exactly say *function is missing the closing brace*. Instead, the message states *unexpected end of file found*. You need to be able to interpret each message's meaning, depending on the given circumstance. In the case of the function's missing closing brace, the compiler searched through the entire source file to locate a matching closing brace for the function. The *unexpected end of file found* message was raised because the end of the file was reached before the compiler found the closing brace.

You can jump quickly to the line that raised the build error by double clicking on the compiler error message in the Output window. The ability to jump quickly to the line that raised a build error is one of the most useful debugging features in the Visual C++ IDE. Figure 9-4 shows the compiler error message from the Output window in Figure 9-3, along with the Text Editor window containing the source code file. After double-clicking on the compiler error message in the Output window, the cursor is placed in the line in the source file that raised the error—in this case the end of the file—and a blue arrow points to the line to identify it.

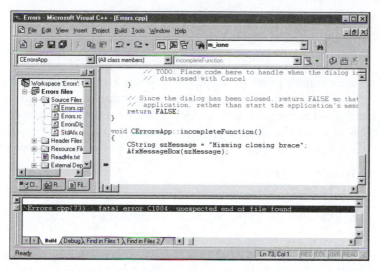

Figure 9-4   Jumping to a statement that raised a compiler error message

9

Let's consider another example of error messages that do not exactly identify the cause of an error. The `dResult = dAmount * dPercentage;` statement in the following code causes an error because it cannot locate the dPercentage and dAmount variables. The dPercentage and dAmount variables are not global because they are declared inside the variableDeclarations() function. Therefore, they are not visible to the calculatePercentage() function, which causes the error. Although the `dResult = dAmount * dPercentage;` statement generates the error since it attempts to access variables that are local to another function, the real bug in the code is that the dPercentage and dAmount variables must be declared at a global level.

```
void variableDeclarations() {
     double dPercentage = .25;
     double dAmount = 1600;
}
void calculatePercentage() {
     double dResult;
     dResult = dAmount * dPercentage;
}
```

Warning messages occur for any potential problems that might exist in your code, but that are not serious enough to cause a compiler error message. One of the more common warning messages you might see occurs when you declare a variable, but do not use it in your program. For example, consider the following code:

```
void calculateProfits() {
     int iPayRate = 15;
     int iNumHours = 40;
     double dGrossPay;
     double dNetPay = (iPayRate * iNumHours) / .20;
}
```

Because the dGrossPay variable is never used, the following warning message appears in the Output window:

```
warning C4101: 'dGrossPay' : unreferenced local variable
```

An unused variable is not really a problem in a C++ program. However, the compiler issues a warning about any unused variables and other unused programming elements in order to help you write cleaner and more efficient code. Although an unused variable will not cause problems, other types of issues that generate warning messages could cause problems. For example, consider the following modified version of the calculateProfits() function:

```
void calculateProfits() {
    int iPayRate = 15;
    int iNumHours = 40.5;
    double dNetPay = (iPayRate * iNumHours) / .20;
}
```

The statement `int iNumHours = 40.5;` causes a more serious warning message because it attempts to assign a floating-point value to an integer variable. This statement will not prevent the program from compiling, but it will result in the loss of data. For this reason, Visual C++ raises the following warning message:

```
warning C4244: 'initializing' : conversion from 'const
double' to 'int', possible loss of data
```

The number and severity of warning messages displayed in the Output window is determined by the Warning Level setting in the C/C++ tab of the Project Settings dialog box. Figure 9-5 lists the warning levels and describes what they mean.

Warning Level	Description
None	All warning messages are turned off
Level 1	Displays very severe warning messages
Level 2	Displays less severe warning messages
Level 3	Displays moderately severe warning messages
Level 4	Displays information warnings
Warnings as Errors	Treats all warnings as errors

Figure 9-5   Warning levels

Until you are a more experienced programmer, you should leave your warning level set to the default setting of Level 3. You may even want to consider setting your warning level to Warnings as Errors, which will help you write better code by forcing you to fix all code that raises warnings. If you want to adjust your warning level, select Settings from the Project menu, and then click on the C/C++ tab in the Project Settings dialog box. Warning levels are set with the Warning level drop-down list box and the Warnings as errors check box. Figure 9-6 shows an example of the C/C++ tab in the Project Settings dialog box.

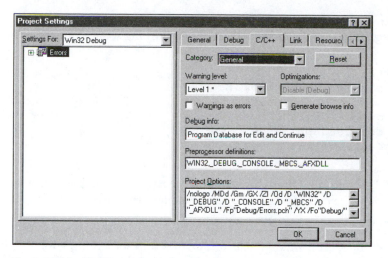

Figure 9-6   C/C++ tab in the Project Settings dialog box

Next, you will use build messages to help locate bugs in the Moving Estimator program.

To use build messages to help locate bugs in the Moving Estimator program:

1. Create a Chapter.09 folder in your Visual C++ Projects Folder.

2. Copy the **MovingEstimatorWithBugs** folder from the Chapter.09 folder on your Data Disk to the Chapter.09 folder in your Visual C++ Projects folder.

3. Open the **MovingEstimator** project from the MovingEstimatorWithBugs folder in your Visual C++ Projects folder and select Settings from the Project menu. Click on the C/C++ tab in the Project Settings dialog box and make sure that the warning level in the Warning level drop-down list box is set to Level 3. Click **OK** to close the dialog box.

4. Build the project. You should receive six error messages and a single warning message.

5. Scroll to the top of the message list in the Output window and start with the first message, which reads as follows:

```
error C2628: 'CMovingEstimatorDlg' followed by 'char' is
illegal (did you forget a ';'?)
```

6. Double-click on the error message and the MovingEstimator.cpp file should open with the **static char THIS_FILE[] = __FILE__;** statement highlighted. It is not readily obvious from the preceding error message, but the compiler does not recognize the class declaration. The problem is that a semicolon does not follow the class declaration's closing brace. Since the compiler could not locate the class declaration's closing semicolon in the declaration file, it continued searching in the

implementation file until it found one. Fix the problem by opening the **MovingEstimatorDlg.h** file and adding the missing semicolon, as follows:

```
...
private:
    double dMileageCost;
    double dLaborCost;
    double dFlightsCost;
    double dAppliancesCost;
    double dPianosCost;
};
```

7. Rebuild the project. This time you should receive two compiler error messages and a warning error message. The first compiler error message reads as follows:

```
error C2181: illegal else without matching if
```

8. The preceding error message tells you that there is something wrong with an **if** statement. Double-click on the error message and the **MovingEstimator.cpp** file will open with the offending **else** statement highlighted. The problem is that the preceding **if** statement is missing a closing brace. Fix the problem by adding the closing brace as follows:

```
if (nResponse == IDOK) {
    // TODO: Place code here to handle when the dialog is
    //  dismissed with OK
}
else if (nResponse == IDCANCEL) {
    // TODO: Place code here to handle when the dialog is
    //  dismissed with Cancel
}
```

9. Rebuild the project again. You should receive the following error message:

```
error C4716: 'CMovingEstimatorApp::InitInstance'
: must return a value
```

10. The preceding error message occurs because the InitInstance() function does not include a return statement. Double-click on the preceding error message and the InitInstance() function's closing brace is highlighted. Fix the problem by adding the statement **return FALSE;** before the InitInstance() function's closing brace.

11. Rebuild the project again. You should receive a single warning message that is similar to the following:

```
warning C4552: '*' : operator has no effect; expected
operator with side-effect
```

12. Double-click on the warning message and the statement **m_iPounds * .15;** in the setLaborCost() function is highlighted. This statement is incomplete and should assign the result of the multiplication operation to the dLaborCost data member. Modify the statement so that it reads **dLaborCost = m_iPounds * .15;**.

13. Rebuild the project a final time and you should receive no more build messages. However, do not try to use the program yet since it still contains plenty of bugs.

BASIC DEBUGGING TECHNIQUES

Although Visual C++ contains a variety of advanced debugging tools, which you will learn about later in this chapter, using advanced debugging tools for simple types of bugs can be overkill. If you know that a bug in your program is being caused by a complicated program design that includes derived classes, inherited functions, and other advanced techniques, then you should use Visual C++'s advanced debugging tools. If you are fairly certain, however, that the bug in your program is being caused by something simple, such as a variable being assigned the wrong value at some point, then you can use some basic debugging tools with which you are already familiar to help you find the error. These basic debugging tools include tracing console application errors with output statements, using comments, and analyzing your logic.

Tracing Console Application Errors with Output Statements

If you are unable to locate a bug in your program using error messages, or if the bug is a logic error that does not generate error messages, then you must trace your code. **Tracing** is the examination of individual statements in an executing program. Although you will use Visual C++'s built-in tracing tools later, one of the simplest tracing tools you can use is an output statement (cout) in a console application. You use output statements placed at different points in your program to print the contents of a variable, an array, or the value returned from a function. Using this technique, you can monitor values as they change during program execution. Output statements are especially useful when you want to trace a bug in your program by analyzing a list of values.

Be aware that you can also use console applications to code from MFC programs. Although you cannot actually use MFC classes in a console application, you can use console applications to test the code contained in an MFC program. For example, you may have a function in an MFC program that you want to test separately from the MFC program itself in order to be sure that it is operating correctly. For example, quickly viewing a list of variable values in a console application window is a simple, yet effective, technique for testing many types of code. Once you are sure the code is operating correctly, you can then plug it back into your MFC program. Simplified, temporary programs that are used for testing functions and other code are called **driver programs**. Driver programs do not have to be elaborate; they can be as simple as a main() function and the function you are testing. They allow you to isolate and test an individual function without having to worry about user interface elements, derived-MFC classes, and other programming constructs that form your application's functionality as a whole.

A testing technique that is essentially the opposite of driver programs is the use of stub functions. **Stub functions** are empty functions that serve as placeholders (or "stubs") for a

9

program's actual functions. Typically, a stub function returns a hard-coded value that represents the result of the actual function. Using stub functions allows you to check for errors in your program from the ground up. You start by swapping stub functions for the actual function definition. Each time you add the actual function definition, you rebuild and test the program. You repeat the process for each function in your program. This technique allows you to isolate and correct bugs within functions, or to correct bugs that occur as a result of how an individual function operates within your program as a whole.

For an example of how to trace a bug using output statements, examine the function in Figure 9-7, which calculates weekly net pay, rounded to the nearest integer. The function is syntactically correct and does not generate an error message. However, it is not returning the correct result, which should be 484.776. Instead, the function is returning a value of 5.16911e+006.

```
double calculatePay() {
    double dPayRate = 20;
    double dNumHours = 40;
    double dGrossPay = dPayRate * dNumHours;
    double dFederalTaxes = dGrossPay * .06794;
    double dStateTaxes = dGrossPay * .0476;
    double dSocialSecurity = dGrossPay * .062;
    double dMedicare = dGrossPay * .0145;
    double dNetPay = dGrossPay - dFederalTaxes;
    dNetPay *= dStateTaxes;
    dNetPay *= dSocialSecurity;
    dNetPay *= dMedicare;
    return dNetPay;
}
```

Figure 9-7   calculatePay() function with a logic error

To trace the problem, you place the function in a driver program and add an output statement at the point in the program where you think the error may be located. For example, the first thing you might want to check in the calculatePay() function is whether the dGrossPay variable is calculating correctly. To check whether the program calculates dGrossPay correctly, place an output statement in the function following the calculation of the dGrossPay variable, as shown in the driver program in Figure 9-8.

```
#include <iostream.h>
double calculatePay();
void main() {
     double dReturnValue = calculatePay();
cout << "value returned from calculatePay(): "
     << dReturnValue << endl;
}
double calculatePay() {
     double dPayRate = 20;
     double dNumHours = 40;
     double dGrossPay = dPayRate * dNumHours;
cout << "dGrossPay is " << dGrossPay << endl;
     double dFederalTaxes = dGrossPay * .06794;
     double dStateTaxes = dGrossPay * .0476;
     double dSocialSecurity = dGrossPay * .062;
     double dMedicare = dGrossPay * .0145;
     double dNetPay = dGrossPay - dFederalTaxes;
     dNetPay *= dStateTaxes;
     dNetPay *= dSocialSecurity;
     dNetPay *= dMedicare;
     return dNetPay;
}
```

9

Figure 9-8   calculatePay() function with an output statement in a driver program

 It is helpful to place output statements that are used to trace program execution at a different level of indentation in order to clearly distinguish them as not being part of the actual function.

Because the dGrossPay variable calculates correctly as 800, start checking the dNetPay variable by moving the output statement down a few lines. You continue with this technique until you discover the error. The calculatePay() function does not perform properly because the lines that add the dStateTaxes, dSocialSecurity, and dMedicare variables to the dNetPay variable are incorrect. They use the multiplication assignment operator (*=) instead of the subtraction assignment operator (-=). A correct version of the function is shown in Figure 9-9.

An alternative to using a single output statement is to place multiple output statements throughout your code to check values as the code executes. For example, you could trace the calculatePay() function using multiple output statements as shown in Figure 9-10. Output statements are placed throughout the function to track the values assigned to the dGrossPay and dNetPay variables. Using the output shown in Figure 9-11, you can then evaluate each variable in the calculatePay() function as values change throughout the function's execution.

```
double calculatePay () {
     double dPayRate = 20;
     double dNumHours = 40;
     double dGrossPay = dPayRate * dNumHours;
     double dFederalTaxes = dGrossPay * .06794;
     double dStateTaxes = dGrossPay * .0476;
     double dSocialSecurity = dGrossPay * .062;
     double dMedicare = dGrossPay * .0145;
     double dNetPay = dGrossPay - dFederalTaxes;
     dNetPay -= dStateTaxes;
     dNetPay -= dSocialSecurity;
     dNetPay -= dMedicare;
     return dNetPay;
}
```

Figure 9-9   Corrected version of the calculatePay() function

```
#include <iostream.h>
double calculatePay();
void main() {
     double dReturnValue = calculatePay();
cout << "value returned from calculatePay(): "
     << dReturnValue << endl;
}
double calculatePay() {
     double dPayRate = 20;
     double dNumHours = 40;
     double dGrossPay = dPayRate * dNumHours;
cout << "dGrossPay is " << dGrossPay << endl;
     double dFederalTaxes = dGrossPay * .06794;
     double dStateTaxes = dGrossPay * .0476;
     double dSocialSecurity = dGrossPay * .062;
     double dMedicare = dGrossPay * .0145;
     double dNetPay = dGrossPay - dFederalTaxes;
cout << "dNetPay minus federal taxes is "
     << dNetPay << endl;;
     dNetPay *= dStateTaxes;
cout << "dNetPay minus state taxes is "
     << dNetPay << endl;
     dNetPay *= dSocialSecurity;
cout << "dNetPay minus social security is "
     << dNetPay << endl;
     dNetPay *= dMedicare;
cout << "dNetPay minus Medicare is "
     << dNetPay << endl;
     return dNetPay;
}
```

Figure 9-10   calculatePay() function with multiple output statements

Figure 9-11 Output of calculatePay() function in a driver program

Later in this chapter, you will use more sophisticated tools for tracing the values of variables as they change throughout a program's execution. However, the important thing you should learn from the output statement technique is that tracing gives you an opportunity to evaluate variables at different points in your program in order to locate the cause of an error.

Next, you will use output statements to help locate bugs in the Moving Estimator program's calcTotalEstimate() function. The calcTotalEstimate() function should return a total of the dMileageCost, dLaborCost, dFlightsCost, dAppliancesCost, dPianosCost, and m_iExtras variables. However, you need to be sure that the calculations are being performed properly before you can confidently include the function in the Moving Estimator program. The calcTotalEstimate() function is a very simple function, but, it serves the purpose of demonstrating how to use a driver program to debug a function.

To use output statements to help locate bugs in the Moving Estimator program's calcTotalEstimate() function:

1. Return to the Moving Estimator project in Visual C++ and open the **MovingEstimatorDlg.cpp** file in the Text Editor window.

2. Highlight the calcTotalEstimate() function and copy it to the Clipboard by selecting **Copy** from the **Edit** menu or by pressing **Ctrl+C**.

3. Create a new empty Win32 Console Application project named **FunctionCheck**. Save the project in the **Chapter.09** folder in your Visual C++ Projects folders. Once the project is created, add a C++ source file named **FunctionCheck**.

4. Type the processing directive that gives the program access to the iostream library: **#include <iostream.h>**.

5. Press **Enter** and type the function prototype for the calcTotalEstimate() function: **double calcTotalEstimate();**. In this version, the function returns a double value for testing purposes instead of being declared with a void data type.

6. Add the following main() function, which calls the calcTotalEstimate() function and prints its return value:

```
void main() {
    double dReturn;
    dReturn = calcTotalEstimate();
    cout << "calcTotalEstimate() returned "
        << dReturn << endl;
}
```

7. Paste the **calcTotalEstimate()** function, which you copied from the Moving Estimator program, from the Clipboard. Modify its header declaration as follows so that it does not include the reference to the CMovingEstimatorDlg class and so that it returns a double value:

```
double calcTotalEstimate()
{
...
}
```

8. The m_dTotal variable should be assigned the combined values of the six other variables. Therefore, if each of the other variables contains a value of 100, the m_dTotal variable should be assigned a total value of 600. To test how the calculations perform under these conditions, add the following declarations and assignments for each variable. In the MFC version of the program, the data members are declared in the interface file, and they receive their values from the dialog box controls.

```
double calcTotalEstimate() {
double m_dTotal = 0;
double dMileageCost = 100;
double dLaborCost = 100;
double dFlightsCost = 100;
double dAppliancesCost = 100;
double dPianosCost = 100;
double m_iExtras = 100;
    m_dTotal = dMileageCost;
    m_dTotal += dLaborCost;
    m_dTotal = dFlightsCost;
    m_dTotal = dAppliancesCost;
    m_dTotal += dPianosCost;
    m_dTotal += m_iExtras;
}
```

9. Next, add to the calcTotalEstimate() function output statements that print the value of the m_dTotal data member each time it is assigned a new value, along with a statement that returns the m_dTotal variable:

```
double calcTotalEstimate() {
...
    m_dTotal = dMileageCost;
cout << "m_dTotal after adding dMileageCost "
    << m_dTotal << endl;
```

```
         m_dTotal += dLaborCost;
  cout << "m_dTotal after adding dLaborCost "
       << m_dTotal << endl;
         m_dTotal + dFlightsCost;
  cout << "m_dTotal after adding dFlightsCost "
       << m_dTotal << endl;
         m_dTotal + dAppliancesCost;
  cout << "m_dTotal after adding dAppliancesCost "
       << m_dTotal << endl;
         m_dTotal += dPianosCost;
  cout << "m_dTotal after adding dPianosCost "
       << m_dTotal << endl;
         m_dTotal += m_iExtras;
  cout << "m_dTotal after adding m_iExtras "
       << m_dTotal << endl;
         return m_dTotal;
}
```

10. Build and execute the program. Your output should resemble Figure 9-12.

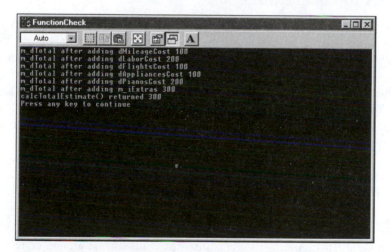

Figure 9-12   Output of FunctionCheck project

You can see from the output statement in the main() function that the calcTotalEstimate() function did not return a value of 600. Instead, it returned a value of 300. Looking back over the individual output statements that printed the value of m_dTotal each time it was assigned a new value, you can see that dFlightsCost and dAppliancesCost values were not added to the m_dTotal value, but instead replaced it. As you probably already noticed, the two statements that assign these values to the m_dTotal value used the assignment operator instead of the += operator. Although this is a very simple example, it does demonstrate how output statements can help you analyze a variable's changing values.

11. Press any key to close the console window.

12. Reopen the **MovingEstimator** project and, if necessary, open the **MovingEstimatorDlg.cpp** file in the Text Editor window.

13. Modify the **calcTotalEstimate()** function so that the statements that assign the dFlightsCost and dApplicancesCost values to the m_dTotal value use += operators instead of the assignment operator, as follows, and then rebuild the program:

```
void CMovingEstimatorDlg::calcTotalEstimate()
{
    m_dTotal = dMileageCost;
    m_dTotal += dLaborCost;
    m_dTotal += dFlightsCost;
    m_dTotal += dAppliancesCost;
    m_dTotal += dPianosCost;
    m_dTotal += m_iExtras;
}
```

Using Comments to Locate Bugs

Another method of locating bugs in a C++ program is to comment out lines that you think might be causing the problem. You can comment out individual lines that might be causing the error, or comment out all lines except the lines that you know work. When you receive an error message, start by commenting out only the statement specified by the error message's line number. Rebuild and execute the program, and see if you receive another error. If you receive additional error messages, then comment out those statements as well. Once you eliminate the error messages, examine the commented out statements for the cause of the bug.

 The cause of an error in a particular statement is often the result of an error in a preceding line of code.

The last five statements in Figure 9-13 are commented out since they generate compiler error messages stating that dYearlyIntrest is not defined. The problem with the code is that the dYearlyInterest variable is incorrectly spelled as dYearlyIntrest, lacking an *e*, in several of the statements. Commenting out the lines isolates the problem statements.

Although the error in Figure 9-13 might seem somewhat simple, it is typical of the types of errors you will encounter. Often you will see the error right away and not need to comment out code or use any other tracing technique. However, when you have been staring at the same code for long periods of time, simple spelling errors, like yearlyIntrest, are not always easy to spot. Commenting out the lines you know are giving you trouble is a good technique for helping you isolate and correct even the simplest types of bugs.

```
        double dAmount = 100000;
        double dPercentage = .08;
        cout << "The interest rate for a loan "
             << " in the amount of " << dAmount
             << " is " << dPercentage << endl;
        double dYearlyInterest = dAmount * dPercentage;
//      cout << "The amount of interest for one year is "
//      << dYearlyIntrest << endl;
//      double dMonthlyInterest = dYearlyIntrest / 12;
//      cout << "The amount of interest for one month is "
//          << dMonthlyInterest << endl;
//      double dDailyInterest = dYearlyInterest / 365;
//      cout << "The amount of interest for one day is "
//          << dDailyInterest << endl;
```

Figure 9-13   Code using comments to trace errors

Provided that you are working with console applications, you can combine the output state-ment and comment debugging techniques to aid in your search for errors. Figure 9-14 uses the calculatePay() function as an example of how to use comments combined with an output statement to trace errors. You know that the `var grossPay = payRate * numHours;` statement is the last statement in the function that operates correctly. Therefore, all of the lines following that statement are commented out. You then use an output statement to check the value of each statement, removing comments from each statement in a sequential order, and checking and correcting syntax as you go.

```
double calculatePay() {
        double dPayRate = 20;
        double dNumHours = 40;
        double dGrossPay = dPayRate * dNumHours;
cout << "dGrossPay is " << dGrossPay << endl;
//      double dFederalTaxes = dGrossPay * .06794;
//      double dStateTaxes = dGrossPay * .0476;
//      double dSocialSecurity = dGrossPay * .062;
//      double dMedicare = dGrossPay * .0145;
//      double dNetPay = dGrossPay - dFederalTaxes;
//      dNetPay *= dStateTaxes;
//      dNetPay *= dSocialSecurity;
//      dNetPay *= dMedicare;
//      return dNetPay;
}
```

Figure 9-14   calculatePay() function with comments and an output statement to trace program execution

Next, you will use comments to help locate bugs in the Moving Estimator program.

To use comments to help locate bugs in the Moving Estimator program:

1. First, run the Moving Estimator program and enter **10000** in the Distance in miles edit box. After you enter the number, press your **Tab** key to call the edit box's ON_EN_KILLFOCUS message handler. An incorrect value of –9.2559631349 is assigned to the Moving estimate box. In order to locate the code that is causing this problem, you will add comments to the calcTotalEstimate() function.

2. Close the Moving Estimator program.

3. In the calcTotalEstimate() function, add comment lines as follows to all of the statements except the first statement, which assigns the dMileageCost data member to the m_dTotal variable. When you are finished, rebuild and execute the program.

```
void CMovingEstimatorDlg::calcTotalEstimate()
{
     m_dTotal = dMileageCost;
//   m_dTotal += dLaborCost;
//   m_dTotal += dFlightsCost;
//   m_dTotal += dAppliancesCost;
//   m_dTotal += dPianosCost;
//   m_dTotal += m_iExtras;
}
```

4. Enter **10000** in the Distance in miles edit box again and press **Tab**. The correct value of 12500 is assigned to the Moving estimate box. Therefore, the problem is not with the dMileageCost data member. Close the Moving Estimator program.

5. Remove the comment line from the **m_dTotal += dLaborCost;** statement, and then rebuild and execute the program.

6. Enter **10000** in the Distance in miles box, press **Tab**, and then enter **500** in the Weight in pounds edit box and press **Tab**. The Weight in pounds edit box's ON_EN_KILLFOCUS message handler executes and assigns a value of 12575 to the Moving estimate box. At 15 cents a pound, the total cost of 500 pounds is $75. Adding 75 to the Distance in miles amount of 12500 results in 12575. Therefore, the program is functioning correctly so far. Close the Moving Estimator program.

7. Remove the comment line from the **m_dTotal += dFlightsCost;** statement, and then rebuild and execute the program. Enter **10000** in the Distance in miles box, and press **Tab**. This time, the Moving estimate box is assigned the incorrect value of –9.2559631349. The program functioned correctly until you tried to assign the dFlightsCost value to the m_dTotal variable. Since the incorrect number resulted before you entered a number into the # of flights edit box, the problem lies with the initialization of the variable. Close the Moving Estimator program.

8. If you scroll up to the CMovingEstimateDlg class's constructor, you will see that there is no initialization statement for the dFlightsCost data member. Add a statement that initializes the dFlightsCost data member's value to 0, as follows:

```
CMovingEstimatorDlg::CMovingEstimatorDlg(CWnd* pParent
/*=NULL*/): CDialog(CMovingEstimatorDlg::IDD, pParent)
{
    dMileageCost = 0;
    dLaborCost = 0;
    dFlightsCost = 0;
    dAppliancesCost = 0;
    dPianosCost = 0;
...
```

9. Remove the remainder of the comments from the statements in the calcTotalEstimate() function, and then rebuild and execute the program. Enter **10000** into the Distance in miles edit box, **500** into the Weight in pounds edit box, and **2** into the # of flights of stairs edit box. Be sure to press **Tab** after you enter the value into the # of flights of stairs edit box. The correct value of 12675 should be assigned to the Moving estimate edit box, as shown in Figure 9-15. Do not enter any numbers into the window's other edit boxes since the program still contains some errors.

9

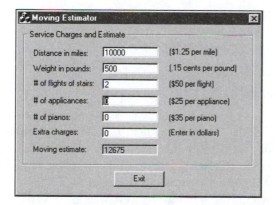

Figure 9-15   Moving Estimator program after correcting the data member initialization error

10. Click **Exit** to close the window.

You might be wondering how to decide where to begin looking for a bug. How do you know to place comments in the calcTotalEstimate( ) function, or use output statements in a driver program, or use any of the other tools you will examine in this chapter? The answer is that it depends on the program. Every program you write, or rewrite, will be different. You need to determine the most logical place to start debugging based on the design of your program. With the Moving Estimator program, you could have started looking in any of the member functions, or even in the interface file itself. However, since the program should result in the calculation of a single number, you started at the "top" by first analyzing the number assigned to the m_dTotal variable in the calcTotalEstimate( ) function. If the error you were receiving could not be located in the calcTotalEstimate( ) function, you could have directed your efforts to the functions that assign values to the variables used by the calcTotalEstimate( ) function. And if that had not worked, you would have begun examining the interface files and other more basic parts of the MFC program.

Analyzing Your Logic

At times, errors in your code will be logic problems that are difficult to spot using tracing techniques. When you suspect that your code contains logic errors, you must analyze each statement on a case-by-case basis. For example, the following code contains a logic flaw that prevents it from functioning correctly.

```
bool bDisplayAlert = false;
CString szConditionTrue = "no condition";
if (bDisplayAlert == true)
    szConditionTrue = "condition is true";
    AfxMessageBox(szConditionTrue);
```

If you were to execute the preceding code, you would always see the message box, although it should not appear since the bDisplayAlert variable is set to false. If you examine the **if** statement more closely, you will see that the **if** statement ends after the string is assigned to the szConditionTrue variable. The AfxMessageBox() function following the variable assignment is not part of the **if** structure since the **if** statement does not include a set of braces to enclose the lines it executes when the conditional evaluation returns true. The AfxMessageBox() function will also display the value *no condition* since the statement that assigns the value *condition is true* to the conditionTrue variable is bypassed when the **if** statement's conditional expression evaluates to false. For the code to execute properly, the **if** statement must include braces as follows:

```
bool bDisplayAlert = false;
CString szConditionTrue = "no condition";
if (bDisplayAlert == true) {
    szConditionTrue = "condition is true";
    AfxMessageBox(szConditionTrue);
}
```

The following code shows another example of an easily overlooked logic error using a **for** statement.

```
int iCount = 0;
for (iCount = 1; iCount < 6; ++iCount);
     cout << iCount << endl;
```

The code should print the numbers 1 through 5 to the screen. However, the line **for (iCount = 1; iCount < 6; ++ iCount);** contains an ending semicolon, which marks the end of the **for** loop. The loop executes five times and changes the value of count to 6, but does nothing else since there are no statements before its ending semicolon. The line **cout << iCount << endl;** is a separate statement that executes only once, printing the number 6 to the screen. The code is syntactically correct, but does not function as you anticipated. As you can see from these examples, it is easy to overlook very minor logic errors in your code.

THE VISUAL C++ DEBUGGER

Many high-level programming languages have debugging capabilities built directly into their development environment. These built-in debugging capabilities provide sophisticated commands for tracking errors. Up to this point, you have learned how to interpret error messages and correct the statements that cause the errors. As helpful as they are, error messages are useful only in resolving syntax and run-time errors. You have also learned some techniques that assist in locating logic errors. Examining your code manually is usually the first step to take when you have a logic error, or you may use a driver program to track values assigned to a function's variables. These techniques work fine with smaller programs. However, when you are creating a large program that includes multiple derived classes and functions, logic errors can be very difficult to spot. For instance, you might have a function that instantiates objects from several different classes. Each instantiated object might then call member functions or use data members from its base class or from other indirect base classes. Attempting to trace the logic and flow of such a program using simple tools such as output statements can be difficult. Visual C++ provides a program called the **debugger** that contains several tools that can help you trace each line of code, creating a much more efficient method of finding and resolving logic errors.

 Any error messages that are generated while you are debugging an application are printed to the Debug tab of the Output window.

You start the debugger by selecting one of the commands on the Start Debug submenu on the Build menu. You will use several of the commands on the Start Debug submenu shortly. Using the Start Debug submenu commands along with several other techniques allows you to enter and work in break mode. **Break mode** temporarily suspends, or pauses, program execution so that you can monitor values and trace program execution. Once the debugger is started, the Build menu becomes the Debug menu, the Debug toolbar appears, and several debugging windows appear at the bottom of the IDE window. Figure 9-16 shows an example of the IDE with the debugger started.

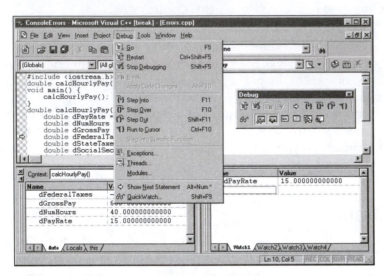

Figure 9-16   IDE with the debugger started

 This text instructs you to use the Debug menu to execute commands. However, many of the commands are also available as icons on the Debug toolbar.

Build Configurations

To use the Visual C++ debugger, you need to build a Win32 Debug release of your program. A **Win32 Debug build** contains additional information that is required by the debugger tools. You can also create a Win32 Release build. A **Win32 Release build** does not contain any debugging information. By default when you first create a project, it is set to compile as a Win32 Debug build. Win32 Debug build is the default setting so that you have debugging information available to you while you are developing your application. Visual C++ places a debug build of your program, along with a .pdb file that contains the debugging information, in a folder named Debug in your project's main folder. In spite of its helpfulness during development, the extra debugging information found in a Win32 Debug build slows down your program and makes it unnecessarily large. Once you have completed writing and debugging your application, you create a Win32 Release build, which contains only the files necessary for your program to run and doesn't contain the extra debugging information. Visual C++ places a release build of your program in a folder named Release in your project's main folder, along with various settings and information files that are required by the release build. You distribute the files in the Release folder to your clients.

Although you need to build a Win32 Debug release of your program to use the Visual C++ debugger, some bugs do not surface until you build and run a release version of your program. Therefore, you should periodically build and test your code using a Win32 Release build in order to identify any bugs that do not appear in Win32 Debug builds. To change the build setting for your project, select the Set Active Configuration command from the Build menu to display the Set Active Project Configuration dialog box, shown in Figure 9-17.

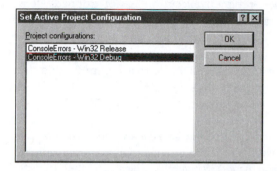

Figure 9-17   Set Active Project Configuration dialog box

Next, you will make sure your project is set to build a Win32 Debug version.

To make sure your project is set to build a Win32 Debug version:

1. Select **Set Active Configuration** from the **Build** menu. The Set Active Project Configuration dialog box appears.

2. In the Set Active Project Configuration dialog box, select **MovingEstimator – Win32 Debug** and click the **OK** button.

Tracing Program Execution with Step Commands

The Step Into, Step Over, and Step Out commands on the Debug menu are used for tracing program execution once you enter break mode. The **Step Into** command executes an individual line of code and then pauses until you instruct the debugger to continue. This feature gives you an opportunity to evaluate a program's flow and structure as it is being executed.

As you use the Step Into command to move through code, the debugger stops at each line within every function. When stepping through a program to trace a logical error, it is convenient to be able to skip functions that you know are working correctly. The **Step Over** command allows you to skip function calls. The program still executes the function that you step over, but it appears in the debugger as if a single statement executes.

The **Step Out** command executes all remaining code in the current function. If the current function is called from another function, all remaining code in the current function executes and the debugger stops at the next statement in the calling function.

You can also trace program execution with the Run to Cursor command on the Debug menu. When you select the **Run to Cursor command**, the program runs normally until it reaches the statement where your cursor is located, at which point the program enters break mode. You can then use the Step Into, Step Over, and Step Out commands to continue tracing program execution. The Run to Cursor command is useful if you are sure that your program is functioning correctly up to a certain point in the code.

When a program enters break mode, program execution is not stopped—it is only suspended. To resume program execution after entering break mode, select Go from the Debug menu. The Go command ends the debugging session and executes the rest of the program normally. You can also end a debugging session and halt program execution by selecting the Stop Debugging command from the Debug menu. Note that before starting the debugger, you should always manually save your C++ source file since certain types of errors that you may encounter in the debugger, such as memory errors, can cause Visual C++ to crash.

 Although you can make changes to code in break mode, they will not take effect while the program is executing. You must end program execution (using the Go or Stop Debugging commands), rebuild the project, and then start the program again.

Next, you will practice tracing program execution using the step commands.

To practice tracing program execution:

1. Return to the **MovingEstimatorDlg.cpp** file in the Text Editor window.

2. Locate the OnKillfocusMiles() message handler and place the insertion point anywhere in the statement that reads `setMileageCost();`.

3. Point to the **Start Debug** submenu on the **Build** menu and select **Run to Cursor**. The program starts running and displays the Moving Estimator dialog window. Enter a value in the Distance in miles edit box and press the **Tab** key. As soon as you press Tab, program execution enters break mode and a yellow arrow in the margin of the Text Editor window points to the next statement to be processed, as shown in Figure 9-18.

 When you select the Run To Cursor command, the debugger executes all statements before the line that your cursor is in. The statement in the line containing your cursor is the next statement to be processed.

4. Select **Step Into** from the **Debug** menu. The debugger processes the current statement and transfers control to the setMileageCost() function. The yellow arrow points to the setMileageCost() function's opening brace.

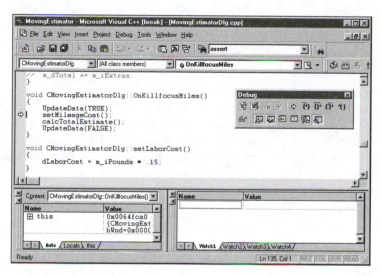

Figure 9-18   Moving Estimator program in break mode

Most of the commands on the Debug menu can also be executed using keyboard shortcuts or buttons on the Debug toolbar. Each command's keyboard shortcut is listed to the right of the command on the Debug menu. To display a ToolTip for a specific Debug toolbar button, hold your pointer over the desired button.

5. Select **Step Into** from the **Debug** menu again. The yellow arrow moves to the only statement in the function, `dMileageCost = m_iMiles * 1.25;`. Select the **Step Into** command again to execute the statement, and then a final time to end the function. Control is transferred back to the OnKillfocusMiles() function.

6. Once control returns to the OnKillfocusMiles() function, execute the **Step Into** command to transfer control to the calcTotalEstimate() function.

7. Because you already know that the calcTotalEstimate() function works correctly, select the **Step Out** command from the **Debug** menu. The rest of the statements in the calcTotalEstimate() function execute normally, and control is transferred back to the onKillfocusMiles() function.

8. The next statement to execute calls the UpdateData() function. If you were to step into this function, the MFC base class from which the UpdateData() function derives would open and you could step through its code. Instead, select the **Step Over** command from the **Debug** menu. The debugger executes the UpdateData() function and highlights the OnKillfocusMiles() function's closing brace.

9. Finally, select **Stop Debugging** from the **Debug** menu to halt debugging and program execution.

The Debug menu also contains an additional command, Show Next Statement, to assist in tracing program execution. The Show Next Statement command highlights the next statement to be executed.

Another method of tracing program execution in the Visual C++ debugger involves inserting breakpoints into code. A **breakpoint** is a position in the code at which program execution enters break mode. You add a breakpoint to your code using the Insert/Remove Breakpoint button on the Build toolbar or by right-clicking a statement and selecting Insert/Remove Breakpoint from the Shortcut menu. Once a program is paused at a breakpoint, you can use the Step Into, Step Over, Step Out, and Run to Cursor commands to trace program execution, or you can use the Go or Stop Debugging commands to complete program execution and run to the next breakpoint. Multiple breakpoints provide a convenient way to pause program execution at key positions in your code where you think there could be a bug.

Next, you will practice using breakpoints.

To practice using breakpoints:

1. Return to the **MovingEstimatorDlg.cpp** file in the Text Editor window.

2. In the OnKillfocusMiles() funtion, place the insertion point anywhere in the statement that reads `UpdateData(TRUE);` and select the **Insert/Remove Breakpoint** button (which resembles a small hand) on the **Build** toolbar, or right click the `UpdateData(TRUE);` statement and select **Insert/Remove Breakpoint** from the **Shortcut** menu. A red circle appears in the left margin of the Text Editor window next to the line containing the breakpoint.

3. Add another breakpoint in the line that reads `UpdateData(FALSE);`. Figure 9-19 shows how the Text Editor window appears with the two breakpoints.

```
//  m_dTotal += dPianosCost;
//  m_dTotal += m_iExtras;
}

void CMovingEstimatorDlg::OnKillfocusMiles()
{
    UpdateData(TRUE);
    setMileageCost();
    calcTotalEstimate();
    UpdateData(FALSE);
}

void CMovingEstimatorDlg::setLaborCost()
{
    dLaborCost = m_iPounds * .15;
}

void CMovingEstimatorDlg::OnKillfocusPounds()
{
    UpdateData(TRUE);
```

Figure 9-19   Breakpoints in the Text Editor window

4. Point to the **Start Debug** submenu on the **Build** menu and select **Go**. The program starts running and displays the Moving Estimator dialog window. Enter a value in the Distance in miles edit box and press the **Tab** key. As soon as you

press Tab, program execution enters break mode and pauses at the first break-point. A yellow arrow appears in margin of the Text Editor window on top of the red circle that marks the breakpoint.

5. Select **Go** from the **Debug** menu. The statements between the two breakpoints execute, and then program execution pauses at the second breakpoint.

6. Select **Stop Debugging** from the **Debug** menu to halt debugging and program execution.

If you are having trouble setting breakpoints in a program, you can hard code them using the DebugBreak() function for non-MFC programs and the AfxDebugBreak() function for MFC programs. If you use either one of these functions, be sure to remove them before you create a Win32 Release build.

To remove breakpoints from a file:

1. Place the insertion point anywhere in the line containing the first breakpoint and select the **Insert/Remove Breakpoint** button on the **Build** toolbar, or right click the `UpdateData(TRUE);` statement and select **Remove Breakpoint** from the **Shortcut** menu.

9

Instead of removing a breakpoint, you can enable and disable it by right click-ing the statement containing the breakpoint and selecting Enable/Disable Breakpoint from the Shortcut menu. A disabled breakpoint appears as a white circle in the left margin of the Text Editor window.

2. Repeat Step 1 to remove the second breakpoint in the file.

You can add and remove breakpoints using the Breakpoints dialog box. To access the Breakpoints dialog box, select Breakpoints from the Edit menu. You can also use the Breakpoints dialog box to set the conditions for which a pro-gram should pause at a breakpoint. For example, you can set a breakpoint to occur only when the contents of a variable match a specific value.

TRACING VARIABLES AND EXPRESSIONS WITH DEBUG WINDOWS

As you trace program execution using step commands and breakpoints, you might also need to trace how variables and expressions change during the course of program execution. For example, you might have a statement that reads `resultNum = firstNum / secondNum`. You know this line is causing a divide-by-zero error, but you do not know exactly when secondNum is being changed to a 0 value. The ability to trace program execution and learn the exact location at which secondNum is being changed to a 0 value allows you to pinpoint the cause of the logic problem. The debugger contains several tools that you can use during break mode to help you trace and analyze variables and expressions. These tools include debugging windows that help you analyze the value of variables during program execution, and the Call Stack window, which helps you trace the calls to your program's functions.

In addition to using the debug windows to learn the value of a variable during program execution, in break mode you can learn the value of a variable by holding your mouse over the variable. An information bubble, similar to a ToolTip, will display the variable's current value. You can also learn the result of an expression by highlighting the expression and holding your mouse over it.

The Variables Window

The Variables window displays three tabs: Auto, Locals, and this, that monitor variables as you step through a program in break mode. In any of these tabs, the most recently modified variable is highlighted in red. If the Variables window does not automatically display when you start the debugger, you can manually display it by pointing to Debug Windows on the View menu and selecting Variables.

The debugger also includes three windows: Memory, Registers, and Disassembly, that are normally required for debugging purposes. The Memory window allows you to view the contents of specific memory locations. The Registers and Disassembly windows are used for debugging at the assembly language level.

Using the Auto Tab

If you are stepping through a program and execute a statement that declares int iSampleVariable =1;, iSampleVariable comes into scope. When you reach the end of a block in which a variable is declared, the variable goes out of scope. The **Auto tab** of the Variables window displays variables that have been initialized within the *current* scope. You use the Auto tab to monitor variables within a specific context, such as during the execution of a function. For example, consider the following version of the calculatePayFunction(). If you are stepping through the function and stop on the bolded statement, the Auto tab will appear similar to the example shown in Figure 9-20. Notice that only the dNumHours and dPayRate variables have been initialized. The large exponential number that you see assigned to the dGrossPay variable has no meaning except to inform you that the dGrossPay variable has not been initialized.

```
double calcHourlyPay() {
    double dPayRate = 20;
    double dNumHours = 40;
    double dGrossPay = dPayRate * dNumHours;
    double dFederalTaxes = dGrossPay * .06794;
```

```
        double dStateTaxes = dGrossPay * .0476;

        double dSocialSecurity = dGrossPay * .062;

        double dMedicare = dGrossPay * .0145;

        double dNetPay = dGrossPay - dFederalTaxes;

        dNetPay *= dStateTaxes;

        dNetPay *= dSocialSecurity;

        dNetPay *= dMedicare;

        return dNetPay;

}
```

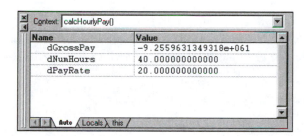

Figure 9-20   Auto tab

The Auto tab helps you see how different values affect program execution. As you step through code in break mode, you can change the value of a variable in the Auto window by clicking once on the value in the Value column, entering a new value, and pressing Enter. Changing a value in break mode changes the value only for the current instance of program execution.

Using the Locals tab

The **Locals tab** of the Variables window displays all local variables within the currently executing function, regardless of whether they have been initialized. The Locals tab helps you see how different values in the currently executing function affect program execution. You use the Locals tab when you need to be able to see all of a function's variables, regardless of whether they have been assigned a value. You can change the value of a variable in the Locals tab by clicking once on the value in the Value column, entering a new value, and pressing Enter. Figure 9-21 shows how the Locals tab appears when you step through the calculatePay() function and pause at the bolded line. Even though only the dNumHours and dPayRate variables have been initialized, all of the function's variables are listed in the Locals tab.

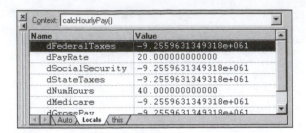

Figure 9-21   Locals tab

At the top of the Locals tab is a drop-down list box containing all of the functions from which the current function was called. To display another function's variables, select the function from the list.

Using the this Tab

The **this tab** of the Variables window displays variables and other information associated with the current `this` reference. For example, you may have a CStocks class that contains a member function named getTotalValue() as follows:

```
double CStocks::getTotalValue(int iShares,
    double dCurPrice) {
    iNumShares = iShares;
    dCurrentPricePerShare = dCurPrice;
    dCurrentValue = iNumShares * dCurrentPricePerShare;
    return dCurrentValue;
}
```

If you step through the preceding getTotalValue() function and examine the this tab of the Variables window, it will appear similar to Figure 9-22.

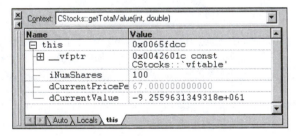

Figure 9-22   The this tab

As with the Auto tab and the Locals tab, you can change the value of a variable in the this tab by clicking once on the value in the Value column, entering a new value, and pressing Enter.

Next, you will practice tracing variables with the Variables window and the Auto, Locals, and this tabs.

To practice tracing variables with the Variables window and the Auto, Locals, and this tabs:

1. Open the **MovingEstimator.cpp** file in the Text Editor window.

2. In the InitInstance() function, add a breakpoint to the statement that reads **CMovingEstimatorDlg dlg;**.

3. Open the **MovingEstimatorDlg.cpp** file in the Text Editor window.

4. In the calcTotalEstimate() function, add a breakpoint to the statement that reads **m_dTotal = dMileageCost;**.

5. Execute the program by pointing to the **Start Debug** submenu on the **Build** menu and selecting **Go**. The program starts running and pauses at the **CMovingEstimatorDlg dlg;** statement in the InitInstance() function.

6. Click the **Auto** tab in the Variables window. You should see the dlg object and the this reference listed in the Name column. The value column displays the memory address where each variable is stored. Recall that the Auto tab displays variables that have been initialized within the current scope. The dlg variable refers to the instantiated CMovingEstimatorDlg object. In the case of an MFC application, the this reference refers to the application itself, which is in the current scope.

If the Variables window does not automatically display after you start the program, manually display it by pointing to Debug Windows on the View menu and selecting Variables.

7. Expand the **this** reference by clicking the **plus** symbol to the left of the name. You will see all of the variables within the application scope, including data members that are inherited and initiated by the MFC base classes. You will also see references, pointers, and objects such as function names, with plus symbols next to their names. Clicking a plus symbol next to an object name will display all of the variables local to that object. The Locals tab and the this tab also contain this reference entries since the application itself is within the scope of all three tabs. In fact, the this reference is the only entry contained in the this tab.

8. Click the **Locals** tab in the Variables window. The Locals tab also contains the dlg object and the this reference. It also contains the nResponse variable, which is the only local variable in the function. (In fact, it is the only local variable in the entire program.) Since the nResponse variable has not yet been initialized, it contains an unusable value.

9. Now click the **this** tab in the Variables window. You can see that the only entry in the tab is the reference.

10. Select the **Go** command from the **Debug** menu, and the Moving Estimator dialog window appears. Enter **10000** in the Distance in miles edit box and press the **Tab** key. As soon as you press Tab, program execution enters break mode again and pauses at the second breakpoint you set on the **m_dTotal = dMileageCost;** statement in the calcTotalEstimate() function in the MovingEstimatorDlg.cpp file.

11. Click the **Auto** tab in the Variables window. Notice that the Auto tab contains two variables which are within the calcTotalEstimate() function's scope: dMileageCost and m_dTotal. The dMileageCost variable was assigned its value of 12,500 from the setMileageCost() function. The m_dTotal variable has not yet been assigned a value, so its initial value of 0 is displayed.

12. Select the **Step Into** command. Notice that the m_dTotal variable has now been assigned *12500* from the dMileageCost variable. The value of the m_dTotal variable in the value column of the Auto tab appears in red because it was the last value to be updated. Also, notice that a new variable, dLaborCost, has come into scope.

13. Select **Stop Debugging** from the **Debug** menu to halt program execution.

The Watch Window

The **Watch window** is used for monitoring and changing specific variables that you enter. Unlike the tabs in the Variables window, which automatically show the values of variables according to the current scope, you must manually enter the variables into the Watch window that you want to monitor. You can enter the name of a variable into the Watch window and monitor how the variable changes during the course of program execution. You use the Watch window when you are interested in monitoring only specific variables. You can also enter expressions in the Watch window and observe how their values change as the program executes. For example, if you place the expression `dPayRate * 1.5` in the Watch window, its value changes as the dPayRate variable changes.

If the Watch window does not automatically appear when you start the debugger, you can manually display it by pointing to the Debug Windows submenu on the View menu, and selecting Watch. Figure 9-23 shows an example of the Watch window.

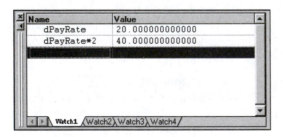

Figure 9-23   The Watch window

You enter variable names and expressions directly into a row in the Watch window, or you can use your mouse to drag a variable or expression onto the Watch window from the Text Editor window or from one of the tabs on the Variables window.

QuickWatch

Another way of watching variables is by using QuickWatch. **QuickWatch** is a dialog box that you can use to quickly examine the value of a single variable or expression. Once you are in break mode, you can display QuickWatch by selecting QuickWatch from the Debug menu. You can then enter a variable name or expression in the Expression edit box and click the Recalculate button to view its value. Alternatively, after entering a variable name or expression in the QuickWatch Expression edit box, you can add it to the Watch window by clicking the Add Watch button. QuickWatch is of somewhat limited use because it is a modal dialog box. You must close it in order to continue debugging your application. However, you may find it useful for quickly retrieving a value or calculating an expression. Figure 9-24 shows an example of the QuickWatch window.

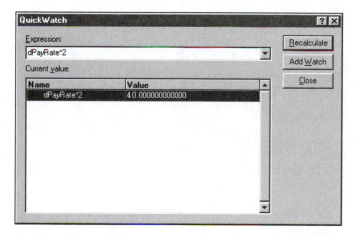

Figure 9-24   QuickWatch window

 You can also view the values of variables or expressions by highlighting them in the Text Editor window and by selecting QuickWatch from the Debug menu. The highlighted variable or expression will be added to the QuickWatch window for you.

Next, you will use the Watch window and the QuickWatch dialog box to find a bug in the Moving Estimator program.

To use the Watch window and the QuickWatch dialog box to find a bug in the Moving Estimator program:

1. First, remove all of the breakpoints from the Moving Estimator program by selecting **Breakpoints** from the **Edit** menu. The Breakpoints dialog box appears. The breakpoints you set are listed in the Breakpoints list at the bottom of the dialog box. Click the **Remove All** button, then click the **OK** button. The Breakpoints dialog box is shown in Figure 9-25.

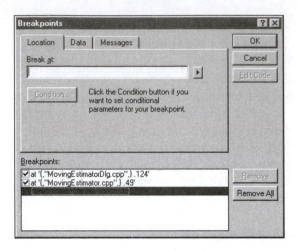

Figure 9-25   Breakpoints dialog box

2. Return to the **MovingEstimatorDlg.cpp** file in the Text Editor window.

3. Next, rebuild and run the Moving Estimator program, and enter the following data into each of the edit boxes.

```
Distance in miles: 10000
Weight in pounds: 500
# of flights of stairs: 2
# of appliances: 3
# of pianos: 1
Extra charges: 100
```

4. After you enter the preceding numbers, the Moving estimate edit box displays a value of 12785. However, you can tell by doing the math manually that the value should be 12885. Since you have already corrected the Distance in miles, Weight in pounds, and # of flights of stairs calculations, you will start by examining the # of appliances calculation. You will examine the two values required by the appliances calculation: the m_iAppliances data member, which receives its value from the dialog box via the UpdateData() function, and the dAppliancesCost data member, which receives the result of the calculation. First, close the Moving Estimator program, and then enter a breakpoint on the **dAppliancesCost = m_iAppliances * 25;** statement in the setAppliancesCost() function, and then select the **Go** command from the **Start Debug** submenu on the **Build** menu. The program starts to execute and displays the Moving Estimator window.

5. Enter the values from Step 3 into the Distance in miles edit box, Weight in pounds edit box, # of flights of stairs edit box, and the # of appliances edit box. Press your **Tab** key after entering the value into the # of appliances edit box and the program enters break mode and pauses on the **dAppliancesCost = m_iAppliances * 25;** statement.

6. Before stepping through the function, use the QuickWatch dialog box to examine the values contained in the m_iAppliances and dAppliancesCost data members by selecting **QuickWatch** from the **Debug** menu. When the QuickWatch dialog box appears, enter **m_iAppliances** in the Expression box and click the **Recalculate** button. The Current value list should display the correct value of *3* for the m_iAppliances variable. Now, check the result that should be returned by the function by typing **m_iAppliances * 25** in the Expression box and clicking the **Recalculate** button. The correct value of *75* should display in the Current value list. This is the value that should be assigned to the dAppliancesCost data member when the calculation finishes. Click the **Close** button to close the QuickWatch dialog box.

7. Select the **Step Into** command to execute the function's calculation statement.

8. Place your cursor anywhere within the dAppliancesCost data member and open the QuickWatch dialog box. The dAppliancesCost data member should be automatically entered into the QuickWatch dialog box and the correct value of *75* should be displayed in the Current value list. Therefore, the problem does not appear to be with the appliances cost calculation. Click the **Close** button to close the QuickWatch dialog box.

9. Select **Stop Debugging** from the **Debug** menu.

10. Remove the breakpoint from the **dAppliancesCost = m_iAppliances * 25;** statement in the setAppliancesCost() function.

11. Next, you will examine the two values required by the piano calculation: the m_iPianos data member, which receives its value from the dialog box via the UpdateData() function, and the dPianosCost data member, which receives the result of the calculation. Enter a breakpoint on the **dFlightsCost = m_iPianos * 35;** statement in the setPianosCost() function, and then select the **Go** command from the **Start Debug** submenu on the **Build** menu. The program starts to execute and displays the Moving Estimator window.

12. Enter the values from Step 3 into the Distance in miles edit box, Weight in pounds edit box, # of flights of stairs edit box, # of appliances edit box, and the # of pianos edit box. Press your **Tab** key after entering the value into the # of pianos edit box and the program enters break mode and pauses on the **dFlightsCost = m_iPianos * 35;** statement.

13. Now, place your cursor in the Name column of the Watch window and type **m_iPianos**. Press your **Enter** key and type **dPianosCost** in the second row of the Watch window. The **m_iPianos** data member should have a value of *1,* and the **dPianosCost** data member should have a value of *0*. Since the cost to move a single piano is $35, the dPianosCost data member should update to *35* after executing the statement in the function. Figure 9-26 shows the Watch window after entering the two variables.

9

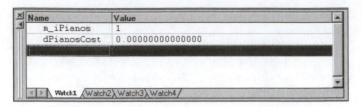

Figure 9-26   Watch window with the m_iPianos and dPianosCost data members

14. Select the **Step Into** command to execute the statement. Notice that the dPianosCost variable is not updated to *35* after executing the statement. If you are observant, you have probably already noticed that the setPianosCost() function's single **dFlightsCost = m_iPianos * 35;** statement incorrectly assigns the result of the calculation to the dFlightsCost variable—not the dPianosCost variable.

15. Select **Stop Debugging** from the **Debug** menu and remove the breakpoint from the **dFlightsCost = m_iPianos * 35;** statement.

16. Modify the incorrect statement in the setPianosCost() function so that it reads as follows:

    dPianosCost = m_iPianos * 35;

17. Rebuild and execute the program, and then enter the values from Step 3. The program should now function correctly.

THE CALL STACK WINDOW

When you are working with a C++ program that contains multiple functions, the computer must remember the order in which functions are executed. For example, if you have a main() function that calls an accountsPayable() function that calls an accountsReceivable() function, the computer must remember to return to the accountsPayable() function once the accountsReceivable() function finishes executing, and then return to the main() function once the accountsPayable() function finishes executing. Similarly, if the accountsReceivable() function calls a depositFunds() function after it has been called by the accountsPayable() function, then the computer must remember to return to the accountsReceivable() function when the depositFunds() function finishes executing, then return to the accountsPayable() function once the accountsReceivable() function finishes executing, and finally return to the main() function after the accountsPayable() function finishes executing. The **call stack** refers to the order in which functions execute in a program. Each time a program calls a function, the function is added to the top of the call stack, then removed once it finishes executing.

The ability to view the contents of a call stack is very useful when tracing logic errors in large programs with multiple functions. For example, you might have a variable that is passed as an argument among several functions. At some point, the variable is being assigned the wrong value. Viewing the call stack, along with using tracing and other debug windows, makes it easier to locate the specific function causing the problem. When you enter break mode to debug a program, functions are automatically added to and removed from the Call Stack window as you step through your program. You display the call stack when you are in break mode by selecting Call Stack from the Debug Windows submenu on the View menu.

Next, you will step through some of the functions in the Moving Estimator program to observe the contents of the Call Stack window.

To step through some of the functions in the Moving Estimator program to observe the contents of the Call Stack window:

1. Open the **MovingEstimator.cpp** file in the Text Editor window.

2. Place your cursor in the **CMovingEstimatorDlg dlg;** statement and select the **Run to Cursor** command by pointing the **Start Debug** on the **Build** menu and selecting **Run to Cursor**. The program starts executing and then enters break mode when it encounters the **CMovingEstimatorDlg dlg;** statement.

3. Display the Call Stack window by clicking the **Call Stack** window command on the **Debug Windows** submenu on the **View** menu. The Call Stack window includes several function calls required by the system, including the call to the inherited MFC WinMain() function. At the top of the call stack is the last function call to the InitInstance() function.

4. Select the **Step Into** command to execute the **CMovingEstimatorDlg dlg;** statement. Because you are instantiating a new object, control transfers to the CMovingEstimator class's constructor function, which is added to the Call Stack. Your Call Stack window should resemble Figure 9-27, although there may be some additional items on the Call Stack depending on your system.

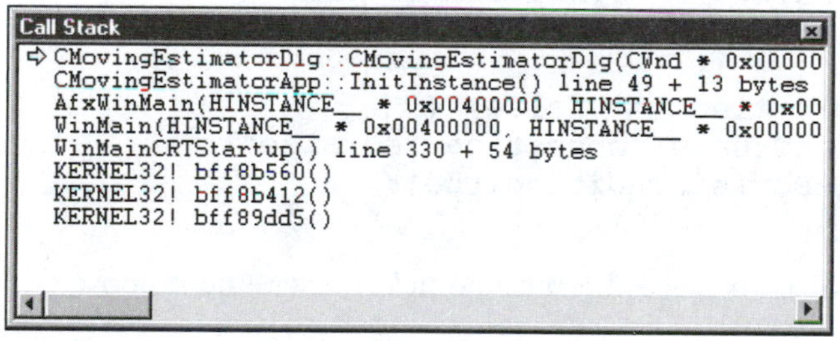

Figure 9-27   Call Stack window in the Moving Estimator program

5. Select the **Step Out** command and the constructor function finishes executing. Control is transferred back to the InitInstance() function, and the constructor function call is removed from the Call Stack window. Functions will continue to be added and removed from the Call Stack window in this manner for the duration of the program.

6. Select **Stop Debugging** from the **Debug** menu to end debugging mode.

C++ LANGUAGE BUGS AND DEBUGGING RESOURCES

If you have tried everything you can think of to fix a bug in your program, consider the possibility that you might be encountering one of the known bugs in Visual C++. Bugs can occur with Visual C++'s implementation of the C++ language or with the Visual C++ application itself. One of the known C++ bugs involves a special data type known as a sized integer. The **__int64 sized integer data type** is used for declaring integer variables that are composed of 64-bits. You declare a __int64 size integer variable the way you declare other data types, using a statement similar to `__int64 iNumber = 100;`. However, when you attempt to use an __int64 variable with the insertion operator, <<, you will receive a compiler error message. For example, consider the following code:

```
void main() {
    __int64 myNumber = 100;
    cout << myNumber << endl;
```

The preceding code *should* function correctly; there is nothing wrong with the syntax or underlying logic. However, it will produce a compiler error message because of the known sized integer bug. This bug will more than likely be remedied in the next release of Visual C++. For now, the preceding code generates the following compiler error warning:

```
error C2593: 'operator <<' is ambiguous
```

Another known bug involves the Visual C++ application itself and the use of breakpoints with `else if` statements. If you set a breakpoint on the bolded `else if` statement in the following code, the Visual C++ debugger will *not* stop there, even though it is supposed to.

```
bool bDisplayAlert = false;
CString szConditionTrue = "no condition";
if (bDisplayAlert == true) {
    szConditionTrue = "condition is true";
    AfxMessageBox(szConditionTrue);
}
else if (bDisplayAlert == false) {
    szConditionTrue = "condition is false";
    AfxMessageBox(szConditionTrue);
}
```

A solution to this problem is to place the breakpoint on a statement above or below the `else if` statement.

To see a list of known bugs in Visual C++ (as well as other Microsoft development tools), visit the MSDN Bug Center at *http://msdn.microsoft.com/bugs/*. You can view lists of known bugs and suggested workarounds. You can also view a list of "perceived bugs," which appear to be bugs to some users, but are really part of Visual C++'s design. If you find what appears to be an undocumented bug in Visual C++, you can submit a bug report at *http://support.microsoft.com/support/visualc/report/default.asp*. But before you submit a bug report, be sure that the problem does not already exist in the bug list and be sure that you can reproduce the bug. Sometimes a problem may occur because your computer is out of memory or you are experiencing other system problems. Microsoft would certainly have its hands full if it received a bug report every time a programmer received an error in his or her application that was caused by a faulty computer or system problem.

Note that the manufacturer of a software program is not always the first to know about a bug in its product. Innovative users often discover bugs first, and then report them to a program's creator. These users also usually love to share their bug discoveries with other users. Take advantage of the many Visual C++ programmers who are often more than happy to help you solve a problem or track down a bug. You can find help on many different Web sites, in newsgroups, and in the special forums of Internet service providers such as CompuServe, Prodigy, and America Online. Figure 9-28 lists some Internet debugging resources, including Microsoft sites.

Resource	Address
MSDN Online	http://msdn.microsoft.com
Microsoft's Visual C++ Page	http://msdn.microsoft.com/visualc
Visual C++ Developers Journal	http://www.vcdj.com
MFC Frequently Asked Questions	http://mfcfaq.stingray.com/
Microsoft's Visual C++ Frequently Asked Questions	http://msdn.microsoft.com/visualc/technical/techfaq.asp
C/C++ Newsgroups	alt.comp.lang.learn.c-c++ comp.lang.c comp.lang.c++ comp.std.c++ ctdl.lang.c ctdl.lang.c++ fiu.lang.c fiu.lang.c++

Figure 9-28   Visual C++ debugging resources on the Internet

 Before participating in a newsgroup, be sure you read the Frequently Asked Questions and understand the ground rules for posting and responding to messages. Usually, a newsgroup's ground rules are listed in a Frequently Asked Questions document.

The addresses in Figure 9-28 are current as of December 2000. As you access the addresses, keep in mind that the Internet is an ever-changing place. Just like other businesses, Web sites may change their addresses over time or close altogether.

CHAPTER SUMMARY

❒ Syntax errors occur when you enter code that the compiler does not recognize.

❒ If your Visual C++ program encounters a problem while it is executing, the problem is called a run-time error.

❒ Logic errors are problems in the design of a program that prevent it from running as you anticipate it will run.

❒ There are two main types of build messages: compiler error messages and warning messages.

❒ Compiler error messages occur for any syntax errors in a program.

❒ Compiler error messages should be used only to find the general location of an error in a program and not as the exact indicator of an error.

❒ Warning messages occur for any potential problems that may exist in your code, but that are not serious enough to cause a compiler error message.

❒ The number and severity of warning messages displayed in the Output window is determined by the Warning Level setting on the C/C++ tab of the Project Settings dialog box.

❒ Tracing is the examination of individual statements in an executing program.

❒ One of the simplest tracing tools you can use is an output statement (cout) in a console application.

❒ Simplified, temporary programs that are used for testing functions and other code are called driver programs.

❒ Stub functions are empty functions that serve as placeholders (or "stubs") for a program's actual functions.

❒ You can use comments in your code to help locate bugs.

❒ At times, errors in your code will be logic problems that are difficult to spot using tracing techniques.

❒ Visual C++ provides a program called the debugger that contains several tools that can help you trace each line of code, creating a much more efficient method of finding and resolving logic errors.

❒ Break mode temporarily suspends, or pauses, program execution so that you can monitor values and trace program execution.

❒ A Win32 Debug build contains additional information that is required by the debugger tools.

❒ A Win32 Release build does not contain any debugging information.

❒ By default, a project is set to compile as a Win32 Debug build when you first create a project.

❏ The Step Into, Step Over, and Step Out commands on the Debug menu are used for tracing program execution once you enter break mode.

❏ The Step Into command executes an individual line of code and then pauses until you instruct the debugger to continue.

❏ The Step Over command allows you to skip function calls.

❏ The Step Out command executes all remaining code in the current function.

❏ When you select the Run to Cursor command, the program runs normally until it reaches the statement where your cursor is located, at which point the program enters break mode.

❏ When a program enters break mode, program execution is not stopped—it is only suspended.

❏ A breakpoint is a position in the code at which program execution enters break mode.

❏ The Auto tab of the Variables window displays variables that have been initialized within the current scope.

❏ The Locals tab of the Variables window displays all local variables within the currently executing function, regardless of whether they have been initialized.

❏ The this tab of the Variables window displays variables and other information associated with the current this reference.

❏ The Watch window is used for monitoring and changing specific variables that you enter.

❏ QuickWatch is a dialog box that you can use to quickly examine the value of a single variable or expression.

❏ The call stack refers to the order in which functions execute in a program.

❏ Each time a program calls a function, the function is added to the top of the call stack, then removed once it finishes executing.

❏ If you have tried everything you can think of to fix a bug in your program, consider the possibility that you may be encountering one of the known bugs in Visual C++.

REVIEW QUESTIONS

1. _____ errors occur when you enter code that the compiler does not recognize.

    a. Application

    b. Logic

    c. Run-time

    d. Syntax

2. If a program encounters a problem while a program is executing, that problem is called a(n) _____ error.

   a. application

   b. logic

   c. run-time

   d. syntax

3. _____ errors are problems in the design of a program that prevent it from running as you anticipate.

   a. Application

   b. Logic

   c. Run-time

   d. Syntax

4. Which of the following statements would cause a syntax error?

   a. `cout << "" <<;`

   b. `AfxMessageBox("Hello World")`

   c. `return TRUE;`

   d. `CMainWindow curWin;`

5. Which of the following functions would cause a run-time error?

   a.
   ```
   double calcMarginPercent() {
       double dGrossProfit = 100;
       double dNetProfit = 100;
       double dMargin = dGrossProfit - dNetProfit;
       double dMarginPercent = dMargin / dGrossProfit;
   }
   ```

   b.
   ```
   double calcMarginPercent() {
       double dGrossProfit = 200;
       double dNetProfit = 100;
       double dMargin = dGrossProfit - dNetProfit;
       double dMarginPercent = dMargin / dGrossProfit;
   }
   ```

   c.
   ```
   double calcMarginPercent() {
       double dGrossProfit = 200;
       double dNetProfit = 100;
       double dMargin = dGrossProfit - dNetProfit;
       double dMarginPercent = dMargin / dGrossProfit;
   }
   ```

```
d. double calcMarginPercent() {
      double dGrossProfit = 0;
      double dNetProfit = 100;
      double dMargin = dGrossProfit - dNetProfit;
      double dMarginPercent = dMargin / dGrossProfit;
   }
```

6. Which of the following if statements is logically incorrect?

a.
```
if (count < 5)
    cout << count << endl;
```

b.
```
if (count =< 5)
    cout << count << endl;
```

c.
```
if (count = 5);
    cout << count << endl;
```

d.
```
if (count = 5) {
    cout << count << endl;
}
```

7. Which of the following statements would cause a compiler error message?

a. `int iNumber = 3.12;`

b. `double = 3.12;`

c. `float = 3.12;`

d. `bool = 3.12`

8. Which of the following statements would cause a compiler warning message?

a. `int iNumber = 3.12;`

b. `double = 3.12;`

c. `float = 3.12;`

d. `bool = 3.12`

9. What is the most severe compiler warning level?

a. Level 1

b. Level 2

c. Level 3

d. Level 4

10. _____ refers to the examination of individual statements in an executing program.

a. Trailing

b. Tracing

c. Tracking

d. Commenting

11. Simplified, temporary programs that are used for testing functions and other code are called _____.

    a. test kits

    b. stub functions

    c. driver programs

    d. dynamic link libraries

12. Which of the following code structure prints the text *Hello World* five times?

    a.
```
for (var count = 1; count < 6; ++count);
       cout << "Hello World" << endl;
       cout << "Hello World" << endl;
       cout << "Hello World" << endl;
       cout << "Hello World" << endl;
       cout << "Hello World" << endl;
```

    b.
```
for (var count = 0; count < 6; ++count)
       cout << "Hello World" << endl;
```

    c.
```
for (var count = 0; count < 6; ++count) {
       cout << "Hello World" << endl;
   }
```

    d.
```
for (var count = 0; count < 6; ++count);
       cout << "Hello World" << endl;
```

13. _____ mode temporarily suspends, or pauses, program execution so that you can monitor values and trace program execution.

    a. Break

    b. Stop

    c. Suspend

    d. Wait

14. Which build version do you use when debugging a program?

    a. Win32 Debug

    b. Win32 Check

    c. Debug Release

    d. Build Release

15. Which build version do you use when distributing a program?

    a. Win32 Complete

    b. Win32 Release

    c. Final Release

    d. Build Release

16. Which debugger command executes the next line of code?

   a. Step Into

   b. Step Out

   c. Step Over

   d. Continue

17. Which debugger command executes all the statements in the next function?

   a. Step Into

   b. Step Out

   c. Step Over

   d. Continue

18. Which debugger command executes the rest of the commands in a function and moves to the next statement following the statement that called the current function?

   a. Step Into

   b. Step Out

   c. Step Over

   d. Continue

19. Which debugger command proceeds with the normal execution of a program?

   a. Continue

   b. Proceed

   c. Exit Debug

   d. Go

20. A(n) _____ is a statement in the code at which program execution enters break mode.

   a. stop marker

   b. breakpoint

   c. pause position

   d. interrupt

21. The _____ tab of the Variables window displays all local variables within the currently executing function, regardless of whether they have been initialized.

   a. Auto

   b. Locals

   c. this

   d. Scope

22. The _____ window is used for monitoring and changing specific variables that you enter.

    a. Trace

    b. Immediate

    c. Variables

    d. Watch

23. The order in which functions execute in a program is the _____.

    a. execution chain

    b. procedure heap

    c. call stack

    d. method batch

EXERCISES

1. Manually locate and correct the syntax errors in the following code:

```cpp
#include <iostream.h>;
char* cityLocation(int iAmericanCity);
main()
{
    int iCity = 0;
    char* szState;
    cout << "Enter a number to find the state
        where a city is located. << endl;
    cout << "1. Boston" <<;
    cout << "2. Chicago" << endl;
    cout << "3. Los Angeles" << endl;
    cout << "4. Miami" << endl;
    cout << "5. Providence" << endl << endl;
    cin >> iCity;
    cout << endl;
    szState = cityLocation(iCity);
    cout << szState << endl << endl;
}
char* cityLocation(int iAmericanCity) {
    switch (iAmericanCity)
        case 1:
            return "Boston is in Massachusetts";
            break;
        case 2:
            return "Chicago is in Illinois";
            break;
        case 3:
            return "Los Angeles is in California";
            break;
```

```
                    case 4
                        return "Miami is in Florida";
                        break;
                case 5:
                        return "Providence is in Rhode Island";
                        break;
            default:
                        return "You did not select one of the five
        cities!";
            }
```

2. The following code should output the two statements within the **if** statement. Instead, it only prints the single statement contained in the **else** clause. Identify the error and rewrite the code:

```
int iNum = 5;
if (iNum = 6) {       // CONDITION EVALUATES TO 'TRUE'
    cout << "The condition evaluates to true." << endl;
    cout << "iNum is equal to 5." << endl;
}
else
    cout << "The condition is false." << endl;
}
```

9

3. The following code should print the values *1*, *2*, *4*, and *5* to the screen. Instead, the code prints only *1* and *2* to the screen. Find the error in code and make the appropriate modification(s).

```
for(int ctCount = 1; ctCount <=5; ++ctCount) {
    if(ctCount == 3)
            break;
    cout << ctCount << endl;
}
```

4. The following code should print the days of the week. Instead, only Tuesday through Sunday are printed, and an indecipherable value is printed after *Sunday*. Locate the bugs and make the appropriate changes.

```
#include <iostream.h>
void main() {
    char* szDaysOfWeek[7];
    szDaysOfWeek[0] = "Monday";
    szDaysOfWeek[1] = "Tuesday";
    szDaysOfWeek[2] = "Wednesday";
    szDaysOfWeek[3] = "Thursday";
    szDaysOfWeek[4] = "Friday";
    szDaysOfWeek[5] = "Saturday";
    szDaysOfWeek[6] = "Sunday";
    int ctCount = 1;
    do {
            cout << szDaysOfWeek[ctCount] << endl;
            ++ctCount;
```

```
            } while (ctCount <= 7);
            cout << endl;
        }
```

5. Many advanced programming languages, including C++, include a feature known as exception handling, which allows programs to handle errors as they occur in the execution of a program. Search the MSDN Library for exception-handling topics and explain how you would use exception handling in your projects.

6. Locate the Debugging Techniques, Problems, and Solutions topic in the MSDN Library and study some of the advanced debugging techniques available in Visual C++. How can you apply some of the advanced debugging techniques to the programs you develop?

7. Programs created with MFCs have an additional tool available, the TRACE macro, that can be used for tracing the value of variables as a program executes. Search the MSDN Library for information on the TRACE macro. How do you use the TRACE macro? Since MFC programs do not use console windows, where is the output from the TRACE macro written to?

8. Another debugging tool that can be used with MFC programs is the ASSERT macro, which allows you to test the validity of an expression. Search the MSDN Library for information on the ASSERT macro. Why would you use the ASSERT macro in your programs? Describe a scenario in which you would use the ASSERT macro to test your program before releasing it.

9. The MFC TRACE macro and the ASSERT macro are only used for debugging purposes. What happens if you create a Win32 Release build of a project that includes these macros? Are they compiled with the release build? Search the MSDN Library for your answer.

10. Visual C++ also gives you the option of compiling and linking your project from the command line. How do you go about building a project from the command line? What additional debugging features, if any, exist for command-line compilation? Refer to the Compiling and Linking topic in MSDN Library for your answer.

11. One of the most important aspects of creating a good program is the design and analysis phase of the project. Conducting a good design and analysis phase is critical to minimizing bugs in your program. Search the Internet or your local library for information on this topic. Then explain how you should handle the design and analysis phase of a software project.

12. Equally important to minimizing bugs during software development is the testing phase. Search the Internet or your local library for information on software testing. Then design a plan for thoroughly testing your Visual C++ programs. How would you use driver programs and stub functions in your testing plan?

13. Visit Microsoft's Bug Center at http://msdn.microsoft.com/bugs/ and study the different types of bugs and errors in Visual C++ that are currently known. Write an analysis of the different categories of bugs and include information such as the category of error and what sort of fix, if any, exists for each bug.

14. The Chapter.09 folder on your Data Disk contains copies of some of the projects you created earlier in this text. However, all of the programs contain errors. Use any of the debugging skills you have learned in this chapter to correct the errors. You may review earlier chapters to see how each program should function—but *do not* do so to copy or review the correct syntax. Use these exercises as an opportunity to test and improve your debugging skills. The projects for you to correct are as follows:

- Chapter2_HelloWorld
- Chapter3_ChemistryQuizFinal
- Chapter4_RetirementPlanner
- Chapter5_BuildingEstimator
- Chapter6_ConversionCenter
- Chapter7_Calculator
- Chapter8_Calculator

9

CHAPTER

10

WORKING WITH DOCUMENTS AND VIEWS

In this chapter you will learn:

◆ About documents and views

◆ About document interfaces

◆ How to work with the CView class

◆ How to work with the CDocument Class

◆ About document templates

◆ About common dialog boxes

◆ How to store data

PREVIEW: THE INVOICE PROGRAM

In this chapter, you will work with an Invoice program to learn how to use documents with MFC programs. The Invoice program allows you to create individual invoices that you can save to a disk file, the same way you can save document or spreadsheet files from programs such as Word or Excel.

To preview the Invoice program:

1. Create a **Chapter.10** folder in your Visual C++ Projects folder.

2. Copy the **Chapter10_Invoice** folder from the Chapter.10 folder on your Data Disk to the Chapter.10 folder in your Visual C++ Projects folder, and then open the Invoice project in Visual C++.

3. Click on the **FileView** tab in the Workspace window and expand the Source Files folder, if necessary. The Invoice.cpp file is the definition file for the program's application class, and the MainFrm.cpp file is the definition file for the frame class. Notice the InvoiceDoc.cpp and InvoiceView.cpp files. These are the definition files for the CInvoiceDoc and CInvoiceView classes that give the MFC program its ability to work with documents. The CInvoiceDoc class derives from the CDocument class and is used for managing and storing a document's data. The CInvoiceView class derives from the CView class and is used for displaying to a user the data that is managed and stored by the CInvoiceDoc class.

4. Open the **InvoiceDoc.cpp** file. If you scroll through the file, you will see some typical MFC functions. You will also see an OnNewDocument() function, a Serialize() function, and a DeleteContents() function. The OnNewDocument()

function executes each time the user creates a new document. To reinitialize the data each time a new document is created, the OnNewDocument() function calls the DeleteContents() function, which reinitializes the class's data members. The Serialize() function is what actually writes and reads a document's data to and from a disk file. Figure 10-1 shows the OnNewDocument(), Serialize(), and DeleteContents() functions.

```cpp
BOOL CInvoiceDoc::OnNewDocument()
{
    DeleteContents();
    if (!CDocument::OnNewDocument())
        return FALSE;
    return TRUE;
}
void CInvoiceDoc::Serialize(CArchive& ar)
{
    if (ar.IsStoring())
    {
        ar << m_dAmount1; ar << m_dAmount2;
        ar << m_dAmount3; ar << m_szDescription2;
        ar << m_szDescription1; ar << m_szDescription3;
        ar << m_iQuantity1; ar << m_iQuantity2;
        ar << m_iQuantity3; ar << m_dRate1;
        ar << m_dRate2; ar << m_dRate3;
        ar << m_dTOTAL; ar << m_szDate;
        ar << m_szCustomer; ar << m_szInvoice;
        ar << m_szTerms;
    }
    else
    {
        ar >> m_dAmount1; ar >> m_dAmount2;
        ar >> m_dAmount3; ar >> m_szDescription2;
        ar >> m_szDescription1; ar >> m_szDescription3;
        ar >> m_iQuantity1; ar >> m_iQuantity2;
        ar >> m_iQuantity3; ar >> m_dRate1;
        ar >> m_dRate2; ar >> m_dRate3;
        ar >> m_dTOTAL; ar >> m_szDate;
        ar >> m_szCustomer; ar >> m_szInvoice;
        ar >> m_szTerms;
    }
}
void CInvoiceDoc::DeleteContents()
{
    m_dAmount1 = 0.0; m_dAmount2 = 0.0;
    m_dAmount3 = 0.0;
    m_szDescription2 = _T("");
    m_szDescription1 = _T("");
    m_szDescription3 = _T("");
```

Figure 10-1 InvoiceDoc.cpp

```
        m_iQuantity1 = 0; m_iQuantity2 = 0;
        m_iQuantity3 = 0; m_dRate1 = 0.0;
        m_dRate2 = 0.0; m_dRate3 = 0.0;
        m_dTOTAL = 0.0; m_szDate = _T("");
        m_szCustomer = _T(""); m_szInvoice = _T("");
        m_szTerms = _T("");
        CDocument::DeleteContents();
}
```

Figure 10-1   InvoiceDoc.cpp (continued)

5. Next, open the **InvoiceView.cpp** file. The CInvoiceView class displays a document's data, which is stored in the CInvoiceDoc class. If you scroll through the file, you will see a number of member functions that give the program its functionality, along with some typical MFC functions. You will also see an OnUpdate() function. The OnUpdate() function updates the display in the window if any of the data in the CInvoiceDoc changes. Notice that the statements in the function's body use a CInvoiceDoc class pointer (pDoc) to a function named GetDocument(). The GetDocument() function allows classes derived from CView to communicate with their associated classes that are derived from CDocument. Figure 10-2 shows the OnUpdate() function.

10

```
void CInvoiceView::OnUpdate(CView* pSender, LPARAM lHint,
CObject* pHint)
{
    CInvoiceDoc* pDoc = GetDocument();
    m_dAmount1 = pDoc->m_dAmount1;
    m_dAmount2 = pDoc->m_dAmount2;
    m_dAmount3 = pDoc->m_dAmount3;
    m_szDescription1 = pDoc->m_szDescription1;
    m_szDescription2 = pDoc->m_szDescription2;
    m_szDescription3 = pDoc->m_szDescription3;
    m_iQuantity1 = pDoc->m_iQuantity1;
    m_iQuantity2 = pDoc->m_iQuantity2;
    m_iQuantity3 = pDoc->m_iQuantity3;
    m_dRate1 = pDoc->m_dRate1;
    m_dRate2 = pDoc->m_dRate2;
    m_dRate3 = pDoc->m_dRate3;
    m_dTOTAL = pDoc->m_dTOTAL;
    m_szDate = pDoc->m_szDate;
    m_szCustomer = pDoc->m_szCustomer;
    m_szInvoice = pDoc->m_szInvoice;
    m_szTerms = pDoc->m_szTerms;
    UpdateData(FALSE);
}
```

Figure 10-2   OnUpdate() function

6. Build and execute the Invoice program. The program allows you to enter three lines of billing information. Enter some data in the document. After you enter numbers into the Quantity and Rate edit boxes, the values in the Amount boxes and the TOTAL box recalculate when each edit box loses focus. After entering data, select the **Save** command from the program's **File** menu. A typical Windows Save dialog box, which is a common dialog box, appears. Save the invoice as Invoice001 in the Chapter.10 folder in your Visual C++ projects folder and then close the Invoice program.

7. Open the Invoice program again, and select the **Open** command on the **File** menu to reopen the invoice you just saved. Alternatively, you can select the file name from the list of most recently opened files at the bottom of the File menu.

After you select the file name, you will receive a dialog box asking if you want to save the current invoice (named Untitled). Click the **No** button and the document you just saved should open in the Invoice program and display the data you entered in the preceding step. Figure 10-3 shows an example of the Invoice program window.

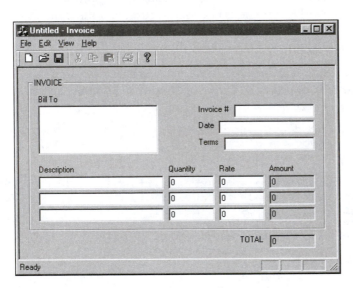

Figure 10-3 Invoice program window

8. Click the Close button to close the Invoice program window.

INTRODUCTION

So far, all of the projects you have created performed some sort of calculation or task that was applicable only to the current application session. For example, the console application-based Chemistry Quiz, Retirement Planner, Conversion Center, and Building Estimator programs gathered information from the user, returned a result, and then exited. Even the

Windows-based Calculator and Moving Estimator programs simply returned a result to the user that existed only until the program closed.

A very important missing piece of the application puzzle is the ability to store data that you can retrieve later. The Chemistry Quiz, for instance, would be much more useful if you could store each student's test results. The Moving Estimator program would be much more valuable if you could save moving estimates for different customers. With the current application, you could enter information for one customer, calculate the results, write the information down on a piece of paper, and then re-enter new information for another customer. But this is the Information Age—you should not need to manually write information on a piece of paper. Instead, you should be able to save that information to a computer's hard drive. As another example, consider the Invoice program you will create in this chapter. What good would the Invoice program be if you could not save the data you entered? Your only alternative would be to print a hard copy of each invoice that you would then store in a filing cabinet. If you had to store a hard copy, then you might as well use a typewriter to fill in a preprinted form, or even write your invoice information onto the preprinted form by hand. It is worth noting that not all applications need to have the ability to save different sets of data. For instance, you would not normally need to enter or save different sets of data for the simple Calculator programs you have created. However, the ability to enter and save different sets of data would certainly add to the functionality of other programs, such as the Chemistry Quiz and Moving Estimator programs.

The MFC applications you have worked with in the last two chapters have been dialog based in that dialog boxes control the entire functionality of the program. More powerful, and often more useful, MFC applications are usually document based. A **document** is a file that is associated with a particular application and that contains different sets of data depending on your program's functionality and each user's needs. Users can create their own documents within a document-based application that they can later reopen for viewing or editing. You have probably worked with many document-based applications. Microsoft Word and Excel are both document-based applications that you may have seen or worked with at one time or another. Documents do not necessarily need to be complex like the word processing documents you use with Word or the spreadsheet documents you use with Excel. Instead, a document can consist of a simple set of data, such as the customer information you enter into the Moving Estimator program.

In this chapter, you will learn how to create document-based MFC applications that users can use to open and save their own files. Before you actually create a document-based application using AppWizard, you need to understand the basics of documents and views.

DOCUMENTS AND VIEWS

When you first learned how to work with MFC programming in Chapter 8, you briefly reviewed how to create a window class based on the CFrameWnd class, which creates a simple window with a frame, title bar, control menu, and control buttons. With the exception of dialog-based applications, almost all MFC programs include a window class derived from the CFrameWnd class. The windows displayed by classes that derive from the CFrameWnd class are referred to as frame windows. To refresh your memory on the CFrameWnd class, Figure 10-4 shows a basic MFC program that includes an application class and a window class derived from the CFrameWnd class. The most significant parts of the window class are the class header declaration that derives the class from the CFrameWnd class, and the Create() function that creates the window itself when an object of the window class is instantiated. The window is then displayed by calling the ShowWindow() function from the application class's InitInstance() function using an instantiated object of the window class. Figure 10-5 shows the frame window displayed by the basic MFC application.

```
// BasicApp.h
#include <afxwin.h>
class CBasicApp : public CWinApp {
public:
    CBasicApp();
    virtual ~CBasicApp();
    virtual BOOL InitInstance();
};
// BasicApp.cpp
#include "BasicApp.h"
#include "BasicFrameWnd.h"
CBasicApp::CBasicApp () {
}
CBasicApp::~CBasicApp () {
}
BOOL CBasicApp::InitInstance() {
    m_pMainWnd = new CBasicFrameWnd;
    m_pMainWnd->ShowWindow(m_nCmdShow);
    m_pMainWnd->UpdateWindow();
    return TRUE;
}
CBasicApp theAppObject; // global object
// BasicFrameWnd.h
#include <afxwin.h>
class CBasicFrameWnd : public CFrameWnd {
public:
    CBasicFrameWnd();
    virtual ~CBasicFrameWnd();
};
// CBasicFrameWnd.cpp
#include "BasicFrameWnd.h"
CBasicFrameWnd::CBasicFrameWnd () {
    Create(NULL, "Basic MFC Program");
}
CBasicFrameWnd::~CBasicFrameWnd () {
}
```

Figure 10-4 Basic MFC application with a frame window

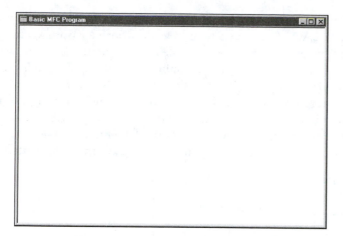

Figure 10-5   Basic MFC program window

There are many similarities in appearance between the dialog windows you have created and frame windows—remember that both the CDialog class and the CFrameWnd class derive from the CWnd class. However, you need to understand an important difference between dialog-based applications and applications based on the CFrameWnd class. Whereas a dialog-based application is used for creating applications that perform some sort of calculation or task that is applicable only to the current application session, applications based on the CFrameWnd class are document based. A **document-based application** allows users to read and write to documents that are associated with the application.

Whereas dialog windows contain controls that are used for interacting with your program's functionality, a frame window provides a "frame" around one or more views of a document. To understand what this means, you need to understand the MFC document/view architecture. The **MFC document/view architecture** separates a program's data from the way that data is displayed and accessed by users. A program's data (the document) is *managed and stored* by a class derived from the **CDocument class**. How a document-based program's data is *displayed* to the user is controlled by one or more classes derived from the **CView class**. In simpler terms, CDocument manages and stores a program's data, while CView displays it. Although CDocument and CView are separate classes that do not derive from each other, the classes you derive from them will communicate with each other, as illustrated in Figure 10-6.

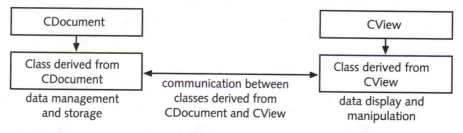

Figure 10-6   Relationship between CDocument and CView classes

10

CDocument and CView classes are added to an MFC program in addition to an application class derived from CWinApp, and a window class derived from CFrameWnd. Although Windows applications can include multiple CDocument classes, most include only a single CDocument class to contain the application's data. With many types of Windows applications today, however, you can simultaneously view the same data in several different ways. Therefore, your MFC programs may include multiple CView classes for displaying and manipulating the data contained in a single CDocument class. Each view is just a different way of looking at the same data. Figure 10-7 illustrates the concept of multiple CView classes that display and manipulate the data contained in a single CDocument class.

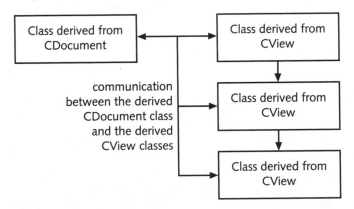

Figure 10-7   Relationship between CDocument class and multiple CView classes

Note that the data stored in a CDocument class can be displayed and manipulated by multiple CView classes. However, a CView class can display and manipulate only the data from a single CDocument class.

As an example of document/view architecture, consider Microsoft Excel, which is a typical Windows spreadsheet application that employs the document/view architecture. Although you will not be creating anything quite so ambitious, a spreadsheet application provides one of the best ways to illustrate the document/view architecture since it can present the same data in multiple formats. Modern spreadsheet programs allow you to enter data into a table (the spreadsheet) and then present the data as pie charts, bar charts, and so on. The Excel spreadsheet represents the "document" portion of the program, while each chart represents a "view." Figure 10-8 shows an example of a simple Excel spreadsheet containing several charts that graphically display portions of the spreadsheet data.

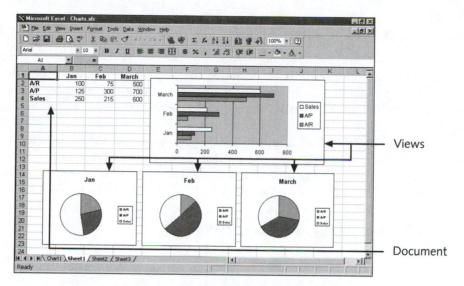

Figure 10-8   Excel "document" and "views"

You are not required to use document/view architecture in your document-based MFC programs; you can actually turn off document/view architecture support when you use AppWizard to build a document-based application. However, by enabling document/view architecture, your document-based MFC applications automatically inherit a wide range of document functionality that allows you to read and write documents, use print and print preview functions, and perform other types of document-specific tasks. Automatically inheriting this functionality means you do not have to manually write much of the code that is required by document-based applications; Visual C++ generates the code for you. Document-based MFC programs that are created without document/view architecture do not automatically inherit document functionality. You can add these features by hand, although doing so can be a tedious task, especially for a beginner.

As you start examining the specifics of how to build a document-based application, keep in mind that you will use AppWizard and ClassWizard to generate much of the application. The code generated by AppWizard and ClassWizard was designed by some of the best software engineers in the world and can be somewhat complex. Because Visual C++ generates this code for you, you will not examine every single segment of code in detail. Instead, you will focus on learning to find the hooks in the generated code that you can use to build your own applications.

You should ultimately understand the code created by AppWizard and ClassWizard. The more you understand about the intricacies of MFC programming, the better your own programs will be.

DOCUMENT INTERFACES

Current Windows programming supports two models for document-based applications: single document interface and multiple document interface. The **single document interface**, or **SDI**, allows users to have only one document open at a time. The **multiple document interface**, or **MDI**, allows users to have multiple documents open at the same time. The Notepad text editor application that is part of Windows is an example of an SDI program. Examples of MDI applications include Excel and Visual C++. You can usually tell that an application is an MDI application if it includes a Window option in the menu bar. Figure 10-9 shows an example of the single document that is available in Notepad, and Figure 10-10 shows an example of Word with multiple documents open.

Figure 10-9   Notepad single document interface

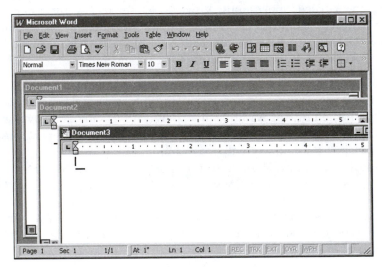

Figure 10-10   Word multiple document interface

In this text, the focus is on creating SDI applications, and you will pursue that focus for two important reasons. First, some experts consider MDI applications to be difficult for new and intermediate users to learn. Second, future versions of Windows, and therefore Windows software development, will more than likely focus on documents and content, rather than on applications.

When an application allows users to open multiple documents, it forces them to focus on the application instead of focusing on the document with which they are working. For example, rather than simply searching for a window containing the document they are editing, users must first search for the application, and then search within the application for the window containing their document. In this type of situation, the central item is the application; it is an application-centric situation.

A "document-centric" application provides a different approach. Rather than focusing on the application, document-centric applications focus on the content being displayed or manipulated by the application. An example of a document-centric application, and one of the most commonly used SDI applications today, is the Web browser. Rather than opening Web pages (documents) in multiple windows within the same Web browser instance, users must either replace the current Web page with a new one or open the new Web page in a separate instance of the Web browser. This allows Internet users to focus on the content of their Web pages rather than on the Web browser.

10

THE CVIEW CLASS

Earlier you learned that a frame window provides a "frame" around one or more views of a document. You display a window created from a class derived from CView *within* a frame window. This means the CView window is a child of a frame window. The CView window completely covers the frame window's client area, but does not cover visual interface elements such as the title bar or scroll bars. Figure 10-11 illustrates this concept.

You may wonder why view windows are necessary at all. Why not just display document data and interface controls directly in the frame window? The answer is that using view windows allows you to display multiple views within the same window. If you want to show a different view of data and you only have a single frame window, then you need to replace the existing view with the view you want to see—you would not be able to see both views of the data simultaneously. With view windows, you can divide the frame's client area into different views, depending on the needs of your program. For example, you may have a program that tracks company sales by region. In one view of the program you can display the sales numbers for each region; in a second view you can display the same data graphically in a pie chart, as illustrated in Figure 10-12. You are working with the same data in both views—you are just choosing to display the data graphically in the second view.

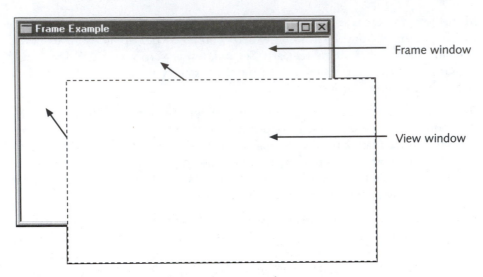

Figure 10-11   Frame window and view window

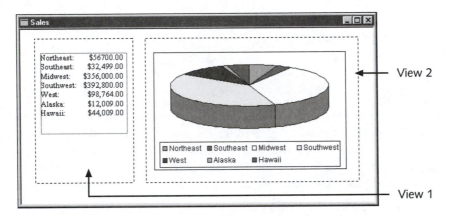

Figure 10-12   Multiple views in a frame window

 Do not confuse a multiple document interface with multiple views of the same document. The multiple document interface allows you to open multiple, separate documents within the same program, while multiple views allow you to display multiple views of a single document.

In this chapter, you will not actually create projects with more than one view. You still need to understand, however, that the reason for using the document/view architecture is that it allows you to separate your program's data from how it is displayed. Multiple views allow you to display the same data in multiple formats if necessary.

CView Child Classes

When you create a document-based application, you can base your view class on CView or on one of the classes that derive from CView, which are described in Figure 10-13. The classes that derive from CView are used for creating more specialized view windows. In this chapter, you will use the CEditView and CListView classes.

Class	Description
CCtrlView	Creates view windows that use tree, list, and rich edit controls
CDaoRecordView	Displays OLE DB database records in dialog-box controls
CEditView	Creates a simple text editor
CFormView	Creates a view window that is similar to a dialog-box window and that can be edited in the Dialog Editor
CHTMLView	Displays HTML documents
CListView	Creates a view window that uses list controls
COLeDBRecordView	Displays DAO database records in dialog-box controls
CRecordView	Displays database records in dialog-box controls
CRichEditView	Creates a view window that uses rich edit controls
CScrollView	Provides scrolling support to view windows
CTreeView	Creates a view window that uses tree controls

Figure 10-13   CView child classes

Next, you will start creating a simple Text Editor SDI application based on the CEditView class.

To start creating a simple Text Editor SDI application based on the CEditView class:

1. Using the MFC AppWizard (exe) option, create a new project named **SimpleTextEditor**. Save the project in the **Chapter.10** folder in your Visual C++ Projects folder.

2. AppWizard executes and starts to walk you through the steps involved in creating an MFC program. In Step 1, select **Single document** from the application choices as shown in Figure 10-14. Be sure to leave the **Document/View architecture support?** check box selected and the language combo box set to **English**. Then click **Next**.

3. In Step 2, leave the data support option set to **None** as shown in Figure 10-15, and click **Next**. Data support options are used for databases, which you will examine in the next chapter.

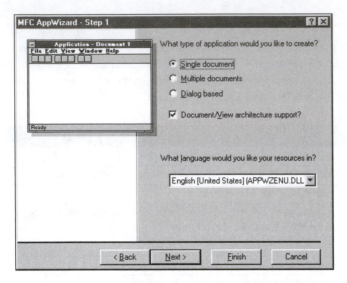

Figure 10-14   MFC AppWizard - Step 1

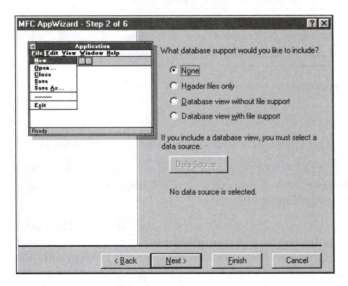

Figure 10-15   MFC AppWizard - Step 2 of 6

4. In Step 3, the first set of options allows you to select your project's compound document support options. A compound document contains data of different formats, such as graphics, sound files, video files, spreadsheets, and so on. Because you will not be using data in different formats, leave the compound document support option set to **None**. The two other types of support that you can select are Automation and ActiveX Controls. Automation allows your program to

control objects created in other programs, and allows other programs to control your program's objects. **ActiveX controls** are objects that are placed in Web pages or inside programs created with COM-enabled programming languages. (You first learned about COM in Chapter 8.) Make sure the **Automation** check box is cleared, and clear the **ActiveX Controls** checkbox, as shown in Figure 10-16. Click the **Next** button to continue.

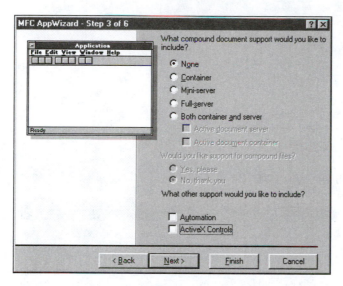

Figure 10-16   MFC AppWizard - Step 3 of 6

5. In Step 4, clear the **Printing and print preview** checkbox, but leave the **Docking toolbar**, **Initial status bar**, and **3D controls** checkboxes selected as shown in Figure 10-17. By default, the number of files displayed in a document-based application's most recently used file list is set to four, which is fine for the program you are creating.

6. Click the **Advanced** button in the Step 4 panel to display the Advanced Options dialog box, which contains two tabs: Document Template Strings and Window Styles. Both tabs of the Advanced Options dialog box are shown in Figure 10-18 as they should appear once you select the appropriate options.

10

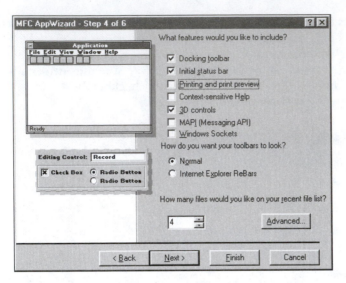

Figure 10-17   MFC AppWizard - Step 4 of 6

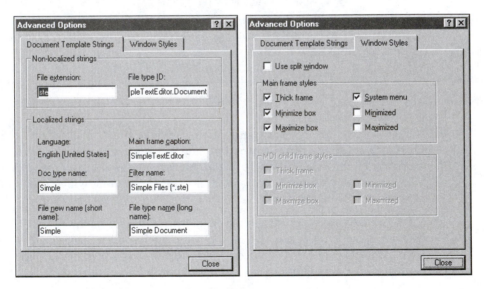

Figure 10-18   Advanced Options dialog box

The Document Template Strings tab of the Advanced Options dialog box contains various text boxes for customizing the document settings in a document-based application. A description of each text box in the Document Template Strings tab is listed in Figure 10-19. The options in the Window Styles tab are used for determining the style of the application window and are self-explanatory. For example, clicking the Maximize box checkbox adds a maximize box to the application window.

Text Box	Description
File extension	Designates a file extension to use with files created from your program
File type ID	Identifies the document type in the System Registry
Main frame caption	Sets the text that will appear in the application's main title bar
Doc type name	Designates the document type under which a file can be grouped
Filter name	Determines the file type and extension that appear in the Open and Save dialog box
File new name (short name)	Determines the name that will appear in the New dialog box if the application supports more than one file type
File type name (long name)	Designates the file type name in the System Registry and used with an Automation server program as the Automation object's long file name

Figure 10-19   Text box descriptions in the Document Template Strings tab of the Advanced Options dialog box

7. In the Document Template Strings tab, type **ste** (for **s**imple **t**ext **e**ditor) in the File Extension box. Any files saved from the Text Editor program will be saved with an extension of .ste. Notice as you are typing the file extension that the Filter Name text box changes to reflect the new file extension. Modify the Main frame caption text box to read **Text Editor Program**. Leave the rest of the options as they are in the Document Template Strings tab, as well as all the options in the Windows Styles tab. Click the **Close** button to close the Advanced Options dialog box, and then press the **Next** button to proceed to Step 5 of AppWizard.

8. Leave the default options in Step 5 of AppWizard, shown in Figure 10-20, as they are and click the **Next** button.

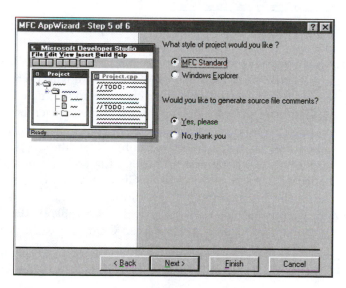

Figure 10-20   MFC AppWizard - Step 5 of 6

If you are using the Professional or Enterprise edition of Visual C++, you will see a third option in Step 5 asking whether you would like to use the MFC library as a shared DLL or a statically linked library. Select the As a shared DLL option.

9. Step 6 of AppWizard, shown in Figure 10-21, lists the names that will be assigned to each class in the Text Editor program. The Base class drop-down list box also displays the child classes of the CView class upon which you can base the application. Select **CEditView** from the Base class drop-down list box and click the **Finish** button. When the New Project Information dialog box displays, click the **OK** button to create the project.

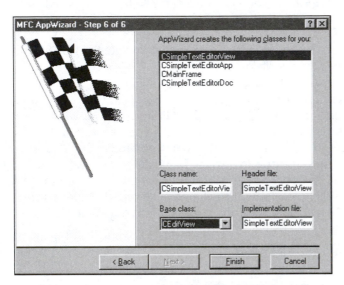

Figure 10-21   MFC AppWizard - Step 6 of 6

Once AppWizard finishes creating your program, open the FileView tab of the Workspace window and examine the files that were created. AppWizard should have created two classes with which you are already familiar: an application class named CSimpleTextEditor and a frame class named CMainFrm. (As you look at the file names, remember that the naming convention in MFC programming is to exclude the *C* that precedes class names from the text file names when they are saved. Therefore, SimpleTextEditor.cpp is the file containing the CSimpleTextEditor class definition.) Although the code in these classes is more complex than the basic MFC program you saw in Chapter 8, the classes still perform the same task of creating and instantiating the application and frame window of an MFC program. AppWizard also creates a CView class named CSimpleTextEditorView that derives from CEditView and a CDocument class named CSimpleTextEditorDoc.

Open the SimpleTextEditorView.h file in your Text Editor window and examine the code. An example of the class declaration portion of the file is shown in Figure 10-22.

```cpp
class CSimpleTextEditorView : public CView {
protected: // create from serialization only
     CSimpleTextEditorView();
     DECLARE_DYNCREATE(CSimpleTextEditorView)
// Attributes
public:
     CSimpleTextEditorDoc* GetDocument();
// Operations
public:
// Overrides
     // ClassWizard generated virtual function overrides
     //{{AFX_VIRTUAL(CSimpleTextEditorView)
     public:
     virtual void OnDraw(CDC* pDC);  // overridden to
                                     // draw this view
     virtual BOOL PreCreateWindow(CREATESTRUCT& cs);
     protected:
     //}}AFX_VIRTUAL
// Implementation
public:
     virtual ~CSimpleTextEditorView();
#ifdef _DEBUG
     virtual void AssertValid() const;
     virtual void Dump(CDumpContext& dc) const;
#endif
protected:
// Generated message map functions
protected:
     //{{AFX_MSG(CSimpleTextEditorView)
          // NOTE - the ClassWizard will add
          //    and remove member functions here.
          //     DO NOT EDIT what you see in these
               blocks of generated code !
     //}}AFX_MSG
     DECLARE_MESSAGE_MAP()
};
```

Figure 10-22   SimpleTextEditorView.h

You should recognize the usual constructor, destructor, PreCreateWindow(), AssertValid(), Dump(), and DECLARE_MESSAGE_MAP declarations that are found in all CWnd-derived classes that are generated by AppWizard.

The DECLARE_DYNCREATE() macro dynamically creates an object from data stored in a file. You will learn about the DECLARE_DYNCREATE() macro later in this chapter.

Next, you will build the Simple Text Editor program and examine its functionality.

To build the Simple Text Editor program and examine its functionality:

1. Build and execute the program. Even though you have not written any of your own code, the program is a complete and functional text-editing program.

2. Examine the program's menu and toolbars. All of the commands on both the menu bar and toolbar are functional. Enter some text into the document area, and then use Cut, Copy, and Paste commands to manipulate the text. Open one of the menus and move your cursor over each command without selecting it. Notice that a description of each command appears in the status bar at the bottom of the program window. If you hold your mouse over a toolbar button, you will also see a ToolTip for each button. AppWizard automatically creates basic menu and toolbar commands for you. You will learn how to create and modify menus and toolbars in the next chapter. Figure 10-23 shows an example of the Simple Text Editor program window.

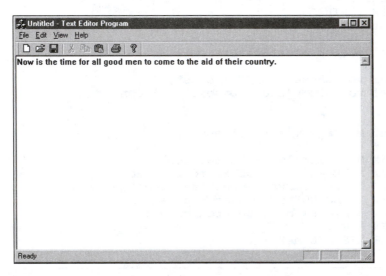

Figure 10-23   Simple Text Editor program window

3. Next, save the document by selecting **Save** from the **File** menu. Save the file as **text1** in the Chapter.10 folder in your Visual C++ Projects folder. After you save the file, select the New command from the File menu to create a new document. If you want to reopen the file you just saved, you can select Open from the File menu, or select the file name from the list of most recently opened files at the bottom of the File menu.

 If you try to close the program without saving the document, you will see a message box prompting you to save the file, just like you see in most other document-based Windows applications.

4. Close the Simple Text Editor program window.

The Simple Text Editor program requires no further programming on your part since AppWizard automatically created most of its functionality. However, more advanced programs such as the Invoice program require that you add custom code. Next, you will start building the Invoice program.

To start creating the Invoice program:

1. Create a new project named **Invoice** using the MFC AppWizard (exe) option. Be sure to create the project in a new workspace, and not within the existing SimpleTextEditor workspace, by clicking the **Create a new workspace** radio button. Save the project in the **Chapter.10** folder in your Visual C++ Projects folder.

2. AppWizard executes and starts to walk you through the steps involved in creating an MFC program. In Step 1, select **Single document** from the application choices. Be sure to leave the **Document/View architecture support?** check box selected. Then click **Next**.

3. In Step 2, leave the data support option set to **None** and click **Next**.

4. In Step 3, leave the compound document support option set to **None** and clear the **ActiveX Controls** checkbox. Click the **Next** button to continue.

5. In Step 4, clear the **Printing and print preview** checkbox, but leave the **Docking toolbar**, **Initial status bar**, and **3D controls** checkboxes selected.

6. Click the **Advanced** button in the Step 4 panel to display the Advanced Options dialog box.

7. In the Document Template Strings tab, type **inv** in the File extension box. Any files saved from the Invoice program will be saved with an extension of .inv. Leave the rest of the options as they are in the Document Template Strings tab, as well as all the options in the Windows Styles tab. Click the **Close** button to close the Advanced Options dialog box, and then press the **Next** button to proceed to Step 5 of AppWizard.

8. Leave the default options in Step 5 of AppWizard as they are and click the **Next** button.

9. In Step 6 of AppWizard, select **CFormView** from the Base class drop-down list box and click the **Finish** button. When the New Project Information dialog box displays, click the **OK** button to create the project. Because the Invoice program is based on the CFormView class, AppWizard opens the program's form view window in the dialog editor after you click the OK button to create the project. Because they are so similar to dialog windows, you can use the dialog editor to add controls to a form view window.

Next, you will add controls to the Invoice program's view window, along with DDX data members for each control. Figure 10-24 shows an example of how the controls in the window should be placed. You should already be familiar with the Edit Box controls. Two new

10

controls that you have not yet added to a project are the Static Text control and the Group Box control (although you saw them in the Moving Estimator program in the last chapter). Static Text controls are simply unchanging text boxes that you use to add instructions and labels to your interface. Group Box controls are used for visually "grouping" other controls together in a window. Both types of controls are used only for enhancing the visual design of your windows. Do your best when designing the form, and be sure to check your work using the Test command on the Layout menu.

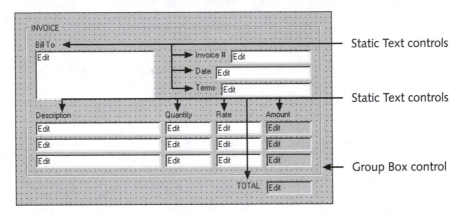

Figure 10-24   Invoice program controls

To add controls to the Invoice program's view window, along with DDX data members for each control:

1. After AppWizard finishes creating the Invoice program window, Visual C++ should automatically open the Dialog Editor. If the Dialog Editor does not open automatically, then use the Resource tab on the Workspace window to open the IDD_INVOICE_FORM dialog resource. (The IDD_INVOICE_FORM resource ID is automatically assigned by AppWizard.) Add Static Text controls, Edit Box controls, and a Group Box control to the window using the captions shown in Figure 10-24.

2. Open the **Properties** window for the **Bill To** edit box and change its resource ID in the General tab to **IDC_CUSTOMER**. Click the **Styles** tab in the Properties window and select the **Multiline** and **Want return** check boxes.

3. Use the table shown in Figure 10-25 to modify the resource IDs for the rest of the Edit Box controls. Also, make the Amount boxes and TOTAL box read-only.

Edit Box Control	Resource ID
Invoice #	IDC_INVOICE
Date	IDC_DATE
Terms	IDC_TERMS
Description (first line)	IDC_DESCRIPTION1
Description (second line)	IDC_DESCRIPTION2
Description (third line)	IDC_DESCRIPTION3
Quantity (first line)	IDC_QUANTITY1
Quantity (second line)	IDC_QUANTITY2
Quantity (third line)	IDC_QUANTITY3
Rate (first line)	IDC_RATE1
Rate (second line)	IDC_RATE2
Rate (third line)	IDC_RATE3
Amount (first line)	IDC_AMOUNT1
Amount (second line)	IDC_AMOUNT2
Amount (third line)	IDC_AMOUNT3
TOTAL	IDC_TOTAL

Figure 10-25   Button captions and resource IDs

4. When you are finished adding the controls to the dialog resource, open **ClassWizard**, click the **Member Variables** tab, and select CInvoiceView in the Class name combo box. Add DDX data members for each of the controls using the variable names and data types shown in Figure 10-26. For example, for the IDC_CUSTOMER resource ID, select **IDC_CUSTOMER** in the Control IDs list, and click the **Add Variable** button. The Add Member Variable dialog box appears. In the Add Member Variable dialog box, type **m_szCustomer** as the name of the variable. Leave the value in the Category drop-down list box as **Value** and the value in the Variable type drop-down list box as **CString**. Click the **OK** button to close the Add Member Variable dialog box, and then repeat the operation for the other resource IDs shown in Figure 10-26.

Resource ID	Variable Name	Data Type
IDC_CUSTOMER	m_szCustomer	CString
IDC_INVOICE	m_szInvoice	CString
IDC_DATE	m_szDate	CString
IDC_TERMS	m_szTerms	CString
IDC_DESCRIPTION1	m_szDescription1	CString
IDC_DESCRIPTION2	m_szDescription2	CString
IDC_DESCRIPTION3	m_szDescription3	CString
IDC_QUANTITY1	m_iQuantity1	int
IDC_QUANTITY2	m_iQuantity2	int
IDC_QUANTITY3	m_iQuantity3	int
IDC_RATE1	m_dRate1	double
IDC_RATE2	m_dRate2	double
IDC_RATE3	m_dRate3	double
IDC_AMOUNT1	m_dAmount1	double
IDC_AMOUNT2	m_dAmount2	double
IDC_AMOUNT3	m_dAmount3	double
IDC_TOTAL	m_dTOTAL	double

Figure 10-26   DDX data member names and types

CView Member Functions

A view class is responsible for graphically displaying a document's data and for handling the manipulation of that data according to user requests. For example, if the document class contains a data member containing a stock price, then it is up to the view class to display that stock price to the user. Additionally, if the user changes the displayed stock price and clicks a button named Update Stock, then it is also up to the view class to update that data in the document class.

The CView class contains various functions for displaying and manipulating data. The primary CView class member functions that you use to display and manipulate data are as follows:

- OnDraw()
- GetDocument()
- OnUpdate()

One of the most important functions in the CView class is the OnDraw() function, which is used to graphically display and print a document's data. For the Text Editor program, you do not need to worry about displaying the document's data since the display of a text file is handled automatically by the CEditView class. You also do not need to worry about the

OnDraw() function for the Invoice program since the Invoice program is based on the CFormView class, which uses the Dialog Editor to create the user interface. Therefore, you will not learn about the OnDraw() function, and several other important functions including OnPrint(), until the next chapter in this text. Note that since the OnDraw() function is declared as a pure virtual function in the CView base class, you must override it in any classes that derive from CView.

The GetDocument( ) Function

The **GetDocument( ) function** returns a pointer to the document associated with a view. If you examine the header file for the CSimpleEditorView class, you will see that the GetDocument() function is declared in the public section and returns a pointer data type of the document class, CSimpleTextEditorDoc. A pointer to the document is automatically created in the inherited m_pDocument data member. Remember, you will never actually see the m_pDocument data member declared or defined in your document-based program since it has already been declared and defined in a base class.

The GetDocument() function returns a pointer to the m_pDocument data member that you can use anywhere in the view class when you need to access the document's data. For example, if you have a member function in the document class named setStockPrice() that modifies the value of a double data member, you can call that function from the view class using the following statement:

```
GetDocument()->setStockPrice(120.5);
```

Rather than calling the GetDocument() function directly, you can assign it to a pointer variable of your document class's type, and then call the pointer variable. Calling a function repeatedly is not as efficient as calling a function once. Therefore, if you know you will need to use a pointer to a document repeatedly in any given instance (such as within the body of a function), then it is usually more efficient to call the GetDocument() function once and assign its return value to a pointer variable. You can then use the pointer variable in place of the GetDocument() function. For example, the preceding call to the setStockPrice() function could also be accomplished using the following pDoc pointer:

```
CSimpleTextEditorDoc* pDoc = GetDocument();
pDoc->setStockPrice(120.5);
```

You will actually find two definitions of the GetDocument() function in your view classes: a debug version and a release build version. The debug version of the GetDocument() function is defined in the view class's definition file and uses the ASSERT() macro and IsKindOf() function to verify the validity of the document pointer. The ASSERT() macro is used for identifying program errors during development, while the IsKindOf() function determines if an object belongs to a particular class, or if it derives from a specific class. Once

10

the pointer is verified, it is cast to your document class data type and returned. The following code is an example of the debug version of the GetDocument() function:

```
CSimpleTextEditorDoc* CSimpleTextEditorView::GetDocument()
//    non-debug version is inline
{
    ASSERT(m_pDocument->IsKindOf(RUNTIME_CLASS(
        CSimpleTextEditorDoc)));
    return (CSimpleTextEditorDoc*)m_pDocument;
}
```

The release build version of the GetDocument() macro is defined as an inline function in the view class declaration file, within a pair of #ifndef and #endif preprocessor directives immediately following the class definition. The release build version does not include the ASSERT() macro or IsKindOf() function and simply returns the pointer to the m_pDocument data member after casting it to the document class data type, as follows:

```
#ifndef _DEBUG  // debug version in
                    // SimpleTextEditorView.cpp
inline CSimpleTextEditorDoc*
    CSimpleTextEditorView::GetDocument()
    { return (CSimpleTextEditorDoc*)m_pDocument; }
#endif
```

Using the #ifndef preprocessor directive is identical to using the #if preprocessor directive with the defined constant expression to determine which portions of a file to compile depending on the result of a conditional expression. For example, the statement #if !defined(STOCKS_H) could also be written as #ifndef STOCKS_H. Using the #if preprocessor directive and the defined constant expression, however, is the preferred method. AppWizard uses the #ifndef preprocessor directive to define the GetDocument() function in order to provide backward compatibility with previous versions of C++.

Next, you will add message map functions to the CInvoiceView class along with an updateDataMembers() function that will call the GetDocument() function. The message map functions will use the EN_KILLFOCUS message. Each time a control loses focus, its EN_KILLFOCUS message map function will call the UpdateData() function to update the CInvoiceView class's DDX data members. For the Quantity and Rate controls, the message map functions will also calculate the Amount and TOTAL control values. Then, each message map will call the updateDataMembers() function, which will use the GetDocument() function to update the CInvoiceDoc class's data members from the CInvoiceView class's DDX data members.

To add message map functions to the CInvoiceView class along with an updateDataMembers() function:

1. Use ClassWizard's Message Maps tab to add the following EN_KILLFOCUS message map functions to the CInvoiceView class. The name of each message map function's resource ID is contained in a comment line above each function.

For example, to add the OnKillfocusCustomer() message map function, first start **ClassWizard**, click the **Message Maps** tab, and select CInvoiceView in the Class name combo box. Select **IDC_CUSTOMER** in the Object IDs list and **EN_KILLFOCUS** in the Messages list. Then click the **Add Function** button. The Add Member Function dialog box appears. In the Add Member Function dialog box, accept the suggested name of OnKillfocusCustomer and click the **OK** button. Click the **Edit Code** button in ClassWizard. The InvoiceView.cpp file opens to the OnKillfocusCustomer() handler function. Replace the // TODO comment with the following bolded code in the OnKillfocusCustomer() function. Repeat these steps for the rest of the message map functions.

```
// IDC_CUSTOMER
void CInvoiceView::OnKillfocusCustomer() {
    UpdateData(TRUE);
    updateDataMembers();
}
// IDC_INVOICE
void CInvoiceView::OnKillfocusInvoice() {
    UpdateData(TRUE);
    updateDataMembers();
}
// IDC_DATE
void CInvoiceView::OnKillfocusDate() {
    UpdateData(TRUE);
    updateDataMembers();
}
// IDC_TERMS
void CInvoiceView::OnKillfocusTerms() {
    UpdateData(TRUE);
    updateDataMembers();
}
// IDC_DESCRIPTION1
void CInvoiceView::OnKillfocusDescription1() {
    UpdateData(TRUE);
    updateDataMembers();
}
// IDC_DESCRIPTION2
void CInvoiceView::OnKillfocusDescription2() {
    UpdateData(TRUE);
    updateDataMembers();
}
// IDC_DESCRIPTION3
void CInvoiceView::OnKillfocusDescription3() {
    UpdateData(TRUE);
    updateDataMembers();
}
```

10

```
                    // IDC_QUANTITY1
                    void CInvoiceView::OnKillfocusQuantity1() {
                         UpdateData(TRUE);
                         m_dAmount1 = m_iQuantity1 * m_dRate1;
                         m_dTOTAL = m_dAmount1 + m_dAmount2 + m_dAmount3;
                         UpdateData(FALSE);
                         updateDataMembers();
                    }
                    // IDC_QUANTITY2
                    void CInvoiceView::OnKillfocusQuantity2() {
                         UpdateData(TRUE);
                         m_dAmount2 = m_iQuantity2 * m_dRate2;
                         m_dTOTAL = m_dAmount1 + m_dAmount2 + m_dAmount3;
                         UpdateData(FALSE);
                         updateDataMembers();
                    }
                    // IDC_QUANTITY3
                    void CInvoiceView::OnKillfocusQuantity3() {
                         UpdateData(TRUE);
                         m_dAmount3 = m_iQuantity3 * m_dRate3;
                         m_dTOTAL = m_dAmount1 + m_dAmount2 + m_dAmount3;
                         UpdateData(FALSE);
                         updateDataMembers();
                    }
                    // IDC_RATE1
                    void CInvoiceView::OnKillfocusRate1() {
                         UpdateData(TRUE);
                         m_dAmount1 = m_iQuantity1 * m_dRate1;
                         m_dTOTAL = m_dAmount1 + m_dAmount2 + m_dAmount3;
                         UpdateData(FALSE);
                         updateDataMembers();
                    }
                    // IDC_RATE2
                    void CInvoiceView::OnKillfocusRate2() {
                         UpdateData(TRUE);
                         m_dAmount2 = m_iQuantity2 * m_dRate2;
                         m_dTOTAL = m_dAmount1 + m_dAmount2 + m_dAmount3;
                         UpdateData(FALSE);
                         updateDataMembers();
                    }
                    // IDC_RATE3
                    void CInvoiceView::OnKillfocusRate3() {
                         UpdateData(TRUE);
                         m_dAmount3 = m_iQuantity3 * m_dRate3;
                         m_dTOTAL = m_dAmount1 + m_dAmount2 + m_dAmount3;
                         UpdateData(FALSE);
                         updateDataMembers();
                    }
```

2. Next, use the WizardBar to add to the CInvoiceView class a member function named updateDataMembers(). Create the function with a return type of **void** and **Public** access. Leave the Static and Virtual check boxes unselected. After the function is created, add the following statements that transfer the values from the CInvoiceView class to the data members in the CInvoiceDoc class.

```
void CInvoiceView::updateDataMembers()
{
    CInvoiceDoc* pDoc = GetDocument();
    pDoc->m_dAmount1 = m_dAmount1;
    pDoc->m_dAmount2 = m_dAmount2;
    pDoc->m_dAmount3 = m_dAmount3;
    pDoc->m_szDescription1 = m_szDescription1;
    pDoc->m_szDescription2 = m_szDescription2;
    pDoc->m_szDescription3 = m_szDescription3;
    pDoc->m_iQuantity1 = m_iQuantity1;
    pDoc->m_iQuantity2 = m_iQuantity2;
    pDoc->m_iQuantity3 = m_iQuantity3;
    pDoc->m_dRate1 = m_dRate1;
    pDoc->m_dRate2 = m_dRate2;
    pDoc->m_dRate3 = m_dRate3;
    pDoc->m_dTOTAL = m_dTOTAL;
    pDoc->m_szDate = m_szDate;
    pDoc->m_szCustomer = m_szCustomer;
    pDoc->m_szInvoice = m_szInvoice;
    pDoc->m_szTerms = m_szTerms;
}
```

The OnUpdate() Function

Another important CView member function is the OnUpdate() function. Each view class inherits an **OnUpdate() function** that is called each time the document class changes or whenever the document class executes an UpdateAllViews() function. The OnUpdate() function allows all of the view windows in an application to display the most current data. The UpdateAllViews() function is a member function of CDocument and causes each view window's OnUpdate() function to execute in order to allow each view to display the most recent data. Note that you execute the UpdateAllViews() function from a derived CDocument class, not a derived CView class. The inherited default OnUpdate() function does not automatically update its view. You must write your own definition of the OnUpdate() function, which uses the GetDocument() function to retrieve the most recent data values from the document object, and then display those values in the view window. For example, if you have a Stocks program that includes a view window named CStocksView that is based on CFormView, you could write the following OnUpdate() function to display the most recent values when the document window executes its UpdateAllViews() function. The code uses the CStocksDoc class's member functions to retrieve the most recent data member values, which are then assigned to DDX data members. The UpdateData() function then copies each DDX data member's value to its associated dialog control. The first statement in the body of the function instantiates a new pointer named pDoc and assigns to it the pointer that is returned from the GetDocument() function. The other statements use the new pDoc pointer to call member functions of the CStocksDoc class.

```
void CStocksView::OnUpdate(CView* pSender,
    LPARAM lHint, CObject* pHint) {
    CStocksView* pDoc = GetDocument();
    m_iNumShares = pDoc->getNumShares();
    m_dCurrentValue = pDoc->getCurrentValue();
    m_dPricePerShare = pDoc->getPricePerShare();
    UpdateData(FALSE);
}
```

Note that each inherited function in the MFC hierarchy requires a slightly different header declaration. Additionally, almost all of the inherited functions in the MFC hierarchy are virtual. Recall that a virtual function instructs the compiler to decide at run time which version of an overridden function to call. Rather than memorize each function declaration or search in the MSDN Library for the function declaration you need, you can use the WizardBar's Add Virtual Function command to quickly add a virtual function declaration to your class. If you open a class declaration or definition file in the Text Editor window and select Add Virtual Function from the WizardBar, the New Virtual Override dialog box displays a list of virtual functions you can add to your program, along with a list of virtual functions that have already been added to your program. You can then select one of the dialog box's buttons to add or edit a virtual function. Figure 10-27 shows the New Virtual Override dialog box for the CSimpleTextEditorView class.

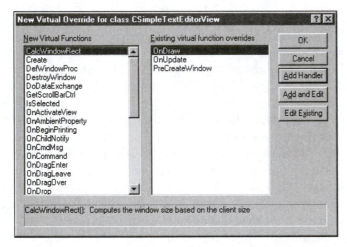

Figure 10-27   New Virtual Override dialog box for the CSimpleTextEditorView class

Next, you will add an OnUpdate() function to the Invoice program's CView class. Each time the user creates a new document, the controls in the Invoice program's form need to be reset to their original values. In the next section, you will learn how to reset the document member's data values using the document class's inherited OnNewDocument() function. To display the reset values in the form, you must create an OnUpdate() function, which is called automatically after the OnNewDocument() function executes.

To add an OnUpdate() function to the Invoice program's CView class:

1. Be sure you have InvoiceView.cpp or InvoiceView.h open in the Text Editor window and select **Add Virtual Function** from the **WizardBar** to display the New Virtual Override dialog box.

2. Select **OnUpdate** from the **New Virtual Functions** list and click the **Add and Edit** button. The new function is created and your cursor moves to the function definition.

3. Modify the OnUpdate() function definition as follows to copy the values of the CInvoiceDoc class's data members to the CInvoiceView class's DDX data members. The last statement in the function passes a value of FALSE to the UpdateData() function to update the controls in the dialog window.

```
void CInvoiceView::OnUpdate(CView* pSender,
    LPARAM lHint, CObject* pHint) {
    CInvoiceDoc* pDoc = GetDocument();
    m_dAmount1 = pDoc->m_dAmount1;
    m_dAmount2 = pDoc->m_dAmount2;
    m_dAmount3 = pDoc->m_dAmount3;
    m_szDescription1 = pDoc->m_szDescription1;
    m_szDescription2 = pDoc->m_szDescription2;
    m_szDescription3 = pDoc->m_szDescription3;
    m_iQuantity1 = pDoc->m_iQuantity1;
    m_iQuantity2 = pDoc->m_iQuantity2;
    m_iQuantity3 = pDoc->m_iQuantity3;
    m_dRate1 = pDoc->m_dRate1;
    m_dRate2 = pDoc->m_dRate2;
    m_dRate3 = pDoc->m_dRate3;
    m_dTOTAL = pDoc->m_dTOTAL;
    m_szDate = pDoc->m_szDate;
    m_szCustomer = pDoc->m_szCustomer;
    m_szInvoice = pDoc->m_szInvoice;
    m_szTerms = pDoc->m_szTerms;
    UpdateData(FALSE);
}
```

10

THE CDOCUMENT CLASS

One aspect of working with programs created with AppWizard that is a little hard to get used to is that most of the work is already done for you. The Simple Text Editor program, for instance, is a complete and functioning program. To create a useful program, however, you still must do some work. For example, with more advanced programs such as the Invoice program, you need to do some additional coding since Visual C++ does not automatically know what type of data you want to read from and write to a file. Once AppWizard creates your derived document class, you must perform the following tasks:

- Create data members to temporarily hold the data for the current document.
- Override the CDocument class's member functions to customize the creating, loading, and saving mechanisms of the document/view architecture.
- Override CDocument's Serialize() member function in order to read the document's data from and write the document's data to a file.

In this section, you will learn how to create data members to temporarily hold the data for the current document and how to override some of the CDocument class's member functions to customize the creating, loading, and saving mechanisms of the document/view architecture. Later in the chapter, you will learn how to override CDocument's Serialize() member function in order to read the document's data from, and write the document's data to, a file. Keep in mind that data members stored in a CDocument-derived class and the inherited CDocument member functions are designed to work with the Serialize() member function in order to read information from, and write information to, a file.

CDocument Data Members

You create data members in the CDocument class by adding declarations for each data member to the interface file, the same way you create data members in other classes. You can then initialize each data member in the class constructor and use appropriate *set* and *get* member functions to manipulate each data member.

One of the main differences between CDocument and other types of classes is that you call the *set* and *get* member functions from the view class using the GetDocument() function. For example in the Stocks program, a view class would use the GetDocument() function to call a document class's setStockPrice() and getStockPrice() member functions in order to set and retrieve the values of a stock price data member using the following statements:

```
GetDocument()->setStockPrice(120.5);
GetDocument()->getStockPrice();
```

You must add data members to the Invoice program's derived CDocument class for each of the controls on the Invoice form. Next, you will add data members to the Invoice program's CInvoiceDoc class, which derives from CDocument. To keep things simple, you will use the same names for the CInvoiceDoc class that you used for the CInvoiceView class. Also, you will declare the data members as public so that they can be easily accessed from the CInvoiceView class.

To add data members to the Invoice program's CInvoiceDoc class:

1. Because you are using the same data member names for the CInvoiceView and CInvoiceDoc classes, the easiest way to add the data members to the CInvoiceDoc class is to copy the data member declarations from the CInvoiceView class. First, open **InvoiceView.h** in the Text Editor window. Locate the following data member declarations in the public section and copy them to the Clipboard. Note that the data members in your InvoiceView.h file may be in a different order than shown below.

```
double      m_dAmount1;
double      m_dAmount2;
double      m_dAmount3;
CString     m_szDescription2;
CString     m_szDescription1;
CString     m_szDescription3;
int         m_iQuantity1;
int         m_iQuantity2;
int         m_iQuantity3;
double      m_dRate1;
double      m_dRate2;
double      m_dRate3;
double      m_dTOTAL;
CString     m_szDate;
CString     m_szCustomer;
CString     m_szInvoice;
CString     m_szTerms;
```

2. Open the **InvoiceDoc.h** file in the Text Editor window and paste the data member declarations into the first public section.

CDocument Member Functions

Although many of the CDocument member functions are called automatically by the framework, you can override each of the functions to customize how your application creates, loads, and saves documents. Figure 10-28 lists some of the functions that are inherited from the CDocument class that programmers commonly override.

The function names in Figure 10-28 that are preceded by *On* are called automatically by the framework. For example, the OnOpenDocument() function is called automatically when the user selects the Open command from the File menu. Similarly, the OnSaveDocument() function is called when the user selects the Save or Save As commands from the File menu. If you want to perform any sort of special processing when one of these events occurs, you can override any of the functions in your derived CDocument class. The only functions from which AppWizard automatically provides overridden implementations are the OnNewDocument() and Serialize() functions, since the OnNewDocument() function is one of the most commonly overridden functions and the Serialize() function is necessary for reading data from, and writing data to, files.

10

Function	Description
DeleteContents()	Used to reinitialize a CDocument object's data members
OnCloseDocument()	Called by the MFC framework when the File Close command executes
OnNewDocument()	Called by the MFC framework when the File New command executes
OnOpenDocument()	Called by the MFC framework when the File Open command executes
OnSaveDocument()	Called by the MFC framework when the File Save command executes
Serialize()	Used for reading data from and writing data to a file
SetModifiedFlag()	Determines if a document has been modified since the last time it was saved
UpdateAllViews()	Causes each view window's OnUpdate() function to execute in order to allow each view to display the most recent data

Figure 10-28   Common CDocument member functions

Figure 10-29 shows the Simple Text Editor program's derived CDocument class, SimpleTextEditorDoc.h. Notice the overridden OnNewDocument() and Serialize() functions.

When a user creates a new document in an SDI application, MFC reuses the same document object. This is not a problem in the Simple Text Editor program since the CEditView class automatically reinitializes the document object for you. With other types of programs, however, you need to override the DeleteContents() function to reinitialize the document object's data members each time a new document is created. For example, a user of the Invoice program may enter values into the program's fields, save the document, and then select New from the File menu. Because the program reuses the same document object, the values contained in the document class's data members will be displayed in the fields, unless you reinitialize the data members using the DeleteContents() function. You call the DeleteContents() function from the OnNewDocument() function. The following code shows an example (from the Stocks program) of the OnNewDocument() function definition that is created automatically by the framework.

```
BOOL CStocksDoc::OnNewDocument()
{
    if (!CDocument::OnNewDocument())
        return FALSE;
    // TODO: add reinitialization code here
    // (SDI documents will reuse this document)
    return TRUE;
}
```

```
class CSimpleTextEditorDoc : public CDocument {
protected: // create from serialization only
     CSimpleTextEditorDoc();
     DECLARE_DYNCREATE(CSimpleTextEditorDoc)
// Attributes
public:
// Operations
public:
// Overrides
     // ClassWizard generated virtual function overrides
     //{{AFX_VIRTUAL(CSimpleTextEditorDoc)
     public:
     virtual BOOL OnNewDocument();
     virtual void Serialize(CArchive& ar);
     //}}AFX_VIRTUAL
// Implementation
public:
     virtual ~CSimpleTextEditorDoc();
#ifdef _DEBUG
     virtual void AssertValid() const;
     virtual void Dump(CDumpContext& dc) const;
#endif
protected:
// Generated message map functions
protected:
     //{{AFX_MSG(CSimpleTextEditorDoc)
          // NOTE - the ClassWizard will add and remove
          member functions here.
          //    DO NOT EDIT what you see in these blocks of
          generated code !
     //}}AFX_MSG
     DECLARE_MESSAGE_MAP()
};
```

Figure 10-29   SimpleTextEditorDoc.h

Notice in the preceding code the hooks that are provided for you in the form of comments. You replace the comments with any initialization code required by your program. For example, the following code shows the same OnNewDocument() function with the hook comments replaced by a call to the DeleteContents() function. The DeleteContents() function reinitializes the data members of the Stocks class to 0.

```
BOOL CStocksDoc::OnNewDocument()
{
     if (!CDocument::OnNewDocument())
          return FALSE;
     DeleteContents();
     return TRUE;
}
```

```
void CStocksDoc::DeleteContents()
{
    m_iNumShares = 0;
    m_dCurrentValue = 0;
    m_dPricePerShare = 0;
    CDocument::DeleteContents();
}
```

When you use the WizardBar to add the virtual DeleteContents() function to your derived CDocument class, the function definition that is created for you automatically includes a call to the CDocument base class's DeleteContents() function with the statement `CDocument::DeleteContents();`. Although the CDocument class's default implementation of the DeleteContents() function does nothing, it is included in the preceding code in order to help you recognize the DeleteContents() function that the WizardBar creates for you. In your overridden implementations of the DeleteContents() function, you can safely delete the `CDocument::DeleteContents();` statement.

Next, you will override the DeleteContents() function in the CInvoiceDoc class.

To override the DeleteContents() function in the CInvoiceDoc class:

1. Select **Add Virtual Function** from the **WizardBar** to display the New Virtual Override dialog box.

2. Select **DeleteContents** from the **New Virtual Functions** list and click the **Add and Edit** button. The new function is created and your cursor is moved to the function definition.

3. Add the following bolded statements to the DeleteContents() function to reinitialize the data members:

```
void CInvoiceDoc::DeleteContents() {
    m_dAmount1 = 0.0;
    m_dAmount2 = 0.0;
    m_dAmount3 = 0.0;
    m_szDescription2 = _T("");
    m_szDescription1 = _T("");
    m_szDescription3 = _T("");
    m_iQuantity1 = 0;
    m_iQuantity2 = 0;
    m_iQuantity3 = 0;
    m_dRate1 = 0.0;
    m_dRate2 = 0.0;
    m_dRate3 = 0.0;
    m_dTOTAL = 0.0;
    m_szDate = _T("");
    m_szCustomer = _T("");
    m_szInvoice = _T("");
```

```
        m_szTerms = _T("");
        CDocument::DeleteContents();
    }
```

4. Finally, add to the OnNewDocument() function a call to the new DeleteContents() function as follows:

```
BOOL CInvoiceDoc::OnNewDocument()
{
    DeleteContents();
    if (!CDocument::OnNewDocument())
        return FALSE;
    return TRUE;
}
```

Two CDocument functions that you should call in almost every document-based application are the SetModifiedFlag()and UpdateAllViews() functions. The **SetModifiedFlag() function** is used by the MFC framework to determine if a document has been modified since the last time it was saved. The **UpdateAllViews() function** causes each view window's OnUpdate() function to execute in order to allow each view to display the most recent data. Passing a single value of NULL to the UpdateAllViews() function informs the system that all views in the program should be updated. When you change a document's data, you pass to the SetModifiedFlag() function a value of TRUE to indicate that the document needs to be saved. If users attempt to close the document or open a new document without saving, and the SetModifiedFlag() function has been called with a value of TRUE, they will receive a dialog box prompting them to save their changes. With the Simple Text Editor program, you do not need to call the SetModifiedFlag() when a user makes changes to a document since it is already called internally by the CEditView class. For other types of document-based programs, however, you need to call the SetModifiedFlag() manually. You should follow each SetModifiedFlag() call with a call to UpdateAllWindows(). For example, you may have a *set* function named setPricePerShare() in a CDocument class named CStocksDoc that sets the value of a data member named m_dPricePerShare. Once you assign a new value to the m_dPricePerShare data member, you call the SetModifiedFlag() and UpdateAllViews()functions, as follows:

```
void CStocksDoc::setPricePerShare(double dPrice) {
    m_dPricePerShare = dPrice;
    SetModifiedFlag(TRUE);
    UpdateAllViews(NULL);
}
```

Next, you will modify the Invoice program's OnNewDocument() function and add the SetModifiedFlag()and UpdateAllViews() functions to the updateDataMembers() function. Because the Invoice program includes only a single view, you do not actually need the UpdateAllViews() function. However, it is good practice to always include the UpdateAllViews() function anytime you change the data in a CView class in case you decide to add additional views to a program later.

10

To add the SetModifiedFlag() and UpdateAllViews()functions to the updateDataMembers() function:

1. Open the **InvoiceView.cpp** file in the Text Editor window.

2. Add the following bolded SetModifiedFlag() and UpdateAllViews() functions to the updateDataMembers() function:

```
void CInvoiceView::updateDataMembers() {
    CInvoiceDoc* pDoc = GetDocument();
    ...
    pDoc->m_szInvoice = m_szInvoice;
    pDoc->m_szTerms = m_szTerms;
    pDoc->SetModifiedFlag(TRUE);
    pDoc->UpdateAllViews(NULL);
}
```

DOCUMENT TEMPLATES

You may be wondering how the framework knows how the different classes that make up a document-based application should work together. A **document template** defines the relationship between a document-based program's frame, document, and view classes. When you first create a document-based application, AppWizard automatically creates a document template in the application class's InitInstance() function based on one of two classes: CSingleDocTemplate or CMultiDocTemplate. The CSingleDocTemplate class is used for SDI applications, and the CMultiDocTemplate is used for MDI applications. If you open the Simple Text Editor program's SimpleTextEditor.cpp file in the Text Editor window and examine its InitInstance() function, you will see the following code, which is used for defining the document template. Because the Simple Text Editor program is an SDI application, the code uses the CSingleDocTemplate class.

```
CSingleDocTemplate* pDocTemplate;
pDocTemplate = new CSingleDocTemplate(
    IDR_MAINFRAME,
    RUNTIME_CLASS(CSimpleTextEditorDoc),
    RUNTIME_CLASS(CMainFrame),     // main SDI frame window
    RUNTIME_CLASS(CSimpleTextEditorView));
AddDocTemplate(pDocTemplate);
```

The first statement in this code segment creates a pointer named pDocTemplate. The second statement creates a new CSingleDocTemplate object and assigns it to the pDocTemplate pointer. The first parameter for the CSingleDocTemplate class constructor is the resource ID for the application's menu. (You will learn about menus shortly.) For the last three constructor parameters, you pass the names of the document, frame, and view classes to the RUNTIME() macro. The **RUNTIME() macro** returns a CRunTimeClass structure for each class. The framework uses the **CRunTimeClass structure** to obtain class information at run time. The last statement in the preceding code, AddDocTemplate(pDocTemplate);, adds the document template to a list of documents that are available to the application.

For the simple SDI applications you are creating in this text, you do not need to make any modifications to the document template. Some document-based applications, however, are designed to work with more than one type of document. That is why the preceding code includes the statement `AddDocTemplate(pDocTemplate);` to add the document template to a list of documents available to the application. For example, an accounting program, which might include your Invoice program, may have the ability to open and save other types of documents in addition to Invoice documents, such as Accounts Payable and Accounts Receivable documents. For these types of applications, you would need to add additional document templates for each of the different document types.

When the RUN TIME() macro returns a CRunTimeClass structure for the document, frame, and view classes, it is actually creating the class objects dynamically at run time. Normally, class objects are declared and created during compilation. It is necessary to create these document-based class objects dynamically at run time, however, since stored information, such as a document's data, cannot be known prior to run time. For the RUN TIME() macro to function, the document, view, and frame classes must each include the DECLARE_DYNCREATE() macro in its header file, and the IMPLEMENT_DYNCREATE() macro in its implementation file. The **DECLARE_DYNCREATE() and IMPLEMENT_DYNCREATE() macros** allow classes to be created dynamically at run time. These macros are also required for the data storage technique of serialization. The DECLARE_DYNCREATE() macro requires the name of a class as its single argument. The IMPLEMENT_DYNCREATE() macro requires two arguments: the name of a class and its base class. If you examine the Simple Text Editor program's document, view, and frame classes, you will see that each class's header file includes a DECLARE_DYNCREATE() macro and each class's implementation file includes an IMPLEMENT_DYNCREATE() macro. For example, the SimpleTextEditorDoc.h file includes the following DECLARE_DYNCREATE() macro declaration:

```
DECLARE_DYNCREATE(CSimpleTextEditorDoc)
```

Additionally, the SimpleTextEditorDoc.cpp file includes the IMPLEMENT_DYNCREATE() macro definition below:

```
IMPLEMENT_DYNCREATE(CSimpleTextEditorDoc, CDocument)
```

COMMON DIALOG BOXES

You may have noticed that most Windows applications use the same dialog boxes for certain functions. For example, the File Open and File Save dialog boxes are identical across many Windows applications. There was a time in Windows programming when creators of programs had to design their own implementations for standard dialog boxes such as the File Open and File Save dialog boxes. You can imagine the additional time required to create each standard dialog box, as well as the confusion among users when they were presented with different versions of dialog boxes, such as the File Open dialog box, in different Windows applications. To make the development of Windows programs easier, and to provide a uniform interface for standard dialog box types, the

Windows API now includes several standard dialog boxes, called **common dialog boxes**, that you can use in your applications. Common dialog boxes work in concert with documents and views. MFC provides a set of classes for instantiating and manipulating common dialog boxes in your programs. Figure 10-30 lists the Windows common dialog boxes and the associated MFC dialog classes.

Dialog Box	Description	MFC Class
Color	Displays a list of available colors and allows users to create custom colors	CColorDialog
Find	Finds designated text	CFindReplaceDialog
Font	Changes fonts, point sizes, and other typeface information	CFontDialog
Open	Opens a file from disk	CFileDialog
Print	Prints a file	CPrintDialog
Page Setup	Formats the setup of a document page	CPageSetupDialog
Replace	Finds and replaces designated text	CFindReplaceDialog
Save As	Saves a file to disk	CFileDialog

Figure 10-30   Windows common dialog boxes

Using one of the common dialog boxes in your program is fairly simple. All you need to do is instantiate an object of the dialog class, and then use the inherited DoModal() function in an `if` statement to display the dialog box, the same as for the dialog-based applications you worked with in past chapters. For example, to add the Font dialog box in your program, you can use the following statements and `if` structure:

```
CFontDialog dlg;
int nResponse = dlg.DoModal();
if (nResponse == IDOK) {
    // OK button statements
}
else if (nResponse == IDCANCEL) {
    // Cancel button statements
}
```

The preceding code displays the common Font dialog box shown in Figure 10-31.

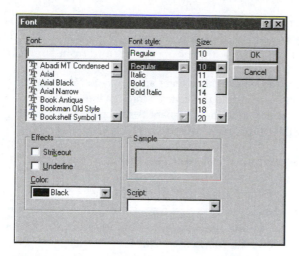

Figure 10-31   Common Font dialog box

Using common dialog boxes becomes more difficult when you want to customize one of the dialog boxes, and when you need to write code that handles pressing the OK button. For example, you may want to add a Read Only check box control to the Open dialog box. Or, you may need to add code that applies font styles to selected text when the user presses OK in the Font dialog box. Customizing common dialog boxes or writing code to process a dialog box's functionality when the user presses the OK button are beyond the scope of this book; refer to the MSDN Library for information about these advanced topics.

Document-based applications automatically inherit prewritten common dialog functions from the CDocument class for several of the common dialog boxes. When AppWizard creates your document class, it does not include any implementations for the common dialog functions. Instead, the framework automatically calls the functions from the CDocument base class. If you run the Simple Text Editor program, add text to a document, and then select Save from the File menu, you will be presented with the Save dialog box, which you can use to save the document. Similarly, you can use the Open command on the File menu to execute the Open dialog box to open an existing file. Note that these dialog boxes and their functionality were made available to you automatically; you did not need to instantiate any common dialog objects when you created the Text Editor program.

STORING DATA

For a document-based application to be useful, you must be able to make the application's data persistent. **Persistence** refers to the ability for data to continue to exist after the program closes. The process of storing data to, and retrieving data from, a persistent storage medium is called **serialization**. (The process of retrieving data stored in a disk file is sometimes referred to as *deserialization*.) For your purposes, "storage medium" refers to disk files, although the term can also refer to other types of storage such as memory locations. With serialization, you store objects rather than just text or numbers. In this chapter, the objects you store will be the simple data member variables (which are objects) in the document classes. However, you can store much more complex objects derived from large classes.

The data storage concepts discussed in this chapter apply only to MFC applications. Data storage for console applications is handled through the C++ iostream class library. To learn how to add data storage capabilities to console application programs, search the MSDN Library index for *iostream class library reference*.

Although the behind-the-scenes mechanics that MFC uses to enable serialization is rather complex, you need to perform only a few tasks to save your documents to disk. The serialization capabilities in MFC programming are stored in the CObject class. You may recall from Chapter 8 that the CObject class is the base class for all MFC classes. Therefore, almost any MFC program can support serialization. In addition to deriving from the CObject class, basic serialized classes must also include the following:

- the DECLARE_SERIAL() macro
- an empty, default constructor
- an overridden Serialize() function

When you build a document-based MFC program with AppWizard, the preceding requirements are automatically added to the document, view, and frame classes. The only thing you need to do is add code to the Serialize() function to store and retrieve data. The **Serialize() function** reads and writes data to and from a disk file.

Serialized classes also require the IMPLEMENT_SERIAL macro, which the MFC framework automatically provides for you. The **IMPLEMENT_SERIAL macro** defines the code and various functions needed by a serialized class. If you create a serialized MFC class without using the framework, you must manually add the IMPLEMENT_SERIAL macro to your class definition file. For more information, look for IMPLEMENT_SERIAL in the MSDN Library's index.

In the Simple Text Editor program, serialization techniques are handled automatically by the CEditView class. For other types of document-based classes, such as classes created from CView, AppWizard adds the following overridden Serialize() function to the derived CView class:

```
void CExampleDoc::Serialize(CArchive& ar)
{
    if (ar.IsStoring())
    {
        // TODO: add storing code here
    }
    else
    {
        // TODO: add loading code here
    }
}
```

Notice that the Serialize() method accepts as its argument a single reference named "ar" to a CArchive object. The **CArchive class** is used for writing and reading data to and from a storage medium. You can think of CArchive as an intermediary between your program and a disk file.

Now, examine the `if...else` structure in the Serialize() function's body. The Serialize() function is called in one of two circumstances: when the document is being saved or when it is being retrieved. The conditional statement in the `if` statement uses the CArchive class's IsStoring() function to see if the document is being saved. If the IsStoring() function returns true, then the `if` statement executes and stores the data. However, if the IsStoring() function returns false, then the `else` statement executes and retrieves the data.

To actually write to and read from a disk file, you use the CArchive object within the `if` and `else` structure's command blocks along with the insertion operator (<<) and the extraction operator (>>) and the document class's data members. Recall that you used the insertion and extraction operators with console applications. However, instead of writing to the output stream and reading from the input stream, when used with serialization, the insertion and extraction operators write to and read from a CArchive object. The CArchive object internally handles the storage of data to, and retrieval of data from, the disk file. The CStocksDoc document class example you examined earlier in this chapter includes several data members. To write the CStocksDoc document class's data members to a disk file and read them from a disk file, you modify the Serialize() function as follows:

```
void CExampleDoc::Serialize(CArchive& ar)
{
    if (ar.IsStoring())
    {
        ar << m_iNumShares;
        ar << m_dCurrentValue;
        ar << m_dPricePerShare;
    }
    else
    {
        ar >> m_iNumShares;
        ar >> m_dCurrentValue;
        ar >> m_dPricePerShare;
    }
}
```

In the preceding code, the CArchive object and insertion operators in the `if` statement store the contents of the data members to a disk file. The CArchive object and extraction operators in the `else` statement read the objects from the disk file and assign them to the appropriate data member.

Next, you will modify the Invoice program's Serialize() function so the program can save documents to disk.

To modify the Invoice program's Serialize() function so the program can save documents to disk:

1. Open the **InvoiceDoc.cpp** file in the Text Editor window and locate the Serialize() function.

2. Add to the Serialize() function the following bolded statements that write the CInvoiceDoc class's data members to, and read them from, disk files.

```cpp
void CInvoiceDoc::Serialize(CArchive& ar)
{
    if (ar.IsStoring())
    {
        ar << m_dAmount1;
        ar << m_dAmount2;
        ar << m_dAmount3;
        ar << m_szDescription2;
        ar << m_szDescription1;
        ar << m_szDescription3;
        ar << m_iQuantity1;
        ar << m_iQuantity2;
        ar << m_iQuantity3;
        ar << m_dRate1;
        ar << m_dRate2;
        ar << m_dRate3;
        ar << m_dTOTAL;
        ar << m_szDate;
        ar << m_szCustomer;
        ar << m_szInvoice;
        ar << m_szTerms;
    }
    else
    {
        ar >> m_dAmount1;
        ar >> m_dAmount2;
        ar >> m_dAmount3;
        ar >> m_szDescription2;
        ar >> m_szDescription1;
        ar >> m_szDescription3;
        ar >> m_iQuantity1;
        ar >> m_iQuantity2;
        ar >> m_iQuantity3;
        ar >> m_dRate1;
        ar >> m_dRate2;
        ar >> m_dRate3;
        ar >> m_dTOTAL;
        ar >> m_szDate;
        ar >> m_szCustomer;
        ar >> m_szInvoice;
        ar >> m_szTerms;
    }
}
```

3. Finally, rebuild and execute the Invoice program. Test the program to see if it functions properly by saving a document, creating a new document, and then by reopening the document you saved.

4. When you are finished testing the program, close the Invoice program window.

CHAPTER SUMMARY

❑ A document is a file that is associated with a particular application and contains different sets of data depending on your program's functionality and each user's needs.

❑ Applications that are based on the CFrameWnd class are document based.

❑ A document-based application allows clients to read from and write to documents that are associated with the application.

❑ The MFC document/view architecture separates a program's data from the way that the data is displayed and accessed by users.

❑ A program's data (the document) is managed and stored by a class derived from the CDocument class.

❑ A program's data is displayed to the user by one or more classes derived from the CView class.

❑ With document-based applications, CDocument and CView classes are added to an MFC project, in addition to an application class derived from CWinApp and a window class derived from CFrameWnd.

❑ The data stored in a CDocument class can be displayed and manipulated by multiple CView classes. However, a CView class can only display and manipulate the data from a single CDocument class.

❑ By enabling document/view architecture, your document-based MFC applications automatically inherit a wide range of document functionality that allows you to read and write documents, use print and print preview functions, and perform other types of document-specific tasks.

❑ The single document interface, or SDI, allows users to have only one document open at a time.

❑ The multiple document interface, or MDI, allows users to have multiple documents open at the same time.

❑ When you create a document-based application, you can base your view class on CView or one of its derived classes.

❑ A view class is responsible for graphically displaying a document's data and for handling the manipulation of that data according to user requests.

10

❑ The GetDocument() function is used for returning a pointer to the document associated with a view.

❑ The debug version of the GetDocument() function is defined in the view class's definition file and uses the ASSERT() macro and IsKindOf() function to verify the validity of the document pointer.

❑ The release build version of the GetDocument() macro is defined as an inline function in the view class declaration file, in an #ifndef directive immediately following the class definition. The release build version does not include the ASSERT() macro or IsKindOf() function, and simply returns the pointer to the m_pDocument data member after casting it to the document class data type.

❑ Each view class inherits an OnUpdate() function that is called each time the document class changes or whenever the document class executes an UpdateAllViews() function.

❑ You can use the WizardBar's Add Virtual Function command to quickly add a virtual function declaration to your class.

❑ The OnNewDocument() function is called when a user creates a new document.

❑ When a user creates a new document in an SDI application, MFC reuses the same document object.

❑ You need to override the DeleteContents() function to reinitialize the document object's data members each time a new document is created. You call the DeleteContents() function from the OnNewDocument() function.

❑ The SetModifiedFlag() function is used by the MFC framework to determine if a document has been modified since the last time it was saved.

❑ The UpdateAllViews() function causes each view window's OnUpdate() function to execute in order to allow each view to display the most recent data.

❑ A document template defines the relationship between a document-based program's frame, document, and view classes. The CSingleDocTemplate class is used for SDI applications, and the CMultiDocTemplate is used for MDI applications.

❑ The RUNTIME() macro returns a CRunTimeClass structure for each class. The framework uses the CRunTimeClass structure to obtain class information at run time.

❑ The DECLARE_DYNCREATE() and IMPLEMENT_DYNCREATE() macros allow classes to be created dynamically at run time.

❑ The Windows API includes several standard dialog boxes, called common dialog boxes, that you can use in your applications.

❑ Persistence refers to the ability for data to continue to exist after the program closes.

❑ The process of storing data to, and retrieving data from, a persistent storage medium is called serialization.

❑ The Serialize() function reads data from, and writes data to, a disk file.

- ☐ The CArchive class is used for writing data to, and reading data from, a storage medium.

- ☐ The Serialize() function is called in one of two circumstances: when the document is being saved or when it is being retrieved.

REVIEW QUESTIONS

1. A _____ refers to a file that is associated with a particular application and that contains different sets of data depending on your program's functionality and each user's needs.

   a. receptacle

   b. container

   c. document

   d. collection

2. Whereas a dialog-based application is used for creating applications that perform some sort of calculation or task that is applicable only to the current application session, applications that are based on the CFrameWnd class _____.

   a. do not perform calculations

   b. are document based

   c. do not use dialog controls

   d. class based

3. CDocument manages and stores a program's data, while CView _____ it.

   a. archives

   b. files

   c. deletes

   d. displays

4. A CDocument class can be associated with _____ CView classes.

   a. zero

   b. one

   c. two

   d. any number of

5. A CView class can be associated with _____ CDocument classes.

   a. zero

   b. one

   c. two

   d. any number of

10

6. Which of the following statements is correct?

   a. You are required to use document/view architecture in your document-based MFC programs.

   b. You are not required to use document/view architecture in your document-based MFC programs.

   c. MFC programs created with the document/view architecture are of little value.

   d. Programs that are created with the document/view architecture do not automatically inherit the document functionality that allows you to read and write documents, use print and print preview functions, and perform other types of document-specific tasks.

7. What does SDI stand for?

   a. Single Document Interface

   b. Separate Document Instantiation

   c. Subroutine Design Information

   d. Special Document Integration

8. What does MDI stand for?

   a. Multiple Document Interface

   b. Multiple Document Instantiation

   c. Minimal Design Integration

   d. Maximum Dynamic Interface

9. Where do you display a class instantiated from CView?

   a. Within the application window

   b. Within a dialog window

   c. Within a CDocument window

   d. Within a frame window

10. Which subclass of CView creates a text editor program?

    a. CFormView

    b. CEditView

    c. CCtrlView

    d. CHTMLView

11. Which subclass of CView creates a window that can be edited in Dialog Editor?

    a. CFormView

    b. CEditView

    c. CCtrlView

    d. CHTMLView

12. Which version of the GetDocument() function is used with a program's release build?

    a. The inline version defined in the declaration file of the CView-derived class

    b. The version defined in the definition file of the CView-derived class

    c. The inline version defined in the declaration file of CDocument-derived class

    d. The version defined in the definition file of the CDocument-derived class

13. An OnUpdate() function is called each time the document class changes or whenever the document class executes an _____ function.

    a. Refresh()

    b. UpdateViews()

    c. UpdateAllViews()

    d. Update()

14. Which Visual C++ tool can you use to quickly override a virtual function in an MFC class?

    a. ClassView

    b. AppWizard

    c. The Add Virtual Function command

    d. The Add Member Function command

15. Which of the following tasks is not required in order for a class derived from CDocument to write data to, and read data from, files?

    a. Create a WinMain() function

    b. Create data members to temporarily hold the data for the current document

    c. Override the CDocument class's member functions to customize the creating, loading, and saving mechanisms of the document/view architecture

    d. Override CDocument's Serialize() member function in order to read and write the document's data to and from a file

16. The AppWizard automatically provides overridden implementations for the CDocument class's _____ and Serialize() functions.

    a. OnOpenDocument()

    b. OnNewDocument()

    c. OnCloseDocument()

    d. DeleteContents()

17. Which of the following functions is used for reinitializing a CDocument class's data members when the user creates a new document?

    a. OnOpenDocument()

    b. OnNewDocument()

    c. OnCloseDocument()

    d. DeleteContents()

10

18. When a user creates a new document in an SDI application, MFC _____.

    a. reuses the same document object

    b. creates a new document object

    c. builds an array of document objects

    d. copies the original document object's data members to a new document object

19. The _____ function is used by the MFC framework to determine if a document has been modified since the last time it was saved.

    a. ChangedDocument()

    b. CleanDocument()

    c. LastModified()

    d. SetModifiedFlag()

20. Document templates are based on one of two classes: the CSingleDocTemplate or _____.

    a. CVariedDocTemplate

    b. CPluralDocTemplate

    c. CMultiDocTemplate

    d. CManyDocTemplate

21. The _____ macro returns a CRunTimeClass structure for each class.

    a. IMPLEMENT_SERIAL

    b. RUNTIME()

    c. DECLARE_DYNCREATE()

    d. IMPLEMENT_DYNCREATE()

22. _____ refers to the ability for data to continue to exist after the program closes.

    a. Persistence

    b. Stability

    c. Dynamism

    d. Continuance

23. The process of storing data to and retrieving data from a persistent storage medium is referred to as _____.

    a. encryption

    b. serialization

    c. compilation

    d. interpretation

24. Which of the following is required in a serialized class?

    a. An overridden OnFileSave() function

    b. An overridden DeleteContents() function

    c. An empty, default constructor

    d. An empty, default destructor

25. Which function of the CArchive class checks to see if a document is being stored?

    a. OnStoreFile()

    b. OnSaveFile()

    c. IsSaving()

    d. IsStoring()

26. Which operators are used with a CArchive object to write data to a disk file?

    a. <<

    b. >>

    c. ++

    d. <-

27. Which operators are used with a CArchive object to read data from a disk file?

    a. <<

    b. >>

    c. ++

    d. <-

10

EXERCISES

1. Assume you have a document-based MFC program that saves contact information to files. The program gathers five pieces of information—first name, last name, address, city, state, ZIP, and telephone—and stores each piece of information in data members named m_szFirst, m_szLast, m_szAddress, m_szCity, m_szState, m_szZip, and m_szPhone. Modify the following member function named updateInfo() so that it reads data values from a document object named CContactsDoc and assigns the values to the view class's data members. For simplicity, assume that both the view class and the document class use the same variable names for the data members.

```
void CContactsView::updateInfo() {
}
```

2. Modify the following OnUpdate() function for the CContactsView class so that controls in the program's dialog window are reset to the original values when the user creates a new document.

```
void CContactsView::OnUpdate(CView* pSender,
    LPARAM lHint, CObject* pHint)
{

    // TODO: Add your specialized code here and/or
        call the base class

}
```

3. Modify the following OnNewDocument() function and DeleteContents() function so that the document class's data members are reinitialized to their original values when a user creates a new document.

```
BOOL CContactsDoc::OnNewDocument() {
    if (!CDocument::OnNewDocument())
        return FALSE;
    return TRUE;
}
void CContactsDoc::DeleteContents() {
    // TODO: Add your specialized code here and/or
        call the base class
    CDocument::DeleteContents();
}
```

4. Modify the UpdateInfo() function from exercise 1 so that it marks the program as modified and updates any other document views.

5. Write the skeleton code to instantiate a CColorDialog dialog box.

6. Modify the following Serialize() function in the Contacts program's CContactsDoc class so that the data members listed in exercise 1 are written to and read from disk files.

```
void CContactsDoc::Serialize(CArchive& ar)
{
    if (ar.IsStoring())
    {
    }
    else
    {
    }
}
```

7. Create a document-based version of the BugReport program you created in Chapter 8 that is used as a software development bug report. Save each bug report as a separate document.

8. Create a document-based version of the Interview application you created in Chapter 8 that is used for tracking, documenting, and managing the process of interviewing candidates for professional positions. Save each prospective employee's interview as a document.

9. Create a document-based version of the math quiz program for a sixth grade class that you created in Chapter 8. Save each student's score as a separate document.

10. Create a document-based version of the Retirement Planner program you created in Chapter 4 that saves individual retirement scenarios as separate documents.

11. Another persistence technique that you may want to explore on your own involves a special Windows database known as the System Registry. The System Registry stores Windows system information along with initialization and configuration information for individual applications. Look for the System Registry topic in the MSDN Library and redesign the Invoice program so that the most recently used invoice number is stored in the System Registry. Each time you open the Invoice program, it should retrieve the invoice number from the System Registry, increment it by one, and then display the new number in the Invoice # edit box. The number stored in the System Registry should only be updated when the user saves a new invoice.

10

11

DESIGNING THE VISUAL INTERFACE

In this chapter you will learn:

♦ About the Graphics Device Interface

♦ How to draw in a window

♦ How to work with graphic object classes

♦ How to work with menus and commands

♦ How to work with toolbars and buttons

PREVIEW: THE STOCK CHARTING PROGRAM

You will work with a simple Stock Charting program in this chapter in order to demonstrate how to draw graphic objects and how to add menus and toolbar commands to an application. The Stock Charting program, allows you to track a stock's value over a five-day period (Monday through Friday) using three separate charts: a line chart, a column chart, and a scatter chart. The charts in the Stock Charting program are simplified versions of the types of charts you may have seen in Microsoft Excel. Although the Stock Charting program would not be very useful in a real-world setting because of its limitations, it will give you a good idea of how to add and manipulate graphic objects in programs.

To preview the Library Database application:

1. Create a **Chapter.11** folder in your Visual C++ Projects folder.

2. Copy the **Chapter11_StockCharting** folder from the Chapter.11 folder on your Data Disk to the Chapter.11 folder in your Visual C++ Projects folder, and then open the StockCharting project in Visual C++.

3. Click on the **FileView** tab in the Workspace window and expand the Source Files folder. The project contains several classes with which you are familiar, including an application class, a frame class, a view class, and a document class. Open the CStockChartingView class's implementation file, **StockChartingView.cpp**, in the Text Editor window.

4. Locate the **OnDraw() function** in the StockChartingView.cpp file. You use the OnDraw() function to add graphic objects to an application's device context. A device context is a special data structure that stores information about the text and graphics displayed by an application. For the Stock Charting program, all of the code that adds graphic objects to the program's window is contained in the

OnDraw() function. Figure 11-1 shows only portions of the Stock Charting program's OnDraw() function since the function is too lengthy to list here. The first few statements following the function header are used for converting the stock values entered by a user to the pixels scale of the charts. Now, notice the CPen and CBrush statements. CPen objects determine the style and color of lines, while CBrush objects control the color and pattern displayed in closed objects such as rectangles and circles. Also, notice the many statements that use the pDC pointer. The pDC pointer is a handle to the device context that you use to draw graphic objects on the screen. Finally, notice the **switch** statement toward the bottom of the function. The **switch** statement determines which chart to display according to the value in an enum variable named m_Chart. (You will learn about enum data types later in this chapter.) Code within each **case** label adds the appropriate graphic objects to the device context, depending on the selected chart.

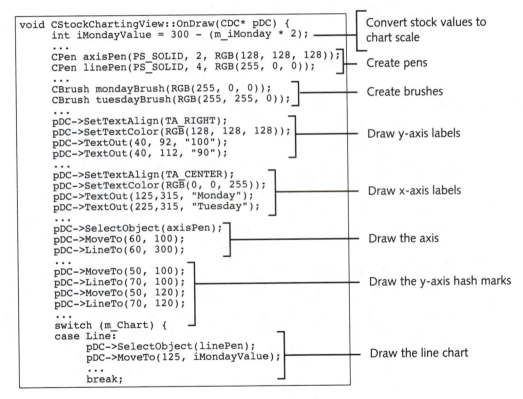

```
void CStockChartingView::OnDraw(CDC* pDC) {            ⌐ Convert stock values to
    int iMondayValue = 300 - (m_iMonday * 2);        ─┘ chart scale
    ...
    CPen axisPen(PS_SOLID, 2, RGB(128, 128, 128));   ⌐
    CPen linePen(PS_SOLID, 4, RGB(255, 0, 0));       ─┘ Create pens
    ...
    CBrush mondayBrush(RGB(255, 0, 0));              ⌐ Create brushes
    CBrush tuesdayBrush(RGB(255, 255, 0));           ─┘
    ...
    pDC->SetTextAlign(TA_RIGHT);                     ⌐
    pDC->SetTextColor(RGB(128, 128, 128));            │ Draw y-axis labels
    pDC->TextOut(40, 92, "100");                      │
    pDC->TextOut(40, 112, "90");                     ─┘
    ...
    pDC->SetTextAlign(TA_CENTER);                    ⌐
    pDC->SetTextColor(RGB(0, 0, 255));                │ Draw x-axis labels
    pDC->TextOut(125,315, "Monday");                  │
    pDC->TextOut(225,315, "Tuesday");                ─┘
    ...
    pDC->SelectObject(axisPen);                      ⌐
    pDC->MoveTo(60, 100);                             │ Draw the axis
    pDC->LineTo(60, 300);                            ─┘
    ...
    pDC->MoveTo(50, 100);                            ⌐
    pDC->LineTo(70, 100);                             │ Draw the y-axis hash marks
    pDC->MoveTo(50, 120);                             │
    pDC->LineTo(70, 120);                            ─┘
    ...
    switch (m_Chart) {
    case Line:
        pDC->SelectObject(linePen);                  ⌐
        pDC->MoveTo(125, iMondayValue);               │ Draw the line chart
        ...                                           │
        break;                                       ─┘
```

Figure 11-1 Stock Charting program's OnDraw() function

```
        case Column:
            pDC->SelectObject(columnPen);
            pDC->SelectObject(mondayBrush);
            pDC->Rectangle(80, iMondayValue, 170, 300);      ]——— Draw the column chart
            ...
            break;
        case Scatter:
            pDC->SelectObject(scatterPen);
            pDC->SelectObject(mondayBrush);
            pDC->Ellipse(120, iMondayValue - 5, 130,         ]——— Draw the scatter chart
                iMondayValue + 5);
            ...
            break;
    }
}
```

Figure 11-1   Stock Charting program's OnDraw() function (continued)

5. Build and execute the program. The default chart type is the line chart, with each stock value set to a default value of 0. Try entering some new values in each of the edit boxes. When you exit each edit box, an EN_KILLFOCUS event occurs, which executes event handlers that update the associated graphical value in the chart. Now, open the **View** menu. Notice the three commands at the bottom of the menu that you can use to change the type of displayed chart. Display the column chart and scatter chart by selecting their associated commands on the View menu. Now, examine the toolbar. At the right end of the toolbar are buttons that represent each chart type. Try clicking each button to display its associated chart. Both the menu commands and toolbar buttons execute the same WM_COMMAND messages used for command button events. Figure 11-2 shows an example of the Stock Charting program with the column chart displayed.

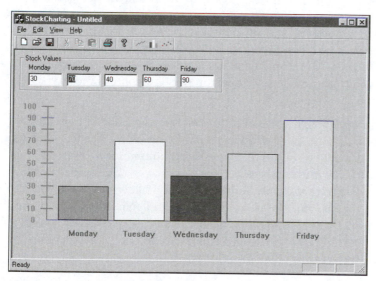

Figure 11-2   Stock Charting program with the column chart displayed

6. Press the **Close** button to close the Stock Charting program window.

INTRODUCTION

The first programs you created in this text were simple console applications that included little in the way of a visual interface, other than the text that was output to the screen. As your studies of Visual C++ have progressed, you have learned how to create Win32 applications that include basic Windows operating system elements such as dialog controls and command buttons. This chapter brings you the next level of application development by introducing several techniques for designing the visual interface. The techniques you will learn include how to draw in an application window, how to modify the application window itself, and how to add menu commands and toolbar buttons to your application. Be aware, however, that you will learn only the basics of visual interface design. Nevertheless, you should learn enough in this chapter to be able to explore more advanced interface topics on your own.

THE GRAPHICS DEVICE INTERFACE

At one time or another in your work with Windows operating systems, you have probably come across the term device driver. A **device** is a generic term that refers to a particular piece of computer hardware, such as a monitor or printer. A **device driver** is a specialized type of program that allows the Windows operating system to communicate with a particular device. Many different types of devices, produced by numerous manufacturers, exist for personal computers. For Windows to communicate with a particular device, a driver must exist for it. Drivers for popular devices are available as part of the Windows operating system itself, while drivers for new or relatively obscure devices are usually available from the manufacturer of the device. Note that many types of drivers exist, including drivers that control a computer's drives and input devices such as a mouse and keyboard. When you write a Windows application, however, you do not need to add any code to your program for directly communicating with the drivers for individual devices. If that were the case, then to write a Windows program, you would need to include code for the thousands of devices that are available today. Instead, the Windows operating system controls most types of devices by using drivers behind the scenes.

When designing a visual interface, you need to concern yourself with how the visual portion of your program displays on output devices such as monitors, printers, and plotters. The **graphics device interface**, or **GDI**, manages communication with different types of Windows graphical device drivers. In essence, the GDI acts as a translation layer between your application and the device to which it outputs. The GDI allows Windows applications to be device-independent by mapping the visual portion of an application to the appropriate output required by a given device driver. For example, monitors are available in different resolutions and color settings. A VGA monitor's resolution, for instance, is 640 columns by 480 rows of pixels, while a Super VGA monitor's resolution is 1,024 columns by 768 rows of pixels.

Additionally, some monitors can display only 256 colors, while other monitors can display millions of colors. The GDI manages the mapping of an application's visual interface to the appropriate resolution for any given monitor, and maps color values to a monitor's nearest available color. Similarly, the output to printers and plotters requires different mappings, depending on the type of printer or plotter you are using. Figure 11-3 illustrates how the GDI translates between Windows applications and devices.

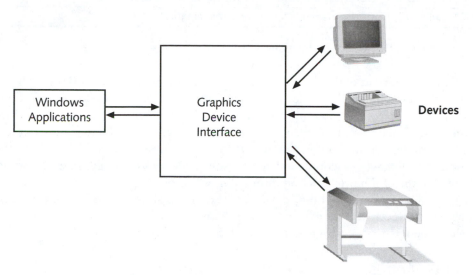

Figure 11-3   GDI translation between Windows applications and devices

One of the most important parts of the GDI as it relates to the design of a visual interface is the device context, which you will examine next.

Device Contexts

To draw in an application window, you must do so through a device context. A **device context** is a Windows GDI data structure that stores information about the text and graphics displayed by an application. When your application runs on a given device, the GDI translates the information stored in the device context to the format of the device driver. Essentially, you "draw" your text and graphics into the device context and then hand the device context off to the GDI, which translates the device context to the appropriate device driver when necessary. You can actually think of the device context as a canvas that you can use to paint the visual elements of your program. The data structure that represents a device context is created and manipulated by the classes listed in Figure 11-4.

11

Class	Description
CDC	The base class for device contexts, used for directly accessing and modifying an application's drawing information
CPaintDC	Represents an application's display information
CClientDC	Represents the client area of a window
CWindowDC	Represents the whole application window, including its frame
CMetaFileDC	Enables drawing into a Windows metafile

Figure 11-4   Device context classes

The most important of the device context classes listed in Figure 11-4 is the CDC class; this is the base class for the other device context classes. The framework automatically instantiates a CDC object for you and supplies you with a pointer to the object in the inherited OnDraw() function. You use the CDC object pointer in the OnDraw() function to directly add and modify drawing information in the device context. You will learn about the CDC class and OnDraw() functions shortly. For now, understand that all drawing output is performed in the OnDraw() function through the CDC object pointer. You do not usually need to work directly with the other device context classes since the framework manages them for you. However, you should understand the use of each device context class in case you need to design a more advanced user interface in the future.

Mapping Modes

Recall that you reference a window's pixels with x-axis and y-axis coordinates, beginning in the upper-left corner of a screen or window at an x-axis position of 0 and a y-axis position of 0. Pixel measurements are usually written in the format x, y, which means that the starting point, or point of origin, in the upper-left corner of the screen is written as position 0, 0. As you move right from the upper-left corner of the screen along the x-axis, or down along the y-axis, the pixel measurements increase. Therefore, a pixel position that is 100 pixels to the right along the x-axis and 200 pixels down on the y-axis is written as 100, 200. A device context uses this manner of measuring pixel positions as its default measurement system, or mapping mode. A **mapping mode** is a coordinate system that determines the units and scaling orientation in a device context. Figure 11-5 illustrates the default measurement system.

Mapping modes begin with a prefix of *MM_*, followed by a description of the mapping mode. The default mapping mode illustrated in Figure 11-5 is named MM_TEXT. Figure 11-6 lists the eight mapping modes you can use in applications.

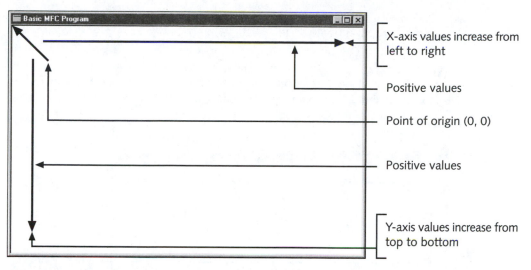

Figure 11-5 Default measurement system

Mapping Mode	Description
MM_ANISOTROPIC	Units of measure are mapped to application-specific values. Axes are scaled independently. Orientation of x and y axes are user defined.
MM_HIENGLISH	Units of measure are mapped to 0.0001 inches. X-axis values increase from left to right. Y-axis values decrease from top to bottom.
MM_HIMETRIC	Units of measure are mapped to 0.01 millimeters. X-axis values increase from left to right. Y-axis values decrease from top to bottom.
MM_ISOTROPIC	Units of measure are mapped to application-specific values. Axes are scaled identically. Orientation of x and y axes are user defined.
MM_LOENGLISH	Units of measure are mapped to 0.01 inches. X-axis values increase from left to right. Y-axis values decrease from top to bottom.
MM_LOMETRIC	Units of measure are mapped to 0.1 millimeters. X-axis values increase from left to right. Y-axis values decrease from top to bottom.
MM_TEXT	Units of measure are mapped to one pixel. X-axis values increase from left to right. Y-axis values increase from top to bottom.
MM_TWIPS	Units of measure are mapped to one twip, which is equal to 1/20th of a printer's point or 1/1440 inches. X-axis values increase from left to right. Y-axis values decrease from top to bottom.

Figure 11-6 Mapping Modes

All mapping modes begin with a point of origin of $0, 0$ in the upper-left corner of the screen or window. However, for all of the mapping modes except MM_TEXT (the default), MM_ISOTROPIC, AND MM_ANISOTROPIC, the values along the y-axis decrease instead of increase as you move away from the point of origin. Therefore, a pixel position that is 100 pixels to the right along the x-axis and 200 pixels down on the y-axis is written as

100, −200 using any of the mapping modes other than MM_TEXT, MM_ISOTROPIC, AND MM_ANISOTROPIC. Figure 11-7 illustrates how y-axis values decrease as you move away from the point of origin.

 You can change a mapping mode's point of origin from 0, 0 to another value using the SetViewportOrg() API function or the SetViewportOrg() member function of the CDC class.

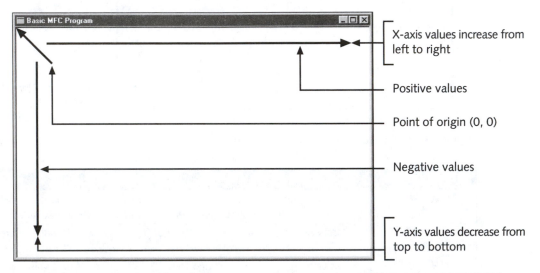

Figure 11-7   Axis values for all mapping modes except MM_TEXT, MM_ISOTROPIC, AND MM_ANISOTROPIC

As mentioned previously, the default mapping mode is MM_TEXT. If you want to change the mapping mode in your application, then you need to execute the SetMapMode() function of the CDC class, which you will learn about shortly. Although, there will be times when you will want to use a mapping mode other than MM_TEXT, the default mapping mode of MM_TEXT is sufficient for your studies in this chapter. For instance, you may need to use a more exact unit of measure than pixels. Additionally, if you are configuring a document to print, it is much easier to use the MM_LOENGLISH mapping mode. Since the MM_LOENGLISH mapping mode uses inches as its unit of measure, it is much easier to use when calculating where your document should print on an 8 ½" by 11" sheet of paper. If you were to use the MM_TEXT mapping mode, which uses pixels as its unit of measure, then you would need to convert the pixels to inches in order to accurately gauge your printing coordinates.

Working with Color

Although computer systems can display anywhere from 256 to millions of colors, the display of colors is the result of combining just three primary colors, red, blue, and green. Graphical computer systems, such as Windows, use the **red**, **green**, **blue**, or **RGB**, **color system** for specifying colors. You create individual colors in the RGB color system using the **RGB()** **macro**. The color created with an RGB() macro is sometimes referred to as an **RGB** **triplet**. The syntax for using the RGB() macro is RGB(red, green, blue). Each of the three parameters in the RGB() macro can accept an integer value ranging from 0 to 255, which indicates the intensity to use for each color. A value of 0 indicates that the color you are creating should include the minimum intensity of a primary color, while a value of 255 indicates that the color should include the maximum intensity of a primary color. By combining different intensities of the red, green, and blue primary colors, you can come up with millions of different hues. You create primary colors of red, green, or blue by using a full intensity value of 255 for one of the primary colors, but values of 0 for the other primary colors. For example, to display the color red, you use the RGB() macro as follows: RGB(255, 0, 0). Black is represented by the minimum intensities for each primary color using the statement RGB(0, 0, 0). White is represented by the maximum intensities for each primary color using the statement RGB(255, 255, 255). Figure 11–8 lists RGB color values for some common colors.

Color	Red Intensity	Green Intensity	Blue Intensity
Red	255	0	0
Green	0	255	0
Blue	0	0	255
White	255	255	255
Black	0	0	0
Light Gray	192	192	192
Dark Gray	128	128	128
Yellow	255	255	0
Cyan	0	255	255
Magenta	255	0	255

Figure 11-8   Common RGB color values

Even though you can come up with millions of colors with the RGB color system, the number of colors that can actually be displayed depends on the color capabilities of individual hardware devices such as monitors and printers.

Several of the device context functions that you will use in this chapter require RGB color parameters. For instance, the CreatePen() function, which is used for designating line thickness and color, requires an RGB color value as its third parameter. One way to pass the RGB color value to a function is to pass an RGB() macro, along with your desired color intensities, as the function argument. The following example shows how to pass a blue RGB color as the third parameter of the CreatePen() function using the RGB() macro. For now, do not worry about how the CreatePen() function works since you will examine it in detail later in this chapter.

```
CPen m_CurPen;
m_CurPen.CreatePen(PS_SOLID, 2, RGB(0, 0, 255));
```

You can also declare your own color variable using the Win32 **COLORREF data type**. You create a color variable by assigning the RGB triplet returned from the RGB() macro to a variable of the COLORREF data type. The following code shows another version of the CreatePen() function, but this time a COLORREF variable named blueColor is passed as the CreatePen() function's third parameter instead of an RGB() macro:

```
CPen m_CurPen;
COLORREF blueColor = RGB(0, 0, 255);
m_CurPen.CreatePen(PS_SOLID, 2, blueColor);
```

 Once you create a COLORREF variable, you can extract the intensity value of each primary color using the GetRValue(), GetGValue(), and GetBValue() macros.

DRAWING IN A WINDOW

Although you have added dialog controls to some of the programs you have created, you have not actually drawn graphic objects in any of your windows. Graphic objects refers to lines, rectangles, and circles that you add to a device context. You can create lines, rectangles, and circles using different colors, line thickness, and fills. (Fills refer to colors and patterns that you apply to the interior of closed images such as rectangles and circles.) You can also draw text graphic objects into a device context that are similar to the Static Text controls you have added to dialog windows. Unlike Static Text controls, however, you can use different fonts and colors to format the text you draw into a device context. Figure 11-9 shows an example of some of the graphic objects that you can display in a window through the device context.

Next, you will start creating the Stock Charting program. You will derive the program's CView class from the CFormView class in order to be able to use dialog controls in the application window. Later, you will add graphic objects to the same window containing the dialog controls.

To start creating the Stock Charting program:

1. Create a new project named **StockCharting** using the MFC AppWizard (exe) option. Save the project in the **Chapter.11** folder in your Visual C++ Projects folder.

2. AppWizard executes and starts to walk you through the steps involved in creating an MFC program. In Step 1, select **Single document** from the application choices. Leave the **Document/View architecture support?** check box selected and click the **Next** button.

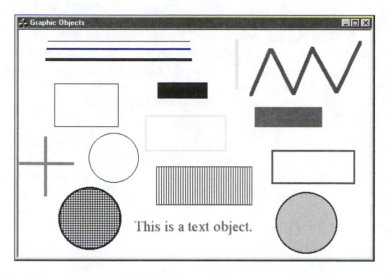

Figure 11-9   Graphic objects

3. In Step 2, leave the data support option set to **None** and click the **Next** button.

4. In Step 3, leave the compound document support option set to **None** and clear the **ActiveX Controls** checkbox. Click the **Next** button to continue.

5. In Step 4, click the **Advanced** button to display the Advanced Options dialog box. In the Window Styles tab of the Advanced Options dialog box, select the **Maximized** check box. Leave the rest of the options in the Window Styles tab set to their defaults and then click the **Close** button.

6. Accept the default options in Steps 4 and 5.

7. In Step 6, select **CFormView** from the Base class drop-down list box and click the **Finish** button. When the New Project Information dialog box displays, click the **OK** button to create the project.

Next, you will add dialog controls to the CStockChartingView class's dialog window. You will add five Edit Box controls to the dialog window in which users can enter the stock value for each day of the week that they are charting a stock. You will also add command buttons that you will temporarily use to change the displayed chart type. Later, you will delete the command buttons after adding menu commands and toolbar buttons that will change the displayed chart type.

In some situations, you may want to limit the values that users can enter into controls. For example, in the Stock Charting program, the y-axis of each chart has a scale that begins with 0 and ends at 100. Therefore, users can only enter stock values between 0 and 100. A mechanism called dialog data validation, or DDV, which is related to DDX, assists in the validation of data when you exchange values between controls and variables, allowing you to limit the values users can enter. When you add DDX data members using the Member Variables tab in ClassWizard, certain data types, such as integer and floating point data types, support

DDV by allowing you to set the minimum and maximum values that users can enter into a control, such as an Edit Box. For the stock value Edit Box controls in the Stock Charting program, you want to allow users to enter only values between 0 and 100. Once you call the UpdateData() function to exchange values between your dialog controls and their associated DDX data members, DDV checks to make sure that users entered values that are within the range you specified. For the stock value Edit Box controls, you will use the int data type, which supports DDV.

You may wonder why you are using int data types when stock values often include decimal portions. The device context functions you use to plot each value on the charts require that you pass integer values, not floating-point values. You could allow users to enter floating-point values, and then round off each value and cast it to the int data type. However, that would make your code unnecessarily complex. Remember, your purpose in this chapter is to study drawing functionality. Therefore, you will use the int data type.

To add dialog controls to the CStockChartingView class's dialog window:

1. After AppWizard finishes creating the StockCharting program window, Visual C++ should automatically open the Dialog Editor. If the Dialog Editor does not open automatically, use the ResourceView tab on the Workspace window to open the **IDD_STOCKCHARTING_FORM** dialog resource.

2. Delete the Static Text control that reads
   TODO: Place form controls on this dialog..

3. Modify your dialog window so that it matches Figure 11-10.

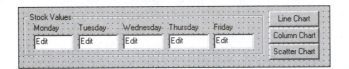

Figure 11-10   Stock Charting dialog controls

4. Use the table shown in Figure 11-11 to modify the resource IDs for each of the dialog controls.

5. When you are finished adding the controls to the dialog resource, open **ClassWizard** and click the **Member Variables** tab. Add DDX data members for each of the stock value Edit Box controls using the variable names and data types shown in Figure 11-12. Also, set the minimum and maximum values for each DDX data member to 0 and 100, respectively. DDV will use these values to validate the numbers entered by users. Figure 11-13 shows an example of the ClassWizard Member Variables tab after creating each DDX data member and setting its minimum and maximum DDV values.

Control	Resource ID
Monday	IDC_MONDAY
Tuesday	IDC_TUESDAY
Wednesday	IDC_WEDNESDAY
Thursday	IDC_THURSDAY
Friday	IDC_FRIDAY
Line Chart	ID_DRAW_LINE_CHART
Column Chart	ID_DRAW_COLUMN_CHART
Scatter Chart	ID_DRAW_SCATTER_CHART

Figure 11-11 Dialog control resource IDs

Resource ID	Variable Name	Data Type
IDC_MONDAY	m_iMonday	int
IDC_TUESDAY	m_iTuesday	int
IDC_WEDNESDAY	m_iWednesday	int
IDC_THURSDAY	m_iThursday	int
IDC_FRIDAY	m_iFriday	int

Figure 11-12 DDX data member names and types

11

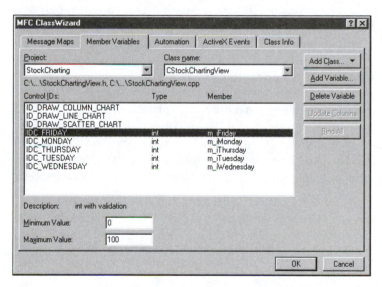

Figure 11-13 ClassWizard Member Variables tab after creating each DDX data member and setting its minimum and maximum DDV values

The ability to draw into a device context is controlled by two functions: OnPaint() and OnDraw(). First, you will learn about the OnPaint() function.

Understanding the OnPaint( ) Function

All Windows applications must provide an event handler for the WM_PAINT message. The **WM_PAINT message** informs an application that its window must be redrawn, or *repainted*. Events that generate WM_PAINT messages include when a user resizes a window or when part of a window that is obscured by another window becomes visible again. A WM_PAINT message is also generated by the UpdateWindow() function, which the framework calls when an MFC program first executes. Calling the UpdateWindow() function allows an application to initially draw the contents of its windows. The message handler function for the WM_PAINT message is named **OnPaint()**, and is inherited from the CWnd class. The framework automatically provides the OnPaint() function for handling any WM_PAINT messages it receives, as follows.

```
void CView::OnPaint() {
    // standard paint routine
    CPaintDC dc(this);
    OnPrepareDC(&dc);
    OnDraw(&dc);
}
```

The first statement in the OnPaint() function, `CPaintDC dc(this);`, declares an object named dc of the CPaintDC class. The dc object is the handle you will use to access an application's device context. Note that the CPaintDC device context class can only be used when responding to a WM_PAINT message. One of the requirements in an event handler that responds to a WM_PAINT message is that the handler must execute the BeginPaint() function at construction time, and the EndPaint() function at destruction time. The constructor and destructor for the CPaintDC class automatically handle the calls to these functions. The second statement in the OnPaint() function, `OnPrepareDC(&dc);`, is used for adjusting attributes of the device context. The default implementation of the OnPrepareDC() function does nothing. However, in order to handle special display and print capabilities such as pagination of multi-page documents, you override the OnPrepareDC() function in your derived CView class. The last statement in the OnPaint() function, `OnDraw(&dc);`, calls a function named OnDraw() and passes to it the address of the dc (device context) object.

You will never actually see the OnPaint() message handler in your programs since it is well hidden by the framework. Also, you will not normally need to override the OnPaint() message handler in your programs. Since the OnPaint() message handler is hidden and you don't need to override it, you may be wondering where you add code that adds graphic objects to your window. You actually add your graphic object code to the OnDraw() function.

Overriding the OnDraw()Function

You use the **OnDraw() function**, which is inherited from the CView base class, to manage an application's device context. Essentially, the WM_PAINT message causes the OnPaint() event handler to execute, which, in turn, causes the OnDraw() function to execute. The most confusing part about drawing graphic objects through the device context is that the WM_PAINT message must go through the OnPaint() event handler to execute the OnDraw() function. You may think it would be easier to simply override the OnPaint() event handler and forget the OnDraw() function altogether. In fact, you can override the OnPaint() event handler and add all of your drawing code to the overridden function, if you so choose. However, graphic objects are not just displayed on the screen—they are also displayed in print preview and printed. The OnPaint() event handler prepares a "generic" device context that you can use for your graphic objects. Because it needs to be generic, the OnPaint() function cannot provide specific preview and printing functionality. This is one of the main reasons that the OnPaint() event handler is hidden by the framework. The OnDraw() function, on the other hand, is used for adding specific functionality for the display and printing of graphic objects.

Next, you will override the OnDraw() function by adding a skeleton version of the function to the CStockChartingView class using the Add Virtual Function command from the WizardBar. The skeleton version of the overriden OnDraw() function that you add to the CStockChartingView class will not actually contain any functionality yet. You will add functionality to the OnDraw() function shortly.

To override the OnDraw() function:

1. Open the **StockChartingView.cpp** file in the Text Editor window.

2. Select **Add Virtual Function** from the **WizardBar** to display the New Virtual Override dialog box.

3. Select **OnDraw** from the **New Virtual Functions** list, and then click the **Add and Edit** button. The new function is created and your cursor is moved to the function definition.

The following code shows the OnDraw() function skeleton that you just added to the CStockChartingView definition file.

```
void CStockChartingView::OnDraw(CDC* pDC) {
    // TODO: Add your specialized code here and/or call
    // the base class
}
```

Notice that CDC* pDC is declared in the function header, creating an object pointer named pDC of the CDC class. You will use the **pDC pointer** as a handle for accessing the application's device context. Recall that when the OnPaint() function called the OnDraw() function, it passed the dc object as an argument. However, the dc object, which represents the device context, was created using the CPaintDC device context class. But, remember that the CPaintDC device context class is used only when responding to a WM_PAINT message. Therefore, the device context that was created with the CPaintDC class is passed to an object of the CDC class. Because the CDC class is the base class for the other device context classes, an object of the CDC class can be used to store an object of one of its derived classes. The passing of the pDC pointer to access an application's device context is illustrated in Figure 11-14.

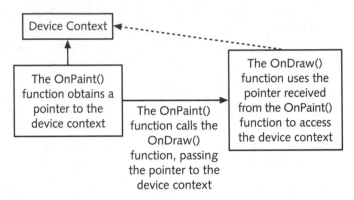

Figure 11-14   Passing of the pDC pointer to access an application's device context

Updating the Display

Before exploring individual drawing commands, you need to understand how to update the device context display—an important aspect of drawing. As you know, the OnDraw() function executes when the WM_PAINT message is generated, which occurs automatically when an application first loads or when the application window needs to be redrawn. However, what if you want to modify or replace your application's displayed graphic objects based on user input or program functionality?

To modify or replace the graphic objects that are already displayed in a device context, you must first call the Invalidate() function. The **Invalidate() function** notifies the update region that the window needs to be erased. The **update region** identifies portions of a window that need to be repainted. If an application's update region is not empty, then Windows generates a WM_PAINT message. The window is erased when the BegPaint() function executes in the OnPaint() handler. The OnPaint() handler then calls the OnDraw() function to update the display.

 You can also notify the update region that only portions of a window need to be erased using the InvalidateRect() and InvalidateRgn() functions. The InvalidateRect() function identifies a given rectangle as needing to be repainted. The InvalidateRgn() function identifies a specific region within a window as needing to be repainted.

If you do not call the Invalidate() function to erase the device context before adding new graphic objects, then any new graphic objects you add will be placed directly on top of the old graphic objects. For example, the Stock Charting program loads the line chart by default. If you were to select the column chart and then the scatter chart without first erasing the device context with the Invalidate()function, the column chart would be placed on top of the original line chart, and then the scatter chart would be placed on top of the other two charts, as shown in Figure 11-15.

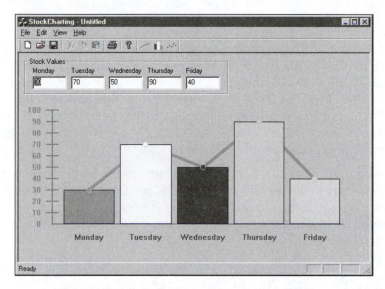

Figure 11-15   Stock Charting program without calls to the Invalidate() function

There are several methods for modifying and replacing graphic objects in the device context once you erase the window using the Invalidate() function. For the Stock Charting program, you will use a **switch** statement in the OnDraw() function to check the value of an enumerated variable that determines which of the charts to display.

The **enumerated**, or **enum**, data type allows you to create a variable to which only a series of predefined constant values can be assigned. You declare an enum variable using the syntax enum {*value1, value2, value3, ...} variable_name;*. The values between the braces are known as *enumerators* and are used for symbolically representing a value. Each enumerator receives an integer value, starting with 0 for the first enumerator. For example, to create an enum variable named daysOfWeek that contains enumerators for each day of the week, you use a declaration statement similar to the following:

```
enum {Sunday, Monday, Tuesday, Wednesday, Thursday, Friday,
Saturday, Sunday} daysOfWeek;
```

The daysOfWeek variable can only be assigned one of the enumerators in the declaration list, which are *Sunday* through *Monday*. If you attempt to assign any other value to the daysOfWeek variable, you will receive a compile error. Note that each value, Sunday through

Monday, only represents an integer value, starting with 0. For example, if you assign the value *Tuesday* to the daysOfWeek variable using the statement `daysOfWeek = Tuesday;`, the daysOfWeek variable is really being assigned a value of *2*.

Each enumerator assigned to an enum variable is really a constant. In fact, instead of using an enum data type, you could just create the daysOfWeek variable as an int data type and create each of the enumerators as constants using a statement similar to `const int Sunday = 0;`. However, assigning related groups of symbolic identifiers to the same variable makes your code easier to work with.

The main reasons for using the enum data type are to limit the number of values that can be assigned to a variable and to logically organize groups of related constants. Another important use for the enum data type is to allow you to use meaningful labels within a `switch` statement. Recall that each `case` label in a `switch` statement must be a constant value of an integer data type. Therefore, using a `case` label similar to `case "Monday":` is illegal since the label is not an integer data type or a constant value. However, if you use an enum data type like the daysOfWeek variable, the statement `case Monday:` is legal since the Monday enumerator is a constant integer value of 1.

You will use an enum variable within a `switch` statement in the Stock Charting program to determine which chart to display. The enum variable you create for the Stock Charting program will be named m_Chart and will contain constants for each of the chart types: Line, Column, and Scatter. Next, you will create the m_Chart enum variable and `switch` statement in the Stock Charting program.

To create the m_Chart enum variable and `switch` statement in the Stock Charting program:

1. Open the **StockChartingView.h** file in the Text Editor window.

2. Add the following bolded enum variable declaration to the first protected section, following the `DECLARE_DYNCREATE(CStockChartingView)` statement:

```
protected:
    CStockChartingView();
    DECLARE_DYNCREATE(CStockChartingView)
    enum {Line, Column, Scatter} m_Chart;
```

3. Next, open the **StockChartingView.cpp** file in the Text Editor window.

4. Replace the `// TODO: add construction code here` comment in the class constructor with the following bolded statement to initialize the m_Chart variable to *Line*:

```
CStockChartingView::CStockChartingView()
    : CFormView(CStockChartingView::IDD) {
    //{{AFX_DATA_INIT(CStockChartingView)
    m_iFriday = 0;
    m_iMonday = 0;
    m_iThursday = 0;
    m_iTuesday = 0;
```

```
        m_iWednesday = 0;
       //}}AFX_DATA_INIT
        m_Chart = Line;
   }
```

5. Next, locate the OnDraw() function and replace the **// TODO: Add your specialized code here and/or call the base class** comment with the following bolded **switch** statement. As you progress through the chapter, you will add code to each **case** label that draws the graphic objects for each chart type.

```
void CStockChartingView::OnDraw(CDC* pDC) {
    switch (m_Chart) {
        case Line:
            // TODO: add line chart code here
            break;
        case Column:
            // TODO: add column chart code here
            break;
        case Scatter:
            // TODO: add scatter chart code here
            break;
    }
}
```

Working with the CDC Class

Recall that the CDC class and its derived classes are used for accessing an application's device context. In addition to being the base class for other device context classes, the CDC class also contains all of the functions you need to draw in the device context. Later in this chapter, you will learn how to use some special graphics classes to change the display and formatting of drawn objects, but the CDC class is what you use to actually draw the objects. More specifically, to access the drawing functions in the CDC class, you use the pDC pointer that is passed to the OnDraw() function.

The CDC class contains many functions for drawing and for working with the device context in general. The CDC topic in the MSDN Library provides a complete listing of CDC member functions. In this chapter, you will only work with the functions that you need to draw primitive graphic objects such as lines, rectangles, and circles, as well as functions for outputting text to the screen.

Drawing Lines

You use the **LineTo() function** to draw lines in the device context. The LineTo() function accepts two arguments: the x-coordinate and the y-coordinate of the line's ending position. You append the LineTo() function to the pDC pointer using the indirect member selection operator as follows: **pDC->LineTo(x, y)**. A line's starting position is drawn according to the current position. The **current position** is the starting point for any line or curve drawing function. The default current position is the mapping mode's point of origin, 0, 0.

Therefore, to draw a line from the point of origin to position 100, 75 using the default MM_TEXT mapping mode, you modify the OnDraw() function as shown in the following code. Figure 11-16 shows the output.

```
void CGraphicsExampleView::OnDraw(CDC* pDC) {
    pDC->LineTo(100, 50);
}
```

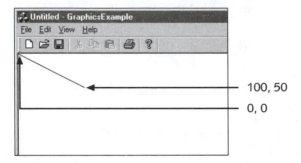

Figure 11-16   Output of a single LineTo() function

After you execute the LineTo() function, the x and y parameters you passed to it become the new current position. The following code shows how to create two connecting lines using the LineTo() function. Figure 11-17 shows the output.

```
void CGraphicsExampleView::OnDraw(CDC* pDC) {
    pDC->LineTo(100, 50);
    pDC->LineTo(150, 25);
}
```

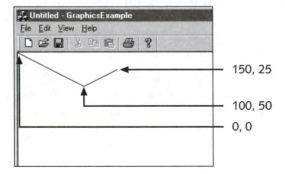

Figure 11-17   Output of two LineTo() functions

If you don't want your lines to start at the origin, 0, 0, you use the **MoveTo() function** to manually change the current position. You pass to the MoveTo() function an x parameter and a y parameter specifying the new current position. The following code shows a modified version of the OnDraw() function that uses LineTo() functions to draw a star. The first drawing statement calls the MoveTo() function to move the current position to 75, 255, which is the star's lower left point. Then, each of the LineTo() functions draws a segment of the star. Figure 11-18 shows the output.

```cpp
void CGraphicsExampleView::OnDraw(CDC* pDC) {
    pDC->MoveTo(75, 225);
    pDC->LineTo(150, 50);
    pDC->LineTo(225, 225);
    pDC->LineTo(50, 100);
    pDC->LineTo(250, 100);
    pDC->LineTo(75, 225);
}
```

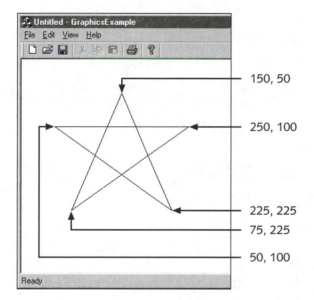

Figure 11-18   OnDraw() function that uses the MoveTo() functions and LineTo() functions to draw a star

Next, you will use LineTo() and MoveTo() functions to draw the axis for the Stock Chart program.

To use LineTo() and MoveTo() functions to draw the axis for the Stock Chart program:

1. Return to the **StockChartingView.cpp** file in the Text Editor window.

2. Above the **switch** statement, add the following bolded statements to the OnDraw() function. The first bolded statement moves the current position to 60, 100, which is the point at which you will start drawing the y-axis. The second

statement adds the y-axis by drawing a line to 60, 300, and the third statement adds the x-axis by drawing a line to 575, 300.

```
void CStockChartingView::OnDraw(CDC* pDC) {
    pDC->MoveTo(60, 100);
    pDC->LineTo(60, 300);
    pDC->LineTo(575, 300);
    switch (m_Chart) {
    ...
}
```

3. Next, above the `switch` statement, but after the statement `pDC->LineTo (575, 300);`, add the following bolded statements to draw the hash marks along the y-axis. Hash marks appear along the y-axis every twenty pixels. Since the hash marks do not connect like the x-axis and y-axis, you must use a MoveTo() function to move the current position before drawing each hash mark.

```
void CStockChartingView::OnDraw(CDC* pDC) {
    ...
    pDC->MoveTo(50, 100);
    pDC->LineTo(70, 100);
    pDC->MoveTo(50, 120);
    pDC->LineTo(70, 120);
    pDC->MoveTo(50, 140);
    pDC->LineTo(70, 140);
    pDC->MoveTo(50, 160);
    pDC->LineTo(70, 160);
    pDC->MoveTo(50, 180);
    pDC->LineTo(70, 180);
    pDC->MoveTo(50, 200);
    pDC->LineTo(70, 200);
    pDC->MoveTo(50, 220);
    pDC->LineTo(70, 220);
    pDC->MoveTo(50, 240);
    pDC->LineTo(70, 240);
    pDC->MoveTo(50, 260);
    pDC->LineTo(70, 260);
    pDC->MoveTo(50, 280);
    pDC->LineTo(70, 280);
    switch (m_Chart) {
    ...
}
```

4. Build and execute the program. None of the program's functionality has been built yet, but you should see the axis lines as shown in Figure 11-19.

5. Close the Stock Charting program window.

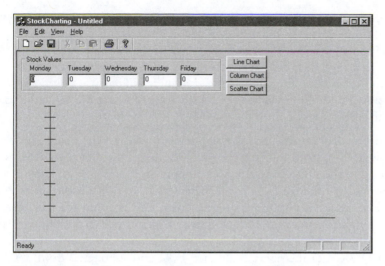

Figure 11-19 Stock Charting program axis lines

Next, you will use LineTo() and MoveTo() functions to create the Stock Chart program's line chart. Before creating the line chart, however, you need to understand the mathematics required to convert the numbers entered by users into values that correspond to the chart's grid system. The MM_TEXT mapping mode increases as you move *down* the screen, which is the opposite of how your chart works. Values on your chart increase as you move *up* the chart. Additionally, the x-axis and y-axis are not placed at the screen's 0 positions. As a consequence, the values a user enters do not directly correspond to values on the chart. You need some way to convert the users' values to the chart's values.

The x-values on the line chart are always placed at exact positions, 100 units apart. Monday's x-value is 125, Tuesday's x-value is 225, Wednesday's x-value is 325, Thursday's x-value is 425, and Friday's x-value is 525, as illustrated in Figure 11-20. These values are determined within the program and are not gathered from users, so you don't need to worry about fixing them.

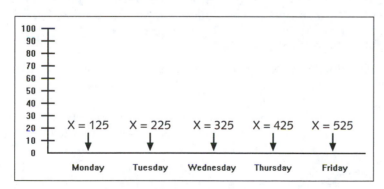

Figure 11-20 X-axis values

The value you are really gathering from the user is the y-axis value, which represents the stock price. The 0 position on the y-axis is drawn at 300 pixels from the top of the window, and the 100 position on the y-axis is drawn at 100 pixels from the top of the window. Therefore, the y-axis displayed on screen is situated on a 200-pixel grid (300-100), that increases when you travel *down* the screen, instead of increasing as you go up the screen like your chart is supposed to do. You will need to do some math to get the value the user enters (from 0 to 100) to map correctly onto the y-axis.

Essentially, each dollar that a user enters is equal to two pixels on the chart grid. Therefore, the first thing you need to do is multiply the value the user enters by 2 in order to get the value to correspond to the 200-pixel grid. After multiplying the stock value by 2, you need to account for the fact that the mapping mode increases as you move down the screen, while your chart's value increases as you move up the screen. You account for this difference by subtracting the multiplied value from the 0 position, which is drawn at 300 pixels from the top of the screen. You will create local variables in the OnDraw() function and assign to them the values in the DDX data members, multiplied by 2 and subtracted from 300. The following code shows the local variable declaration and assignment you will add to the OnDraw() function for the Monday stock value:

```
int iMondayValue = 300 - (m_iMonday * 2);
```

Next, you will add to the OnDraw() function code that converts the stock values and displays the line chart.

To add to the OnDraw() function code that converts the stock values and displays the line chart:

1. Return to the **StockChartingView.cpp** file in the Text Editor window.

2. Immediately after the opening brace of the OnDraw() function, add the following bolded variable declarations and assignments that convert the stock values:

```
void CStockChartingView::OnDraw(CDC* pDC) {
    int iMondayValue = 300 - (m_iMonday * 2);
    int iTuesdayValue = 300 - (m_iTuesday * 2);
    int iWednesdayValue = 300 - (m_iWednesday * 2);
    int iThursdayValue = 300 - (m_iThursday * 2);
    int iFridayValue = 300 - (m_iFriday * 2);
    pDC->MoveTo(60, 100);
```

3. Next, replace the **// TODO: add line chart code here** comment in the **switch** statement's Line **case** label with the following statements. The first statement moves to the x-axis position of 125 and the y-axis position of the value assigned to the iMondayValue variable in the preceding step. Each subsequent statement then draws a line using the next stock value's associated local variable.

```
switch (m_Chart) {
    case Line:
        pDC->MoveTo(125, iMondayValue);
        pDC->LineTo(225, iTuesdayValue);
        pDC->LineTo(325, iWednesdayValue);
        pDC->LineTo(425, iThursdayValue);
```

```
        pDC->LineTo(525, iFridayValue);
        break;
...
```

Before you can display the line chart, you need to add some message handlers to give the program its functionality. For each of the Edit Box controls, you will add EN_KILLFOCUS message handlers that update the chart after the user enters a new value into one of the controls and moves to another control. You will also add to the ID_DRAW_LINE_CHART resource ID a BN_CLICKED message handler that updates the display with the line chart when the user clicks the Line Chart command button.

To add message handlers (or message handler functions) to the Stock Charting program:

1. Use ClassWizard's Message Maps tab to add the following EN_KILLFOCUS message handler functions to the CStockChartingView class for each of the Edit Box controls. The name of each message map function's resource ID is contained in a comment line above each function. The first statement in each function transfers the values in each control to its associated DDX data member. The Invalidate() function then erases the device context and raises a WM_PAINT message, which executes the OnDraw() function.

```
// IDC_MONDAY
void CStockChartingView::OnKillfocusMonday() {
    UpdateData(TRUE);
    Invalidate(TRUE);
}
// IDC_TUESDAY
void CStockChartingView::OnKillfocusTuesday() {
    UpdateData(TRUE);
    Invalidate(TRUE);
}
// IDC_WEDNESDAY
void CStockChartingView::OnKillfocusWednesday() {
    UpdateData(TRUE);
    Invalidate(TRUE);
}
// IDC_THURSDAY
void CStockChartingView::OnKillfocusThursday() {
    UpdateData(TRUE);
    Invalidate(TRUE);
}
// IDC_FRIDAY
void CStockChartingView::OnKillfocusFriday() {
    UpdateData(TRUE);
    Invalidate(TRUE);
}
```

2. Next, to the CStockChartingView class, add the following BN_CLICKED message handler function for the ID_DRAW_LINE_CHART resource ID. The function contains the same statements as the Edit Box control function handlers, but it also contains a statement that assigns the m_Chart variable a value of *Line*

11

to inform the **switch** statement in the OnDraw() function to display the line chart. The BN_CLICKED message handler for the ID_DRAW_LINE_CHART resource ID will be necessary later when you want to redisplay the line chart after displaying the column or scatter charts.

```
void CStockChartingView::OnDrawLineChart() {
    UpdateData(TRUE);
    m_Chart = Line;
    Invalidate(TRUE);
}
```

3. Rebuild and execute the program. You will not see a line chart at first since the chart starts at a default value of 0. Enter values in the edit boxes and see if the chart updates correctly. Figure 11-21 shows the line chart after entering some values.

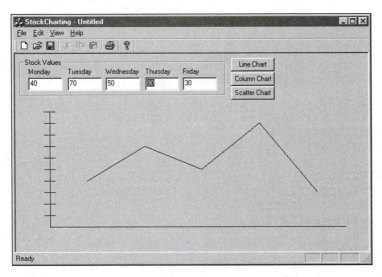

Figure 11-21   Line chart after entering values

4. Close the Stock Charting program window.

Drawing Rectangles

You draw rectangles into the device context using the **Rectangle() function**. The Rectangle() function accepts four parameters: x1, y1, x2, and y2. The x1 and y1 parameters represent the rectangle's upper left corner, and the x2 and y2 parameters represent the rectangle's lower right corner. The following OnDraw() function with a Rectangle() statement draws the rectangle shown in Figure 11-22:

```
void CGraphicsExampleView::OnDraw(CDC* pDC) {
    pDC->Rectangle(50, 50, 200, 200);
}
```

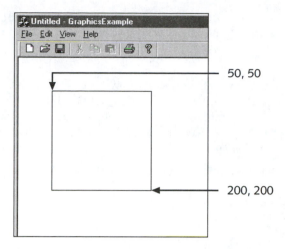

Figure 11-22   Output of a Rectangle() statement

There are many CDC functions for creating and manipulating rectangles. Later in this section, you will learn how to change a rectangle's line style and how to fill its interior with different colors or patterns.

Next, you will use rectangles to create the Stock Charting program's column chart. For determining the height of each rectangle (the height of each rectangle represents the value entered into each edit box), the column chart uses the same local stock variables that are declared and assigned values at the beginning of the OnDraw() function. However, you will use these local variables only to set each rectangle's y1 parameter, which represents the height of each rectangle. The x1, x2, and y2 parameters for each rectangle are set to permanent values. For example, the statement that creates the rectangle for the Monday stock value is written as follows:

```
pDC->Rectangle(80, iMondayValue, 170, 300);
```

To use rectangles to create the Stock Charting program's column chart:

1. Return to the **StockChartingView.cpp** file in the Text Editor window.

2. Replace the **// TODO: add column chart code here** comment in the **switch** statement's Column **case** label with the following statements. Each statement uses the Rectangle() function to draw one of the chart's columns. The x1, x2, and y2 parameters are permanently set for each rectangle. However, each function determines the height of each column with an associated local stock variable as the y1 parameter.

```
switch (m_Chart) {
...
    case Column:
        pDC->Rectangle(80, iMondayValue, 170, 300);
        pDC->Rectangle(180, iTuesdayValue, 270, 300);
        pDC->Rectangle(280, iWednesdayValue, 370, 300);
```

```
        pDC->Rectangle(380, iThursdayValue, 470, 300);
        pDC->Rectangle(480, iFridayValue, 570, 300);
    break;
```
...

3. Next, to the CStockChartingView class, add the following BN_CLICKED message handler function for the ID_DRAW_COLUMN_CHART resource ID. The function contains the same statements as the message handler function you added for the ID_DRAW_LINE_CHART resource ID, except that the m_Chart variable is assigned a value of *Column*.

```
void CStockChartingView::OnDrawColumnChart()
{
    UpdateData(TRUE);
    m_Chart = Column;
    Invalidate(TRUE);
}
```

4. Rebuild and execute the program. Click the **Column Chart** button and enter some values to see if the chart updates correctly. Then, click the **Line Chart** button. The line chart should appear and display the same values that the column chart displayed. Figure 11-23 shows an example of the column chart after entering some values.

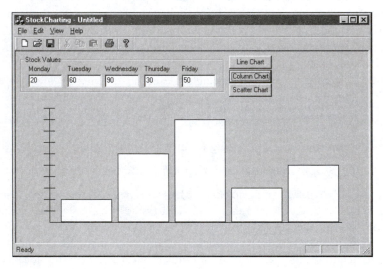

Figure 11-23   Column chart after entering values

5. Close the Stock Charting program window.

Drawing Ellipses

In geometry, an ellipse is the mathematical term for an oval or circle. You use the **Ellipse() function** to draw ovals and circles in a device context. As with the Rectangle() function, the Ellipse() function accepts four parameters: x1, y1, x2, and y2. Instead of representing actual points on the ellipse, the x1, y1, x2, and y2 parameters represent the upper left and lower right positions of the ellipse's bounding rectangle. The **bounding rectangle** determines the height and width of an ellipse. An oval or circle contained by a bounding box will be created to fill the height and width of the bounding box. You do not actually see the bounding rectangle; it is more of a conceptual element for containing an oval or circle. Figure 11-24 illustrates an ellipse's bounding rectangle.

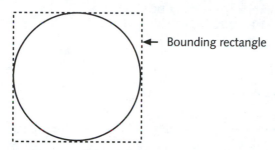

Figure 11-24   Ellipse's bounding rectangle

If you set the x1 and y1 parameters of the Ellipse() function to 0, then the ellipse's bounding rectangle will start in the upper left corner of the client window. The following OnDraw() function contains a single Ellipse() function whose x1 and y1 parameters are set to 0. Figure 11-25 shows the output.

```
void CGraphicsExampleView::OnDraw(CDC* pDC) {
    pDC->Ellipse(0, 0, 100, 100);
}
```

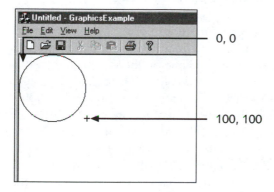

Figure 11-25   OnDraw() function with a single Ellipse() function

To create a perfect circle, the height and width of an ellipse's bounding box must be equal. To create a bounding box with an equal height and width, the value returned when you subtract the x1 parameter from the x2 parameter must be equal to the value that is returned

11

when you subtract the y1 parameter from the y2 parameter. For example, the statement `Ellipse(50, 100, 150, 200);` creates a circle since both the height and the width are equal to 100. If the height and width of an ellipse's bounding box are not equal, then the ellipse will be an oval. For example, the statement `Ellipse(50, 100, 150, 300);` creates an oval since the width is equal to 100, but the height is equal to 200. The following OnDraw() function creates the two ellipses shown in Figure 11-26. The first ellipse is an oval, and the second ellipse is a circle.

```
void CGraphicsExampleView::OnDraw(CDC* pDC) {
    pDC->Ellipse(10, 10, 300, 50);
    pDC->Ellipse(50, 100, 150, 200);
}
```

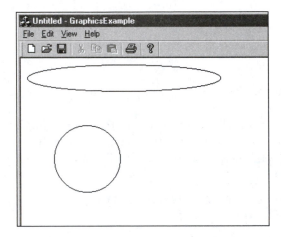

Figure 11-26   OnDraw() function with two Ellipse() statements

Next, you will create the Stock Charting program's scatter chart. You will use ellipses to represent each individual value plotted on the scatter chart. The scatter chart code uses the local stock variables to calculate the placement of each ellipse on the y-axis. However, the calculations are slightly different from those for the line and column charts. Each local stock variable represents the exact position of each stock value on the y-axis. In addition, you want each ellipse on the scatter chart to be a circle that is ten pixels in diameter. To calculate the width of the bounding rectangle for each ellipse, you will hard-code the x1 and x2 parameters. To set the y-axis parameters so that the height of the ellipse is equal to 10, you will subtract 5 from the local variable to determine the y1 parameter, but add 5 to the local variable to determine the y2 parameter. For example, the statement that creates the ellipse for the Monday stock value is written as follows:

```
pDC->Ellipse(120, iMondayValue - 5, 130, iMondayValue + 5);
```

To create the Stock Charting program's scatter chart:

1. Return to the **StockChartingView.cpp** file in the Text Editor window.

2. Replace the **// TODO: add scatter chart code here** comment in the **switch** statement's Scatter **case** label with the following statements. Each statement uses the Ellipse() function to draw one of the chart's circles. The x1 and x2 parameters are permanently set for each ellipse. To determine the height of each ellipse, each function subtracts a value of 5 from an associated local stock variable for the y1 parameter and adds a value of 5 to the same associated local stock variable.

```
switch (m_Chart) {
...
    case Scatter:
        pDC->Ellipse(120, iMondayValue - 5, 130,
            iMondayValue + 5);
        pDC->Ellipse(220, iTuesdayValue - 5, 230,
            iTuesdayValue + 5);
        pDC->Ellipse(320, iWednesdayValue - 5, 330,
            iWednesdayValue + 5);
        pDC->Ellipse(420, iThursdayValue - 5, 430,
            iThursdayValue + 5);
        pDC->Ellipse(520, iFridayValue - 5, 530,
            iFridayValue + 5);
        break;
}
```

3. Next, to the CStockChartingView class add the following BN_CLICKED message handler function for the ID_DRAW_SCATTER_CHART resource ID. The function contains the same statements as the message handler functions you added for the charts, except that the m_Chart variable is assigned a value of *Scatter*.

```
void CStockChartingView::OnDrawScatterChart() {
    UpdateData(TRUE);
    m_Chart = Scatter;
    Invalidate(TRUE);
}
```

4. Rebuild and execute the program. Click the **Scatter Chart** button. Notice that when you first view the Scatter Chart, each of the ellipses is set to a value of 0, and they are therefore lined up with the x-axis. Next, enter some values to see if the chart updates correctly. Then, try clicking the other two charts. Each chart should appear and display the same values that the scatter chart displayed. Figure 11-27 shows an example of the scatter chart after entering some values.

11

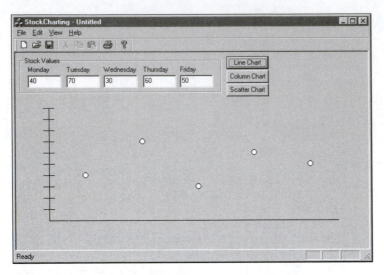

Figure 11-27   Scatter chart after entering values

> 5. Close the Stock Charting program window.

Outputting Text

You add text to the device context using the **TextOut() function**. The TextOut() function accepts three parameters using the syntax `pDC.TextOut(x, y, string)`. The *x* and *y* parameters represent the horizontal and vertical coordinates at which you want to place the text according to the mapping mode, and the *string* parameter is a CString variable or a literal string containing the text you want to be displayed. For example, in the following OnDraw() function, the text Sample Text is assigned to a CString variable named szText. The TextOut() function displays the contents of the szText variable at position 100, 100 in the device context. Figure 11-28 shows the output.

```
void CGraphicsExampleView::OnDraw(CDC* pDC) {
    CString szText = "Sample Text";
    pDC->TextOut(100, 100, szText);
}
```

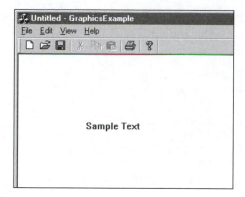

Figure 11-28   OnDraw() function with a single TextOut() statement

 Modifying the default font that Windows uses to display text graphic objects is a surprisingly difficult operation that is beyond the scope of this book. If you would like more information on how to modify the font for text objects, refer to the CFont class topic in the MSDN Library.

The CDC class contains several functions for manipulating text objects. Two of the CDC text functions you will use in this chapter are the SetTextAlign() function and the SetTextColor() functions. The **SetTextAlign() function** sets the horizontal text alignment for text objects. You append the SetTextAlign() function to the pDC pointer with a member selection operator, just like you do for other CDC functions. To set the alignment you want, you pass to the SetTextAlign() function one of the alignment values listed in Figure 11-29. The TA_LEFT, TA_CENTER, and TA_RIGHT values align text according to the TextOut() function's x-value. The TA_BASELINE, TA_BOTTOM, and TA_TOP values align text according to a text object's bounding rectangle.

Value	Description
TA_BASELINE	The text aligns according to the baseline of the text.
TA_BOTTOM	The text aligns at the bottom edge of the bounding rectangle.
TA_CENTER	The text aligns with the center of the bounding rectangle.
TA_LEFT	The text aligns on the left edge of the bounding rectangle.
TA_RIGHT	The text aligns on the right edge of the bounding rectangle.
TA_TOP	The text aligns at the top edge of the bounding rectangle.

Figure 11-29   SetTextAlign() function alignment values

When you use the TextOut() function, a bounding rectangle is created for the text, similar to the bounding rectangle that is created for ellipses. In order to set text alignment, you must call the SetTextAlign() function before you call any TextOut() statements. Any TextOut() statements that follow a SetTextAlign() function will use that SetTextAlign() function's alignment setting until another SetTextAlign() function is called in the code. For example, the following code includes several SetTextAlign() and TextOut() function calls. Each call to a SetTextAlign() function changes the alignment for any TextOut() objects that follow. Figure 11-30 shows the output.

```
void CGraphicsExampleView::OnDraw(CDC* pDC) {
    pDC->SetTextAlign(TA_LEFT);
    pDC->TextOut(200, 50, "Left Alignment");
    pDC->SetTextAlign(TA_CENTER);
    pDC->TextOut(200, 100, "Center Alignment");
    pDC->SetTextAlign(TA_RIGHT);
    pDC->TextOut(200, 150, "Right Alignment");
}
```

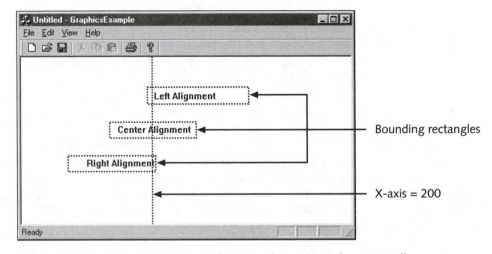

Figure 11-30   Output of SetTextAlign() and TextOut() function calls

The **SetTextColor()** function sets the color of any text objects displayed with the TextOut() function. You pass to the SetTextColor() function an RGB color value using either the RGB() macro or a COLORREF variable. Any TextOut() statements that follow a SetTextColor() function will use that SetTextColor() function's color setting until another SetTextColor() function is called in the code. For example, the following code displays three text objects. The first text object is set to a light gray color value, the second text object is set to a dark gray color value, and the third text object is set to black. Figure 11-31 shows the output.

```
pDC->SetTextColor(RGB(192, 192, 192));
pDC->TextOut(50, 50, "Light Gray Text");
pDC->SetTextColor(RGB(128, 128, 128));
pDC->TextOut(50, 100, "Dark Gray Text");
pDC->SetTextColor(RGB(0, 0, 0));
pDC->TextOut(50, 150, "Black Text");
```

Figure 11-31   Output of SetTextColor() and TextOut() function calls

Next, you will add the axis labels to the Stock Charting program. The y-axis labels are right-aligned and set to dark gray. The x-axis labels are center-aligned and set to blue.

To add the axis labels to the Stock Charting program:

1. Return to the **StockChartingView.cpp** file in the Text Editor window.

2. Immediately above the `switch` statement in the OnDraw() function, add the following bolded statements, which draw the y-axis labels. The first statement sets the text alignment to right, the second statement sets the text color to dark gray, and the rest of the statements draw the text labels.

```
void CStockChartingView::OnDraw(CDC* pDC) {
...
    pDC->SetTextAlign(TA_RIGHT);
    pDC->SetTextColor(RGB(128, 128, 128));
    pDC->TextOut(40, 92, "100");
    pDC->TextOut(40, 112, "90");
    pDC->TextOut(40, 132, "80");
    pDC->TextOut(40, 152, "70");
    pDC->TextOut(40, 172, "60");
    pDC->TextOut(40, 192, "50");
    pDC->TextOut(40, 212, "40");
    pDC->TextOut(40, 232, "30");
    pDC->TextOut(40, 252, "20");
    pDC->TextOut(40, 272, "10");
    pDC->TextOut(40, 292, "0");
    switch (m_Chart) {
    ...
}
```

11

3. Next, above the switch statement in the OnDraw() function, immediately following the code you added in Step 2, add the following bolded statements to draw the x-axis labels. The SetTextAlign() function changes the text alignment to center and the SetTextColor() function changes the text color to blue.

```
void CStockChartingView::OnDraw(CDC* pDC) {
...
    pDC->SetTextAlign(TA_CENTER);
    pDC->SetTextColor(RGB(0, 0, 255));
    pDC->TextOut(125,315, "Monday");
    pDC->TextOut(225,315, "Tuesday");
    pDC->TextOut(325,315, "Wednesday");
    pDC->TextOut(425,315, "Thursday");
    pDC->TextOut(525,315, "Friday");
    switch (m_Chart) {
    ...
}
```

4. Rebuild and execute the program. Figure 11-32 shows how the new axis labels appear before entering any stock values.

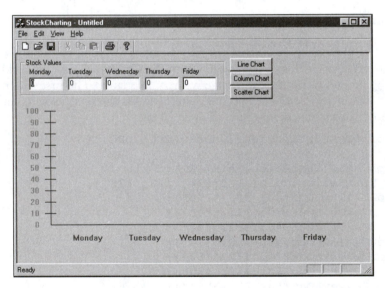

Figure 11-32   Stock Charting program after adding axis labels

5. Close the Stock Charting program window.

GRAPHIC OBJECT CLASSES

MFC includes several GDI classes for modifying the display of the graphic objects that you add to a device context. Some of the display elements you can select with the GDI classes include the size and colors of lines, the color and patterns used to fill the interiors of closed objects, and the fonts used to display text objects. The two graphic classes you will learn about in this chapter are the CPen and CBrush classes.

Working with Pens

When you draw any type of object that includes lines, you use a pen to draw those lines. A **pen** is an object created with the CPen class that determines a line's style, thickness, and color. You control the formatting of a pen with constructor functions. There are two constructors for creating a pen: a default constructor and a parameterized constructor. If you use the default constructor, then you must call the CreatePen() function to initialize the pen object. The **CreatePen() function** initializes a new pen with style, width, and color values. The syntax for using the CreatePen() function is as follows:

```
CPen variable;
variable.CreatePen(style, width, color);
```

The parameterized constructor uses a simpler syntax to declare and initialize a pen object in the same statement as follows:

```
CPen variable(style, width, color);
```

Notice that you do not use the CreatePen() function with the parameterized constructor. Rather, the parameterized constructor for the CPen class calls the CreatePen() function for you.

The first parameter you pass when creating a new CPen object is the style parameter. The style parameter determines the line style (solid, dashed, and so on) with which you want to draw. Figure 11-33 lists some of the common style values you can pass to the style parameter.

Style	Description
PS_SOLID	Creates a solid line
PS_DASH	Creates a dashed line
PS_DOT	Creates a dotted line
PS_DASHDOT	Creates a line with alternating dashes and dots
PS_DASHDOTDOT	Creates a line with alternating dashes and double dots
PS_INSIDEFRAME	Creates a line that does not extend outside of an object's bounding rectangle
PS_NULL	Creates a pen that draws a blank line

Figure 11-33   Common pen styles

The CPen object width parameter determines the width of a line. If you pass a value of 0 to the width parameter, then the line thickness will always be one pixel wide, regardless of the mapping mode that is currently in use. However, if you pass a value of 1 or higher, then the line thickness will be set to the units of the mapping mode you are using, using the passed number. For example, if you pass a value of 3 and you are using a mapping mode of

11

MM_TEXT, then the line thickness will be three pixels wide. If you are using a mapping mode of MM_LOENGLISH (which measures its units in increments of .03 inches), then the line thickness will be .03 inches wide.

The last CPen object parameter, color, determines the line color using an RGB color value.

 The dashed and dotted pen styles listed in Figure 11-33 work only if the CPen object width parameter is set to a value of 1. If you pass a value larger than 1 to the width parameter, then the PS_SOLID pen style will be used, regardless of which style parameter you pass to the CPen object.

Even though you declare and initialize a CPen object, the pen will not be applied to the device context until you pass the new object to the SelectObject() function. The **SelectObject() function** loads an object into the device context. In more simplified terms, you can think of the device context as being an artist. For your device context "artist" to use a different pen, you must use the SelectObject() function to actually hand it a new pen. The pen you last applied to the device context, using the SelectObject() function, will be used for all line drawing until you select a new pen into the device context. The following code shows how to use the CPen object to draw some lines that have different styles, thickness, and color. Figure 11-34 shows the output.

```
CPen solidPen(PS_SOLID, 1, RGB(0, 0, 0));
pDC->SelectObject(solidPen);
pDC->MoveTo(25, 50);
pDC->LineTo(300, 50);
CPen dashedPen(PS_DASH, 1, RGB(0, 0, 0));
pDC->SelectObject(dashedPen);
pDC->MoveTo(25, 75);
pDC->LineTo(300, 75);
CPen dottedPen(PS_DOT, 1, RGB(0, 0, 0));
pDC->SelectObject(dottedPen);
pDC->MoveTo(25, 100);
pDC->LineTo(300, 100);
CPen thickPen(PS_SOLID, 3, RGB(0, 0, 0));
pDC->SelectObject(thickPen);
pDC->MoveTo(25, 125);
pDC->LineTo(300, 125);
CPen thickerPen(PS_SOLID, 6, RGB(0, 0, 0));
pDC->SelectObject(thickerPen);
pDC->MoveTo(25, 150);
pDC->LineTo(300, 150);
CPen lightGrayThickPen(PS_SOLID, 6,
    RGB(192, 192, 192));
pDC->SelectObject(lightGrayThickPen);
pDC->MoveTo(25, 175);
pDC->LineTo(300, 175);
CPen darkGrayThinPen(PS_SOLID, 1,
    RGB(128, 128, 128));
```

```
pDC->SelectObject(darkGrayThinPen);
pDC->MoveTo(25, 200);
pDC->LineTo(300, 200);
```

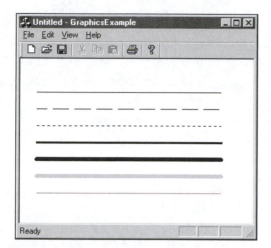

Figure 11-34 Pen examples

 Although the preceding code and figure use LineTo() functions for simplicity's sake, you can also use pens with rectangles, ellipses, and other types of objects.

Next, you will add some pens to the Stock Charting program that you will use to add different line styles and line colors to the program's graphical elements.

To add some pens to the Stock Charting program:

1. Return to the **StockChartingView.cpp** file in the Text Editor window.

2. First, in the OnDraw() function, immediately following the statements that convert the user's values into the chart's coordinate system, declare and initialize some pens. All of these pens use a solid border style. The axisPen is two pixels wide and dark gray, and will be used for the axis lines. The linePen is four pixels wide and red, and will be used for the line that is drawn by the line chart. The columnPen pen is one pixel wide and black, and will be used for the borders of the rectangles displayed by the column chart. The scatterPen is also one pixel wide and will be used for the borders of the ellipses in the scatter chart. The scatterPen is set to light gray so that the borders of the ellipses match the color of the dialog window—you want each ellipse to appear as a solid color on the scatter chart, with no visible border.

```
void CStockChartingView::OnDraw(CDC* pDC) {
    // Convert stock values to chart scale
    ...
    int iFridayValue = 300 - (m_iFriday * 2);
    CPen axisPen(PS_SOLID, 2, RGB(128, 128, 128));
    CPen linePen(PS_SOLID, 4, RGB(255, 0, 0));
    CPen columnPen(PS_SOLID, 1, RGB(0, 0, 0));
    CPen scatterPen(PS_SOLID, 1, RGB(192, 192, 192));
```

3. Press **Enter** and add the statement **pDC->SelectObject(axisPen);** to select the axisPen into the device context.

4. To select the linePen into the device context, add the following bolded statement as the first statement in the **switch** statement's Line label :

```
...
case Line:
    pDC->SelectObject(linePen);
    pDC->MoveTo(125, iMondayValue);
...
```

5. To select the columnPen into the device context, add the following bolded statement as the first statement in the **switch** statement's Column label:

```
...
case Column:
    pDC->SelectObject(columnPen);
    pDC->Rectangle(80, iMondayValue, 170, 300);
...
```

6. To select the scatterPen into the device context, add the following bolded statement as the first statement in the **switch** statement's Scatter label:

```
...
case Scatter:
    pDC->SelectObject(scatterPen);
    pDC->Ellipse(120, iMondayValue - 5, 130,
        iMondayValue + 5);
...
```

7. Rebuild and execute the program. Since the initial stock values are set to 0, you will see the red line that plots the values on the line chart visible along the x-axis. Figure 11-35 shows how the program with the new pens appears after entering some values for the line chart.

8. Close the Stock Charting program window.

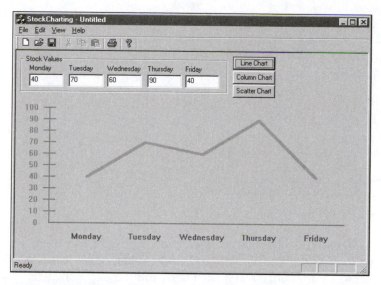

Figure 11-35   Line Chart after adding pens to the Stock Charting program

Working with Brushes

When you draw any type of closed object, such as rectangles or ellipses, you can select the formatting of the brush that you use to fill those objects. A **brush** is an object created with the CBrush class that determines the color and pattern that is drawn in the interior of a closed object. As with the CPen class, there are multiple methods of constructing a brush. You will use the same method of constructing and initializing a brush with CBrush constructors that you used with the CPen class. The CBrush class, however, includes several overloaded constructors that allow you to construct brushes using different attributes; you will learn about two of those constructors. The first overloaded constructor creates a brush that fills an object with a solid color. The second overloaded constructor creates a brush that fills an object with a predefined pattern in a selected color.

The syntax for creating a brush that fills an object with a solid color is CBrush *variable(color);*. You pass to the constructor an RGB color using the RGB macro or COLORREF macro. For example, to create a brush named darkGrayBrush(), you use the statement `CBrush darkGrayBrush(RGB(128, 128, 128));`. Once you create a brush, you must select it into the device context using the SelectObject() function. The brush you last applied to the device context using the SelectObject() function will be used for all fills until you select a new brush into the device context. For example, the following code draws the two circles displayed in Figure 11-36:

```
CBrush darkGrayBrush(RGB(128, 128, 128));
pDC->SelectObject(darkGrayBrush);
pDC->Ellipse(25, 25, 100, 100);
CBrush lightGrayBrush(RGB(192, 192, 192));
pDC->SelectObject(lightGrayBrush);
pDC->Ellipse(125, 25, 200, 100);
```

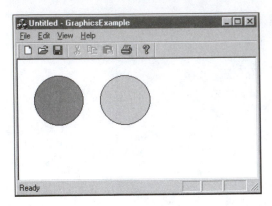

Figure 11-36 Circles filled by colored brushes

The syntax for creating a brush that fills an object with a predefined pattern in a selected color is CBrush *variable(pattern, color)*;.The value for the *pattern* parameter can be any of the predefined values listed in Figure 11-37, and the *color* parameter is simply an RGB color with which you want to draw the pattern.

Value	Description
HS_BDIAGONAL	Downward 45 degree crosshatch
HS_CROSS	Horizontal and vertical crosshatch
HS_DIAGCROSS	45 degree crosshatch
HS_FDIAGONAL	Upward 45 degree crosshatch
HS_HORIZONTAL	Horizontal crosshatch
HS_VERTICAL	Vertical crosshatch

Figure 11-37 Brush pattern values

The following code draws the same circles from the previous example, but this time using the CBrush class that creates patterns. The brush pattern applied to the first circle is HS_HORIZONTAL, and the brush pattern applied to the second circle is HS_CROSS. Figure 11-38 shows the output.

```
CBrush darkGrayBrush(HS_HORIZONTAL, RGB(128, 128, 128));
pDC->SelectObject(darkGrayBrush);
pDC->Ellipse(25, 25, 100, 100);
CBrush lightGrayBrush(HS_CROSS, RGB(192, 192, 192));
pDC->SelectObject(lightGrayBrush);
pDC->Ellipse(125, 25, 200, 100);
```

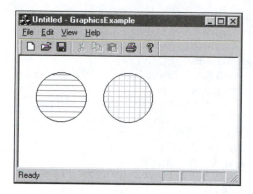

Figure 11-38   Circles filled by patterned and colored brushes

Next, you will add some colored brushes to the Stock Charting program that you will use to fill in the rectangles on the column chart and the ellipses on the scatter chart.

To add some colored brushes to the Stock Charting program:

1. Return to the **StockChartingView.cpp** file in the Text Editor window.

2. First, define the following brushes that you will apply to the rectangles in the column chart and the ellipses in the scatter chart. Each brush corresponds to a weekly stock. Add the brushes to the OnDraw() function after the code that defines the pens, which you added in the previous set of steps.

```
void CStockChartingView::OnDraw(CDC* pDC)
{
    ...
    CPen axisPen(PS_SOLID, 2, RGB(128, 128, 128));
    CPen linePen(PS_SOLID, 4, RGB(255, 0, 0));
    CPen columnPen(PS_SOLID, 1, RGB(0, 0, 0));
    CPen scatterPen(PS_SOLID, 1, RGB(192, 192, 192));
    CBrush mondayBrush(RGB(255, 0, 0));
    CBrush tuesdayBrush(RGB(255, 255, 0));
    CBrush wednesdayBrush(RGB(0, 0, 255));
    CBrush thursdayBrush(RGB(0, 255, 0));
    CBrush fridayBrush(RGB(0, 255, 255));
    pDC->SelectObject(axisPen);
    ...
```

3. Next, add the following bolded statements to the Column and Scatter `case` labels in the `switch` statement. Each statement selects the appropriate brush into the device context, depending on which column or ellipse is to be drawn next.

```
...
case Column:
    pDC->SelectObject(columnPen);
    pDC->SelectObject(mondayBrush);
    pDC->Rectangle(80, iMondayValue, 170, 300);
    pDC->SelectObject(tuesdayBrush);
```

```
        pDC->Rectangle(180, iTuesdayValue, 270, 300);
        pDC->SelectObject(wednesdayBrush);
        pDC->Rectangle(280, iWednesdayValue, 370, 300);
        pDC->SelectObject(thursdayBrush);
        pDC->Rectangle(380, iThursdayValue, 470, 300);
        pDC->SelectObject(fridayBrush);
        pDC->Rectangle(480, iFridayValue, 570, 300);
        break;
    case Scatter:
        pDC->SelectObject(scatterPen);
        pDC->SelectObject(mondayBrush);
        pDC->Ellipse(120, iMondayValue - 5, 130,
            iMondayValue + 5);
        pDC->SelectObject(tuesdayBrush);
        pDC->Ellipse(220, iTuesdayValue - 5, 230,
            iTuesdayValue + 5);
        pDC->SelectObject(wednesdayBrush);
        pDC->Ellipse(320, iWednesdayValue - 5, 330,
            iWednesdayValue + 5);
        pDC->SelectObject(thursdayBrush);
        pDC->Ellipse(420, iThursdayValue - 5, 430,
            iThursdayValue + 5);
        pDC->SelectObject(fridayBrush);
        pDC->Ellipse(520, iFridayValue - 5, 530,
            iFridayValue + 5);
        break;
```

4. Rebuild and execute the program. Enter some values and check the column and scatter charts to see if the rectangles and ellipses display in color. Figure 11-39 shows an example of the Column chart after entering some values.

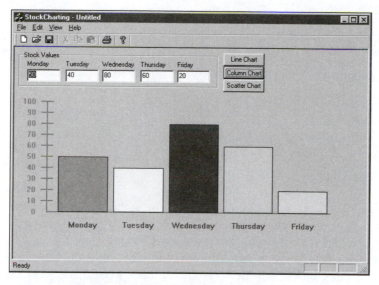

Figure 11-39 Column chart after applying brushes

5. Close the Stock Charting program window.

MENUS AND COMMANDS

For the rest of this chapter, you will learn how to execute commands using the menu and toolbar. Menus and toolbars are not exactly part of the device context, but they are important to the design of a Windows application's visual interface.

You have probably already noticed that AppWizard creates a menu for you whenever you build an MFC application. Menus are essential components of Windows applications. They allow you to execute commands that are contained within menus of choices. You can actually think of the commands on a menu as being very similar to the command buttons that you have used in dialog windows. Instead of being represented by a button, however, commands on a menu are represented by descriptive text.

In Visual C++, you use the Menu Editor to design and edit menus. If you click on the ResourceView tab in the Workspace window and expand the Menu folder, you will see the IDR_MAINFRAME resource that AppWizard automatically creates for you. By default, the menu resource includes File, Edit, View, and Help menus, with prewritten commands, such as the Copy and Paste commands, on the Edit menu. Figure 11-40 shows an example of the IDR_MAINFRAME menu resource in the Menu Editor, with the Edit menu displayed.

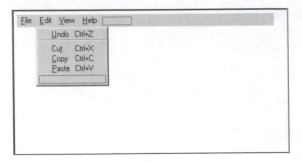

Figure 11-40   Menu Editor

Notice in Figure 11-40 that there is an empty box to the right of the Help menu. You use this empty box to add a new menu to the menu resource. If you click the empty menu box to select it and display its Properties window, you can set a caption for the new menu window, along with various style elements. Also notice the empty box at the bottom of the Edit menu. You use this empty box to add new command items to a menu. After clicking the empty box to select it, you use the Properties window to set the command elements, the same as you do for menus. The Properties window for each menu command also contains an ID drop-down list box in which you can enter or select a resource ID for a menu command. You can then use a COMMAND message and an associated message handler function to execute the functionality required by a command.

 You can move menus and commands by positioning your mouse cursor on an element, holding your left mouse button, and then dragging the element to a new position. To delete an existing command, highlight the command you want to delete and press your Delete key.

Menus and commands usually have an accelerator key associated with them. An **accelerator key** is an underlined character in a menu or command caption that defines a keystroke sequence that you can use to open a menu or select a command without using your mouse. For menus themselves, you open the menu by holding down the Alt key and pressing the underlined character on your keyboard. Once you open a menu, you can select a command by pressing its accelerator key. For example, most File menus include an Exit command. Notice in the preceding sentence that the F in File and the x in Exit are underlined. To open a File menu, you press Alt and the letter F. To select the Exit command once the File menu is opened, you simply press x.

You use the Properties window to define an accelerator key in your menus and commands by placing an ampersand (&) in the caption before the letter you want to use as the accelerator key. For example, if you want to add a Delete command to the Edit menu, you click the empty box at the bottom of the Edit menu and display the Properties window. In the Properties window, you select or define a resource ID, select any styles you want, and then type an ampersand (&) and the letter you want to use as an underlined accelerator key in the Caption box.

When you highlight a menu command, most programs usually display some text in the application's status bar that describes the command's purpose. For any new menu commands, you use the Prompt text box in the Properties window to set the text you want displayed in the status bar. Figure 11-41 shows an example of the Properties window for a new Delete command on the Edit menu. The menu command uses the letter *D* as an accelerator key and places the text *Deletes the current selection* in the application's status bar. Notice in the Edit menu that the *D* is underlined in the Delete command caption.

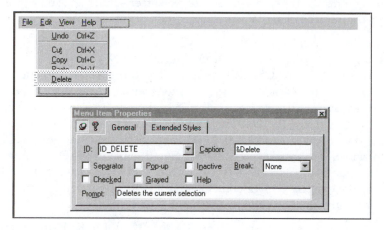

Figure 11-41   Adding a new menu command

Next, you will modify the Stock Charting program's View menu so that it includes commands to display each chart type.

To modify the Stock Charting program's View menu so that it includes commands to display each chart type:

1. First, open the **IDD_STOCKCHARTING_FORM** resource in the Dialog Editor and delete the Line Chart, Column Chart, and Scatter Chart command buttons.

2. Next, click the **ResourceView** tab in the **Workspace** window, if necessary, and then expand the **Menu** folder. Double-click the **IDR_MAINFRAME** resource ID to display the menu in the Menu Editor.

3. Expand the **View** menu in the Menu Editor and click the empty box at the bottom of the menu. Display the object's Properties window and click the **Separator** check box. The Separator check box adds a visual element to menus that groups related commands. After you click the Separator check box, a new empty box appears at the bottom of the View menu.

4. Click the new empty box at the bottom of the View menu and display its Properties window. In the ID drop-down list box, type **ID_DRAW_LINE_CHART** as the menu command's resource ID. Type a caption of **&Line Chart** and add a prompt of **Displays the line chart**.

11

5. Click the new empty box at the bottom of the View menu and display its Properties window. In the ID drop-down list box, type **ID_DRAW_COLUMN_CHART** as the menu command's resource ID. Type a caption of **&Column Chart** and add a prompt of **Displays the column chart**.

6. Click the new empty box at the bottom of the View menu and display its Properties window. In the ID drop-down list box, type **ID_DRAW_SCATTER_CHART** as the menu command's ID. Type a caption of **Sc&atter Chart** and add a prompt of **Displays the scatter chart**. When you are finished, press **Enter**.

7. Use ClassWizard to map the COMMAND messages for the ID_DRAW_LINE_CHART, ID_DRAW_COLUMN_CHART, and ID_DRAW_SCATTER_CHART resource IDs to the handler functions you created earlier for the command buttons. After you start ClassWizard, be sure that the **CStockChartingView** class is selected in the Class name combo box. For the line chart, click the **ID_DRAW_LINE_CHART** resource ID in the Object ID's list and then click the **COMMAND** message in the Messages list. Click the **Add Function** button and accept the suggested name of **OnDrawLineChart** for the function name. The ID_DRAW_LINE_CHART resource ID will be mapped to the existing OnDrawLineChart() function, that you created earlier. Repeat these steps for the column chart and scatter chart.

8. Finally, delete the existing message maps for the BN_CLICKED functions—you will not need them anymore since you have deleted the command buttons with which they were associated. You delete an existing message map by clicking on an item in the Member functions list at the bottom of the Message Maps tab in ClassView, and then by clicking the **Delete Function** button.

 As you delete a message map, you will receive an ominous message warning you that you must manually remove the implementation of the associated function. DO NOT manually remove the functions since you have associated them with COMMAND messages for the menu commands. Click Yes to continue.

9. Click **OK** to close Class Wizard.

10. Rebuild and execute the program. Test the new commands and see if they open each of the chart types correctly. Make sure the status bar text and accelerator commands function correctly.

11. Close the Stock Charting program window.

TOOLBARS AND BUTTONS

Menus and toolbars are closely related. In fact, a menu is a special type of a toolbar. Instead of having text commands like menus, however, toolbars execute commands using graphical icons known as **buttons**. When you work with toolbars, you assign resource IDs to toolbar buttons, and then use COMMAND messages to map each button to a handler function. This procedure is almost identical to how you map menu commands to handler functions. The main difference is that a menu is text based, while a toolbar is graphical.

You design and edit toolbars in Visual C++ using the Toolbar Editor. If you click the ResourceView tab in the Workspace window and expand the Toolbar folder, you will see the IDR_MAINFRAME resource. This is the same resource ID used by the menu resource. If you open the IDR_MAINFRAME resource in the Toolbar Editor, you will see several buttons already created for you, such as the Edit and Paste buttons. Buttons such as the Edit and Paste buttons execute the exact same commands as their counterparts on the Edit menu. Figure 11-42 shows an example of the toolbar resource in the Toolbar Editor.

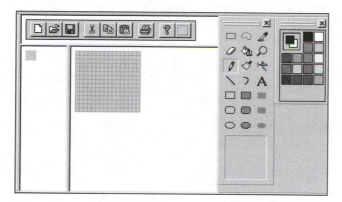

Figure 11-42 Toolbar Editor

At the far right of the toolbar is an empty button that you use to design a new button. The left portion of the Toolbar Editor, beneath the toolbar itself, displays a preview of the button you are editing. To the right of the preview window is where you design the button. Notice that the Toolbar Editor includes graphic controls and a color palette that you can use to design toolbar buttons. When you design a button, you color in the individual pixels that make up the button. You can see the individual pixels for the empty toolbar button in the preview window in Figure 11-42. By default, the New button appears when you first open the Toolbar Editor. You can edit another existing button by clicking it to display it in the editing area. Once you have created a new button or edited an existing button, you use the Properties window to set the button elements, the same as for menus and commands. After associating a button with a resource ID, you can use a COMMAND message and an associated message handler function to execute the functionality required by the button.

 You can move a button on the toolbar by clicking it with your left mouse button and dragging it to a new position while holding the left mouse button down. To delete an existing button, click and hold your left mouse button over the button you want to delete, drag the button off the toolbar, and then release your mouse button.

When you move your mouse over a toolbar button, many applications display a prompt in the status bar, the same as when you highlight a menu command. You use the Prompt text box in the Properties window to set the text you want displayed in the status bar for any toolbar buttons, the same as for menu commands. Although toolbars and buttons do not use accelerator keys, they usually have an associated ToolTip. As you should know, a ToolTip is a short description that appears when you hold your pointer over a button. You create a ToolTip by appending to the status bar text a \n and the text you want displayed in the ToolTip. Figure 11-43 shows an example of the Properties window for a new Delete button. The text in the Prompt edit box is *Deletes the current selection\nDelete*. This sets the status bar text to *Deletes the current selection* and the ToolTip to *Delete*.

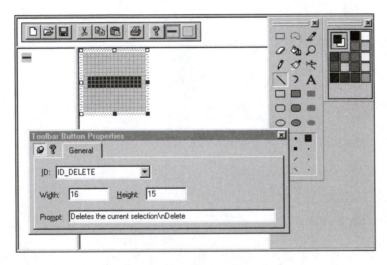

Figure 11-43   Toolbar button Properties window

Next, you will add to the Stock Charting program toolbar buttons that display the different chart types.

To add to the Stock Charting program toolbar buttons that display the different chart types:

1. Click on the **ResourceView** tab in the **Workspace** window, and then expand the **Toolbar** folder. Double-click the **IDR_MAINFRAME** resource ID to display the toolbar in the Toolbar Editor.

2. The New button should be highlighted when you first open the Toolbar Editor. Click the empty button at the far right of the toolbar, and use Figure 11-44 as a model to design a button that displays the line chart.

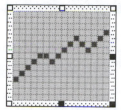

Figure 11-44   Line chart button

3. When you are finished designing the line chart button, display its Properties window. In the ID drop-down list box, select the **ID_DRAW_LINE_CHART** resource ID that you created earlier. Replace the default text that appears in the Prompt edit box with **Displays the line chart\nLine Chart**.

4. Click the new empty button at the far right of the toolbar and design a button for the column chart, using Figure 11-45 as a model.

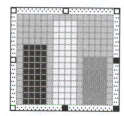

Figure 11-45   Column chart button

5. When you are finished designing the column chart button, display its Properties window. In the ID drop-down list box, select the **ID_DRAW_COLUMN_CHART** resource ID that you created earlier. Enter **Displays the column chart\nColumn Chart** in the Prompt edit box for the status bar and ToolTip text.

6. Click the new empty button at the far right of the toolbar and design a button for the scatter chart, using Figure 11-46 as a model.

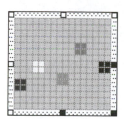

Figure 11-46   Scatter chart button

7. When you are finished designing the scatter chart button, display its Properties window. In the ID drop-down list box, select the **ID_DRAW_SCATTER_CHART**

11

resource ID that you created earlier. Enter **Displays the scatter chart\nScatter Chart** in the Prompt edit box for the status bar and ToolTip text.

8. Rebuild and execute the program. Test the new toolbar buttons and see if they open each of the chart types correctly. Make sure the status bar prompts and the ToolTips for each button function correctly.

 Since toolbar buttons execute the same COMMAND message that menu commands do, you only need one message map function to handle the functionality of a menu command and toolbar button that share the same resource ID. Since you already created COMMAND message maps for the resource IDs when you created the menu commands, you do not need to add any new message maps after creating the toolbar buttons.

9. Close the Stock Charting program window.

CHAPTER SUMMARY

- You refer to a particular piece of computer hardware, such as a monitor or printer, as a device.

- A device driver is what allows the Windows operating system to communicate with a particular device.

- The graphics device interface, or GDI, manages communication with different types of Windows graphical device drivers.

- A device context is a Windows GDI data structure that stores information about the text and graphics displayed by an application.

- The CDC class is the base class for device context classes.

- A mapping mode is a coordinate system that determines the units and scaling orientation in a device context. The default mapping mode is MM_TEXT.

- If you want to change the mapping mode in your application, you execute the SetMapMode() function of the CDC class.

- Graphical computer systems, such as Windows, use the red, green, blue, or RGB, color system for specifying colors.

- You create individual colors in the RGB color system using the RGB() macro. The color created with an RGB() macro is sometimes referred to as an RGB triplet.

- You can declare your own color variable using the Win32 COLORREF data type.

- The WM_PAINT message informs an application that its window must be redrawn, or repainted.

❑ The message handler function for the WM_PAINT message is named OnPaint(), and is inherited from the CWnd class.

❑ You use the OnDraw() function, which is inherited from the CView base class, to manage an application's device context.

❑ You use the pDC pointer as a handle for accessing the application's device context.

❑ The Invalidate() function notifies the update region that the window needs to be erased.

❑ The update region identifies portions of a window that need to be repainted.

❑ The enumerated, or enum, data type allows you to create a variable to which only a series of predefined constant values can be assigned.

❑ You use the LineTo() function to draw lines in the device context.

❑ The current position is the starting point for any line- or curve-drawing function.

❑ You use the MoveTo() function to manually change the current position.

❑ You draw rectangles in a device context with the Rectangle() function.

❑ You use the Ellipse() function to draw ovals and circles in a device context.

❑ The bounding rectangle determines the height and width of an ellipse.

❑ To create a perfect circle, the height and width of an ellipse's bounding box must be equal.

❑ You add text to the device context using the TextOut() function.

❑ The SetTextAlign() function sets the horizontal text alignment for text objects.

❑ The SetTextColor() function sets the color of any text objects displayed with the TextOut() function.

❑ Any TextOut() statements that follow a SetTextColor() function will use that SetTextColor() function's color setting until another SetTextColor() function is called in the code.

❑ A pen is an object created with the CPen class that determines a line's style, thickness, and color.

❑ The CreatePen() function initializes a new pen with style, width, and color values.

❑ The SelectObject() function loads an object into the device context.

❑ The pen you last applied to the device context using the SelectObject() function will be used for all line drawing until you select a new pen into the device context.

❑ A brush is an object created with the CBrush class that determines the color and pattern that is drawn in the interior of a closed object.

11

❑ The brush you last applied to the device context using the SelectObject() function will be used for all fills until you select a new brush into the device context.

❑ You design and edit menus in Visual C++ using the Menu Editor.

❑ An accelerator key is an underlined character in a menu or command caption that defines a keystroke sequence that you can use to open a menu or select a command without using your mouse.

❑ Toolbars execute commands using graphical icons known as buttons.

❑ You design and edit toolbars in Visual C++ using the Toolbar Editor.

❑ You create a ToolTip by appending to the status bar text a \n and the text you want displayed in the ToolTip.

REVIEW QUESTIONS

1. In Windows terminology, you refer to a particular piece of computer hardware, such as a monitor or printer, as a(n) _____.

   a. implement

   b. appliance

   c. tool

   d. device

2. The Windows operating system communicates with its computer hardware using a _____.

   a. hardware operator

   b. transmission facilitator

   c. communicator

   d. device driver

3. What does GDI stand for?

   a. Good Development Initiative

   b. Graphics Device Interface

   c. General Documentation Information

   d. Geared Delivery Integrator

4. What is the device context?

   a. An MFC dynamic link library

   b. A Visual C++ program

   c. A Windows GDI data structure

   d. A Windows API function call

5. What is the base class for device context classes?

a. CDC

b. CClientDC

c. CPaintDC

d. CWindowDC

6. What is the CDC object pointer in the OnDraw() function used for?

a. To perform serialization for graphical objects

b. To store information for a derived CDocument class

c. To directly add and modify drawing information in the device context

d. The OnDraw() function does not contain a CDC object pointer

7. What is the default mapping mode?

a. MM_TWIPS

b. MM_TEXT

c. MM_LOENGLISH

d. MM_HIENGLISH

8. Where is the point of origin for all mapping modes?

a. The upper-left corner of the screen or window

b. The upper-right corner of the screen or window

c. The lower-left corner of the screen or window

d. The lower-right corner of the screen or window

9. Which of the following RGB() macros returns the full intensity of the color blue?

a. RGB(255, 0, 0)

b. RGB(0, 255, 0)

c. RGB(255, 0, 255)

d. RGB(0, 0, 255)

10. Which of the following RGB() macros returns the color black?

a. RGB(0, 0, 0)

b. RGB(255, 255, 255)

c. RGB(0, 255, 0)

d. RGB(128, 128, 128)

11. What is the correct Win32 data type that you use to declare your own color variable?

a. COLOR

b. COLORRGB

c. COLORPRIMARY

d. COLORREF

11

12. Which of the following messages informs an application that its window needs to be redrawn?

   a. PAINT

   b. WM_PAINT

   c. DRAW

   d. REDRAW

13. The _____ function notifies the update region that the window needs to be erased.

   a. Validate()

   b. Invalidate()

   c. Clear()

   d. OnPaint()

14. What is the correct syntax for drawing a line from the current position of 0, 0 to 100, 50?

   a. LineTo(100, 50)

   b. pDC.LineTo(100, 50)

   c. pDC->LineTo(100, 50)

   d. pDC->LineTo(0, 0, 100, 50)

15. Which of the following functions do you use to move the current position?

   a. MoveTo()

   b. CurrentPosition()

   c. GetPosition()

   d. SetPosition()

16. You draw rectangles into the device context using the _____ function.

   a. Rect()

   b. Rectangle()

   c. Polygon()

   d. Square()

17. You use the _____ function to draw ovals and circles in a device context.

   a. Circle()

   b. Oval()

   c. Round()

   d. Ellipse()

18. How do you set the size of an oval or circle?

    a. By setting the height and width of its bounding rectangle

    b. By passing a starting position, along with the oval or circle's circumference

    c. By passing the object's center point, along with its radius. For ovals, you must also pass an array containing x, y pairs representing the dimensions of the oval's curvature

    d. By passing eight x, y pairs representing equal positions on the oval or circle's circumference

19. You add text to the device context using the _____ function.

    a. Print()

    b. Write()

    c. Text()

    d. TextOut()

20. The _____ function sets the horizontal text alignment for text objects.

    a. TextAlign()

    b. SetTextAlign()

    c. Justify()

    d. Align()

21. Which of the following values do you use with the correct function for horizontal text alignment to align a text object within the center of its bounding rectangle?

    a. 3

    b. CENTER

    c. ALIGN_CENTER

    d. TA_CENTER

22. Which of the following functions sets the color of text objects?

    a. Color()

    b. TextColor()

    c. SetTextColor()

    d. Foreground()

23. Which is the correct syntax for declaring a pen object named curPen that is two pixels wide, dashed, and red?

    a. `CPen curPen(PS_DASH, 2, RGB(255, 0, 0));`

    b. `CPen variable(2, PS_DASH, RGB(255, 0, 0));`

    c. `CPen variable(RGB(255, 0, 0), 2, PS_DASH);`

    d. `CPen variable(2, RGB(255, 0, 0), PS_DASH);`

11

24. The _____ function selects an object into the device context.

    a. DCObject()

    b. SetObject()

    c. GetObject()

    d. SelectObject()

25. What is the correct syntax to create a black brush named hatchBrush with an HS_CROSS pattern?

    a. `CBrush hatchBrush(HS_CROSS);`

    b. `CBrush hatchBrush(HS_CROSS, RGB(0, 0, 0));`

    c. `CBrush hatchBrush(RGB(0, 0, 0), HS_CROSS);`

    d. `CBrush hatchBrush(RGB(0, 0, 0), HS_CROSS, TRUE);`

26. Which special character do you use in the Prompt box for a menu or command resource to designate a character in a text string as the menu or command's accelerator key?

    a. @

    b. &

    c. %

    d. #

27. What special character(s) do you use to separate status bar text from ToolTip text in the Prompt box of a toolbar button's Properties window?

    a. &

    b. $

    c. \n

    d. /t

28. Which message is generated by both menu commands and toolbar buttons?

    a. BN_CLICKED

    b. WM_PAINT

    c. COMMAND

    d. EN_CHANGE

EXERCISES

1. Use LineTo() and MoveTo() functions to create a drawing program that displays your initials in large block letters.

2. Modify the line chart of the Stock Charting program so that each line segment is connected by a solid black circle.

3. Study the CFonts topic and the Text and Fonts topic in the MSDN Library to learn how to manipulate the typefaces displayed by text objects. Modify the axis labels in the Stock Charting program so that they use a serif typeface such as Times New Roman.

4. Add text labels for each stock value in the Stock Charting program that appear above the appropriate element in each chart. For example, if the Monday stock value is 80, then add a text object above the Monday column in the column chart that reads *$80*.

5. Add an overlay chart to the Stock Charting program. An overlay chart combines both a column chart and a line chart.

6. Modify the brush for the column chart of the Stock Chart program so that each column uses a different pattern.

7. Add a bar chart to the Stock Charting program. A bar chart differs from a column chart in that each rectangle increases in value from left to right instead of from bottom to top as do column charts. Since the scale for a bar chart progresses from left to right, so you will need to create a new coordinate system for the bar chart's grid.

8. Add controls to the Stock Chart program that you can use to compare two stock values. In other words, you will want to display the values for two stocks simultaneously in the Stock Charting program. Modify the line, column, and scatter charts so that they display both sets of values. Use a single color on the charts for each stock, such as a blue line for one stock and a red line for another stock. As another example, make all of the columns of the column chart for the first stock blue and make all of the columns for the second stock red.

9. Create a program that draws different types of objects based on a selection the user makes in an Objects menu, or by clicking a toolbar button. Study the CDC class's member functions and include other object types in addition to the lines, rectangles, and ellipses you studied in this chapter. Create two additional menus: Lines and Fills. On the Lines menu, allow the user to select different line styles, sizes, and colors for the displayed object. On the Fills menu, allow the user to select different patterns and colors for the selected object.

10. You may have seen menu commands that include a check mark when that command's feature is currently active. You add a check mark next to a menu item using the SetCheck() function of the CCmdUI class along with the ON_UPDATE_COMMAND_UI message handler. Search the MSDN Library for information on these topics and see if you can add a check mark next to the currently visible chart in the View menu of the Stock Charting program.

11

CHAPTER
12

CONNECTING TO DATABASES

In this chapter you will learn:

- About basic database structure
- About database management systems
- About structured query language
- How to connect to databases with MFC
- How to link dialog controls to database fields
- How to sort and filter records
- How to add and delete records

PREVIEW: THE LIBRARY DATABASE PROGRAM

In this chapter, you will work with a Library Database application that demonstrates how to use MFC to access databases. The Library Database application stores information about fiction and nonfiction books, including the book title, author name, and publisher. Although the program is fairly simple, it demonstrates how you could write a much larger program that might actually be used by a library, for a corporate documentation database, or as an order entry database for a book vendor.

To preview the Library Database application:

1. Create a **Chapter.12** folder in your Visual C++ Projects folder.

2. Copy the **Chapter12_LibraryDatabase** folder from the Chapter.12 folder on your Data Disk to the Chapter.12 folder in your Visual C++ Projects folder, and then open the LibraryDatabase project in Visual C++.

3. Click the **FileView** tab in the Workspace window and expand the Source Files folder. The project contains several classes with which you are familiar, including an application class, a frame class, a view class, and a document class. The project also contains a class named CLibraryDatabaseSet, which is used for managing the information in a database.

4. Open the **LibraryDatabaseSet.cpp** file in the Text Editor window. If you scroll through the file, you will see some typical MFC functions. You will also see a DoFieldExchange() function, which is used for exchanging data between data members in the view class and records in the database. Figure 12-1 shows the LibraryDatabaseSet.cpp file's DoFieldExchange() function.

```
void CLibraryDatabaseSet::DoFieldExchange(CFieldExchange* pFX)
{
    //{{AFX_FIELD_MAP(CLibraryDatabaseSet)
    pFX->SetFieldType(CFieldExchange::outputColumn);
    RFX_Text(pFX, _T("[BookID]"), m_BookID);
    RFX_Text(pFX, _T("[Title]"), m_Title);
    RFX_Text(pFX, _T("[Author]"), m_Author);
    RFX_Text(pFX, _T("[Publisher]"), m_Publisher);
    RFX_Int(pFX, _T("[Genre]"), m_Genre);
    RFX_Text(pFX, _T("[Description]"), m_Description);
    //}}AFX_FIELD_MAP
}
```

Figure 12-1   DoFieldExchange() function

5. You cannot build and execute the program until you configure your system to recognize the database. However, Figure 12-2 shows an example of the Library Database application window.

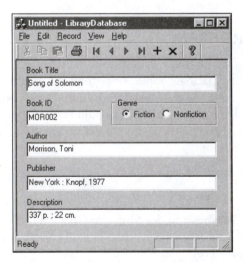

Figure 12-2   Library Database application window

The descriptions and publishing information for the records in the Library Database application were downloaded from the Library of Congress Online Catalog. If you would like to view the Library of Congress Online Catalog, visit *http://catalog.loc.gov/webvoy.htm*.

UNDERSTANDING DATABASES

The goal of this chapter is to learn how to use MFC to read, write, and modify database information. To accomplish this goal, it helps to first understand how databases work. Formally defined, a **database** is an ordered collection of information from which a computer program can quickly access information. You can probably think of many databases from your everyday life. For example, your address book is a database. So is the card file containing recipes in a kitchen. Other examples of databases include a company's employee directory and a file cabinet containing client information. Essentially, any information that can be organized into ordered sets of data, then quickly retrieved, can be considered a database. A collection of hundreds of baseball cards thrown into a shoebox is not a database, since an individual card cannot be quickly or easily retrieved (except by luck). However, if the baseball card collection was organized in binders by team, and then further organized according to each player's field position or batting average, then it could be considered a database since you could quickly locate a specific card.

The information stored in computer databases is actually stored in tables similar to spreadsheets. Each row in a database table is called a record. A **record** in a database contains a single complete set of related information. Each recipe in a recipe database, for instance, is a single database record. Each column in a database table is called a field. **Fields** are the individual pieces of information stored in a record. Examples of fields that might exist in a recipe database include ingredients, cooking time, cooking temperature, and so on. Database fields are created using data types, the same as C++ variables. In fact, the data types of many database programs are very similar to C++ data types. For instance, common data types that are found in many databases include string, integer, floating-point, and Boolean.

To summarize, you can think of databases as consisting of tables, which consist of records, which consist of fields. Figure 12-3 shows an example of an employee directory for programmers at an application development company. The database consists of five records, one for each employee. Each record consists of seven fields: Last_Name, First_Name, Address, City, State, Zip, and Extension.

Last_Name	First_Name	Address	City	State	Zip	Extension
Blair	Dennis	204 Spruce Lane	Brookfield	MA	01506	x305
Hernandez	Louis	68 Boston Post Road	Spencer	MA	01562	x412
Miller	Erica	271 Baker Hill Road	E. Brookfield	MA	01515	x291
Morinaga	Scott	17 Ashley Road	N. Brookfield	MA	01535	x177
Picard	Raymond	1113 Oakham Road	New Braintree	MA	01531	x213

Figure 12-3   Employee directory database

The database in Figure 12-3 is an example of a flat-file database, one of the simplest types of databases. A **flat-file database** stores information in a single table. For simple collections of information, flat-file databases are usually adequate. With large and complex collections of information, flat-file databases can become unwieldy. A better solution for large and complex databases is a relational database. A **relational database** stores information across multiple related tables. Although you will not actually work with a relational database in this chapter, understanding how they work is helpful since relational databases are among the most common in use today.

Two other types of database systems you may encounter are hierarchical databases and network databases.

Relational databases consist of one or more related tables. In fact, large relational databases can consist of dozens or hundreds of related tables. Although relational databases may consist of many tables, you create relationships within the database by working with two tables at a time. One table in a relationship is always considered to be the primary table, while the other table is considered to be the related table. A **primary table** is the main table in a relationship that is referenced by another table. A **related**, or **child table** references a primary table in a relational database. Tables in a relationship are connected using primary and foreign keys. A **primary key** is a field that contains a unique identifier for each record in a primary table. A **foreign key** is a field in a related table that refers to the primary key in a primary table. Primary and foreign keys are what link records across multiple tables in a relational database.

There are three basic types of relationships within a relational database: one-to-one, one-to-many, and many-to-many. A **one-to-one relationship** exists between two tables when a related table contains exactly one record for each record in the primary table. You create one-to-one relationships when you want to break information into multiple, logical sets. It is important to understand that information in the tables in a one-to-one relationship can usually be placed within a single table. However, you may want to break the information into multiple tables to better organize the information into logical sets. Another reason for using one-to-one relationships is that they allow you to make the information in one of the tables confidential and accessible only by certain individuals. For example, you might want to create a personnel table that contains basic information about an employee, similar to the information in the table in Figure 12-3. Yet, you might also want to create a payroll table that contains confidential information about each employee's salary, benefits, and other types of compensation, and that can be accessed only by the Human Resources and Accounting departments. Figure 12-4 shows two tables, Employees and Payroll, with a one-to-one relationship. The primary table is the employee information table from Figure 12-3. The related table is a payroll table that contains confidential salary and compensation information. Notice that each table contains identical numbers of records; one record in the primary table corresponds to one record in the related table. The relationship is achieved by adding a primary key to the Employees table and a foreign key to the Payroll table.

Employees table

ID	Last_Name	First_Name	Address	City	State	Zip	Extension
101	Blair	Dennis	204 Spruce Lane	Brookfield	MA	01506	x305
102	Hernandez	Louis	68 Boston Post Road	Spencer	MA	01562	x412
103	Miller	Erica	271 Baker Hill Road	E. Brookfield	MA	01515	x291
104	Morinaga	Scott	17 Ashley Road	N. Brookfield	MA	01535	x177
105	Picard	Raymond	1113 Oakham Road	New Braintree	MA	01531	x213

Payroll table

ID	Start_Date	Pay_Rate	Health_Coverage	Year_Vested	401K
101	1998	$21.25	No Coverage	NA	No
102	1993	$28.00	Family Plan	1998	Yes
103	1996	$24.50	Individual	NA	Yes
104	1991	$36.00	Family Plan	1996	Yes
105	1992	$31.00	Individual	1997	Yes

Figure 12-4   One-to-one relationship

A **one-to-many relationship** exists in a relational database when one record in a primary table has many related records in a related table. You create a one-to-many relationship in order to eliminate redundant information in a single table. Primary and foreign keys are the only pieces of information in a relational database table that should be duplicated. Breaking tables into multiple related tables in order to reduce redundant and duplicate information is called **normalization**. The elimination of redundant information (normalization) reduces the size of a database and makes the data easier to work with. For example, consider the table in Figure 12-5. The table lists each programmer's primary and other programming languages. Notice that each programmer's name is repeated for each programming language with which he or she is familiar. This repetition is an example of redundant information that can occur in a single table.

ID	Last_Name	First_Name	Programming_Language
101	Blair	Dennis	C
101	Blair	Dennis	C++
102	Hernandez	Louis	C
102	Hernandez	Louis	C++
102	Hernandez	Louis	Fortran
103	Miller	Erica	C
103	Miller	Erica	C++
103	Miller	Erica	Fortran
103	Miller	Erica	Java
104	Morinaga	Scott	C
104	Morinaga	Scott	Fortran
104	Morinaga	Scott	Java
105	Picard	Raymond	C
105	Picard	Raymond	Fortran

Figure 12-5   Table with redundant information

A one-to-many relationship provides a more efficient and less redundant method of storing this information in a database. Figure 12-6 shows the same information organized into a one-to-many relationship.

12

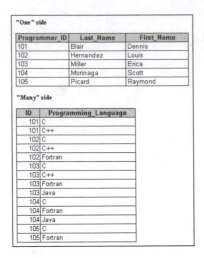

"One" side

Programmer_ID	Last_Name	First_Name
101	Blair	Dennis
102	Hernandez	Louis
103	Miller	Erica
104	Morinaga	Scott
105	Picard	Raymond

"Many" side

ID	Programming_Language
101	C
101	C++
102	C
102	C++
102	Fortran
103	C
103	C++
103	Fortran
103	Java
104	C
104	Fortran
104	Java
105	C
105	Fortran

Figure 12-6   One-to-many relationship

The "many" side of a one-to-many relationship is sometimes used as the primary table. In these cases, the relationship is often referred to as a many-to-one relationship.

Although Figure 12-6 is an example of a one-to-many relationship, the tables are not normalized since the Programming Language field contains duplicate values. Recall that primary and foreign keys are the only pieces of information in a relational database that should be duplicated. To further reduce repetition, you could organize the "many" table in Figure 12-6 into another one-to-many relationship. However, a better choice is to create a many-to-many relationship. A **many-to-many relationship** exists in a relational database when many records in one table are related to many records in another table. Consider the relationship between programmers and programming languages. Each programmer can work with many programming languages, while each programming language can be used by many programmers. To create a many-to-many relationship, you must use a junction table since most relational database systems cannot work directly with many-to-many relationships. A **junction table** creates a one-to-many relationship for each of the two tables in a many-to-many relationship. A junction table contains foreign keys from the two tables in a many-to-many relationship, along with any other fields that correspond to a many-to-many relationship. Figure 12-7 contains an example of a many-to-many relationship between a Programmers table and a Programming Languages table. The Programmers table contains a primary key named Programmer_ID, and the Programming Languages table contains a primary key named Language_ID. A junction table named Programming Experience contains two foreign keys corresponding to the Programmer_ID primary key in the Programmers table, and to the Language_ID in the Programming Languages table. The Programming Experience junction table also contains a field named Years_Experience. You add records to the Programming Experience junction table to build a list of the years that each programmer has been working with a particular programming language.

Programmers table

Programmer_ID	Last_Name	First_Name
101	Blair	Dennis
102	Hernandez	Louis
103	Miller	Erica
104	Morinaga	Scott
105	Picard	Raymond

Programming Languages table

Language_ID	Programming_Language
10	C
11	C++
12	Fortran
13	Java

Programming Experience junction table

Programmer_ID	Language_ID	Years_Experience
101	10	5
101	11	4
102	10	3
102	11	2
102	12	3
103	10	2
104	12	3
104	13	5
105	11	3

Figure 12-7   Many-to-many relationship

Database Management Systems

With a grasp of basic database design, you can now begin to consider how to create and manipulate databases. An application or collection of applications used to create, access, and manage a database is called a **database management system**, or **DBMS**. Database management systems run on many different platforms, ranging from personal computers, to client-server systems, to mainframes. Different database management systems exist for different types of database formats. A database management system that stores data in a flat-file format is called a **flat-file database management system**. A database management system that stores data in a relational format is called a **relational database management system**, or **RDBMS**. Other types of database management systems include hierarchical and network database management systems. Some of the more popular relational database management systems you may have heard of include Oracle, Sybase, Informix, and DB2 for mainframes, and Access, FoxPro, and Paradox for PCs.

Database management systems perform many of the same functions as other types of applications you might have worked with, such as word processing and spreadsheet programs. For example, database management systems create new database files and contain interfaces that allow users to enter and manipulate data. One of the most important functions of a database management system is the structuring and preservation of the database file's structure. Additionally, a database management system must ensure that data is stored correctly in a database's tables, regardless of the database format (flat-file, relational, hierarchical, or network). In relational databases, the database management system ensures that the appropriate information is entered according to the relationship structure in the database tables. Many DBMS systems also have security features that can be used to restrict user access to specific types of data.

Two other important aspects of database management systems are their querying and reporting capabilities. A **query** is a structured set of instructions and criteria for retrieving, adding, modifying, and deleting database information. A **report** is the formatted, printed output of a database table or the results of a query. Most database management systems use a **data manipulation language**, or **DML**, for creating queries. Different database management systems support different data manipulation languages. However, **structured query language**, or **SQL** (pronounced like the word *sequel*), has become somewhat of a standard data manipulation language among many database management systems.

12

Many database management systems make it easier for users to create queries by hiding the data manipulation language behind a user interface. Figure 12-8 shows an example of Access's query design screen. Users can create queries by dragging fields from the table objects in the upper portion of the screen to the criteria grid in the bottom portion of the screen. Behind the scenes, Access creates the SQL code shown in Figure 12-9. SQL is Access's data manipulation language.

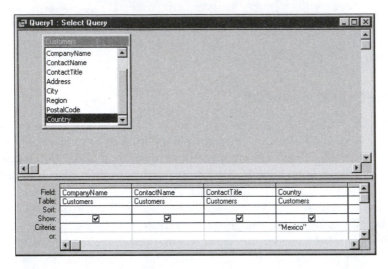

Figure 12-8   Access query design screen

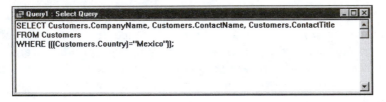

Figure 12-9   Access SQL code

Although working with an interface to design queries is fine for end users, to programmatically manipulate the data in a database, you must learn the database management system's data manipulation language. For example, when accessing databases with MFC, you must use a data manipulation language. Because SQL is the underlying data manipulation language for many database management systems, you will learn more about SQL later in this section so that you can better understand how MFC communicates with database management systems.

 Many database management systems also use a data definition language, or DDL, for creating databases, tables, fields, and other components of a database.

It is important to understand that even though many database management systems support the same database format (flat–file, relational, hierarchical, or network), each database management system is an individual application that creates its own proprietary file types. For example, even though Access and Paradox are both relational database management systems, Access creates its database files in a proprietary format with an extension of .mdb, while Paradox creates its database files in a proprietary format with an extension .db. Although both Paradox and Access contain filters that allow you to import each other's file formats, the database files are not completely interchangeable between the two programs. This situation occurs for most database management systems: They can *import* each other's file formats, but they cannot directly *read* each other's files.

In today's environment, it is often necessary for an application, such as an MFC program, to access multiple databases created in different database management systems. For example, a company may need an MFC application that simultaneously accesses a large legacy database written in dBase and a newer database written in Oracle. Converting the large dBase database to Oracle would be cost-prohibitive. On the other hand, the company cannot continue using the older dBase database since its needs have grown beyond the older database's capabilities. Still, the company must be able to access the data in both systems. To allow easy access to data in various database formats, Microsoft came up with the open database connectivity standard. **Open database connectivity**, or **ODBC**, allows applications that are written to comply with the ODBC standard to access any data source for which there is an ODBC driver. ODBC uses SQL commands (known as ODBC SQL) to allow an ODBC-compliant application to access a database. Essentially, an ODBC application connects to a database for which there is an ODBC driver and then executes ODBC SQL commands. Then, the ODBC driver translates the SQL commands into a format that the database can understand.

12

Structured Query Language

IBM invented SQL in the 1970s as a way of querying databases for specific criteria. Since then, SQL has been adopted by numerous database management systems running on mainframes, minicomputers, and PCs. In 1986 the American National Standards Institute (ANSI) approved an official standard for the SQL language. In 1991 The X/Open and SQL Access Group created a standardized version of SQL known as the Common Applications Environment (CAE) SQL draft specification. Even with two major standards available, however, most database management systems use their own version of the SQL language. ODBC SQL corresponds with the X/Open and SQL Access Group's CAE SQL draft specification. Therefore, an ODBC driver for a specific database management system must support ODBC SQL.

 If you ever work directly with an individual database management system, keep in mind that the ODBC SQL you learn in this chapter may not correspond directly to that database management system's version of SQL.

SQL uses fairly easy-to-understand statements to execute database commands. SQL statements are composed of keywords that perform actions on a database. Figure 12-10 lists several SQL keywords that are common to most versions of SQL.

Keyword	Description
FROM	Specifies the tables from which to retrieve or delete records
SELECT	Returns information from a table
WHERE	Specifies the conditions that must be met for records to be returned from a query
ORDER BY	Sorts the records returned from a table
INSERT	Inserts a new row into a table
INTO	Determines the table into which records should be inserted
DELETE	Deletes a row from a table
UPDATE	Saves changes to fields in a record

Figure 12-10   Common SQL keywords

The simple SQL statement SELECT * FROM Programmers selects all records (using the asterisk * wildcard) from the Programmers table. The following code shows a more complex SQL statement that selects the Last_Name and First_Name fields from the Programmers table if the record's City field is equal to Spencer. The results are then sorted by the Last_Name and First_Name fields using the ORDER BY keyword.

```
SELECT Last_Name, First_Name FROM Programmers
WHERE City = "Spencer" ORDER BY Last_Name, First_Name
```

SQL table or field names that include spaces are enclosed in brackets. For example, if the Last_Name and First_Name field names in the preceding code included spaces instead of underscore characters, you would write the statement as follows:

```
SELECT [Last Name], [First Name] FROM [Programmers]
WHERE [City] = "Spencer" ORDER BY [Last Name], [First Name]
```

By default, the framework automatically places brackets around field names, even if they do not include spaces. For this reason, in any SQL statements you see in this chapter, brackets surround table and field names.

The MFC framework handles much of the work involved in assembling an SQL string. Therefore, for basic MFC database programs, you do not usually need to use any full SQL statements such as SELECT * FROM [Programmers]. However, you do need to understand how an SQL statement works since you will often need to define the parts of an SQL statement. Additionally, certain operations involving databases require that you write your own SQL statements. For example, later in this chapter you will learn how to narrow the record set returned from a database using the inherited m_strFilter data member. You must assign SQL statements to the m_strFilter data member using a statement similar to the following:

```
m_strFilter = "[Programming_Language] = 'C' OR 'C++'";
```

Refer to the MSDN Library for comprehensive information on ODBC SQL.

CONNECTING TO DATABASES WITH MFC

You connect to databases with MFC using ODBC or Data Access Objects. You have already learned that ODBC allows applications that are written to comply with the ODBC standard to access any data source for which there is an ODBC driver. **Data Access Objects**, or **DAO**, is a set of classes that provide access to databases created with the Microsoft Jet (for *Joint engine technology)* database engine. The **Jet database engine** is a DBMS technology that Microsoft Access uses to interact with and manipulate the database files (with an extension of .mdb) it creates. Because the Jet database engine does most of the work in Access, you will often see Access databases referred to as Jet databases. DAO allows programming tools such as Visual Basic to directly interact with Access (Jet) databases through the Jet database engine.

You can also use DAO to access ODBC-compliant databases. However, using DAO to access ODBC-compliant databases adds an additional processing layer to your program, as shown in Figure 12-11. For complex applications, the additional ODBC layer may cause your program to run slower than database applications that directly use ODBC to access ODBC-compliant databases. To state the concept illustrated in Figure 12-11 more simply, DAO needs ODBC to access ODBC-compliant databases, but ODBC does not need DAO to access ODBC-compliant databases.

12

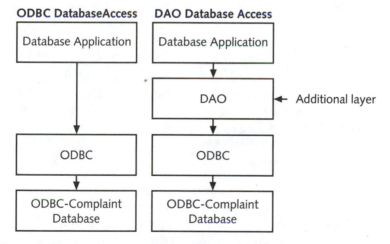

Figure 12-11   Additional layer involved when using DAO to access and ODBC-compliant database

Jet and DAO, however, are much more efficient if your database application needs to work only with Access databases. ODBC can also work with Access databases since Access is ODBC-compliant, but not as efficiently as when you use DAO and the Jet database engine.

Therefore, a rough rule of thumb is to use DAO when your program needs to work only with Access databases, but use ODBC when your program needs to work with other types of ODBC-compliant databases.

Future versions of Visual C++ are also expected to support database access using ActiveX Data Objects. **ActiveX Data objects**, or **ADO**, is a Microsoft database connectivity technology that allows programming tools to access ODBC and OLE DB-compliant databases. **OLE DB** is a data source connectivity standard promoted by Microsoft as a successor to ODBC. One of the primary differences between OLE DB and ODBC is that ODBC supports access only to relational databases, while OLE DB provides access to both relational databases and non-relational data sources, such as spreadsheet programs. ADO and OLE DB are part of Microsoft's Universal Data Access strategy for providing access to data, regardless of its storage format.

While you are learning about DAO verses ODBC, you should note that Access, and another popular DBMS, Paradox, are considered to be "desktop" database applications, not suited for large, enterprise-wide database systems that companies rely on for managing their businesses. Access and Paradox have their uses—both Access and Paradox databases are fairly easy to create and manage on a small scale. For mission-critical database applications, however, most companies use professional-strength, ODBC-compliant databases such as Oracle, Sybase, or Informix. In this chapter, you will learn about the ODBC method of accessing databases with MFC so that you can study database connectivity on a professional scale.

To create an ODBC database application, you must perform the following steps:

1. Create a Data Source Name to locate and identify the database.

2. Run AppWizard to create the basic framework of an ODBC database application.

3. Add controls and code to display and manipulate the records in a database.

Next, you will learn how to create a Data Source Name to locate and identify the database and how to run AppWizard to create the basic framework of an ODBC database application. Later in this chapter, you will examine the steps involved in adding controls and code to display and manipulate the records in a database.

Creating the Data Source Name

To make it easier to access ODBC-compliant databases on 32-bit Windows operating systems, such as Windows NT and Windows 98, you create a Data Source Name to locate and identify the database. A **Data Source Name**, or **DSN**, contains configuration information that Windows operating systems use to access a particular ODBC-compliant database. The DSNs to which you can connect in a Windows environment are installed and managed using the ODBC Administrator utility in Control Panel. There are three types of DSNs: system, user, or file. The system DSN enables all users logged onto a server to access a database. A user DSN restricts database access to authorized users only. A file DSN creates a file-based data source, with an extension of .dsn, that can be shared among users. You will create a user DSN in this chapter.

To create the Library Database program, you will work with an existing Microsoft Access database named Library.mdb. Because Access databases are ODBC-compliant, you can access them in an MFC program using either ODBC or DAO. The Library.mdb database consists of a single table named Books, with a primary key named BooksID. Next, you will create a user DSN for the Library.mdb database file.

The following steps were created on a computer running Windows 98. The Control Panel options may appear different to you if you are running a different version of Windows.

To create a user DSN for the Library.mdb database file:

1. Copy the **Library.mdb** file from the Chapter.12 folder on your Data Disk to the **Chapter.12** folder in your Visual C++ Projects folder.

2. Click the Windows **Start** menu, and then select **Control Panel** from the Settings folder.

3. Depending on how your desktop is configured, click or double-click the **ODBC** icon in the Control Panel window. If you are using Windows 2000, you will need to select the **Administrative Tools** folder in Control Panel to access the **ODBC** icon.

Depending on your version of Windows, the ODBC icon in the Control Panel window may have a different caption. For example, in Windows 98, the caption for the ODBC icon reads *ODBC Data Sources (32bit)*.

12

4. In the ODBC Data Source Administrator window, select the **User DSN** tab, if necessary. Figure 12-12 shows the User DSN tab.

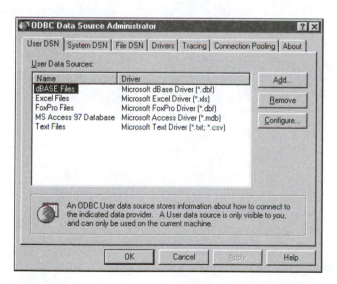

Figure 12-12   User DSN tab in the ODBC Data Source Administrator window

602   Chapter 12   Connecting to Databases

5. Click the **Add** button on the User DSN tab to display the Create New Data Source dialog box, as shown in Figure 12-13.

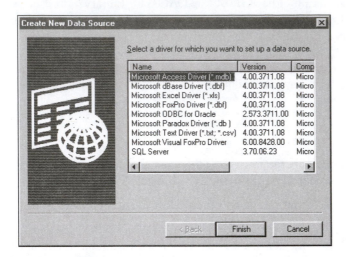

Figure 12-13   Create New Data Source dialog box

6. In the Create New Data Source dialog box window, select **Microsoft Access Driver (*.mdb)** and click the **Finish** button. The ODBC Microsoft Access Setup dialog box appears.

7. In the ODBC Microsoft Access Setup dialog box, type **Library** as the Data Source Name, and then click the **Select** button. In the Select Database dialog box that appears, select the **Library.mdb** file from the Chapter.12 folder in your Visual C++ Projects folder and click **OK**. The Select Database dialog box will close. Your ODBC Microsoft Access Setup dialog box should appear similar to Figure 12-14.

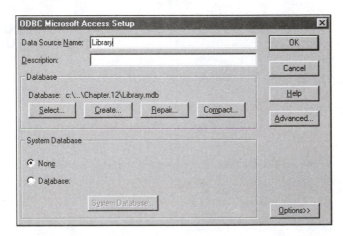

Figure 12-14   ODBC Microsoft Access Setup dialog box

8. Click **OK** to close the Microsoft Access Setup dialog box, and then click **OK** to close the ODBC Data Source Administrator window. Finally, close **Control Panel**.

Creating an ODBC Database Application

The functionality that allows MFC to access ODBC-compliant databases is contained in the classes listed in Figure 12-15. AppWizard derives classes for you from the ODBC database classes, and the framework manages almost all of the function calls and data members required to connect to an ODBC database. However, you need to understand which classes are used in an MFC ODBC database application in order to be able to customize the application for your own needs.

Class	Description
CDatabase	Manages a connection to a database
CDBException	Returns exceptions for any failures that occur when managing records in an ODBC database
CFieldExchange	Manages the exchange of data between dialog controls and their associated fields in a database record, similar to DDX which handles the exchange of values between controls and variables
CRecordset	Represents the records returned from a database
CRecordView	Displays in dialog-box controls the database records associated with a CRecordset object; derived from Cview

Figure 12-15 ODBC classes

All ODBC database applications begin with the CDatabase class. The CFieldExchange class manages the exchange of information between your application and the database. The framework hides all of the details of the CDatabase and CFieldExchange classes from you, so you will not spend any time learning about them. The framework automatically calls the CDBException class for any failures that occur when managing records in an ODBC database. The CDBException class is part of Visual C++'s exception handling capabilities. You will not explore the CDBException class since exception handling is an advanced topic, which this text does not cover.

 Exception handling is an advanced technique that allows programs to handle errors as they occur during the execution of a program.

The classes you need to explore include the CRecordSet and CRecordView classes. The CRecordset class represents records returned from a database, and the CRecordView class displays those records in a dialog-style window that you can edit with the Dialog Editor. Before you can actually display the records represented by the CRecordset class, you must add controls to the CRecordView's dialog window for each field you want to display. Then, you must bind each control to its associated fields in the database record set. You will learn how to create data-bound controls in the next section.

 The CRecordView class is very similar to the CFormView class you used in Chapter 10.

You can create two types of CRecordset objects: a snapshot or a dynaset. A **snapshot** is a static view of the records in a database. Any changes made to the database after you run your application, whether the changes are made by other users or by other CRecordset objects in your application, will not be reflected in your application's record set. In comparison, a **dynaset** is a dynamic record set that displays the most recent changes to a database each time you move from one record to another in a database application. Essentially, a snapshot queries the database only once when your application first executes. In contrast, a dynaset queries the database when an application first executes *and* each time a user moves to a different record. Snapshots are usually faster than dynasets since your application only needs to query the database once. Dynasets, however, are necessary in multi-user environments in which users need to work with a database's most current information. For example, a company may use a database to record inventory levels for items they sell. A sales associate could use the database to check if there is sufficient inventory to fill an order for a particular item, and then update the database with the current inventory level once he or she has filled the order. In order for one sales associate to see the most recent changes to inventory levels made by other sales associates, the inventory database needs to be created as a dynaset.

Because we will not use the Library Database application in a multi-user environment, you will create its CRecordset objects as a snapshot. Next, you will use AppWizard to create the Library Database project.

To use AppWizard to create the Library Database project:

1. Create a new project named **LibraryDatabase** using the MFC AppWizard (exe) option. Save the project in the **Chapter.12** folder in your Visual C++ Projects folder.

2. AppWizard executes and starts to walk you through the steps involved in creating an MFC program. In Step 1, select **Single document** from the application choices. Be sure to leave the **Document/View architecture support?** check box selected. Then click **Next**.

3. As shown in Figure 12-16, Step 2 of AppWizard prompts you for the type of database support you want in your application. The first option, *None*, creates the application without database support. The second option, *Header files only*, adds basic database support to an application, but does not create any of the database classes. If you select the *Header files only* option, then you must manually derive your own classes from the database-specific classes. The third option, *Database view*

without file support, creates an application that can read and write information to and from a database, but does not include support for additional files created with serialization. The fourth option, *Database view with file support*, creates an application that can read information from and write information to a database, and includes support for additional serialized files. Because the Library Database application does not need to work with any files other than the database itself, select **Database view without file support**, the third option and click the **Data Source** button to display the Database Options dialog box.

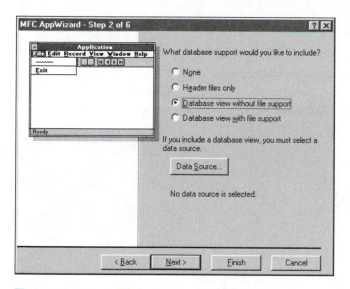

Figure 12-16 MFC AppWizard - Step 2 of 6

4. The Database Options dialog box allows you to select the type of database and the data source with which you want your database application to work. The ODBC option should be selected by default. In the drop-down list box next to the ODBC option, select **Library**, which is the DSN you created for the Library.mdb file in the previous set of steps. Also, be sure the Recordset type is set to **Snapshot**. Figure 12-17 shows how your Database Options dialog box should look. Once you are finished setting the dialog box options, click the **OK** button. After clicking the OK button, you should see the Select Database Tables dialog box.

5. The Select Database Tables dialog box allows you to select the tables from the database that you want to make available to your database application. As shown in Figure 12-18, the Library.mdb database contains a single table named Books. Click once with your mouse to select the table, and then click the **OK** button. After clicking the OK button, you will be returned to Step 2 of AppWizard. Click the **Next** button to move to Step 3.

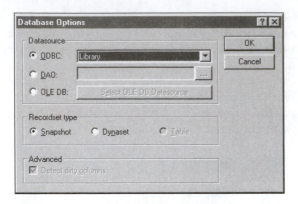

Figure 12-17   Database Options dialog box

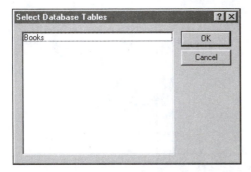

Figure 12-18   Select Database Tables dialog box

6. In Step 3, leave the compound document support option set to **None** and clear the **ActiveX Controls** checkbox. Click the **Next** button to continue.

7. Accept the default options in Steps 4, 5, and 6. When the New Project Information dialog box displays after clicking the Finish button in Step 6, click the **OK** button to create the project.

Once AppWizard finishes creating your program, open the FileView tab of the Workspace window and examine the files that were created. AppWizard should have created three classes that you are already familiar with: an application class named CLibraryDatabase, a frame class named CMainFrm, and a document class named CLibraryDatabaseDoc. AppWizard will have also created a CLibraryDatabaseSet class and a CLibraryDatabaseView class. Next, you will examine the CRecordset and CRecordView classes.

The CRecordset Class

The CRecordset class represents the records returned from a database. The CLibraryDatabaseSet class that AppWizard built for you derives from the CRecordset class. Figure 12-19 shows the CLibraryDatabaseSet class declaration file.

```
class CLibraryDatabaseSet : public CRecordset {
public:
    CLibraryDatabaseSet(CDatabase* pDatabase = NULL);
    DECLARE_DYNAMIC(CLibraryDatabaseSet)
// Field/Param Data
    //{{AFX_FIELD(CLibraryDatabaseSet, CRecordset)
    CString   m_BookID;
    CString   m_Title;
    CString   m_Author;
    CString   m_Publisher;
    int   m_Genre;
    CString   m_Description;
    //}}AFX_FIELD
// Overrides
    // ClassWizard generated virtual function overrides
    //{{AFX_VIRTUAL(CLibraryDatabaseSet)
    public:
    virtual CString GetDefaultConnect(); // Default
                                     connection string
    virtual CString GetDefaultSQL();    // default SQL
                                     for Recordset
    virtual void DoFieldExchange(CFieldExchange* pFX);
    // RFX support
    //}}AFX_VIRTUAL
// Implementation
#ifdef _DEBUG
    virtual void AssertValid() const;
    virtual void Dump(CDumpContext& dc) const;
#endif
};
```

Figure 12-19   LibraryDatabaseSet.h

One of the first things you should notice is the data member declarations that AppWizard created in the public section of the declaration file. A data member has been created that corresponds to each field in the database. Notice that for the name of each data member, AppWizard uses the name of each field in the database, prefixed with m_ to identify the variables as MFC variables. AppWizard also declares each data member using the corresponding data type for each field in the database. For example, the Author field is a text string field in the Library.mdb database. The corresponding data member in the CLibraryDatabaseSet class is named m_Author and is declared with a data type of CString using the statement: CString m_Author;. MFC handles the exchange of values between CRecordset data members and their corresponding fields in a database using a mechanism called **record field exchange**, or **RFX**. RFX is very similar to MFC's DDX mechanism, which handles the exchange of values between controls and variables. Whereas DDX uses the DoDataExchange() function to handle the exchange of values between controls and variables, RFX uses the DoFieldExchange() function to handle the exchange of values between

12

CRecordset data members and their corresponding fields in a database. You will see the following declaration for the DoFieldExchange() function in the LibraryDatabaseSet.h file:

```
virtual void DoFieldExchange(CFieldExchange* pFX);
```

In the LibraryDatabaseSet.cpp file, you will see the following definition for the DoFieldExchange() function:

```
void CLibraryDatabaseSet::DoFieldExchange(
     CFieldExchange* pFX) {
     //{{AFX_FIELD_MAP(CLibraryDatabaseSet)
     pFX->SetFieldType(CFieldExchange::outputColumn);
     RFX_Text(pFX, _T("[BookID]"), m_BookID);
     RFX_Text(pFX, _T("[Title]"), m_Title);
     RFX_Text(pFX, _T("[Author]"), m_Author);
     RFX_Text(pFX, _T("[Publisher]"), m_Publisher);
     RFX_Int(pFX, _T("[Genre]"), m_Genre);
     RFX_Text(pFX, _T("[Description]"), m_Description);    //}
}AFX_FIELD_MAP
}
```

You do not normally need to modify the DoFieldExchange() function since it is under the control of ClassWizard and the framework. However, you should be aware that the statements within the DoFieldExchange() function are what enable the transfer of values between a derived CRecordset class's data members and the fields in a database.

AppWizard automatically creates the mapping between the CLibraryDataBaseSet data members and their corresponding fields for the RFX mechanism. You can view the mappings in the Member Variables tab in ClassWizard, as shown in Figure 12-20.

The next thing to understand in the CLibraryDatabaseSet class is the constructor: **CLibraryDatabaseSet(CDatabase* pDatabase = NULL);**. Notice the parameter for the constructor, **CDatabase* pDatabase = NULL**, which passes a pointer to a CDatabase object named pDatabase. Recall that the CDatabase class manages a connection to a database. Assigning a value of NULL to the pDatabase pointer in the CLibraryDatabaseSet class constructor informs the framework to automatically construct a CDatabase object for you and to connect your program to the database.

For database applications with more than one CRecordset class, if a CDatabase object and connection already exist for a database, the framework will pass a pointer to an existing database rather than create and connect to a new CDatabase object. Creating and connecting to a database object is resource-intensive, so it is much more efficient to work with a single database object instead of working with multiple database objects.

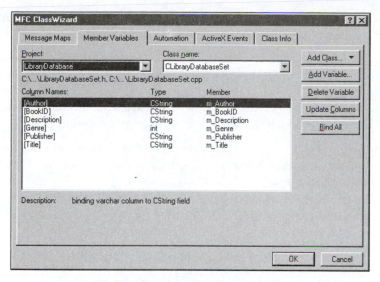

Figure 12-20   Mappings in ClassWizard between the CLibraryDataBaseSet data members and their corresponding RFX fields

If you examine the LibraryDatabaseSet.cpp file, you will see the following definition for the class constructor:

```
CLibraryDatabaseSet::CLibraryDatabaseSet(CDatabase* pdb)
    : CRecordset(pdb) {
    //{{AFX_FIELD_INIT(CLibraryDatabaseSet)
    m_BookID =   _T("");
    m_Title = _T("");
    m_Author = _T("");
    m_Publisher = _T("");
    m_Genre = 0;
    m_Description = _T("");
    m_nFields = 6;
    //}}AFX_FIELD_INIT
    m_nDefaultType = snapshot;
}
```

Notice that the CDatabase object pointer named pdb is passed to the constructor for the CRecordset base class. Also notice that the data members representing fields in the database table are initialized to default values. The initial values assigned to each data member will be quickly replaced with values in the database fields once the framework calls the RFX DoFieldExchange() function. Finally, notice the definition for the m_nDefaultType data member, which determines whether you want the CRecordset object to be a snapshot or a dynaset. Since you selected snapshot when you ran AppWizard, the m_nDefaultType data member is defined using the statement `m_nDefaultType = snapshot;`. However, if you had selected dynaset the statement would read `m_nDefaultType = dynaset;`. You can

12

modify the statement manually after running AppWizard if you change your mind about what type of CRecordset object you want to use.

After the constructor for a CRecordset class executes, the framework automatically calls the inherited Open() function of the CRecordset class. You will not see a declaration or definition for the Open() function in your classes that derived from CRecordset since the framework uses the base class version of the function. However, you should be aware of the Open() function since it does much of the work in setting up the connection to a database.

When you pass a value of NULL to the pDatabase pointer in the derived CRecordset class constructor, the Open() function constructs a new CDatabase object and then calls the GetDefaultConnect() function to connect to the database. AppWizard created an overridden version of the GetDefaultConnect() function for you that specifies the necessary information to connect to your database. If you examine the LibraryDatabaseSet.cpp file, you will find the following GetDefaultConnect() function definition:

```
CString CLibraryDatabaseSet::GetDefaultConnect() {
    return _T("ODBC;DSN=Library");
}
```

The GetDefaultConnect() function contains a single statement `return _T("ODBC; DSN=Library");` that uses the special _T() data mapping function to return a text string that identifies the type of database (ODBC) and the DSN to connect to, in this case the Library DSN you created earlier. The database information string is returned to the Open() function, which uses it to connect to the database.

After the Open() function connects to the database by calling the GetDefaultConnect() function, it calls the GetDefaultSQL() function, which returns a string that the Open() function uses to build the default SQL statement that is executed against the database. If you examine the LibraryDatabaseSet.cpp file, you will find the following overridden GetDefaultSQL() function definition that is automatically supplied by AppWizard:

```
CString CLibraryDatabaseSet::GetDefaultSQL() {
    return _T("[Books]");
}
```

The single statement in the GetDefaultSQL() function also uses the special _T() data mapping function to return a text string to the Open() function that contains the name of the table that you selected when you ran AppWizard. Notice that the table name in the returned string is in SQL format. Once the Open() function receives the string, it constructs a SQL statement that simply returns all of the records in the tables you specified when you ran AppWizard.

If you want the default SQL statement to be more explicit, you can modify the string returned by the GetDefaultSQL() function. For example, if you want the records returned from the database to be sorted by the Author field, then you can modify the return statement in the GetDefaultSQL() function as follows:

```
return _T("[Books] ORDER BY [Books].[Author]");
```

The preceding statement is only one method of sorting the records returned from an SQL query. Note that the GetDefaultSQL() function is used only to sort records when they are first returned from the database. You will see another method of sorting later in this chapter that you can use at any point in your program. For your version of the Library Database application, leave the GetDefaultSQL() function set to its default value of returning only the table name to the Open() function.

One final item about the CRecordset class that needs to be pointed out is where an object of the class is instantiated in a database application. An object of a derived CRecordset class is actually instantiated in the application's document class. This way, when you instantiate an object of the document class in the application class's InitInstance() function, an object of a derived CRecordset class is also instantiated. If you examine the LibraryDatabaseDoc.h file, you will see the following CLibraryDatabaseSet object declared in the public section:

```
CLibraryDatabaseSet m_libraryDatabaseSet;
```

The CRecordView Class

The CRecordView class, which derives from CView, displays records from the CRecordset class in a dialog-style window that you can edit with the Dialog Editor. Figure 12-21 shows the Library Database application's CLibraryDatabaseView class declaration file that AppWizard derived from CRecordView.

```
class CLibraryDatabaseView : public CRecordView {
protected: // create from serialization only
    CLibraryDatabaseView();
    DECLARE_DYNCREATE(CLibraryDatabaseView)
public:
    //{{AFX_DATA(CLibraryDatabaseView)
    enum{ IDD = IDD_LIBRARYDATABASE_FORM };
    CLibraryDatabaseSet* m_pSet;
    // NOTE: the ClassWizard will add data members here
    //}}AFX_DATA
// Attributes
public:
    CLibraryDatabaseDoc* GetDocument();
// Operations
public:
// Overrides
    // ClassWizard generated virtual function overrides
    //{{AFX_VIRTUAL(CLibraryDatabaseView)
    public:
    virtual CRecordset* OnGetRecordset();
    virtual BOOL PreCreateWindow(CREATESTRUCT& cs);
    protected:
    virtual void DoDataExchange(CDataExchange* pDX);
                        // DDX/DDV support
```

Figure 12-21 LibraryDatabaseView.h

```
        virtual void OnInitialUpdate(); // called first time
                                        //    after construct
        virtual BOOL OnPreparePrinting(CPrintInfo* pInfo);
        virtual void OnBeginPrinting(CDC* pDC,
            CPrintInfo* pInfo);
        virtual void OnEndPrinting(CDC* pDC,
            CPrintInfo* pInfo);
        //}}AFX_VIRTUAL
// Implementation
public:
        virtual ~CLibraryDatabaseView();
#ifdef _DEBUG
        virtual void AssertValid() const;
        virtual void Dump(CDumpContext& dc) const;
#endif
protected:
// Generated message map functions
protected:
        //{{AFX_MSG(CLibraryDatabaseView)
            // NOTE - the ClassWizard will add and remove
                member functions here.
        //      DO NOT EDIT what you see in these blocks
                of generated code !
        //}}AFX_MSG
        DECLARE_MESSAGE_MAP()
};
```

Figure 12-21   LibraryDatabaseView.h (continued)

Notice in the first public section in Figure 12-21 that the CLibraryDatabaseView declares a
pointer named m_pSet of the CLibraryDatabaseSet class. It is through the m_pSet pointer
that a CRecordView class communicates with its associated CRecordset class. However, as
shown in the following code, the m_pSet pointer is initially assigned a value of NULL in the
CLibraryDatabaseView class constructor:

```
CLibraryDatabaseView::CLibraryDatabaseView()
    : CRecordView(CLibraryDatabaseView::IDD) {
    //{{AFX_DATA_INIT(CLibraryDatabaseView)
        // NOTE: the ClassWizard will add member
            initialization here
    m_pSet = NULL;
    //}}AFX_DATA_INIT
    // TODO: add construction code here
}
```

Now, notice the OnInitialUpdate() function that is declared in the LibraryDatabaseView.h
file. The OnInitialUpdate() function is derived from CView and is called by the framework
after the view is first attached to the document, but before the view is displayed. It is in the
OnInitialUpdate() function that you assign to the m_pSet variable a pointer to the derived
CRecordset associated with a derived CRecordView class. The following code shows the

OnInitialUpdate() function that AppWizard defined for you in the CLibraryDatabaseView definition file:

```
void CLibraryDatabaseView::OnInitialUpdate() {
    m_pSet = &GetDocument()->m_libraryDatabaseSet;
    CRecordView::OnInitialUpdate();
    GetParentFrame()->RecalcLayout();
    ResizeParentToFit();
}
```

Recall that an object of a derived CRecordset class is instantiated in an application's document class. The CRecordset object that was declared in the document class for the Library Database application was named m_libraryDatabaseSet. Observe that in the first statement in the preceding code, the m_pSet variable is assigned a pointer to the libraryDatabaseSet using the GetDocument() function of the CView class. Essentially, a CRecordView class communicates with its CRecordset class *through* the application's document class using the GetDocument() function. The second statement in the OnInitialUpdate() function calls the OnInitialUpdate() function for the CRecordView base class, while the last two statements adjust the size of the frame window to the CRecordView dialog window.

 You learned in Chapter 10 that the GetDocument() function allows classes derived from CView to communicate with their associated document classes.

One final requirement for the m_pSet variables involves the pure virtual OnGetRecordset() function. In order to assign a pointer to a recordset object, a database application must override the OnGetRecordset() function and return a pointer to the m_pSet variable. The following code shows the OnGetRecordset() function that AppWizard defined in the Library Database application's CLibraryDatabaseView definition file:

```
CRecordset* CLibraryDatabaseView::OnGetRecordset() {
    return m_pSet;
}
```

LINKING DIALOG CONTROLS TO DATABASE FIELDS

The reason you spent so much time learning about the m_pSet pointer in the last section is that the m_pSet pointer is necessary for the CRecordView class's dialog window to communicate with the CRecordset class's data members. First, you need to add controls to a derived CRecordView class's dialog window. Then, you use the m_pSet pointer to map each control's resource ID to a data member in the derived CRecordset class. You map a control to a CRecordset data member using the MessageVariables tab in ClassWizard, the same as when you map standard dialog controls to a derived CView class's data members. The derived CRecordView class's DDX mechanism will then automatically handle the exchange of data between the dialog controls and the derived CRecordset class's data members. For example,

12

in the next exercise you will create a control with a resource ID of IDC_AUTHOR that will display the name of an author from the current record of the Library database. You will map the IDC_AUTHOR resource ID to the m_Author data member of the CLibraryDatabaseSet class using the m_pSet pointer. Within the CLibraryDatabaseView class's DoDataExchange() function, you will see the following statement, which DDX uses to manage the exchange of information:

```
DDX_FieldText(pDX, IDC_AUTHOR,
        m_pSet->m_Author, m_pSet);
```

The derived CLibraryDatabaseSet class's RFX mechanism will then handle the data exchange between the class's data members and fields in the database. In short, the DDX mechanism handles data exchange between the dialog controls and a derived CRecordset class's data members, while the RFX mechanism handles data exchange between a derived CRecordset class's data members and a database's fields. Figure 12-22 illustrates how data is exchanged across a database application.

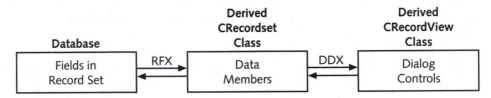

Figure 12-22 Data exchange across database application

Next, you will add dialog controls to the CLibraryDatabaseView class's dialog window to display the fields in the Library Database program. You will use a new type of dialog control, Radio Button controls, to select a book's genre of fiction or nonfiction. A radio button appears as a small empty circle; when selected, it appears to be filled with a black dot. A radio button is usually contained within a group of other radio buttons, and you can select only one of the grouped radio buttons at a time. Figure 12-23 shows an example of a group of four radio buttons.

The term *radio button* comes from car radios that have a group of push buttons, each of which is set to a radio station. In the same manner that you can select only one car radio button at a time, you can select only one Radio Button control contained within a group of other radio buttons.

What type of platform do you use?

- ○ Windows 95/98/2000
- ○ Windows NT
- ○ UNIX
- ○ Macintosh

Figure 12-23 Radio buttons

When used with a database, a single group of related radio buttons is used to represent a set number of choices that users can place in a single field. For example, you can enter only one of the four platform types in the database associated with the radio button group shown in Figure 12-23. In the code, you do not use a radio button's associated string, such as *Windows NT*, to refer to the radio button. Rather, you use an integer value that is associated with each radio button that is part of a group. The first radio button in a radio button group is represented by a 0, and each subsequent control in the group is represented by the next higher number. Therefore, the Macintosh control in Figure 12-23 is represented in a database field as the number 3.

Radio Button controls are recognized as being in the same group when the first control in the group has the Group check box selected in its Radio Button Properties window. All radio buttons that follow are recognized as part of the same group until Visual C++ encounters another Radio Button control with its Group check box selected, which starts a new group. Additionally, the resource ID property of the first Radio Button control in a group is used to represent *all* of the Radio Button controls in the group; any resource IDs you assign to other controls in the group will be ignored. When used with a database, you associate the first Radio Button control's resource ID with a CRecordset data member. The framework will automatically recognize which control in the group is selected and enter its integer value into the associated database field. Conversely, the framework will also read each integer value in the database field that is associated with a radio button group and select the appropriate radio button when its record is displayed.

To add to the CLibraryDatabaseView class's dialog window dialog controls that will display the fields in the Library Database program:

1. Open the CLibraryDatabaseView class's dialog resource window, **LibraryDatabase.rc**, in the Dialog Editor.

2. Delete the Static Text control that reads **TODO: Place form controls on this dialog.**.

3. Modify your dialog window so that it matches Figure 12-24.

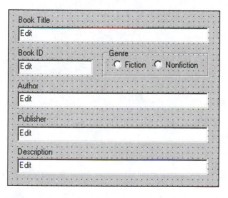

Figure 12-24   Library Database dialog controls

4. Open the **Properties** window for the Book Title edit box and set its resource ID to **IDC_TITLE**.

12

5. Open the **Properties** window for the Book ID edit box and set its resource ID to **IDC_BOOKID**.

6. Open the **Properties** window for the Fiction radio button control and set its resource ID to **IDC_GENRE**. Also, click the **Group** check box to designate the Fiction radio button as the first button in the IDC_GENRE group.

7. Open the **Properties** window for the Author edit box and set its resource ID to **IDC_AUTHOR**.

8. Open the **Properties** window for the Publisher edit box and set its resource ID to **IDC_PUBLISHER**.

9. Open the **Properties** window for the Description control and set its resource ID to **IDC_DESCRIPTION**.

Next, you will map the dialog control resource IDs to their associated field data members in the CLibraryDatabaseSet class.

To map the dialog control resource IDs to their associated field data members in the CLibraryDatabaseSet class:

1. Open **Class Wizard** and click the **Member Variables** tab. You will see six resource IDs listed for the controls you placed in the dialog box. (Remember that the two Radio Button controls are both represented by the single IDC_GENRE resource ID.)

2. With the IDC_AUTHOR resource ID selected, click the **Add Variable** button to display the Add Member Variable dialog box. The Member variable name box will contain m_ as a prefix for the new variable. Instead of typing a variable name, click the arrow to the right of the Member variable name box. You will see a list of the field data members in the CLibraryDatabaseSet class, including m_pSet pointer, as shown in Figure 12-25.

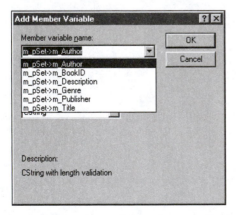

Figure 12-25   Add Member Variable dialog box

3. Select **m_pSet->m_Author** as the variable name to map to the IDC_AUTHOR control and click the **OK** button.

4. Repeat Steps 2 and 3 to map the rest of the dialog control resource IDs to their associated field data members in the CLibraryDatabaseSet class. When you are through, click **OK** to close the ClassWizard dialog box.

5. When you are through mapping dialog control resource IDs to their associated field data members, build and execute the project. The program should open to the first record, which is for the book *Of Mice and Men*.

6. The framework automatically added a Record menu and toolbar buttons that you can use to navigate to the first, previous, next, and last records in the database. The framework also automatically added the code that manages the navigation functions associated with the menu commands and toolbar buttons for moving to and displaying each record in the record set. Practice navigating through the database using the menu and toolbar buttons. To see the navigation function performed by each button, hold your mouse over a button to display its ToolTip.

7. The framework also manages any updates you need to make to records in the database. Whenever you make changes to a record, the framework updates the record in the database when you move to another record in the record set—you do not need to manually save a record when you make changes. For practice, move to the record for the book *Tender is the Night*. The book's author is incorrectly entered as *Hemingway, Ernest* when it should be *Fitzgerald, F. Scott*. In addition, the book's genre should be *Fiction*, not *Nonfiction*. Make these changes to the record and then move to the previous record using either the Record menu or the toolbar. Then, immediately move back to the *Tender is the Night* record. The changes you made to the record should be visible.

8. Close the Library Database program window.

MANIPULATING RECORD SETS

You will often want to give users of your program the ability to manipulate record sets returned from a database. Two of the most common ways of manipulating record sets are sorting and filtering. Sorting presents database records in alphanumeric order based on a field in the record set. Filtering uses a given criterion to narrow records that the user can see. For example, suppose you have a sales database that lists revenue for each state in the United States. You can filter the sales database so that only the records for California and New York are visible. Sorting and filtering do not change any data, nor do they change the number of records in the returned record set. Rather, sorting and filtering determine how the records are presented to the user and what records are visible to the user. First, you will learn about sorting.

12

Sorting

One way to sort records when they are first returned from a database, as you saw earlier in the chapter, involves modifying the return statement in the GetDefaultSQL() function. The following code uses the ORDER BY clause to sort the record set by the Author field in the Books table.

```
CString CLibraryDatabaseSet::GetDefaultSQL() {
return _T(" [Books] ORDER BY [Books].[Author]");
}
```

The GetDefaultSQL() function is useful only for defining initial SQL criteria for the record set you want to be returned from a database.

When you derive a class from CRecordset, the derived class inherits a data member named m_strSort. You dynamically sort the records in a record set by assigning the field name by which you want to sort to the m_strSort data member. The framework uses the field name in the m_strSort data member to construct an ORDER BY SQL statement to execute against the database. You assign values to the m_strSort data member from a CRecordView class using the m_pSet pointer to the associated CRecordset class. One way to use the m_strSort data member is in the OnInitialUpdate() function that runs when the application first executes. For example, the following modified version of the CLibraryDatabaseView class's OnInitialUpdate() function assigns the Author field to the m_strSort data member, which causes the database records to be sorted by author names when the program first executes:

```
void CLibraryDatabaseView::OnInitialUpdate() {
    m_pSet = &GetDocument()->m_libraryDatabaseSet;
    m_pSet->m_strSort = "[Author]";
    CRecordView::OnInitialUpdate();
    GetParentFrame()->RecalcLayout();
    ResizeParentToFit();
}
```

Using the m_strSort data member in the OnInitialUpdate() function is essentially the same as adding an ORDER BY clause to the return statement in the GetDefaultSQL() function. For users to dynamically sort the records in the Library Database application, you need to add message handlers that assign the field to sort by to the m_strSort data member.

To use the m_strSort data member after the record set has been returned from the database, you must close the open record set using the Close() function inherited from the CRecordset class, assign a field name to the m_strSort data member, and then reopen the record set with the Open() method. Finally, you call the UpdateData() function to update the data displayed in the CRecordView class's dialog controls. For example to dynamically sort the Library Database application's record set by the Author field, you would add a message handler to the CLibraryDatabaseView class that executes the following statements:

```
m_pSet->Close();
m_pSet->m_strSort = "[Author]";
m_pSet->Open();
UpdateData(FALSE);
```

You may have noticed with the Library Database application that records are displayed in the numeric order of the BooksID field. This means that records are displayed in the order that they were added to the Books table, which isn't very useful to your users. Next, you will modify the Library Database application so that users can sort on author name and book title. You will add to the Record menu commands that execute each sort type.

To modify the Library Database application so that users can sort on author name and book title:

1. Open the Library Database application's menu in the Menu Editor.

2. Add a **separator**, a **Sort by Author** command, and a **Sort by Title** command to the Record menu, as shown in Figure 12-26. Modify the Sort by Author command's resource ID to **ID_AUTHOR_SORT** and set its Prompt text to **Sort the record set by author name**. Then, modify the Sort by Title command's resource ID to **ID_TITLE_SORT** and set its Prompt text to **Sort the record set by book title**.

Figure 12-26   Adding new sort commands

3. Use ClassWizard's Message Maps tab to add to the CLibraryDatabaseView class the following COMMAND message map function for the ID_AUTHOR_SORT resource ID:

```
void CLibraryDatabaseView::OnAuthorSort()
{
    m_pSet->Close();
    m_pSet->m_strSort = "[Author]";
    m_pSet->Open();
    UpdateData(FALSE);
}
```

4. Use ClassWizard's Message Maps tab to add to the CLibraryDatabaseView class the following COMMAND message map function for the ID_TITLE_SORT resource ID:

```
void CLibraryDatabaseView::OnTitleSort()
{
    m_pSet->Close();
    m_pSet->m_strSort = "[Title]";
    m_pSet->Open();
    UpdateData(FALSE);
}
```

5. Rebuild and execute the program. Test the Sort by Author and Sort by Title commands on the Record menu to be sure the sort functions are working correctly.

Filtering

Filtering works almost the same as sorting. Instead of using the m_strSort data member, you use the m_strFilter data member, which is also inherited from CRecordset. As with the m_strSort data member, you assign values to the m_strFilter data member from a CRecordView class using the m_pSet pointer to the associated CRecordset class. Instead of simply assigning a field name to the m_strFilter data member, you must also add an assignment statement that tells the framework how you want to filter the record set. The framework uses the assignment statement in the m_strFilter data member to construct a WHERE SQL statement to execute against the database. You must also close and reopen the record set using the Close() and Open() functions, the same as with the m_strSort data member. For example, you would use the following code to filter the records in the Library Database application so that only records in which the Author field is equal to *Hemingway, Ernest* are returned:

```
m_pSet->Close();

    = "[Author] = 'Hemingway, Ernest'";

m_pSet->Open();
```

Be sure *not* to include the WHERE clause in the text string you assign to the m_strFilter data member. For example, the following assignment statement is incorrect:

```
m_pSet->m_strFilter
        = "WHERE [Author] = 'Hemingway, Ernest'";
```

When you filter records, the possibility exists that no records may match the filter expression that you assign to the m_strFilter data member. To be sure that there are records to display to the user, you use the GetRecordCount() function that is inherited from CRecordset to count the number of records in the record set. If the GetRecordCount() function returns a value of 0, then no records matched the filter expression. The following code shows how to use the GetRecordCount() function within the example that filters for books by Hemingway. If the GetRecordCount() function returns a value of 0, then a message box informs the user that no matching records were found, the record set is closed, the m_strFilter data member is assigned an empty string, and then the record set is reopened. Assigning an empty string to the m_strFilter data member removes any previously assigned filter expression and instructs the framework to return the entire record set.

```
m_pSet->Close();
m_pSet->m_strFilter
        = "[Author] = 'Hemingway, Ernest'";
m_pSet->Open();
int iNumRecords = m_pSet->GetRecordCount();
```

```
if (iNumRecords == 0) {
    AfxMessageBox("No matching records found.");
    m_pSet->Close();
    m_pSet->m_strFilter = "";
    m_pSet->Open();
}
UpdateData(FALSE);
```

Next, you will modify the Library Database application so users can filter records based on the type of book they are interested in. You will add commands to the Record menu that apply each filter. The filter will be applied to the Genre field in the Books table. Recall that Radio Button controls store integer values in database fields, starting with a value of 0 for the first control in a group. Because the Genre field is controlled by a radio button group, the first value in the group, Fiction, is stored as 0 in the database, while the second value, Nonfiction, is stored as the number 1. To filter the Library database to return only Fiction titles, you use the filter `m_pSet->m_strFilter = "[Genre] = 0";`. To filter the Library database to return only Nonfiction titles, you use the filter `m_pSet->m_strFilter = "[Genre] = 1";`. Finally, to reset the database to show all titles, you pass an empty string to the filter using the statement `m_pSet->m_strFilter = "";`.

To modify the Library Database application so users can filter records based on the type of book they are interested in:

1. Open the Library Database application's menu in the Menu Editor.

2. To the Record menu, add a **separator**, a **Show Fiction Titles** command, a **Show Nonfiction Titles** command, and a **Show All Titles** command, as shown in Figure 12-27. Modify the Show Fiction Titles command's resource ID to **ID_SHOW_FICTION,** and set its Prompt text to **Show fiction titles only**. Then modify the Show Nonfiction Titles command's resource ID to **ID_SHOW_NONFICTION,** and set its Prompt text to **Show nonfiction titles only**. Finally, modify the Show All Titles command's resource ID to **ID_SHOW_ALL** and set its Prompt text to **Show all titles**.

Figure 12-27 Adding new filter commands

3. To filter the database by fiction titles, use ClassWizard's Message Maps tab to add to the CLibraryDatabaseView class the following COMMAND message map function for the ID_SHOW_FICTION resource ID :

```
void CLibraryDatabaseView::OnShowFiction()
{
    m_pSet->Close();
    m_pSet->m_strFilter = "[Genre] = 0";
    m_pSet->Open();
    int iNumRecords = m_pSet->GetRecordCount();
    if (iNumRecords == 0) {
        AfxMessageBox("No matching records found.");
        m_pSet->Close();
        m_pSet->m_strFilter = "";
        m_pSet->Open();
    }
    UpdateData(FALSE);
}
```

4. To filter the database by nonfiction titles, use ClassWizard's Message Maps tab to add to the CLibraryDatabaseView class the following COMMAND message map function for the ID_SHOW_NONFICTION resource ID:

```
void CLibraryDatabaseView::OnShowNonfiction()
{
    m_pSet->Close();
    m_pSet->m_strFilter = "[Genre] = 1";
    m_pSet->Open();
    int iNumRecords = m_pSet->GetRecordCount();
    if (iNumRecords == 0) {
        AfxMessageBox("No matching records found.");
        m_pSet->Close();
        m_pSet->m_strFilter = "";
        m_pSet->Open();
    }
    UpdateData(FALSE);
}
```

5. Finally, to remove any filters, use ClassWizard's Message Maps tab to add to the CLibraryDatabaseView class the following COMMAND message map function for the ID_SHOW_ALL resource ID:

```
void CLibraryDatabaseView::OnShowAll()
{
    m_pSet->Close();
    m_pSet->m_strFilter = "";
    m_pSet->Open();
    int iNumRecords = m_pSet->GetRecordCount();
```

```
        if (iNumRecords == 0) {
            AfxMessageBox("No matching records found.");
            m_pSet->Close();
            m_pSet->m_strFilter = "";
            m_pSet->Open();
        }
        UpdateData(FALSE);
    }
```

6. Rebuild and execute the program. Test the Show Fiction, Show Nonfiction, and Show All Titles commands on the Record menu to be sure the filters are being applied correctly.

ADDING AND DELETING RECORDS

So far the Library Database application is quite functional. It allows users to modify existing records and sort and filter by different fields. However, it has two very big shortcomings in that you cannot add new records or delete existing records. For some types of databases, you may not want to allow users to add or delete records. For example, if the Library Database application was available to users in a public library, you would not allow those users to add or delete records in the database. But suppose that the Library Database application is available only to library personnel who catalog and organize the library's collections of books and other media. Library personnel would certainly need to be able to add and delete records to and from the database.

Due to the many different methods of designing an interface for a database application (using menu commands, toolbars, controls, and so on), the framework does not automatically create an option for adding records to a database. Additionally, the framework does not create an option for deleting records due to the complexity of table relationships across relational databases. Therefore, it is up to you to write code for adding records to and deleting records from your database. In this section, you will write code that adds and deletes records for the Library Database application. Keep in mind that all databases are different and that the code listed in this section for adding and deleting records to an ODBC database may not necessarily work with other types of databases. However, the techniques you learn in this section are a good starting point for writing your own code that adds and deletes records for other types of databases.

Adding Records

The starting point for adding a new record is the AddNew() function that is derived from CRecordset. The **AddNew() function** prepares a new database record by setting the new record's field values to NULL. You then call the UpdateData() function with a value of FALSE to "clear" the dialog controls by assigning them values of NULL. You write your own message handler function to execute the AddNew() member function and the UpdateData() function, along with any other code required for your new records. The following code shows an example of a message handler function definition for the CLibraryDatabaseView class named OnRecordAdd()that executes the AddNew() function:

```
void cLibraryDatabaseView::OnRecordAdd() {
    m_pSet->AddNew();
    m_bAddRecord = TRUE;
    UpdateData(FALSE);
}
```

In the preceding code, notice the m_bAddRecord data member that is assigned a value of TRUE. Unlike updates to existing records, the framework does not automatically update new records that are created with the AddNew() function. Instead, to save the new record to the database, you set your own user-defined (not inherited) Boolean variable to a value of TRUE as a flag that you will use in the OnMove() function (which you learn about next). You can use any Boolean variable name you like, but names such as m_bAddRecord, m_bAddMode, and m_bAddNew are common.

The framework automatically updates a record in the Library Database application (and in most types of database applications) when the user moves to a new record. The process of updating database records is managed by the CRecordView class's **OnMove() function**. However, in order to *save* a *new* record, you must override the CRecordView class's OnMove() function in your derived class. The following code shows a typical example of an overridden OnMove() function for the cLibraryDatabaseView class. The example includes two new functions that derive from CRecordset: the Update() function and the Requery() function. The **Update() function** saves new records to the database and is required in order to complete a new record operation that is started with the AddNew() function. The **Requery()** function updates a database application's record set.

```
void cLibraryDatabaseView::OnMove() {
    if (m_bAddRecord) {
        UpdateData(TRUE);
        m_pSet->Update();
        m_pSet->Requery();
        UpdateData(FALSE);
        m_bAddRecord = FALSE;
        return TRUE;
    }
    else
        return CRecordView::OnMove(nIDMoveCommand);
}
```

The conditional expression in the preceding OnMove() function's if statement checks to see whether the user-defined m_bAddRecord data member is set to TRUE, indicating that the current record is a new record. The first statement in the if statement executes the UpdateData() function with a value of TRUE to copy the dialog control values to their associated data members in the CLibraryDatabaseSet class. Then, the m_pSet->Update(); statement executes to save the new record to the database. Next, the Requery() function executes and updates the record set stored in the m_pSet pointer. The UpdateData() function executes again, but this time with a value of FALSE, to copy the updated values from the CLibraryDatabaseSet data members back into their associated dialog controls. Finally, the m_bAddRecord data member is assigned a value of FALSE and the OnMove() function returns a value of TRUE. Since the `else` statement executes for existing records, it calls the CRecordView base class version of the OnMove() function to allow the framework to automatically handle any updates.

Next, you will modify the Library Database application so that it creates new records when the user clicks an Add Record command on the Record menu.

To modify the Library Database application so that it creates new records:

1. Open the **LibraryDatabaseView.h** file in the Text Editor window.

2. Add the following bolded data member declaration to the first protected section of the file:

```
class CLibraryDatabaseView : public CRecordView
{
protected: // create from serialization only
     CLibraryDatabaseView( );
     DECLARE_DYNCREATE(CLibraryDatabaseView)
     BOOL m_bAddRecord;
...
```

3. Next, open the **LibraryDatabaseView.cpp** file and add the following bolded statement to the constructor that initializes the m_bAddRecord data member to FALSE:

```
CLibraryDatabaseView::CLibraryDatabaseView( )
     : CRecordView(CLibraryDatabaseView::IDD)
{
     //{{AFX_DATA_INIT(CLibraryDatabaseView)
     m_pSet = NULL;
     //}}AFX_DATA_INIT
     // TODO: add construction code here
     m_bAddRecord = FALSE;
}
```

4. Open the Library Database application's menu in the Menu Editor.

5. To the Record menu, add a **separator** and an **Add New Record** command, as shown in Figure 12-28. Modify the Add New Record command's resource ID to **ID_RECORD_ADD** and set its Prompt text to **Add a new record**.

12

Figure 12-28   Adding the Add New Record command

6. Use ClassWizard's Message Maps tab to add to the CLibraryDatabaseView class the following COMMAND message map function for the ID_RECORD_ADD resource ID to add a new record to the database:

```
void CLibraryDatabaseView::OnRecordAdd()
{
    m_pSet->AddNew();
    m_bAddRecord = TRUE;
    UpdateData(FALSE);
}
```

7. Select **Add Virtual Function** from the **WizardBar** to display the New Virtual Override dialog box.

8. Select **OnMove** from the **New Virtual Functions** list, and then click the **Add and Edit** button. The new function is created and your cursor is moved to the function definition.

9. Modify the OnMove() function definition as follows

```
BOOL CLibraryDatabaseView::OnMove(UINT nIDMoveCommand)
{
    if (m_bAddRecord) {
        UpdateData(TRUE);
        m_pSet->Update();
        m_pSet->Requery();
        UpdateData(FALSE);
        m_bAddRecord = FALSE;
        return TRUE;
    }
    else
        return CRecordView::OnMove(nIDMoveCommand);
}
```

10. Rebuild and execute the program. Select the **Add New Record** command from the Record menu to create a new record and add the following information to the fields:

```
Book Title:     The Bridges of Madison County
Book ID:        WALLER001
Genre:          Fiction
Author:         Waller, Robert James
Publisher:      Thorndike, Me. : Thorndike Press, 1992
Description:    184 p. (large print) : ill. ; 23 cm.
```

11. After you finish entering the record, select any of the navigation commands to save the record to the database. Because the newly created record was added to the end of the database, you can review it by selecting the Last Record command on the Record menu or on the toolbar.

Deleting Records

Deleting records from a database is much simpler than adding them. Your two primary tasks are to call the Delete() and the MoveNext() functions that are inherited from the CRecordset class. The CRecordset class's **Delete() function** deletes the currently displayed record. Once you delete the current record, you use the **MoveNext() function** to navigate to the next record in the record set. Typically, you delete records using a message handler function named OnRecordDelete(), as follows:

```
void cLibraryDatabaseView::OnRecordDelete() {
    m_pSet->Delete();
    m_pSet->MoveNext();
}
```

The preceding function is sufficient for deleting a record. However, if the record you delete is the last record in the record set, then calling the MoveNext() function after deleting the record will move you past the end of the database, which means you will not have a valid record selected. In order to prevent this type of problem from occurring, you call the IsEOF() and MoveLast() functions after you call the MoveNext() function. The **IsEOF() function,** inherited from CRecordset, returns a value of TRUE if your position in the record set is at the end of the file. If the IsEOF() function does return a value of TRUE, then you should call the **MoveLast() function,** inherited from CRecordset, to navigate back to the last record in the record set, using code similar to the following:

```
if (m_pSet->IsEOF())
    m_pSet->MoveLast();
```

One more precaution you should take when deleting records is to check whether all of the records in the record set have been deleted, and then to clear the fields left over from the last visible record. After you execute the MoveLast() function, you should call the IsBOF() and SetFieldNull() functions. The **IsBOF() function,** inherited from CRecordset, returns a value of TRUE if your position in the record set is at the beginning of the file. If the IsBOF() function returns a value of TRUE after you execute the MoveLast() function, then your record set is empty. If your record set is empty, you should call the SetFieldNull() function, which is also inherited from CRecordset. The **SetFieldNull() function** receives a single parameter of NULL, which it uses to set all field data members in a derived CRecordset class to

12

NULL. After executing the SetFieldNull() function, you should call the UpdateData() function with a value of FALSE to clear the values displayed in the dialog controls. The following code shows how to write the IsBOF() and SetFieldNull() functions:

```
if (m_pSet->IsBOF())
    m_pSet->SetFieldNull(NULL);
```

The following code shows a completed version of the OnRecordDelete() function.

```
void cLibraryDatabaseView::OnRecordDelete() {
    m_pSet->Delete();
    m_pSet->MoveNext();
    if (m_pSet->IsEOF())
        m_pSet->MoveLast();
    if (m_pSet->IsBOF())
        m_pSet->SetFieldNull(NULL);
    UpdateData(FALSE);
}
```

Next, you will modify the Library Database application so that it can delete existing records.

To modify the Library Database application so that it can delete existing records:

1. Open the Library Database application's menu in the Menu Editor.

2. Add a **Delete Current Record** command to the Record menu, as shown in Figure 12-29. Modify the Delete Current Record command's resource ID to **ID_RECORD_DELETE** and set its Prompt text to **Delete the current record**.

Figure 12-29   Adding the Delete Current Record command

3. Use ClassWizard's Message Maps tab to add to the CLibraryDatabaseView class the following COMMAND message map function for the ID_RECORD_DELETE resource ID to delete the current record from the database:

```
void CLibraryDatabaseView::OnRecordDelete()
{
    m_pSet->Delete();
    m_pSet->MoveNext();
```

```
        if (m_pSet->IsEOF())
            m_pSet->MoveLast();
        if (m_pSet->IsBOF())
            m_pSet->SetFieldNull(NULL);
        UpdateData(FALSE);
    }
```

4. Rebuild and execute the program. Move to the last record in the database, which is the record for *The Bridges of Madison County,* the book you added in the last set of steps. Select the **Delete Current Record** command from the **Record** menu to delete the record for *The Bridges of Madison County.* After you delete the record, you will see <DELETED> displayed in each of the deleted record's fields. Select the **Previous Record** command from the **Record** menu to move to the previous record, which should be *A Brief History of Time.*

5. Close the Library Database program window.

CONCLUSION

Your goal in the study of programming, or of any technology subject for that matter, should not be memorizing facts and syntax. Your goal should be comprehending and understanding how things work. If you forget everything else you learned in this text, remember this: The best programmers in the world do not necessarily know all the answers. Rather, they know where to *find* the answers. Build yourself a library of reference books that you can use to find the answers you need.

12

CHAPTER SUMMARY

❑ A database is an ordered collection of information from which a computer program can quickly access information.

❑ A record in a database contains a single complete set of related information.

❑ The individual pieces of information stored in a record are called fields.

❑ A flat-file database stores information in a single table.

❑ A relational database stores information across multiple related tables.

❑ A one-to-one relationship exists between two tables when each record in a related table contains exactly one record for each record in the primary table.

❑ A one-to-many relationship exists in a relational database when one record in a primary table has many related records in a related table.

❑ Breaking tables into multiple related tables in order to reduce redundant and duplicate information is called normalization.

❑ A many-to-many relationship exists in a relational database when many records in one table are related to many records in another table.

❑ A junction table contains a one-to-many relationship to each of the two tables in a many-to-many relationship.

❑ An application or collection of applications used to create, access, and manage a database is called a database management system, or DBMS.

❑ A query is a structured set of instructions and criteria for retrieving, adding, modifying, and deleting database information.

❑ A report is the formatted, printed output of a database table or the results of a query.

❑ Most database management systems utilize a data manipulation language, or DML, for creating queries.

❑ Structured query language (SQL) has become a standard data manipulation language among many database management systems.

❑ Open database connectivity, or ODBC, allows applications that are written to comply with the ODBC standard to access any data source for which there is an ODBC driver.

❑ You connect to databases with MFC using ODBC or Data Access Objects.

❑ Data Access Objects, or DAO, is a set of classes that provides access to databases created with the Microsoft Jet (for Joint engine technology) database engine.

❑ The Jet database engine is a DBMS technology that Microsoft Access uses to interact with and manipulate the database files (with an extension of .mdb) it creates.

❑ Use DAO when your database application only needs to work with Access databases, but use ODBC when you need your program to work with other types of ODBC-compliant databases.

❑ A Data Source Name, or DSN, contains configuration information that Windows operating systems use to access a particular ODBC-compliant database.

❑ All ODBC database applications begin the CDatabase class, which manages the connection to a database.

❑ The CFieldExchange class manages the exchange of information between your application and the database.

❑ The CRecordset class represents records returned from a database.

❑ The CRecordView class displays database records in a dialog-style window that you can edit with the Dialog Editor.

❑ A snapshot is a static view of the records in a database.

□ A dynaset is a dynamic record set that displays the most recent changes to a database each time you move from one record to another in a database application.

□ MFC handles the exchange of values between CRecordset data members and their corresponding fields in a database using a mechanism called record field exchange, or RFX.

□ The GetDefaultConnect() function specifies the information needed to connect to your database.

□ The GetDefaultSQL() function returns a string that the Open() function uses to build the default SQL statement that is executed against the database.

□ The CRecordView class uses the m_pSet pointer to communicate with its associated CRecordset class.

□ The OnInitialUpdate() function is derived from CView and is called by the framework after the view is first attached to the document, but before the view is displayed.

□ You sort a record set by assigning the field name you want to sort by to the m_strSort data member.

□ You filter a record set by assigning a value to the m_strSort data member.

□ The AddNew() function prepares a new database record by setting the new record's field values to NULL.

□ The process of updating database records is managed by the CRecordView class's OnMove() function.

□ The Update() function saves new records to the database and is required in order to complete a new record operation that is started with the AddNew() function.

□ The Requery() function updates a database application's record set.

□ The Delete() function deletes the currently displayed record.

□ The MoveNext() function navigates to the next record in the record set.

□ The IsEOF() function returns a value of TRUE if your position in the record set is at the end of the file.

□ The MoveLast() function navigates to the last record in the record set.

□ The IsBOF() function returns a value of TRUE if your position in the record set is at the beginning of the file.

□ The SetFieldNull() function sets all field data members in a derived CRecordset class to NULL.

12

REVIEW QUESTIONS

1. What is the correct term for the individual pieces of information that are stored in a database record?

   a. element

   b. field

   c. section

   d. container

2. How many tables does a flat-file database consist of?

   a. 1

   b. 2

   c. Any number of tables

   d. A flat-file database does not consist of tables

3. What is the name of one table's primary key when it is stored in another table?

   a. key symbol

   b. record link

   c. foreign key

   d. unique identifier

4. Breaking tables into multiple related tables in order to reduce redundant and duplicate information is called _____.

   a. normalization

   b. redundancy design

   c. splitting

   d. simplification

5. A _____ relationship exists between two tables when each record in a related table contains exactly one record for each record in the primary table.

   a. one-to-none

   b. one-to-one

   c. one-to-many

   d. many-to-many

6. A _____ relationship exists in a relational database when one record in a primary table has many related records in a related table.

   a. one-to-none

   b. one-to-one

   c. one-to-many

   d. many-to-many

7. A _____ relationship exists in a relational database when many records in one table are related to many records in another table.

   a. one-to-none

   b. one-to-one

   c. one-to-many

   d. many-to-many

8. A _____ contains a one-to-many relationship to each of two tables in a many-to-many relationship.

   a. union database

   b. flat-file link

   c. junction table

   d. bridge table

9. An application or collection of applications used to create, access, and manage a database is called _____.

   a. a shell program

   b. a mainframe system

   c. a database management system

   d. three-tier client server design

10. Most database management systems use a form of _____ for their data manipulation languages.

   a. C syntax

   b. C++ syntax

   c. Structured Query Language

   d. ActiveX Data Objects

11. Which of the following statements is true about DAO?

   a. DAO can only access Microsoft Jet engine databases.

   b. DAO can only access ODBC databases.

   c. DAO can access both Microsoft Jet engine databases and ODBC.

   d. DAO is not used for accessing databases.

12. A _____ contains configuration information that Windows operating systems use to access a particular ODBC-compliant database.

   a. Dynamic Link Library

   b. SQL container

   c. ODBC interface unit

   d. Data Source Name

12

13. Which class manages the connection to an ODBC database?

    a. CDatabase

    b. CFieldExchange

    c. CODBCDB

    d. CODBCDatabase

14. Which of the following is the type of CRecordset object that displays the most recent changes to a database each time you move from one record to another in a database application?

    a. snapshot

    b. dynaset

    c. recordset

    d. DBRecordset

15. Which of the following is the type of CRecordset object that displays a static view of the records in a database?

    a. snapshot

    b. dynaset

    c. recordset

    d. DBRecordset

16. What is the name of the mechanism that MFC uses to handle the exchange of values between CRecordset data members and their corresponding fields in a database?

    a. recordset field exchange or RFE

    b. database field exchange or DFE

    c. dynamic data exchange or DDX

    d. record field exchange or RFX

17. What specific function in a derived CRecordset class handles the exchange of values between CRecordset data members and their corresponding fields in a database?

    a. UpdateData()

    b. DoDataExchange()

    c. DoFieldExchange()

    d. Update()

18. Which of the following is the correct header syntax for the constructor for a derived CRecordset class named CInventorySet?

   a. `CInventorySet::CInventorySet(CDatabase* pdb) : CRecordset(pdb)`

   b. `CInventorySet::CInventorySet(CDatabase* pdb)`

   c. `CInventorySet::CInventorySet(CDatabase* pdb) : CRecordset()`

   d. `CInventorySet::CInventorySet()`

19. Which of the following data members that are inherited from CRecordset determine the database access type of CRecordset object?

   a. m_nDefaultType

   b. m_pSet

   c. m_nType

   d. m_nDefault

20. Which inherited CRecordset function connects a database application to the database?

   a. GetDatabase()

   b. DefaultConnect()

   c. GetDefaultConnect()

   d. Connect()

21. In what class is an object of a derived CRecordset function instantiated?

   a. The derived CRecordset class itself

   b. The application class

   c. The frame class

   d. The document class

22. In what function do you assign to the m_pSet variable a pointer to the derived CRecordset associated with a derived CRecordView class?

   a. The derived CRecordView constructor function

   b. The OnInitialUpdate() function

   c. The DoFieldExchange() function

   d. The DoDataExchange() function

12

23. You have a group of four radio buttons in a database application and the second radio button in the group is labeled with the value *Choice B*. When a user clicks the Choice B radio button, what value will be stored in the associated database field?

    a. 0

    b. 1

    c. 2

    d. Choice B

24. Which property in the Properties window identifies the first button in a group of radio buttons?

    a. Group

    b. Group Box

    c. Radio Group

    d. Radio

25. How do you refer to a CRecordset data member named m_Product from a database application's associated CRecordView class?

    a. m_Product

    b. CRecordView::m_Product

    c. CRecordView->m_Product

    d. m_pSet->m_Product

26. You sort the records in a record set by assigning the field name you want to sort by to the _____ data member.

    a. m_Order

    b. m_strAlpha

    c. m_Sort

    d. m_strSort

27. You filter the records in a record set by assigning the values you want to filter by to the _____ data member.

    a. m_Narrow

    b. m_strRefine

    c. m_Filter

    d. m_strFilter

28. Which of the following is the correct string for a filter that narrows a record set to include only records where the State field is equal to Massachusetts?

    a. "WHERE [State] = 'Massachusetts'"

    b. "State = 'Massachusetts'"

    c. "WHERE [State] = Massachusetts"

    d. "[State] = 'Massachusetts'"

29. The _____ function prepares a new database record by setting the new records field values to NULL.

    a. New()

    b. NewRecord()

    c. AddNew()

    d. Insert()

30. What virtual function must you override in order to complete the process of adding a record to a database?

    a. OnLoad()

    b. UpdateAll()

    c. OnSave()

    d. OnMove()

31. The _____ function saves new records to the database and is required in order to complete a new record operation that is started with the AddNew() function.

    a. Insert()

    b. Commit()

    c. Save()

    d. Update()

32. The _____ function updates a database application's record set.

    a. Update()

    b. Requery()

    c. Read()

    d. Refresh()

12

33. The CRecordset class's _____ function deletes the currently displayed record.

   a. RemoveRecord()

   b. Remove()

   c. DeleteRecord()

   d. Delete()

34. Which code should you add to a function that deletes a record in order to be sure a valid record is displayed in the event that a user deletes the last record in a record set?

   a. `if (m_pSet->IsEOF())`
      `m_pSet->MoveNext();`

   b. `if (m_pSet->IsEOF())`
      `m_pSet->MoveLast();`

   c. `if (m_pSet->IsEOF())`
      `m_pSet->Last();`

   d. `if (m_pSet->IsEND())`
      `m_pSet->MoveLast();`

35. Which code should you add to a function that deletes a record in the event that a user has deleted all of the records in a record set?

   a. `if (m_pSet->IsBOF())`
      `m_pSet->SetFieldNull(NULL);`

   b. `if (m_pSet->IsBOF())`
      `m_pSet->MoveFirst();`

   c. `if (m_pSet->IsBEGINNING())`
      `m_pSet->MoveLast();`

   d. `if (m_pSet->IsBOF())`
      `m_pSet->SetFieldNull();`

EXERCISES

1. Redesign the following table into a one-to-many relationship.

Employee_ID	Last_Name	First_Name	Hourly_Pay	Department
EMP001	Smith	Lucille	$32.50	Marketing
EMP002	Perez	Frank	$40.00	Legal
EMP003	Okayabashi	Mike	$22.00	Accounting
EMP004	Korso	Anthony	$28.00	Accounting
EMP005	Singh	Tasneem	$37.00	Legal

2. Redesign the following table into a many-to-many relationship.

Employee_ID	Last_Name	First_Name	Project_ID	Hours_On_Project
EMP001	Smith	Lucille	100-002	Marketing
EMP002	Perez	Frank	200-056	Legal
EMP003	Okayabashi	Mike	300-010	Accounting
EMP004	Korso	Anthony	300-010	Accounting
EMP005	Singh	Tasneem	200-056	Legal
EMP003	Okayabashi	Mike	300-012	Accounting
EMP001	Smith	Lucille	100-003	Marketing
EMP005	Singh	Tasneem	200-056	Legal

3. Let us assume that you have an ODBC database with a table named Courses that contains two fields, Course_Name and Student_Name. Write an SQL statement that selects just the Course_Name fields from the Courses table and sorts the records by the Course_Name field.

4. Modify the SQL statement in the preceding step so that statements selects all of the fields from the Courses table. Also, sort the returned records by both the Course_Name and the Student_Name fields.

5. Modify the following derived CRecordset class constructor so that it opens the database as a dynaset.

```
CEmployeesSet::CEmployeesSet(CDatabase* pdb)
    : CRecordset(pdb) {
    //{{AFX_FIELD_INIT(CTest4Set)
    m_Employee_ID = _T("");
    m_Last_Name = _T("");
    m_First_Name = _T("");
    m_Hourly_Pay = 0;
    m_Department = _T("");
    m_nFields = 5;
    //}}AFX_FIELD_INIT
    m_nDefaultType = snapshot;
}
```

6. Modify the following GetDefaultSQL() function so that only records where the Shares field in the Stocks table are equal to 100.

```
CString CInvestmentsSet::GetDefaultSQL()
{
    return _T("[Stocks]");
}
```

12

7. Add a statement to the following OnInitialUpdate() function so that the database is sorted by the Net_Revenue field.

```
void CCorporationsView::OnInitialUpdate()
{
    m_pSet = &GetDocument()->m_CorporationsSet;
    CRecordView::OnInitialUpdate();
    GetParentFrame()->RecalcLayout();
    ResizeParentToFit();
}
```

8. Write a message handler function named OnPriceSort() for a Real Estate database application that sorts a record set by the Listing_Price field.

9. Write a message handler function named OnLocationFilter()for a Real Estate database application that filters a record set by the Property_Location field.

10. Add a dialog window to the Library Database application that allows users to filter the record set by a specific author's name.

11. Add the appropriate code to the following OnRecordAdd()and OnMove() functions to add new records to a database:

```
void cProductsView::OnRecordAdd() {
...
}
BOOL CProductsView::OnMove(UINT nIDMoveCommand) {
    // TODO: Add your specialized code here
         and/or call the base class
    return CRecordView::OnMove(nIDMoveCommand);
}
```

12. The following OnRecordDelete() function deletes the current record from a database. Add the appropriate code to display a valid record in the event that a user deletes the last record in the database. Also, add code that clears the fields left over from the last visible record in the event that a user deletes all of the records from the database.

```
void cLibraryDatabaseView::OnRecordDelete() {
    m_pSet->Delete();
    m_pSet->MoveNext();
}
```

13. Database design techniques include the process of being able to identify and design five normalization levels: first normal form, second normal form, third normal form, fourth normal form, and fifth normal form. Search the Internet or visit your local library for information on these techniques and describe how to identify and design each normalization level.

Index